THE UN FRIENDLY RELATIONS DECLARATION AT 50

The year 2020 marks the seventy-fifth anniversary of the United Nations Organization, and the fiftieth anniversary of the UN Friendly Relations Declaration, which states the fundamental principles of the international legal order. In commemoration, some of the world's most prominent international law scholars from all continents have come together to offer a comprehensive study of the fundamental principles of international law. Each chapter in this volume reflects decades of experience, work and reflection by the most authoritative voices of the field. At the same time, the book is an invitation to end narrow specialisation and re-engage with the wider body of rules and processes that lie at the foundations of the international legal order.

Jorge E. Viñuales holds the Harold Samuel Chair at the University of Cambridge and is a Fellow of the Lauterpacht Centre for International Law and of Clare College. He is also a Member (*Associé*) of the *Institut de Droit International*. At Cambridge, he founded and directed the Cambridge Centre for Environment, Energy and Natural Resource Governance (C-EENRG). Professor Viñuales has published many studies on international law, and he has wide experience as counsel, expert and adjudicator.

The UN Friendly Relations Declaration at 50

AN ASSESSMENT OF THE FUNDAMENTAL PRINCIPLES OF INTERNATIONAL LAW

Edited by

JORGE E. VIÑUALES

University of Cambridge

CAMBRIDGE
UNIVERSITY PRESS

CAMBRIDGE
UNIVERSITY PRESS

University Printing House, Cambridge CB2 8BS, United Kingdom

One Liberty Plaza, 20th Floor, New York, NY 10006, USA

477 Williamstown Road, Port Melbourne, VIC 3207, Australia

314–321, 3rd Floor, Plot 3, Splendor Forum, Jasola District Centre, New Delhi – 110025, India

79 Anson Road, #06-04/06, Singapore 079906

Cambridge University Press is part of the University of Cambridge.

It furthers the University's mission by disseminating knowledge in the pursuit of education, learning, and research at the highest international levels of excellence.

www.cambridge.org
Information on this title: www.cambridge.org/9781108483810
DOI: 10.1017/9781108652889

First published 2020

Printed in the United Kingdom by TJ International Ltd, Padstow Cornwall

A catalogue record for this publication is available from the British Library.

ISBN 978-1-108-48381-0 Hardback

To my teachers, colleagues and students

The editor gratefully acknowledges financial support from the Lauterpacht Centre for International Law, Cambridge.

Contents

Contributors

(in alphabetical order)

Georges Abi-Saab – Emeritus Professor of International Law at the Graduate Institute of International and Development Studies, Geneva; former Judge ad hoc of the International Court of Justice; former Judge of the Appeal Chamber of the International Criminal Tribunals for the Former Yugoslavia (ICTY) and for Rwanda (ICTR); former Chairman of the WTO Appellate Body; Member of the Institut de Droit International.

Laurence Boisson de Chazournes – Professor of International Law and International Organization at the University of Geneva; Member of the Institut de Droit International.

Olivier Corten – Professor of International Law and Director of the Centre de droit international et de sociologie appliquée au droit international at the Université libre de Bruxelles; Member (Associé) of the Institut de Droit International.

Pierre-Marie Dupuy – Emeritus Professor of International Law at the Université de Paris 2, Panthéon-Assas, and at the Graduate Institute of International and Development Studies, Geneva; Chair of Public International Law at the European University Institute, Florence (2000–8); Member of the Institut de Droit International.

Leslie-Anne Duvic-Paoli – Lecturer in Law at the Dickson Poon School of Law, King's College London.

Guillaume Futhazar – Senior Research Fellow at the Max Planck Institute for Comparative Public Law and International Law, Heidelberg.

Shotaro Hamamoto – Professor of the Law of International Organizations at the Graduate School of Law, Kyoto University.

Bing Bing Jia – Professor of International Law at the School of Law, Tsinghua University; Member of the Curatorium of the Hague Academy of International Law.

Ville Kari – PhD candidate at the Faculty of Law, University of Helsinki; Visiting Researcher at the Lauterpacht Centre for International Law, Cambridge.

Marcelo G. Kohen – Professor of International Law at the Graduate Institute of International and Development Studies, Geneva; Member and Secretary-General of the Institut de Droit International.

Martti Koskenniemi – Professor of International Law at the Faculty of Law, University of Helsinki; Director of the Erik Castrén Institute of International Law and Human Rights; Fellow of the British Academy; Member (Associé) of the Institut de Droit International.

Jürgen Kurtz – Professor of International Economic Law at the European University Institute, Florence.

Samuel Moyn – Henry R. Luce Professor of Jurisprudence at Yale Law School and Professor of History at Yale University.

Umut Özsu – Associate Professor of Law and Legal Studies at Carleton University, Canada.

Anne Peters – Director at the Max Planck Institute for Comparative Public Law and International Law, Heidelberg; Professor at the Universities of Heidelberg, Freie Universität Berlin and Basel (Switzerland), and William W. Cook Global Law Professor at the University of Michigan.

Eibe Riedel – Emeritus Professor of German and Comparative Public Law, European and International Law at the University of Mannheim, Germany; Former Member and Vice-Chair of the UN Committee on Economic, Social and Cultural Rights, Geneva from 1997 to 2012.

Jason Rudall – Assistant Professor of International Law, Grotius Center for International Legal Studies, Leiden University.

Dire Tladi – Professor of International Law at the Department of Public Law, University of Pretoria; Member of the UN International Law Commission and Special Rapporteur on the topic Peremptory Norms of General International Law (*jus cogens*); Member (Associé) of the Institut de Droit International.

Tullio Treves – Emeritus Professor of International Law at the University of Milan; Former Judge at the International Tribunal for the Law of the Sea; Member of the Institut de Droit International; Member of the Curatorium of the Hague Academy of International Law; International Law Consultant, Curtis, Mallet-Prevost, Colt & Mosle LLP.

Jorge E. Viñuales – Harold Samuel Professor of Law and Environmental Policy at the University of Cambridge; Fellow of the Lauterpacht Centre for International Law and of Clare College, Cambridge; Member (Associé) of the Institut de Droit International.

Michael Waibel – Professor of International Law at the University of Vienna; Former Co-Deputy Director of the Lauterpacht Centre for International Law, Cambridge, from 2015 to 2019; Nomura Visiting Professor of International Financial Systems, Harvard Law School, 2019.

Abbreviations

BBNJ	marine biological diversity of areas beyond the limits of national jurisdiction
BIT	bilateral investment treaty
CESCR	Committee on Economic, Social and Cultural Rights
CISG	Convention on Contracts for the International Sale of Goods (1980)
CITES	Convention on International Trade in Endangered Species of Wild Fauna and Flora (1973)
CRAMRA	Convention on the Regulation of Antarctic Mineral Resource Activities (1988)
DSU	Dispute Settlement Understanding
ECHR	Convention for the Protection of Human Rights and Fundamental Freedoms (1950)
ECOSOC	Economic and Social Council
ECtHR	European Court of Human Rights
EIA	environmental impact assessment
FET	fair and equitable treatment
FSB	Financial Stability Board
FTA	free trade agreement
GAL	Global Administrative Law
GATS	General Agreement on Trade in Services (1994)
GATT	General Agreement on Tariffs and Trade (1947)
HRC	UN Human Rights Committee
IACtHR	Inter-American Court of Human Rights
ICC	International Criminal Court
ICCPR	International Covenant on Civil and Political Rights (1966)
ICESCR	International Covenant on Economic, Social and Cultural Rights (1966)
ICJ	International Court of Justice
ICRC	International Committee of the Red Cross
ICSID	International Centre for Settlement of Investment Disputes
ICTR	International Criminal Tribunal for Rwanda
ICTY	International Criminal Tribunal for the Former Yugoslavia
ILA	International Law Association
ILC	International Law Commission
ILO	International Labour Organization
IMF	International Monetary Fund

ISA	International Seabed Authority
ITLOS	International Tribunal for the Law of the Sea
ITO	International Trade Organization
IWG	Intergovernmental Working Group
MEA	multilateral environmental agreements
NAM	Non-Aligned Movement
NIEO	New International Economic Order
PCA	Permanent Court of Arbitration
PCIJ	Permanent Court of International Justice
SD	self-determination
SPS	Application of Sanitary and Phytosanitary Measures
TBT	Technical Barriers to Trade
TRIPS	Trade-Related Aspects of Intellectual Property Rights
UNCIO	United Nations Conference on International Organization (1945)
UNCITRAL	United Nations Commission on International Trade Law
UNCLOS	United Nations Convention on the Law of the Sea (1982)
UNCTAD	United Nations Conference on Trade and Development
UNESCO	United Nations Educational, Scientific and Cultural Organization
UNFCCC	United Nations Framework Convention on Climate Change (1992)
UNGA	United Nations General Assembly
UPR	Universal Periodic Review
VCLT	Vienna Convention on the Law of Treaties (1969)
WHO	World Health Organization
WTO	World Trade Organization
WTO-DSB	World Trade Organization Dispute Settlement Body

Introduction

The Fundamental Principles of International Law – An Enduring Ideal?

Jorge E. Viñuales

I AN INAUSPICIOUS ANNIVERSARY

The year 2020 marks the seventy-fifth anniversary of the establishment of the United Nations Organisation, the cornerstone of the post-war international order, and the fiftieth anniversary of the 1970 Friendly Relations Declaration,[1] which provided the canonical formulation of seven foundational principles of international law. Yet, the current international context seems largely inauspicious for genuine celebration. Although the world order engineered by the victorious powers after the Second World War has faced daunting challenges in the past,[2] what is particularly disquieting about the present situation is that the challenges come, to a significant extent, from the main proponent and guarantor of the post-war rules-based international order, the United States, in the absence of any comparable stabilising forces. Whether it is the inward reflexes and blame game of major countries in reacting to a global pandemic,[3] or the use of force by Russia for the annexation of Crimea[4] or its interference in electoral processes in the United States, France, Italy and the UK,[5] or the trade war triggered by the United States against China and the EU,[6] or its withdrawal from the Paris Agreement on Climate Change,[7] or China's defiance of the basic rules of the law of the sea to assert its power within a 'nine dash' line in the South China

[1] Declaration on Principles of International Law Concerning Friendly Relations and Co-operation among States in Accordance with the Charter of the United Nations, UNGA Res 2625 (XXV) (24 October 1970), Annex [Friendly Relations Declaration].

[2] See KJ Holsti, *Peace and War: Armed Conflicts and International Order, 1648–1989* (Cambridge University Press, 1991), ch 11 (describing the complexification of war and listing fifty-eight conflicts which occurred in the forty years after the adoption of the UN Charter); JJ Mearsheimer, 'Back to the Future: Instability in Europe after the Cold War' (1990) 15 *International Security* 5; JL Gaddis, 'International Relations Theory and the End of the Cold War' (1992–93) 17 *International Security* 5; S Huntington, 'The Clash of Civilizations?' (1993) 73(3) *Foreign Affairs* 22; G Lundestad, *East, West, North, South: Major Developments in International Relations since 1945* (5th edn, Sage, 2005).

[3] See I Bremmer, 'China and America's Blame Game Over COVID-19 Hurts Everyone', *Time Magazine* (26 March 2020).

[4] For two accounts see T Grant, 'Annexation of Crimea' (2015) 109 *American Journal of International Law* 68; A Grigas, *Beyond Crimea: The New Russian Empire* (Yale University Press, 2016).

[5] See E Brattberg and T Maurer, 'Russian Election Interference: Europe's Counter to Fake News and Cyber Attacks', Carnegie Endowment for International Peace, 23 May 2018; B Sander, 'Democracy under Influence: Paradigms of State Responsibility for Cyber Influence Operations in Elections' (2019) 18 *Chinese Journal of International Law* 1.

[6] See J Weiler, 'Black Lies, White Lies and Some Uncomfortable Truths in and of the International Trading System', *EJIL: Talk!*, 25 July 2018.

[7] See L Rajamani, 'Reflections on the US withdrawal from the Paris Climate Change Agreement', *EJIL: Talk!*, 5 June 2017.

Sea,[8] all these cases go beyond mere controversy over the applicability of a principle to a given situation and constitute open defiance of the letter and/or spirit of the very principles that have served, since 1945, as the normative standards determining the lawfulness of international action.

From a legal standpoint, the diversity and complexity of the issues is daunting. What is the meaning of sovereignty in a world where in a few months a localised viral outbreak can become a global pandemic paralysing the world,[9] or of human rights in a context where even in wealthy countries inequality is laid bare by the blatant differences in access to medical treatment?[10] Is interference with presidential elections or with the Brexit referendum through private companies manipulating social media a violation of the classical principles of non-intervention or of sovereign equality?[11] Is a group with an identifiable cultural tradition (such as indigenous peoples in Brazil or first nations in the United States or Quebec in Canada or, still, Catalonia in Spain) entitled to exercise self-determination and become an independent State, even beyond a decolonisation context?[12] Is cyberwarfare or international terrorism or the poisoning of Russian ex-agents in the territory of the UK a prohibited use of force or a violation of non-intervention or of sovereign equality?[13] Is a restrictive migration policy leaving migrant boats adrift in the Mediterranean without help, preventing them from docking and even restricting the possibility for civil society organisations to offer help consistent with the (extraterritorial) obligation to protect human rights?[14] Are the unilateral sanctions imposed by Saudi Arabia, Bahrain, the United Arab Emirates and Egypt against Qatar a violation of the principles of non-intervention, sovereign equality or human rights?[15] Is the abandonment by the Egyptian government of its claims over two islands in favour of Saudi Arabia in disregard of the collective rights enshrined in the Egyptian Constitution a violation of the right of self-determination of the Egyptian people?[16] Is the market restructuring required by international financial institutions as a condition for a loan to a developing country or the austerity required by European institutions as a condition for financial assistance to Greece[17] or, still, the focus of the International Criminal Court on African States consistent with the principle of non-intervention?[18] Is the triggering of a trade war against specific countries or regional organisations consistent with the principles underlying non-discrimination in trade relations?[19] Is the manipulation of currency exchanges to gain a competitive trade advantage consistent with the principles governing international monetary

8 See D Guilfoyle, 'The South China Sea Award: How Should We Read the UN Convention on the Law of the Sea?' (2018) 8 *Asian Journal of International Law* 51.

9 See J Gibney, 'The Coronavirus Won't Kill Globalization', *Bloomberg Opinion* (22 March 2020).

10 See Human Rights Watch, 'US: Address Impact of Covid-19 on Poor: Virus Outbreak Highlights Structural Inequalities' (19 March 2020).

11 See Sander (n 5).

12 See N Cornago, 'Beyond Self-Determination: Norms Contestation, Constituent Diplomacies and the Co-Production of Sovereignty' (2017) 6 *Global Constitutionalism* 327.

13 See GP Corn and R Taylor, 'Sovereignty in the Age of Cyber' (2017) 111 *AJIL Unbound* 207.

14 See M Martin, 'Prioritising Border Control over Human Lives: Violations of the Rights of Migrants and Refugees at Sea', Euro-Mediterranean Human Rights Network Policy Brief (June 2014).

15 See A Hofer, 'Sanctioning Qatar Continued: The United Arab Emirates Is Brought before the ICJ', *EJIL: Talk!*, 22 June 2018.

16 See G Le Moli, 'The President of The Republic et al. v. Ali Ayyoub et al.' (2019) 113 *American Journal of International Law* 4.

17 See V Paliouras, 'The Right to Restructure Sovereign Debt' (2017) 20 *Journal of International Economic Law* 115.

18 See KJ Heller, 'Radical Complementarity' (2016) 14 *Journal of International Criminal Justice* 637; C de Vos, S Kendall and C Stahn (eds), *Contested Justice: The Politics and Practice of International Criminal Court Interventions* (Cambridge University Press, 2015).

19 See Ch Bown and D Irwin, 'Trump's Assault on the Global Trading System: And Why Decoupling from China Will Change Everything' (September/October 2019) 98(5) *Foreign Affairs*.

or trade relations?[20] Is the ability of foreign investors to challenge public policy measures in the countries where they operate before ad hoc arbitration tribunals composed of private individuals consistent with the sovereign prerogatives of States, human rights or the prevention of environmental harm?[21] Is the failure to achieve complete nuclear disarmament[22] or to raise the level of ambition in mitigating climate change[23] a violation of the duty to co-operate?

One could multiply the examples, but the main underlying point is similar: in the present political context, the foundational principles of the international legal order face daunting challenges, some of which could be existential. Such challenges are of various orders. In some cases, such as the threats arising from the digital revolution or from massive environmental degradation, it is the unanticipated character of the threats or of their scale that challenges the ability of one or more principles to frame them. In other cases, such as the attempted secession of minorities, currency manipulation or trade wars, the nature of the threat was anticipated but the formulation of the relevant principles either left the matter unsettled or did not anticipate other related shortcomings in the implementation machinery (e.g. the deadlock in the appointment of World Trade Organization (WTO) Appellate Body members). Yet in other cases, such as the forceful assertion of territorial claims on the basis of legally unrecognised arguments or blatant violations of the principle of non-refoulement, the actions are clearly unlawful and the main challenge comes precisely from the open defiance of well-established principles.

This is the general context in which, together with the distinguished contributors who kindly accepted my invitation to join this project, we decided to re-examine the past, present and possible futures of the fundamental principles on which the international legal order is based. Seven of them are expressly stated in the Friendly Relations Declaration. Others, such as protection of human rights; the duty to co-operate in the economic, social and cultural fields; or the non-appropriation of Outer Space are mentioned in an embryonic form in the preamble of the Declaration or as part of one of the seven principles. And others, such as prevention of environmental harm or the principles of international humanitarian law, are not referred to in the wording of the Declaration but may be considered as a necessary implication or a subsequent extension of it.

However, it would be inaccurate to conclude from these observations that the Friendly Relations Declaration contains, in condensed manner, 'all' the fundamental principles of international law. As discussed in the contributions in this volume,[24] the Declaration is best seen as the culmination of a period in which the principles of the UN Charter were reappropriated by a now much more diverse international community of States, a community that, over time, had been expanded from Christian States, over to 'civilised' States and, in 1945, to all 'peace-loving' countries,[25] including a large number of 'New Nations'.[26] By contrast, matters of

[20] See RW Staiger and AO Sykes, '"Currency Manipulation" and World Trade' (2010) 9 *World Trade Review* 583.

[21] See JE Viñuales, 'Sovereignty in Foreign Investment Law' in Z Douglas, J Pauwelyn and JE Viñuales (eds), *The Foundations of International Investment Law* (Oxford University Press, 2014), ch 11.

[22] See G Nystuen, S Casey-Maslen and A Golden Bersagel (eds), *Nuclear Weapons under International Law* (Cambridge University Press, 2014).

[23] See R Falkner, 'The Paris Agreement and the New Logic of International Climate Politics' (2016) 92 *International Affairs* 1107.

[24] See the chapter by L-A Duvic-Paoli and JE Viñuales in this volume.

[25] See BVA Röling, *International Law in an Expanded World* (Brug-Djambatan, 1960).

[26] See D Kay, 'The Politics of Decolonization: The New Nations and the United Nations Political Process' (1967) 21 *International Organization* 786.

environmental protection, the formulation of which was only starting in the early 1970s, were excluded from the Declaration, both in its actual wording and in its spirit, which gave pre-eminence to self-determination and sovereign equality, with the attendant implications for the exploitation of natural resources. It may be useful to recall a resolution, entitled 'Development and Environment', which was adopted on the initiative of Brazil, one year after the adoption of the Friendly Relations Declaration and less than a year before the Stockholm Declaration on the Human Environment,[27] and whose last paragraph 'reiterate[d] the primacy of independent economic and social development as the main and paramount objective of international co-operation, in the interests of the welfare of mankind and of peace and world security'.[28] Developing countries expressed great reluctance for any interference with development for the sake of preventing pollution. They only accepted this idea later, in the process triggered by the 1992 Rio Conference on Environment and Development and still ongoing today.

Yet, far from superseded, the principles formulated in the Friendly Relations Declaration, suitably complemented by some other instruments expressing principles not fully fleshed out in 1970, remain the main synthesis so far achieved on the foundations of the rules-based international order. It is from this perspective that the re-examination undertaken in this volume must be understood. Such re-examination is, however, only a part of a wider project, with a wider goal, which I would like to introduce briefly before explaining the place of this volume within it.

II AN ENDURING IDEAL?

'Love is so short, and forgetting is so long', wrote Chilean poet Pablo Neruda in one of his most memorable works.[29] This fact of life, however discomforting to those who face it, harbours some hope when applied to ideals and possibly to their expression through principles.

An intriguing study of how the collective memory of 'cultural objects' – the continued and shared attention to events and people – evolves over time[30] suggests that this process follows two different phases. Once attention to a cultural object has reached its peak, there is first a rapid and steep decline but, at some point, the slope becomes less and less steep and settles in a slow and gentle declining trajectory over a period of decades. This trajectory, which the authors of the study apply to objects as diverse as academic papers (in physics), songs, films and even celebrity, is explained by the different nature of the phenomena driving attention. The surge in attention to a cultural object and the subsequent sudden decline is driven by 'communicative memory', namely contemporary human interactions (direct 'word of mouth' communication of information among contemporaries). This driver of collective memory is powerful but short-lived. Instead, the slower and gentler decline in attention of the second phase is driven by 'cultural memory' – that is, the recording of information through a range of means or, in other words, the penetration of the cultural object in more stable written or physical supports and cultural strata.

27 Declaration of the United Nations Conference on the Human Environment, Stockholm, 16 June 1972, UN Doc A/CONF.48/14/Rev.1, 2 et seq.

28 Development and Environment, UNGA Res 2849 (XXVI) (20 December 1971), para 11.

29 'Es tan corto el amor, y es tan largo el olvido', poema 20, *Veinte poemas de amor y una canción desesperada* (Editorial Nacimiento, 1924). I borrow the analogy with Neruda's writings from the editorial 'How We Forget' (2018) 564 *Nature* 162. The references in this section follow those provided in this editorial, which first sparked my interest in the dynamics and processes of collective memory decay.

30 C Candia et al, 'The Universal Decay of Collective Memory and Attention' (2019) 3 *Nature Human Behaviour* 82–91.

This trajectory of collective memory decay is largely but not universally applicable to all cultural objects.

Whether an extrapolation to the realm of 'normative events' is permitted is a matter that would require sustained attention and possibly a methodology similar to that employed by the authors of the study. Yet, a tentative parallel between those cultural objects and 'normative events', such as a statement of principles, is heuristically useful. It provides an intuitive explanation of how certain subjects, topics or questions attract high levels of attention in international legal circles for a short period of time and then slowly fade away, their subsequent existence being dictated by the extent to which they have been recorded in more stable supports, such as writings, textbooks, curricula, areas of practice in governmental, non-governmental and private institutions, and the like. It also signals a curious and unexpected manner of bringing together historical, including critical, and positivistic accounts of international law as complementing accounts of collective memory decay, the former revisiting the 'genealogy' of the first phase (communicative memory) and the latter focusing on the consolidation of the second phase (cultural memory). This basic observation defines the broad contours of the research programme within which this volume was conceived, which I will further explain below. For present purposes, such a tentative extrapolation of the dynamics of collective memory to the 'normative event' represented by the negotiation and adoption of the Friendly Relations Declaration may explain the notable loss of interest regarding this instrument since the 1970s and our (international lawyers) role, as architects, vehicles and agents in this process.

The process leading to the adoption of the Friendly Relations Declaration attracted, quite understandably, substantial attention in the 1960s[31] and the 1970s.[32] In 1972, two sets of Hague

[31] See eg JN Hazard, 'The Sixth Committee and New Law' (1963) 57 *American Journal of International Law* 604–13; LT Lee, 'The Mexico City Conference of the United Nations Special Committee on Principles of International Law Concerning Friendly Relations and Co-Operation among States' (1965) 14 *International & Comparative Law Quarterly* 1296–310; M Decleva, 'Le dichiarazioni di principi delle Nazioni unite' [1965] *Annuario di Diritto Internazionale* 63–79; M Nawaz et al (eds), *The Legal Principles Governing Friendly Relations and Co-Operation among States in the Spirit of the United Nations Charter* (Sijthoff, 1966); E McWhinney, 'The "New" Countries and the "New" International Law: The United Nations' Special Conference on Friendly Relations and Cooperation among States' (1966) 60 *American Journal of International Law* 1–33; O Asamoah, *The Legal Significance of the Declarations of the General Assembly of the United Nations* (Manchester University Press, 1966) 46 et seq; W Friedmann, *The Changing Structure of International Law* (Columbia University Press, 1966); P-H Houben, 'Principles of International Law Concerning Friendly Relations and Co-Operation among States' (1967) 61 *American Journal of International Law* 703–36; R Bierzanek, 'Legal Principles of Peaceful Co-Existence and Their Codification' (1966–67) 1 *Polish Yearbook of International Law* 17–44; V Pechota, 'Principles of International Law Concerning Friendly Relations and Cooperation among States in Accordance with the Charter of the UN' (1967–68) 37/38 *Hague Yearbook of International Law (formerly AAA)*; S Bastid, 'Observations sur une "étape" dans le développement progressif et la codification des principes du droit international' in *Recueil d'études de droit international en hommage à Paul Guggenheim* (IUHEI/Faculté de Droit de l'Université de Genève, 1968) 132–45; M Virally, 'Le Rôle des "principes" dans le développement du droit international' in *Recueil d'études de droit international en hommage à Paul Guggenheim* (IUHEI/Faculté de Droit de l'Université de Genève, 1968) 531–54.

[32] See eg R Higgins, 'The United Nations and Law-Making: The Political Organs' (1970) *ASIL Proceedings* 37–48; P Raton, 'Travaux de la Commission juridique de l'Assemblée générale des Nations Unies (XXVe session)' (1970) 16 *Annuaire français de droit international* 514–51; K Obradovic, 'Quelques réflexions sur le projet de Déclaration relative aux principes du droit international touchant les relations amicales et la coopération entre les Etats' (1970) *Jugoslovenska revija za medjunarodno parvo* 2–3; R Rosenstock, 'The Declaration of Principles of International Law concerning Friendly Relations: a Survey' (1971) 65 *American Journal of International Law* 713–35; K Kolesnik, 'Tuzmuhamedov, Deklaracija principov mirnogo sosuäcestvovanüa' (1971) 6 *Sovetskoe gosudarstvo i parvo*; M Sahovic, *Principles of International Law Concerning Friendly Relations and Co-Operation* (Oceana, 1972); B zu Dohna, *Die Grundprinzipien des Völkerrechts über die freundschaftlichen Beziehungen und die Zusammenarbeit zwischen den Staaten* (Duncker & Humblot, 1973); JA Frowein, 'Freundschaft und Zusammenarbeit unter den Staaten. Die UN-resolution über freundschaftliche Beziehungen als Ausdruck wichtiger Strömungen im heutigen Völkerrecht' (1973) 28 *Europa-Archiv* 70–76; I Sinclair, 'Principles of International Law Concerning Friendly

Lectures were devoted to the principles of the Declaration in the same year and volume,[33] which is highly exceptional. The works published during this period were, in most cases, authored by those who, in a senior or junior capacity, were involved in the Special Committee which drafted the Declaration. This observation would render plausible the hypothesis of a rise in interest in the Declaration not only as a result of the stakes underlying the process but also of the amplification provided by the interplay of communicative memory – that is, the very exchanges and debates within the international law community (academic and diplomatic) of those years. Thereafter, attention declined, first steeply and then following a slower and gentler declining trajectory,[34] interrupted by some major restatements of the value of the Declaration, mainly the reliance of the International Court of Justice (ICJ) in its 1986 judgment in the *Nicaragua* case[35] and, of course, the new dawn offered by the demise of the Soviet Union and the end of the Cold War.[36] Since then, the Friendly Relations Declaration has largely dropped out of sight, almost gone missing, from the writings and teachings of the current generation of international law scholars, even from textbooks,[37] with the notable exception of the debate over the 'constitutionalisation' of international law.[38] Most principles have received individually significant

Relations and Co-Operation among States' in M Nawaz (ed), *Essays on International Law in Honour of Krishna Rao* (Sijthoff, 1975) 107–40.

33 See G Arangio-Ruiz, 'The Normative Role of the General Assembly of the United Nations and the Declaration of Principles of Friendly Relations' (1972) 137 *Recueil des Cours* 419–742 (subsequently revised as: G Arangio-Ruiz, *The United Nations Declaration on Friendly Relations and the System of the Sources of International Law* (Sijthoff, 1979)); M Sahovic, 'Codification des principes du droit international des relations amicales et de la coopération entre les Etats' (1972) 137 *Recueil des Cours* 243–310.

34 See eg F Anjak, *La Codification des principes de la coexistence pacifique: le comité spécial des principes de droit international touchant les relations amicales et la coopération entre les états conformément à la Charte des Nations-Unies* (Office des publications universitaires, 1980).

35 See *Military and Paramilitary Activities in and against Nicaragua (Nicaragua* v *United States of America)*, Merits, Judgment, ICJ Reports 1986, 14 [*Nicaragua* case], paras 188, 191, 228, 264 (prohibition of the use of force), 212–13, 251–52 (sovereign equality) and 202–9, 264 (non-intervention).

36 Since the 1990s, the main contribution on the Friendly Relations Declaration is C Warbrick and V Lowe (eds), *The United Nations and the Principles of International Law, Essays in Memory of Michael Akehurst* (Routledge, 1994). The explanation why the volume is devoted to the Declaration is stated as follows: 'The essays collected in this volume re-examine the Declaration of Principles of International Law Governing Friendly Relations between States. The Declaration embodies the fundamental values of the international system and is the nearest thing that states have to an international constitution. The great changes in the international system since 1989 hold out the prospect for the reinvigoration of the Charter, perhaps for a new system of international legal relations, and make the reconsideration of the Declaration in these essays particularly timely.' The brief but illuminating chapter by G Abi-Saab to the *Melanges Virally*, published in 1991, highlights a forgotten aspect of the contribution of M Virally, who was the French representative in the Special Committee which drafted the Friendly Relations Declaration. See G Abi-Saab, 'La Reformulation des principes de la charte et la transformation des structures juridiques de la communauté internationale' in *Le droit international au service de la paix, de la justice et du développement: mélanges Michel Virally* (Pedone, 1991) 1–8.

37 With the exception of a full chapter devoted to the fundamental principles of international law, although not specifically to their statement in the Friendly Relations Declaration, in A Cassese, *International Law* (Oxford University Press, 2001), ch 3.

38 On this line of work, which has attracted particular attention from German-speaking scholars, see: P-M Dupuy, 'The Constitutional Dimension of the Charter of the United Nations Revisited' (1997) 1 *Max Planck Yearbook of United Nations Law* 1–33; R Kolb, 'La Structure constitutionnelle du droit international public' [2001] *Canadian Yearbook of International Law* 69; T Cottier and M Hertig, 'The Prospects of 21st Century Constitutionalism' (2003) 7 *Max Planck Yearbook of United Nations Law* 261; A Peters, 'Compensatory Constitutionalism: The Function and Potential of Fundamental International Norms and Structures' (2006) 19 *Leiden Journal of International Law* 579; A Emmerich-Fritsche, *Vom Völkerrecht zum Weltrecht* (Duncker & Humblot, 2007); O Diggelmann and T Altwicker, 'Is There Something Like a Constitution of International Law? A Critical Analysis of the Debate on World Constitutionalism' (2008) 68 *Zeitschrift für ausländisches öffentliches Recht und Völkerrecht* 623; A Peters, 'Humanity as the A and Ω of Sovereignty' (2009) 20 *European Journal of International Law* 513–44; B Fassbender, *The United Nations Charter as the Constitution of the International Community* (Martinus Nijhoff, 2009); N Krisch, *Beyond Constitutionalism: The*

attention, and the Declaration as such is referenced – albeit often in passing – in major international law textbooks. Yet, interest in it as the synthesis instrument marking the reappropriation of the fundamental principles of international law by the then much wider international community of States, including developing and newly independent countries, has all but waned.

This fate may be explained, as for other cultural objects, by the very dynamics of collective memory, although a more granular and familiar perspective would have to refer to the close links between the Declaration and the Soviet doctrine of peaceful co-existence, now mainly of historical interest, the almost completion – with some significant exceptions – of the decolonisation process, and the rise of a new logic – that of sustainable development – with its own imperatives. But, from the perspective of how international law is studied, understood and taught, something more than the Declaration was lost: namely a general or 'generalist' perspective of international law, a 'big picture' of the interrelations across values and their legal expression in legal norms and processes. For someone sceptical about the trend towards extreme and narrow specialisation, who benefited from the teachings of generalists, the Friendly Relations Declaration is more than a mere resolution or codification statement. It is an attempt at agreeing on and synthesising the foundations of the rules-based international order. Thus, the decay of the collective memory of the Friendly Relations Declaration is, in many ways, the passive acceptance of a false impossibility, namely that in a context characterised by increasing specialisation, it is no longer possible or useful to be a generalist international lawyer. What is left then? '"So perhaps you are an expert on the leech?" asked Zarathustra ... "O Zarathustra," answered the man who was trodden on, "that would be a colossal task, how could I undertake it! But what I am master of and expert on is the leech's *brain* – that is *my* world!"'[39]

A study of the fundamental principles of international law formulated in the Friendly Relations Declaration is, in my mind, a tactical step to explore a more integrative view of a rules-based international order. It is integrative because it attempts to bring together, in an articulate manner, the main technical and intellectual traditions of international law as well as to provide a substantive common ground (the fundamental principles reviewed in this volume) for the integration of specialised knowledge into a general account of international law. The goal, whether it may be qualified as intellectually- or policy-driven, is to bring the study of fundamental principles back to the centre stage of international legal education and, thereby, to refresh or restage our collective memory of why those principles emerged, why they were felt as pressing needs, why we attached so much value to their enactment and placed so much hope in them. We are entering a phase where the common normative foundations of the international legal order are again contested. Our focus must therefore move away from our habits of specialisation and technical dexterity in narrow issues, comfortably sitting on the post-1990 normative consensus, and confront again the normative choices that serve as the foundations of the international legal order, not to

Pluralist Structure of Postnational Law (Oxford University Press, 2010); JA Klabbers, A Peters and G Ulfstein, *The Constitutionalization of International Law* (Oxford University Press, 2011); T Kleinlein, *Konstitutionalisierung im Völkerrecht: Konstruktion und Elemente einer idealistischen Völkerrechtslehre* (Springer, 2011); E-U Petersmann, 'Multilevel Trade Governance in the WTO Requires Multilevel Constitutionalism' in C Joerges and EU Petersmann (eds), *Constitutionalism, Multilevel Trade Governance and International Economic Law* (Hart, 2011) 5–57.

39 F Nietzsche, *Thus Spoke Zarathustra: A Book for Everyone and No One* (RJ Hollingdale tr, Penguin, 1961), pt IV, 'The Leech', 263.

thoughtlessly challenge every normative foundation but to lucidly rebuild a more acceptable synthesis.

III THE FUNDAMENTAL PRINCIPLES OF THE INTERNATIONAL LEGAL ORDER TODAY

The Friendly Relations Declaration is not a complete statement of the fundamental principles (or 'basic principles', as the Declaration calls them) of the international legal order. Some other principles were expressly discussed during the negotiations within the Special Committee that drafted the Declaration, and they were either excluded (e.g. the permanent sovereignty over natural resources, which was deemed to be carefully and adequately formulated in Resolution 1803 (XVII)[40]) or only mentioned in the preamble (e.g. the non-appropriation of Outer Space[41]). For this reason, the chapters in this volume are not confined to the seven principles of the Declaration[42] and cover five other fundamental principles or 'clusters' thereof (human rights protection as a principle,[43] the 'cardinal' principles of international humanitarian law,[44] prevention of environmental harm,[45] the principles governing freedoms in the global commons[46] and the principles governing the global economy[47]). Because the focus of the volume is more on the principles than on its supporting instrument (i.e. the Declaration itself), it also includes chapters focusing on the historical and conceptual foundations of these principles.[48] In this context, perhaps the most difficult aspect of designing the contents of this volume was the identification of the relevant principles. I should therefore state, in this introduction, what I understand by the 'fundamental principles of international law' before further elaborating on their fundamental or foundational character.

The 'fundamental principles of international law' as an object are circumscribed from four main perspectives. First, within the broader category of 'norms' in general, the focus of the volume is on the subcategory of 'principles', which can be understood as a type of norm characterised by their higher generality/abstraction (as compared to 'rules'), their formulation (which combines both prescriptive aspects – commands or prohibitions to be 'obeyed' – and permissive aspects – entitlements that can be 'relied on' or not), their mode of application (which entails a proportionality or value-weighing assessment, rather than a binary compliance/non-compliance outcome), and their functions (which, despite variations in proposed taxonomies, may include the actual regulation of behaviour, the co-ordination of reactions against a

[40] See Report of the Special Committee on Principles of International Law concerning Friendly Relations and Co-operation among States (16 November 1964), A/5746, para 280, referring to Permanent Sovereignty over Natural Resources, UNGA Res 1803 (XVII) (14 December 1962).

[41] Friendly Relations Declaration, preamble, seventh para, '[r]ecalling the established principle that outer space, including the Moon and other celestial bodies, is not subject to national appropriation by claim of sovereignty, by means of use or occupation, or by any other means'.

[42] See the chapters by O Corten (on the prohibition of the use of force), Shotaro Hamamoto (on the peaceful settlement of international disputes), D Tladi (on non-intervention), L Boisson de Chazournes and J Rudall (on co-operation), M Kohen (on self-determination), M Koskenniemi and V Kari (on sovereign equality) and G Futhazar and A Peters (on good faith).

[43] See the chapter by E Riedel on the protection of human rights as a principle.

[44] See the chapter by Bing Bing Jia on the cardinal principles of international humanitarian law.

[45] See the chapter by L-A Duvic-Paoli and JE Viñuales on the prevention of environmental harm.

[46] See the chapter by T Treves on the freedoms and uses of the Antarctic, outer space and marine global commons.

[47] See the chapter by J Kurtz, JE Viñuales and M Waibel on the principles governing the global economy.

[48] See the chapters of G Abi-Saab on the system of the Declaration, of S Moyn and U Özsu on the historical origins of the Declaration and of P-M Dupuy on the Declaration at fifty.

certain conduct, the evaluation of conformity of a certain conduct, the interpretation of other norms, and a value-expressive function). Second, within 'principles', 'foundational' principles perform their value-expressive function in a distinctive manner. They do not only 'recognise' and 'store' value, but they do so for values that define the 'identity' of a legal order, a feature which is itself manifested by the 'architectural' function performed by such values in the definition of the structures and institutions of an order. Third, in international law, the 'fundamental principles' have been identified by the community of States or subsets thereof through initial statements (e.g. the 1941 Atlantic Charter[49]), then formal enactment (specifically Articles 1, 2 and 55 of the UN Charter[50]), and then restatements (a series of declarations and resolutions, most notably the 1970 Friendly Relations Declaration but also several others,[51] and restatements in the jurisprudence of the ICJ[52]). Fourth, these

[49] Joint Declaration of President FD Roosevelt and Prime Minister W Churchill, 14 August 1941, known as the 'The Atlantic Charter'.

[50] Charter of the United Nations, 26 June 1945, Arts 1(2) (referring to 'the principle of equal rights and self-determination of peoples' as a purpose of the organisation), 1(3) (referring to 'international cooperation' inter alia 'in promotion of respect for human rights and for fundamental freedoms for all without distinction as to race, sex, language, or religion', as a purpose of the organisation), 2(1) (stating the 'principle of sovereign equality' of States), 2(2) (stating the requirement to 'fulfil in good faith' the obligations assumed under the Charter), 2(3) (stating the requirement to 'settle their international disputes by peaceful means'), 2(4) (stating the obligation to 'refrain . . . from the threat or the use of force'), 2(7) (stressing that nothing in the Charter 'shall authorize the United Nations to intervene in matters which are essentially within the domestic jurisdiction of any state') and 55 (referring inter alia to the 'principle of equal rights and self-determination of peoples' and the promotion of 'universal respect for, and observance of, human rights and fundamental freedoms for all without distinction as to race, sex, language, or religion').

[51] See, among several other instruments: Universal Declaration of Human Rights, UNGA Res 217A (III) (10 December 1948); Declaration on the Granting of Independence to Colonial Countries and Peoples, UNGA Res 1514 (XV) (14 December 1960); Principles which Should Guide Members in Determining Whether or Not an Obligation Exists to Transmit the Information Called for under Art 73e of the Charter, UNGA Res 1541 (XV) (15 December 1960); UNGA Res 1803 (XVII); Declaration of Legal Principles Governing the Activities of States in the Exploration and Use of Outer Space, UNGA Res 1962 (XVIII) (13 December 1963); Declaration on the Inadmissibility of Intervention in the Domestic Affairs of States and the Protection of Their Independence and Sovereignty, UNGA Res 2131 (XX) (21 December 1965); Declaration of Principles Governing the Sea-Bed and the Ocean Floor, and the Subsoil Thereof, beyond the Limits of Nations Jurisdiction, UNGA Res 2749 (XXV) (17 December 1970); Stockholm Declaration (n 27); Declaration on the Inadmissibility of Intervention and Interference in the Internal Affairs of States, UNGA Res 36/103 (9 December 1981); Manila Declaration on the Peaceful Settlement of Disputes, UNGA Res 37/10 (15 November 1982); Rio Declaration on Environment and Development, 13 June 1992, UN Doc A/CONF.151/26.

[52] See inter alia: (1) on the prohibition of the use of force: *Nicaragua* case (n 35), paras 188, 191, 228, 264; *Legality of the Threat or Use of Nuclear Weapons*, Advisory Opinion, ICJ Reports 1996, 226 [*Legality of Nuclear Weapons*], paras 37–39; *Oil Platforms (Islamic Republic of Iran v United States of America)*, Judgment, ICJ Reports 2003, 161 [*Oil Platforms*], paras 43–78; *Legal Consequences of the Construction of a Wall in the Occupied Palestinian Territory*, Advisory Opinion, ICJ Reports 2004, 136 [*Wall Opinion*], paras 86–87 and 138–39; *Armed Activities on the Territory of the Congo (Democratic Republic of the Congo v Uganda)*, Judgment, ICJ Reports 2005, 168 [*DRC v Uganda*], paras 92–166; (2) on peaceful settlement of disputes: *North Sea Continental Shelf*, Judgment, ICJ Reports 1969, 3 [*North Sea Continental Shelf*], para 83–87; *Nicaragua* case (n 35), paras 290–91; (3) on non-intervention: *Nicaragua* case (n 35), paras 202–9, 264; *DRC v Uganda*, paras 155–65; (4) on co-operation: *Corfu Channel* case, Judgment, ICJ Reports 1949, 4 [*Corfu Channel*], 22–22; *North Sea Continental Shelf*, paras 83–87; *Legality of Nuclear Weapons*, paras 98–103; *Pulp Mills on the River Uruguay (Argentina v Uruguay)*, Judgment, ICJ Reports 2010, 14 [*Pulp Mills*], paras 90–122, 132–50; *Obligation to Negotiate Access to the Pacific Ocean (Bolivia v Chile)*, Judgment of 1 October 2018, ICJ General List No 153 [*Obligation to negotiate*], paras 86–87, 91, 146–47, 152, 158–59, 162, 165–67; (5) on self-determination: *Western Sahara*, Advisory Opinion, ICJ Reports 1975, 12, paras 48–78; *East Timor (Portugal v Australia)*, Judgment, ICJ Reports 1995, 90, para 29; *Wall Opinion*, paras 82, 88, 115–22, 156; *DRC v Uganda*, paras 222–50; *Accordance with International Law of the Unilateral Declaration of Independence in Respect of Kosovo*, Advisory Opinion, ICJ Reports 2010, 403, paras 79–84; *Legal Consequences of the Separation of the Chagos Archipelago from Mauritius in 1965*, ICJ, Advisory Opinion, 25 February 2019, paras 148–53; (6) on sovereign equality: *Corfu Channel*, 35; *Nicaragua* case (n 35), paras 202, 212–13, 251–52; *Jurisdictional Immunities of the State (Germany v Italy: Greece Intervening)*, Judgment, ICJ Reports 2012, 99, paras 57–58; (7) on good faith see: *Nuclear Tests (Australia v France)*, Judgment, ICJ Reports 1974, 253, para 46; *Elettronica Sicula Sp.A (ELSI)*, Judgment, ICJ Reports 1989, 15, 76–77; *Land and Maritime Boundary between*

fundamental principles or clusters thereof are representative of wider non-linear processes of emergence and norm contestation involving other competing concepts and principles, which are of great importance in understanding the origins and evolution of such principles. By way of illustration, a body of competing principles embodying what became known as the 'New International Economic Order' (NIEO)[53] found expression in the 1970s opposing, among others, the principles formulated in the late 1940s to govern international economic relations. The selection of the twelve principles and clusters thereof examined in this volume is designed to take into account such major waves of norm contestation driven by what could be summarily referred to as the North–South divide, Cold War politics and, more recently, the rise of environmental concerns and the digital revolution. The selected principles and clusters thereof are therefore intended not to describe what may appear as a linear or teleological evolution or a cannon set in stone but, quite to the contrary, to take into account these complex processes of norm contestation, with a range of possible outcomes. The 'iceberg' is identified by its 'tip' but the analysis is not confined to the tip; the object is the iceberg.

On the basis of these four considerations, the research object of this volume is given by twelve principles or clusters of principles: prohibition of the use of force, peaceful settlement of international disputes, non-intervention, co-operation, self-determination, sovereign equality, good faith, cardinal principles of international humanitarian law (necessity, distinction, proportionality and humanity), the principle of human dignity, the prevention of environmental harm (prevention, due diligence, co-operation, environmental impact assessment, precaution and sustainable development), the principles governing the global commons (prohibition of appropriation, freedom of use subject to due regard for other uses, and common management), and those principles governing international trade, monetary and investment transactions (sovereign prerogative – to set trade policy, exploit natural resources, and on monetary matters – and constraints on that prerogative – regarding market access, non-discrimination, treatment of aliens, and financial stability). I do not claim that these principles cover every single possible topic or area, but they do underpin, as required by their identity and architectural function, the most major international institutions: the UN Organization; the so-called 'International Bill of Rights';[54] the Hague/Geneva

Cameroon and Nigeria (Cameroon v *Nigeria: Equatorial Guinea intervening)*, Judgment, ICJ Reports 2002, 303 [*Cameroon* v *Nigeria*], paras 36–39; *Obligation to negotiate*, paras 86–87, 91, 146–47, 152, 158–59, 162, 165–67; (8) on human rights: *Corfu Channel*, 22; *Wall Opinion*, paras 86, 102–14, 123, 127–37; *DRC* v *Uganda*, paras 205–21, dispositif para 3; *Questions relating to the Obligation to Prosecute or Extradite (Belgium* v *Senegal)*, Judgment, ICJ Reports 2012, 422, paras 64–70; (9) on humanitarian law: *Nicaragua* case (n 35), paras 215–20, 254–56; *Legality of Nuclear Weapons*, paras 24–32, 46, 52–55, 85–97; *Wall Opinion*, paras 89–101; (10) on prevention of environmental harm: *Legality of Nuclear Weapons*, paras 27–36; *Pulp Mills*, paras 77, 101–2, 144–46, 204; *Certain Activities Carried Out by Nicaragua in the Border Area (Costa Rica* v *Nicaragua) and Construction of a Road in Costa Rica along the San Juan River (Nicaragua* v *Costa Rica)*, Judgment, ICJ Reports 2015, 665, paras 100–12 and 165–68; (11) on freedoms in common areas: *Nicaragua* case, paras 214, 251–53; *Land, Island and Maritime Frontier Dispute (El Salvador/Honduras: Nicaragua intervening)*, Judgment, ICJ Reports 1992, 351, para 419; *Case Concerning Maritime Delimitation and Territorial Question between Qatar and Bahrain (Qatar* v *Bahrain)*, Judgment of 16 March 2001, paras 169 et seq, 195 et seq, 223; *Cameroon* v *Nigeria*, paras 288 et seq; *Maritime Delimitation in the Black Sea (Romania* v *Ukraine)*, Judgment, ICJ Reports 2009, 61, paras 115–22; (12) economic activities: *Nicaragua* case (n 35), paras 244–45, 275–76; *Oil Platforms*, paras 45–52; *DRC* v *Uganda*, para 244.

53 See Declaration on the Establishment of a New International Economic Order, UNGA Res 3201 (1 May 1974); Charter of Economic Rights and Duties of States, UNGA Res 3281 (12 December 1974).

54 This expression is generally used to refer to the Universal Declaration of Human Rights as well as the International Covenant on Civil and Political Rights, 16 December 1966, 999 UNTS 171, and the International Covenant on Economic, Social and Cultural Rights, 16 December 1966, 993 UNTS 3.

Conventions;[55] the Stockholm/Rio Declarations[56] and most multilateral environmental agreements;[57] the WTO system;[58] the Bretton Woods Institutions;[59] and the systems of the Antarctic,[60] Outer Space[61] and the UN Convention on the Law of the Sea.[62]

It is also due to their identity and architectural functions, as modalities of the more general value-expressing function, that the study of fundamental principles can be a vector for a new and more granular synthesis of specialisms, general international law and restated or redefined values. This observation must be placed in the context of the broader goal of refreshing the collective memory of fundamental principles through renewed attention to them in international legal studies. This is also the reason why this volume brings together some of the most prominent figures of international law from different continents, generations but also intellectual traditions and approaches. What these contributors all share is their ability to be generalists and specialists. I am grateful for their commitment to this project, and I hope that their contributions will be an inspiration to the readers of this volume, as they have been for the author of these lines.

[55] See Hague Convention (II) with respect to the Laws and Customs of War on Land and its Annex: Regulations concerning the Laws and Customs of War on Land (29 July 1899); Convention (IV) Respecting the Laws and Customs of War and Land and its annex: Regulations concerning the Laws and Customs of War on Land (18 October 1907) and related Declarations; Geneva Convention for the Amelioration of the Condition of the Wounded and Sick in Armed Forces in the Field (First Geneva Convention), 12 August 1949, 75 UNTS 31; Geneva Convention for the Amelioration of the Condition of Wounded, Sick and Shipwrecked Members of Armed Forces at Sea (Second Geneva Convention), 12 August 1949, 75 UNTS 85; Geneva Convention Relative to the Treatment of Prisoners of War (Third Geneva Convention), 12 August 1949, 75 UNTS 135; Geneva Convention Relative to the Protection of Civilian Persons in Time of War (Fourth Geneva Convention), 12 August 1949, 75 UNTS 287; Protocol Additional to the Geneva Conventions of 12 August 1949, and Relating to the Protection of Victims of International Armed Conflicts, 12 August 1977, 1125 UNTS 3; Protocol Additional to the Geneva Conventions of 12 August 1949, and relating to the Protection of Victims of Non-International Armed Conflicts (Protocol II), 12 June 1977, 1125 UNTS 609.

[56] Stockholm Declaration (n 27); Rio Declaration (n 51).

[57] Treaties affirming the prevention principle or expressing its rationale include: Convention on the Prevention of Marine Pollution by Dumping of Wastes and Other Matter, London, 29 December 1972, (1972) 11 ILM 1294, preamble; Convention for the Protection of the World Cultural and Natural Heritage, Paris, 16 November 1972, (1972) 11 ILM 1358; Convention for the Conservation of Antarctic Seals, London, 1 June 1972, (1972) 11 ILM 251 [Convention on Antarctic Seals]; Convention on International Trade in Endangered Species of Wild Fauna and Flora, Washington, 3 March 1973, 993 UNTS 243; Convention on the Conservation of European Wildlife and Natural Habitats, Berne, 19 September 1979, (1982) UKTS 56 Cmnd 8738; Convention on the Conservation of Migratory Species of Wild Animals, Bonn, 23 June 1979, (1980) 19 ILM 15; Convention on Long-Range Transboundary Air Pollution, Geneva, 13 November 1979, (1979) 18 ILM 1442; Convention on the Conservation of Antarctic Marine Living Resources, Canberra, 20 May 1980, (1980) 19 ILM 841 [CCAMLR]; United Nations Convention on the Law of the Sea, Montego Bay, 10 December 1982, in force 16 November 1994, 1833 UNTS 3 [UNCLOS], Arts 192–94.

[58] See General Agreement on Tariffs and Trade, 30 October 1947, 55 UNTS 194; Agreement establishing the World Trade Organisation, 15 April 1994, 1867 UNTS 154.

[59] See Articles of agreement of the International Monetary Fund: adopted at the United Nations Monetary and Financial Conference, Bretton Woods, New Hampshire, 22 July 1944, as last amended effective 26 January 2016 by the modifications approved by the Board of Governors in Res No 66–2, adopted December 15, 2010; Articles of Agreement of the International Monetary Fund, 27 December 1945, 2 UNTS 39; International Bank for Reconstruction and Development, Articles of Agreement, adopted at the United Nations Monetary and Financial Conference, Bretton Woods, New Hampshire, 22 July 1944, as amended effective 27 June 2012.

[60] Antarctic Treaty, 1 December 1959, 402 UNTS 71; Convention on Antarctic Seals; CCAMLR; Protocol to the Antarctic Treaty on Environmental Protection, 4 October 1991, 30 ILM 1455.

[61] Treaty on Principles Governing the Activities of States in the Exploration and Use of Outer Space, including the Moon and Other Celestial Bodies, 27 January 1967, 610 UNTS 205.

[62] UNCLOS.

1

The System of the Friendly Relations Declaration

*Georges Abi-Saab**

I THE PRINCIPLES IN THE INITIAL DESIGN OF THE UN CHARTER

The UN Charter was designed to institutionalise and project into the future the 'Alliance of the Victorious Powers' of the Second World War, as well as their vision of what the post-war world should be. Such vision harboured great potentialities for the future, but it was largely premised, consciously or unconsciously, on the image and presumed structures of the pre-existing world as reflected in classical international law. This heritage is clearly apparent in Article 2 of the Charter, which lays down the 'principles' of the United Nations.[1]

These principles can be classified in three categories:

1. a 'structural' principle – sovereign equality (Article 2(1)) – in that it defines the legal nature of the treaty-based community created within the United Nations, a community of States which are sovereign and formally equal, in the meaning of classical international law
2. two principles delimiting the competences of the United Nations vis-à-vis Member States (Article 2(7)) and non-Member States (Article 2(6))
3. four principles which impose obligations on Member States, and which can in turn be divided into two sub-categories:
   (a) obligations of Member States vis-à-vis the United Nations, chiefly the duty to fulfil in good faith the obligations that they have undertaken under the Charter (Article 2(2)) and that to assist the United Nations in the performance of its functions (Article 2(5)), which is a particular application of the former duty
   (b) reciprocal obligations between Member States, namely the prohibition of the threat or the use of force (Article 2(4)) and the duty to settle their international disputes peacefully (Article 2(3)).

The conception of the international community and, above all, of its legal organisation, which is enshrined in Article 2, is clearly anchored in classical international law. Regarding the

* This chapter builds on the ideas expounded by the author in some previous work, particularly G Abi-Saab, 'La Reformulation des principes de la Charte et la transformation des structures juridiques de la communauté internationale' in *Le droit international au service de la paix, de la justice et du développement. Mélanges Michel Virally* (Pedone, 1991) 1–8.

[1] The Preamble of the Charter starts with 'We the peoples of the united nations'; and ends with 'have agreed to the present Charter . . . and do hereby establish an international organization to be known as the United Nations'. Thus, when the name United Nations or its initials UN are used they refer to the Organisation as such, unless the context indicates a reference to the membership of that Organisation as a whole.

'community' envisaged by the Charter, although the United Nations has a universal vocation, such universality is qualified. Its starting point is provided by the Alliance of Victorious Powers, which the United Nations seeks to extend. But potential aggressors, such as the former enemy States, so long as they have not been reformed, and States with similar regimes, are seen as bellicose by their very nature and hence kept *extra muros*. By contrast, the community is open to 'peace-loving' States (Article 4(1)), but there is no expectation that it will become universal immediately or in the short run. This explains the introduction of Article 2(6) of the Charter as well as the interest that this provision received at the time.[2] It also explains the old controversy as to whether the law of the Charter should be seen as general international law or, rather, as the special law of a more integrated 'community' within the broader international 'society', in which case the articulation between such 'special' law and general international law would have to be elucidated.

Whatever the answers given to such questions, the system of international law that emerges from Article 2 is no different, in its structure and characteristics, from classical international law ensuing from the Peace of Westphalia, namely the 'international law of co-existence', to borrow Wolfgang Friedman's expression.[3] This law came about as a result of the collapse of an international community, that of the 'World State of Medieval Christendom':[4] a feudal hierarchical community of values based on religion and common heritage and kept together at its apex by the 'double allegiance' to pope and emperor. But the advent of the age of discoveries and the emergence of strong polities challenging the authority of the emperor, comforted by the Reformation contesting the authority of the pope, led to the Wars of Religion. These, like all ideological wars, were total wars in the sense that the object of each belligerent was the annihilation of the adversary or its conversion to its own ideology. But when they realised that this was unattainable, they had to find a way out that allowed their co-existence in spite of their divisions. Whence the Peace of Westphalia that shuttered the hierarchical structure by recognising the prince as sovereign – that is, as having the last word in his polity. But for the system to be sustainable, each prince had to recognise the same status to the other princes, regardless of differences in size, power or ideology, namely the principle of formal equality, from which emerged the image of States as opaque billiard balls that only touch from the outside. This new system did not assume any community between its subjects except in having minimal rules of the game between potentially antagonistic units that permitted each to play and win at the expense of the others; a perfect zero-sum game. The alpha and omega of that system of law is thus the State, which the law takes as a given, acknowledging it as its very foundation, consecrated by the principle of 'sovereign equality' from which all other principles and rules are derived.

Indeed, in the overall logic of classical international law, there is only one general obligation, the respect for the sovereignty of others and, more specifically, of the spatial and functional bounds of such sovereignty, which is most clearly infringed when force is used against it. It is, of course, true that the assertion of the prohibition of the use of force had never been as categorical as in Article 2(4) of the Charter. But the rule was already undergoing a process of consolidation that had started well before and, in all events, it was a corollary of the respect for sovereignty. Article 2(3) of the Charter is, in turn, a corollary of the prohibition of the use of force. If force

[2] That provision was the only one in Article 2 that was considered as a 'legal revolution' by the standards of classical international law; as it was interpreted by some, e.g. Kelsen, as extending the jurisdiction of the Organisation beyond its conventional community of States.

[3] W Friedmann, *The Changing Structure of International Law* (Columbia University Press, 1964).

[4] P Vinogradoff, *Historical Types of International Law: Lectures Delivered in the University of Leiden* (Bibliotheca Visseriana, 1923) 1–70.

cannot be used to settle international disputes, then such settlement must be sought through peaceful means.

Similarly, respect for sovereignty can only become operational if the spatial and functional bounds of sovereignty are defined. This explains the obsession of classical international law with the delimitation of the respective ambits of sovereignties and the definition of international law, at least since Vattel,[5] as a law of allocation and delimitation of competencies among its subjects. This is reflected in Article 2 of the Charter in the two paragraphs which address the powers of the United Nations vis-à-vis non-Member States (Article 2(6)) and Member States (Article 2(7)). The latter merely restates, in terms of jurisdiction, the obligation of the United Nations to respect the sovereignty of Member States.

Moreover, if the only general obligation resulting from the 'sovereign equality' postulate is an obligation of abstention, that is not to say that States cannot voluntarily undertake other obligations, whether to perform or to abstain from a certain conduct. But if they do so, they have to discharge their obligations in good faith, including those obligations arising from their participation in an international organisation. And that is precisely what is stated in Article 2, paragraphs (2) and (5) of the Charter.

Hitherto, we are not very far from Westphalia. But it would be a truncated reading of Article 2 if we stopped at that. For, in order to discover the full potentialities of this article and its possible role as a 'juncture' between the past and the vision of the future of the drafters of the Charter, it has to be read in the context of Article 1, which sets out the purposes of the United Nations, and in the pursuit of which 'the Organization and its Members' are enjoined to 'act in accordance with' the principles of Article 2. There is thus a symbiotic relationship between the two provisions.

Article 1 lays down a blueprint of a three-layered strategy of sustainable peace.[6] It responds rapidly and most forcefully to the highest urgencies of the threat to peace and breaches of peace, while proceeding progressively on a longer timescale to address the deep roots of tensions and conflicts that lead to such emergencies. Thus, the first and paramount purpose (Article 1(1)) is the maintenance of international peace and security; which is normal for an organisation born out of war. What is more remarkable is the way it has conceived this task by representing peace as a 'common and indivisible good' in which everyone, and above all the United Nations itself, has an interest, hence a standing to act in order to protect it, preventively through the system of pacific settlement of disputes in Chapter VI of the Charter and, correctively, by the system of collective security of Chapter VII. The second purpose of the United Nations (Article 1(2)), that can be called perfecting the international system, seeks to improve the environment and framework within which international relations unfold and to enhance their stability and predictability. It is pursued by various means and, first, by the development of 'international co-operation in the political field' with which the Charter associates the encouragement of 'progressive development of international law and codification' (Article 13(1)(a)), in order to develop friendly and confident relations among nations. The third purpose – reaching for the socio-economic and other substantive sources of conflict – is to promote international co-operation in other areas, such as the economic, social and cultural fields, as well as that of human rights. The fourth purpose – which is of a different organizational nature – is to use the United Nations itself as an arena and framework for such co-operation in all these fields.

[5] E de Vattel, *Le Droit des gens, ou principes de la loi naturelle appliqués à la conduite et aux affaires des Nations et des Souverains* (1758).

[6] G Abi-Saab, 'The Role of International Law in the Peace Strategy of the Charter' in *Is Universality in Jeopardy?: Report of a Symposium Organized by the United Nations in Connection with the Commemoration of the Fortieth Anniversary of the Organization (Geneva, 16–17 December 1985)* (UN, 1987) 35–49.

Thus, starting from the principles of Article 2, and the initial doubly partial community of the Victorious Powers of the Second World War (in terms of membership) around the Charter regime of maintenance of peace and security (in terms of subject matter), the diligent pursuit of the purposes of Article 1 was to extend co-operation to all fields of international relations. In other words, according to the initial design of the Charter, through the creation of a 'security community',[7] the United Nations would have provided the appropriate framework for the progressive integration of international society, by multiplying and deepening the areas of co-operation among its expanding membership so as to bring it to a point where it may be globally called the 'international community', governed by a community-centred law, the 'law of co-operation' to be discussed below.

II THE ORIGINS OF THE FRIENDLY RELATIONS DECLARATION

Much has been written on the process that started in 1960 leading to the adoption, in 1962, by the UN General Assembly of Resolution 1815 (XVII),[8] and culminating in the adoption by consensus of the 'Declaration on Principles of International Law concerning Friendly Relations and Co-operation among States in accordance with the Charter of the United Nations' on 24 October 1970, at the session commemorating the twenty-fifth anniversary of the United Nations.[9] My purpose here is not to review this process, which is examined later in this volume,[10] but to draw attention to two aspects of this process, namely its genesis and trigger, and the contemporaneous understanding of what the process meant.

The question of examining the basic principles of international law within the process of 'progressive development of international law and its codification' (Article 13(1) of the UN Charter) was raised for the first time during the XV session of the UN General Assembly, in 1960, within its Sixth (Legal) Committee and, more specifically, during the Committee's review of the report of the twelfth session of the International Law Commission (ILC). The discussion was triggered by the strong criticism levelled by several delegates from the socialist bloc regarding the work of codification and progressive development in general, its slow pace, inefficient methods, meagre results and, above all, the political reasons why key questions relating to international peace and security, such as the definition of aggression, had been removed in favour of minor questions such as arbitral procedure. The criticism had itself a strongly political tone. The Soviet delegate, Mr Morozov, observed for example that:

> The reasons for that disturbing situation were not technical but political. The proposal to define aggression had been opposed in the International Law Commission and the Sixth Committee by the United States and its allies, so that they would be left free to pursue their policy of aggression in Korea, Egypt, China, the Congo, Algeria and elsewhere. Those same Powers were trying to prevent principles categorically condemning colonialism and proclaiming the right of all peoples to exploit their natural resources as they saw fit from being included in the covenants

[7] The term 'security community' was coined by Karl Deutsch in KW Deutsch et al, *Political Community and the North Atlantic Area* (Princeton University Press, 1957). It refers to a community within which conflicts are settled exclusively by peaceful pre-established methods.

[8] Consideration of Principles of International Law Concerning Friendly Relations and Co-operation among States in Accordance with the Charter of the United Nations, UNGA Res 1815 (XVII) (18 December 1962), A/RES/1815 (XVII).

[9] Declaration on Principles of International Law Concerning Friendly Relations and Co-operation among States in Accordance with the Charter of the United Nations, UNGA Res 2625 (XXV) (24 October 1970), Annex [Friendly Relations Declaration]. See the bibliographic survey provided in the Introduction by JE Viñuales in this volume.

[10] See the chapter by S Moyn and U Özsu in this volume.

> of human rights. Thus, the importance of international law was being ignored, and the Sixth Committee was no longer fulfilling its proper function.[11]

The criticism concerned, more specifically, the UN Office of Legal Affairs, which was perceived to be pro-Western and also, significantly, the approach taken with regard to the work on State responsibility. According to Morozov:

> The International Law Commission had confined itself to dealing with the international responsibility of the State for injuries caused in its territory to the person or property of aliens. That was not in accordance with the instructions given the Commission under resolution 799 (VIII). There was no justification for so narrow an attitude, for the imperialist States were daily interfering in the internal affairs of other States, and it was therefore indispensable that the principles of international law relating to illegal acts committed by States should be codified. Consequently, the draft articles called for study on a very broad basis.[12]

The two issues were thus combined. The then Director of the Codification Division and Secretary ex officio of the ILC, Dr Liang (from 'nationalist' China), was criticised for his narrow approach and partial attitude, such as involving Harvard Law School, a private Western institution, in the work of the ILC on State Responsibility. Such an initiative, likely undertaken at the behest of the first Special Rapporteur on this issue, Mr Garcia Amador from Cuba, was denounced as partial and beyond the Secretariat's mandate.[13] The same criticism was quickly endorsed by delegates from African, Asian and Latin American States. We should remember that 1960 was Africa's year in the United Nations when seventeen new members were admitted, sixteen African States and Cyprus. Those, as other newly independent States, harboured strong grievances against classical international law which justified and legitimated their subjugation and exploitation. They wanted to effectively participate in the development of a renewed international law purified of archaic and unjust institutions, more inclusive and equitable.[14]

The upshot of these strong criticisms was an equally strong call for a revision and reorientation of the work on the 'progressive development of international law and its codification' towards matters far more topical and crucial for an international society marked by the Cold War and decolonisation. In the words of Morozov, the ILC 'should first of all give priority to the principles governing the relations between States', which would include 'the principles governing State responsibility in the event of violation of national sovereignty and of the right

[11] Morozov (USSR), A/C.6/SR.651 (XV), para 5.

[12] ibid, para 9.

[13] Czernik (Czecholslovakia), A/C.6/SR.655 (XV), para 4. It seems that this incident was what most irked the Socialist delegates, and it may have served as the trigger for this scaling controversy. The first Special Rapporteur, FV Garcia Amador (Cuba), appointed in 1955, had done post-graduate studies at Harvard Law School. It was probably on his suggestion that the UN Secretariat sought formally the collaboration of the School. Anecdotally, I had personal exposure to this episode, but from a very different angle, which I described in another context as follows: 'there are many stories I can tell you, starting again from my days at Harvard Law School, where I worked for some time as a research assistant to Professors Sohn and Baxter in a project on the rules of state responsibility for injuries to aliens. We had one article each, as we were many students working on it ... We had to compile all the precedents of nineteenth century and early-twentieth-century mixed arbitral commissions, etcetera. At the same time, I was very interested in the subject of domestic jurisdiction in economic affairs, and went frequently to the United Nations where delegates were discussing permanent sovereignty over natural resources. After several months' work on the research project, I abandoned what I did; didn' t even claim for work done; as I thought that law should go forward, not backward': 'A Conversation with Georges Abi-Saab' (2017) 111 *ASIL Proceedings* 211, 218. The work undertaken by Sohn and Baxter on State responsibility was an extension of the codification tradition initiated by Manley O Hudson for the League of Nations' Hague Codification Conference of 1930.

[14] See G Abi-Saab, 'The Newly Independent States and the Rules of International Law: An Outline' (1962) 8 *Howard Law Journal* 95.

of peoples to self-determination'.[15] We see clearly the juncture between the old and the new, to which I alluded earlier in the context of Article 2 of the Charter. The starting point for the Soviet delegate and the other critics from Socialist countries was clearly a classical one:

> The codification of such principles would be a step forward in the direction of codification of rules of international law calculated to foster the peaceful coexistence of States with different political and economic systems, and would at the same time rouse the United Nations from its torpor in regard to legal matters.[16]

After much discussion regarding which principles would be included in the work, a question on which the nature of the process (progressive development, codification, mere interpretation of pre-existing norms) depended, a consensus was reached to focus on the principles of Article 2 while adding two other principles, derived from Article 1(3) on 'purposes', the duty to co-operate and self-determination, in a set of seven 'basic' principles to be treated.[17]

Thus, embedding the exercise in the pre-existing principles (whether in Article 2 or Article 1) of the Charter turned it into an exercise in authentic interpretation, although the Friendly Relations Declaration strikes a balance between different views.[18] But much more important is the fact that by reformulating the initial set of principles, some of their latent potentialities were given expression, considering the fact that the partial 'community' initially envisaged at the time of the adoption of the Charter had expanded to englobe a large majority of the States by 1970, which required a reformulation of the principles.

It is this reformulation that must be brought to light, which I hope to do by examining the Friendly Relations Declaration from a double point of view. The first focuses on the internal architecture of the Declaration and the articulation of the different principles included therein with one another. The second looks at the Declaration, taken as a whole, from an external point of view as an important landmark depicting the state of the international legal system and the international community underlying it at that moment in time.

III THE ARCHITECTURE AND SIGNIFICANCE OF THE FRIENDLY RELATIONS DECLARATION

Unlike Article 2 of the UN Charter, the principles of the Friendly Relations Declaration are no longer formulated essentially from the perspective of the relations between the United Nations and States (Members or non-Members), but exclusively in inter-State terms, namely as principles of general international law rather than the special law of a conventional community. Paradoxically, as I shall discuss later, this effort to formulate the principles exclusively in inter-State terms revealed the impossibility of confining international law, as it had evolved by then, only to such a set-up.

[15] Morozov (USSR), A/C.6/SR.651 (XV), para 10.

[16] ibid.

[17] See P-H Houben, 'Principles of International Law Concerning Friendly Relations and Co-Operation among States' (1967) 61 *American Journal of International Law* 703.

[18] The preamble of the Declaration refers to the 'progressive development and codification of the following principles'. However, in its conclusive 'general part', it recalls that '[n]othing in this Declaration shall be construed as prejudicing in any manner the provisions of the Charter or the rights and duties of Member States under the Charter or the rights of peoples under the Charter, taking into account the elaboration of these rights in this Declaration'. Finally, the Declaration concludes that 'the principles of the Charter which are embodied in this Declaration *constitute* basic principles of international law' (emphasis added). This means that the General Assembly considered them *lex lata*, which accredits the characterisation of the Declaration as an authentic interpretation, reflecting the contemporaneous understanding of these principles by the totality of the membership, as fleshed out or elaborated in the Declaration in the light of the previous twenty-five years of practice and reflection.

Yet, the main contribution of the Friendly Relations Declaration is not found at this purely formal level or even in the elaboration of each principle, but in the overall architecture of the Declaration and the careful balance it strikes amongst the different principles.

This observation is not meant to belittle the substantial contribution of the Declaration to the specific formulation of the principles, though nothing in such formulation is to 'be construed as prejudicing in any manner the provisions of the Charter'.[19] As noted earlier, the objective of the exercise progressively crystallised into providing an authentic interpretation of the principles of the Charter in the light of the experience gained during the first twenty-five years of the United Nations. Some of the latent potentialities of the Charter took form in practice and in the perception of States. The principles became more concrete and tangible with the specification, from case to case but also through normative resolutions adopted by the General Assembly, of their legal reach and consequences. The principles thus emerged from the legal 'limbo' to which they had been confined in the classical international law of the nineteenth and early twentieth centuries, namely that of postulates so general and abstract that, while commanding widespread support, they could only perform an axiological and logical/integrative function of the system as a whole but not any concrete regulative function of State conduct.

The practice of the United Nations and of States not only gave vent to certain potentialities of the UN Charter, including those in Article 2, it also correlated these principles in the sense of situating them in relation to each other and allocating them respective weights in consequence. It is this correlation, distilled from twenty-five years of practice, which the Friendly Relations Declaration endeavoured to capture and reflect. As before, we can ask what conception of the international community and its legal organisation emerges from the Declaration, and to what extent it differs from that distilled initially from Article 2 of the UN Charter.

At first sight, there seems to be no radical change. The principle of sovereign equality keeps its role of structural principle. But little is added to its content and understanding as compared with 1945. The Declaration merely replicates the formal (or purely definitional) implications of this principle which appeared already in the *travaux préparatoires* of the Charter, adding however a more substantial one (letter (e), which provides that '[e]ach State has the right freely to choose and develop its political, social, economic and cultural systems'). Another even more substantial implication, namely the recognition of permanent sovereignty over natural resources, was proposed but finally left out due to disagreement not over its inclusion or its content but over its specific formulation.

By contrast, the main corollary of the general obligation to respect sovereign equality – namely the prohibition of the use of force or, when surreptitious, the principle of non-intervention – received substantial elaboration in the Declaration. The different situations of prohibited use of force as well as the legal consequences of such use ('crime against the peace', responsibility, illegality of occupation and annexation, obligation of non-recognition) are articulated in detail (they were further specified in 1974 with the adoption of UN General Assembly Resolution 3314 (XXIX) on the 'Definition of Aggression'[20]). The same exercise was conducted for situations amounting to unlawful intervention in matters within the domestic jurisdiction of States. On the other hand, little if anything is added to the substantive understanding of the principle of peaceful settlement of international disputes or that of good faith.

Yet, the examination of the Friendly Relations Declaration, taken as a whole, leaves the impression that the central place formerly held by the principle of sovereign equality in Article

[19] Friendly Relations Declaration, operative para 2.
[20] Definition of Aggression, UNGA Res 3314 (XXIX) (14 December 1974), A/RES/3314.

2 of the UN Charter has waned. This is because it is relativised and, to some extent, counterbalanced by the two remaining principles of the Declaration transposed from Article 1 on the purposes of the UN, namely 'the principle of equal rights and self-determination of peoples' and 'the duty of States to co-operate with one another in accordance with the Charter'. These were not new as they already existed as potentialities in the Charter, in the sense that their normative components could be found therein, but without being explicitly put together and articulated. In the twenty-five years between the UN Charter and the adoption of the Friendly Relations Declaration, however, they acquired a greater coherence, visibility and practical importance, which made possible their inclusion in the Declaration as fully fledged principles.

The principle of equal rights and self-determination of peoples features in the UN Charter (already under the label 'principles') as the basis of friendly relations among nations, the development of which is one of the United Nations' purposes (Article 1(2)), as well as of the international co-operation underpinning such friendly relations (Article 55). The Friendly Relations Declaration moves a step further from the Charter in that it makes self-determination not only a foundational component but also a sufficiently concrete principle from which rights and obligations can be directly derived. The more this principle becomes operational the more it reveals its potential for disrupting the architecture of classical international law, which takes the State as its starting and final point and unique centre of gravity. The principle overtakes the States in two different directions. The holder of self-determination, now understood as an actual right, is not the State but another entity, a 'people'. This is an infra-State entity in that it is formally and effectively subject to the power of a State against which the right to self-determination is asserted. But the State is overtaken in an opposite direction as well. For what can be the legal rationale of such right, which would have been an intolerable transgression of the sovereignty of the latter State in the logic of classical international law, if not a public interest superior to States: that of the community of States as a whole, which gives priority to a certain collective value over the individual interests of its members. This, in turn, means that such right can be claimed *from* and *by* the international community, and that it could neither exist nor operate in a purely inter-State context.

The other principle transposed from Article 1 that emerges in the Friendly Relations Declaration is the 'duty to co-operate', which despite its innocuous appearance, harbours a potentially disruptive effect in its inner logic. The UN Charter imposes on Member States the duty to give the United Nations 'any assistance in any action it takes in accordance with' the Charter (Article 2(5)), particularly in the context of collective security. But in its reformulation in the Friendly Relations Declaration, this duty is no longer conceived as a treaty-based obligation, which is limited *ratione personae* and *ratione materiae*, but as a general international law obligation. In the logic of classical international law, the only general obligation was that of respect for the sovereignty of others or, in other words, of non-trespass on their territorial and functional ambits. It was an obligation of abstention, consistent with the formal equality among States, which makes abstraction of any real differences among them. After all, the abstention of the elephant and of the mouse is the same, but obviously the action of each of them is not. Yet, the duty to co-operate is not one of abstention but one of action, even of joint action, which implies an allocation of tasks according to the respective needs and capabilities of different States, as well as a certain degree of oversight over the discharge of such tasks. These are the characteristics of the other variety of international law, 'the law of cooperation' according to Friedmann.[21]

[21] See Friedmann (n 3). For further discussion of this dichotomy see G Abi-Saab, 'Whither the International Community?' (1998) 9 *European Journal of International Law* 248.

In contrast to the 'law of co-existence', which aimed at keeping the antagonistic members of a shuttered community 'peacefully apart', the law of co-operation aims at 'bringing' States 'actively together'[22] in a community around a perceived collective interest or value that cannot be promoted and protected at all or adequately by unilateral action.

It is true that the formulation of the duty to co-operate in the Friendly Relations Declaration is succinct and cautious, and that the only clause that goes beyond what is expressly stated in the Charter ('States *should* co-operate in the promotion of economic growth throughout the world, especially that of developing countries') uses the term 'should' (although the French version keeps the prescriptive form 'doivent'). But the very logic of the duty goes beyond the classical conception of sovereign equality in two main ways: first, by challenging the postulate of 'formal' equality; and, second, by piercing, in so doing, the opaque veil of sovereignty of the 'billiard ball' State in classical international law in order to take into consideration the real disparities among and within States for the allocation of the respective rights and obligations entailed by the duty to co-operate.

Thus, the Friendly Relations Declaration, while echoing the initial vision of the structure of the international community enshrined in the UN Charter, with sovereign equality as its pivotal norm and its two necessary – and sufficient – consequences, the prohibition of the use of force and of intervention, qualifies this structure by making a leap beyond the purely inter-State framework in two directions: on the one hand, it reaches for the very sources of the legitimacy of State power (rather than starting from the State as such as a premise); on the other hand, it imposes a positive obligation of action (co-operation) which pierces the State shell and takes into account the real situation and sources of inequality within and among States, thus extending the ambit of international legal regulation to the intra-State level.

The legal structure of the international community, as it emerges from the Friendly Relations Declaration, reveals a community in transition between two different ages, undergoing a difficult phase of evolution, worked up by two fundamentally different logics, competing for the domination of the whole province of international law. One is well established and fully elaborated, but is somewhat overtaken and struggling breathlessly to keep pace with the tremendously fast and complex evolution of events and ideas that marked the world since 1945. The other is young and vigorous, but still seeking its way and its fields of expansion into the areas abandoned or left vacant by the older logic as well as in the new expanses opened by the prodigious evolution of the world. The balance between these two logics is dynamic and unstable, and its evolution is not linear but subject to constant readjustments, which could, in certain conjunctures, give place to tectonic movements in the underlying architecture of the legal system.

The UN Charter reflected the old logic, but it contained, perhaps unconsciously and in embryonic form, the promise of the new one. The Friendly Relations Declaration of 1970, integrating twenty-five particularly eventful years of practice and maturation of ideas, went a long way in fulfilling this promise, giving expression to the latter logic, particularly in its reformulation of self-determination and, to a lesser extent, the duty to co-operate, while seemingly preserving the leading role of the older logic.

[22] D Mitrany, *A Workable Peace System* (Royal Institute of International Affairs, 1943).

IV LOOKING AHEAD

At the time of writing these lines, fifty years after the adoption of the Friendly Relations Declaration, the analysis that I had proposed in 1991, shortly after the end of the Cold War,[23] seems to find support in the evolution of the international legal system, with one major caveat. I would like to end this chapter with some brief observations on both the analysis and the caveat.

The new logic given vent in the Friendly Relations Declaration benefited from the acceleration and the intensification of the double process of overtaking and penetration of the State. The State shell became increasingly translucid veering to transparent not only in practice, owing to the information and communication revolution as well as economic globalisation; but also legally, with the increasing penetration of international law in matters hitherto reserved to the domestic jurisdiction of States. In the first years of the 1990s, one of the basic tenets of sovereign equality, the right of states freely to choose their political and economic organisation (as well as the correlative tenet of permanent sovereignty over natural resources and economic activity), was even called into question by what some saw as the emergence of a 'democratic' principle or entitlement[24] and the so-called Washington consensus, which dictated the supposedly correct economic model that had to be followed.[25] Some rushed to announce the 'end of history',[26] with the triumph of 'liberal' or rather 'market democracy'; an oxymoron that masks the new faces of hegemony.

But doubtful doctrines and policies beget doubtful responses; and here comes the caveat, for since the early 2000s, the older logic seems to have been reinvigorated and to progressively gain ground. As noted in the introduction to this volume, the current international context seems inauspicious for a genuine celebration of the principles enshrined in the Friendly Relations Declaration, some of which being now openly challenged in various forms, whether through the unlawful annexation of territory, targeted killings, cyberattacks or other forms of blatant intervention, etc.

This swing of the pendulum is but a repositioning of the two logics, away from the brief lull that some mistakenly took, in the early 1990s, for a stable and final equilibrium. But the two logics remain fully at play. The classical logic has found expression in the reclusive and egoistic policies of some States in the military and economic fields, which defy the very essence of the international law of co-operation and aimed at imposing their hegemony. But the logic of co-operation has also found powerful expression in the renewed claims against inequality and in the

[23] Abi-Saab (n *) 7–8.

[24] T Franck, 'The Emerging Right to Democratic Governance' (1992) 86 *American Journal of International Law* 46.

[25] See the chapter by J Kurtz, JE Viñuales and M Waibel in this volume. This model recalls the 'open door policy' that Western powers imposed in the nineteenth and early twentieth centuries (with echoes in the mandate system of the League of Nations) on the few formally independent non-Western States (mainly serving as buffers between their colonial empires) and practised in some of their colonies (to avert colonial wars between themselves); a policy that laid bare the natural resources and markets of those non-Western countries and colonial territories to the exploitation of foreign economic interests.

[26] F Fukuyama, *The End of History and the Last Man* (Free Press, 1992), restating an adapted version of the Hegelian thesis. Ironically enough, it was the adepts of economic liberalism who were then advocating the 'withering away of the State', a basic tenet of Marxist doctrine. But giving free reign to the market as sole principle of social-economic organisation, without social-public control, leads to the worst kind of social Darwinism. This is not, however, the only type of social organisation compatible with material globalisation. Anecdotally, during the celebration in 1998 of the fiftieth anniversary of the GATT, Fidel Castro was asked what he thought of globalisation. His answer was 'what do I think of the law of gravity?', referring to material or technological aspects of globalisation. But he immediately added 'I am all for the globalisation of solidarity.'

accumulation of sufficient normative substance for the formulation of two fully fledged principles on the protection of human rights and the environment, which, at the time of the Declaration, were treated as mere fields of co-operation. Thus, the dialectical struggle between the two logics continues in their competition over the possible legal responses to the present concerns of humanity.

In the face of an increasingly pressing demand for governance of a highly complex and accelerating technological revolution and economic globalisation as well as for adequate protection against global threats such as pandemics, global warming and transnational terrorism, we observe, on the one hand, a strong centripetal push towards collective global responses to such global needs and challenges. But we also observe, on the other hand, the pull of centrifugal atavistic reflexes of falling back into oneself, with the hope of coming out better, albeit at the expense of the others. Yet, to borrow a definition of the Common Law, humanity usually ends up 'stumbling into wisdom', but not before exhausting the alternatives.

2

The Historical Origins and Setting of the Friendly Relations Declaration

Samuel Moyn and Umut Özsu

I INTRODUCTION

The 1970 Friendly Relations Declaration is a peculiar document.[1] This is so even by comparison to the battery of legally non-binding but rhetorically charged and politically resonant General Assembly resolutions with which the non-aligned world created through decolonisation attempted to craft a new international order in the decades after the Second World War. Consisting of seven basic concepts of contemporary international law, the 1970 resolution purports to map the rules, norms and practices that States and international lawyers are willing to recognise as necessary for a real commitment to 'friendly relations'. It spells out with varying degrees of clarity and specificity a host of propositions, many of which had already found at least partial expression in multilateral treaties, UN resolutions and rules of customary international law prior to October 1970, when the resolution was finally adopted formally. The result is a lengthy and at times unwieldy document cobbled together through a series of complex negotiations – an instrument that is more a patch-and-mend aggregation of bits and pieces of conceptual furniture than it is a crystalline conceptual blueprint for the new world orders envisioned by the greater and lesser powers of the 1960s.

This chapter revisits the Friendly Relations Declaration's negotiating history, situating it in a broader account of the legal, political, economic and conceptual developments that informed the Declaration's preparation. While mindful of the limitations of official UN records, edited with technocratic decorum by international civil servants and only seldom strictly verbatim transcriptions of actual discussions, it is our view that these summary records, which are often remarkably detailed and intricate, help to reveal the basic structural parameters within which competition between distinct visions of world order were articulated during the course of the Declaration's negotiations. Most of these negotiations were organised around rivalries between a 'First World' struggling by the end of the 1960s with an overproduction-induced decline in the rate of profit and the effective end of the post-war cycle of capital accumulation, a 'Second World' of socialist industrialisation hampered by ageing Stalin-era bureaucratic apparatuses, and a 'Third World' that was largely non-aligned and comprised in the main of countries established through imperial withdrawal or liberation struggle. The official records illuminate the points of

[1] Declaration on Principles of International Law Concerning Friendly Relations and Co-operation among States in Accordance with the Charter of the United Nations, UNGA Res 2625 (XXV) (24 October 1970), Annex [Friendly Relations Declaration].

contact and rupture, lines of agreement and disagreement, that brought these blocs together to make the Declaration.

Formally speaking, the story of the Friendly Relations Declaration begins in 1961, when the General Assembly's Sixth Committee – the UN organ responsible for considering legal matters, producing draft conventions and participating in the process of 'codification and progressive development' that also occupied the International Law Commission – began to take steps toward its preparation.[2] In 1963 the General Assembly authorised the constitution of a special committee that would breathe life into the UN Charter's opaque references to 'friendly relations' – an expression this instrument never defined clearly and satisfactorily[3] – and draft what would eventually become the 1970 declaration.[4] This committee represented a range of different States and alliances (China was the largest power to be excluded), and it undertook extensive deliberations over the course of the next seven years, holding six rounds of negotiations, in 1964, 1966, 1967, 1968, 1969 and 1970.[5] These involved intense, fractious and exceptionally wide-ranging rounds of bargaining, with countless proposals, amendments and counter-proposals being considered in connection with seven legal principles: non-intervention, sovereign equality, inter-State co-operation, peaceful dispute settlement, the prohibition against the threat or use of force, equal rights and self-determination of peoples, and bona fides fulfillment of obligations under the Charter. The content and scope of each of these concepts was – and has always been – deeply contested. That they overlap in numerous ways complicated the negotiations, as did the fact that both the Cold War and competition within the Non-Aligned Movement (NAM) continued unabated during the 1960s. The committee thus found itself discussing such developments as the Vietnam War, the Congo crisis, the Biafran War, the 1967 Arab–Israeli War, and colonial wars in Portuguese Angola, Guinea and Mozambique.[6] In addition to a large number of treaties and other legal instruments, from the 1885 Treaty of Berlin to the 1963 Partial Test Ban Treaty, the committee also considered contemporaneous General Assembly resolutions, chief among them the 1960 Declaration on the Granting of Independence to Colonial Countries and Peoples,[7] the 1962 Declaration on Permanent Sovereignty over Natural Resources,[8] the 1963 Declaration on the Elimination of All Forms of Racial Discrimination,[9] and the 1965 Declaration on the Inadmissibility of Intervention in the Domestic Affairs of States and the Protection of Their Independence and Sovereignty.[10] Among the noted international lawyers who served as delegates to the committee and constructed

[2] See esp UNGA Res 1686 (XVI) (18 December 1961). See also UNGA Res 1815 (XVII) (18 December 1962).
[3] UN Charter, Arts 1(2), 14, 55.
[4] UNGA Res 1966 (XVIII) (16 December 1963).
[5] See Report of the Special Committee on Principles of International Law concerning Friendly Relations and Co-operation among States, UN Doc A/5746 (1964) [Report I]; Report of the Special Committee on Principles of International Law concerning Friendly Relations and Co-operation among States, UN Doc A/6230 (1966) [Report II]; Report of the Special Committee on Principles of International Law concerning Friendly Relations and Co-operation among States, UN Doc A/6799 (1967) [Report III]; Report of the Special Committee on Principles of International Law concerning Friendly Relations and Co-operation among States, UN Doc A/7326 (1968) [Report IV]; Report of the Special Committee on Principles of International Law concerning Friendly Relations and Co-operation among States, UN Doc A/7619 (1969) [Report V]; Report of the Special Committee on Principles of International Law concerning Friendly Relations and Co-operation among States, UN Doc A/8018 (1970) [Report VI].
[6] Interestingly, one report registers a dispute as to whether debates about such conflicts should be recorded in it. A proposal from the US delegation that they not be recorded was set aside after the Soviets voiced strong objections. Report III, paras 476 (US), 478 (USSR).
[7] UNGA Res 1514 (XV) (14 December 1960).
[8] UNGA Res 1803 (XVII) (14 December 1962).
[9] UNGA Res 1904 (XVIII) (20 November 1963).
[10] UNGA Res 2131 (XX) (21 December 1965). See also UNGA Res 2160 (XXI) (30 November 1966).

arguments on the basis of these precedents were Gaetano Arangio-Ruiz (Italy), Hans Blix (Sweden), Jorge Castañeda (Mexico), Mohammed el-Baradei (Egypt), Taslim Elias (Nigeria), Milan Šahović (Yugoslavia), Stephen Schwebel (United States), Ian Sinclair (United Kingdom) and Michel Virally (France).

We argue that the Declaration's seven principles ought to be understood as belonging to two groups. The first group comprises non-intervention, sovereign equality and the prohibition against the threat or use of force. These principles were associated first and foremost with the drive to reinforce and consolidate State sovereignty, including, centrally, the sovereignty of newly independent States arising from the post-1945 wave of decolonisation in Asia, Africa, Oceania and the Caribbean. They were distinguished by a commitment not simply to de jure sovereignty, understood as 'legal' or 'political' independence, but also to 'economic' independence, if not unconditionally then at least to an important degree. By contrast, the second group of principles consists of inter-State co-operation, peaceful dispute settlement, and good faith satisfaction of obligations under the Charter. These principles were associated with a desire to expand the depth and scope of international co-operation, injecting increased solidarism into an international order conventionally conceived in largely anarchical terms, with each State going to great lengths to defend its territorial and jurisdictional autonomy, at its most extreme in the kind of presumption against restrictions on sovereignty that the Permanent Court of International Justice posited as a foundational principle in its 1927 *Lotus* judgment.[11] Crucially, the principle of equal rights and self-determination of peoples acted as a kind of free-floating principle, dovetailing with both groups and understood as a means of bolstering State sovereignty and forging transnational solidarity alike, with potentially destabilising implications that needed to be contained to preserve the State system's structural integrity.

The chapter analyses the relation between these two groups of principles in light of the dynamic tension between sovereignty and solidarity that underwrote so much of the international law of post-1945 decolonisation. The principles of non-intervention, sovereign equality and the prohibition against the threat or use of force were grounded in a sovereigntist approach to international law and world order. For their part, the principles of inter-State co-operation, peaceful dispute settlement, and good faith satisfaction of obligations were informed to a significant degree by the rhetoric of co-operation and interdependence, which circulated widely at the time and left a particularly important mark on legal instruments prepared at the behest of socialist and non-aligned States. To be sure, conceptual relations between the two sets of principles were always close, and the boundary between them was anything but impermeable. Yet an analytical distinction can and should be drawn, as it speaks to the fact that the Declaration was understood by nearly all delegates as an attempt to manage what Columbia University law professor Wolfgang Friedmann termed the transition from the 'international law of co-existence' to the 'international law of co-operation'.[12]

At root, the Declaration was a product of a decades-long push by socialist States, newly independent States, and national liberation movements to transform and radicalise the international law that had been restructured after the Second World War. Its final form did not always reflect the desires of these States and movements, particularly since the committee's deliberative procedure was premised upon the search for consensus.[13] But it was nevertheless an

[11] *Case of the SS 'Lotus' (France v Turkey)*, PCIJ Rep Ser A, No 10 (1927).

[12] Wolfgang Friedmann, *The Changing Structure of International Law* (Columbia University Press, 1964).

[13] For consideration of this procedure, see eg Report II, paras 37, 350 (Sweden), 352 (US), 571 (Lebanon); Report VI, para 223 (UK).

outgrowth of this commitment to update and revise international law. Still, it is important to note that, far from jettisoning existing international law in its entirety, this transformative project preserved important elements of it. Writing in the pages of the *Revue égyptienne de droit international* in 1973, Georges Abi-Saab, the Egyptian lawyer and professor who had already established himself as one of the leading Third World jurists of his generation, explained that newly independent States had developed a dual strategy in regard to international law after securing independence. Having 'realized that while certain rules of the existing international legal order – such as those regulating State succession and State responsibility – are not compatible with their interests, others – such as the principles of sovereign equality, non-intervention and prohibition of threat or use of force – provide them, as the weaker members of the international community, with a much needed protection', Third World States had come 'to adopt a more eclectic attitude': 'instead of rejecting the system as a whole, they claimed the right to re-examine its rules and to retain only those which are compatible with their interests'.[14]

With the 1970 declaration the Third World scored some important points, argued Abi-Saab in the same piece, pointing in particular to 'the recognition for the first time by the West of self-determination as a legal right', the 'wide definition given to the principle of non-intervention to include political and economic pressure', and 'the explicit enunciation of the prohibition of territorial acquisition by force and the obligation not to recognise it as valid legal title'.[15] As Abi-Saab noted, Western powers had often resisted the push to articulate new conceptions of international law rooted in the Charter, only with more conceptual specificity and legal significance, at the outset of negotiations. The Declaration's acclamation against this initial resistance, Abi-Saab argued, showed that international law held promise for a new era of decolonised States.[16] The kind of international law the Third World sought to cultivate would anchor itself in positivist models of national sovereignty in cases where the new States' freedom of action in regard to internal socio-economic development was jeopardised. However, it would also underscore the need for broader understandings of transnational solidarity where 'common interests and collaborative efforts' were thought necessary to effect a more just and equitable global distribution of rights and resources.[17] The 1970 declaration, adopted in the year of the Charter's twenty-fifth anniversary,[18] was the formal validation of this approach, writ into the record of international law with equal parts conservatism and reformist imagination.

II THE DECLARATION IN GLOBAL CONTEXT

For a time in the 1960s and 1970s, one domain in which the global South's enthusiastic struggle in 'world-making' manifested itself was the attempt to transform international law.[19] Although this struggle was ultimately circumvented by great power politics and newer forms of

[14] Georges Abi-Saab, 'The Third World and the Future of the International Legal Order' (1973) 29 *Revue égyptienne de droit international* 27, 38. This paper was originally presented at a conference at Princeton University in June 1972 on the future of the international legal order. It does not appear in Cyril E Black and Richard A Falk (eds), *The Future of the International Legal Order*, 4 vols (Princeton University Press, 1969–72).

[15] Abi-Saab (n 14) 48.

[16] ibid 40.

[17] ibid 59–62.

[18] Report VI, paras 96 (Chile), 158 (Yugoslavia), 238 (Japan).

[19] Adom Getachew, *Worldmaking After Empire: The Rise and Fall of Self-Determination* (Princeton University Press, 2019). This section of the essay follows here and there Samuel Moyn, 'The High Tide of Anticolonial Legalism', *Journal of the History of International Law* (forthcoming).

international law and international organisation, it was a crucial moment. It merits attention in its own right, and as the essential context for the Friendly Relations Declaration.

In recent years, much scholarly effort has been expended on revealing the imperial context of the history of international law, from the early modern period to the twentieth century. Puzzlingly, though, very little has been written on the decolonising moment for the field as a whole. The decolonising moment in the history of international law, generally unstudied amid an accumulating literature on the co-constitutive relations between law and imperialism, therefore deserves attention. After all, there is no way to register the fate of international law in its relation to a world of unequal power and wealth if the hopes attached to its attempted decolonisation are omitted.[20] The international lawyers who drove the project of decolonising international law and who came into their own during the 1960s and 1970s, both intellectually and professionally, belonged to a transnational generation of elite specialists. As Abi-Saab has recently put it, among them were representatives of new States who were 'Third World intellectuals', and who typically regarded themselves as insider-outsiders to a hoary enterprise whose plausibility had to be tested and might remain wanting. As they themselves recognised, posing the question of whether international law was in principle open to a decolonising renovation left them 'like Robinson Crusoe, shipwrecked on a desert island', seeking others who were similarly situated and willing to operate in a metropolitan language to generate a common discussion.[21]

One particularly important point of convergence was the shared belief that developments in the 1960s had the potential to transform international law in light of the decolonisation project – precisely as the negotiations around the Declaration kicked off. 'There is no doubt about it', Dutch international lawyer B. V. A. Röling wrote as the decade opened, that 'the traditional law of nations is a law of European lineage'.[22] But now it would have to be given up for something untraditional. Was it possible, Röling wondered, for a Europe that had 'gambled away its power and prestige in European wars' to 'demand or even expect that its law will continue to be

[20] A decade ago, one of us wrote that 'the decolonization of international law' had been neglected in the booming literature on the field's history, 'in spite of much interest in the imperial context of legal thought in earlier eras'. Samuel Moyn, *The Last Utopia: Human Rights in History* (Harvard University Press, 2010) 320. The situation has improved, but the evaluation remains fundamentally sound. Martti Koskenniemi's field-redefining *The Gentle Civilizer of Nations: The Rise and Fall of International Law 1870–1960* (Cambridge University Press, 2001) features empire but omits decolonisation, as does Jennifer R Pitts's excellent *Boundaries of the International: Law and Empire* (Cambridge University Press, 2018). Antony Anghie's landmark *Imperialism, Sovereignty, and the Making of International Law* (Cambridge University Press, 2005) devotes a full chapter to decolonisation, but the book is not intended as a sustained study of its (many and varied) legal implications. A brilliant theoretical venture, Sundhya Pahuja's *Decolonising International Law: Development, Economic Growth, and the Politics of Universality* (Cambridge University Press, 2011) is not intended as a history per se. One notable example of a study that does focus squarely on decolonisation, though, is Matthew Craven, *The Decolonization of International Law: State Succession and the Law of Treaties* (Cambridge University Press, 2007). Note that several new collections relating to decolonisation and international law have recently become available. See Luis Eslava, Michael Fakhri and Vasuki Nesiah (eds), *Bandung, Global History, and International Law: Critical Pasts and Pending Futures* (Cambridge University Press, 2017); Jochen von Bernstorff and Philipp Dann (eds), *The Battle for International Law: South-North Perspectives on the Decolonization Era* (Cambridge University Press, 2019); (2019) 21 *Journal of the History of International Law* 161–329 (special issue on 'Revisiting State Socialist Approaches to International Criminal and Humanitarian Law'). See also several chapters in Martti Koskenniemi, Walter Rech and Manuel Jiménez Fonseca (eds), *International Law and Empire: Historical Explorations* (Oxford University Press, 2017). See further Umut Özsu, *Completing Humanity: The International Law of Decolonization, 1960–82* (Cambridge University Press, forthcoming).

[21] Georges Abi-Saab, 'The Third World Intellectual in Praxis: Confrontation, Participation, or Operation Behind Enemy Lines?' (2016) 37 *Third World Quarterly* 1957, 1958.

[22] BVA Röling, *International Law in an Expanded World* (Djambatan, 1960) 10.

universally respected'?[23] Or could 'only a revised law be capable of winning that world-wide respect without which no world community can prosper, now that the community within which that law will be carried out has expanded quantitatively and changed qualitatively?'[24] Röling's answer to the first question was resoundingly negative.[25] And fortunately, a 'common law of mankind', as Wilfred Jenks – legal advisor to and later director-general of the International Labour Organization – called it, was emerging from the chrysalis of an international law largely of, by, and for white Christian States.[26] The principal reason was quite simply that a small portion of humans had devised international law. The vast expansion in the number of States – in 1960 itself sixteen entered the United Nations from Africa alone – mandated change. From the turn of the twentieth century to 1960, the number of widely recognised States had already grown exponentially, and the majority of this growth had materialised in the decade and a half since 1945 – when the number of European States actually declined (the Baltic countries had disappeared, while Malta would secure its independence in 1964) as that of African and Asian States skyrocketed.

This growth in the number of States – which has doubled since 1960 – redefined the entitlement of their peoples to count in the first place, as the criterion of eligibility for entrance into the world of States shifted radically. However honoured in the breach, the nineteenth-century expansion from 'Christian' to 'civilised' States as the community of subjects of international law, primarily a cosmetic alteration in language but still permitting some inclusionary gestures towards non-Christian peoples, already portended a flexibility that would now have to be stretched even further to accommodate the global explosion of subjectivity. The UN Charter had gone so far as to drop the criterion of 'civilisation' for inclusion, allowing all 'peace-loving' States membership.[27] Yet what was at stake – neither before nor after the high tide of anti-colonial legalism – was not 'globalisation' or the expansion of the geographical scope of international law, which imperialism had long since accomplished. Rather, as Abi-Saab noted in 1962, this 'revolutionary process' concerned its new authorship, and therefore its potentially new content. 'It is undeniable', he observed, 'that contemporary international law found its origin in the Christian Commonwealth of Europe.' Even so, 'saying that the field of international law has expanded' counted as a gross error since 'international law already covered the whole world' thanks to centuries of empire. 'The basic change', he concluded, 'is the transformation of very large parts of the globe, mostly in Africa and Asia, from objects to subjects of international law.'[28]

Transformation on this scale and over such a short period of time itself constituted an experiment, or trial, that could well have failed. 'The newly independent states are not the legislators of the world', Abi-Saab acknowledged in 1962.[29] But with numerical strength they were not powerless, and the bipolar structure of the Cold War afforded them a certain opening.

[23] ibid 13.

[24] ibid 13.

[25] ibid 15–16. Röling's was the first in a book series he co-edited with his fellow dissenting judge of the Tokyo War Crimes Tribunal, India's Radhabinod Pal, entitled 'Contributions to the Progressive Development of International Law'. On their role there see David Cohen and Yuma Totani, *The Tokyo War Crimes Tribunal: Law, History, and Jurisprudence* (Cambridge University Press, 2018), chs 11–13.

[26] C Wilfred Jenks, *The Common Law of Mankind* (Praeger, 1958). On Jenks's time at the ILO see Guy F Sinclair, *To Reform the World: International Organizations and the Making of Modern States* (Cambridge University Press, 2017) 105–6.

[27] UN Charter, Art 4. On this see also Röling (n 22), chs 3–5.

[28] Georges M Abi-Saab, 'The Newly Independent States and the Rules of International Law: An Outline' (1962) 8 *Howard Law Journal* 95, 97–98.

[29] ibid 100.

It was unclear whether a system that 'claims the allegiance of nations which had no part in building it up, and which either have never known, or no longer accept, the fundamental beliefs and sentiments on which it was originally founded' would continue to prove 'alien' to new participants or would instead come to be accepted as an endeavour in which they had a stake or even a sense of co-origination. So wondered Oxford jurist James Brierly, one of the leading anglophone international lawyers of his time, in the last revision of his *The Law of Nations* in 1955, the year of his death.[30] Decolonisation posed the problem of whether seizing tools of power and authority within an international legal system organised around exploitation and subordination could facilitate that system's transformation into one designed for co-operation, co-ordination and possibly even collective emancipation. The question appeared to many at the time to be an open one.

In general, Third World States favoured the General Assembly, where they controlled a majority during an era in which the Security Council was paralysed by ideological and geopolitical deadlock. Observers of the early stages of the process often concluded that the activism of the new States had vindicated the competence of the United Nations generally and the General Assembly in particular to make new law.[31] At the root of the new approaches to treaty, custom and other forms of international law that these States struggled to cultivate was the momentous claim that such law should follow from, and track the interests of, self-determining peoples and the sovereign States they constituted. For post-colonial States, self-determination made their sovereignty without condition. It was not the case – as it sometimes is today – that sovereignty was premised upon responsibility to higher principles (such as human rights). Rather, an international law undergoing decolonisation would first and foremost need to impose responsibility on former masters to cease and desist from empire. Sovereignty 'for the Asians has often had the connotation of an absolute authority of almost mystical quality', Indonesian international lawyer J. J. G. Syatauw contended in a 1961 treatise growing out of his Yale doctorate.[32] It 'is the most treasured possession of the newly independent States', echoed Surya Prakash Sinha, the first Indian national to become a US law professor, in 1965: 'On the one hand, it makes them the master of their own house and, on the other hand, it provides them with a legal shield against foreign incursions or attempts thereat by stronger States.'[33] This emphasis was itself an old affair. The basic response of politico-economically weaker States to the international law they inherited – notably illustrated in the legal and political actions of Latin American States, and also of the Soviet Union before the Second World War – had long been to double down on sovereignty and to emphasise once again its foundational character in international law. Since a

[30] JL Brierly, *The Law of Nations: An Introduction to the International Law of Peace* (5th edn, Clarendon Press, 1955) 44.

[31] See eg Rosalyn Higgins, *The Development of International Law through the Political Organs of the United Nations* (Oxford University Press, 1963); Michel Virally, 'Droit international et décolonisation devant les Nations Unies' (1963) 9 *Annuaire français de droit international* 508, esp 533–41. In the early 1960s RP Anand was an enthusiastic supporter of the ICJ as an agent of renovation, while others were sceptical in view of the procedure for appointing judges and the depressing outcome of the long-running *South West Africa* cases. See RP Anand, 'Rôle of the "New" Asian-African States in the Present International Legal Order' (1962) 56 *American Journal of International Law* 383. Meanwhile, Radhabinod Pal, in some respects the godfather of decolonising international lawyers, was closely watched for his activities in the ILC. See eg Radhabinod Pal, 'Future Role of the International Law Commission in a Changing World' (1962) 9 *United Nations Review* 31; Radhabinod Pal, 'International Law in a Changing World' in C Wilfred Jenks et al (eds), *International Law in a Changing World* (Oceana, 1963) 89.

[32] JJG Syatauw, *Some Newly Established Asian States and the Development of International Law* (Springer, 1961) 225.

[33] S Prakash Sinha, 'Perspective of the Newly Independent States on the Binding Quality of International Law' (1965) 14 *International and Comparative Law Quarterly* 121, 127.

non-interventionist posture could help to lock in hard-won gains, decolonisation's new States laid 'great stress on the otherwise dwindling concept of national sovereignty'.[34]

The Friendly Relations Declaration's ratification of the formal equality of sovereignty spoke to a passionate desire to reaffirm that principle, and dismay about its incomplete status and practical ineffectiveness. Generally traced back to Emer de Vattel, who had applied it inconsistently beyond the European monarchies, the principle was viewed by Third World jurists as having since suffered abandonment and abuse. In his two-part chronicle of this process and its legacy, R. P. Anand, the US-educated doyen of international legal studies in India, explained that while it had been affirmed in the 1943 Moscow Declaration and UN Charter, the principle of sovereign equality sat rather uneasily with the reality of increased concentration of real power on the international legal plane, notably the Security Council's domination by five States that were more equal than the rest and the General Assembly's relegation to a frequently marginal and symbolic role. Anand therefore agreed with Canadian-American jurist and Princeton professor Percy Corbett that the Charter's recognition of sovereign equality amounted to 'a striking manifestation of the persisting appeal of face-saving phrases in international politics'.[35] However, Anand hoped, the Friendly Relations Declaration project might now yield the final expulsion of these remnants of colonialist hierarchy from the corpus of accepted international law.[36]

Recognition of self-determination and sovereignty meant that non-interference in a decade of transnationalised war rose to the forefront of negotiations for the Friendly Relations Declaration. After all, these negotiations began in the shadow of the Algerian War, while their latter stages coincided with the escalation by the United States and its allies of the Vietnam War, which also wrought havoc in Cambodia and Laos. After 1965 international lawyers the world over struggled even more than usual with the meaning of statehood, especially the status of civil war and national liberation. For Third World international lawyers, the violence of American intervention in what they generally understood to be a national liberation struggle propelled them to lend credence to insurgencies that claimed the mantle of States-in-the-making, and also to forbid great power interventions.

Ultimately, though, this project of decolonising international law would be meaningful only insofar as it succeeded in transforming the exploitative relations that linked North to South and improving the lives of the world's poor. 'A status of economic under-development', Friedmann noted in 1963, 'will produce certain attitudes and approaches toward international law ... The community of outlook will last as long as a community of interests.'[37] Among the first fruits of the new States' growing confidence was the General Assembly's recognition of the principle of 'permanent sovereignty over natural resources' in 1962.[38] This articulation of economic self-determination – the right of each people and State to own and exploit the natural resources of its

[34] RP Anand, 'Attitude of the Asian-African States Toward Certain Problems of International Law' (1966) 15 *International and Comparative Law Quarterly* 55, 69.

[35] RP Anand, 'Sovereign Equality of States in International Law – Part I' (1966) 8 *International Studies* 213, 241 (citing PE Corbett, *Law and Society in the Relations of States* (Harcourt, Brace & Co, 1951) 264–65, and synthesising a rich prior literature on the topic).

[36] RP Anand, 'Sovereign Equality of States in International Law – Part II' (1966) 8 *International Studies* 386, 399–402 (on the Friendly Relations Declaration project).

[37] Wolfgang Friedmann, 'The Position of Underdeveloped Countries and the Universality of International Law' (1963) 2 *Columbia Society of International Law Bulletin* 5, 6, 9.

[38] UNGA Res 1803 (XVII). The path to the principle began a decade earlier. See Integrated Economic Development and Commercial Agreements, UNGA Res 523 (VI) (12 January 1952); Right to Exploit Freely Natural Wealth and Resources, UNGA Res 626 (VII) (21 December 1952). For a good contemporaneous discussion see Karol N Gess, 'Permanent Sovereignty over Natural Resources: An Analytical Review of the United Nations Declaration and Its

territory, regardless of colonial-era agreements – was not to make it into the Friendly Relations Declaration's affirmation of sovereign equality, let alone prove the first inkling of a new international economic order. Indeed, it never escaped the opprobrium that advanced capitalist States and private investors imposed on it. But in the 1960s the assertion of permanent sovereignty over natural resources looked like a breakthrough use of international law to advance post-colonial ends. As Christopher Dietrich has shown, Arab jurists such as Mohammed Bedjaoui and Muhammad Mughraby dreamt big about resource sovereignty's capacity to make major inroads in global hierarchy (especially for those States with oil and gas buried under the ground).[39] 'Self-determination' could mean expulsion not just of political masters but of 'foreign' economic interests.

Having begun with the United Nations's proclamation of its first 'development decade', the 1960s did not live up to expectations.[40] Many development economists, international lawyers and UN officials were impressed by the work of Raúl Prebisch and Hans Singer, both of whom argued that the price of commodities produced in the global South had experienced a long-term decline relative to the price of manufactured goods, produced largely in the global North.[41] None of this would find direct expression in the Friendly Relations Declaration. But the debates that made the Declaration cannot be understood independent of the resulting pressure to reinvent 'co-operation' from an anodyne concept not far from co-existence to one that entailed the renovation and socialisation of international law in a welfarist spirit.[42]

The proposals mooted during the post-1945 wave of decolonisation were varied, ranging from the idea of a legal obligation for wealthy countries to meet a specified minimum of foreign aid to more aggressive price control schemes to counter the deterioration of the terms of trade studied by Prebisch, Singer and others. Yet meeting the long-term goal of economic equality of States was always the desired bottom line, the ultimate measure of what 'sovereign equality' should mean. This objective was too radioactive to find clear expression in the Friendly Relations Declaration project, but in the same timeframe the Group of 77, NAM, UN Conference on Trade and Development, and a variety of other international organisations and fora facilitated discussions that led to the General Assembly's formal inauguration of the New International Economic Order project in two key resolutions on 1 May 1974.[43] This was the high tide of anti-

Genesis' (1964) 13 *International and Comparative Law Quarterly* 398. For a comprehensive recent analysis see Nico Schrijver, *Sovereignty over Natural Resources: Balancing Rights and Duties* (Cambridge University Press, 1997).

39 Christopher RW Dietrich, *Oil Revolution: Anticolonial Elites, Sovereign Rights, and the Economic Culture of Decolonization* (Cambridge University Press, 2017) 150–6. More generally, Dietrich comments, '[t]he union of development economics to the international law of decolonization centralized the anticolonial elite experience' (30).

40 For one reflection of early hopes about the US role in developing the world, see Louis Henkin, 'Les Nations nouvelles: le droit international et leur besoin d'assistance' (1960) 38 *Revue de droit international, de sciences diplomatiques et politiques* 422.

41 Raúl Prebisch, *The Economic Development of Latin America and Its Principal Problems* (United Nations Department of Economic Affairs, 1950), UN Doc E/CN.12/89/Rev.1; Hans W Singer, 'The Distribution of Gains Between Investing and Borrowing Countries' (1950) 40 *American Economic Review* 473. See further John Toye and Richard Toye, 'The Origins and Interpretation of the Singer-Prebisch Hypothesis' (2003) 35 *History of Political Economy* 437.

42 Much of this pressure was applied by socialist and non-aligned States. For useful contextualisation, see Milan Šahović, 'Codification des principes du droit international des relations amicales et de la coopération entre les États' (1972) 137 *Recueil des Cours* 243, 260 et seq.

43 Declaration on the Establishment of a New International Economic Order, UNGA Res 3201 (S-VI) (1 May 1974); Programme of Action on the Establishment of a New International Economic Order, UNGA Res 3202 (S-VI) (1 May 1974). See further Charter of Economic Rights and Duties of States, UNGA Res 3281 (XXIX) (12 December 1974). On this link between the Friendly Relations Declaration and the NIEO instruments, see esp Mohammed Bedjaoui, *Towards a New International Economic Order* (Holmes & Meier, 1979) 154; Georges Abi-Saab, Progressive Development of the Principles and Norms of International Law Relating to the New International Economic Order: Report of the Secretary-General, UN Doc A/39/504/Add.1 (1984), paras 130–32 et seq.

colonial legalism – a legalism both positivistic and committed to 'socialising' international law, prepared to leverage conventional legal forms but also keen to distance itself from conventional legal formalism.

III THE SOVEREIGNTIST DECLARATION

Considered as a package, the principles of non-intervention, sovereign equality and the prohibition against the threat or use of force broach questions about the meaning and scope of State sovereignty. Aside from the principle of self-determination, which proved to be exceptionally complicated, the prohibition on force consumed more of the special committee's time and energy than any other principle.[44] Often considered to be 'the most important' principle of the lot, it was touted as a 'corner-stone of the contemporary international legal order and of the co-operation, friendly relations and peaceful co-existence of States'.[45] As late as the committee's final round of meetings in 1970, agreement had been reached on neither it nor the principle of self-determination.[46] This was hardly surprising, seeing as how the question of how international law would govern coercive violence had been a fixture of debates about the future of the world order spearheaded by the United Nations since its inception in 1945. While Article 2(4) of the Charter famously prohibited the threat or use of force, Article 51, linchpin of the crucial Chapter VII, affirmed an equally important exception for action undertaken urgently for reasons of individual or collective self-defence.

How 'force' was to be understood now, decades of experience with the post-war settlement having been accumulated in the interim, was a matter of some import, particularly in light of the open wars then raging from Congo to Palestine and Rhodesia to Vietnam (not to mention clandestine conflicts such as the one that left its mark in Cuba, with the US-backed counter-revolutionary invasion at Bay of Pigs in 1961).[47] The complexity of the 'present world situation' and the destructive power of large nuclear arsenals added to the controversy.[48] As much as all delegates knew that the Declaration would typically be regarded as legally non-binding,[49] they were also aware that it would have a significant degree of symbolic power, particularly in the global South. In this sense, that it would contribute to the further development of rules of customary international law favourable to national liberation movements and newly independent countries, however crucial in its own right, was almost secondary in importance to the broader political influence it would exert. Using or threatening force, understood narrowly in the form of conventional military action or more capaciously to include a variety of less visible forms of coercive violence, struck at the heart of debates about the nature and limits of State sovereignty in an international legal order with no single superordinate authority and therefore requiring robust networks of horizontal collaboration.

[44] On the latter principle see the chapter by O Corten in this volume.

[45] Report III, para 29; Report II, para 31. See also Report IV, para 29.

[46] Report VI, paras 22, 35. On the relationship between the two principles see also Report II, para 141.

[47] For a sense of how such issues were addressed, see eg Report III, para 41.

[48] Report IV, paras 39, 42.

[49] Gaetano Arangio-Ruiz, a noted international lawyer, would later draw upon his experience as an Italian delegate to examine the legal status of this and other General Assembly resolutions. See Gaetano Arangio-Ruiz, *The UN Declaration on Friendly Relations and the System of the Sources of International Law* (Sijthoff & Noordhoff, 1979), chs 1–2. For an interesting argument that the Declaration, 'the most important single statement representing what the Members of the United Nations agree to be the law of the Charter on these seven principles', is somewhere between mere recommendation and legally binding instrument, though somewhat 'closer to the latter', see Robert Rosenstock, 'The Declaration of Principles of International Law Concerning Friendly Relations: A Survey' (1971) 65 *American Journal of International Law* 713, 714.

To a significant degree, the debate about force turned on the question of how to read the Charter, which marked a significant advance from the Drago Doctrine, the League of Nations Covenant and the 1928 Kellogg-Briand Pact, to take but a few of the traditional landmarks cited by delegates during the negotiations.[50] Article 2(4) enjoined UN Member States to 'refrain in their international relations from the threat or use of force against the territorial integrity or political independence of any State, or in any other manner inconsistent with the Purposes of the United Nations'. Nearly every component of this formulation – 'threat', 'use', 'State', 'force', 'territorial integrity', 'political independence' and 'international relations' – became an object of controversy in the committee.[51]

The meaning of the word 'force' was unsurprisingly the centrepiece of this debate. On the one hand, most advanced capitalist countries sought to confine the term to 'armed force', this being understood in the sense of both conventional armed attack and the commission of terroristic acts and incitements to civil strife in other States.[52] They argued that this was in accord with the letter and spirit of the Charter, and that a Brazilian effort to have economic and political measures integrated into a prohibition on force had been defeated at the 1945 San Francisco Conference.[53] On the other hand, most socialist and non-aligned States sought to broaden it to encompass economic, political and other forms of coercion in inter-State relations, noting that this would give fullest effect to the Charter's purposes and principles, not to mention the term 'force' itself, with the hope of encouraging international law's progressive development.[54] In addition to being concordant with the general approach taken at the 1955 Bandung Conference and recent meetings of non-aligned States in Cairo, Belgrade and elsewhere, it would accord with the 1965 declaration on intervention, which also prohibited economic, political and related forms of coercion.[55]

Some argued that express support for disarmament and a clear condemnation of war propaganda, including first-strike nuclear war policies, should be included in the text,[56] and some

[50] Report I, para 33; Report II, para 31; Report III, para 30. The Drago Doctrine – named after Luis María Drago, the Argentine foreign minister who first propounded it in late 1902 – repudiated the legality of military force to recover debts from Latin American States. So seriously was it taken by US jurists and policy-makers that it ultimately became the first document to be reproduced in the supplement to the first issue of the *American Journal of International Law*; see Luis M Drago, Note From the Argentine Ministry of Foreign Relations and Worship, 29 December 1902, reproduced in (1907) 1 *American Journal of International Law Supplement* 1. The Covenant enjoined League Member States 'to respect and preserve as against external aggression the territorial integrity and existing political independence' of all other member States, stating that '[i]n case of any such aggression or in case of any threat or danger of such aggression the Council shall advise upon the means by which this obligation shall be fulfilled'. Covenant of the League of Nations Adopted by the Peace Conference at Plenary Session, signed 28 April 1919, Art 10, reproduced in (1919) 13 *American Journal of International Law Supplement* 128, 131–32. States parties to the Pact of Paris, or Kellogg-Briand Pact, renounced war and committed themselves to peaceful dispute settlement; see General Treaty for Renunciation of War as an Instrument of National Policy, signed 27 August 1928, 94 LNTS 57.

[51] Report I, paras 36–46.

[52] ibid, paras 29 (UK), 106; Report II, para 27 (Australia, Canada, UK, US); Report III, paras 23 (Australia, Canada, UK, US), 24 (UK); Report IV, paras 23 (Australia, Canada, UK, US), 24 (UK), 51, 119 (UK).

[53] Report I, paras 49–51, 55, 59–63; Report II, para 67.

[54] Report I, paras 27 (Czechoslovakia), 28 (Yugoslavia), 31 (Ghana, India and Yugoslavia), 48, 57–58, 106; Report II, paras 25 (Czechoslovakia), 26 (Algeria, . . .), 28 (Chile), 66, 71–74; Report III, paras 22 (Czechoslovakia), 26 (Algeria, . . .), 52; Report IV, paras 22 (Czechoslovakia), 26 (Algeria, . . .), 50, 52–54. The Czechoslovak proposal spoke of 'other form of pressure', and the joint non-aligned proposal of 'other forms of pressure', while the Yugoslav proposal made note of 'pressure, whether by military, political, economic, or any other means'.

[55] Report II, para 76; UNGA Res 2131 (XX). For useful synopses of the points of contention in regard to the meaning of 'force', see Report III, paras 55–56; Report IV, para 28.

[56] Report I, paras 27 (Czechoslovakia), 95, 99–100, 106; Report II, paras 29 (Italy, Netherlands), 83–84, 105–6; Report III, paras 25 (Italy, Netherlands), 27 (Argentina, . . .), 64, 79–80; Report IV, paras 25 (Italy, Netherlands), 27 (Argentina, . . .), 59–60, 78–79.

chose to express greater concern about States facilitating terrorism and organising armed bands and irregular volunteer forces.[57] First World delegates felt comfortable restricting the legality of force to decisions made by duly authorised UN organs and circumstances in which the 'inherent' right of self-defence was engaged, tellingly also making allowance for 'regional agencies' (like the North Atlantic Treaty Organization).[58] By contrast, Second and Third World representatives omitted the reference to such agencies but included the right of peoples to self-defence 'against colonial domination, in the exercise of their right to self-determination'.[59] This last point naturally proved controversial, and was rejected by many First World delegates on the grounds that commitment to decolonisation and self-determination neither justified nor necessitated armed rebellion, particularly since it engaged the ambiguities of traditional conceptions of 'just war'.[60] This stance provoked a ferocious response in 1968, when the Soviet delegation to the fourth round of negotiations dropped all pretence of diplomatic decorum and condemned 'supporters of colonialism' for the committee's failure to reach agreement on the question of force.[61]

One point of debate, seemingly inconsequential but substantively crucial, was whether the prohibition of force applied across not simply settled territorial boundaries but also 'international lines of demarcation'. A joint proposal from Australia, Canada, the United Kingdom and the United States – all settler-colonial States – favoured the inclusion of such a reference,[62] and was defended on the basis that 'most of the situations which had necessitated peace-keeping operations by the United Nations had arisen precisely in connexion with international lines of demarcation', which were instituted to 'put an end to the use of force and to permit the application of the peaceful methods of settlement provided for in the Charter'.[63] However, representatives of other States questioned whether this was merely a way of assimilating armistice lines into the category of territorial borders and thereby bringing them within the purview of the norm of territorial inviolability.[64] This would have had wide-ranging consequences for divided territories like Cyprus, Israel–Palestine, Kashmir, and Vietnam, effectively ratifying changes on the ground brought about through the actions of those States most capable of effecting such change.

Given the level of controversy surrounding the threat or use of force, an observer of the negotiations might have been forgiven for believing the question of non-intervention to be a comparatively straightforward one.[65] Many international lawyers believed the prohibition against

[57] Report I, paras 29 (UK), 106; Report II, paras 27 (Australia, Canada, UK, US), 29 (Italy, Netherlands); Report IV, paras 23 (Australia, Canada, UK, US), 24 (UK), 61. However, the American delegation did argue for the legality of 'hot pursuit'. Report I, para 117 (US). The Italian-Dutch proposal was an exception in that it did both.

[58] Report I, para 29 (UK); Report II, para 27 (Australia, Canada, UK, US); Report IV, paras 23 (Australia, Canada, UK, US).

[59] Report I, paras 27 (Czechoslovakia), 28 (Yugoslavia), 31 (Ghana, India and Yugoslavia), 83–85, 106; Report III, paras 26 (Algeria, . . .), 101–2; Report IV, paras 22 (Czechoslovakia), 26 (Algeria, . . .), 103, 106–7, 110, 121 (USSR), 123 (Syria).

[60] Report I, paras 86–89, 106; Report III, para 104; Report IV, paras 104–5, 108, 119 (UK), 131 (Australia). For astute analysis of contemporaneous debates about competing interpretations of 'just war', see Jessica Whyte, 'The "Dangerous Concept of the Just War": Decolonization, Wars of National Liberation, and the Additional Protocols to the Geneva Conventions' (2018) 9 *Humanity* 313.

[61] Report IV, para 121 (USSR).

[62] Report II, paras 27 (Australia, Canada, UK, US), 94–97; Report IV, paras 23 (Australia, Canada, UK, US), 24 (UK). This proposal came to receive support from certain Latin American delegations. See Report III, para 27 (Argentina, . . .); Report IV, para 27 (Argentina, . . .).

[63] Report III, para 71. See also Report IV, para 67.

[64] Report III, para 70.

[65] On non-intervention see the chapter by D Tladi in this volume.

intervention in matters falling within domestic jurisdiction to be firmly established in the UN Charter and relevant customary international law. That this was not in fact the case became clear shortly after the special committee began to turn its attention to the question.

Like the debate about force, the debate about intervention was organised around shifting relations between advanced capitalist countries on the one hand and socialist and non-aligned countries on the other. At the outset of the negotiations, the first group argued that the content and scope of the term 'intervention' could not be determined definitively given the realities of an increasingly networked world. As the British and Americans put it during the first round of negotiations in 1964, 'in an interdependent world, it is inevitable and desirable that States will be concerned with and will seek to influence the actions and policies of other States, and that the objective of international law is not to prevent such activity but rather to ensure that it is compatible with the sovereign equality of States and self-determination of their peoples'.[66] Partly with an eye to the ongoing war in Vietnam, where the United States and its allies sought to justify their intervention on the grounds that they had been invited to do so by Saigon, they also stressed that a State which had been subject to unlawful intervention had the right to request and receive aid from third States.[67] By contrast, formal proposals from socialist and non-aligned States – Czechoslovakia, Ghana, Guatemala, India, Lebanon, Mexico, Syria, the United Arab Republic and Yugoslavia – condemned direct and indirect forms of interference in the internal or external affairs of other States, including reliance upon coercive pressure in order to subvert governments, gain commercial or diplomatic advantages, compel acquiescence in new arrangements or otherwise alter social, economic or political systems.[68] Interestingly, though, First World States gave ground on this point over time. While retaining the claim that a certain measure of 'influence' was unavoidable and even necessary in an interdependent world, they accepted language that condemned 'subversive activities' in other States and underscored the right of every State to choose its social, economic and political system and safeguard its territorial integrity and political independence.[69] Again, the 1965 resolution on intervention was referenced widely in these discussions, though with varying degrees of fidelity.[70]

A number of ancillary debates took place on the matter of intervention. At times the negotiations branched out to the question whether intervention by States could be read into the Charter, given that Article 2(7), its most salient provision, repudiated intervention by the United Nations, not by Member States themselves. Most delegations thought that the Charter prohibited both forms of intervention, though not all delegations were persuaded equally.[71] At other points the discussion focused on whether it would be advisable or prudent to provide an explicit definition of 'intervention', and also, to some degree, of 'domestic jurisdiction'. Most socialist and non-aligned delegates believed that it would be best to define 'intervention', and also to enumerate its various modes and forms, whereas most First World States held that this

[66] Report I, paras 205 (UK), 207 (US).
[67] ibid. See also Report III, para 42.
[68] Report I, paras 203 (Czechoslovakia), 204 (Yugoslavia), 208 (Mexico), 209 (Ghana, India, Yugoslavia), 292; Report II, paras 276 (India, . . .), 277 (Ghana), 278 (India, . . .); Report III, para 304 (Czechoslovakia).
[69] Report II, paras 279 (Australia, . . .), 331; Report III, paras 303 (Australia, . . .), 306 (UK).
[70] Report II, paras 282 (UAR), 283 (Chile), 284 (Chile, UAR), 285 (Australia, . . .), 286 (Czechoslovakia), 287 (Czechoslovakia), 292–300, 343 (France), 344 (Japan), 345 (Czechoslovakia), 346 (Italy), 348 (UK), 349 (Guatemala), 350 (Sweden), 351 (Australia), 352 (US); Report III, paras 303 (Australia, . . .), 304 (Czechoslovakia), 307 (Argentina, . . .), 321–31, 352, 466.
[71] Report I, paras 215–27, 292.

would be 'unwise and unprofitable', given that 'extending it would stultify the growth of international co-operation, and restricting it would leave States without protection against very real dangers'.[72] Unsurprisingly, an important point of contention proved to be the question whether intervention could ever be permitted, and if so which conditions might justify the extension of such permission. Some States favoured strict adherence to the general rule of non-intervention, arguing that constraining the freedom of States to undertake such action ensured international law's authority, while others pointed to apartheid policies in South Africa and denials of self-determination in territories still awaiting decolonisation to argue that intervention might be allowed under certain circumstances.[73]

Finally, the principle of sovereign equality completed the sovereigntist dimensions of the Friendly Relations Declaration's preparatory work, and ultimately also of the Declaration's final form.[74] Since all delegations were committed to the formal equality of States, the debate on this score concerned the degree to which this commitment reflected acceptance of each State's right to adhere to whichever social, economic and political systems it liked, as well as its right to dispose of its natural resources and wealth as it saw fit. During the first round of negotiations, proposals from Czechoslovakia, Ghana, India, Mexico and Yugoslavia underlined both points; the leading First World proposal, however, did not, its proponent – the United Kingdom – being joined by Australia, Japan, the United States and other States in expressing doubts about the suggested language and casting doubt on any right of nationalisation unfettered by 'international law' and existing agreements.[75] Unsurprisingly, some socialist and non-aligned States leveraged broadly Marxian arguments about the gap between formal juridical equality and real material equality, a bare assertion of de jure equality being a far cry from the achievement of de facto equality.[76] While sovereignty need not be fetishised, others observed, States by and large remained 'both the creators of the rules of international law and the entities to which these rules were addressed', and sovereignty was therefore 'the basis and *raison d'être* of international law'.[77]

By the second and third rounds of negotiations, in 1966 and 1967 respectively, ample agreement had emerged, including on the right of each State to decide on its own social, economic and political systems, but the question of including language relating to resource sovereignty in the text of the principle remained unresolved, with the result that socialist and non-aligned delegates continued to press the matter.[78] Once again, the debate circled around the thorny relation between State sovereignty and international law. Some insisted that international law was a product of sovereign power, such power being an unconditioned fact rather than something constituted through legal recognition, while others stressed that States might voluntarily accept certain restrictions on their freedom and subordinate themselves to a superordinate system of inter-State rules without thereby surrendering their sovereignty.[79]

[72] ibid, paras 230–44 (quotation 231), 292.
[73] ibid, paras 245–49, 292; Report II, paras 322–24.
[74] On sovereign equality see the chapter by M Koskenniemi and V Kari in this volume.
[75] Report I, paras 294 (Czechoslovakia), 295 (Yugoslavia), 296 (UK), 97 (Ghana, India, Mexico, Yugoslavia), 317–19, 328–31, 339.
[76] ibid, paras 310, 346 (UAR), 351 (Nigeria).
[77] ibid, para 337.
[78] Report II, paras 356, 358 (Czechoslovakia), 359 (Cameroon), 362 (UAR), 363 (Kenya), 364 (Ghana), 376, 379; Report III, paras 448 (Czechoslovakia), 451 (Kenya).
[79] Report II, paras 384–88; Report III, paras 428, 434. The *locus classicus* of the second argument is *Case of the SS 'Wimbledon' (Britain et al* v *Germany)*, PCIJ Rep Ser A, No 1 (1923), 25 ('the right of entering into international engagements is an attribute of State sovereignty').

The question whether reference should be made to the principle of permanent sovereignty over natural resources in the text of the principle – and, if so, the conditions under which it would apply and the amount of compensation to which investors would be entitled in the event of expropriation and nationalisation – lent additional concreteness and significance to otherwise vague talk of 'sovereign equality'.

Ultimately, the Declaration's final adopted form reflected these points of convergence and divergence. On the key question of force, the Declaration reaffirmed the Article 2(4) prohibition on the threat or use of force against the territorial integrity and political independence of States, or in any other manner inconsistent with the Charter's purposes.[80] In addition to condemning war propaganda and wars of aggression, the Declaration's first principle stressed the need for a treaty of general disarmament and repudiated forceful reprisals, unlawful occupations, forceful acquisitions of territory, the use of force against peoples seeking self-determination and direct and indirect support for terrorist and subversive organisations. Most socialist and non-aligned States had either pressed these claims or were willing to tolerate their recognition in the text. However, their most important claims were rejected in the final text. No definition of 'force' was offered. The text of the principle made no mention of economic, political or other forms of coercion. It explained that States are under an obligation to refrain from threatening or using force in regard to 'international lines of demarcation, such as armistice lines, established by or pursuant to an international agreement to which it is a party or which it is otherwise bound to respect', though it also made it clear that this should not 'be construed as prejudicing the positions of the parties concerned with regard to the status and effects of such lines under their special regimes or as affecting their temporary character'. Finally, and most revealingly, it did not recognise the right of liberation movements to have recourse to force against colonial rule or occupation. However, while wars of national liberation were not recognised as permissible uses of force per se, the Declaration would frame the principle of self-determination in such a way as to achieve a broadly similar result.[81]

Matters were somewhat more favourable to socialist and non-aligned positions on the question of intervention, enshrined in the Declaration's third principle.[82] The Declaration's final text rejected direct and indirect forms of interference in the internal or external affairs of other States; condemned the use of coercive pressure in inter-State relations to extract concessions or gain political, economic or other advantages; and confirmed that peoples could not be stripped of their 'national identity' and their right to choose their own political, economic and social systems. The availability of the 1965 non-intervention resolution proved decisive here, and it helped to consolidate support for many of the views held by the socialist and non-aligned camps.

As for the sixth principle, which concerned sovereign equality, the final text confirmed the Charter's blanket affirmation of formal juridical equality, and also underscored the right of each State to select its own economic, political and social systems. However, it made no reference of any kind to issues of resource sovereignty.[83] All States were equal in law, at least so long as they were not equal in fact.

80 All references in this paragraph are to Friendly Relations Declaration, first principle.
81 Abi-Saab (n 14) 43–45, 47–48. We discuss the principle of self-determination below.
82 The references that follow are to Friendly Relations Declaration, third principle.
83 The references in this paragraph are to Friendly Relations Declaration, sixth principle.

IV THE SOLIDARIST DECLARATION

Bundled together like the principles that comprise the Declaration's sovereigntist part, the principles that States are duty-bound to settle their disputes peacefully, co-operate in accord with the UN Charter, and fulfil Charter obligations in good faith come together to form an integral part of the Declaration's conceptual architecture, one marked above all by commitment to 'solidarity'. The negotiations whereby these principles came to be integrated into the Declaration's broader conceptual framework, acting as a counterpoint to its strong support for a capacious understanding of State sovereignty, were not nearly as fractious as the negotiations required to finalise the text of the sovereigntist principles. They took considerably less time to prepare, and delegates to the committee did not generally have their legal and diplomatic skills stretched to the same degree. Yet disagreements did occur, and they were nearly always reflective of differences between advanced capitalist countries on the one hand and socialist and non-aligned countries on the other.

The idea that States would settle their disputes peacefully was the subject of sustained discussion at the first meeting of the special committee in 1964. A British proposal, to which Canada, France, Guatemala, Netherlands and the United States suggested a number of amendments, made explicit reference to the International Court of Justice (ICJ) as a potential adjudicative institution of last resort, and also recommended that recourse be had to negotiation, mediation, arbitration, adjudication in court or some other means of resolving the dispute peacefully.[84] An independent Japanese proposal lent support to the former point,[85] while an independent Czechoslovak proposal (the Czechoslovak delegation framed this principle as 'the corner-stone of international law') agreed on the latter.[86] A Yugoslav proposal omitted both elements, but underscored the importance of resolving disputes 'on a basis of sovereign equality and without the use of any form of pressure' while discouraging States from aggravating unresolved disputes.[87] This last proposal was subsequently rolled into a joint non-aligned draft, put forward by Ghana, India and Yugoslavia. Notably, this joint proposal enjoined disputant States – including those embroiled in disagreements with respect to territorial frontiers – to engage in 'direct negotiations' before trying other peaceful means of conciliation or adjudication, including submitting the matter to the ICJ, a body the United Nations was also encouraged to ensure would represent 'more fully and equitably the main forms of civilization and the principal legal systems of the world'.[88] This last point reflected long-standing concerns in the global South about the neutrality and legitimacy of the 'World Court', an institution whose reputation among newly decolonised peoples had already been tarnished by its handling of the ongoing *South West Africa* proceedings, especially in the few years after the epoch-making judgment in 1966 that so bitterly disappointed Third World observers by deciding that Ethiopia and Liberia did not have legal standing in the question of South-West Africa's status.[89]

[84] Report I, para 131 (UK).
[85] ibid, para 136 (Japan).
[86] ibid, para 129 (Czechoslovakia); Report II, paras 158 (Czechoslovakia), 264 (Czechoslovakia). Czechoslovak representatives used the same language in their correspondence with UN officials. Jiří Hájek, Permanent Representative of Czechoslovakia to the United Nations, to U Thant, UN Secretary-General, 1 June 1965, Ref No 989, United Nations Archives, New York City.
[87] Report I, para 130 (Yugoslavia).
[88] ibid, para 137 (Ghana, India, Yugoslavia).
[89] The Court was split eight to seven, the casting vote being that of President Percy Spender, an Australian judge. *South West Africa (Ethiopia* v *South Africa; Liberia* v *South Africa)*, Second Phase, Judgment, ICJ Reports 1966, 6. See also Declaration of President Percy Spender, ICJ Reports 1966, 49.

Subsequent proposals from various other States, nearly all belonging to the NAM, emphasised one or another combination of these elements, with one Chilean proposal boldly – but vaguely – demanding that dispute resolution 'be based on justice'.[90]

At root, the disagreements following from these and other proposals were relatively limited in scope and duration. Some tried to distinguish disputes of a specifically 'legal' character from disputes of a more broadly 'political' character.[91] A more consequential point concerned the means of dispute settlement. While some delegates preferred 'direct negotiations' between disputants, voicing anxieties about third parties being compelled to enter the fray and thereby destabilising the international legal order as a whole, others pointed to the ICJ and other international institutions, which they thought to be better placed to determine what had happened 'objectively and impartially' and resolve the dispute in a way that made it less likely to recur or continue.[92] Some delegates preferred to cast the principle of peaceful dispute settlement as the culmination of nearly a century of institution-building on the international plane, not to mention various efforts to contain, regulate or even outlaw war.[93] But others noted that the mistrust inspired in new States by third-party dispute settlement mechanisms 'was due in large measure to the antiquated, inequitable, fragmentary and uncertain character of many of the rules comprising the body of substantive rules of existing international law', arguing that these States 'now considered those rules unjust, though formally sanctioned by international law, thus creating a dichotomy between international legality and justice, the inevitable result of which was that such States preferred to resort to political action rather than submit their disputes to arbitration or compulsory judicial settlement'.[94]

The idea that States should co-operate in accord with the UN Charter took even less time and energy to finalise. As usual, a number of proposals were floated for the wording. A joint First World proposal, for instance, emphasised the duty of all States to co-operate with the United Nations to achieve 'universal respect for, and observance of, human rights, fundamental freedoms for all without distinction as to race, sex, language or religion' – language which was ultimately incorporated into the final text in slightly modified form.[95] More fantastically, a Czechoslovak proposal stressed that States should '[r]efrain from any discrimination in their relations with other States, in particular discrimination by reason of differences in political, economic and social systems or in levels of economic development'.[96] Again, some delegates emphasised that 'co-operation', however construed, would need to be anchored in sovereign equality, and stressed specifically economic modes of interdependence geared toward developmental concerns.[97] Some made mention of the question whether the duty to co-operate was an obligation pursuant to customary international law, international treaty law, both or some other source of international law altogether.[98]

As for the notion that States are under a duty to satisfy in good faith their Charter obligations, it too proved relatively easy. There was, of course, some disagreement. A joint non-aligned

[90] See eg Report II, paras 159 (Dahomey, . . .), 160 (Chile), 161 (Algeria, . . .); Report III, paras 371 (Dahomey, . . .), 372 (Chile, . . .), 373 (Algeria, . . .).
[91] See eg Report I, para 145.
[92] ibid, paras 156–78, 191–93; Report II, paras 211–20; Report III, paras 384–93.
[93] Report I, paras 140–41; Report II, paras 265 (Sweden).
[94] Report I, paras 195–96. See also Report II, para 260 (Burma), 269 (Dahomey).
[95] Report II, para 416 (Australia, . . .); Report III, paras 116 (Australia, . . .), 121 (Canada), 158–59, 164 (US), 166 (UK), 167 (USSR), 168 (Japan), 169 (Kenya), 170 (France).
[96] Report II, para 415 (Czechoslovakia); Report III, paras 115 (Czechoslovakia), 145–50.
[97] See eg Report II, paras 420–22, 425–29, 440–43; Report III, para 123 (Algeria, . . .).
[98] Report II, paras 433, 435–37; Report III, paras 136–41.

proposal departed from others in echoing growing efforts to secure legal recognition for international *jus cogens* (efforts that would yield Article 53 of the 1969 Vienna Convention on the Law of Treaties) by suggesting language purporting to invalidate any treaty that violated the Charter.[99] Tellingly, whereas socialist and non-aligned proposals required States to fulfil obligations flowing from treaties they had 'concluded freely and on the basis of equality', a formulation that excluded unequal treaties and many capitulations and other concessionary instruments, a British–American proposal stated flatly that such treaty-based obligations 'may not be lawfully avoided on grounds of incompatibility with either national law or national policy', a formulation that excluded many nationalisation and expropriation schemes.[100] Both this question and related questions about *jus cogens* (and its implications for general ideas of *pacta sunt servanda* and *rebus sic stantibus*) and the legal status of the concept of good faith were discussed.[101]

When all was said and done, the final text of the Declaration reflected these debates in a variety of different ways. The second of the seven listed principles mandated that States would settle their disputes without endangering international peace and security, recommending for this purpose 'negotiation, inquiry, mediation, conciliation, arbitration, judicial settlement, resort to regional agencies or arrangements or other peaceful means of their choice'.[102] It did not refer to the ICJ as such, but it did include language expressly repudiating acts that might aggravate already volatile international situations. Notably, it also made a point of stressing sovereign equality, tethering the duty to pursue peaceful dispute settlement to the need to respect sovereignty, particularly in regard to 'free choice of means' of resolving disputes. Thus, States were expected to be peaceful, but it was ultimately within their power to decide how best to keep the peace. Internationalism, manifested in a commitment to peace, was at root grounded in sovereignty. How precisely concrete disputes were to be settled remained unclear, though, with the final text of the second principle offering no guidance as to the sequence in which dispute settlement techniques were to be tried.

The idea that States were legally obligated to engage in 'co-operative' behaviour in accordance with the Charter, the basis of the Declaration's fourth principle, was formulated so as to be 'irrespective of the differences in their political, economic and social systems', language which socialist and non-aligned delegates consistently pressed to have included in the Declaration (and many other legal instruments at the time).[103] As is so often the case, the trouble here was one primarily of imprecision. The final text invited States to 'co-operate in the promotion of economic growth throughout the world, especially that of the developing countries', and also to co-operate on a variety of other registers, including social, cultural, scientific and technological matters. But it also made sure to encourage them to 'conduct their international relations in the economic, social, cultural, technical and trade fields in accordance with the principles of sovereign equality and non-intervention'. As with the second principle, this suggested a certain relation of subordination: the requirement of co-operation appeared in some sense to be

[99] Report II, para 524 (Burma, . . .); Report III, para 238 (Burma, . . .). On the international legal history of *jus cogens* see Umut Özsu, 'An Anti-Imperialist Universalism? *Jus Cogens* and the Politics of International Law' in Martti Koskenniemi, Walter Rech and Manuel Jiménez Fonseca (eds), *International Law and Empire: Historical Explorations* (Oxford University Press, 2017) 295.

[100] Report II, paras 523 (Czechoslovakia), 524 (Burma, . . .), 525 (UK, US); Report III, paras 237 (Czechoslovakia), 239 (US, UK), 240 (UK), 242 (Algeria, . . .). See further Report II, paras 547–58.

[101] Report II, paras 526–43; Report III, paras 244–84.

[102] This and subsequent references are to Friendly Relations Declaration, second principle.

[103] This and subsequent references are to Friendly Relations Declaration, fourth principle.

secondary to the imperative of upholding State sovereignty, though the inclusion of language stressing observance of 'human rights and fundamental freedoms' did push back on that tendency to some degree.

The final text's seventh and final principle was easily the most nebulous of all.[104] It simply affirmed the duty of all States to fulfil in good faith the legal obligations they incurred from the UN Charter, and also from applicable international treaties and customary international law. It did not attempt to clarify what precisely counted as 'good faith fulfillment', nor did it try to lend additional clarity to the question of what to do when Charter obligations appeared to conflict. Crucially, it did not include the idea, proposed by socialist and non-aligned States, that the principle relate only to those obligations that flowed from treaties 'concluded freely and on the basis of equality', the US delegation welcoming the committee's decision to exclude such language on the basis of its 'inherently subjective character', which 'could endanger the stability of treaties and consequently of international peace'.[105] The Friendly Relations Declaration's tactical ambiguity – the opacity characteristic of both diplomatic deal-making and legal abstraction – was nowhere more clearly evident. The Declaration celebrated 'co-operation' – but without so much as attempting to define the term.

V THE SELF-DETERMINATIVE DECLARATION

The debate about self-determination, one of the two principles that caused the committee the most trouble, found expression in a number of issue-specific discussions. A key issue in regard to which different proposals were offered concerned the status of territories administered by colonial or other foreign authorities. Were these territories simply part of the metropolitan power's own territory, as overseas provinces (as in the case of Portuguese Macau) or *départements* (as the French claimed in Algeria until 1962)? Or did they instead enjoy a wholly distinct and separate legal status under international law?

The question was anything but trivial. Among other things, according a stronger degree of independent legal personality to foreign-held territories typically bolstered claims to collective self-determination. It also reinforced the argument – famously examined at close quarters by Charles Alexandrowicz – that formal independence simply led to the 'reversion' of a sovereignty that had never been extinguished, rather than the creation of a wholly 'new' State.[106] First World delegates tended to hold the view that self-government, and therefore the right of self-determination, might express itself in a number of different forms, one of which was formal incorporation into the metropolitan State.[107] For their part, socialist and non-aligned delegates

[104] The references that follow are to Friendly Relations Declaration, seventh principle.

[105] Report III, para 287 (US); and also paras 291 (UK noting that such language 'might be taken to apply to certain controversial questions relating to treaty succession'), and 300 (France). The UAR expressed regret that 'the smaller countries had not found greater support' in this respect, as did many other socialist and non-aligned States; see Report III, paras 288 (Yugoslavia), 289 (UAR), 290 (Czechoslovakia), 292 (USSR), 293 (Syria), 294 (Algeria), 295 (Nigeria), 297 (Kenya), 298 (Madagascar), 299 (Cameroon).

[106] Charles H Alexandrowicz, 'New and Original States: The Issue of Reversion to Sovereignty' (1969) 45 *International Affairs* 465, 471 et seq. See, more generally, Charles H Alexandrowicz, *The Law of Nations in Global History*, ed David Armitage and Jennifer Pitts (Oxford University Press, 2017), pt 4. The argument was crucial in the context of debates about the law of State succession to treaties; see Craven (n 20).

[107] Report II, para 459 (US); Report III, para 176 (UK); Report IV, paras 137 (US), 139 (UK); Report V, paras 140 (US), 142 (UK).

argued that foreign-held territories were possessed of an independent legal status – a status they had never relinquished and of which they could not now be deprived.[108]

A different but no less explosive issue was the extent to which peoples under colonial subjugation had a right to wage armed struggle in pursuit of independence. The legal question here was one of first-order importance: could armed struggle in the name of self-determination be justified by reference to the Charter's permission of self-defensive force, or, in the alternative, on the basis of relevant rules of customary international law?[109] The second of these two alternatives was the more persuasive of the two, but also the more puzzling. Many international lawyers hailing from the Third World, like their counterparts from the socialist world, had long made a point of questioning the normative basis of customary international law – a body of rules they tended to characterise as Eurocentric in provenance and constitution, and therefore as lacking universal applicability. Yet newly independent States also invested deeply in the General Assembly resolution mechanism, leveraging their numerical weight in that body to push through a lengthy and impressively wide-ranging series of resolutions on self-determination, most famously the 1960 decolonisation resolution.[110] Socialist and non-aligned delegates were keenly aware that such resolutions conferred a significant degree of legal legitimacy upon liberation movements, from Palestine to Rhodesia,[111] and they consistently argued that armed struggle needed to be understood as a logical extension of self-determination if this right were to mean anything under conditions of colonial occupation and foreign domination. Their counterparts in the First World warned of the dangers of sweeping statements about national liberation movements,[112] and underscored the need to combat terrorism, forestall rebellion and maintain general respect for law and order.[113]

Another issue that proved troublesome was the relationship between self-determination and human rights. While there was no effective opposition to the claim that the two concepts were related, at least in some sense, it was unclear how precisely this relation was to be parsed. Complicating matters was the fact that 'human rights' had often come to take on a preponderantly civic-political form, with the struggle over what eventually became the two 1966 human rights instruments – the entitlements enshrined in the Covenant on Civic and Political Rights were detached from and would quickly prove more effective than those enshrined in the Covenant on Economic, Social and Cultural Rights – demonstrating that an individualistic approach generally enjoyed the upper hand, particularly in the global North. Although self-determination had been characterised as a human right, appearing as such in the first provision

[108] Report II, paras 26 (Algeria, . . .), 116–17, 401, 457 (Czechoslovakia), 458 (Algeria, . . .); Report III, paras 177 (Algeria, . . .), 215; Report IV, paras 86, 136 (Algeria, . . .), 140 (Algeria, . . .), 184; Report V, paras 139 (Algeria, . . .), 143 (Algeria, . . .), 145 (Czechoslovakia, . . .), 174.

[109] Support of self-defensive force for such peoples was extensive among socialist and non-aligned delegates: Report I, paras 27 (Czechoslovakia), 28 (Yugoslavia), 31 (Ghana, India and Yugoslavia); Report II, paras 25 (Czechoslovakia), 26 (Algeria, . . .), 136–42, 457 (Czechoslovakia), 458 (Algeria, . . .), 497; Report III, paras 101–3, 207–8; Report IV, paras 22 (Czechoslovakia), 26 (Algeria, . . .), 103, 106–7, 115 (Cameroon), 121 (USSR), 123 (Syria), 136 (Algeria, . . .), 140 (Algeria, . . .), 175; Report V, paras 29 (Czechoslovakia), 34 (Algeria, . . .), 109–13, 120 (Czechoslovakia), 121 (Kenya), 123 (USSR), 130 (Romania), 138 (Czechoslovakia), 139 (Algeria, . . .), 143 (Algeria, . . .), 145 (Czechoslovakia, . . .), 167.

[110] On the implications for the debate about force see Report I, paras 83–89; Report II, paras 112, 138; Report IV, para 104; Report VI, para 92. See also UNGA Res 1514 (XV), paras 2, 4–5.

[111] For these and other analogues see Report VI, para 209 (Syria).

[112] Report III, para 187.

[113] See eg Report I, para 29 (UK); Report II, paras 27 (Australia, Canada, UK, US), 29 (Italy, Netherlands), 114, 144–51; Report III, paras 104, 208; Report IV, paras 28, 85, 105, 119 (UK), 131 (Australia); Report V, para 165; Report VI, paras 234–35 (UK).

of both 1966 covenants,[114] the idea of collective liberation did not always sit well with entitlements to personal privacy, which were also elevated to the status of universal human rights.[115] The British delegation repeatedly linked self-determination to 'universal respect for and observance of human rights and freedoms'.[116] But if this position was intended in part as a challenge to socialist States' claims of moral superiority, it also provided socialist and non-aligned States with an opportunity to point out that foreign administration and 'inhuman practices such as apartheid' violated self-determination and human rights alike.[117] It was during the 1970s that international human rights secured their real operational breakthrough, congealing in the work of well-resourced non-governmental organisations like Amnesty International and gaining significant footholds in the foreign and domestic policies of a great many States. But the muddy legal and conceptual links between self-determination and human rights in the 1960s made for protracted debate within the committee.[118]

At the end of the day, the principle that resulted from these negotiations articulated a kind of *via media* solution to the problem of self-determination. Since blanket, across-the-board recognition of the right to self-determination would jeopardise the stability of an international system that had yet to adjust to the pace of the post-war wave of decolonisation, collective self-determination was to be subject only to a conditional form of universalisation. The substantive outcome was a set of paragraphs that effectively granted some, but not all, 'peoples' the right to determine their own fates.

The Declaration's fifth principle emphasised that it was necessary to 'promote friendly relations and co-operation among States', and that this in turn made it necessary to 'bring a speedy end to colonialism, having due regard to the freely expressed will of the peoples concerned'.[119] It confirmed that self-determination and fundamental human rights could not be upheld if 'alien subjugation, domination and exploitation' were allowed to persist. Further, self-determination could find expression in a range of different legal and institutional arrangements: the establishment of an independent sovereign State, free association with or integration into an existing State, or the 'emergence into any other political status freely determined' by the relevant 'people'. In this respect, the principle accepted a proposal made by British and American delegates,[120] who also succeeded in securing incorporation of language linking self-determination to human rights with a statement that '[e]very State has the duty to promote through joint and separate action universal respect for and observance of human rights and fundamental freedoms in accordance with the Charter'. The complexity of the settlement that was formalised in the fifth principle also yielded an express repudiation of all attempts to strip a 'people' (a term the Declaration did not define) of its right to self-determination, as well as attempts by colonial powers to deprive the territories they administered of their legally distinct

[114] International Covenant on Economic, Social and Cultural Rights, signed 16 December 1966, 993 UNTS 3, Art 1; International Covenant on Civil and Political Rights, signed 16 December 1966, 999 UNTS 171, Art 1 [ICCPR].

[115] ICCPR, Art 17.

[116] Report III, para 176 (UK); Report IV, para 139 (UK); Report V, para 142 (UK).

[117] Report II, para 495. See also para 489.

[118] For the argument about the centrality of the 1970s to international human rights movements, see especially Moyn (n 20). For studies of earlier invocations of self-determination as a human right, see Roland Burke, *Decolonization and the Evolution of International Human Rights* (University of Pennsylvania Press, 2013); Steven LB Jensen, *The Making of International Human Rights: The 1960s, Decolonization, and the Reconstruction of Global Values* (Cambridge University Press, 2016); Meredith Terretta, 'Anticolonial Lawyering, Postwar Human Rights, and Decolonization Across Imperial Boundaries in Africa' (2017) 52 *Canadian Journal of History* 448.

[119] All references in this and the following paragraphs are to Friendly Relations Declaration, fifth principle.

[120] Report II, para 459 (US); Report III, para 176 (UK); Report IV, paras 137 (US), 139 (UK); Report V, paras 140 (US), 142 (UK).

status. It did not go so far as to provide for a specific right to use force to resist colonialism or occupation – a right to armed resistance as such. But it did condemn the use of force to deprive peoples of their right to self-determination. And it also confirmed that all peoples enjoy the right to seek and receive assistance in the face of such force.[121]

The crucial portion of the fifth principle – the portion for which the Declaration as a whole has conventionally earned the most references – expressly prohibited efforts to 'dismember or impair, totally or in part, the territorial integrity or political unity of sovereign and independent States conducting themselves in compliance with the principle of equal rights and self-determination of peoples . . . and thus possessed of a government representing the whole people belonging to the territory without distinction as to race, creed or colour'. No State had the right to engage in activities that might lead to 'the partial or total disruption of the national unity and territorial integrity of any other State or country', it explained, and all States were under an obligation to refrain from such activities. This evasive language, casting self-determination as a universal right while making it exceptionally difficult for this right to be exercised,[122] has since come to be characterised as a 'safeguard clause' or 'saving clause', and committee delegates themselves referred to it as such.[123] It built upon the Declaration on the Granting of Independence to Colonial Countries and Peoples, the sixth article of which stated that '[a]ny attempt aimed at the partial or total disruption of the national unity and the territorial integrity of a country is incompatible with the purposes and principles of the Charter of the United Nations'.[124] The three-part schematic overview of human rights history sketched by Czech-French jurist Karel Vasak in 1977 would position self-determination at the heart of a group of 'rights of solidarity' that he believed to comprise human rights' 'third generation', the first two corresponding to civic-political and socio-economic and cultural rights respectively.[125] Still, what self-determination actually meant in concrete practice remained as murky as ever.

The Friendly Relations Declaration quickly came to be viewed by many as an authoritative, if admittedly non-binding, statement on the question of self-determination. But the only thing that was clear about the Declaration in this regard was that the right of self-determination was to be subordinated to the need to conserve the integrity and independence of existing States, at least so long as they remained 'possessed of a government representing the whole people belonging to the territory without distinction as to race, creed or colour'. Richard Falk, the Princeton University professor and human rights advocate who first made his name opposing the Vietnam War, would later point to this feature of the Declaration as evidence that the interests of today's 'captive nations', peoples like the Kurds, Tamils and Palestinians, were widely believed to be of lesser value than those of yesterday's 'captive States', the new countries that decolonisation had made possible.[126]

121 Abi-Saab (n 14) 47–48.

122 Exceptionally difficult but not strictly impossible, as was demonstrated recently in the ICJ's assertion that self-determination had crystallised as a norm of customary international law by the late 1960s, and would be confirmed in the Friendly Relations Declaration. See *Legal Consequences of the Separation of the Chagos Archipelago from Mauritius in 1965*, ICJ, Advisory Opinion (25 February 2019), paras 144–61, www.icj-cij.org/en/case/169/advisory-opinions.

123 See eg Report VI, paras 78, 150 (France), 177 (Canada), 261 (US).

124 UNGA Res 1514 (XV), para 6.

125 Karel Vasak, 'A Thirty-Year Struggle: The Sustained Efforts to Give Force of Law to the Universal Declaration of Human Rights' (1977) 30 *UNESCO Courier* 29.

126 Richard Falk, 'The Rights of Peoples (In Particular Indigenous Peoples)' in James Crawford (ed), *The Rights of Peoples* (Clarendon, 1988) 17, 23–27.

VI CONCLUSION

For all of its lack of clarity, perhaps more so than any of the other major resolutions adopted by the General Assembly during the heyday of decolonisation, the Friendly Relations Declaration showcases the complexity of the transition from 'co-existence' to 'co-operation', from an explicitly Eurocentric model of international order premised upon direct and indirect colonialism to an increasingly 'universal' mode of organising legal relations in a formally emancipated world.

Negotiations between advanced capitalist countries and socialist and developing countries, particularly in international environmental law, international development law and the law of the sea, were generally couched as means of facilitating 'dialogue' between North and South, partly in the form of discussions between the Group of 77 and what would before long come to be known as the Group of 7.[127] Official rationales for such endeavours typically stressed the need for international collaboration in the face of systemic concerns about the world economy, the structural integrity that Myres McDougal, Michael Reisman and other associates of the policy-oriented New Haven School like Falk were in the habit of describing as 'world public order',[128] and the capacity of existing legal rules and institutions to foster the construction of a stronger international community, through 'South–South co-operation' as well as increased interaction between North and South.[129] Appeals to 'solidarity' of various stripes had played a central role in the reigning ideology of the French Third Republic, with the concept having secured vocal and effective sponsors in Léon Bourgeois, Léon Duguit and Georges Scelle.[130] Deeply imprecise, with a content that was nothing if not essentially contested, the discourse of 'solidarity' came to be mobilised from the 1950s to the 1980s as part of a series of efforts by political and legal elites in North and South alike to reconfigure the legal architecture of the world. In the case of many international lawyers from formerly French territories, this was facilitated by the fact that they had received training, in law and often also in other disciplines, in France itself.[131]

[127] The Group of 77 was officially formed in 1964; the Group of 7 followed suit in 1975–76.

[128] See esp Myres S McDougal, 'International Law, Power and Policy: A Contemporary Conception' (1953) 82 *Recueil des Cours* 137; Myres S McDougal, Harold D Lasswell and W Michael Reisman, 'Theories about International Law: Prologue to a Configurative Jurisprudence' (1968) 8 *Virginia Journal of International Law* 188. For a later authoritative statement see Harold D Lasswell and Myres S McDougal, *Jurisprudence For a Free Society: Studies in Law, Science and Policy*, 2 vols (Martinus Nijhoff, 1992). For recent reassessment see Hengameh Saberi, 'Yale's Policy Science and International Law: Between Legal Formalism and Policy Conceptualism' in Anne Orford and Florian Hoffmann (eds), *The Oxford Handbook of the Theory of International Law* (Oxford University Press, 2016) 427.

[129] The principal locus for these discussions was the Conference for International Economic Co-operation, convened in the mid-1970s to discuss issues of energy, finance, commodities and economic development. Giuliano Garavini, *After Empires: European Integration, Decolonization, and the Challenge from the Global South 1957–1986* (Richard R Nybakken tr, Oxford University Press, 2012 [2009]), ch 6.

[130] For the general background see JES Hayward, 'The Official Social Philosophy of the French Third Republic: Léon Bourgeois and Solidarism' (1961) 6 *International Review of Social History* 19. For the international law implications, see Koskenniemi (n 20), ch 4.

[131] For the case of Mohammed Bedjaoui see Umut Özsu, '"In the Interests of Mankind as a Whole": Mohammed Bedjaoui's New International Economic Order' (2015) 6 *Humanity* 129. For Charles Chaumont, a key figure, see Emmanuelle Tourme-Jouannet, 'Charles Chaumont's Third-World International Legal Theory' in Jochen von Bernstorff and Philipp Dann (eds), *The Battle for International Law: South-North Perspectives on the Decolonization Era* (Cambridge University Press, 2019) 358; Martti Koskenniemi, 'Regarding "Méthode d'analyse du droit international" by Charles Chaumont (1975–I): Dialectics and International Law' (2015) 50 *Revue belge de droit international* 270. Another important figure here is René-Jean Dupuy, raised in Algeria and a doctoral student under Scelle; see 'René-Jean Dupuy' in Antonio Cassese (ed), *Five Masters of International Law: Conversations with R-J Dupuy, E Jiménez de Aréchaga, R Jennings, L Henkin, and O Schachter* (Hart, 2011) 1.

The Friendly Relations Declaration crystallised an especially significant settlement – a rough compromise of sorts – in this complex process of reconstituting international law to govern a world that was itself undergoing systemic overhaul. In the Declaration's compromise vision, inter-State co-operation complemented sovereignty, enmeshing both new and old States in far-reaching networks of interdependence. Despite complaints by some members of the special committee that it was chiefly 'concerned with the acquisition and preservation of sovereign independence', and that '[t]he over-increasing [sic] interdependence of all peoples was as yet insufficiently reflected in its rules, institutions and practices',[132] the Declaration – an instrument codifying a set of principles that some delegates regarded as rising to the level of *jus cogens* norms[133] – was suffused by a significant amount of solidarism in addition to sovereigntism.

Except to lawyers (and even then only a comparatively small band of international lawyers), none of the abstract ideas canonised in the Friendly Relations Declaration was especially vivid. Yet each of the principles in which these ideas found expression hid numerous drafting controversies, and also certain gains won by the global South along the way, beginning with the fact that the Declaration exists at all. More than any other international legal instrument in circulation at the time, the Declaration confirmed that Western powers also accepted the authority of the principle of collective self-determination of peoples, at least legally. The prohibition on the use of force, though seemingly absolute in one principle, made room for assistance to anti-colonial insurgents, and also some recognition of their legal standing, in another principle. And the Declaration's negotiations captured the Third World's rising agenda of a fairer set of arrangements for global economic distribution, even if the final text barely registered this impulse.

Given these features, the Declaration made for an important contrast not just to the decolonised international law for which many at the time aspired, but also to what has turned out to be its post-Cold War future. The favoured law-making agent of post-colonial States, the General Assembly, eventually found itself marginalised by new expert venues, international entities and multilateral fora (most famously the World Trade Organization). Relatedly, what was given short shrift in the Declaration's seven principles, perhaps most strikingly in light of subsequent legal developments, was the issue of protecting persons in the international system – the 'human rights' that so many have identified as central principles of any coherent and defensible international law – as well as the economic prerogatives of property and contract that a now powerful body of international economic law upholds. Indeed, while few would claim that the principles of co-existence and co-operation born of the Cold War and especially decolonisation are altogether dead, they are arguably more honoured in the breach than in the observance, in part because the priorities of governmental and non-governmental interests have moved so powerfully in the direction of individualistic human rights and neoliberal 'globalisation'.[134]

The innovations of the Friendly Relations Declaration venture take on additional significance today, in a moment of considerable change in the international legal order. In the 1960s the very uncertainties of empire's formal end bred a host of different ideas about the basic

[132] Report VI, para 166 (Netherlands).

[133] Report VI, para 109 (Venezuela) (branding the Declaration the 'most effective contribution to the future codification of principles which were authoritatively regarded as authentic examples of *jus cogens* and, therefore, essential to the maintenance of international peace and security').

[134] cf Samuel Moyn, *Not Enough: Human Rights in an Unequal World* (Harvard University Press, 2018).

purposes and structures of international law, which was often thought to be a key source of assistance to newly decolonised States that found themselves emancipated into a Cold War world in which few other tools appeared to be on offer. That this project failed, and that international legal doctrine came to respond to a rather different set of priorities, is worth considering anew at this juncture, particularly inasmuch as the half-century that has elapsed since the Declaration's adoption has been distinguished above all by growing economic inequality and ecological devastation.

PART I

The Principles of the Friendly Relations Declaration

3

The Prohibition of the Use of Force

Olivier Corten

I INTRODUCTION

The first of the seven principles in the Friendly Relations Declaration provides that:

> States shall refrain in their international relations from the threat or use of force against the territorial integrity or political independence of any State or in any other manner inconsistent with the purposes of the United Nations.[1]

There is nothing surprising in this, remembering that the very objective of this statement of the principles already contained in Article 2 of the UN Charter is 'to secure their more effective application within the international community'.[2] This was a particularly topical issue in 1970 with respect to the prohibition of the use of force. It can hardly be said that this prohibition was uniformly and systematically applied after being solemnly proclaimed in the Charter in 1945. The stringency of the prohibition, presented by many as a major advance in international relations,[3] was soon confronted with the harsh realities of practice: besides major conflicts such as the Korean War (1950–53), the Arab–Israeli wars (especially the Six-Day War in 1967) or the Indochina and then Vietnam war (which was still being waged), the United Nations had already experienced multiple flash points by 1970, from the Cuban missile crisis (1962) to the Soviet interventions in Hungary (1956) and Czechoslovakia (1967), by way of US military operations in Cuba (1961) and the Dominican Republic (1965), and the Suez crisis (1956), not counting the colonial or post-colonial conflicts (such as the Belgian intervention in the Congo in 1960) or other local conflicts.[4] Against this backdrop, it is understandable that, if they were to continue on an idealistic or even utopian course, the UN Member States might as well see the reaffirmation of the outline definition of the prohibition of the use of force as a way to make it more effective.[5] The solemn proclamation of the existence of the rule, which was set out at the time as a

[1] Declaration on Principles of International Law Concerning Friendly Relations and Co-operation among States in Accordance with the Charter of the United Nations, UNGA Res 2625 (XXV) (24 October 1970), Annex [Friendly Relations Declaration].

[2] ibid, preamble.

[3] A Verdebout, 'The Contemporary Discourse on the Use of Force in the Nineteenth Century: a Diachronic and Critical Analysis' (2014) 1 *Journal on the Use of Force and International Law* 223–46.

[4] M Weisburd, *Use of Force: The Practice of States Since World War II* (Pennsylvania University Press, 1997).

[5] See also Declaration on the Enhancement of the Effectiveness of the Principle of Refraining from the Threat or Use of Force in International Relations, annexed to UNGA Res 42/22 (18 November 1987).

peremptory norm of international law (*jus cogens*),[6] thus appeared to be a way to curb the reign of force that it seemed was to characterise international relations.

In strictly legal terms, the point of the text was indeed to go beyond the contrasting viewpoints that had characterised – as they still do – debates about the lawfulness of military interventions conducted in particular instances.[7] With the Friendly Relations Declaration appended to a resolution of the UN General Assembly adopted by consensus, we have an instrument that is meant to reflect the position of the 'international community of States as a whole', to use the expression in Article 53 of the Vienna Convention on the Law of Treaties of 1969. This explains why the International Court of Justice (ICJ) deemed that this Declaration could be used to express the *opinio juris* of States on the matter of the rule prohibiting the use of force.[8] Such an approach makes it possible, the Court maintains, not only to clarify the meaning of this rule but also to reassert its customary character despite practice to the contrary that is commonly encountered in international relations.[9] The text of the Declaration is therefore remarkably interesting in terms both of the establishment of a customary legal rule but also of the interpretation of a treaty, to wit the UN Charter. It is common knowledge that Article 31(3) of the Vienna Convention referred to above prescribes, as a means of interpretation, consideration of 'any subsequent agreement between the parties regarding the interpretation of the treaty or the application of its provisions'. It is incontrovertible that the Friendly Relations Declaration is indeed a 'subsequent agreement between the parties' that can be used to determine the meaning of the relevant provisions of the Charter concerning *jus contra bellum*. Of course, the final paragraph of the part of the Declaration on the non-use of force provides that '[n]othing in the foregoing paragraphs shall be construed as enlarging or diminishing in any way the scope of the provisions of the Charter concerning cases in which the use of force is lawful'. But, as the above-mentioned precedents of the ICJ confirmed, that does not preclude using the Declaration to clarify the meaning of those provisions.[10]

The purpose of this chapter is not to make an exhaustive commentary paragraph by paragraph of the text adopted in 1970. Some of the passages in it are besides not particularly innovative or at any rate are non-controversial. These include the following excerpts:

> A war of aggression constitutes a crime against the peace, for which there is responsibility under international law.
>
> ...
>
> States have a duty to refrain from acts of reprisal involving the use of force.
>
> ...
>
> The territory of a State shall not be the object of military occupation resulting from the use of force in contravention of the provisions of the Charter. The territory of a State shall not be the object of acquisition by another State resulting from the threat or use of force. No territorial acquisition resulting from the threat or use of force shall be recognized as legal. Nothing in the foregoing shall be construed as affecting:

[6] O Corten, *The Law Against War* (Hart, 2010) 200–7.

[7] T Ruys and O Corten (eds), *The Use of Force in International Law: A Case-Based Approach* (Oxford University Press, 2018).

[8] *Military and Paramilitary Activities in and against Nicaragua*, ICJ Reports 1986, 98–101, paras 187–90; *Legal Consequences of the Construction of a Wall in the Occupied Palestinian Territory*, ICJ Reports 2004, 171, para 87; *Armed Activities on the Territory of the Congo (Democratic Republic of the Congo v Uganda)*, ICJ Reports 2005, para 162; see also *Legality of the Threat or Use of Nuclear Weapons*, ICJ Reports 1996, 264, para 102.

[9] *Military and Paramilitary Activities* (n 8), para 186.

[10] See n 8.

(a) Provisions of the Charter or any international agreement prior to the Charter regime and valid under international law; or
(b) The powers of the Security Council under the Charter.

None of these assertions has been fundamentally challenged, with respect to the principles in any case. Debates on them generally concern their application in particular instances, which is a question beyond the ambit of the present commentary.[11]

Other excerpts from the Declaration have, though, given rise to lively debates and are still related today to particularly sensitive issues. Some of these issues concern instead the *scope* of the prohibition of the use of force, such as the issue of non-military force, which has recently become topical again with the question of cyberwarfare. Other issues relate more to certain real or putative *exceptions* to the prohibition, whether self-defence or what is termed the 'right of humanitarian intervention'. Both types of question shall be considered in turn. The objective shall be to determine to what extent the Friendly Relations Declaration made it possible (when it was first adopted) and still makes it possible today to settle some of these debates. To this end, we shall take account of the preparatory works for the Declaration as well as the works that unfolded in parallel and that were to lead in 1974 to the Definition of Aggression appended to UN General Assembly Resolution 3314 (XXIX), which, too, is considered to reflect customary law.[12] With a view to also saying something about the current standing of the Friendly Relations Declaration, it shall be construed with reference to subsequent practice and specifically by taking up other texts that make direct reference to it, be it the Definition of Aggression just mentioned, the Declaration on the Enhancement of the Effectiveness of the Principle of Refraining from the Threat or Use of Force in International Relations adopted in 1987,[13] or the 2005 World Summit Outcome.[14] Generally, the argument that shall be defended is the following: on the scale of the United Nations, texts have continued to have a classical tone, tending to restrict the possibilities of the use of force. Initiatives tending to make the regime more flexible by including new interpretations or new exceptions have never been reflected in the texts with the result that the development of law has remained limited on this particularly sensitive matter.[15]

II THE SCOPE OF THE PROHIBITION

Taking up Article 2(4) of the UN Charter almost word for word, the Friendly Relations Declaration provides that:

> Every State has the duty to refrain in its international relations from the threat or use of force against the territorial integrity or political independence of any State, or in any other manner inconsistent with the purposes of the United Nations.[16]

Two main questions arise from reading the provision. The first relates to the very definition of the notion of 'force'. Should it be confined to military force or more broadly conceived as extending in particular to the economic sphere? The second concerns the expression

[11] See eg A Lagerwall, *Le Principe 'ex injuria non oritur' en droit international contemporain* (Bruylant, 2016).
[12] See n 8.
[13] Annexed to UNGA Res 42/22.
[14] Annexed to UNGA Res 60/1 (24 October 2005).
[15] For further details and developments, see Corten (n 6). Certain parts of the present study are directly inspired from some passages of this book.
[16] Friendly Relations Declaration, second paragraph.

'international relations'. Should it be limited to relations between States or can it be extended to certain actions involving non-State actors? In both cases, the Declaration seems to reflect rather a restrictive position, a position that largely remains current half a century later.

1 *The Meaning of 'Force'*

It is widely known that during the preparatory work on the UN Charter a proposed amendment to include economic force in the wording of its Article 2(4) was dismissed.[17] The text of the Friendly Relations Declaration seems to confirm that 'force', within the meaning of this provision, is to be understood as covering military force only. It reads: 'No State may use or encourage the use of economic, political or any other type of measures to coerce another State in order to obtain from it the subordination of the exercise of its sovereign rights.'[18] However, this statement appears in the third principle: 'concerning the duty not to intervene in matters within the domestic jurisdiction of any State, in accordance with the Charter'. Conversely, no allusion to economic coercion features in the part of the text on the use of force. Admittedly, the debates held before the resolution was adopted reveal a degree of contention among States on this issue,[19] and that contention arose in parallel during the discussions that led to the adoption of the Vienna Convention of 1969 and especially its Article 52 ('Coercion of a State by the threat or use of force'). Some States, and especially those from the global South, came out in favour of extending the provision to economic force while others, mostly Western States, objected to such an extension.[20] In the absence of any consensus on this point and allowing also for subsequent practice which shows that Article 2(4) is invoked essentially to denounce military force (economic force being associated with the principle of non-intervention), it is difficult to go beyond this restrictive interpretation. This does not mean that economic coercion is allowed but rather that its prohibition does not flow specifically from the rule set out in Article 2(4) of the Charter. Beyond the symbolic scope of the debate (can one rely on the principle prohibiting force in addition to the principle of non-intervention?), the legal consequences are essentially of two orders.[21] First, economic coercion cannot readily be used to invalidate a treaty by application of Article 52 of the Vienna Convention (for that matter, there is no precedent to this effect).[22] Next, and here we come back more directly to the domain of *jus contra bellum*, because economic force is not a use of 'force' within the meaning of the Charter, it will never serve as a basis for a right of self-defence, which right only arises in any case in the event of an '*armed* attack' (under the terms of Article 51 of the Charter).

At the same time, the force in question should not be understood in too limited a way. The drafters of the Charter – and this was confirmed on several occasions in the work leading to the adoption of Resolution 2625 (XXV) – meant to widen the prohibition which, under the systems of the Covenant of the League of Nations and the Pact of Paris was limited to the notion of 'war'.[23]

17 A Randelzhofer and O Dörr, 'Article 2(4)' in B Simma et al (eds), *The Charter of the United Nations: A Commentary* (3rd edn, Oxford University Press, 2012) 209.

18 Friendly Relations Declaration, second principle, para 2.

19 *United Nations Yearbook* (1965) 627; (1966) 907–8; (1967) 744; (1968) 826; (1969) 760 and 764.

20 O Corten, 'Article 52' in O Corten and P Klein (eds), *The Vienna Conventions on the Law of Treaties: A Commentary Article by Article* (Oxford University Press, 2011) 1215–11.

21 See O Corten et al, *A Critical Introduction to International Law* (2nd edn, Hart, 2019), ch 5.

22 Corten (n 20) 1209–10.

23 See A Randelzhofer, 'Use of Force' in R Bernhardt (ed), *Max Planck Encyclopaedia of Public International Law*, vol 4 (North-Holland Publishers, 1982) 267; E Giraud, 'L'Interdiction du recours à la force. La théorie et la pratique des Nations Unies' (1963) 67 *Revue générale de droit international public* 511.

The 'force' that was prohibited from then on therefore covers limited military interventions, that fall well short of invasion, massive bombardment or missile launches. But can it be considered that *any and all* executive acts of extraterritorial scope are a violation of the prohibition of the use of force? The question was not raised in the debates before the Friendly Relations Declaration was adopted and the text is silent on the subject. As for practice, allowance for it seems to lead to the following two lessons. On the one side, and case law enshrines this,[24] it does indeed seem that 'force' within the meaning of Article 2(4) does not cover *any and all* acts of violence in international relations: accordingly, the provision is not generally invoked to condemn the abduction of a person (as the *Eichmann* case attests), or certain 'under-cover operations' (as shown by the case of the *Rainbow Warrior*) in the territory of another State, unauthorised intrusion into another State's maritime area or airspace, and (as a knock-on effect) the interception of a foreign aircraft or vessel, not to speak of incidents arising from unintentional acts (such as a State agent inadvertently crossing a border or even the accidental dropping of a bomb on foreign territory).[25] But, on the other side, practice shows all the difficulty in drawing a precise dividing line short of which the characterisation of the use of 'force' would be excluded.[26] It has happened, probably because of a conflict-ridden context between two States, that minor actions are considered to come within the ambit of Article 2(4) of the Charter. Evidence of this includes in particular the abortive operation to rescue US hostages in Tehran undertaken by the United States in 1979 or, more recently, targeted killings in the context of a war against terrorism viewed as the exercise of self-defence on a very large scale. In yet other cases, States fail to agree on any characterisation. In March 2018, the UK authorities accused Russia of using force contrary to the Charter in poisoning two Russian citizens (and injuring a British police officer) in Salisbury and so in UK territory.[27] A brief debate was held in the Security Council and no other State evoked Article 2(4) of the Charter, probably out of concern not to make matters worse.[28] The same difficulties surround the characterisation of what are referred to as 'cyberattacks' – that is, the use of computing resources not just to collect or disseminate information abroad but also, as the case may be, to cause damage there.[29] Practice is very limited on this but there has been much debate on the matter since the 2010s, including within the United Nations.[30] Once again the conclusions are nuanced. On the one hand, it is generally accepted that some cyberattacks could be characterised as a use of force contrary to Article 2(4), at least if they cause damage or effects comparable to those caused by a conventional military attack. As the ICJ emphasised, the provisions of the Charter 'do not refer to specific weapons. They apply to any use of force, regardless of the weapons

[24] *Fisheries Jurisdiction (Spain v Canada)*, ICJ Reports 1998, 466, para 84; Arbitral Tribunal Constituted Pursuant to Article 287, and in Accordance with Annex VII of the UN Convention on the Law of the Sea (Guyana and Suriname), 17 September 2007, para 445.

[25] Corten (n 6) 51–92; ME O'Connell, 'The Prohibition of the Use of Force' in ND White and C Henderson (eds), *Research Handbook on International Conflict and Security Law* (Edward Elgar, 2013) 102–7; comp T Tom Ruys, 'The Meaning of "Force" and the Boundaries of *Jus ad bellum*: Are "Minimal" Uses of Force Excluded from UN Charter Article 2(4)' (2014) 108 *American Journal of International Law* 159–210.

[26] Corten (n 6) 66 et seq.

[27] S/PV8203, 14 March 2018, 2. However, the letter sent to the Security Council does not mention a use of 'force' according to Art 2.4 of the UN Charter, preferring to label the incident as an 'attack', without further precision or explanation (S/2018/218, 13 March 2018).

[28] Several States referred to an 'attack': the USA (S/PV8203, 14 March 2018, 4), France (ibid), Equatorial Guinea (ibid 5), Poland (ibid 6), Sweden (ibid), Ethiopia (ibid 7) the Netherlands (10–11) and the UK itself (ibid 2–3 and 11).

[29] NATO Co-operative Cyber Defence, *The Tallin Manual*, prepared by the international group of experts at the invitation of the NATO Cooperative Cyber Centre of Excellence (general ed Michael Shmitt, Cambridge University Press, 2013); *Tallin Manual* 2.0. (general ed Michael Shmitt, Cambridge University Press, 2017).

[30] K Bannelier and T Christakis, *Cyber-Attacks: Prevention-Reactions: The Role of States and Private Actors* (Les Cahiers de la Défense nationale, 2017).

employed.'[31] The use of 'computer weapons', like biological or chemical weapons, does not therefore rule out the characterisation of force. But on the other hand, it is difficult to determine in each individual case whether the effects are equivalent to those of a use of force. It shall be recalled in this respect that the economic consequences of an embargo, that may be particularly deadly, are generally considered to be excluded, in any event. But in that case, and even if the death of numerous victims does not suffice (think for example of the effects of the embargo on Iraq in the 1990s), when can it be considered that the threshold of 'force' has been reached? It would probably be necessary for the type of act caused by the cyberattack to be similar to military force, such as an explosion or a direct act of physical violence.[32] In the absence of such precedents, it is hard even to give any pointers in this respect.

Accordingly, whether in 1970 or fifty years later, it remains difficult to define the notion of 'force' precisely. The ambivalence underlying the question emerges clearly here. On the one side, extending the scope of the notion seems to strengthen prohibition and so serve as a factor for pacifying international relations. But on the other side reducing the threshold of the field of application of Article 2(4) might lead some States to more readily rely on their right of self-defence, which might encourage military escalation. This dilemma must invariably be taken into account when considering the notion of 'force' within the meaning of the UN Charter and it also concerns the notion of 'international relations' as shall be seen next.

2 *The Meaning of 'International Relations'*

Does an act of terrorism or more generally the action of a non-State actor fall within the scope of Article 2(4) of the Charter? And as a knock-on effect, is such an act liable to trigger a right of self-defence pursuant to Article 51? These particularly topical questions were discussed in depth at the time the Friendly Relations Declaration was adopted. And it is particularly interesting today to remember this before wondering whether the position then adopted – which was rather restrictive as shall be seen – has been subsequently challenged by the United Nations.

Mention must be made first of three situations that have given rise to a reaffirmation of the inter-State character of the rule set out in Article 2(4) of the Charter. First, it was unanimously accepted that the rule was not aimed at acts of violence committed within the territory of a State whether by rebel or secessionist forces or by the authorities themselves. The statement by Australia's representative is significant in this respect:

> [T]he significance of the expression 'in their international relations' in Article 2 (4) of the Charter was that force employed in a civil war fell outside the scope of the provision. Neither international law in general nor the Charter placed any restrictions upon the use of force in the establishment of new internal legal orders. That elaboration of the rule seemed to cover also rebellions which aimed at secession.[33]

No State seems ever to have challenged this assertion; quite the contrary.[34] Accordingly, although it is regulated by various provisions relating to international humanitarian law or

[31] *Legality of the Threat or Use of Nuclear Weapons* (n 8) 244, para 39.

[32] *Tallin Manual* 2.0 (n 29) Rule 69, 330–37.

[33] Australia; A/AC119/SR10, 3 September 1964, at 8–9.

[34] See similar statements made by Guatemala, A/AC119/SR14, 8 September 1964, 7; Sweden, A/AC125/SR25, 25 March 1966, 9, para 13; China, A/C.6/SR.875, 15 November 1965, para 5; Central African Republic (A/C.6/SR.884, 29 November 1965, para 27); USA, MM Whiteman, *Digest of International Law* 13 (Department of State Publication, 1968) 358–59.

human rights, and although there is nothing besides to prevent the Security Council from adopting resolutions governing it, civil war remains outside the scope of the prohibition of the use of force.[35] Subsequent practice has not challenged this conception. While the Security Council tends increasingly to adopt resolutions demanding ceasefires or prohibiting violence in internal conflict, it does so on a case-by-case basis, depending on considerations of expediency relating to maintaining peace and international security.[36] Never, though, does it conceive its action as the implementation of a more general rule prohibiting the use of force within States. As for the ICJ, it reiterated in its Opinion on the *Declaration of Independence in respect of Kosovo*, that a secessionist conflict remained outside the field of application of Article 2(4) of the Charter.[37]

Second, some States have suggested extending the prohibition on the use of force in 'international relations' to the repression by a colonial power of a national liberation movement ensuring a people's exercise of its right to self-determination. From this perspective, the oppressed people would supposedly be the victim of an armed attack and would consequently have a right of self-defence. The collective dimension of self-defence might even, in some circumstances, entitle other States to intervene to end the unlawful occupation for which the colonial power is allegedly responsible. As might be expected, this argument, which was supported by the States of the global South and by the States allied to the USSR, was fiercely contested by the Western States.[38] Ultimately, the Friendly Relations Declaration provides that:

> Every State has the duty to refrain from any forcible action which deprives peoples referred to in the elaboration of the principle of equal rights and self-determination of their right to self-determination and freedom and independence.[39]

But we must not be misled by this text. Under no circumstance does it reflect an agreement that a State might be considered the author of an armed attack for the mere reason that it fails to observe a people's right of self-determination, with as a consequence that the people has a right of individual or collective self-defence. No precedent before or after 1970 can be found to this effect.[40] As for the ICJ, it seems indeed to have condemned such reasoning by recalling, in the case concerning the *Wall in the Occupied Palestinian Territory*, the inter-State character of Article 51 of the Charter including in a context characterised by the right of peoples to self-determination.[41]

Third, the debates ahead of the adoption of the Friendly Relations Declaration, and in parallel with the Definition of Aggression, attest to an attempt by certain Western States to extend *jus contra bellum* to certain political entities.[42] The objective was to include entities like South Vietnam whose standing as a State was doubtful. The Soviet Union then stated clearly that 'a definition which was made to apply to political entities without statehood would be

[35] R Pinto, 'Les Règles du droit international concernant la guerre civile' (1965) 114 *Recueil des Cours* 477; J Salmon, 'Internal Aspects of the Right to Self-Determination: Towards a Democratic Legitimacy Principle' in C Tomuschat (ed), *Modern Law of Self-Determination* (Martinus Nijhoff Publishers, 1993) 256.

[36] O Corten, 'La Rébellion et le droit international. Le principe de neutralité en tension' (2014) 374 *Recueil des Cours* 133–51.

[37] *Unilateral Declaration of Independence in respect of Kosovo*, ICJ Reports 2010, 437, para 80.

[38] Corten (n 6) 135–49 (with numerous references cited).

[39] See also a similar text in the Definition of Aggression annexed to UNGA Res 3314 (XXIX) (14 December 1974), Art 7.

[40] Corten (n 6) 142–47.

[41] *Legal Consequences of the Construction of a Wall in the Occupied Palestinian Territory* (n 8) 194, para 139.

[42] Corten (n 6) 151–60.

unacceptable to the Soviet Union also, for reasons of principle'.[43] This position was taken up by all socialist countries, but also by the non-aligned States and even certain Western States.[44] It is not surprising, then, that, in the early 1970s, the United States abandoned the idea of introducing the concept of 'political entity' into the Definition of Aggression,[45] suggesting instead that a clause be added excluding the criterion of recognition, which was quickly accepted.[46] The passage of the Friendly Relations Declaration relating to demarcation lines must be read in this context. It says:

> Every State likewise has the duty to refrain from the threat or use of force to violate international lines of demarcation, such as armistice lines, established by or pursuant to an international agreement to which it is a party or which it is otherwise bound to respect.

The *travaux préparatoires* show that, what was finally in view were the lines separating the territories of two States and not a territorial boundary of any non-State entity.[47] Discussions related essentially to the legal status of those lines and not to that of the entities in question, which were clearly considered to be States.[48] Here again subsequent practice has not challenged this equilibrium. In the case of attempted secessions or other conflicts akin to civil wars, the rules referred to above have continued to prevail. The precedents of Kosovo, South Ossetia or Abkhazia or again of the 'Republic of Transnistria' can be cited in support.[49]

It remains for us to consider a particularly intricate situation which is that of private groups, characterised sometimes as guerrillas, sometimes terrorists or sometimes again as rebels, but who have in common a military capability similar to that of some States. In a situation of the kind, can it be considered that we are faced with a use of force within the meaning of Article 2(4) of the Charter?

The question was debated at great length in the discussions leading up to the Friendly Relations Declaration and then the Definition of Aggression adopted four years later.[50] It resulted in the establishment of a double threshold that can be presented by taking excerpts from these two fundamental texts. The first states that:

> Every State has the duty to refrain from organizing or encouraging the organization of irregular forces or armed bands including mercenaries, for incursion into the territory of another State.
>
> Every State has the duty to refrain from organizing, instigating, assisting or participating in acts of civil strife or terrorist acts in another State or acquiescing in organized activities within its territory directed towards the commission of such acts, when the acts referred to in the present paragraph involve a threat or use of force.

The second characterises aggression as '[t]he *sending by or on behalf of a State* of armed bands, groups, irregulars or mercenaries, which carry out acts of armed force against another State of such gravity as to amount to the acts listed above, *or its substantial involvement therein*'.[51]

[43] A/AC134/SR65, 28 July 1970 in A/AC134/SR52–66, 148.
[44] Corten (n 6) 154.
[45] A/AC134/SR65, 28 July 1970 in A/AC134/SR52–66.
[46] A/AC134/SR59, 22 July 1970 in A/AC134/SR52–66; A/AC134/SR65, 28 July 1970 in A/AC134/SR52–66.
[47] See eg Iran (A/AC134/SR41, 24 March 1969 in A/AC134/SR25–51; A/AC134/SR56, 17 July 1970 in A/AC134/SR52–66).
[48] Bolivia (A/C.6/SR.1160, 26 November 1969, para 1), Netherlands (A/AC.125/SR.101, 22 August 1969), India (A/C.6/SR.1183, 28 September 1970, para 8), Syria (A/AC.125/SR.65, 31 July 1967; Report of the Special Committee on Principles of International Law concerning Friendly Relations and Co-operation among States, Supp No 18, A/8018, 1970, para 207; A/AC.125/SR.109, 19 September 1969).
[49] Corten (n 6) 447–50.
[50] ibid 447–50.
[51] Art 3(g) of the Definition of Aggression (emphasis added).

Readers will have noticed the distinction made between a use of 'force', which covers any support for irregular groups when those groups themselves use force and an 'aggression' which requires the State concerned to 'send' such a group or to be culpable of 'substantial involvement' in its activities. In the first case, there is a violation of the Charter but no armed attack (as in the second) and therefore no right to self-defence on the part of the State incurring the attack. In both situations, we are however in an inter-State perspective: the irregular group cannot as such violate Article 2(4) of the Charter, which is meant for States alone, and for the same reason it cannot be the perpetrator, as such, of an aggression, since aggression can only be conceived of in relations between States. At the same time, the inter-State dimension of the regime does not prevent the condemnation of a State, behind the private group, that supports it or which, if it were proved, used it directly to employ force. The early 1970s saw, then, a compromise reached between the many States which wished purely and simply to ignore violence by private groups and others, essentially Western States, for which all actions by private groups should be attributable to the States harbouring them.[52]

Has this compromise been called into question since, especially after the deadly events of 11 September 2001? Many authors have argued as much.[53] They contend that practice has enshrined a new regime under which private groups (and especially those characterised as terrorists) do indeed use 'force' in international relations, and that use of force should be likened to an 'armed attack' triggering a right of self-defence within the meaning of Article 51 of the Charter. By application of this right, any State that is the victim of a terrorist attack would be authorised to riposte by using force. And such riposte, if it proved necessary to combat the terrorist group, might affect the States harbouring the group or more generally the States in whose territory the group was located. Evidence of this is found in the precedents such as the war in Afghanistan (2001), the war in Lebanon (2006) or more recently the war against Islamic State in Iraq or in Syria (2014). From this perspective, the compromise set out in the texts appended to Resolutions 2615 (XXV) and 3314 (XXIX) was supposedly overturned and replaced by far more extensive possibilities for the use of force. These 'international relations' were therefore defined far more widely than in the Charter, and extended beyond inter-State relations – with, as a consequence, an enhanced right to self-defence.

Doctrinal debates are particularly fierce on this subject and it would be vain to claim to resolve them in the limited context of this chapter. It is worth mentioning, though, the following points which argue in favour of a degree of reluctance to overturn the advances of the Friendly Relations Declaration and the Definition of Aggression.

First, the texts adopted since, far from challenging them, tend to confirm their contents. Thus an International Convention for the Suppression of Acts of Nuclear Terrorism was adopted in 2005, Article 21 of which prescribes that States shall 'carry out their obligations under this Convention in a manner consistent with the principles of sovereign equality and territorial integrity of States and that of non-intervention in the domestic affairs of other States'. Its Article 22 adds:

[52] Corten (n 6) 449–50.

[53] See eg E Wilmshurst, 'The Chatham House Principles of International Law on the Use of Force by States in Self-Defence' (2006) 55 *International & Comparative Law Quarterly* 963–72. C Tams, 'The Use of Force against Terrorists' (2009) 20 *European Journal of International Law* 359–97; M Wood, 'Terrorism and the International Law on the Use of Force' in B Saul (ed), *Research Handbook on International Law and Terrorism* (Edward Elgar, 2014) 195–207; D Bethlehem, 'Principles Relevant to the Scope of a State's Right to Self-Defense against an Imminent or Actual Armed Attack by Nonstate Actors' (2012) 106 *American Journal of International Law* 1–8.

> Nothing in this Convention entitles a State Party to undertake in the territory of another State Party the exercise of jurisdiction and performance of functions which are exclusively reserved for the authorities of that other State Party by its national law.

It is clear from this convention that even if a terrorist group does operate from a State's territory, that does not entitle other States to conduct military action to end that group's activities. Such a right cannot be readily inferred from the Charter itself, at least if one keeps to the declaration of the World Summit 2005. This declaration does not in any way reflect the idea that the development of terrorism has brought about a change in *jus contra bellum*. On the contrary, the heads of State and government 'reiterate[d] the obligation *of all Member States* to refrain in their international relations from the threat or use of force in any manner inconsistent with the Charter'.[54] In another passage of the document, States explicitly affirm that 'the relevant provisions of the Charter are sufficient to address the full range of threats to international peace and security'.[55] No trace of applicability of Charter Articles 2(4) or 51 to terrorist groups can be found in the preparatory documents either, with the high-level panel report for example recalling the inter-State character of this provision.[56] In the same vein, it will be noted that the States of the Assembly of the International Criminal Court defined aggression in 2010 as 'the use of armed force by a State against the sovereignty, territorial integrity or political independence of another State', referring explicitly to the definition appended to UN General Assembly Resolution 3314 (XXIX) and taking up *in extenso* its Article 3(g) cited above.[57] The texts seem therefore to stand by the compromise expressed in that article and in the Friendly Relations Declaration. The perpetration of acts of violence by private actors may bring the rules of *jus contra bellum* into play, but only if a State supports or tolerates such violence (which is enough to evoke a use of force in international relations within the meaning of Article 2(4)) or *a fortiori* if it sends such actors to attack another State (in which case it can be proved there has been an armed attack that triggers the right of self-defence).

Next, the case law of the ICJ remains firmly rooted in this direction. In its opinion concerning the *Wall in the Occupied Palestinian Territory*, handed down in 2004, the Court explicitly affirmed that 'Article 51 of the Charter thus recognizes the existence of an inherent right of self-defence in the case of armed attack by one State against another State' and concluded that it was of 'no relevance in this case'.[58] It is on this basis that it dismissed Israel's argument invoking this provision to justify building the wall as a protective measure against what Israel considered to be terrorist groups. A year later, in the case of *Armed Activities on the Territory of the Congo*, the Court was asked to determine whether Uganda could rely on its right of self-defence to riposte against military actions by irregular Ugandan forces operating from the territory of the Congo. The Court found that it could not, observing that '[t]he attacks did not emanate from armed bands or irregulars sent by the DRC or on behalf of the DRC, within the sense of Article 3(g) of General Assembly resolution 3314 (XXIX) on the Definition of Aggression, adopted on 14 December 1974', and went on to affirm more generally that:

> Article 51 of the Charter may justify a use of force in self-defence only within the strict confines there laid down. It does not allow the use of force by a State to protect perceived security

[54] 2005 World Summit Outcome, A/RES/60/1, 24 October 2005, para 77 (emphasis added).
[55] ibid, para 79.
[56] 'A More Secure World: Our Shared Responsibility', Report of the Secretary-General's High-Level Panel on Threats, Challenges and Change, UN, 2004, A/59/565, 58, para 185; see also ibid 59, para 192.
[57] ICC Statute, Art 8*bis*.
[58] n 8, 194, para 139.

> interests beyond these parameters. Other means are available to a concerned State, including, in particular, recourse to the Security Council.[59]

In the same judgment, the Court cited several times its 1986 decision in the case concerning *Military and Paramilitary Activities*, in which it had affirmed that:

> [W]hile the concept of an armed attack includes the despatch by one State of armed bands into the territory of another State, the supply of arms and other support to such bands cannot be equated with armed attack. Nevertheless, such activities may well constitute a breach of the principle of the non-use of force and an intervention in the internal affairs of a State, that is, a form of conduct which is certainly wrongful, but is of lesser gravity than an armed attack.[60]

To date the Court has consistently maintained an openly restrictive position, both by maintaining the *jus contra bellum* regime within the sphere of inter-State relations and by distinguishing, as do General Assembly Resolutions 2625 (XX) and 3314 (IX), between a simple use of force and an armed attack, depending on the degree of involvement of the State in the activity of the irregular groups. One may regret it or attempt to criticise these precedents by invoking certain isolated dissenting or individual opinions, but the Court's case law is clear on this.

Against the restrictive position regularly reaffirmed in the texts and in case law, the emphasis some commentators place on erratic and ambiguous practice does not carry much weight. While it is true that the war against Afghanistan brought about a widespread (but not unanimous) challenge to the traditional interpretations of Articles 2(4) and 51 of the Charter, other precedents have revealed staunch resistance from the great majority of States. The position of the Non-Aligned Movement (NAM), which was reiterated on several occasions, and notably in the context of the war against Islamic State, is significant in this respect:

> The Movement stressed that the UN Charter contains sufficient provisions regarding the use of force to maintain and preserve international peace and security . . . In addition, and consistent with the practice of the UN and international law, as pronounced by the ICJ, Article 51 of the UN Charter is restrictive and should not be re-written or re-interpreted.[61]

All of these points probably explain the caution shown by much of the legal literature with respect to tendencies to make the provisions of the Charter on the use of force more flexible.[62] In short, the texts adopted by the General Assembly in 1970 and 1974 after long years of discussions cannot be made light of. This is true for the scope of the rule itself, especially the notion of 'force' in 'international relations' as just seen. But it will also have been understood that the debate bears also on the exceptions to the prohibition of the use of force, which leads us to the second part of our exposition.

III EXCEPTIONS TO THE PROHIBITION OF THE USE OF FORCE

It is traditional to consider that there are two exceptions to the prohibition of the use of force: self-defence and coercive action under the aegis of the Security Council. The second exception

[59] *Armed Activities on the Territory of the Congo* (n 8) 54, paras 146–48.

[60] n 8, 126–27, para 247.

[61] NAM, Eighteenth Mid-Term Ministerial Meeting of the Non-Aligned Movement, Baku, 3–6 April 2018, para 27.2. See also, among other similar statements, Seventeenth Summit of Heads of State and Government of the Non-Aligned Movement, Venezuela, 16–18 September 2016, para 25.2.

[62] See the *Institut de droit International* Resolution on Self-Defence, Rhodes Session, 2007; and ILA, Final Report on Aggression and the Use of Force, 2018; more radically, see eg 'A Plea Against an Abusive Conception of Self-Defense as a Response to Terrorism' (text in (2016) 51 *RBDI* 7–30), signed by more than 300 international lawyers.

was not subject to any real debate when the Friendly Relations Declaration was adopted, which, as seen, generally reaffirms the 'powers of the Security Council under the Charter'. At most it was occasionally mentioned that any authorisation should be given expressly,[63] and that, unless such authorisation was given, regional organisations could not decide on coercive action in the territory of another State without its consent.[64] As concerns self-defence, we have already mentioned the input from the Declaration concerning the notion of 'international relations' in connection with non-State actors, with all the consequences it entails for the interpretation of Article 51 of the Charter. Mention remains to be made of the question of 'anticipatory', 'preventive' or 'pre-emptive' self-defence – that is, regardless of the terms used, self-defence that could be exercised in the event of a simple threat and not an armed attack (see section III.1 of this chapter). We shall then examine the debates on another possible exception that is not explicitly mentioned in the Charter, that of an intervention for humanitarian purposes (section III.2 of this chapter). In both cases, it shall be observed that the somewhat restrictive positions that finally prevailed in 1970 were subsequently criticised, without that leading to the consecration of a new interpretation of *jus contra bellum*. Here again, today the Friendly Relations Declaration still appears to accurately represent existing law.

1 *Anticipatory, Preventive or Pre-Emptive Self-Defence*

After 11 September 2001 in particular, the theories that it should be possible to act in self-defence even before an attack is launched regained currency.[65] These theories come in various shapes and sizes. For some, especially in this nuclear era, and in a context marked by the development of the nuisance capacity of terrorist groups, a mere threat should be enough to warrant implementing Article 51 of the Charter.[66] For others, who consider they are protecting the stringency of *jus contra bellum*, only an 'imminent' threat could trigger application of this provision.[67] In both cases, emphasis is placed on the wording of Article 51 which states there is an 'inherent right', which itself refers back to a custom that there has supposedly always been, at any rate since the case of the *Caroline* in the early nineteenth century. The idea is that the Charter is not a 'suicide pact' and that States must be able to defend themselves without having to wait to suffer the effects of an attack. In contradistinction to these theories, others emphasise

[63] Czechoslovakia (A/C.6/S.R.871, 8 November 1965, 203, para 35); Chile (A/AC.125/L.23, 24 March 1966, (h) and A/AC.125/SR.22, 23 March 1966, 13, para 31); Mexico (A/C.6/S.R.886, 1 December 1965, 293, para 34); Sweden (A/AC.125/SR.86, 13 September 1968, 44).

[64] See eg Ukraine (A/C.6/S.R.875, 15 November 1965, 218, para 19); Iran (A/C.6/S.R.882, 24 November 1965, 261, para 18); Sweden (A/C.6/S.R.886, 1 December 1965, 291, para 18); UK (A/AC.119/SR.16, 9 September 1964, 12–13); Argentina, Chile, Guatemala, Mexico and Venezuela (A/AC.125/SR66, 1 August 1967, 7 (and A/AC.125/L.49, III).

[65] T Franck, *Recourse to Force: State Action Against Threats and Armed Attacks* (Cambridge University Press, 2002) 77, 97–107; J Brunnée and SJ Toope, 'Slouching Towards New "Just" Wars: International Law and the Use of Force after September 11th' (2004) 51 *Netherlands International Law Review* 373–76.

[66] M Reisman, 'International Legal Responses to Terrorism' (1999) 22 *Houston Journal of International Law* 17–19; AD Sofaer, 'On the Necessity of Pre-Emption' (2003) 14 *European Journal of International Law* 209–26; R Wedgwood, 'Unilateral Action in the UN System' (2000) 11 *European Journal of International Law* 355.

[67] R Higgins, *The Development of International Law Through the Political Organs of the United Nations* (Oxford University Press, 1963) 199; R Hofmann, 'International Law and the Use of Military Force Against Iraq' (2002) 45 *German Yearbook of International Law* 31; J Brumée, 'The Security Council and Self-Defence: Which Way to Global Security?' in N Blokker and N Schrijver (eds), *The Security Council and the Use of Force: A Need for Change?* (Martinus Nijhoff, 2005) 118–19.

the dangers engendered by preventive self-defence, which was invoked in particular by Nazi Germany and Imperial Japan to justify the invasion of Belgium and the Netherlands in May 1940 and the attack on Pearl Harbor in December 1941, respectively.[68] This explains why the allied powers sought to exclude any form of self-defence in the absence of an actual armed attack, which is indicated both by Article 51 and the preparatory work for it.[69] Accordingly, while there is nothing to prohibit a State from triggering a military riposte against an attack that has already begun but not yet born fruit (against a missile launched from the territory of another State, aircraft preparing to take off to attack, or troops heading to cross the border), one cannot rely on a mere 'threat', whether imminent or not (and there are serious problems of definition here), to trigger an armed action. While 'interceptive' self-defence may be accepted, this would not be true of preventive, pre-emptive or anticipatory self-defence, all of which terms should be dismissed as oxymorons.[70]

There is in truth nothing new in this debate. It was begun in the 1950s as part of the work on the Definition of Aggression, and then continued until the adoption of Resolutions 2625 (XXV) and 3314 (XXIX). It was then given fresh impetus in the 2000s in the discussions preceding the adoption of UN General Assembly Resolution 60/1 (2005 World Summit). Although the texts of these instruments give little indication as to the interpretation of Charter Article 51 that prevailed, a glance at the discussions before their adoption is particularly instructive.

The proposal to accept preventive self-defence in international law was first made during the debates concerning the Definition of Aggression in the early 1950s, in the context of the nuclear arms race. That proposal was defended by the Netherlands,[71] Greece,[72] Belgium,[73] China,[74] Panama,[75] Peru[76] and Colombia.[77] These arguments, though, are far from having convinced all the States that were then UN members, with socialist (USSR,[78] Ukraine,[79] Belarus,[80] Poland,[81] Romania,[82] Czechoslovakia[83]), African or Asian (Egypt,[84] Iran,[85] Syria[86]),

68 German memorandum to Belgium and the Netherlands, May 1940; Japan, 1941, *Keesing's Contemporary Archives*, 1940–1943, 4923.
69 Corten (n 6) 414–16.
70 ibid 406–43.
71 A/C.6/SR.337, 28 November 1952, para 6; A/C.6/SR.410, 28 October 1954, paras 40–42 and 46; A/C.6/SR.417, 8 November 1954, para 19.
72 A/C.6/SR.279, 7 January 1952, para 10.
73 A/C.6/SR.287, 15 January 1952, paras 27, 28, 29; A/C.6/SR.290, 16 January 1952, 60–61 and 65; but see A/C.6/SR.409, 28 October 1954, para 15.
74 A/C.6/SR.329, 19 November 1952, para 6; A/C.6/SR.417, 8 November 1954, para 31; A/C.6/SR.337, 28 November 1952, para 42–43; A/C.6/SR.1168, 3 December 1969, 387, para 24.
75 A/C.6/SR.403, 14 October 1954, para 25.
76 A/C.6/SR.528, 4 November 1957.
77 A/C.6/SR.532, 13 November 1957.
78 A/C.6/SR.288, 16 January 1952, paras 21 and 34; A/C.6/SR.341, 4 December 1952, para 14; A/C.6/SR.414, 3 November 1954, paras 33 and 37.
79 A/C.6/SR.290, 18 January 1952, para 3.
80 A/C.6/SR.411, 29 October 1954, para 15; A/C.6/SR.528, 4 November 1957.
81 A/C.6/SR.292, 19 January 1952, para 24; A/C.6/SR.406, 20 October 1954, para 39; A/C.6/SR.415, 4 November 1954, paras 22 and 24.
82 A/C.6/SR.520, 22 October 1957, para 11; A/C.6/SR.1349, 3 November 1972, para 50.
83 A/C.6/SR.413, 3 November 1954, paras 10–11; A/C.6/SR.418, 9 November 1954, para 46; A/C.6/SR.524, 29 October 1957; see also A/AC.134/SR.19, 2 July 1968 in A/AC.134/SR.1–24.
84 A/C.6/SR.291, 19 January 1952, paras 10–11; A/C.6/SR.414, 3 November 1954, para 2.
85 A/C.6/SR.405, 18 October 1954, paras 3 and 5; A/C.6/SR.416, 5 November 1954, para 32.
86 A/C.6/SR.517, 14 October 1957.

Latin American (Chile,[87] Mexico,[88] Paraguay[89]), or Western countries (Norway,[90] or even France[91] and at that time the UK[92]) opposing the idea of preventive self-defence. The controversy continued into the 1960s. The UK, for example, then evoked 'the intent of the framers of the Charter, who had it clearly in mind that the protection afforded by Article 51 should apply only in the case of an unlawful *threat* or use of armed force'.[93] But other States adopted an entirely different position, like Mexico which affirmed that:

> [according to some] the right of self-defence could be exercised not only in the event of armed attack but also when the military potential of a State and the aggressive intentions it betrayed gave grounds for thinking that it would perpetrate an attack. The answer to that argument was that armed attack was armed attack and nothing else ... To return to the inherent right of self-defence, it was only permitted under Article 51 in the event of armed aggression, to the exclusion of any other act, including provocation.[94]

At that time, a similar balance of power setting a minority of States favourable to preventive self-defence against a majority that were highly critical of it could be observed. In the main, the first group comprised Western States[95] and the second socialist,[96] Third World[97] and Latin American[98] States. The distinction, though, was not a radical one, with several Western States

[87] A/C.6/SR.281, 9 January 1952, para 28; see also A/C.6/SR.290, 18 January 1952, paras 56–57.
[88] A/C.6/SR.408, 25 October 1954, para 32.
[89] A/C.6/SR.419, 10 November 1954, para 15.
[90] A/C.6/SR.413, 3 November 1954, para 30.
[91] AC Kiss, *Répertoire de la Pratique française en matière de droit international public*, vol 6 (CNRS, 1969) 63, No 84; see also ibid 72, No 100 and 101.
[92] A/C.6/SR.412, 1 November 1954, para 10; A/C.6/SR.416, 5 November 1954, paras 18–28.
[93] A/AC.125/SR.65, 31 July 1967, 6.
[94] A/AC.119/SR.9, 3 September 1964, 12 and 11.
[95] United Kingdom (A/C.6/S.R.805, 5 November 1963, para 7; A/AC.125/SR.65, 31 July 1967; A/AC.134/SR.85, 9 February 1971 in A/AC.134/SR.79–91, 50; but see also A/C.6/S.R.761, 16 November 1962, 147, para 13); Australia (A/C.6/S.R.817, 21 November 1963, para 23; but see A/AC.119/SR.10, 3 September 1964, 11); Norway (A/AC.134/SR.67, 30 July 1970 in A/AC.134/SR.67–78; but see A/C.6/SR.1208, 27 October 1970, para 43); Greece (A/C.6/SR.1208, 27 October 1970, para 6); Belgium (A/C.6/SR.1351, 6 November 1972, para 1).
[96] Czechoslovakia (A/C.6/S.R.871, 8 November 1965, para 35; A/AC.125/SR.62, 26 July 1967; A/C.6/S.R.1086, 4 December 1968, para 30); USSR (A/AC.134/SR.67, 30 July 1970 in A/AC.134/SR.67–78; A/C.6/SR.1272, 2 November 1971, para 8; A/C.6/SR.1351, 6 November 1972, para 33); Romania (A/C.6/SR.1164, 1 December 1969, para 9); Yugoslavia (A/C.6/SR.1167, 3 December 1969, para 25; A/AC.134/SR.87, 11 February 1971 in A/AC.134/SR.79–91); Bulgaria (A/AC.134/SR.33, 12 March 1969 in A/AC.134/SR.25–51; A/AC.134/SR.57, 20 July 1970 in A/AC.134/SR.52–66, 46).
[97] Ceylon (A/C.6/S.R.805, 5 November 1963, para 21; Sri Lanka (A/C.6/SR.1478, 16 October 1974, para 56); Indonesia (A/C.6/S.R.809, 12 November 1963, para 8); Philippines (A/C.6/S.R.823, 2 December 1963, para 4); Mongolia (A/C.6/S.R.935, 22 November 1966, para 24; A/C.6/SR.1274, 3 November 1971, para 37; A/C.6/SR.1169, 3 December 1969, para 4; A/C.6/SR.1474, 11 October 1974, para 12); Ethiopia (A/C.6/S.R.936, 22 November 1966, para 40); Syria (A/AC.125/SR.88, 16 September 1968; Report of the Special Committee on Principles of International Law concerning Friendly Relations and Co-operation among States, Supp No 18, A/8018, 1970, para 207; A/AC.134/SR.70, 4 August 1970 in A/AC.134/SR.67–78); Jordan (A/C.6/SR.1271, 1 November 1971, para 14); Dahomey (A/C.6/SR.1075, 20 November 1968, para 33); Sudan (A/C.6/SR.1078, 22 November 1968, para 2; A/AC.134/SR.47, 27 March 1969 in A/AC.134/SR.25–51); Iraq (A/C.6/SR.1167, 3 December 1969, para 16; A/C.6/SR.1202, 16 October 1970, para 19; A/C.6/SR.1348, 2 November 1972, para 12; A/AC.134/SR.39, 21 March 1969 in A/AC.134/SR.25–51; A/AC.134/SR.47, 27 March 1969 in A/AC.134/SR.25–51; A/AC.134/SR.67, 30 July 1970 in A/AC.134/SR.67–78; A/C.6/SR.1271, 1 November 1971, para 22); Congo-Brazzaville (A/C.6/SR.1169, 3 December 1969, para 84); Gabon (A/C.6/SR.1205, 22 October 1970, para 36); UAR (A/AC.134/SR.22, 5 July 1968 in A/AC.134/SR.1–24; A/AC.134/SR.64, 27 July 1970 in A/AC.134/SR.52–66); Algeria (A/AC.134/SR.86, 10 February 1971 in A/AC.134/SR.79–91); Iran (A/AC.134/SR.41, 24 March 1969 in A/AC.134/SR.25–51); Pakistan (A/C.6/SR.1207, 27 October 1970, para 20; A/C.6/SR.1347, 1 November 1972, para 6); Lebanon (A/C.6/SR.1212, 30 October 1970, para 28); Egypt (A/C.6/SR.1269, 27 October 1971, para 17; A/C.6/SR.1483, 23 October 1974, para 28); Kenya (A/C.6/SR.1350, 3 November 1972, 231, para 32); Nigeria (A/C.6/SR.1351, 6 November 1972, para 20).
[98] Peru (A/C.6/S.R.765, 23 November 1962, para 22); Cuba (A/C.6/S.R.820, 27 November 1963, para 22; A/C.6/S.R.893, 8 December 1965, para 36; A/C.6/S.R.1091, 10 December 1968, para 41; A/C.6/SR.1479, 18 October 1974, para 41;

also criticising the notion, as illustrated notably[99] by this declaration by Spain: '[it] was clear that only when a country has first been attacked could it exercise its legitimate right of self-defence under Article 51. Any possibility of legalizing preventive war was out of the question.'[100] In this context, it is understandable that the proponents of preventive self-defence have progressively given up wanting to have their view prevail within the General Assembly. The text of the Friendly Relations Declaration contains, then, nothing that might be interpreted to this effect, whereas the text on the Definition of Aggression, inasmuch as it defines aggression as the use (and not the threat of use) of force, does seem to rule out any possibility of preventive self-defence.

Whereas it remained largely muted during the 1980s and 1990s, the debate was revived after the events of 11 September in the context of the preparation for the sixty years of the United Nations. In his report, based on the work of a High-Level Panel which had made a similar finding,[101] the Secretary-General affirmed that:

> Imminent threats are fully covered by Article 51, which safeguards the inherent right of sovereign States to defend themselves against armed attack. Lawyers have long recognized that this covers an imminent attack as well as one that has already happened.[102]

Just months from the 2005 World Summit, the argument of preventive self-defence, admittedly limited to the case of an imminent threat, was thus proposed to all States. The Secretary-General enshrined in part the arguments of the Bush administration which had defended the same interpretation of positive international law in a reference document published in September 2002.[103] Was the balance of power observed in the 1970s about to be tipped? It would be an exaggeration to claim as much. All told, a dozen States at most have clearly supported the position defended by the Panel and then by the UN Secretary-General: the USA,[104]

see also A/C.6/SR.1076, 21 November 1968, para 8; A/C.6/SR.1206, 26 October 1970, para 70; A/C.6/SR.1273, 2 November 1971, para 32; A/C.6/SR.1349, 3 November 1972, para 28; A/C.6/SR.1441, 19 November 1973, para 30); Panama (A/C.6/S.R.824, 2 December 1963, para 8); Uruguay (A/C.6/S.R.997, 14 November 1967, para 25; A/AC.124/SR.74, 7 August 1970 in A/AC.134/SR.67–78); Mexico (A/AC.119/SR.9, 3 September 1964; A/C.6/S.R.1095, 13 December 1968, para 36; A/AC.125/SR.22, 23 March 1966, para 20; A/AC.134/SR.6, 11 June 1968 in A/AC.134/SR.1–24; A/C.6/SR.1165, 2 December 1969, para 35; A/C.6/SR.1074, 19 November 1968, para 22; A/C.6/SR.1075, 20 November 1968, para 24); Chile (A/AC.125/L.23, 24 March 1966, g: A/AC.125/SR.22, 23 March 1966, para 31; A/AC.125/SR.66, 1 August 1967; A/C.6/SR.1167, 3 December 1969, para 11; A/AC.134/SR.15, 26 June 1968 in A/AC.134/SR.1–24; A/C.6/SR.1276, 4 November 1971, para 34); Jamaica (A/C.6/SR.1077, 22 November 1968, para 24); Ecuador (A/C.6/SR.1078, 22 November 1968, para 36; A/AC.134/SR.10, 17 June 1968 in A/AC.134/SR.1–24; A/AC.134/SR.58, 21 July 1970 in A/AC.134/SR.52–66; A/C.6/SR.1273, 2 November 1971, para 22); Guyana (A/AC.134/SR.33, 12 March 1969 in A/AC.134/SR.25–51, 54; A/AC.134/SR.95, 1 March 1972 in A/AC.134/SR.79–91, 37).

99 See also France (A/C.6/SR.1166, 2 December 1969, para 3); Sweden (A/C.6/SR.1079, 25 November 1968, para 6); and Italy (A/AC.134/SR.47, 27 March 1969 in A/AC.134/SR.25–51, 203; see also A/AC.134/SR.70, 4 August 1970 in A/AC.134/SR.67–78, 54–61).

100 Representative of Spain (A/AC.134/SR.9, 14 June 1968 in A/AC.134/SR.1–24, 101).

101 'A More Secure World' (n 56), paras 188–89.

102 Report of the Secretary-General, 'In Larger Freedom: Towards Development, Security and Human Rights for All', A/59/2005, 24 March 2005, 33, para 124.

103 The National Security Strategy of the United States of America, September 2002, 15.

104 US Reactions to UN Secretary-General's High-Level Panel Report, 'Contemporary Practice of the United States' (2005) 99 *American Journal of International Law* 495; see also, Statement by Ambassador Patrick Kennedy, US Representative for United Nations Management and Reform, on the Report of the High Level Panel on Reform, in an Informal Meeting of the General Assembly, 31 January 2005; The National Security Strategy of the USA, March 2006, 'Contemporary Practice of the United States' (2006) 100 *American Journal of International Law* 690; USA, A/59/PV87, 7 April 2005, 23.

the UK,[105] Australia,[106] Israel,[107] Uganda,[108] Morocco,[109] Liechtenstein,[110] Switzerland[111] and Korea,[112] with Russia adopting an ambiguous position.[113] By contrast, a vast majority of States denied any possibility of recognising the legality of preventive self-defence. Alongside positions by States from various parts of the world,[114] mention must be made of the position of the NAM of 117 States that published several documents commenting on the reports cited, taking up several times a passage about Charter Article 51 by which:

> The Non-Aligned Movement emphasizes that Article 51 of the UN Charter is restrictive and recognizes 'the inherent right of individual or collective self-defence if an armed attack occurs against a Member of the United Nations'. This Article should not be re-written or reinterpreted. This is supported by the practice of the UN and in accordance with international law pronounced by the International Court of Justice, the principal judicial organ of the UN, concerning this question. The Non-Aligned Movement stresses its deep concern over the intention of a group of States to unilaterally re-interpret or re-draft the existing legal instruments, in accordance with their own views and interests. NAM reemphasises that the integrity of international legal instruments must be maintained by Member States.[115]

After recalling the document from which an excerpt has just been cited, the movement's representative asserted in the debates in the General Assembly that: 'The member countries of NAM, which represent almost two thirds of the membership of this Organization, have noted that generally the ideas and observations submitted by NAM have not been taken into

[105] A/59/PV.85, 5 April 2005, 26; see also 'United Kingdom Materials on International Law', 2001, 691; (2002) 73 *British Yearbook of International Law* 853–55; (2003) 74 *British Yearbook of International Law* 767 and 769; (2004) 75 *British Yearbook of International Law* 822–23 and 825–26; (2005) 76 *British Yearbook of International Law* 902.

[106] UNGA, 7 April 2005, Plenary Exchange on the Secretary-General's Report, 'In Larger Freedom', Statement by HE Mr John Dauth LVO Ambassador and Permanent Representative of Australia to the UN, Australian Mission to the United Nations.

[107] Informal Meeting of the GA on the Draft Outcome of the High-Level Plenary Meeting of the GA (14–16 September 2005), Statement by HE Ambassador Dan Gillerman, Permanent Representative of Israel to the UN (emphasis added); see also United Nations Reforms – Position Paper of the Government of Israel, 1 July 2005.

[108] 'With regard to security threats, a state is entitled to use force in self-defence in the event of actual or imminent attack. This principle is within the ambit of the Charter of the United Nations *and should be clearly reflected in the outcome document*' (emphasis added): Statement by HE Mr Francis K Butagira, Ambassador and Permanent Representative of the Republic of Uganda to the United Nations to the Tenth Informal High-Level Plenary Meeting of the GA of September 2005, New York, 1 July 2005, Permanent Mission of Uganda to the UN.

[109] Echange de vues sur les recommandations contenues dans le rapport du groupe de personnalités de haut niveau sur les menaces, les défis et le changement, New York, 31 January 2005.

[110] Statement by HE Christian Wanaweser, 27 January 2005, informal meeting of the UNGA, Permanent Mission of the Principality of Liechtenstein to the UN, para 9.

[111] Chapter author's translation. Permanent Mission of Switzerland to the United Nations, Fifty-Ninth Session of the UNGA, informal consultations, points 45 and 55 of the agenda; Report of the Secretary-General, 'In Larger Freedom' (n 102), Cluster II (Freedom from Fear); Declaration of HE Mr Peter Maurer, Permanent Representative of Switzerland to the United Nations, New York, 21 April 2005; see also 'La Pratique suisse en matière de droit international public' (2002) 12 *Revue suisse de droit international et de droit européen* 643; contra, 'La Pratique suisse en matière de droit international public' (2001) 11 *Revue suisse de droit international et de droit européen* 599; A/59/PV.86, 6 April 2005.

[112] Report of the Secretary-General, 'In Larger Freedom' (n 102), Cluster II (Freedom from Fear).

[113] Ministry of Foreign Affairs of the Russian Federation, Information and Press Department, Russian MFA Information and Press Department Commentary Regarding a Russian Media Question Concerning Possible Preventive Strikes at Terrorists' Bases, 3 February 2005.

[114] See eg Statement by Ambassador Wang Guangya on the Report of the High-Level Group, 27 January 2005.

[115] Comments of the Non-Aligned Movement on the Observations and Recommendations contained in the Report of the High-Level Panel on Threats, Challenges and Change (A/59/565 and A/59/565CORR.1), New York, 28 February 2005, paras 23–24.

consideration in the Secretary-General's report.'[116] This is a criticism that applies perfectly well to the position defended in the report on Article 51 of the UN Charter.[117]

Ultimately it can be seen that the general trend that prevailed when the Friendly Relations Declaration and the Definition of Aggression were first drawn up has not fundamentally altered. In the absence of any precedent in which preventive self-defence might have been accepted (whether Israel's military actions in the Iraqi locality of Osirak in 1981 or the Syrian base of Al-Kibbar in 2007, or certain military actions in Syria in 2015), and because case law is silent on this point, it is difficult not to abide by the restrictive interpretation resulting from the express terms of Article 51 of the UN Charter ('if an armed attack occurs') – that is, a restrictive interpretation maintained by a majority of States after it was adopted.[118] This is a point that is relevant for appraising another debate, that bearing on the existence of a 'right of humanitarian intervention'.

2 A '*Right of Humanitarian Intervention*'?

While the UN Charter does not enshrine any right of humanitarian intervention, it does not rule one out either. That at least is what some authors claim for whom Article 2(4) leaves the door open to military action to protect human rights in other States' territory.[119] Such action would not be directed 'against the territorial integrity or political independence of any State, or in any other manner inconsistent with the Purposes of the United Nations', to take up the terms of the prohibition as expressed in the provision. An *a contrario* interpretation of the wording of the Charter of this kind is far from having won over most scholars. Many point out that a military intervention in a State's territory without its consent plainly calls into question its political independence and territorial integrity. Moreover, it is then added, the drafters of the Charter meant to strengthen and not attenuate the prohibition by mentioning the objective of the use of force referred to.[120] Lastly no convention protecting human rights (including the Convention on the Prevention and Punishment of the Crime of Genocide) or international humanitarian law contains any provision suggesting that their violation would confer a right to act militarily to enforce them. In this respect, the Security Council alone would have the power to authorise a use of force pursuant to Chapter VII of the UN Charter.

How is the Friendly Relations Declaration to be understood in this context? Plainly the text does seem to condemn any humanitarian intervention. It says that '[e]very State has the duty to refrain from the threat or use of force to *violate the existing international boundaries of another State* or as a means of solving international disputes'.[121] Accordingly merely crossing a border is a violation of the prohibition of the use of force. We are faced with an objective criterion which does not depend on allowance for the subjective criterion of the aim pursued by the actors involved. Unless it can be grounded on one of the exceptions expressly recognised in the Charter

[116] 5 April 2005, A/59/PV.85, 16.

[117] See also Jamaica (on behalf of the G77), 5 April 2005, A/59/PV.85, 18.

[118] Corten (n 6) 435–41.

[119] F Teson, *Humanitarian Intervention: An Inquiry into Law and Morality* (2nd edn, Transnational Publishers, 1997) 150–51; B Lepard, *Rethinking Humanitarian Intervention* (Pennsylvania Univ Press, 2002) 344–45.

[120] Giraud (n 23) 512–13; CHM Waldock, 'The Regulation of the Use of Force by Individual States in International Law' (1952) 81(2) *Recueil des Cours* 493; I Brownlie, 'The Use of Force in Self-Defence' (1961) 64 *British Yearbook of International Law* 233–36; JF Murphy, *The United States and the Rule of Law in International Affairs* (Cambridge University Press, 2004) 159; I Brownlie and CJ Apperley, 'Kosovo Crisis Inquiry: Memorandum on the International Law Aspects' (2000) 49 *International & Comparative Law Quarterly* 884–85, paras 33–36.

[121] Emphasis added.

(self-defence or Security Council authorisation), an operation of the kind must therefore be presumed to be unlawful.

That impression is confirmed upon examination of the debates that preceded the adoption of Resolutions 2625 (XXV) and 3314 (XXIX), which showed great reluctance by the international community of States as a whole to admit such a justification in contemporary international law. Two points should be set out in this respect.

First, an impressive number of States from all regions of the world were keen to emphasise that the use of force knew only two exceptions: self-defence or military action under the aegis of the Security Council.[122] It could admittedly be retorted that, by the argument of the *a contrario* interpretation of Article 2(4), the right of humanitarian intervention is not an 'exception' to the prohibition of the use of force, but is simply not covered by the prohibition. Careful examination of States' declarations shows, however, that what they had to say was plainly intended to dismiss the arguments predicated on the legitimacy of the purpose of a military intervention, whether humanitarian or other. The term 'exception' is not used in a technical sense but in its very general meaning, the idea being quite simply to identify the situations in which a use of force would be countenanced.[123] The dismissal of a third possible exception must therefore be understood in a broad sense as countering any justification or argument legitimising a use of force that is not expressly provided for in the UN Charter.[124]

As a second point, it must be pointed out that the *a contrario* interpretation of Article 2(4) has been repeatedly criticised during the debates that took place in the United Nations. This is

[122] France (A/C.6/S.R.1179, 24 September 1970, para 9; A/C.6/SR.1077, 22 November 1968, para 19; A/C.6/SR.1077, 22 November 1968, para 19); Spain (A/C.6/S.R.813, 18 November 1963, para 8); Cuba (A/C.6/S.R.820, 27 November 1963, para 22; A/C.6/S.R.893, 8 December 1965, para 36; A/C.6/S.R.1091, 10 December 1968, para 41); Philippines (A/C.6/S.R.823, 2 December 1963, para 4); India (A/AC.119/SR.3, 31 August 1964); Argentina (A/AC.119/SR.3, 31 August 1964); Czechoslovakia (A/C.6/S.R.871, 8 November 1965, para 35); Mali (A/C.6/S.R.882, 24 November 1965, para 28); Mexico (A/C.6/S.R.886, 1 December 1965, paras 34 and 37; A/C.6/32/SR.65, 7 December 1977, para 5); Cyprus (A/C.6/S.R.892, 7 December 1965, para 18); Bolivia (A/C.6/S.R.1004, 21 November 1967, para 25); Australia (A/C.6/S.R.1178, 23 September 1970, para 38); Portugal (A/C.6/S.R.1182, 25 September 1970, para 3); Guatemala (A/AC.119/SR.14, 8 September 1964); Nigeria (A/AC.119/SR.4, 31 August 1964; A/AC.119/SR.7, 2 September 1964); Iran (A/C.6/SR.329, 19 November 1952, para 43; A/C.6/SR.416, 5 November 1954, para 34); Sweden (A/C.6/SR.332, 22 November 1952, para 9); Netherlands (GA, Supp No 16 (A/3574), New York, 1957, para 208); Iraq (A/AC.77/L.8/Rev.1); Mexico, Paraguay, Peru and Dominican Republic (A/AC.77/L.11); Belgium (A/C.6/SR.514, 7 October 1957); Syria (A/C.6/SR.517, 14 October 1957); Guatemala (A/C.6/SR.520, 22 October 1957); Ecuador (A/AC.134/SR.58, 21 July 1970 in A/AC.134/SR.52–66); Bulgaria (A/C.6/SR.519, 18 October 1957); Guyana (A/AC.134/SR.65, 28 July 1970 in A/AC.134/SR.52–66); Italy (A/AC.134/SR.18, 1 July 1968 in A/AC.134/SR.1–24; A/AC.134/SR.64, 27 July 1970 in A/AC.134/SR.52–66); Ghana (A/AC.134/SR.37, 18 March 1969 in A/AC.134/SR.25–51; A/C.6/SR.1169, 3 December 1969, para 45); Canada (A/AC.134/SR.45, 26 March 1969 in A/AC.134/SR.25–51); Afghanistan (A/C.6/SR.1206, 26 October 1970, para 49); Greece (A/C.6/SR.1208, 27 October 1970, para 3); Uruguay (A/AC.134/SR.95, 1 March 1972 in A/AC.134/SR.79–91); Romania (A/C.6/SR.1207, 27 October 1970, para 25); Egypt (A/C.6/SR.1269, 27 October 1971, para 13); Haiti (A/C.6/SR.1443, 20 November 1973, para 17); FRG (A/C.6/SR.1478, 16 October 1974, para 19); Brazil (A/C.6/32/SR.65, 7 December 1977, para 28); Bangladesh (A/C.6/34/SR.21, 18 October 1979, para 13); Algeria (A/36/415, 8 September 1981); DRC (A/C.6/37/SR.35, 3 November 1982, para 1); Jordan (A/C.6/37/SR.39, 8 November 1982, para 67); Cape Verde (A/C.6/38/SR.17, 17 October 1983, para 88); Kenya (A/C.6/39/SR.17, 11 October 1984, para 68); Chile (A/C.6/42/SR.18, 9 October 1987, para 27); Botswana (A/C.6/42/SR.21, 13 October 1987, para 47). See also Switzerland, then a non-Member State; 'La Pratique suisse en matière de droit international public' (1983) 39 *Annuaire de suisse droit international* 248.

[123] See eg Bahamas (A/C.6/36/SR.10, 2 October 1981, para 23); Ecuador (A/C.6/S.R.1003, 20 November 1967, para 53); Israel (A/C.6/S.R.767, 27 November 1962, para 15); Yugoslavia (A/C.6/S.R.753, 5 November 1962, para 31); China (A/C.6/S.R.818, 21 November 1963, para 6); Columbia (A/C.6/S.R.929, 11 November 1966, para 8); or Panama (A/C.6/SR.403, 14 October 1954, para 27; A/C.6/SR.406, 20 October 1954, para 8).

[124] See also France, 'Pratique française du droit international' (1964) 10 *Annuaire français de droit international* 950; and Institut de droit international, 'Declaration on the Use of Force, 2 September 2003' (2003) 36 *Revue belge de droit international* 573–74, and commentaries by J Salmon, ibid 566–72.

hardly surprising for States that were traditionally careful to maintain the full stringency of the prohibition of the use of force, such as the Third World States,[125] socialist States[126] and Latin American States.[127] However, several Western States too took up the same positions, as attested to for example[128] by this statement from the US representative: '[I]f the Members of the United Nations must refrain in their international relations from the threat or use of force against the territorial integrity of any State, it was obvious that they were bound to respect the frontiers of other States.'[129] Such declarations can be explained in part by the concern to rule out arguments based on the legitimacy of national liberation struggles that were then regularly advanced, or by a challenge to the 'Brezhnev doctrine'.[130] Against this backdrop, Western States preferred to insist on the prohibition set out in Article 2(4), condemning any argument predicated on the legitimacy of motives. In doing so they indirectly but clearly dismissed any idea of a right of humanitarian intervention.

At the time there was little doubt that the right of humanitarian intervention was very largely rejected by States. This probably explains why it was not really called for either during debates in the United Nations or in particular precedents. In 1986 the ICJ clearly ruled out the idea that military action might be justified by the protection of human rights:

> [W]hile the United States might form its own appraisal of the situation as to respect for human rights in Nicaragua, the use of force could not be the appropriate method to monitor or ensure such respect ... the argument derived from the preservation of human rights in Nicaragua cannot afford a legal justification for the conduct of the United States ...[131]

After the Cold War ended, practice was to evolve towards greater centralisation of the use of force. The Security Council began to authorise certain military operations with humanitarian objectives, be it in Somalia, Bosnia-Herzegovina, Rwanda or East Timor. The war begun in 1999 against Yugoslavia to end exactions in Kosovo was from this point of view a tipping point as it was begun without UN authorisation.[132] A few States revived the doctrine of the right of humanitarian intervention in this context initially without much success. However, the question was raised in the United Nations and it quickly appeared that the classical position that had been consecrated in the Friendly Relations Declaration was not to be called into question, as attested for example by this declaration of 24 September 1999 by the Group of 77, an organisation that speaks for 132 UN Member States:

[125] Madagascar (A/AC.119/SR.9, 3 September 1964, 17–18); India (A/C.6/SR.418, 9 November 1954, para 13); China (A/C.6/SR.417, 8 November 1954, para 31).

[126] See eg USSR (A/AC.119/SR.43, 2 October 1964).

[127] Chile (A/C.6/S.R.1092, 11 December 1968, para 31; A/AC.125/L.23, 24 March 1966, (e) and A/AC.125/SR.22, 23 March 1966, para 31); Mexico (A/C.6/S.R.806, 6 November 1963, para 17; A/C.6/42/SR.17, 8 October 1987, para 8); Ecuador (A/C.6/S.R.1183, 28 September 1970, para 35); and Brazil (A/C.6/34/SR.18, 16 October 1979, para 41).

[128] See also UK (A/C.6/S.R.805, 5 November 1963, para 8); Netherlands (A/C.6/SR.410, 28 October 1954, para 32); and Israel (A/C.6/SR.412, 1 November 1954, para 35).

[129] A/AC.119/SR.42, 2 October 1964, 7; see also A/C.6/S.R.808, 11 November 1963, para 19; A/AC.119/SR.3, 31 August 1964; A/AC.134/SR.59, 22 July 1970 in A/AC.134/SR.52–66; MM Whiteman, *Digest of International Law*, vol 13 (Department of State Publication, 1968) 358.

[130] See the views expressed by UK (Report of the Special Committee on Enhancing the Effectiveness of the Principle of Non-Use of Force in International Relations, Supp No 41 (A/36/41), 1981, para 161.

[131] *Military and Paramilitary Activities* (n 8) 134–35, para 268.

[132] M Kohen, 'L'Emploi de la force et la crise du Kosovo: vers un nouveau désordre juridique international' (1999) 32 *Revue belge de droit international* 123–48.

> The Ministers stressed the need to maintain clear distinctions between humanitarian assistance and other activities of the United Nations. *They rejected the so-called right of humanitarian intervention, which has no basis in the UN Charter or in international law.*[133]

Other similar texts were adopted by the NAM[134] and then by the Islamic Conference Organisation.[135] Against this backdrop it is not surprising that the Final Summit Declaration, when evoking 'responsibility to protect', limited this to military action under the aegis of the Security Council, pursuant to Chapter VII of the Charter:

> The international community, through the United Nations, also has the responsibility to use appropriate diplomatic, humanitarian and other peaceful means, in accordance with Chapters VI and VIII of the Charter, to help to protect populations from genocide, war crimes, ethnic cleansing and crimes against humanity. In this context, we are prepared to take collective action, in a timely and decisive manner, *through the Security Council, in accordance with the Charter, including Chapter VII,* on a case-by-case basis and in cooperation with relevant regional organizations as appropriate, should peaceful means be inadequate and national authorities are manifestly failing to protect their populations from genocide, war crimes, ethnic cleansing and crimes against humanity . . .[136]

A *contrario*, it is clear that no right of humanitarian intervention was recognised, no more in 2005 than thirty-five years earlier, in the Friendly Relations Declaration.[137]

IV CONCLUDING OBSERVATIONS

The adoption of Resolution 2625 (XXV) on the Principles of International Law concerning Friendly Relations and Co-operation among States in accordance with the Charter of the United Nations marked an important milestone in the history of the prohibition on the use of force. The text indeed brought several clarifications about the scope and interpretation of certain essential provisions of the UN Charter, particularly Articles 2(4) and 51. It is therefore not surprising that the ICJ referred to the Declaration as an instrument codifying customary international law, in the *Military and Paramilitary Activities* (1986) and in the *Armed Activities* (2005) cases.

More specifically, the Declaration is particularly relevant in assessing four classical problems in relation to the use of force: the meaning of 'force', the use of force by (or against) non-State actors, preventive self-defence and humanitarian intervention. For each of those domains, the

[133] Declaration given on the occasion of the thirty-fifth anniversary of the creation of the 'Group of 77', paras 69 and 70 (emphasis added).

[134] Final Document, Ministerial Conference, Cartagena (Columbia) 8–9 April 2000, para 11; see also Declaration of Durban: 'humanitarian assistance should be neutral and impartial, be provided at the request of the country concerned, and fully respect its territorial integrity and sovereignty' (Declaration adopted after the XIIth Summit in Durban, 3 September 1998, para 63); Statement by Rastam Mohd Isa, Permanent Representative of Malaysia to the UN, in his capacity as Chairman of the Coordinating Bureau of the NAM, on behalf of the NAM, at the Fourth Informal Meeting of the Plenary of the Fifty-Ninth Session of the General Assembly, 27 January 2005, para 16; see also Special Meeting of the Ministers of Foreign Affairs of the NAM, Doha, Qatar, 13 June 2005, Declaration, NAM/2005/SFMM/05, para 18; and Statement by Chairman of the Coordinating Bureau of the NAM on behalf of the NAM, 21 June 2005, para 4 g; Ministerial Meeting of the Coordinating Bureau of the Non-aligned Movement, Putrajaya, Malaysia, 27–30 May 2006, Final Document, para 208.

[135] Final Communiqué of the Twenty-Seventh Session of the Islamic Conference of Foreign Ministers, Kuala Lumpur, Malaysia, para 79.

[136] A/RES/60/1 of 24 October 2005 (emphasis added); see also 'A More Secure World' (n 56) 65–66, para 199–203; and Report of the Secretary-General, 'In Larger Freedom' (n 102) 39, para 125.

[137] N Hajjami, *La Responsabilité de protéger* (Bruylant, 2013).

debates preceding the adoption of the text has been analysed in depth. It appeared that several delegations tried to introduce some broad interpretations of the UN Charter, resulting from the evolution of international relations. However, most of those broad interpretations were rejected, the majority of States being reluctant to offer new arguments to the intervening States, in the context of several military interventions characteristic of the Cold War (Vietnam war, USSR intervention in Czechoslovakia, . . .). The adoption of the Declaration rather seems to illustrate the prevalence of a restrictive conception of the prohibition of the use of force, sticking to the text of Articles 2(4) and 51.

But is this restrictive conception still dominant today? As we have seen, the debates about the meaning of 'force', the use of force by or against non-State actors, the existence of a preventive self-defence or a possible right to humanitarian intervention, did not end with the adoption of the Declaration. Once adopted, the text was interpreted differently by States or other actors, if not challenged on some occasions. Other instruments were adopted and then used to interpret certain provisions of the Declaration: the definition of aggression (1974) or of the crime of aggression (2010), and the World Summit Outcome Declaration (2005). Here again, a debate arose about the opportunity to accept a flexible interpretation of the prohibition to use force, in the name of the protection either of certain values (such as, in particular, the concept of 'responsibility to protect') or of the security of States threatened or attacked by terrorist activities. Still, a majority of States preferred to repeat that the relevant provisions of the UN Charter were 'restrictive and should not be re-written or re-interpreted' (to use the formula repeatedly used by the NAM and cited above).

Finally, confronted with erratic practice that is particularly influenced by political factors, allowance for the major texts adopted by all of the UN Member States proves especially valuable. While the legal literature on *jus contra bellum* often concentrates on the particularly intricate interpretation of specific precedents of military intervention, it often tends to overlook consideration of the major resolutions adopted by the General Assembly. Yet these resolutions, particularly if illuminated by the debates before and after their adoption, are highly significant. They show that States in their very large majority are not ready to accept interpretations tending to make the regime of prohibition of the use of force laid down in the UN Charter in 1945 more flexible. In this respect, a study of the Friendly Relations Declaration is entirely meaningful today.

4

Peaceful Settlement of International Disputes

Shotaro Hamamoto

I INTRODUCTION

In the Friendly Relations Declaration,[1] the principle of peaceful settlement of international disputes is stipulated immediately after the principle relating to the prohibition of the threat or the use of force.[2] This is evidently not a coincidence. As pointed out in the Report of the Special Committee in 1964, 'the principle of peaceful settlement appear[s] as the logical corollary of the injunction to refrain from the threat or use of force' and '[t]he history of international law and international relations show[s] that the two principles ... developed side by side'.[3]

An early attempt to limit the power to use force which embodied the close relation between the two principles was the Hague Convention on the Limitation of Employment of Force for Recovery of Contract Debts, adopted at the second Hague Peace Conference in 1907. Its Article 1 provides:

> The Contracting Powers agree not to have recourse to armed force for the recovery of contract debts claimed from the Government of one country by the Government of other country as being due to its nationals. This undertaking is, however, not applicable when the debtor State refuses or neglects to reply to an offer of arbitration, or, after accepting the offer, prevents any compromise from being agreed on, or, after the arbitration, fails to submit to the award.[4]

The text indicates that the settlement of disputes by way of arbitration is the precondition for the obligation to refrain from using force to apply. A similar linkage is found also in the Covenant of the League of Nations, adopted in 1919 (Article 13(2)).[5] It follows that it was difficult to speak of an 'obligation' to seek peaceful settlement of disputes at that time, recourse to war being not prohibited. Thus, Article 1 of the 1907 Convention for the Pacific Settlement of International Disputes[6] provides that the Contracting Powers agree 'to use their best efforts' to ensure the peaceful settlement of international disputes.

[1] Declaration on Principles of International Law Concerning Friendly Relations and Co-operation among States in Accordance with the Charter of the United Nations, UNGA Res 2625 (XXV) (24 October 1970), Annex.

[2] On the prohibition of the use of force see the chapter by O Corten in this volume.

[3] Report of the Special Committee, 1964, UN Doc A/5746, 82, para 139.

[4] Convention between the United States and Other Powers Respecting the Limitation of the Employment of Force for the Recovery of Contract Debts, 18 October 1907, 36 *Statutes at Large* 2241.

[5] Covenant of the League of Nations, 28 June 1919, 225 Parry 195.

[6] Hague Convention for the Pacific Settlement of International Disputes, 18 October 1907, (1908) 2 *American Journal of International Law Supplement* 43.

With the gradual consolidation of the prohibition of the use of force, however, the status of the peaceful settlement of disputes as a precondition for recourse to war was bound to change. For example, in the 1928 General Treaty for Renunciation of War as an Instrument of National Policy,[7] the renunciation of war (Article I) and the principle of peaceful settlement of disputes (Article II) are juxtaposed without being linked to each other. Whether a dispute is peacefully settled or not, disputing parties are not allowed to resort to war under the Treaty. If peaceful settlement of disputes is no longer a precondition for the recourse to war, since the latter is prohibited anyway, what is its status under international law? The 1928 Treaty gives no answer to this question.

The 1945 Charter of the United Nations furnishes, for its part, a clear answer. The use or threat of force is prohibited under Article 2(4). In the preceding paragraph, the Charter stipulates an obligation to settle international disputes by peaceful means (Article 2(3)). That the peaceful settlement of international disputes is an obligation under international law is reaffirmed by the Friendly Relations Declaration, various other General Assembly resolutions[8] and by the *Nicaragua* judgment of the International Court of Justice (ICJ).[9]

From a purely logical point of view, the prohibition of the use or threat of force does not necessarily result in an obligation to settle international disputes by peaceful means. However, 'the principle of peaceful settlement of disputes. . . is inseparable from the principle of refraining from the threat or use of force'.[10] This is because the effectiveness of the latter depends, at least to a certain extent, on that of the former. A State that considers that its vital rights have been infringed by another State might be tempted to use force to rectify the situation if the latter does not accept to peacefully settle the dispute. It is therefore reasonable that the Friendly Relations Declaration enunciates the principle of peaceful settlement of disputes immediately after that of the prohibition of the use or threat of force.

The second principle of the Friendly Relations Declaration was conceived under this historical context. This chapter first explains the basic elements this principle, as envisaged in the Friendly Relations Declaration, and it then examines later developments of issues relating to international dispute settlement not envisaged in the Friendly Relations Declaration.

II BASIC ELEMENTS ENVISAGED IN THE FRIENDLY RELATIONS DECLARATION

1 *'Obligation' to Peacefully Settle International Disputes*

While there is no doubt about the positive character of the obligation to peacefully settle international disputes,[11] the content of the obligation remains unclear. It is impossible to impose upon States an obligation requiring the achievement of settlement of disputes. Any inter-State dispute has at least two disputing parties, each of which is sovereign. A dispute cannot therefore

[7] Treaty Between the United States and Other Powers Providing for the Renunciation of War as an Instrument of National Policy, 27 August 1928, 94 LNTS 57.

[8] See particularly the Manila Declaration on the Peaceful Settlement of Disputes, UNGA Res 37/10 (15 November 1982), para 2; Solemn Appeal to States in Conflict to Cease Armed Action forthwith and to Settle Disputes between Them through Negotiations, UN Doc A/RES/40/9, para 2.

[9] *Military and Paramilitary Activities in and against Nicaragua (Nicaragua* v *United States of America)*, Merits, Judgment, ICJ Reports 1986, 14, 145, para 290.

[10] Declaration on the Enhancement of the Effectiveness of the Principle of Refraining from the Threat or Use of Force in International Relations, UN Doc A/RES/42/22, para 16.

[11] *North Sea Continental Shelf*, Judgment, ICJ Reports 1969, 3, paras 83–87; *Nicaragua* case (n 9), paras 290–91.

be settled without agreement between all disputing parties. States are thus required, under the obligation of peaceful settlement of disputes, to *seek* settlement of disputes (Article 33, UN Charter; Friendly Relations Declaration, second principle, para. 2) 'in good faith and in a spirit of co-operation'.[12] However, this obligation to seek settlement does not necessarily require States to actively seek settlement. As observed in a number of territorial disputes, States may wish to leave their dispute as it stands, agreeing to disagree.[13]

2 *Obligation of Non-Aggravation*

The Friendly Relations Declaration provides that 'States ... shall refrain from any action which may aggravate the situation so as to endanger the maintenance of international peace and security' (second principle, para. 4). The Manila Declaration, adopted by the UN General Assembly in 1982, also requires States not to take 'any action whatsoever which may... impede the peaceful settlement of the dispute'.[14]

An important question is whether the adoption of countermeasures is compatible with the obligation of non-aggravation of the situation or the dispute. Although 'any taking of countermeasures may lead to an unfortunate spiral of further countermeasures', it is difficult to say that *any* countermeasure is incompatible with the obligation, for '[a]ny other view ... would be tantamount to conferring privileges on a wrong-doer'.[15] However, in an admittedly rare situation where there are:

> necessary [procedural] means to achieve the objectives justifying the counter-measures, it must be admitted that the right of the Parties to initiate such measures disappears. In other words, the power of a tribunal to decide on interim measures of protection ... leads to the disappearance of the power to initiate counter-measures ... to the extent that the tribunal so provides as an interim measure of protection.[16]

3 *Free Choice of Means*

Article 33(1) of the UN Charter provides that '[t]he parties to any dispute ... shall ... seek a solution by ... peaceful means of their own choice'. The Friendly Relations Declaration links the principle of free choice of means to the sovereign equality of States (second principle, para. 5). Every State is expected to know means of settlement that are appropriate to the circumstances and the nature of the dispute, but no State is under an obligation to accept a specific means of dispute settlement selected by another State.

It evidently follows that a dispute remains unsettled as long as the parties to the dispute cannot agree on the means of the settlement of their dispute. However, even in the situation where a dispute is thus perpetuated, States 'shall refrain from any action which may aggravate the situation so as to endanger the maintenance of international peace and security' (second

[12] Manila Declaration (n 8), para 5.

[13] This is a frequent occurrence in relation to disputed energy deposits, which are jointly developed without settling the question of sovereignty or delimitation. See D Ong, 'Joint Development of Common Offshore oil and Gas Deposits: "Mere" State Practice or Customary International Law?' (1999) 93 *American Journal of International Law* 771.

[14] Manila Declaration (n 8), para 8.

[15] C Tomuschat, 'Article 2(3)', B Simma et al (eds), *The Charter of the United Nations: A Commentary* (3rd edn, Oxford University Press, 2012) 197, MN 41–42.

[16] *Case Concerning the Air Service Agreement of 27 March 1946 between the United States of America and France*, Decision of 9 December 1978, RIAA, vol XVIII, 417, 445–46, para 96.

principle, para. 4) and from resorting to the use or threat of force, and continue to be under the duty 'to seek a settlement of the dispute by other peaceful means agreed upon by them' (second principle, para. 2).

4 Dispute Settlement as Friendly Act

The Friendly Relations Declaration states that '[r]ecourse to, or acceptance of, a settlement procedure freely agreed to by States with regard to existing or future disputes to which they are parties shall not be regarded as incompatible with sovereign equality' (second principle, para. 5). A similar statement is made in the Manila Declaration: 'Recourse to judicial settlement of legal disputes, particularly referral to the ICJ, should not be considered an unfriendly act between States' (para. 5). Article 48(2) of the 1907 Convention for the Pacific Settlement of International Disputes sets forth a similar rule from the standpoint of a dispute settlement organ.[17]

In practice, States who find themselves respondents in judicial or arbitral proceedings commenced by unilateral applications do not state usually that such applications are unfriendly acts. For example, when the Philippines instituted arbitration against China under Annex VII of the UN Convention on the Law of the Sea (UNCLOS), China issued a vehemently critical but well-measured statement:

> China does not consider submission by agreement of a dispute to arbitration as an unfriendly act. In respect of disputes of territorial sovereignty and maritime rights, unilateral resort to compulsory arbitration against another State, however, cannot be taken as a friendly act, when the initiating State is fully aware of the opposition of the other State to the action and the existing agreement between them on dispute settlement through negotiations.[18]

Whether an act is deemed 'unfriendly' or 'inimical', but not unlawful, may be relevant from the perspective of the adoption of so-called 'Unilateral Coercive Measures' (UCMs).[19] Whereas resort by one party to dispute settlement cannot constitute a basis for the adoption of a countermeasure (which is premised on a prior unlawful act), it can provide a basis for some UCMs in the form of retorsions (i.e. inimical but lawful acts). In practice, international dispute settlement has become 'normalised' to a degree that certain categories of disputes are considered – at least by reasonable government administrations – as routine. Such has been the case of trade disputes.[20]

5 Sovereign Equality and Settlement of International Disputes

In the *travaux préparatoires*, sovereign equality was discussed mostly in the context of the free choice of means of settlement.[21] However, another problem, which is more serious in practical

[17] '[Les Puissances contractantes] Elles déclarent que le fait de rappeler aux Parties en conflit les dispositions de la présente Convention, et le conseil donné, dans l'intérêt supérieur de la paix, de s'adresser à la Cour Permanente, ne peuvent être considérés que comme actes de bons offices.'

[18] Position Paper of the Government of the People's Republic of China on the Matter of Jurisdiction in the South China Sea Arbitration Initiated by the Republic of the Philippines, 7 December 2014, www.fmprc.gov.cn/nanhai/eng/snhwtlcwj_1/t1368895.htm, para 90.

[19] On the types of measures encompassed by the term UCM see G Le Moli and JE Viñuales, 'Today as Yesterday? Unilateral Coercive Measures and Human Dignity' (2019) 18 *Chinese Journal of International Law*, 437.

[20] See generally the chapter by J Kurtz, JE Viñuales and M Waibel in this volume.

[21] Report of the Special Committee, 1966, UN Doc A/6230, paras 179, 188, 258

terms, started to attract attention in relation to the equality of States. It is related to the cost of judicial or arbitral proceedings.

It is well known that States have to be ready to bear considerable costs to cover remuneration of counsel, preparation of documents and so on to submit a dispute to an international court or tribunal.[22] Although usually far less expensive than military activities, all such costs could be prohibitive for a number of developing States.[23] Accordingly, if every State legally enjoys an equal treatment before an international court, its door may in fact be closed to less fortunate ones.

To alleviate such de facto inequality between potential disputing parties, various funds have been established. The oldest of such funds is the Secretary-General's Trust Fund to Assist States in the Settlement of Disputes through the ICJ, which was created in 1989.[24] Its terms of reference, referring to the Friendly Relations Declaration to reiterate the importance of peaceful settlement of international disputes, explain the raison d'être of the Trust Fund:

> The cost which may be incurred by proceedings of the International Court of Justice is a factor which may in some instances discourage States from resorting to it . . . The administrative costs of the Court are borne by the United Nations. However, as in arbitration, the parties must remunerate their counsel, reimburse, where applicable, the costs of their agents, experts and witnesses and bear the expense of the preparation of memorials and counter-memorials. The total costs may be considerable.[25]

Financial assistance is provided to States for expenses incurred in connection with a dispute submitted to the ICJ by way of a special agreement or a dispute in which preliminary objections, if they have been filed, have been rejected by the Court or definitively withdrawn by the party or the parties concerned. Although an application for financial assistance from the Fund may be submitted by any State that has access to the ICJ,[26] it shall be considered in light of the financial needs of the requesting State.[27] As of 2019, the Trust Fund received applications from nine States, to which certain amounts of financial assistance were granted.[28] Similar trust funds have been created for the Permanent Court of Arbitration (PCA)[29] and the International Tribunal for the Law of the Sea (ITLOS).[30] Despite limitations of such trust funds, they certainly represent a first step to reduce the de facto inequality between States in the access to international courts and tribunals.

However, financial inequality is not the sole element of factual inequality that could reduce sovereign equality into a nominal principle regarding access to international courts and tribunals. While some States may have rich experience and intellectual resources regarding

[22] See A Miron, 'Le Coût de la justice internationale: enquête sur les aspects financiers du contentieux interétatique' (2014) 60 *Annuaire français de droit international* 241.

[23] See D Vignes, 'Aide au développement et assistance judiciaire pour le règlement des différends par la Cour internationale de justice' (1989) 35 *Annuaire français de droit international* 321.

[24] UN Doc A/44/PV43, 7–11.

[25] Revised Terms of Reference, Guidelines and Rules of the Secretary-General's Trust Fund to Assist States in the Settlement of Disputes through the International Court of Justice, UN Doc A/59/372, para 4. The original terms of reference was adopted in 1989. UN Doc A/44/PV43.

[26] Revised Terms of Reference (n 25), para 8.

[27] ibid, para 11.

[28] UN Doc A/47/444, paras 7–8; A/56/456, paras 5–7; A/59/372, paras 4–5; A/63/229, paras 4–5; A/69/337, para 4; A/71/339, para 4.

[29] Permanent Court of Arbitration Financial Assistance Fund for Settlement of International Disputes, Terms of Reference and Guidelines, as approved by the Administrative Council on 11 December 1995, https://pca-cpa.org/wp-content/uploads/sites/6/2016/02/Financial-Assistance-Fund-for-Settlement-of-International-Disputes.pdf.

[30] International Tribunal for the Law of the Sea Trust Fund, Terms of Reference, UN Doc A/RES/55/7, Annex I.

international litigation and arbitration, many do not. It is difficult to expect that the latter could assess the strengths and weaknesses of a case, prepare the defence and establish the strategy and course of action before the court or the tribunal as efficiently as the former. States can and do outsource their defence to external counsel but that requires financial resources and at least a certain degree of expertise to select – and manage – competent and suitable external counsel.

The Advisory Centre on WTO Law (ACWL) is an interesting experiment in this respect. It is an international organisation independent of the World Trade Organization (WTO) established under a multilateral treaty.[31] Its purpose is 'to provide legal training, support and advice on WTO law and dispute settlement procedures to developing countries, in particular to the least developed among them, and to countries with economies in transition' (Article 2(1) of the Agreement). To this end, the ACWL provides legal advice on WTO law, supports parties and third parties in WTO dispute settlement proceedings and trains government officials in WTO law (Article 2(2)).

III DEVELOPMENTS NOT ENVISAGED IN THE FRIENDLY RELATIONS DECLARATION

1 Blurring Boundary between Judicial Settlement and Arbitration

The Friendly Relations Declaration was adopted at a time when the ICJ was least used in its history. After the final judgment of the *Barcelona Traction* case handed down in 1970,[32] there was no contentious case pending before the Court. It received a request from the Security Council for an advisory opinion with respect to Namibia, but after rendering its advisory opinion in 1971,[33] the Court once again saw no case in its docket. In the dispute settlement clauses of the Vienna Convention on the Law of Treaties,[34] the ICJ was mentioned only in relation to *jus cogens*, while States had been able to agree on protocols that, though optional, set forth an obligation for States to settle disputes by peaceful means including the settlement before the ICJ, with respect to the Vienna Convention on Diplomatic Relations and the Vienna Convention on Consular Relations, adopted some years before.[35] A number of studies carried out to find causes of this indifference of States toward the Court pointed out the antipathy or hostility among developing States to the Court aroused by its 1966 judgment of the *South West Africa* cases.[36]

A number of studies were carried out to 'revitalise' the Court in academia as well as in the General Assembly.[37] The Court itself bent its efforts to increase its appeal through successive amendments of the Rules of Court. One of such efforts was to make the use of chambers more attractive for States. Under the Statute of the Court, it was not clear whether the disputing parties should be allowed to have a say in the composition of the chamber (Article 26(2)). The original Rules of Court, adopted in 1946, required the President of the Court to ascertain the views of the

[31] Agreement establishing the Advisory Centre on WTO Law, www.acwl.ch/basic-documents/.

[32] *Barcelona Traction, Light and Power Company, Limited*, Judgment, ICJ Reports 1970, 3.

[33] *Legal Consequences for States of the Continued Presence of South Africa in Namibia (South West Africa) notwithstanding Security Council Resolution 276 (1970)*, Advisory Opinion, ICJ Reports 1971, 16.

[34] Vienna Convention on the Law of Treaties, 23 May 1969, 1155 UNTS 331 [VCLT], Art 66(a).

[35] Optional Protocol to the Vienna Convention on Diplomatic Relations, concerning the Compulsory Settlement of Disputes, 18 April 1961, 500 UNTS 241; Optional Protocol to the Vienna Convention on Consular Relations, concerning the Compulsory Settlement of Disputes, 24 April 1963, 596 UNTS 487.

[36] *South West Africa*, Second Phase, Judgment, ICJ Reports 1966, 6.

[37] See eg H Mosler and R Bernhardt (eds), *Judicial Settlement of International Disputes* (Springer, 1974); L Gross (ed), *The Future of the International Court of Justice*, 2 vols (Oceana, 1976); UNGA Res 2733 (XXV) (16 December 1970).

parties only as regards the number of judges constituting the chamber (Article 71(3)). The Rules were revised in 1972, during the period of inactivity of the Court, and they included a new Article 26(1), which required the President to consult the parties concerning the composition of the chamber. The 1978 revision slightly modified the language, requiring the President to 'ascertain' the views of the parties regarding the composition of the chamber. Jiménez de Aréchaga, then judge at the Court, stated that it was difficult to suppose that the Court would not elect judges in accordance with the parties' views, as that would force the parties to walk out of the Court.[38] Although often criticised,[39] the de facto power of the disputing parties to select judges constituting the chamber is generally considered to be inevitable,[40] and the ITLOS Statute – not the Rules – legalised the power of the disputing parties: Article 15(2) provides that the composition of the tribunal must be approved by the parties.

Judgments given by chambers shall be considered as rendered by the Court or by the Tribunal (Article 27, ICJ Statute; Article 15(4), ITLOS Statute). However, since the composition of the chamber needs to be approved de facto (in the case of the ICJ) or de jure (in the case of the ITLOS) by the disputing parties, the difference between judicial settlement and arbitration becomes blurred at least with respect to ICJ or ITLOS chambers.[41]

2 *Proliferation of International Courts and Tribunals*

After the end of the Cold War, many international courts and tribunals came into existence, to an extent that 'judicialisation' of international law became a subject of debate.[42] Of particular importance from the perspective of inter-State dispute settlement were the creation of the ITLOS (in 1996), the constitution of a number of tribunals constituted under Annex VII of UNCLOS[43] (since 1999) and the establishment of the WTO-DSB (WTO Dispute Settlement Body)[44] (in 1995).

The period immediately following the end of the Cold War also saw an exponential development of international courts and tribunals whose proceedings involve individuals and juridical persons: the creation of the International Criminal Tribunal for the Former Yugoslavia (ICTY) (1993),[45] the International Criminal Tribunal for Rwanda (ICTR) (1995),[46] the International Criminal Court (ICC) (2002)[47] and the African Court on Human and Peoples'

38 See E Jiménez de Aréchaga, 'The Amendments to the Rules of Procedure of the International Court of Justice' (1973) 67 *American Journal of International Law* 1, 3.

39 Dissenting Opinion of Judge Morozov, *Delimitation of the Maritime Boundary in the Gulf of Maine Area, Constitution of Chamber,* Order of 20 January 1982, ICJ Reports 1982, 11; Dissenting Opinion of M El-Khani, ICJ Reports 1982, 12.

40 See S Oda, 'Further Thoughts on the Chambers Procedure of the International Court of Justice' (1988) 82 *American Journal of International Law* 556, 558–59.

41 See E McWhinney, 'Special Chambers within the International Court of Justice: The Preliminary, Procedural Aspect of the Gulf of Maine Case' (1985) 12 *Syracuse Journal of International Law and Commerce* 1, 6; T Sugihara, 'Kokusai Siho Saiban no Chii to Kino [Status and Functions of International Judicial Settlement]' in K Hirobe (ed), *Kokusaiho to Kokunaiho* [*International Law and Domestic Law*] (Keiso Shobo, 1991) 505, 516 [in Japanese].

42 SFDI, *La Juridictionnalisation du droit international* (Pedone, 2003). For an overview of the debate see P-M Dupuy and JE Viñuales, 'The Challenge of 'Proliferation': An Anatomy of the Debate' in C Romano, K Alter and Y Shany (eds), *The Oxford Handbook of International Adjudication* (Oxford University Press, 2013) 135–57.

43 United Nations Convention on the Law of the Sea, 10 December 1982, 1833 UNTS 397.

44 Agreement establishing the World Trade Organization, 15 April 1994, 1867 UNTS 154, Annex II: Annex: Understanding on rules and procedures governing the settlement of disputes.

45 UN Security Council Res S/RES/827 (1993) of 25 May 1993.

46 UN Security Council Res S/RES/955 (1994) of 8 November 1994.

47 Rome Statute of the International Criminal Court, 17 July 1998, 2187 UNTS 3.

Rights (1998),[48] as well as the recognition of individuals' direct access to the European Court of Human Rights (ECtHR) (1998)[49] and the mushrooming of treaty-based investor–State arbitral tribunals (since 1990).[50] These international courts and tribunals involving individuals and juridical persons are not mentioned in the Friendly Relations Declaration, which is quite understandable given the absence of such courts or tribunals at that time, though the creation of international criminal tribunals was already envisaged in Article VI of the Genocide Convention.[51] While it is true that these courts and tribunals either do not deal with inter-State disputes at all (international criminal tribunals) or only to a limited extent (human rights courts and investment tribunals), their activities are tightly related to international dispute settlement. The ICTY and the ICTR were created under situations constituting a threat to international peace and security and their establishment was expected to contribute to the restoration and maintenance of peace.[52] The ICC was established to put an end to impunity for the perpetrators of the most serious crimes of concern to the international community, which threaten the peace, security and well-being of the world.[53] Human rights courts and investment arbitral tribunals deal with disputes between individuals or juridical persons and States, which could turn into inter-State disputes.[54]

3 *Fear of Fragmentation of International Law*

The proliferation of international courts and tribunals was perceived to be a double-edged sword. According to Gilbert Guillaume, the then President of the ICJ:

> Proliferation has led to a significant increase in the number of cases coming before courts in an increasing number of fields, thus contributing to the development of international law and to its enrichment. This is a phenomenon which one is bound to welcome.
>
> Nonetheless, the proliferation of international courts engenders serious risks of inconsistency within the case law.[55]

He was particularly concerned that the ITLOS might develop a line of jurisprudence that would be different from that of the ICJ.[56]

However, the courts and tribunals tend to refer to decisions taken by other courts and tribunals to buttress or confirm their decisions. Notably, the ICJ stated in the *Diallo* judgment that, when interpreting human rights treaties, it 'should ascribe great weight to' or 'must take due

[48] Protocol to the African Charter on Human and Peoples' Rights on the Establishment of an African Court on Human and Peoples' Rights, 9 June 1998, OAU Doc OAU/LEG/MIN/AFCHPR/PROT.1 rev.2 (1997).

[49] Protocol No 11 to the Convention for the Protection of Human Rights and Fundamental Freedoms, restructuring the control machinery established thereby, 11 May 1994, ETS No 155.

[50] See the chapter by J Kurtz, JE Viñuales and M Waibel in this volume.

[51] Convention on the Prevention and Punishment of the Crime of Genocide, 9 December 1948, 78 UNTS 277.

[52] Preamble, S/RES/827 (1993); S/RES/955 (1994).

[53] Preamble, Rome Statute.

[54] '[F]undamental freedoms … are the foundation of justice and peace in the world': preamble, the ECHR. It is well known that investor–State arbitration was introduced to 'depoliticise' investment disputes. The ICSID was thus established to reduce the likelihood of unresolved conflicts between host countries and investors in a manner which would eliminate the risk of a confrontation of the host country and the national State of the investor. A Broches, 'The Convention on the Settlement of Investment Disputes between States and Nationals of Other States' (1972) 136(2) *Recueil des Cours* 331, 343.

[55] 'The Proliferation of International Judicial Bodies', Speech by His Excellency Judge Gilbert Guillaume, President of the International Court of Justice, to the Sixth Committee of the General Assembly of the United Nations, 27 October 2000, www.icj-cij.org/files/press-releases/1/3001.pdf.

[56] See his reference (ibid) to the provisional measures order in the *Southern Bluefin Tuna* case.

account of the interpretation adopted by the independent body that was established specifically to supervise the application of the treaties.[57] The ITLOS also considers that:

> [d]ecisions of international courts and tribunals, referred to in article 38 of the Statute of the ICJ, are of particular importance in determining the content of the law applicable to maritime delimitation under articles 74 and 83 of the [United Nations] Convention [on the Law of the Sea][58]

and pays much attention to the jurisprudence of other courts, particularly the ICJ. This practice of cross-reference led Shunji Yanai, the then President of the ITLOS, to state that:

> ITLOS, ICJ and arbitral tribunals have dealt with a significant number of disputes over law of the sea matters since UNCLOS entered into force, but it would appear that judges and arbitrators carefully study the judgments and arbitral awards handed down in similar cases by other courts or tribunals and the feared 'fragmentation' has not occurred.[59]

Although it happens that courts and tribunals arrive at diametrically opposite conclusions,[60] it is certainly excessive to see any fragmentation of international law caused by the proliferation of international courts and tribunals. This non-occurrence of 'fragmentation' of international law is something which one is bound to welcome. However, paradoxically, that could put the *raison d'être* of certain courts or tribunals in question. If the same result would be obtained at any court or tribunal, why do we need more than one?

4 *Concern about the Democratic Legitimacy of International Courts and Tribunals*

The proliferation of international courts and tribunals has been accompanied by the expansion of the field of their activities and their intensification. Any decision of an international court or tribunal has some implications for nationals of the disputing parties and perhaps also for other people. However, the development of ever-increasing international norms that become more and more intrusive into domestic policy-making, together with the increasing number of decisions taken by international courts and tribunals, has led domestic policy-making to be far more exposed to their influence than before. Coupled with the evolution of the idea of democracy after the Cold War, the democratic legitimacy of international courts and tribunals started to be questioned.

The ICJ, whose legitimacy is rarely contested on the inter-State plane except during a certain period following the 1966 *South West Africa* judgment, is no exception to this phenomenon. In *Breard*, Paraguay argued that the United States had failed to inform Breard, a national of

[57] *Armadou Sadio Diallo (Republic of Guinea* v *Democratic Republic of the Congo)*, Judgment, ICJ Reports 2010, 639, 664, paras 66–67. The Court further referred to the jurisprudence of the European Court of Human Rights and the Inter-American Court of Human Rights to confirm the interpretation of the relevant provisions of the African Charter on Human and Peoples' Rights, para 68.

[58] *Delimitation of the maritime boundary in the Bay of Bengal (Bangladesh/Myanmar)*, Judgment, 14 March 2012, ITLOS Reports 2012, 4, 56, para 184.

[59] S Yanai, 'Rule of Law over the Seas and Oceans', United Nations Convention on the Law of the Sea at 30, International Conference, Yeosu, Republic of Korea, 12 August 2012, www.itlos.org/fileadmin/itlos/documents/statements_of_president/yanai/Yeosu_Korea_UNCLOS_at_30_11-13_Aug_2012__2_.pdf, 3.

[60] The most famous example is the 'quarrel' between the ICJ and the ICTY concerning the standard of attribution of acts of private persons to the State. *Prosecutor* v *Tadić*, IT-94-1-A, Judgment, 15 July 1999, paras 115–45; *Application of the Convention on the Prevention and Punishment of the Crime of Genocide (Bosnia and Herzegovina* v *Serbia and Montenegro)*, Judgment, ICJ Reports 2007, 43, 206–11, paras 396–407.

Paraguay who was then on death row in a prison in Virginia, of his right to request that the relevant consular office of Paraguay be advised of his arrest and detention, and to communicate with that office. In response to a request made by Paraguay upon the filing of the case, the ICJ indicated, as a provisional measure, that the United States should take all measures at its disposal to ensure that Breard was not executed pending the final decision in the proceeding before the Court.[61] In light of the provisional measures order rendered by the Court, the US Secretary of State requested that the Governor of Virginia stay the execution of Breard.[62] The Governor, however, decided not to stay the execution and Breard was executed. The Governor issued a press statement:

> I am concerned that to delay Mr. Breard's execution so that the International Court of Justice may review this matter would have the practical effect of transferring responsibility from the courts of the Commonwealth and the United States to the International Court ... Indeed, the safety of those residing in the Commonwealth of Virginia is not the responsibility of the International Court of Justice. It is my responsibility and the responsibility of law enforcement and judicial officials throughout the Commonwealth. I cannot cede such responsibility to the International Court of Justice.[63]

This unfortunate pattern of events was repeated in the later similar cases, namely *La Grand*[64] and *Avena*.[65]

A similar argument was mobilised by the Italian Constitutional Court against the judgment in *Jurisdictional immunities of the State*, in which the ICJ found that Italy had violated its obligation to respect the immunity which Germany enjoyed by allowing civil claims to be brought against it based on violations of international humanitarian law committed by the German Reich during the Second World War.[66] In face of the judgment, the Italian Constitutional Court held that Italian domestic statutes obliging the State to comply with judgments of the ICJ were unconstitutional to the extent that it obliged Italian courts to comply with the judgment of the ICJ in *Jurisdictional immunities of the State*, by emphasising the democratic nature of the right to judicial protection recognised under the Italian Constitution.[67]

The legitimacy of international courts and tribunals are more frequently put into question with respect to human rights, where they are by definition bound to deal with domestic measures taken by the local State. The most conspicuous illustrations in this respect are the reactions in the United Kingdom to the judgments in *Hirst* v. *UK (No. 2)* and *Greens and MT* v. *UK*. In *Hirst* v. *UK (No. 2)*, the ECtHR found that the blanket ban on the right of a convicted prisoner to vote imposed by UK law constituted a violation of Article 3 of the Protocol (Right to free elections).[68] In *Greens and MT* v. *UK*, the Court found the respondent State had failed to execute the *Hirst* judgment and held that the respondent State was under an obligation to enact

61 *Vienna Convention on Consular Relations (Paraguay* v *United States of America)*, Provisional Measures, Order of 9 April 1998, ICJ Reports 1998, 248, para 41.

62 Digest of United States Practice in International Law, 1991–1999, 313–14.

63 ibid 318.

64 *La Grand (Germany* v *United States of America)*, Memorial of the Federal Republic of Germany, 16 September 1999, vol 1, para 2.16.

65 Submission of Mexico in response to the Written Observations of the United States of America, Request for Interpretation of the Judgment of 31 March 2004 in the *Case Concerning Avena and Other Mexican Nationals (United Mexican States* v *United States of America)*, 17 September 2008, para 19.

66 *Jurisdictional Immunities of the State (Germany* v *Italy: Greece intervening)*, Judgment, ICJ Reports 2012, 99.

67 Corte costituzionale, Sentenza N 238, anno 2014, Considerato in diritto, 3.4.

68 *Hirst* v *UK (No 2)*, Appl No 74025/01, GC, 6 October 2005.

the required legislation to comply with the Convention.[69] In response to these judgments, the UK House of Commons adopted, by an overwhelming majority, a resolution declaring:

> this House ... is of the opinion that legislative decisions of this nature should be a matter for democratically-elected lawmakers; and supports the current situation in which no prisoner is able to vote except those imprisoned for contempt, default or on remand.[70]

The Inter-American Court of Human Rights has also been under criticism for being anti-democratic. The Court, in its judgment in *Yean and Bosico Girls* v. *Dominican Republic*, declared that the respondent State had violated the right to nationality (Article 20, American Convention on Human Rights) by failing to grant nationality to the applicants of Haitian origin born in the respondent State on the ground that their fathers were Haitian migratory workers and were considered to be in transit.[71] This judgment was later confirmed in *Expelled Dominicans and Haitians* v. *Dominican Republic*.[72] Following the latter, the President of the Dominican Republic issued a statement that these judgments threatened the democratic values of Dominican society because they questioned the legitimately constituted powers of the State.[73]

As is the case with human rights courts, treaty-based investment arbitration, which examines the compatibility of domestic measures with investment treaties concluded by the host State, has become the frequent target of criticism for being anti-democratic. The Independent Expert on the democratic and equitable international order, appointed by the Human Rights Council of the United Nations, sounded the alarm in his report in 2015:

> Indeed, investor State dispute settlement poses a particular challenge to the democratic order, particularly when Governments that have been democratically elected to carry out specific social policies have been sued by investors precisely because of those democratically mandated policies.[74]

Similar concerns have been raised by States.[75]

5 *Diversity of Judges/Arbitrators*

The legitimacy of international courts and tribunals has not been put into question only from a democratic perspective. Already in the 1960s and 1970s, when a number of developing States seriously questioned the legitimacy of the ICJ, they alleged that the composition of the Court was unjustifiably favourable to developed States, particularly the Permanent Members of the Security Council.[76] Although such frustration among developing States was one of the reasons for which the ITLOS was established under the UNCLOS,[77] the geographical distribution of judges has evolved along with the gradual increase of African and Asian Member States in the United Nations, and there is no strong voice questioning the legitimacy of the ICJ in terms of the

[69] *Greens and MT* v *UK*, Appl Nos 60041/08 and 60054/08), 23 November 2010.

[70] The motion was adopted by 234:22. Hansard, HC Deb, vol 523, col 585–86 (10 February 2011).

[71] *The Girls Yean and Bosico* v *Dominican Republic*, Judgment of 8 September 2005, paras 152, 174, 260.

[72] *Expelled Dominicans and Haitians* v *Dominican Republic*, Judgment of 28 August 2014.

[73] https://presidencia.gob.do/noticias/el-gobierno-dominicano-rechaza-la-sentencia-de-la-corte-interamericana-de-derechos-humanos.

[74] UN Doc A/70/285.

[75] See eg UN Doc A/CN.9/WG.III/WP.176, para 11.

[76] See IFI Shihata, 'The Attitude of New States toward the International Court of Justice' (1965) 19 *International Organization* 216.

[77] JE Noyes, 'The International Tribunal for the Law of the Sea' (1998) 32 *Cornell International Law Journal* 109, 119.

geographical diversity on the bench.[78] The same observation applies to other 'universal' courts and tribunals such as the ITLOS,[79] the WTO Appellate Body[80] and the ICC.[81]

However, the geographical imbalance in the composition of investment tribunals has become a subject of critical debates. According to the ICSID, 48% of the arbitrators, conciliators and ad hoc Committee Members appointed (appointments by parties and by ICSID) in cases for the period ending 30 June 2019 were from Western Europe, 20% from North America, 11% from South and East Asia and the Pacific, 11% from South America, 4% from the Middle East and North Africa, 2% from Eastern Europe and Central Asia, 2% from Central America and the Caribbean, and 2% from Sub-Saharan Africa. This result is particularly noteworthy if it is compared with the geographic distribution of disputes: 8% from Western Europe, 4% from North America, 7% from South and East Asia and the Pacific, 22% from South America, 12% from the Middle East and North Africa, 26% from Eastern Europe and Central Asia, 6% from Central America and the Caribbean, and 15% from Sub-Saharan Africa.[82]

If the lack of geographical diversity is a phenomenon unique to investment arbitration, that of gender diversity is rather a universal one. As of 2019, the percentage of women amounts to 20% on the ICJ (3 out of 15) and 10% on the ITLOS (2 out of 21). In the WTO Appellate Body, there was only one woman when it had the full seven members in 2017 (14%). The situation is even more imbalanced, though only slightly, in investment arbitration, where 11% of the arbitrators are women according to the ICSID statistics.[83]

However, the gender imbalance on the bench of international courts and tribunals has started to be rectified. The Rome Statute of the ICC, adopted in 1998, provides, in Article 36(8)(a)(iii), that the States parties shall take into account the need for a fair representation of female and male judges. In addition, the Assembly of States parties to the Rome Statute adopted a resolution that requires each State party to vote for a minimum number of candidates of each gender.[84] Thirty-three per cent of the ICC judges are women (6 out of 18). A similar mechanism has been established in 2001 by the Protocol to the African Charter on Human and Peoples' Rights on the Establishment of an African Court on Human and Peoples' Rights, which provides that due consideration shall be given to adequate gender representation in the nomination process of judges of the African Court. As of 2019, more than half of the judges (6 out of 11) are women. Finally, the Parliamentary Assembly of the Council of Europe, which elects judges of the ECtHR,[85] established a similar system in 2004.[86] The current rule is stipulated in Resolution 1841 (2011), which provides that the Assembly should decide from single-sex lists of candidates (submitted by a State party) when the candidates belong to the sex which is under-represented in the Court (i.e. the sex to which under 40 per cent of the total number of judges belong), or in exceptional circumstances where a Contracting Party has taken all the necessary and appropriate steps to ensure that the list contains candidates of both sexes meeting the requirements of

[78] Art 9 of the ICJ Statute does not speak of geographical distribution but refers to 'the representation of the main forms of civilization and of the principal legal systems of the world'.
[79] See Arts 2(2) and 3(2) of the ITLOS Statute.
[80] Art 17(3) of the WTO DSU does not refer to geographical distribution but provides that '[t]he Appellate Body membership shall be broadly representative of membership in the WTO'.
[81] See Art 36(8)(a) of the Rome Statute.
[82] The ICSID Caseload-Statistics, Issue 2019–2.
[83] ibid.
[84] Res ICC-ASP/3/Res 6, 10 September 2004, para 20(c).
[85] Art 22, ECHR.
[86] Resolutions 1366 (2004), 1426 (2005) and 1627 (2008) of the Parliamentary Assembly of the Council of Europe.

paragraph 1 of Article 21 of the European Convention on Human Rights. Thirty-two per cent of the ECtHR judges are women (15 out of 47).

With respect to investment arbitration, where the lack of diversity of adjudicators is blatantly clear, States have started to cope with the problem. In Working Group 3 of the United Nations Commission on International Trade Law (UNCITRAL), which has been working on possible reform of investor–State dispute settlement, States share the view that the current lack of diversity in decision-makers in this field contributes to the undermining of the legitimacy of the regime of investor–State dispute settlement and decided to develop reforms in order to respond to concerns about the lack of appropriate diversity.[87]

Why is diversity important? While geographical diversity may well be required in light of sovereign equality, the necessity of gender diversity is difficult to explain from a State-centric point of view. Although it is said that diverse decision-makers are more likely to avoid cognitive biases and group-think in decision-making, there are no empirical studies that would point out that female judges decide cases differently from male judges.[88] Diversity on the bench is required because it is considered to be a desirable objective in and of itself.[89]

6 *Standard of Ethics for Judges/Arbitrators*

Although Article 16 of the ICJ Statute provides that '[n]o member of the Court may exercise … any other occupation of a professional nature', members of the Court frequently take part in inter-State arbitrations. For example, two of the five arbitrators were judges of the ICJ in *UK-France Delimitation of the Continental Shelf* (André Gros and Humphrey Waldock)[90] and in *Eritrea-Yemen Maritime Delimitation* (Stephen M. Schwebel and Rosalyn Higgins).[91] According to the Court:

> That occasional practice goes back to the origins of the Permanent Court of International Justice. Not only is it in conformity with the Statute of the Court; the repeated endorsement by the international organs and by the States that have appointed Members of the Court as arbitrators shows their awareness of the contribution that the Members of the Court may, by this function, make to the development of international law, and of the benefits deriving therefrom for all institutions concerned. The practice, which involves a very limited number of judges for very limited periods, has no adverse effect on the pace of the work of the Court or the total precedence given to that work by its Members.[92]

However, with the proliferation of international courts and tribunals, particularly due to the flourishing of investment arbitration, this 'occasional' or 'limited' practice became almost permanent and extensive. A report of the Committee on Procedure of International Courts and Tribunals of the International Law Association (ILA) points out two problems in this respect:

[87] UN Doc A/CN.9/964, paras 92, 98.

[88] Boyd, Epstein and Martin indicate that female judges decide cases differently from male judges only in cases with a salient gender dimension. CL Boyd, L Epstein and AD Martin, 'Untangling the Causal Effects of Sex on Judging' (2004) 54 *American Journal of Political Science* 389–411.

[89] G Kaufmann-Kohler and M Potestà, 'The Composition of a Multilateral Investment Court and of an Appeal Mechanism for Investment Awards', CIDS Supplemental Report, 15 November 2017, para 46.

[90] RIAA, vol XVIII, 3.

[91] RIAA, vol XXII, 336.

[92] Report of the International Court of Justice, 1 August 1995–31 July 1996, UN Doc A/51/4, para 199.

> First, '[m]embers of the Court shall be bound... to hold themselves permanently at the disposal of the Court'[93] ... If judges are perceived to be unable to give 'the fullest precedence to their supervening duties as members of the Court' due to other activities, the legitimacy of the Court will be weakened. Second, arbitrator work gives rise to an ethical problem of conflict-of-interest. Whether the judge is appointed by the investor or by the State, the participation of that judge in a subsequent proceeding at the Court in which that State appears would give rise to a perception of bias. Since the judge would need to self-recuse, the Court would be deprived of his/her service.[94]

In face of mounting criticism,[95] the President of the ICJ declared at the General Assembly in 2018:

> Members of the Court have come to the decision, last month, that they will not normally accept to participate in international arbitration. In particular, they will not participate in investor-State arbitration or in commercial arbitration. However, ... the Court ... will, if the circumstances so warrant, authorize its Members to participate in inter-State arbitration cases. Even in such exceptional cases, a Member of the Court will only participate, if authorized, in one arbitration procedure at a time... Members of the Court, will, however, decline to be appointed as arbitrators by a State that is a party in a case pending before the Court, even if there is no substantial interference between that case and the case submitted to arbitration. This is essential to place beyond reproach the impartiality and independence of Judges in the exercise of their judicial functions.[96]

ITLOS judges also frequently participate in inter-State arbitration, particularly in the UN Convention on the Law of the Sea of 1982 (UNCLOS) Annex VII arbitrations. This is not considered to be problematic since such arbitrations constitute part of the UNCLOS dispute settlement system.[97] Participation of ITLOS judges in Annex VII arbitrations is expected to contribute to achieving and maintaining the consistency of jurisprudence regarding UNCLOS.

The flourishing of investment arbitration has created another new type of problem called 'double-hatting', involving arbitrators in an investment arbitration simultaneously serving as counsel in another investment arbitration. The practice of double-hatting, though not widespread across the entire spectrum of investor–state dispute settlement cases,[98] is certainly not exceptional. Double-hatting causes no problem and is even encouraged in commercial arbitration, but raises concerns in the context of investment arbitration on the ground that arbitrators (appear to) have the possibility of deciding on an issue in one manner to benefit a party that they represent as counsel in another arbitration case,[99] because it is well-known that an arbitral award or decision rendered on the basis of an investment treaty may affect later arbitral tribunals even if the latter are constituted on the basis of different investment treaties. Since the practice of

93 Art 23(3), ICJ Statute.

94 ILA, Committee on Procedure of International Courts and Tribunals, Interim Report, 1 May 2018, 23–24.

95 See in particular N Bernasconi-Osterwalder and M Dietrich Brauch, 'Is "Moonlighting" a Problem? The Role of ICJ judges in ISDS', November 2017, www.iisd.org/sites/default/files/publications/icj-judges-isds-commentary.pdf.

96 Speech by HE Abdulqawi A Yusuf, President of the International Court of Justice, on the Occasion of the Seventy-Third Session of the United Nations General Assembly, 25 October 2018, 12.

97 ILA, Committee on Procedure of International Courts and Tribunals, Interim Report, 1 May 2018, 24.

98 UN Doc A/CN.9/WG.III/WP.151, para 34.

99 UN Doc A/CN.9/964, para 72.

double-hatting is difficult to regulate under existing rules on the conflict of interests,[100] the UNCITRAL has started to consider elaborating a new set of rules for this purpose.[101]

IV CONCLUSION

At the time of the adoption of the Friendly Relations Declaration, international law relating to the peaceful settlement of international disputes was at its lowest point in the post-Second World War period due to the Cold War and the distrust of the ICJ entertained by developing States following its *South West Africa* judgment in 1966. It is thus not surprising at all that the second principle on the peaceful settlement of disputes is no more than a restatement of the law containing few innovative elements.

However, the international community observed a spectacular development of international courts, tribunals and quasi-judicial organs after the end of the Cold War and such proliferation of judicial organs produced a new set of problems that were not foreseen or envisaged in the Friendly Relations Declaration. Many of them were born out of the zeitgeist of the post-Cold War period – that is, democracy, transparency and fairness in social relations.

[100] J Dunoff et al, 'Lack of Independence and Impartiality of Arbitrators', Academic Forum on ISDS Concept Paper, Spring 2019, 8–9.

[101] UN Doc A/CN.9/964, para 83.

5

The Duty Not to Intervene in Matters within Domestic Jurisdiction

*Dire Tladi**

I INTRODUCTION

The period leading up to the fiftieth anniversary of the Declaration on the Principles of International Law concerning Friendly Relations and Co-operation among States was characterised by numerous claims of intervention by one State levelled against another State or group of States. The case of alleged Russian involvement in the presidential elections of the United States, the decision by some States to recognise a rival government in Venezuela, the provision of arms to fighting groups in Saudi Arabia in the conflict in the Yemen are but some recent examples. These claims raise the question of the scope, content and status of the duty of non-intervention in matters within the domestic jurisdiction of any State.[1]

As the Declaration explicitly states, the principles in the Declaration 'in their interpretation and application . . . are interrelated and each principle should be seen in the context of the other principles'.[2] This is certainly true but perhaps even more true of the principle of non-intervention. As will be illustrated in this chapter, the principle of non-intervention is, in some ways, the golden thread that runs through the Declaration. It is intimately connected with other principles and provides a connection amongst them. For example, the principle that States shall refrain from the use of force[3] is a concrete example of the principle of non-intervention since the use of force is, in general, a form of intervention. At the same time, the principle of non-intervention is a consequence of both the principle of sovereign equality of States[4] and the right of self-determination.[5] Yet, as central as the duty of non-intervention in the domestic affairs of other States is to the Declaration, it remains less understood and open to (mis)interpretation than the other principles in the Declaration.[6] Part of the difficulty of pinning down the contours

* This chapter was written during time spent at the University of California Irvine on a Fulbright Scholarship. I am grateful for the research assistance of Francesca Allegra, JD class of 2021 (UCI).

[1] Philip Kunig, 'The Prohibition of Intervention' in *Max Planck Encyclopedia of Public International Law* (April 2008), para 1 ('The principle of non-intervention is an international legal norm whose violation is often alleged and which is proclaimed under completely different circumstances. As a result, the exact meaning of the principle remains unclear.').

[2] See the chapter by P-M Dupuy in this volume.

[3] See the chapter by O Corten in this volume.

[4] See the chapter by M Koskenniemi and V Kari in this volume.

[5] See the chapter by MG Kohen in this volume.

[6] See for discussion James N Rosenau, 'The Concept of Intervention' (1968) 22 *Journal of International Affairs* 165, 166 who makes the following observation: 'Ambiguous and contradictory formulations characterise the voluminous moral, legal and strategic writings on the subject, and as a result intervention has come to be treated as synonymous

of intervention – or better yet, the contours of the prohibition of intervention, since not all intervention is prohibited – is the normative and ethical questions that are often intrinsically intertwined with cases of intervention on the ground.[7] Should States stand by while atrocities are being committed? Under what circumstances would the Friendly Relations Declaration allow intervention for *iusta cause* – just cause?

This chapter explores the contours and status of the duty of non-intervention in international law. It does this by first describing its relationship, not only with other principles in the Declaration but also other principles of international law, including as reflected in the UN Charter and then seeking to situate the principle of non-intervention in modern practice. In the next section, the chapter situates the duty of non-intervention in the context of general international law and other principles of the Declaration. Thereafter different forms of intervention are assessed against the principle of non-intervention, focusing in particular on modern forms of intervention. This assessment is not only intended to evaluate the consistency of these forms of intervention with the Declaration but also to understand what they tell us about the attitudes of States to this principle – fifty years after the adoption of the Declaration.

II THE DUTY OF NON-INTERVENTION: SETTING THE CONTEXT

1 *Relationship with Other Principles in the Declaration*

The principles included in the Friendly Relations Declaration are intended to reflect and build on the principles and purposes of the Charter. This is clear from the very title of the Declaration – Declaration on Principles of International Law concerning Friendly Relations and Co-operation among States *in Accordance with the Charter of the United Nations*. This notion that the principles are reflected in the Charter is sprinkled throughout the text of the Resolution to which the Declaration is annexed, as well of the Declaration itself.[8] The preamble of the Resolution, for example, declares that the adoption of the Declaration would contribute to 'promoting the rule of law among nations and particularly the universal application of the principles embodied in the Charter'. It is unsurprising, therefore, that in general the principles contained in the Declaration refer back to the Charter.[9] The first principle concerning the prohibition of the use force, for example, has a catch-all description 'in any manner inconsistent with the purposes of the United Nations', and describes the use of force 'as a violation of the Charter of the United Nations'. Under the second principle, settlement of disputes through peaceful means,[10] States that are party to an international dispute are obliged to, inter alia, 'act in accordance with the purposes and principles of the United Nations'.[11]

with influence.' See also Percy H Winfield, 'The History of Intervention in International Law' (1922–23) 3 *British Yearbook of International Law* 130 ('The subject of intervention is one of the most vaguest branches of international law. We are told that intervention is a right; that it is a crime; that it is a rule; that it is the exception; that it is never permissible at all'). See also Maziar Jamnejad and Michael Wood, 'The Principle of Non-Intervention' (2009) 22 *Leiden Journal of International Law* 345, 380 describing it as 'the important, although obscure, subject of non-intervention', and stating that 'the principle is uncertain in scope'.

7 See eg David Fischer, 'The Ethics of Intervention' (1994) 36 *Survival* 51.

8 See eg UNGA Res/25/2625 (XXV) (24 October 1970), para 1.

9 The precise import of each reference to the Charter is better addressed in the separate chapters dealing with the individual principles in this volume.

10 See the chapter by Shotaro Hamamoto in this volume.

11 See also the principle that States shall fulfil in good faith the obligations assumed by them *in accordance with the Charter*; and the principle of equal rights and self-determination of peoples, which is said described as being

The principle of non-intervention itself is described as being in accordance with the Charter. Yet, unlike all the other principles in the Declaration, the duty of non-intervention does not appear, as such, in any one of the purposes and principles of the Charter.[12] The principle that States shall refrain from the threat or use of force, is drawn from Article 2(4) of the Charter; the principle that States are to settle their disputes by peaceful means is drawn from Articles 1(1) and 2(3); the duty to co-operate is drawn from Article 1(3); the principle of the sovereign equality of States is based on Article 2(1); the principle that States shall fulfil in good faith their obligations is based on 2(2); while the principle of equal rights and self-determination is based on Article 1(2). There is, however, no equivalent provision in the Charter to which the duty of non-intervention can be tied. Although Article 2(7) of the Charter may be referred to, it is different from duty of non-intervention as formulated in the Friendly Relations Declaration in two material ways.[13] First, Article 2(7) is couched not as a duty but rather as a without-prejudice clause. Second, and more importantly, the addressee of Article 2(7) is not States, as is the case with the other principles, but rather the United Nations itself.

The fact that the principle on non-intervention does not appear to be based on any particular provision in the Charter in the same way as the other principles in the Declaration should not be taken to indicate the inferiority of the principle of non-intervention relative to other principles. Quite the contrary. The duty of non-intervention is an integral part of the Charter mosaic and has a deep connection with the other principles in the Declaration and the Charter.[14] The prohibition on the use of force, for example, reflects a distinct form of intervention, military intervention.[15] As Jamnejad and Wood observe, the prohibition on the use of force is 'a specific application of the principle of non-intervention, indeed the most important application of the principle'.[16] Moreover, the text of the principle, having stated that 'No State or group of States' may intervene 'in the internal or external affairs of any other State' proceeds to state that '[c]onsequently, armed intervention' is a violation of international law. The particular relationship between the prohibition on the use force and the principle of non-intervention is succinctly captured by the International Court of Justice (ICJ) in the *Military and Paramilitary Activities* case, where the Court noted that acts of unlawful intervention 'will also, if they directly or indirectly involve the use of force, constitute a breach of the principle of non-use of force in international relations'.[17]

'enshrined in the Charter' and which, the Declaration proclaims, 'every State has a duty to respect . . . in accordance with the provisions of the Charter'.

12 See *Military and Paramilitary Activities in and against Nicaragua (Nicaragua v United States of America)*, Merits, ICJ Reports 1986, 14 para 202 ('this principle is not, as such, spelt out in the Charter').

13 The Charter of the United Nations, Art 2(7): 'Nothing in the present Charter shall authorise the United Nations to intervene in matters which are essentially within the domestic jurisdiction of any State or shall require the Members to submit such matters to settlement under the present Charter; but this principle shall not prejudice the application of enforcement measures under Chapter VII.'

14 Kunig (n 1), para 10, illustrates how connections *can* be made between the duty of non-intervention and specific provisions of the Charter.

15 See Fischer (n 7) esp 52. See also Kunig (n 1), para 10: 'Others derive it [the principle of non-intervention] from Art. 2 (4) . . . '. He notes, correctly however, that the prohibition on the use of force is only one part of the principle. It is in this context, probably more correct to say that Art 2(4) derives from the duty of non-intervention, rather than the other way around. See also Jamnejad and Wood (n 6) 2, 348, stating that there 'is a close relationship between the principle of non-intervention and the rules of international law on the use of force', noting further that 'Many writings on "non-intervention", particularly in earlier times, dealt solely with the law on the use of force.'

16 Jamnejad and Wood (n 6) 348–49.

17 *Military and Paramilitary Activities* case (n 12), para 209. See also *Case Concerning Armed Activities on the Territory of the Congo (Democratic Republic of the Congo v Uganda)*, ICJ Reports 2005, 168, para 164.

It is also easy to see how the principle of the sovereign equality of States is connected to the principle of non-intervention.[18] The rationale for the principle of non-intervention is the sovereign equality of States. One of the elements of sovereignty is the right of the State to freely choose its political, social, economic and cultural systems,[19] a right that would be negatively affected if other States were entitled to intervene in such matters. To this end, Winfield sees the duty of non-intervention as 'an obvious corollary from the state independence rule'.[20] For this reason the Declaration recognises that intervention leads to the 'subordination of the exercise of sovereign rights'.[21] The link between the duty of non-intervention and the right of self-determination is also clear. Intervention, at its core, is intended to influence the State in which intervention is taking place to follow a path preferred by the intervening State in a way that deprives the peoples of the intervened-in State the right to self-determination. This link is made in the elements of self-determination under the Declaration, which states that 'all peoples have the right freely to determine, without *external interference*, their political and to pursue their economic, social and cultural development'.

The connection between the duty of non-intervention and the duty to settle international disputes peacefully is less explicit and less obvious but no less significant.[22] The duty to settle disputes peacefully is the other side of the duty of non-intervention coin. It is the failure to settle disputes in a peaceful manner that often results in intervention, including the use of force. This is also the case with the duty to fulfil obligations in good faith. States intervening in another State often use creative arguments to justify their intervention. The principle of good faith in the fulfilment of obligations, in the context of intervention, would require States to assess whether the intended intervention would be consistent with the rules of international law and obligations incumbent upon it.

The duty of non-intervention is thus a thread that runs throughout the Declaration, raising its head every so often in the context of other principles in the Declaration. Yet, it has a separate and definitive content beyond the other principles to which it is so closely connected.

2 *The Duty of Non-Intervention under International Law*

The principle of non-intervention has a long and contested history which has been described elsewhere.[23] Yet today it is generally accepted that the duty of non-intervention is undeniably a principle of customary international law.[24] In the *Military and Paramilitary Activities* case, the

[18] The International Court of Justice, in the *Military and Paramilitary Activities* case, when substantiating the customary international law basis of the duty of non-intervention referred to its dictum in the *Corfu Channel* case, Merits, ICJ Reports 1949, 4, 35 where it had stated that '[b]etween independent States, respect for territorial sovereignty is an essential foundation of international relations'.

[19] According to the Declaration, sovereign equality includes this aspect as an element: 'Each State has the right freely to choose and develop its political, social, economic and cultural systems.'

[20] Winfield (n 6) 131 and 136.

[21] Compare also the description of intervention in terms of 'threats against the personality of the State' with the inclusion of 'the duty to respect the personality of other States' as an element of the principle of sovereign equality.

[22] Kunig (n 1), para 10, also illustrates how the duty of non-intervention has been linked with Art 2(3) of the UN Charter: 'Others again are convinced that the principle of non-intervention follows from Art. 2(3) of the UN Charter …'.

[23] See eg Winfield (n 6); and Jan H Verzijl, *International Law in Historical Perspective*, vol 1 (Sijthoff, 1968) 236 et seq. See also Kunig (n 1), paras 14 et seq.

[24] See eg Robert Jennings and Arthur Watts, *Oppenheim's International Law*, vol 1 (9th edn, 2008) 428 ('That intervention is, as a rule, forbidden by international law there is no doubt'). See also Kunig (n 1), para 7 and also Jamnejad and Wood (n 6) 380, stating that the 'principle of non-intervention remains well-established in contemporary international law. It is part of customary international law …'.

ICJ declared that it considered the principle 'part and parcel of customary international law'.[25] The Court based its conclusion on resolutions of international organisations, including the Declaration, and examples of State practice.[26] In addition to these, various multilateral treaties recognising the duty of non-intervention have been advanced to support the customary international law status of the prohibition of non-intervention.[27] Moreover, as Jamnejad and Wood observe, 'the principle is often referred to in diplomatic correspondence and protests, and in debates at the United Nations'.[28] In *Armed Activities on the Territory of the Congo*, the Court determined that the provisions of the Declaration were declaratory of customary international law.[29] Although Kunig has referred to the principle as a peremptory norm of general international law (*jus cogens*),[30] there is little evidence that the principle as a whole constitutes *jus cogens*.[31] Certainly the rules relating to the prohibition of the use of force, in particular the prohibition of aggression, are peremptory in nature.[32] However, as explained above, the law on the use of force is only a part of the principle of non-intervention and the fact that there is a peremptory norm relating to the prohibition of the use of force does not mean the whole of the principle of non-intervention has the same status.

While the status of the duty of non-intervention as part of customary international law is hardly contested, its scope and content are less clear. The first paragraph of the third principle in the Declaration, entitled the 'principle concerning the duty not to intervene in matters within the domestic jurisdiction of any State, in accordance with the Charter', which may be seen as a definition of the concept, states as follows:

> No State or group of States has the right to intervene, directly or indirectly, for any reason whatever, in the internal or external affairs of any other State. Consequently, armed intervention and all other forms of interference or attempted threats against the personality of the State or against its political, economic and cultural elements, are in violation of international law.

This definition confirms that the duty of non-intervention is broader than the prohibition on the use of force under Article 2(4) of the Charter and the first principle of the Declaration.[33] What

[25] *Military and Paramilitary Activities* case (n 12), para 202.

[26] ibid. See also UNGA Res 2131 (XX) (21 December 1965) on the Declaration on the Inadmissibility of Intervention in the Domestic Affairs of States and the Protection of their Independence and Sovereignty referred to by the Court.

[27] See eg amongst many other examples, Art 4(g) of the 2000 AU Constitutive Act, which provides for the principle of 'non-interference by any Member State in the internal affairs of another'; Art 2(2)(e) of the 2009 Charter of the Association of Southeast Asian Nations which refers to the principle of 'non-interference in the internal affairs of ASEAN Members States'; Art 4(2) of the 2008 Charter of the Islamic Conference Organisation which provides for the duty of members to 'refrain from interfering in the internal affairs of others'; Art 3 of the 1977 Additional Protocol II to the Geneva Convention.

[28] Jamnejad and Wood (n 6) 347.

[29] *Case Concerning Armed Activities on the Territory of the Congo* (n 17), para 162.

[30] See Kunig (n 1), para 7.

[31] See eg Jamnejad and Wood (n 6) 380.

[32] See para (a) of the Annex to the International Law Commission Draft Conclusions on Peremptory Norms of General International Law (*Jus Cogens*), Report of the International Law Commission, Seventy-First Session, General Assembly Official Records, Supp No 10 (A/74/10). See also para 5 of the commentary to draft conclusion 23 of the Draft Conclusions, which provides other terms used to described the jus cogens prohibition related to the use of force. For a description of the support in practice for the prohibition see Fourth Report of the Special Rapporteur on Peremptory Norms of General International Law (*Jus Cogens*), Dire Tladi, UN Doc A/CN.4/727, paras 62–68. See also Aniel Caro de Beer, *Peremptory Norms of General International Law (Jus Cogens) and the Prohibition of Terrorism* (Brill, 2019) 198–203.

[33] Jennings and Watts (n 24) 429 stating that while 'the customary rules of international law relating to intervention have now to a considerable extent to be considered alongside the more general prohibition of the use or threat of force, intervention is still a distinct concept'.

the duty of non-intervention prohibits is not only 'armed intervention' but also 'all other forms of interference . . . against the personality of the State or against its political, economic and cultural elements'. In the second place, this definition confirms that it is both direct and indirect intervention that is prohibited. Third, the prohibited intervention may be directed at the internal or external affairs of the State.

Although the third principle defines non-intervention as intervention relating to both internal and external affairs, the principle is generally understood as applying to the intervention in domestic affairs. But 'external' must be restricted to those aspects that, though external, are an integral part of sovereignty or the exercise of sovereign rights, such as recognition of foreign governments and votes in international fora. While these are external matters, they fall within what may described as sovereign 'functions of government'.[34] The ICJ, having defined the duty of non-intervention in similar terms (i.e. as intervention in 'internal or external affairs'), proceeded to circumscribe this potentially broad definition by stating that a prohibited intervention is one which bears 'on matters in which each State is permitted, by the principle of State sovereignty, to decide freely'.[35] These matters in which each State is permitted to decide freely include, foreign policy (external affairs) and political, economic and cultural matters (internal affairs). The internal and external policies to which the rule relates can be termed matters of 'domestic jurisdiction'.[36] A policy to breach a rule of international law, though an external affair, is not one that falls to be protected by the duty of non-intervention since States are not 'permitted, by the principle of State sovereignty, to decide freely' on whether to breach international law. A State is thus entitled to intervene, within the strict confines of international law, in matters in which another State is in serious violation of rules of international law – what this means for humanitarian intervention, a form of intervention, is covered in section III of this chapter.

Kunig suggests that the determination of what falls within domestic jurisdiction is difficult because in the current state of the international system most issues traditionally falling under domestic jurisdiction are now covered by treaties.[37] Yet the fact that a matter is covered by a treaty, or even general international law, does not remove the issue from the domestic jurisdiction of the State concerned. What matters is whether the relevant intervention is directed at a matter over which the State concerned retains the sovereign right to decide freely.

The second paragraph under the third principle states that States may not use any 'measures to coerce another State'. Thus, it is not every intervention or attempted intervention that is prohibited by the duty of non-intervention. Intervention is only prohibited under the principle of non-intervention if it is coercive (i.e. it seeks to force a State to adopt a particular position). In other words, the intervention must be intended to *compel* or *force* a State to change its policy or cause action, not through influence or persuasion but through threats or imposition of negative consequences. The intervention must be motivated by a desire to deprive the target State of the sovereign control over the issue in question.[38] The ICJ in the *Nicaragua* case also stated that to fall within the proscribed limits of intervention, State action must be coercive:

[34] See Winfield (n 6) 136.

[35] *Military and Paramilitary Activities* case (n 12) 205.

[36] See Kunig (n 1), para 3.

[37] ibid.

[38] Jennings and Watts (n 24) at 430, note that the intervention should be 'calculated to impose certain conduct or consequences'.

> Intervention is wrongful when it uses methods of coercion in regard to such choices, which must remain free ones. The element of coercion, which defines, and indeed forms the very essence of, prohibited intervention, is particularly obvious in the case of an intervention which uses force, either in the direct form of military action, or in the indirect form of support for subversive or terrorist armed activities within another State.[39]

This requirement is intended to distinguish prohibited intervention from other acts that may touch upon a State's area of sovereign competence, but which are not coercive. For example, a request from one State to another State to support an initiative at a multilateral forum of course relates to an area in which the State being requested has the sovereign right to decide. Similarly, an expression of dissatisfaction at the adoption of a law in a State is related to an area in which the latter State has sovereignty. Offers of assistance in times of crisis naturally also touch upon matters falling within the domestic jurisdiction of the State concerned. Yet these acts, though touching upon matters of domestic jurisdiction, occur regularly in diplomacy, and are not prohibited forms of intervention because they are not coercive and leave intact the concerned State's right to freely exercise its sovereign rights.

III FORMS OF INTERVENTION

1 *General*

To understand the modern concept of intervention under international law, this section will consider different forms of intervention. Following the content of the third principle of the Declaration, the section will assess these different forms of intervention with reference to some events, situations and acts that have been described as intervention. The main elements of intervention described in section II are applied to each of these events, situations and practice with a view to determining whether they can be classified as prohibited interventions under international law. The forms of intervention discussed hereunder are illustrative and non-exhaustive. In particular, military intervention (armed intervention), internal political and democratic intervention and economic coercion, as forms of interventions, are discussed. It is, however, important to emphasise that, as a general rule, any form of intervention which is intended to coerce a State in a matter within the internal or sovereign domain of the targeted State would violate the duty of non-intervention.

2 *Armed Intervention*

2.1 *Overview*

According to the Declaration, the duty of non-intervention includes the prohibition of 'armed intervention'. The Declaration also prohibits States from organising, assisting, fomenting, financing, inciting or tolerating 'subversive, terrorist, or armed activities directed towards the violent overthrow of the regime of another State' or interfering in 'civil strife in another State'. The use of force is described as depriving 'peoples of their national identity' and as a violation of 'their inalienable rights and [of] the principle of non-intervention'. The first principle in the Declaration, which concerns the prohibition on the use of force, is considered in this volume in the chapter by Olivier Corten and is therefore not addressed in this chapter. However, the intersection between the prohibition on the use of force and the duty of non-intervention

[39] *Military and Paramilitary Activities* case (n 12) 205.

described above makes it inevitable that salient forms of armed intervention, such as intervention in civil conflict and humanitarian intervention, may have to be considered.

2.2 *Humanitarian Intervention*

Perhaps no other form of intervention has given rise to as much controversy as 'humanitarian intervention'. Humanitarian intervention, in the sense that it is used here, refers to a unilateral use of armed force in order to protect the population of a third State against egregious violations of rights.[40] The discussions around humanitarian intervention have led to the creation of such concepts as the responsibility to protect and the doctrine that an intervention may be 'illegal but legitimate'. Two cases in recent history illustrate the tensions that arise when armed force is used to aid a population in a third State whose rights are being violated, namely the armed intervention in Kosovo and the intervention in Syria in response to alleged chemical weapons use by the Syrian government.[41]

In 1999 NATO members intervened militarily in Kosovo to stop continuing violations by the forces of the Federal Republic of Yugoslavia against Kosovar Albanians. This armed intervention in Kosovo has resulted in an extensive amount of scholarship.[42] For most scholars, the intervention in Kosovo, though illegal, was to be welcomed as legitimate.[43] This followed the determination by a commission of enquiry, chaired by South African jurist Richard Goldstone, that the intervention was illegal but legitimate.[44]

40 See Tladi (n 32) 15. See also Nikolai Krylov, 'Humanitarian Intervention: Pros and Cons' (1995) 17 *Loyola of Los Angeles International and Comparative Law Review* 365, 366.

41 The tensions that arise from any discussion of humanitarian intervention are well reflected upon by Richard Falk, 'Kosovo, World Order and the Future of International Law' (1999) 93 *American Journal of International Law* 847, 848. Having quoted, and described, the opposing views of Vaclav Havel and Robert Fisk, the latter supporting NATO intervention in Kosovo and the latter opposing it, he the states that a 'difficulty of assessment arises because in crucial respects *both* of these seemingly contradictory positions are persuasive' (emphasis original).

42 Fernando R Tesón, 'Kosovo: A Powerful Precedent for the Doctrine of Humanitarian Intervention' (2009) 1 *Amsterdam Law Forum* 42; Christopher Greenwood, 'Humanitarian Intervention: The Case of Kosovo' (1999) 10 *Finnish Yearbook of International Law* 141; Daniel Franchini and Antonios Tzanakopoulos, 'The Kosovo Crisis – 1999' in Tom Ruys and Olivier Corten (eds), *The Use of Force in International Law: A Case Based Approach* (Oxford University Press, 2018); Jonathan Charney, 'Anticipatory Humanitarian Intervention in Kosovo' (1999) 93 *American Journal of International Law* 834; Bruno Simma, 'NATO, the UN and the Use of Force: Legal Aspects' (1999) 10 *European Journal of International Law* 1; Simon Chesterman, *Just War or Just Peace? Humanitarian Intervention and International Law* (Oxford University Press, 2001).

43 See eg Simma (n 42); Antonio Cassesse, '*Ex iniuria ius oritur*: Are We Moving Towards International Legitimation of Forcible Humanitarian Countermeasures in the World Community?' (1999) 10 *European Journal of International Law* 23; Thomas Franck, *Recourse to Force and State Action against Threats and Armed Attacks* (Cambridge University Press, 2002) 174–91. See, however, advocating that the humanitarian intervention is not only legitimate but legal Harold Koh, 'The War Powers and Humanitarian Intervention' (2016) 53 *Houston Law Review* 971, 1033 et seq. See for a contrary position, Franchini and Tzanakopoulos (n 42) at 620 et seq who question the use of an amorphous concept such as 'legitimacy' in legal issues and Mary Ellen O'Connell, 'Self-Defence, Pernicious Doctrines, Peremptory Norms' in Christian Tams, Mary Ellen O'Connell and Dire Tladi, *Max Planck Triologues on War and Peace*, vol 1: *The Use of Force against Non-State Actors* (Cambridge University Press, 2019) 245 ('Supporters of humanitarian intervention tend to accept that they stand on weak legal grounds and tend to substitute moral arguments as supplementary legal ones. The great suffering of victims is used to argue for a lower quantity of evidence to support reinterpretation, modification or addition to the Charter exceptions for resort to force').

44 See the Independent International Commission on Kosovo, *The Kosovo Report: Conflict, International Response, Lessons Learned* (Oxford University Press, 2000) 4, where the Commission concludes that 'the NATO military intervention was illegal but legitimate. It was illegal because it did not receive prior approval from the United Nations Security Council. However, the Commission considers that the intervention was justified because all diplomatic avenues had been exhausted and because the intervention had the effect of liberating the majority population of Kosovo from a long period of oppression under Serbian rule.'

The legal discourse resulting from the Kosovo intervention and its description as 'illegal but legitimate', together with the failure to act in response to the genocide in Rwanda, led to the emergence of the doctrine of responsibility to protect.[45] While the first and second pillars of responsibility to protect recognise the responsibility of a State to protect its population and requires the international community to assist States in need of assistance respectively, the third pillars foresees the possibility of intervention, including military intervention, if the territorial State is unwilling or unable to protect its population. Intervention on the basis of this third pillar, is subject to authorisation by the UN Security Council.[46] For this reason, responsibility to protect is not, itself, a justification to intervene.[47] The legal justification for coercive intervention, including the use of force, pursuant to the responsibility to protect remains authorisation and not the responsibility to protect.

More recently, the United States, the United Kingdom and France launched airstrikes against a number of facilities in Syria in response to alleged use of chemical weapons by the Syrian government against its own population.[48]

Both the situations in Kosovo and Syria illustrate the doctrinal tensions that can result from the humanitarian intervention, but also the continued relevance of the Declaration in addressing cases of intervention. On the one hand, humanitarian intervention constitutes the use of armed force and violates the territorial integrity of the third State. As such it falls foul of Article 2(4) of the Charter and amounts to an armed intervention as described in the third principle of the Declaration. Nonetheless, some arguments have been made in support of humanitarian intervention. First, it has been argued that it does not fall foul of the prohibition in the Charter since Article 2(4), on its terms, only prohibits the use of force when such force is directed 'against the territorial integrity or political independence of any State, or in any other manner inconsistent with the Purposes of the United Nations'.[49] Second, and flowing from this first argument, it may be argued that the third principle of the Declaration only prohibits intervention in internal matters in which a State retains the rights under international law to freely determine for itself. Since a State is not free to choose to abuse its population, an intervention directed at quelling such abuse cannot be contrary to the duty of non-intervention in third principle of the Declaration.

These arguments aimed at restricting the scope of the prohibition of armed intervention are, however, misleading and unconvincing, at best, and at worst dangerous.[50] The words 'against the territorial integrity or political independence of any State, or in any other manner

[45] See for discussion Mindia Vashakmadze, 'Responsibility to Protect' in Bruno Simma et al (eds), *The Charter of the United Nations: A Commentary*, vol 1 (2012) 1219; Carsten Stahn, 'Responsibility to Protect: Political Rhetoric or Emerging Legal Norm' (2007) 101 *American Journal of International Law* 99.

[46] UNGA 2005 World Summit Outcome, 16 September 2005 (A/RES/60/1), para 139.

[47] Dire Tladi, 'The Intervention in Côte d'Ivoire' in Ruys and Corten (n 42) 793; Aniel de Beer and Dire Tladi, 'The Use of Force against Syria in Response to Alleged Use of Chemical Weapons by Syria: A Return to Humanitarian Intervention?' (2019) 79 *Zeitschrift für Ausländisches Öffentliches Recht und Völkerrecht* 205, 226.

[48] Monica Hakimi, 'The Attack on Syria and the Contemporary *Jus ad Bellum*', *EJILTalk*, www.ejiltalk.org/the-attack-on-syria-and-the-contemporary-jus-ad-bellum/ (15 April 2018), 1–2; de Beer and Tladi (n 47).

[49] Tesón (n 42) 151, who argues that 'genuine humanitarian intervention does not result in territorial conquest or political subjugation'. See further W Michael Reisman and Myres S McDougal, 'Humanitarian Intervention to Protect the Ibos' in Richard B Lillich (ed), *Humanitarian Intervention and the United Nations* (University Press of Virginia, 1973) 177.

[50] See for a rejection Christine Gray, 'The Use of Force for Humanitarian Purposes' in Nigel White and Christian Henderson (eds), *Research Handbook on International Conflict and Security Law* (Edward Elgar, 2013) 230, stating that 'Article 2(4) is an absolute prohibition of the use of force; its concluding words are not to be construed as a loophole allowing the use of force for what states may claim to be benign purposes. These words limit rather than enable the use of force.'

inconsistent with the Purposes of the United Nations' serve only to describe the prohibition – that is, any use of force amounts to a violation of the territorial integrity and political independence of another States – and not to limit its scope. Moreover, the illegality or not of the conduct against which the intervention is (purportedly) directed is irrelevant for the determination of the legality of the intervention. Any response, including a response to intervene, must itself meet the requirement and may therefore not constitute a breach of Article 2(4) of the Charter. This general approach appears clear from the language of the third principle of the Declaration. The third principle prohibits, for example, intervention whether 'directly or indirectly, or *for any reason whatsoever*'.

The approach to humanitarian intervention which has been put forward in this section is also consistent with State practice. I have, elsewhere,[51] described the debate on humanitarian intervention as 'largely passé' on account of the fact that it 'is rejected by a large majority of States'.[52] The G77 – a group of 134 States – and the Non-Aligned Movement – a collective of more 120 States – have consistently rejected the legality of humanitarian intervention.[53] The debates in the UN Security Council have also tended to confirm the general view that, whatever its moral rationale, humanitarian intervention remains illegal under international law. For example, while many States expressed support for the US, UK and French intervention, most of these States did so on purely moral and not legal grounds.[54] Indeed the only State to explicitly pronounce that the intervention was legal has been the United Kingdom.[55] Moreover, many States, including some that generally supported the intervention, questioned (or at least expressed ambivalence about) the legality of the intervention.[56]

2.3 *Participation in Civil Wars*

The third principle in the Declaration also provides that States may not 'participate in civil strife in another State'. For this reason, a State may not intervene to assist an insurrectional movement engaged in a conflict for power with the government of the day. The third principle of the

[51] Admittedly this view was expressed prior to the intervention in Syria in response to chemical weapons.

[52] See Dire Tladi, 'The Use of Force against Non-State Actors, Decline of Collective Security and the Rise of Unilateralism: Whither International Law?' in Tams, O'Connell and Tladi (n 43) 15. See also generally Dire Tladi, 'The Intervention in Côte d'Ivoire' Ruys and Corten (n 42).

[53] See eg G77 Summit decision of 2000, Declaration of the South Summit, Havana, 10–14 April 2000, para 54, just after the Kosovo intervention in which it 'rejected the so-called right of humanitarian intervention', www.g77.org/summit/Declaration_G77Summit.htm. See also Seventeenth Summit of Heads of State and Government of the Non-Aligned Movement of 2016, 180, para 777, http://cns.miis.edu/nam/documents/Official_Document/XVII-NAM-Summit-Final-Outcome-Document-ENGpdf ('*reaffirmed* the Movement's commitment to enhance international cooperation to provide humanitarian assistance in full compliance with the UN Charter and mindful of the relevant UN resolutions, where applicable, in particular 46/182 and in this regard, they reiterated the rejection by the Movement of the so-called "right" of humanitarian intervention, which has no basis either in the UN Charter or in international law').

[54] See generally further 8233th Meeting of the UNSC, S/PV8233 (14 April 2018).

[55] See UK statement, ibid, wherein it stated that any state is permitted under international law, on an exceptional basis, to take measures in order to alleviate overwhelming humanitarian suffering. In language reminiscent of the Kosovo 'illegal but legitimate' mantra, the representative for France took the opportunity to state that the voting reflects the Council's 'understanding' of the action, but did not state that the Council found the action to be legal: 'The result of the voting sends a clear message that the members of the Council understand the circumstances, reason for and objectives of the military action taken yesterday. The Council understands why such action, which has been acknowledged as proportional and targeted, was required.'

[56] See S/PV8233 (n 54). The Russian delegation, for example, described the intervention as '[a]n act of aggression against a sovereign State on the front lines in the fight against terrorism was committed without permission from the Security Council and in violation of the Charter of the United Nations and the norms and principles of international law'; the Chinese representative emphasised that China advocates respect for the sovereignty, independence, unity and territorial integrity of all countries and stated the US, UK and French intervention violated these principles.

Declaration prohibits the provision of assistance to insurrectional movements 'directed at the overthrow of the regime of another State'. Yet, under international law, a recognised government is entitled to request assistance from another to quell uprisings. Thus, South Africa's decision in 2014 to send a military and police contingent to Lesotho at the request of then under-siege Prime Minister of Lesotho, Thomas Thabane, was a lawful intervention at the request of the recognised government in effective control of the territory.[57] Because the intervention was made pursuant to a request by an incumbent government, it was not designed to undermine 'the inalienable right' of a State to freely determine its political destiny. Similarly, the intervention by Uganda in South Sudan in 2013 was consistent with the duty of non-intervention since it was pursuant to an invitation by the recognised government of South Sudan.[58]

In contrast, the intervention by the Russian Federation in aid of the Berkut (a Ukrainian Special Police) and pro-Russian militia in Crimea seeking the secession of Crimea from Ukraine was inconsistent with the duty not to intervene in civil strife since it was not done at the request of the recognised government of Ukraine.[59] Although, the Russian Federation cited invitation by former Ukraine President Viktor Yanukovych, there are at least two reasons why that invitation could not make valid Russia's intervention. First, at the time of the intervention, Yanukoyvich was no longer President of Ukraine and thus no longer in effective control. Second, the request was limited to restoration of order and did not extend to intervention to assist separatists to secure secession. Intervention in another State to assist rebels seeking to oust the recognised government is inconsistent with the explicit terms of the Declaration – 'no State shall organise, assist, foment, finance, incite or tolerate subversive, terrorist or armed activities directed towards the violent overthrow of the regime of another State'. This prohibition has been endorsed by the ICJ.[60] In the context of the ongoing Syrian conflict, assistance given to the Free Syrian Army – a movement aimed at overthrowing the Syrian government – is inconsistent with the duty of non-intervention under customary international law as reflected in the *Nicaragua* case and the Declaration.[61]

While there is little doubt about the illegality of intervention at the request of a rebel movement seeking to oust a recognised government, the question of intervention at the request of the government is complex. While cases where a recognised government is in effective control of its territory, such as the Lesotho and South Sudan cases referred to above, do not create difficulties, other cases where the government has lost control of some or all of its territory raise more controversy. In such cases, the intervention does not affect the right of peoples to freely determine their destiny.[62] In the event of civil war, however, where the government has lost control of some of its territory, supporting one side in the conflict negatively affects the rights of the State (or the people of the State) 'to choose its political, economic, social and cultural

[57] See David Klion, 'South Africa's Cautious Intervention in Lesotho's Political Crisis', 9 September 2014, www.worldpoliticsreview.com/trend-lines/14048/south-africa-s-cautious-intervention-in-lesotho-s-political-crisis.

[58] See Kasaija Phillip Apuuli, 'Explaining the (Il)Legality of Uganda's intervention in the Current South Sudan Conflict' (2014) 23 *African Security Review* 352, 357.

[59] See for discussion Mary Ellen O'Connell, 'The Crisis in Ukraine – 2014' in Ruys and Corten (n 42).

[60] See eg *Military and Paramilitary Activities* case (n 12), paras 195 and 205. See also *Armed Activities on the Territory of the Congo* (n 17) 160, where the Court determined that 'the training and military support given by Uganda to' a rebel group within the DRC was a violation of international law.

[61] See for discussion Tom Ruys, 'Of Arms, Funding and "Non-Lethal Assistance" – Issues Surrounding Third State Intervention in the Syrian Civil War' (2014) 13 *Chinese Journal of International Law* 13, esp 51.

[62] See eg Karine Bannelier and Theodore Christakis, 'The Intervention of France and African Countries in Mali – 2013' in Ruys and Corten (n 42) 819.

system' – or put another way, to determine its future.[63] The Saudi-led intervention in Yemen in 2016 against the Houthi rebel movement at the invitation of the government is an illustration of an intervention that was inconsistent with the duty of non-intervention under international law as reflected in the Declaration.

3 *Intervention in Internal Political or Democratic Processes*

One of the clearest ways in which one State can intervene in the internal affairs of another State is to interfere in the internal political or democratic processes of another State. Internal political or democratic processes represent a fundamental way in which a State (and its people) 'choose its political, economic, social and cultural system' and the interference in such processes is thus contrary to the Declaration. The right of a State and its people to choose their government is a sovereign right and the interference with internal political or democratic processes strikes at the very heart of this right. In the International Law Commission's (ILC) 1949 Declaration on the Rights and Duties of States, the Commission states in this respect that '[e]very State has the right to independence and hence to exercise freely, without dictation by any other States, all its legal powers, including the choice of its own form of government'.[64] Article 41 of the Vienna Convention on Diplomatic Relations, though dealing with diplomats, is of particular relevance here. It states that diplomats 'have a duty not to interfere in the internal affairs of that State'.[65] The commentary to Article 40 of the ILC Draft Articles on Diplomatic Intercourse, on which Article 41 of the Vienna Convention on Diplomatic Relations is based, explains that the purport of this provision is that diplomats 'must not take part in political campaigns'.[66] Thus attempts by one State (or its agents) at inserting itself in the internal political or democratic processes of another State, would amount to a violation of the duty of non-interference.

More direct interference in the internal political and democratic processes will more clearly be contrary to the duty of non-intervention. This explains the highly critical response of several States to the decision by a number of States, including the United States, Austria, the United Kingdom, France, Germany, Colombia, Argentina, Ecuador, Peru, Costa Rica, Paraguay and Spain, to recognise Venezuela's opposition leader, Juan Guaidó, barely two weeks after Venezuela's President Nicolás Maduro had been sworn in for another term.[67] The Prime Minister of Antigua and Barbuda, Gaston Browne, has stated that most States in CARICOM do not accept Juan Guaidó as the interim President and that the decision of some States to recognise him is 'an affront to democracy within the hemisphere' and violates the principles of non-interference,

[63] See for discussion Luca Ferro and Tom Ruys, 'The Saudi-led Military Intervention in Yemen's Civil War – 2015' in Ruys and Corten (n 42) 909.

[64] Art 1 of the 1949 Declaration of the Rights and Duties of States, with Commentaries, *Yearbook of the International Law Commission* (UN, 1949).

[65] Art 41 of the 1961 Vienna Convention on Diplomatic Relations.

[66] Para 2 of Commentary to Draft Art 40 of the 1958 Draft Articles on Diplomatic Intercourse with Commentaries, *Yearbook of the International Law Commission*, vol 2 (UN, 1958).

[67] For a different perspectives of the events see Amanda Macias, 'Maduro Says Venezuela Is Breaking Relations with US, Gives American Diplomats 72 Hours to Leave Country', www.cnbc.com/2019/01/23/venezuela-president-maduro-breaks-relations-with-us-gives-american-diplomats-72–hours-to-leave-country.html; RT, 'Final Countdown: US Diplomats Given 72 Hours to Pull Out of Venezuela', www.rt.com/news/453626–us-embassy-caracas-deadline; Telesure, 'Trump Admin Wants $500M to Fund Intervention in Venezuela', www.telesurenglish.net/news/Trump-Admin-Wants-500M-to-Fund-Its-Intervention-in-Venezuela-20190312–0007.html; Paul Craig, 'Washington Has Never Forgiven Chavez for Nationalising Oil – Economist', https://sputniknews.com/analysis/201903111073124477–venezuela-us-oil-nationalisation/.

non-intervention and sovereignty as well as respecting the sovereignty of States.[68] In a statement read by its chairperson, the Southern African Development Community (SADC), described the recognition of Guaidó as 'attempts … to interfere in the affairs and sovereignty of' Venezuela and as 'violations of principles of international law'.[69] Similar sentiments were expressed by several States during a debate on the situation in Venezuela held in the UN Security Council on 26 January.[70]

Various organs of the US government have accused the Russian Federation of interfering in its 2016 presidential elections. The accusations put forward two forms of interference, namely propaganda aimed at dissuading voters from voting for the Democratic Party candidate and hacking the computer and the electronic systems of the Democratic Party.[71] The Russian Federation has denied these allegations but if it were to be proven that Russia engaged in these acts, this would constitute interference which might amount to a breach of the duty of non-intervention. Whether this alleged action by the Russian authorities, assuming that Russia engaged in these actions, amounts to intervention prohibited under international law depends on whether it was intended to be coercive or to undermine the right of the United States to decide 'on matters in which each State is permitted, by the principle of State sovereignty, to decide freely'.[72] Interference in political elections, to choose a government, clearly undermines this right in the same way that a military intervention to put in place a puppet government would undermine such a right and thus fall foul of the principle of non-intervention.

While these overtly interventionist acts do raise questions of fact and proof, they do not raise legal questions as to whether they constitute intervention. In the case of Russia's alleged interference in the US elections, for example, the question is whether the acts occurred at all and, if they did, whether they can be attributed to Russia. Other cases of potential interference may be more complicated. Does the funding of a political party constitute interference? Does it matter whether the funded party is the ruling party or the opposition? In each of these, it is likely that the funding is intended – and may be effective – to influence the political and economic direction of the foreign State and would thus amount to the 'subordination of the exercise of its sovereign rights' contrary to the third principle of the Declaration. The issues can become even more muddy. Does the funding of non-State entities, whose objectives may be, on the surface,

[68] Jacqueline Charles, 'As Crisis in Venezuela Escalates, Caribbean Nations Take Sides, Haiti Joins US', www.miamiherald.com/news/nation-world/world/americas/haiti/article225070430.html.

[69] SADC Solidarity Statement with the Bolivarian Republic of Venezuela, www.sadc.int/files/8415/4980/4167/Solidarity_statement_with_the_Bolivarian_Republic_of_Venezuela_by_SADC_Chairperson.pdf.

[70] See statements by various statements at the meeting of the UN Security Council on 26 January 2019, UN S/PV8452: the Russian Federation described the actions of the United States and others as 'shameless and aggressive' and stated that these actions were 'aimed at ousting the legitimately elected President of Venezuela', and referred to them as a 'United States strategy to carry out regime change in Venezuela' and 'interference in the internal affairs of another State'; South Africa, for its part, expressed deep concern at what it termed 'a clear attempt, in Venezuela, to circumvent the constitutional legal mechanisms of the country that govern its elections'; Equatorial Guinea, more cautiously, described the situation in Venezuela as 'an internal matter', noting that 'external interference' was unlikely to result in a lasting solution; Kuwait, without stating directly that the recognition of the opposition amounted to intervention, referred to 'the respect [for] the sovereignty of States' and the duty 'not interfere in their internal affairs', as 'principles that govern relations among nations'; China, for its part stated it 'opposes foreign interference in Venezuela's domestic affairs' and that 'the situation in Venezuela is a domestic matter'. Other States, such as the United Kingdom, United States, Germany and Peru, expressed support for recognition of the opposition.

[71] See, for description, Scott Shane and Sheera Frenkel, 'Russian 2016 Influence Operation Targeted African-Americans on Social Media', www.nytimes.com/2018/12/17/us/politics/russia-2016-influence-campaign.html; see also the indictment in *US v Netyksho*, www.documentcloud.org/documents/4598904-Special-Counsel-Indictment-July-13–2018.html.

[72] *Military and Paramilitary Activities* case (n 12) 205.

apolitical, by another State constitute intervention prohibited by customary international law as reflected in the terms of the Declaration? Does it matter whether the funding does not come directly from the foreign State but from a State-funded agency that has some level of independence. Whether these types of funding activities constitute prohibited intervention is a question of fact dependent on several factors, including the intent of the financial support, the operations of the non-State entity supported, the extent to which it is overtly political, the attitude of the State in which the non-State entity operates and, in particular, whether the laws of the State permit the operation of the non-State entity and foreign funding of such non-State entities.[73]

4 *Economic Intervention*

Perhaps no other form of intervention creates controversy like economic coercion. It is clear that the application of economic measures against certain States can constitute intervention prohibited under international law. This much is clear from the third principle of the Declaration under which '[n]o State may use or encourage the use of economic, political or any other type of measure to coerce another' State. The key factor, therefore, lies in whether the economic measure is adopted for the purposes of coercing another State.[74] I pause here to point out that economic measures, even when rising to the level of coercion and thus prohibited under the duty of non-intervention, are not a violation of Article 2(4) of the Charter.[75] It is unnecessary to address this issue since the view that economic coercion amounts to aggression under Article 2(4) 'is a minority one'.[76] It is sufficient only to recall that while there is a close relationship between the prohibition on the use of force and the duty of non-intervention – in particular that the use of force is a particular type of intervention – the two are not synonymous and should not be conflated.

The fact that economic coercion does not amount to the use of force, however, does not mean that it does not fall foul of international law.[77] Moreover, although the ICJ, in the *Military and Paramilitary Activities* case, determined that the economic measures adopted by the United States and directed at Nicaragua, such as the cessation of aid, did not amount to indirect intervention prohibited by international law, this conclusion appeared to be limited to the particular actions of the United States in that case and should not be seen as a general proposition.[78] Yet clearly not all economic measures by one State that are harmful to another State's interest can be said to be a violation of the duty of non-intervention.[79] As with the question of political intervention, the question whether a particular economic measure violates

[73] See generally Jamnejad and Wood (n 6) 369.

[74] See eg Derek Bowett, 'Economic Coercion and Reprisals by States' (1972) *Virginia Journal of International Law* 1, 5. See also Kunig (n 1), para 25 ('In order to determine prohibited economic interventions, it can be of value to look at the motivations of a State and identify the object of the State action').

[75] For a different view see Jordan J Paust and Albert P Blaunstein, 'The Arab Oil Weapon – A Threat to International Peace' (1974) 68 *American Journal of International Law* 410, esp 439 ('Thus, the coercion was of such mounting intensity and efficacy that it can be authoritatively proscribed as a violation of basic Charter goals and of Article 2(4) [of the Charter]').

[76] Richard B Lillich, 'The Status of Economic Coercion under International Law: United Nations Norms' (1977) 12 *Texas International Law Journal* 17, 18.

[77] Derek Bowett, 'International Law and Economic Coercion' (1976) 16 *Virginia Journal of International Law* 245, 246.

[78] *Military and Paramilitary Activities* case (n 12), paras 144–45 ('the Court has merely to say that it is unable to regard such action on the economic plane as is here complained of as a breach of the customary-law principle of non-intervention').

[79] See Kunig (n 1), para 25 ('Economic intervention is a particularly controversial issue, as it is very difficult to draw a line between the legitimate pursuance of a State's own economic interests and illegal pressure put upon another State').

the duty of non-intervention will depend on whether the measure is coercive, which in turn will depend on a number of factors. These include whether the measure, rather than being intended to gain an economic advantage, is intended to direct the political, economic or other policies of the target State in a way that would lead to the 'subordination of the exercise of sovereign rights' of the target State or prevents the latter from choosing 'its political, economic, social or cultural systems'. Other factors that ought to be taken into account are the intensity and effect of the measures.

The range of economic measures adopted by the United States government since 2015 against the government of Venezuela, which are intended to affect the policy and governance of Venezuela and have had a crippling effect on the economy of that country, are likely to amount to intervention prohibited under international law.[80] Other measures which, depending on the application of these factors, may well constitute intervention prohibited by international law, include the diplomatic and economic measures imposed by the Gulf Co-operation States of Bahrain, Kuwait, Oman, Saudi Arabia and the United Arab Emirates against former member Qatar. While formally the measures are presented as part of a response to terrorism, the list of thirteen demands issued to Qatar appear to be directed at its foreign policy and sovereign choices. These demands include, for example, that Qatar should cut ties with Iran and close its diplomatic mission in Tehran and terminate Turkish military presence in Qatar.[81] Given the motive of coercing Qatar into adopting a particular foreign-policy posture and the wide-ranging nature of the measures, including prohibiting the access to airspace and ports, these measures are likely to constitute intervention prohibited by international law and have already been the subject of several proceedings.[82]

5 *When Is Coercive Intervention Permissible under International Law?*

The third principle of the Declaration ends with a 'without prejudice clause':

> Nothing in the foregoing paragraphs shall be construed as affecting the relevant provisions of the Charter relating to the maintenance of international peace and security.

This provision is an application of Article 2(7) of the Charter of the United Nations that provides as follows:

> Nothing contained in the present Charter shall authorize the United Nations to intervene in matters which are essentially within the domestic jurisdiction of any state or shall require the

80 See eg Executive Order 13692 of 8 March 2015, 'Blocking Property and Suspending Entry of Certain Persons Contributing to the Situation in Venezuela'; Executive Order 13808 of 24 August 2017, 'Imposing Additional Sanctions With Respect to the Situation in Venezuela'; Executive Order 13827 of 19 March 2018, 'Taking Additional Steps to Address the Situation in Venezuela'; Executive Order 13835 of 21 May 2018, 'Prohibiting Certain Additional Transactions With Respect to Venezuela'; Executive Order 13857 of 28 January 2019, 'Taking Additional Steps to Address the National Emergency with Respect to Venezuela'.

81 For a list of the demands see *The Guardian*, 'Qatar Given 10 Days to Meet 13 Sweeping Demands by Saudi Arabia', www.theguardian.com/world/2017/jun/23/close-al-jazeera-saudi-arabia-issues-qatar-with-13–demands-to-end-blockade.

82 In an as yet unpublished decision, the Council of the International Civil Aviation Authority has already made a determination on its competence to deal with a complaint by Qatar against the five States. In turn, the five States have filed a joint application appealing the decision with the International Court of Justice. See *Appeal Against a Decision of the ICAO Council Dated 29 June 2018 on Preliminary Objections (Application (A)) (Kingdom of Bahrain, Arab Republic of Egypt, Kingdom of Saudi Arabia and the United Arab Emirates* v *State of Qatar)*, Joint Application of 4 July 2018. Qatar has, for its part filed a dispute at the International Court of Justice under the Convention against the Elimination of Racial Discrimination, *Interpretation and Application of the International Convention on the Elimination of All Forms of Racial Discrimination (the State of Qatar* v *the United Arab Emirates)*, Application of 11 June 2018.

> Members to submit such matters to settlement under the present Charter; but this principle shall not prejudice the application of enforcement measures under Chapter VII.

In the context of non-intervention, the essence of these provisions is to exclude from the scope of the duty of non-intervention, the provisions of the Charter relating to the maintenance of peace and security contained in Chapter VII. The application of Chapter VII enforcement measures almost by definition involves intervention. Such measures, however, would not violate the duty of non-intervention. A State that engages in conduct which would ordinarily constitute intervention, would not be violating the duty of non-intervention if such conduct were carried out pursuant to an authorisation or obligation under a decision of the UN Security Council acting under Chapter VII of the Charter. A typical example is the case of Haiti where an armed intervention at the request of a government no longer in control was effectively done pursuant to a UN Security Council resolution.[83]

As noted above, the prohibition of non-intervention is not, in and of itself, a norm of *jus cogens*. This is not to say that some measures of intervention may not constitute violations of peremptory norms. For example, a measure of armed intervention may rise to the level of aggression or the denial of self-determination, which are both prohibited by peremptory norms.[84] Save for the instances in which a measure of intervention amounts to a breach of a peremptory norm, intervention may be justified on grounds precluding wrongfulness under international law.[85] A State might, for example, plead necessity as a ground for imposing economic measures aimed at coercing a State to stop committing serious crimes of concern to the international community. Two caveats are necessary. First, given the possibility for abuse, the determination of the facts constituting a basis for the ground excluding wrongfulness ought not to be based solely on the unilateral assessment of the State in question. Second, the requirements of the particular ground excluding wrongfulness should be strictly complied with.

Finally, as discussed earlier, in the cases where intervention rises to the level of conflict with peremptory norms of general international law, intervention may be permitted, in the first instance, where there has been an authorisation or an imposition of a duty by the UN Security Council. Second, intervention in such cases would be permitted where the scope of the peremptory norm itself makes provision for such an intervention. The right to use force in self-defence is typical where the peremptory norm in question, the prohibition of aggression, permits the right to use force where the requirements of self-defence are met.

In *Oppenheim's International Law*, Jennings and Watts identify a number of more detailed grounds.[86] These include a State's right to protect its citizens, intervention to prevent a State from committing cruelties against its own population, the right of self-defence, to assist the peoples from securing their right to self-determination and through operation of a treaty. These grounds, however, are nothing more than the application of the grounds identified above. For example, a State seeking to protect its nationals in another State may rely on the ground of

[83] Para 4 of UN Security Council Res 940 (1994) authorised States 'to form a multinational force under unified command and control and, in this framework, to use all necessary means to facilitate the departure from Haiti of the military leadership . . . the prompt return of the legitimately elected President and the restoration of the legitimate authorities of the Government of Haiti'.

[84] See paras (a) and (h) of the Annex to the International Law Commission Draft Conclusions on Peremptory Norms of General International Law (n 32). See also para 12 of the commentary to draft conclusion 23 of the Draft Conclusions, which provides other terms used to described the *jus cogens* norm of self-determination. See Fourth Report of Special Rapporteur on Peremptory Norms (n 32), paras 62–68 (aggression) and 108–15 (self-determination).

[85] Chapter V of Part I of 2001 Articles on Responsibility of States for Internationally Wrongful Acts with Commentaries, *Yearbook of the International Law Commission*, vol 2(1) (UN, 2001).

[86] Jennings and Watts (n 24) 339 et seq.

necessity to intervene. However, such an intervention may not involve the use force which is prohibited as a norm of *jus cogens* and should strictly meet the test of necessity under international law. The same is also true of intervention in a State to stop it from committing atrocities against its population. In this context, the question is often posed whether the international community should stand by and allow mass atrocities to continue. Yet in cases of mass atrocities against a State's own population, intervention may be permitted subject to certain conditions. First, intervention falling short of the use of force or other breach of peremptory norms may be permitted even if such intervention would, but for the mass atrocities, be a violation of the duty of non-intervention. For example, the measures adopted by the Gulf Co-operation States against Qatar described above may be justified if they were in response to the commission of mass atrocities by Qatar. Second, in the case of mass atrocities, intervention, including using armed forces, would be permissible under international law if authorised by the UN Security Council acting under Chapter VII of the Charter as was the case in the situation in Libya.[87]

Intervention to assist peoples in securing their right to self-determination is an application of the rules of peremptory norms according to which there is a duty on States to co-operate to end situations created by the breach of peremptory norms of international law.[88] It is important to emphasise, however, that under the articles of State responsibility, only 'lawful' measures may be implemented, which would exclude armed intervention or other measures inconsistent with peremptory norms of international law.[89] Intervention on the basis of the application of a treaty can also be seen as an application of a ground excluding wrongfulness, namely consent.[90] Intervention on the basis of the Constitutive Act of the African Union may also be justified on the basis of the grounds described above. Intervention under Article 4(h) of the Constitutive Act,[91] for example, could be seen either as the application of consent, since the Constitutive Act is a treaty, or as an application of the Chapter VIII arrangements under the UN Charter on co-operation between the United Nations and regional organisations in the maintenance of international peace and security. On the other hand, intervention under Article 4(j) of the Constitutive Act,[92] in addition to constituting consent, should also be seen as intervention by invitation and subject to constraints outlined in section III.2.3.

IV CONCLUSION

The duty of non-intervention has long been accepted as a principle of customary international law. Nonetheless, commentators have highlighted, up to the present day, its vague scope and content. In many ways, the third principle in the Declaration on the Principles of International Law concerning Friendly Relations and Co-operation among States, which the ICJ has recognised as reflecting customary international law, has provided some detail on the scope of the principle of non-intervention under international law. This chapter has attempted, relying

[87] See UN Security Council Res 1973 (2011).

[88] See Art 41 para 1 of the Articles on State Responsibility (n 85).

[89] See Draft Conclusion 19 of the Draft Conclusions on Peremptory Norms of General International Law and para 3 of the commentary thereto (n 32). See the Third Report of the Special Rapporteur on Peremptory Norms of General International Law (*Jus Cogens*), Dire Tladi, UN Doc A/CN.4/714, para 93.

[90] See Art 20 of the Articles on State Responsibility (n 85).

[91] Art 4(h) of the African Union Constitutive Acts provides the right of the Union to intervene 'in respect of grave circumstances . . .'.

[92] Art 4(j) of the African Union Constitutive Acts provides for 'the right of Member States to request intervention from the Union in order to restore peace and security'.

primarily on the Declaration, to identify some of the key issues in the application of the duty of non-intervention. In sum, there are many different types of measures and conduct that may constitute intervention under international law. As a general matter, the measure must be directed at an issue or decision that falls within the domestic domain of the target State and must be intended to coerce such a State. These requirements, which are mentioned in the first two paragraphs of the third principle of the Declaration, remain relevant for the determination of whether an intervention is lawful or not and can be applied to recent developments, even fifty years after the adoption of the Declaration.

Non-intervention remains a bedrock principle, aimed at promoting the peaceful co-existence among States in a political climate in which States may be tempted to interfere in the domestic affairs of others. It provides a golden thread that ties important principles such as sovereign equality and prohibition of the use of force together, creating a mosaic which, if respected, would lead to a peaceful world order.

6

Co-Operation

Laurence Boisson de Chazournes and Jason Rudall

'Alone we can do so little; together we can do so much.'[1]

I INTRODUCTION

Co-operation is a cornerstone principle of contemporary international law. It is difficult to overstate its reach as it finds expression in many different areas of international legal relations. That said, its gravitation to the heart of international law has been a relatively recent phenomenon. The Declaration on Principles of International Law concerning Friendly Relations and Co-operation among States in accordance with the Charter of the United Nations of 1970 has played an important role in this transition.

Co-operation has gradually gained prominence over the course of the twentieth century, with a clear emphasis on the obligation to co-operate in the aftermath of the Second World War. This led some to consider that international law has evolved from a law of co-existence to a law of co-operation.[2] Wolfgang Friedmann observed that States were increasingly resorting to co-operation, as opposed to conflict, to achieve their objectives. Today, co-operation finds application in matters of peace and security, human rights, international economic relations and international environmental law, amongst many others. While other principles of international law, such as the prohibition on the use of force, the duty of non-intervention and the sovereign equality of States are conceived in a negative sense – that is, they are aimed at restraining certain behaviour – the principle of co-operation is aimed at promoting certain behaviour.[3] Wolfgang Friedmann noted that the development of international co-operation was part of a changing structure in international law 'from an essentially negative code of rule abstention to positive rules of co-operation'.[4] Being positive in nature, the duty to co-operate serves as a tool for the

[1] Attributed to the American author and political activist Helen Keller. See Joseph P Lash, *Helen and Teacher: The Story of Helen Keller and Anne Sullivan Macy* (Da Capo Press, 1980) 489.

[2] See eg Wolfgang Friedmann, *The Changing Structure of International Law* (Stevens, 1964); Georges Abi-Saab, 'Cours général de droit international public (Volume 207)' in *Collected Courses of the Hague Academy of International Law* (Brill, 1987); Georges Abi-Saab, 'Whither the International Community?' (1998) 9 *European Journal of International Law* 248; Pierre-Marie Dupuy, 'International Law: Torn between Coexistence, Co-operation and Globalization: General Conclusions' (1998) 9 *European Journal of International Law* 278.

[3] Piet-Hein Houben, 'Principles of International Law Concerning Friendly Relations and Co-Operation among States' (1967) 61 *American Journal of International Law* 703, 721.

[4] Friedmann (n 2) 62.

realisation of certain aims or values. These aims or values cannot be realised unilaterally and instead require the collective effort of States taking action together.[5]

While international co-operation has only served as a central principle of the international legal order over the last half century, its history can in fact be traced back much further. With the Industrial Revolution and globalisation came the need for international regulation. These economic and regulatory developments meant States became linked to one another and interdependent. This was the reason for the earliest manifestations of economic co-operation between States and international institutions became essential for solving co-ordination and co-operation problems in this context.[6]

An early example of co-operation in international legal relations was the need to ensure freedom of navigation. This led to some of the first legal manifestations of co-operation in the form of regulatory frameworks and institutional structures that were concerned with water-courses.[7] As early as the beginning of the nineteenth century, the regulation of navigation on a number of European rivers became internationalised.[8] Indeed, the Central Commission for Navigation on the Rhine was created in 1815,[9] and the Danube Commissions were set up in 1856.[10] Other basin organisations were established thereafter. Over time these joint bodies saw their mandates enlarged and, as a result, co-operation strengthened.

Beyond these early manifestations over shared natural resources, co-operation was also necessary in other areas where States were increasingly connected. As a result, international administrative unions were formed to co-ordinate State activity and quickly became significant sites of co-operative action. For example, in 1865 the International Telegraph Union was established by the International Telegraph Convention[11] to co-ordinate the use of telecommunication infrastructure and facilitate co-operation on the development of technical standards. Latterly it fostered co-operation regarding satellite orbits and the improvement of telecommunications in the developing world. Similarly, in 1874, the General Postal Union was created and would later become the Universal Postal Union in 1878 to foster co-operation and co-ordination in postal activities.

The trend towards institutionalising co-operative endeavours in legal frameworks and institutions accelerated after the First World War. In 1919, the International Labour Organization (ILO) was established, motivated by the belief that universal and lasting peace could only be achieved if there was social justice.[12] International co-operation was extended from those issues of a technical, administrative or specialised nature to those of a more general and fundamental character, not least the maintenance of international peace and security or the enhancement of

[5] Abi-Saab, 'Whither the International Community?' (n 2).

[6] Eyal Benvenisti, 'The Law of Global Governance (Volume 368)' in *Collected Courses of the Hague Academy of International Law* (Brill, 2013).

[7] Laurence Boisson de Chazournes, *Fresh Water in International Law* (Oxford University Press, 2013); Abi-Saab, 'Whither the International Community' (n 2).

[8] See Boisson de Chazournes (n 7); Claude-Albert Colliard, 'Evolution et aspects actuels du régime juridique des fleuves internationaux (Volume 125)' in *Collected Courses of the Hague Academy of International Law* (Brill, 1968) 417.

[9] See Act of Congress of Vienna, Art CVIII, English translation and further discussion available in Stephen C McCaffrey, *The Law of International Watercourses – Non-Navigational Uses* (Oxford University Press, 2001), 173–74.

[10] General Treaty for the Re-Establishment of Peace between Austria, France, Great Britain, Prussia, Sardinia, Turkey, and Russia (Paris, 30 March 1856) in Parry, vol 114 (1885–86) 409–20.

[11] International Telegraph Convention, 17 May 1865, 130 *Consol. TS* 198.

[12] Preamble, Constitution of the International Labour Organization, 1 April 1919, adopted by the Peace Conference in April 1919. The ILO Constitution became Part XIII of the Treaty of Versailles (28 June 1919).

global welfare.[13] This development occurred with the creation of the League of Nations and the United Nations respectively. Since co-operation was positioned at the heart of the UN Charter and reaffirmed in the Friendly Relations Declaration, the constitutional status of co-operation in the international legal order was placed beyond doubt.

That said, does a general obligation to co-operate exist today? Is the expression of co-operation in the UN Charter and the Friendly Relations Declaration an 'empty shell'?[14] Do the various conceptions of co-operation in particular areas of international law differ and might those contain specific duties to co-operate? This chapter will explore the notion of co-operation and its contours, unpacking its manifestations to understand its scope and operation in contemporary international law.

II INTERNATIONAL CO-OPERATION: FOUNDATIONS OF A CONSTITUTIONAL PRINCIPLE

1 *Co-Operation under the UN Charter*

Article 1(3) of the UN Charter provides that a central objective of the United Nations is to 'achieve international co-operation in solving international problems of an economic, social, cultural, or humanitarian character', while Articles 2, 55 and 56 of the UN Charter go on to provide further for co-operation among States. These provisions work together to further the objectives of the United Nations. The aims of the United Nations as provided for in Article 1 of its Charter are to ensure the maintenance of international peace and security, to pursue international development and to promote and encourage international respect for and enjoyment of human rights and fundamental freedoms.

Under Article 56 of the Charter the notions of 'international co-operation' and 'joint and separate action' are expressed explicitly. The *travaux préparatoires* shed light on the extent to which Member States of the United Nations would be expected to act either within the context of the United Nations or externally to the organisation.[15] Some delegations were concerned with the potential ramifications of including a reference to 'separate action' but other delegates saw little cause for concern.[16] Certain delegations thought there was sufficient protection elsewhere in the Charter to allay fears of interference with the domestic affairs of other States.[17] There is little evidence that any of the delegates were concerned with the positive nature of the obligation of international co-operation, as inclusion of the term 'action' suggests. Given that 'separate action' was left in the revised draft and that draft was so widely accepted, we can surmise that States envisaged a commitment, at the very least to make individual and collective efforts on the diplomatic plane, but perhaps even beyond that.

Reading Articles 1, 55 and 56 together has led some to conclude that these provisions create a binding legal obligation to co-operate in furthering the objectives of the United Nations.[18]

[13] Abi-Saab, 'Whither the International Community?' (n 2) 255.

[14] Jost Delbrück, 'Coexistence, Co-operation and Solidarity in International Law: The International Obligation to Co-operate – An Empty Shell or a Hard Law Principle of International Law? – A Critical Look at a Much Debated Paradigm of Modern International Law' in Holger P Hestermeyer et al (eds), *Coexistence, Co-Operation and Solidarity: Liber Amicorum Rüdiger Wolfrum* (Brill, 2011).

[15] The UNCIO, Committee II, General Assembly, Committee 3: Economic and Social Co-operation, 10 (1945) *Documents of the UN Conference on International Organization* 139–41.

[16] ibid.

[17] ibid.

[18] See eg Bruno Simma and Philip Alston, 'The Sources of Human Rights Law: Custom, *Jus Cogens*, and General Principles' 12 (1988) *Australian Yearbook of International Law* 82, 90, describing the 'authoritative interpretation'

As such, an argument can be made that States have undertaken a commitment to engage in co-operative action for the realisation of human rights, development and international peace and security. That said, the specific content of any general duty to co-operate is undefined by the provisions of the Charter and little guidance is offered by the *travaux préparatoires*. We now turn to subsequent expressions of the general concept for further insights.

2 *Co-Operation in the Friendly Relations Declaration*

Coming twenty-five years after the UN Charter, the Declaration on Principles of International Law concerning Friendly Relations and Co-operation among States in accordance with the Charter of the United Nations of 24 October 1970[19] was an important reaffirmation of the commitments made by States under the Charter.[20] It also provided an opportunity to clarify the content of the principles at the heart of the new international legal order. The provisions of the Friendly Relations Declaration indicate that international co-operation extends to economic, social, cultural and trade fields, as well as those of science and technology. Similarly, international co-operation is connected with the promotion of development. As such, the Declaration confirms and extends the scope of international co-operation. In doing so, the Declaration consolidates the principle of co-operation as central to international legal relations and as having a wide reach across a range of areas where States interact. It also mandates the circumstances under which co-operation should occur.

The Declaration reiterates that States have a duty to co-operate with one another in accordance with the Charter, and goes on to elaborate that such co-operation should occur despite any political, economic or social differences they may have and should be aimed at maintaining international peace and security, promoting economic development, securing respect for human rights and the elimination of racial discrimination and religious intolerance. Furthermore, States are directed to conduct their international relations in the economic, social, cultural, technical and trade fields in accordance with the principles of sovereign equality and non-intervention. Further still, States who are members of the United Nations are under a duty to take joint and separate action in co-operation with the United Nations in accordance with the relevant provisions of the Charter. The Declaration also expresses that States should co-operate in the fields of science and technology as well as for the promotion of international cultural and educational progress.

Despite this elaboration of the areas in which States committed to co-operate, there has been some criticism that this Declaration does not add much additional content to the provisions of the UN Charter concerning co-operation.[21] The Declaration largely repeats what had earlier

approach 'used to arrive at human rights obligations under international law independently of specific treaties'. Simma and Alston also note: 'It consists of treating the Universal Declaration and the body of soft law built upon it as an *authoritative interpretation* of the obligation contained in Articles 55 and 56 of the UN Charter according to which "all Members pledge themselves to take joint and separate action in co-operation with the Organization" in order to achieve "universal respect for, and observance of, human rights and fundamental freedoms for all without distinction as to race, sex, language or religion"' (at 100).

[19] Declaration on Principles of International Law Concerning Friendly Relations and Co-operation among States in Accordance with the Charter of the United Nations, UNGA Res 2625 (XXV) (24 October 1970), UN Doc A/RES/25/2625.

[20] Delbrück (n 14) 7.

[21] See eg Gaetano Arangio-Ruiz, *The UN Declaration on Friendly Relations and the System of the Sources of International Law* (Springer, 1979) 143; Robert Rosenstock, 'The Declaration of Principles of International Law Concerning Friendly Relations: A Survey' (1971) 65(5) *American Journal of International Law* 713, 729.

been set out in the Charter and appears to suggest that little consensus existed around the exact scope of the duty to co-operate.[22]

A review of the *travaux préparatoires* of the Friendly Relations Declaration sheds some light on this. Given the positive nature of the principle, it was difficult to reach consensus on the precise content of co-operation during the 1966 Special Committee meeting.[23] One particularly difficult question was the extent to which the principle of co-operation as expressed under Article 56 of the UN Charter applied to States beyond the United Nations. Socialist countries argued that co-operation was applicable to all States. Non-aligned countries were also of the view that co-operation was universally applicable but that UN Member States could not impose duties on non-members. Western delegations argued that the principle under the Friendly Relations Declaration should be applicable only to UN members. They were also keen to emphasise Articles 55 and 56 of the UN Charter in the Friendly Relations Declaration, which would confirm that Members of the United Nations had an obligation to take joint and separate action in co-operation with the United Nations. However, the Western delegations' proposal did not receive support.

The non-aligned countries' proposal made no mention of the United Nations and simply envisaged co-operation between States.[24] Similarly, a Czech proposal offered a similar approach, as well as stipulating that the aim of co-operation was the maintenance of international peace and security. This proposal also included a provision on non-discrimination that was considered to be important by Socialist countries, namely that 'States have the duty to co-operate with one another irrespective of their different systems' and, as such, should 'refrain from any discrimination in their relations with other States, in particular discrimination by reason of differences in political, economic and social systems or in levels of economic development'.[25]

However, it was not possible to include such language in the final draft given the complexity of the issue, especially in light of trade concerns and the presence of trade preferences for developing countries.[26] Responding to a concern expressed by the Australian representative, the Czech delegate stated that 'obviously no preferences which might be granted to developing countries could be regarded as discrimination'.[27] It is thought that the Czech delegate had in mind an exception that would encompass all developing countries rather than singling any of them out.[28]

The non-aligned countries, in particular Algeria, Burma, Cameroon, India, Kenya, Lebanon, Madagascar, UAR and Yugoslavia (as well as amendments by Chile) put forward a proposal that 'differences in the political, economic and social systems of States as well as in their levels of economic and social development shall not impede international co-operation'.[29] This text was less problematic than that proposed by the Czech delegation. However, it still posed several challenges for Western delegations and therefore did not attract their support.

[22] Philip Alston and Gerard Quinn, 'The Nature and Scope of States Parties' Obligations under the International Covenant on Economic, Social and Cultural Rights' (1987) 9(2) *Human Rights Quarterly* 156, 188.

[23] See also Arangio-Rui (n 21); Rosenstock (n 21).

[24] ibid.

[25] Discussions of the Special Committee on the Friendly Relations Declaration: L.16; Potocny (Czechoslovakia), SR 34, 5.

[26] Rosenstock (n 21) 729–30.

[27] Discussions of the Special Committee on the Friendly Relations Declaration: L.16; Pechota (Czechoslovakia), SR 38, 12.

[28] Houben (n 3) 722.

[29] Discussions of the Special Committee on the Friendly Relations Declaration: L.29; L.30.

The non-aligned proposal ultimately provided that 'States shall co-operate in the promotion of economic growth throughout the world, especially that of the developing countries' and Western countries had also expressed 'a strong belief in the duty to contribute to the solution of the problem of the unequal distribution of the prosperity in the world'.[30] Agreement in the Drafting Committee was achieved around most of this text, and two alternatives were given for part of the text. As such, the following was what the Drafting Committee presented to the Special Committee, with the possibility to vote on the two variants set out:

1. States have the duty to co-operate with one another, irrespective of their different political, economic and social systems, in the various spheres of international relations in order to maintain international peace and security and to promote international economic stability and programs and the general welfare of nations.
2. To this end,
   a) States shall co-operate with other States in the maintenance of international peace and security;
   b) *Alternative I*
   States shall conduct their international relations in the economic, social, technical and trade fields in accordance with the principles of sovereign equality and non-intervention with a view to *realizing* international co-operation free from discrimination based on differences in political, economic or social systems;
   Alternative II
   States shall conduct their international relations in the economic, social, technical and trade fields in accordance with the principles of sovereign equality and non-intervention with a view to *ensuring the realization of* international co-operation free from discrimination based on differences in political, economic or social systems;
   c) States Members of the United Nations have the duty to take joint and separate action in co-operation with the United Nations in accordance with the relevant provisions of the Charter.
3. States should co-operate in the economic, social and cultural fields as well as in the field of science and technology and for the promotion of international cultural and educational progress. States should co-operate in the promotion of economic growth throughout the world, especially that of the developing countries.

Ultimately the alternatives were voted on and the present formulation was adopted:

> States have the duty to co-operate with one another, irrespective of the differences in their political, economic and social systems, in the various spheres of international relations, in order to maintain international peace and security and to promote international economic stability and progress, the general welfare of nations and international co-operation free from discrimination based on such differences.
>
> To this end:
>
> a) States shall co-operate with other States in the maintenance of international peace and security;
> b) States shall co-operate in the promotion of universal respect for, and observance of, human rights and fundamental freedoms for all, and in the elimination of all forms of racial discrimination and all forms of religious intolerance;
> c) States shall conduct their international relations in the economic, social, technical and trade fields in accordance with the principles of sovereign equality and non-intervention;

[30] Houben (n 3) 722.

d) States Members of the United Nations have the duty to take joint and separate action in co-operation with the United Nations in accordance with the relevant provisions of the Charter.

States should co-operate in the economic, social and cultural fields as well as in the field of science and technology and for the promotion of international cultural and educational progress. States should co-operate in the promotion of economic growth throughout the world, especially that of the developing countries.

Interestingly, there is a distinction in the mandatory nature of the paragraphs of this provision. Some set out that States 'have the duty to co-operate', others that States 'shall co-operate', and others again note that States 'should co-operate'. The third paragraph contradicts the mandatory nature of the first paragraph. It has been pointed out that this reflects a negotiated compromise during the drafting of the Declaration in the Special Committee in which Western delegations were reluctant to create any impression that there is a general legal obligation to co-operate.[31] This was in contrast to the position of developing and socialist States, who were in favour of such an obligation.[32]

While the precise meaning of co-operation did not develop much from the UN Charter, particularly as regards the specific behaviour that is expected of States and the form that co-operation should take, it did serve to connect co-operation to other areas of international law and confirm its role in forging international legal relations, particularly between the developed and developing world. Given the centrality of co-operation today, it is easy to critique the Friendly Relations Declaration for not having contributed to the advancement of international co-operation. But the Declaration, along with the UN Charter, in fact crystallised the paradigm shift in the post-Second World War global order from one of predominantly co-existence to one of predominantly co-operation. These two instruments laid the groundwork for international co-operation and became reference points for subsequent expressions of co-operation.

3 *Other General Expressions of Co-Operation*

Many subsequent instruments of a universal nature have referred to international co-operation. These have nevertheless begun to apply co-operation in specific contexts, building on the groundwork of the Friendly Relations Declaration. The Declaration on the Establishment of a New International Economic Order[33] expressed in General Assembly Resolution 3201 of 1974, for example, was adopted during the Cold War and in the aftermath of the process of decolonisation. It emphasises co-operation for economic development. It was similarly expressed in the Charter of Rights and Duties of States in 1974.[34] In this context, States committed to international co-operation for development, co-operation in their economic relations, as well as co-operation in scientific and technological endeavours. Co-operation in international economic relations was perceived as particularly important because States pursuing trade policies that were purely to advance their own national interest could harm the economies of other States or negatively affect the achievement of commonly agreed goals.[35]

[31] Rüdiger Wolfrum, 'Co-operation', *Max Planck Encyclopedia of Public International Law* (April 2008), http://opil.ouplaw.com/view/10.1093/law:epil/9780199231690/law-9780199231690-e1427?prd=EPIL.

[32] ibid.

[33] UNGA Res S-6/3201 (1 May 1974).

[34] UNGA Res 3281 (XXIX) (12 December 1974).

[35] Delbrück (n 14) 11.

In a different way, the Manila Declaration on the Peaceful Settlement of International Disputes of 1982, as well as many conventions that express the principle of the peaceful settlement of international disputes since the Hague Convention on the Peaceful Settlement of International Disputes of 1899, refer to co-operation as a means of avoiding disputes.[36]

International co-operation also plays an important role through Article 41 of the Draft Articles, on the Responsibility of States for Internationally Wrongful Acts. The Draft Articles make it clear that States must co-operate to bring an end to serious violations of international law.[37] The International Law Commission (ILC) noted that international co-operation is among the 'special legal obligations of States' in the context of serious breaches of international law.[38]

General Assembly Resolution 59/204 of 20 December 2004[39] is concerned with '[r]espect for the purposes and principles contained in the Charter of the United Nations to achieve international co-operation in promoting and encouraging respect for human rights and for fundamental freedoms and in solving international problems of a humanitarian character'. In particular, it adds further clarity as to the scope of international co-operation under the UN Charter. For example, it reaffirms in its preamble

> that the promotion and protection of all human rights and fundamental freedoms must be considered a priority objective of the United Nations in accordance with its purposes and principles, in particular the purpose of international co-operation …

The preamble goes on to note that

> the enhancement of international co-operation in the field of human rights is essential for the full achievement of the purposes of the United Nations and that human rights and fundamental freedoms are the birthright of all human beings, the promotion and protection of such rights and freedoms being the first responsibility of Governments.

This preambular language adds interesting contours to the duty of international co-operation. First, the use of terms such as 'enhancement', 'full achievement' and 'first responsibility' lend themselves to the proposition that this General Assembly resolution is a call for more, better and deeper international co-operation. Second, the reference to 'human rights and fundamental freedoms [as] the birthright of all human beings' underlines the universality of human rights and, in this connection, the universal nature of the duty to co-operate so that all human beings may benefit from human rights protection. Similarly, the resolution

> [c]alls upon all States to co-operate fully, through constructive dialogue, to ensure the promotion and protection of all human rights for all and in promoting peaceful solutions to international problems of a humanitarian character …

This illustrates the depth and breadth of the obligation to co-operate to ensure human rights and underlines the positive character of the obligation. Moreover, it brings into sharper focus the roles that co-operation can play in specific areas of international law.

36 Manila Declaration on the Peaceful Settlement of Disputes, UNGA Res 37/10 (15 November 1982).

37 Draft Articles on the Responsibility of States for Internationally Wrongful Acts; *Legal Consequences of the Construction of a Wall in the Occupied Palestinian Territory*, Advisory Opinion, ICJ Reports 2004, 136.

38 Draft Articles on the Responsibility of States for Internationally Wrongful Acts, with commentaries, 114.

39 Respect for the Purposes and Principles Contained in the Charter of the United Nations to Achieve International Co-operation in Promoting and Encouraging Respect for Human Rights and for Fundamental Freedoms and in Solving International Problems of a Humanitarian Character, UNGA Res 59/204 (20 December 2004), UN Doc A/59/503/Add.2.

4 Co-Operation as a Constitutional Principle

These instruments suggest that a minimum duty to engage with other States certainly exists.[40] However, the content of that general duty remains unclear. The developments explored above indicate that co-operation may rely on specific applications for its elaboration and operation. International co-operation is an 'entrenched precept' of the UN Charter system.[41] The Friendly Relations Declaration confirms that the scope of application of the principle of co-operation is broad. International co-operation is provided for in many different manifestations. While co-operation has never been comprehensively defined as a general obligation, obligations to co-operate for the realisation of specific ends – peace and security, human rights, environmental protection or development, for example – remain defined by the regime within which the objectives exist.[42]

General international law provides the basic obligation but it is without specific meaning. As will become evident, particular regimes have gradually contributed to the content of international co-operation and its application within those regimes is tailored to their unique contours. It will thus be shown that different regimes furnish co-operation with different features. In particular contexts, for example, international co-operation can be employed to prompt specific behaviour from States or can lead to the creation of institutions to induce co-operative behaviour. This is in fact a common feature of certain principles of international law.

Principles have many different roles in international law. They can permit new legal ideas, which have been driven by some social need, to emerge.[43] Principles can operate both as sources of law (akin to a statute in municipal law), which is to say that they can lead to the emergence of sub-principles having general application, and as sources of obligation (akin to a contract in municipal law), which is to say that it can operate to create rights and commitments for specific actors.[44] As keystones in the architecture of the international legal order, principles have certain constitutional functions that they perform as well.[45] They serve to unify the international legal system by their application across different fragments of international law. They give flexibility to the international legal system, allowing the law to adjust to the multifaceted nature of the social reality it must regulate, without allowing a fully open-ended system to emerge. In a similar way, they permit the law to evolve and help fill lacunae in legal regulation. Indeed, an effective legal system must combine 'normative closure' with 'cognitive openness', which means the law adjusts to developments in society while at the time having normative force.[46] As such, it ingests certain external norms and also determines its own content according to its internal rules and principles.[47]

Lacunae-filling was one of the major functions that the drafters of the Statute of the International Court of Justice (ICJ) had in mind for general principles of law and the main

[40] See also Wolfrum (n 31).

[41] Michael Nyongesa Wabwile, *Legal Protection of Social and Economic Rights of Children in Developing Countries: Reassessing International Co-operation and Responsibility* (Intersentia, 2010) 92.

[42] Wolfrum (n 31).

[43] Robert Kolb, 'Principles as Sources of International Law (With a Special Reference to Good Faith)' (2006) 53(1) *Netherlands International Law Review* 1, 7.

[44] ibid 11–13.

[45] See ibid 27–36.

[46] Niklas Luhmann, *Social Systems* (Stanford University Press, 1995) 6.

[47] ibid 92–96.

reason they were inserted in the Statute at all.[48] Principles also help in the interpretation of legal norms, just as equity or good faith may be used in the interpretation of specific rules. Principles may be needed to complement the operation of a series of legal rules. A good example here is the way in which the principles of necessity and proportionality are required to operationalise the law on self-defence. Alternatively, in a recent advisory opinion, the ICJ referred to the Friendly Relations Declaration in calling upon States to co-operate with the United Nations to help realise the right of self-determination in completing the decolonisation of Mauritius:

> Since respect for the right to self-determination is an obligation *erga omnes*, all States have a legal interest in protecting that right (*East Timor*; *Barcelona Traction*). The Court considers that, while it is for the General Assembly to pronounce on the modalities required to ensure the completion of the decolonization of Mauritius, all Member States must co-operate with the United Nations to put those modalities into effect. As recalled in the Declaration on the Principles of International Law concerning Friendly Relations and Co-operation among States in accordance with the Charter of the United Nations:
>
> 'Every State has the duty to promote, through joint and separate action, realization of the principle of equal rights and self-determination of peoples, in accordance with the provisions of the Charter, and to render assistance to the United Nations in carrying out the responsibilities entrusted to it by the Charter regarding the implementation of the principle'.
>
> . . .
>
> In response to Question (b) of the General Assembly, relating to the consequences under international law that arise from the continued administration by the United Kingdom of the Chagos Archipelago, the Court concludes that the United Kingdom has an obligation to bring to an end its administration of the Chagos Archipelago as rapidly as possible, and that all Member States must co-operate with the United Nations to complete the decolonization of Mauritius.[49]

Finally, such constitutional principles can play an important role in the negotiation of international instruments as they can help to facilitate compromises. In other words, they 'bridge gaps of interest without yet fixing a precise legal regime',[50] leaving the latter to come into fruition at a later point in time.

The recourse to principles suggests that certain norms may crystallise in the international legal order beyond the usual processes of customary law formation and the conclusion of treaties by States.[51] In a similar way, it has been observed that the drafters of the ICJ Statute envisaged that general principles of law would not simply be those drawn from those existing *in foro domestico*, but that they could also be created anew at the international level. While principles do ultimately require general acceptance and recognition by States, to find application they do not require conclusive evidence of widespread State practice and *opinio juris*.[52] In this way,

48 Béla Vitanyi, 'Les Positions doctrinales concernant le sens de la notion de 'principes généraux de droit reconnus par les nations civilisées' (1982) 86 *Revue générale de droit international public* 259.

49 *Legal Consequences of the Separation of the Chagos Archipelago from Mauritius in* 1965, 25 February 2019, General List No 169, www.icj-cij.org/files/case-related/169/169-20190225-01-00-EN.pdf, paras 180 and 182.

50 Kolb (n 43) 35.

51 See in particular Christian Tomuschat, 'Obligations Arising for States Without or Against their Will (Volume 241)' in *Collected Courses of the Hague Academy of International Law* (Brill, 1994) 195; see also, Oscar Schachter, 'International Law in Theory and Practice: General Course in Public International Law (Volume 178)' in *Collected Courses of the Hague Academy of International Law* (Brill, 1982) 21, 333–42 and 334 (noting that human rights come into existence in a multitude of ways, including beyond the 'usual processes of customary law formation').

52 Simma and Alston (n 18) 105. Similarly, Judge Tanaka in the *South West Africa* cases argued that general principles under Art 38(1)(c) of the ICJ Statute encompassed 'the concept of human rights and of their protection' and that Art 38 (1)(c) 'does not require the consent of States as a condition of the recognition of the general principles'. As such,

Bruno Simma and Philip Alston have noted that 'the development of human rights law principles have always preceded practice'.[53] Indeed, general principles play an important role in the propagation of human rights protection, particularly among the rules of general international law as is evident in the jurisprudence of the ICJ.[54] This serves to illustrate the power of constitutional principles in international law. They can elaborate on State practice and *opinio juris*, allowing for the emergence of more expansive legal norms than individual States may have intended.[55] Given the inherent power of constitutional principles, this is undoubtedly a major reason why some inertia has attached to the development of a general duty to co-operate, as was evident in the negotiations of the Friendly Relations Declaration.[56]

III INTERNATIONAL CO-OPERATION IN SPECIFIC CONTEXTS: SHADES OF A GENERAL DUTY

Having considered the general duty to co-operate, we now turn to consider its particular manifestations to understand how various disciplines have endowed international co-operation with different colours. To highlight how these specific regimes have contributed to the development of international co-operation, it is not necessary to consider all of its particular manifestations. Rather we aim to show that international co-operation has evolved differently in discrete areas of international law, and that each area can contribute a different feature to our general understanding.

1 *The Realisation of Human Rights – Giving Content to Co-operation*

A duty to co-operate to realise certain rights is evident in a number of international instruments and jurisprudence. Chapter IX of the UN Charter is dedicated to 'International Economic and Social Co-operation'. In this context, Article 55 is directed at the United Nations itself, which is committed to promoting 'higher standards of living, full employment, and conditions of economic and social progress and development' (Article 55(a)), 'solutions of international economic, social, health, and related problems; and international cultural and educational co-operation' (Article 55(b)) and 'universal respect for, and observance of, human rights and fundamental freedoms for all without discrimination as to race, sex, language, or religion' (Article 55(c)). Article 56 of the UN Charter contains a concrete obligation for Member States

'[f]rom this kind of source international law could have the foundation of its validity extended beyond the will of States, that is to say, into the sphere of natural law and assume an aspect of its supra-national and supra-positive character'. *South West Africa cases (Ethiopia* v *South Africa; Liberia* v *South Africa)*, Second Phase, Dissenting Opinion of Judge Tanaka, ICJ Reports 1966, 6, 298.

[53] Simma and Alston (n 18) 107.

[54] See eg *Corfu Channel* case, Judgment, ICJ Reports 1949, 4, 22 ('obligations ... based ... on certain general and well-recognized principles' as including 'elementary considerations of humanity'); *Reservations of the Genocide Convention*, Advisory Opinion, ICJ Reports 1951, 15, 23 ('the principles underlying the Convention are principles which are recognized by civilized nations as binding on States, even without any convention obligation'); *Barcelona Traction, Light & Power Co (Belgium* v *Spain)*, Second Phase, ICJ Reports 1970, 3, 32 (*erga omnes* obligations derive 'from the principles and rules concerning the basic rights of the human person'); *United States Diplomatic and Consular Staff in Tehran*, Judgment, ICJ Reports 1980, 3, 42 (to '[w]rongfully deprive human beings of their freedom and to subject them to physical constraint in conditions of hardship is in itself manifestly incompatible with the principles of the Charter of the United Nations, as well as with the fundamental principles enunciated in the Universal Declaration of Human Rights').

[55] See Simma and Alston (n 18).

[56] See section II.2.

of the United Nations to 'take joint and separate action in co-operation with the Organization' on the pledges set out in the previous provision.

The *travaux préparatoires* to Article 56 of the UN Charter, and in particular the notions of 'international co-operation' and 'joint and separate action', reveal some notable features as to what the drafters had in mind when they included the reference to international co-operation in this context:

> The Delegation of the United Kingdom said that there was no doubt in his mind that the Committee had approved a three-fold pledge – for separate action, for joint action, and for co-operation with the Organization ... He then went on to say that co-operation implies joint and separate action.[57]

The standard that the drafters had in mind was joint and separate action. Joint action, both with the United Nations and with each other, but also separate action individually. As such, joint and separate action is intended to mean that States should take steps individually and collectively to assist the United Nations in the realisation of the goals set out in Article 55. It is similarly taken to mean that States should co-operate for the achievement of the United Nations' more general aims, as set out in Article 1 of the UN Charter and explained above. The Friendly Relations Declaration reiterates that States have a duty to co-operate with one another in accordance with the Charter and, more specifically, that members of the United Nations 'have the duty to take joint and separate action in co-operation with the United Nations in accordance with the relevant provisions of the Charter'.

The notions of 'co-operation', 'joint and separate action' and 'assistance' have been elaborated upon in other human rights instruments and their meaning has been elaborated upon by human rights bodies, especially the Committee on Economic, Social and Cultural Rights (CESCR). In fact, Article 2(1) of the International Covenant on Economic, Social and Cultural Rights 1966 (ICESCR) contains one of the strongest formulations of international co-operation under international law. It provides:

> Each State Party to the present Covenant undertakes to take steps, individually and through international assistance and co-operation, especially economic and technical, to the maximum of its available resources, with a view to achieving progressively the full realization of the rights recognized in the present Covenant by all appropriate means, including particularly the adoption of legislative measures.

This provision obliges States to co-operate and assist, particularly by offering economic and technical resources, for the realisation of rights provided for in the Covenant. Beyond diplomatic efforts at co-operation, it also envisages the commitment of resources and assistance. The distinction made in the text between taking steps 'individually' and 'through international assistance and co-operation' is a strong indication that the Covenant binds States as regards people within their own jurisdiction but also commits States to co-operating and assisting in the realisation of such rights in other countries. This indication is further strengthened by having reference to the *travaux préparatoires*, other provisions of the Covenant and the interpretations of the CESCR, as will become evident.

The *travaux préparatoires* of the Covenant show that, as regards the commitment of resources envisaged under Article 2(1), the French delegate on the Drafting Commission stated:

57 The UNCIO (n 15).

> [t]he expression 'their resources' was intended to convey, not that States should, in implementing the rights in question, renounce all progress which was beyond their own resources, but that countries with substantial resources should lend their assistance internationally.[58]

Similarly, recognising the need for developed States to provide assistance to developing States, the Iraqi delegate said that because 'the under-developed countries would be taking on much heavier commitments than the advanced countries ... [t]hey would certainly need international co-operation in discharging their obligations'.[59] The delegate of the United States emphasised that the provision would need 'to indicate the necessity of international co-operation in the matter'[60] and the delegate of Chile was of the view that 'international assistance to under-developed countries had in a sense become mandatory as a result of commitments assumed by States in the United Nations'.[61] All of these statements support the claim that developed countries should commit resources and assistance towards the realisation of socio-economic rights in developing countries.

Turning to the work of the CESCR, which monitors the implementation of the Covenant and adopts General Comments with a view to aiding the interpretation of its provisions, further clarity is offered on the nature of the commitments States must undertake. Interpreting Article 2(1) of the Covenant in its General Comment No. 3 of 1990, the Committee has said of international co-operation and assistance that:

> the phrase 'to the maximum of its available resources' was intended by the drafters of the Covenant to refer to both the resources existing within a State and those available from the international community through international co-operation and assistance. ...
>
> In accordance with Articles 55 and 56 of the Charter of the United Nations, and with the provisions of the Covenant itself, international co-operation for development and thus for the realization of economic, social and cultural rights is an obligation of all States. It is particularly incumbent upon those States which are in a position to assist others in this regard.[62]

States are concretely encouraged to develop an 'active programme of international assistance and co-operation', thereby urging positive individual action and the commitment of national resources for the benefit of developing States. This conception of assistance and co-operation thus goes well beyond diplomatic efforts, and implies a positive other-directed aspect to the obligation. Moreover, the Committee on Economic, Social and Cultural rights has indicated that States can partly discharge the obligation of international assistance by meeting the internationally agreed[63] commitment to set aside a minimum net amount of 0.7 per cent of

[58] Commission on Human Rights, 'Summary Record of the Two Hundred and Thirty-Third Meeting', 2 July 1951, UN Doc E/CN.4/SR.233, 7 UN ESCOR C.4, 8.

[59] Iraq, General Assembly Third Committee, 1203rd Meeting, 17 UN GAOR C.3, UN Doc A/C.3SR.1203 (1962), para 21.

[60] Commission on Human Rights, 'Summary Record of the Two Hundred and Seventieth Meeting', 14 May 1952, UN Doc E/CN.4/SR.270, 8 UN ESCOR C.4, 10.

[61] Chile, General Assembly Third Committee, 1203rd Meeting, 17 UN GAOR C.3, UN Doc A/C.3/SR.1203 (1962), para 10. However, it should be noted that there were several States opposed to the idea that financial assistance to developing states would be rendered mandatory; see eg the statement of Mr Bouquin of France (France, General Assembly Third Committee, 1205th Meeting, 17 UN GAOR C.3, UN Doc A/C.3/SR.1205 (1962), para 12), the statement of Mr Ostrovsky of the USSR (General Assembly Third Committee, 1203rd Meeting, 17 UN GAOR C.3, UN Doc A/C.3/SR.1203 (1962), para 14), or Mr Mantzoulinos of Greece (General Assembly Third Committee, 1204th Meeting 17 UN GAOR C.3, UN Doc A/C.3/SR.1204, para 14).

[62] CESCR, General Comment No 3 on the nature of states parties' obligations (1990), paras 13 and 14.

[63] See eg International Development Strategy for the Second United Nations Development Decade, UNGA Res 2626 (XXV) (24 October 1970), UN Doc A/RES/25/2626.

its gross national product for development assistance.[64] This is yet further evidence that a commitment of resources, particularly by developed countries to developing countries, is expected.

The Committee has also provided States with guidance on how to approach their co-operation and assistance efforts. First, in its General Comment No. 3, the Committee set out that the rights of the disadvantaged, such as women and refugees, and those of marginalised or vulnerable groups, such as children, should be prioritised. Second, they must ensure that 'minimum essential levels' of economic, social and cultural rights are realised. Third, the pace of co-operation to realise these rights must be as expeditious as possible. Fourth, the modalities chosen should be as effective as possible. Finally, all regressive measures should be avoided.[65]

Several other provisions in the Covenant illustrate the action required of States in fulfilling their duties of international assistance and co-operation. For example, Article 11(1) of the Covenant specifically places an obligation on States to ensure the realisation of the right of everyone to an adequate standard of living for themselves and their family, including adequate food, clothing and housing, and to the continuous improvement of living conditions. In this context, co-operation based on free consent is recognised as a means for such realisation. Reiterating similar language to that found in Article 2(1), Article 11 places States under an obligation to 'take appropriate steps to ensure the realization of this right, recognizing to this effect the essential importance of international co-operation based on free consent'. As regards the right to adequate food under Article 11 the CESCR has referred to the role that international co-operation plays in the realisation of this right:

> In implementing this commitment, States parties should take steps to respect the enjoyment of the right to food in other countries, to protect that right, to facilitate access to food and to provide the necessary aid when required. States parties should, in international agreements whenever relevant, ensure that the right to adequate food is given due attention and consider the development of further international legal instruments to that end.[66]

The Committee thus added further colour to the commitment to take joint and separate action in the context of the right to food, and emphasised that co-operating jointly and separately requires positive action to ensure the realisation of the right in other countries.

The importance of positive international action to realise the rights under the Covenant is further reinforced in Article 23. This provision of the Covenant provides for a non-exhaustive list of ways in which international co-operation and assistance may be effected:

> The States Parties to the present Covenant agree that international action for the achievement of the rights recognized in the present Covenant includes such methods as the conclusion of conventions, the adoption of recommendations, the furnishing of technical assistance and the holding of regional meetings and technical meetings for the purpose of consultation and study organized in conjunction with the Governments concerned.

[64] See Olivier de Schutter et al, 'Commentary to the Maastricht Principles on the Extraterritorial Obligations of States in the Area of Economic, Social and Cultural Rights' (2012) 34(4) *Human Rights Quarterly* 1085.

[65] See CESCR (n 62), paras 9–12. See also, CESCR, General Comment No 19 on the right to social security (Article 9 of the Covenant), 4 February 2008, UN Doc E/C.12/GC/19, para 31; CESCR, General Comment No 15 on the right to water (Articles 11 and 12 of the Covenant), 20 January 2003, UN Doc E/C.12/2002/11, para 16; CESCR, General Comment No 14 on the right to the highest attainable standard of health (Article 12 of the Covenant), 11 August 2000, UN Doc E/C.12/2000/4, para 40.

[66] CESCR, General Comment No 12 on the right to adequate food (Article 11), para 36.

This indicates a mix of diplomatic efforts as well as the commitment of resources, such as 'the furnishing of technical assistance'. It indicates the minimum positive action expected under the Covenant, and provisions on specific rights encourage States to go further in terms of committing resources, as is the case with Article 11 and the realisation of the right to an adequate standard of living for everyone.

Article 12 of the Covenant obliges States to 'recognize the right of everyone to the enjoyment of the highest attainable standard of physical and mental health'. Once again, the universal nature of this right is underlined in the provision itself. Interestingly, in a General Comment, the CESCR has added further detail as regards the scope of the commitment to international assistance and co-operation. The Committee set out that:

> To comply with their international obligations in relation to article 12, States parties have to respect the enjoyment of the right to health in other countries, and to prevent third parties from violating the right in other countries, if they are able to influence these third parties by way of legal or political means, in accordance with the Charter of the United Nations and applicable international law. Depending on the availability of resources, States should facilitate access to essential health facilities, goods and services in other countries, wherever possible and provide the necessary aid when required.
>
> ...
>
> For the avoidance of any doubt, the Committee wishes to emphasize that it is particularly incumbent on States parties and other actors in a position to assist, to provide 'international assistance and co-operation, especially economic and technical' which enable developing countries to fulfil their core and other obligations.[67]

Clearly, this is a right which requires international co-operation and assistance, particularly from developed to developing countries, for its realisation.

Similarly, as regards the right to water under the Covenant (Articles 11 and 12), the CESCR has emphasised in its General Comment No. 15 that States should 'facilitate realization of the right to water in other countries'.[68] This General Comment spells out that the obligation includes such positive action as providing water resources, as well as financial, technical and other assistance, when this is necessary for the realisation of the right to water. Moreover, the General Comment speaks of a 'special responsibility' incumbent upon developed States to assist developing States. Emphasising the universal nature of the right to water, the Committee also noted that '[t]he human right to water entitles everyone to sufficient, safe, acceptable, physically accessible and affordable water for personal and domestic uses'.[69]

Turning to the right to education under Article 13 of the Covenant, General Comment No. 13 of the CESCR elaborates that:

> In its General Comment 3, the Committee drew attention to the obligation of all States parties to take steps, 'individually and through international assistance and co-operation, especially economic and technical', towards the full realization of the rights recognized in the Covenant, such as the right to education. Articles 2(1) and 23 of the Covenant, Article 56 of the Charter of the United Nations, Article 10 of the World Declaration on Education for All, and Part I, paragraph 34 of the Vienna Declaration and Programme of Action all reinforce the obligation of

[67] CESCR, General Comment No 14 on the right to the highest attainable standard of health, paras 39 and 45 respectively.

[68] CESCR, General Comment No 15 on right to water (Articles 11 and 12 of the Covenant), para 34.

[69] ibid, para 2.

> States parties in relation to the provision of international assistance and co-operation for the full realization of the right to education.[70]

As is evident from this General Comment, the Committee envisages that international assistance and co-operation would 'especially' take the form of economic and technical support, in terms not only of the right to education but also of other rights under the Covenant.

These General Comments all contribute to the *acquis* of the ICESCR, and help to clarify the nature of rights under it. The text of the obligations discussed and the *acquis* give meaning to the obligations of international co-operation and assistance.[71] These obligations can involve the promotion of rights through diplomatic means, but also the commitment of resources as well as economic and technical support, particularly from developed States to developing countries. The meaning of co-operation has been widened still in the elaboration of the right to development, as will be explored in the next subsection.

2 *Promoting Development under International Law – Widening the Scope of Co-Operation*

A further context in which international co-operation finds expression is in the various declarations and agreements aimed at furthering development. It has been contended that the law of co-operation 'means co-operation among States for the purposes of development to increase the social welfare of the world community'.[72] Development co-operation is understood to include the activities carried out by developed countries to enhance the economic progress of developing countries.[73] Development co-operation may be multilateral in nature where it is conducted through an international organisation or bilateral where it is conducted by individual States in accordance with their own foreign policy.[74] Development co-operation can also be of a financial nature, which might involve the mobilisation of capital through loans, or of a technical nature, which might involve the transfer of knowledge.[75] Early examples of technical assistance are the Technical Assistance Programme that was established by the UN General Assembly through Resolution 200(III) of 4 December 1948. It involved experts being sent on missions to developing countries, granting scholarships and the creation of training and research centres. Various institutions were established to further this endeavour. The UN General Assembly created the UN Programme for Development (UNDP),[76] which was intended to co-ordinate and streamline the various initiatives that were being pursued by different specialised agencies of the United Nations. The UN Conference on Trade and Development (UNCTAD) and the UN Industrial Development Organization (UNIDO) were established to enhance technical co-operation and assistance for the benefit of developing countries. As for financial co-operation, this is typically co-ordinated by institutions linked to the World Bank, such as the International Development Association, which was established in 1960.

In fact, it has long been argued that States should contribute to each other's welfare. In 1758, for example, Vattel observed that '[t]he first general law, which is to be found in the very end of the society of Nations, is that each Nation should contribute as far as it can to the happiness and

70 CESCR, General Comment No 13 on the right to education (Article 13 of the Covenant) at para 56.
71 Wabwile (n 41) 108.
72 Wolfrum (n 31).
73 Antonio Cassese, *International Law* (2nd edn, Oxford University Press, 2005) 518.
74 ibid.
75 ibid 519.
76 UNGA Res 2029–XX (22 November 1965).

advancement of other Nations'.[77] In the 1980s, the universal nature of development and, as a result, the need for collective efforts in its realisation, was underlined by the UN Commission on Human Rights Resolution 6 (XXXVIO). Its paragraph 2 provides that 'the right to development is a human right and that equality of opportunity for development is as much a prerogative of nations as of individuals within nations'.[78] Georges Abi-Saab has argued that the right to development is a collective right which is an 'aggregate of the social, economic and cultural rights ... of all individuals constituting a collectivity. In other words, it is the sum total of a double aggregation of the rights and of the individuals.'[79]

A positive obligation on States to co-operate internationally is provided by the 1986 Declaration on the Right to Development, which recognises that all States are responsible for the realisation of the right to development. Its Article 1 provides that:

> The right to development is an inalienable human right by virtue of which every human person and all peoples are entitled to participate in, contribute to, and enjoy economic, social, cultural and political development, in which all human rights and fundamental freedoms can be fully realized.

Article 3.3 of the Declaration on the Right to Development provides that 'States have the duty to co-operate with each other in ensuring development and eliminating obstacles to development', and Article 4.1 notes that 'States have the duty to take steps, individually and collectively, to formulate international development policies with a view to facilitating the full realization of the right to development.' These provisions, read alongside the preamble of the Declaration that calls for 'international co-operation in solving international problems of an economic, social, cultural or humanitarian nature, and ... promoting and encouraging respect for human rights and fundamental freedoms', provides a basis for the proposition that States are under an affirmative duty to pursue a legislative programme that facilitates realisation of the right to development. That there is a reference to individual and collective action would suggest that States must both take measures themselves through their own domestic policies and engage in co-operative efforts with other countries to this end.

States are responsible for implementing the right to development and the beneficiaries are intended to be individuals in developing countries. It is incumbent on the international community to co-operate to ensure that States fulfil their obligation to realise the right to development. Full realisation of the right to development will require the realisation of many different rights as well as a favourable economic system, improving the rule of law, fundamental institutional change and strengthening the infrastructure of the developing country. All of this may require co-operation and assistance from the international community.[80]

In the earlier Charter of Economic Rights and Duties of States of 1974, its Article 17 underlines the importance of international co-operation in the realisation of development. Indeed, it emphasises that international co-operation for development is both a shared goal and a common duty for States:

[77] Emer de Vattel, *The Law of Nations or the Principles of Natural Law Applied to the Conduct and the Affairs of Nations and of Sovereigns* (1758) in James B Scott (ed), *The Classics of International Law* (Carnegie Institute, 1916) 6.

[78] UN Commission on Human Rights, Res 6 (XXXVIO).

[79] Georges Abi-Saab, 'The Legal Formulation of the Right to Development' in Rene-Jean Dupuy (ed), *The Right to Development at the International Level* (The Hague Academy of International Law, 1980) 164.

[80] Arjun Sengupta, 'Conceptualizing the Right to Development for the Twenty-First Century' in United Nations (ed), *Realising the Right to Development* (UN, 2014), 72–73.

> Every State should co-operate with the efforts of developing countries to accelerate their economic and social development by providing favourable external conditions and by extending active assistance to them, consistent with their development needs and objectives, with strict respect for the sovereign equality of States and free of any conditions derogating from their sovereignty.

In Commitment 9 of the UN World Summit for Social Development,[81] States committed themselves 'to increasingly and/or utilizing more efficiently the resources allocated to social development in order to achieve the goals of the Summit through national action and regional and international co-operation'.[82] Commitment 9 goes on to set out the more concrete ways in which this may be achieved.

The UN Millennium Declaration, which included the Millennium Development Goals and was adopted by the UN General Assembly, also makes an implicit reference to international co-operation:

> In addition to our separate responsibilities to our individual societies, we have a collective responsibility to uphold the principles of human dignity, equality and equity at the global level. As leaders we have a duty therefore to all the world's people, especially the most vulnerable and, in particular, the children of the world, to whom the future belongs.[83]

Furthermore, the Millennium Development Goals made a call to developed countries in a number of areas. Goal 8 stipulated a 'global partnership for development' as well as targets to develop 'an open, rule-based predictable, non-discriminatory trading system' (Target 12) and to meet the needs of the least developed countries (Target 13). In so doing, the Declaration adds yet further colour to our understanding of international co-operation.

International co-operation has played a role in forging approaches to international development, which is called by some the law of development co-operation.[84] This can involve the transfer of official development assistance from industrialised countries to developing countries.[85] It has also assisted in mediating the distinction between the formal equality of sovereign States under international law and the need to ensure material differences in the expected commitments of developing countries, taking into account their capacity. This is also a feature in the context of the protection of the environment, as will be shown in the following subsection.

3 *Co-Operation in International Environmental Law – The Emergence of Transparency and Accountability as Incentives*

The scale and nature of environmental challenges mean that protection of the environment can only occur through international co-operation. The interdependence of States makes co-operation an important tool for solving common problems like damage to the environment.[86] States co-operate to protect global public goods, manage shared resources and solve challenges that can only be achieved through bilateral or multilateral action. Co-operation has many facets

81 UN World Summit for Social Development, 6–12 March 1995, UN Doc A/CONF.166/9.
82 ibid, Commitment 9.
83 United Nations Millennium Declaration, UNGA Res 55/2 (8 September 2000), UN Doc 55/2, at para 2.
84 See Philip Dann, *The Law of Development Co-operation: A Comparative Analysis of the World Bank, EU and Germany* (Cambridge University Press, 2013).
85 ibid 13.
86 Daniel Bodansky, Jutta Brunnée and Ellen Hey, 'International Environmental Law: Mapping the Field' in Daniel Bodansky, Jutta Brunnée and Ellen Hey (eds), *The Oxford Handbook of International Environmental Law* (Oxford University Press, 2008) 8.

in the area of environmental protection. It is aimed at mitigating transboundary risks and emergencies,[87] and is closely connected with the obligation of prevention and the no-harm rule. It also includes, amongst other aspects, the duty to consult and negotiate, and reflects the need for institutional co-operation. The principle has similarly been referred to in many decisions of international courts and tribunals, including the ICJ and the International Tribunal for the Law of the Sea (ITLOS). This case law serves to confirm that co-operation is a fundamental principle at the heart of international law and that States are under an obligation to co-operate in good faith. In the *Pulp Mills* case, for example, the ICJ said:

> [i]t is by co-operating that the States concerned can jointly manage the rules of damage to the environment that might be created by the plans initiated by one or other of them, so as to prevent the damage in question.[88]

The Court went on to elaborate the related obligations to notify, consult and conduct environmental impact assessments (EIAs), in turn giving colour and texture to the obligation of co-operation in this context. Moreover, the Court noted that there was a customary international law obligation to conduct an EIA where a particular project poses a risk to the environment. In a transboundary context, the conduct of an EIA will require co-operation with other States:

> [EIAs] must be notified by the party concerned to the other party. . . This notification is intended to enable the notified party to participate in the process of ensuring that the assessment is complete, so that it can then consider the plan and its effects with a full knowledge of the facts.[89]

In a similar way, the ICJ said of the obligation to give prior notification to the relevant basin organisation that 'the obligation to inform . . . allows for the initiation of co-operation between the Parties which is necessary in order to fulfil the obligation of prevention'.[90] This provides an interesting example of the way in which co-operation connects to other fundamental principles of international environmental law.

In addition to customary international law, an obligation to co-operate has become a regular feature of numerous multilateral environmental agreements (MEAs). The obligation to co-operate is present in a wide range of MEAs. That said, it varies greatly in its precise meaning from one MEA to another. Specific manifestations of the principle might include the exchange of information between States, the conduct of scientific research and systematic observations, prior notification, consultation, prior informed consent, notification in the case of an emergency or emergency assistance, for example.[91] Many instruments also have provisions requiring co-operation in investigating, identifying and avoiding environmental harm. As for the scope of co-operation in international environmental law, this can range from the requirement to offer 'economic and technical assistance' in the context of climate change or the 'exchange of data and information' to protect water resources, amongst others.

The Stockholm and Rio Declarations provide for co-operation as a means of achieving environmental objectives. Principle 24 of the Stockholm Declaration articulates that:

87 Patricia Birnie, Alan Boyle and Catherine Redgwell, *International Law and the Environment* (3rd edn, Oxford University Press, 2009) 137.

88 *Pulp Mills on the River Uruguay (Argentina* v *Uruguay)*, Judgment, ICJ Reports 2010, para 77.

89 ibid.

90 ibid, para 102.

91 See Laurence Boisson de Chazournes et al (eds), *Protection internationale de l'environnement* (Pedone, 2005); David Hunter, Julia Sommer and Scott Vaughan, 'Concepts and Principles of International Environmental Law: An Introduction', *Environment and Trade* (CIEL, UN Environment Programme, 1994).

> [i]nternational matters concerning the protection and improvement of the environment should be handled in a co-operative spirit by all countries, big and small, on an equal footing. Co-operation … is essential to effectively control, prevent, reduce and eliminate adverse environmental effects resulting from activities conducted in all spheres, in such a way that due account is taken of the sovereignty and interests of all States.

Principle 27 of the Rio Declaration provides that:

> States and people shall co-operate in good faith and in a spirit of partnership in the fulfilment of the principles embodied in this Declaration and in the further development of international law in the field of sustainable development.

Moreover, the preamble of the Rio Declaration speaks of 'the creation of new levels of co-operation among States, key sectors of societies and people'. In this way, co-operative efforts should manifest themselves in different forms, at various levels, and with diverse actions through, for example, public–private partnership programmes.[92]

Under framework conventions, international co-operation can serve a particularly important additional purpose. Indeed, it is often inserted to drive the progressive development of framework convention regimes. As for the climate-change regime, the UN Framework Convention on Climate Change 1992 (UNFCCC) refers to co-operation in several provisions, including its preamble and Articles 3, 7 and 9, while the Kyoto Protocol does so in its Article 2(b), and the Paris Agreement in Articles 6, 7, 10 and 12. In fact, the 2030 Agenda for Sustainable Development, which includes the Sustainable Development Goals, explicitly recognises the centrality of co-operation to climate change action as follows:

> [t]he global nature of climate change calls for the widest possible international co-operation aimed at accelerating the reduction of global greenhouse gas emissions and addressing adaptation to the adverse impacts of climate change.[93]

Like the UNFCCC, the Paris Agreement is based on the advancement of a common interest. It recalls that 'climate change is a common concern of humankind'.[94]

International co-operation requires both financial and technical assistance to ensure that developing countries can mitigate and adapt to the effects of climate change. Developed countries have a special responsibility in this context. As for the financial assistance commitments under the Paris Agreement, it is only the developed country parties that are expected to assume them. In accordance with the principle of common but differentiated responsibilities, developed States parties have committed to approximately 100 billion dollars per year. There is a further undertaking to set a new financial assistance objective before 2025.[95]

The Paris Agreement also aims to ensure that there is 'efficient access to financial resources through simplified approval procedures and enhanced readiness support for developing country Parties'.[96] At COP 24, several countries made new commitments in respect of the Adaptation Fund (e.g. Germany, Sweden, Italy, France, Belgium and the European Union).[97] Moreover,

[92] Peter Sand, 'Principle 27: Co-operation in a Spirit of Global Partnership' in Jorge E Viñuales (ed), *The Rio Declaration on Environment and Development: A Commentary* (Oxford University Press, 2015) 622.

[93] Transforming Our World: The 2030 Agenda for Sustainable Development, A/RES/70/1, 21 October 2015, para 31.

[94] Eleventh para of the preamble to the Paris Agreement.

[95] Para 54 of the Decision of the Contracting Parties.

[96] Art 9.9 of the Paris Agreement.

[97] See Adaptation Fund, 'Adaptation Fund Breaks Single-Year Resource Mobilization Record with Nearly US$ 129M in New Pledges Received', www.adaptation-fund.org/adaptation-fund-breaks-single-year-resource-mobilization-record-nearly-us-129m-new-pledges-received/.

Germany and Norway committed to doubling their contribution to the Green Climate Fund.[98] Further still, greater transparency was envisaged through the recently agreed Katowice Rulebook in the context of funding for developing countries.[99] Financial assistance will also form a part of the global stocktake under the Paris Agreement, which is due to take place every five years. Technology development and transfer is similarly intended to help advance the effective implementation of the Paris Agreement. The importance of co-operation in respect of technology is evidenced in its ability to enhance climate change mitigation and adaptation action. In this context, parties are required to 'strengthen co-operative action on technology development and transfer' under Article 10.2 of the Paris Agreement.

An emerging feature of the regime for co-operation on climate change is the importance attached to transparency and accountability. These are essential implementation tools that are intended to give the Paris Agreement its teeth. The Agreement envisages, for example, an 'enhanced transparency framework for action and support'. This includes an augmented reporting mechanism that is concerned with the action and support of States. Developed countries must report on financial, technology transfer and capacity-building support provided to developing country parties under Articles 9, 10 and 11 of the Paris Agreement. This information provided by developed countries will also be subject to a technical expert review. In addition, interestingly, developing countries should report on financial, technology transfer and capacity-building support needed and received under Articles 9, 10 and 11. These elements all suggest a thickening of the institutional structure for the purpose of improving implementation of co-operative efforts in the context of climate action.

Transparency under the Paris Agreement is intended to be comprehensive and information is made available through the Internet to all and any actors. Non-governmental organisations, scientific associations and other actors now have new tools at their disposal, and it will be interesting to see how they take advantage of them. This transparency and accountability to civil society may provide new dimensions to co-operation and a renewed impetus for States to co-operate for the universal realisation of climate goals.

4 *International Co-Operation to Protect Water Resources – the Need for Institutions*

Co-operation for the effective use and management of shared water resources has a long history. This co-operation can take the form of international conventions or institutional structures like basin organisations or river commissions. Indeed, co-operation through institutional structures and mechanisms helps to ensure that international water resources are managed effectively.[100] Co-operation can take various forms in these institutions, from the interaction between different stakeholders to the facilitation of joint activities between States.

Such institutions serve as important mechanisms for dialogue and consultation, which helps to prevent tension that could lead to disputes. When disputes do arise, these institutions can help

[98] See Green Climate Fund, 'GCF Replenishment Wins Strong Endorsement at COP24', www.greenclimate.fund/news/gcf-replenishment-wins-strong-endorsement-at-cop24.

[99] Report of the Conference of the Parties on its Twenty-Fourth Session, held in Katowice from 2 to 5 December 2018, Decision 1/CP.24, FCCC/CP/2018/10/Add.1 (19 March 2019).

[100] Boisson de Chazournes (n 7) 30–31.

to resolve them.[101] Their structure differs from one mechanism to another.[102] Co-operation can take many forms in these legal frameworks, whether in respect of the inter-State co-operation essential to their establishment or the co-operation they facilitate with other stakeholders, such as representatives of local communities. Indeed, the secretariats of basin organisations and commissions can constitute important channels for co-operation between States and other stakeholders.[103]

The scope of co-operation in the context of these institutions has become relatively large over time, while the competencies of basin organisations and commissions have become more varied. If in the beginning their main function concerned navigation and fishing activity, the competence of these organisations has gradually extended to hydro-plants and the production of energy, irrigation activities or environmental protection. Today, their functions can include information collection and dissemination, regulation by the adoption of standards and guidelines, the brokering of negotiations for the development of binding instruments or agreements, or the promotion and execution of joint operational activities.

These organisations also often facilitate the conduct of joint activities, which may be carried out by the organisation itself or by Member States. Therefore, in addition to the aspects of co-ordination necessary to prevent damage to protected interests, these collective frameworks also encourage resource development insofar as this is possible within the jurisdictions of the organisations, and as such add further value to their existence. Many of these mechanisms have a legal personality that allows them to engage directly on the international stage.[104]

The purpose of these bodies is to prevent damage to protected resources through the application of various legal regimes. In this context, the protection of the environment has over time become an important field of activity for these basin organisations and commissions. Several legal instruments and programmes have been adopted or pursued under their auspices, which have strengthened the work of their secretariats in this area. The international commissions for the Rhine and the Danube are particularly notable as they have both adopted instruments and pursued programmes that have helped raise awareness of and reinforce the means of protection offered by these institutions.[105]

The law of shared watercourses highlights that co-operation can take place within the context of institutional structures and mechanisms. River or basin commissions have helped to ensure that international water resources are managed effectively.

[101] See ibid 48–53; Laurence Boisson de Chazournes, *Interactions between Regional and Universal Organizations: A Legal Perspective* (Brill, 2016) 29–31.

[102] See the typology of functions offered by Colliard (n 8) at 421–31; Lucius Caflisch, 'Règles générales du droit des cours d'eau internationaux (Volume 219)' in *Collected Courses of the Hague Academy of International Law* (Brill, 1989) 196–202.

[103] See Mekong River Commission for Sustainable Development, *Public Participation in the Lower Mekong Basin* (Mekong River Commission, 2005), www.mrcmekong.org/assets/Publications/governance/Public-Participation.pdf.

[104] On the status of the Administrative Commission of the River Uruguay, see *Pulp Mills on the River Uruguay (Argentina* v *Uruguay)* (n 98), paras 87, 89.

[105] See Convention on the Protection of the Rhine 1999; Rhine 2020 – Program on the sustainable development of the Rhine (implementing Directive 2000/60/EC of the European Parliament and of the Council of 23 October 2000 establishing a framework for Community action in the field of water policy [2000] OJ L327, 1–73), www.iksr.org/fileadmin/user_upload/Dokumente_en/rhein2020_e.pdf. See also Joint Statement on Guiding Principles for the Development of Inland Navigation and Environmental Protection in the Danube River Basin (with annexes) 2007, www.danubecommission.org/uploads/doc/72/Joint%20Statement/EN/Joint_Statement_FINAL.pdf.

5 *International Co-operation in the Law of the Sea – Towards Community-Based Co-Operation*

International co-operation is an essential component of the UN Convention on the Law of the Sea of 1982 (UNCLOS). In particular, Part XII of UNCLOS requires States to co-operate in the prevention of marine pollution. In the *MOX Plant* case of ITLOS, the Tribunal noted that '[t]he duty to co-operate is a fundamental principle in the prevention of pollution of the marine environment under Part XII of the [UNLCOS], and general international law'.[106] ITLOS has in fact reiterated the fundamental nature of the principle of co-operation in international law on several occasions, in particular the *Southern Bluefin Tuna* cases,[107] the *Case Concerning Land Reclamation by Singapore in and around the Straits of Johor (Malaysia* v. *Singapore)*[108] and the *Request for an Advisory Opinion submitted by the Sub-Regional Fisheries Commission (SRFC)*.[109]

Indeed, UNCLOS requires that States co-operate, at the universal and regional levels, directly or through international organisations, to ensure the protection of the marine environment, the conservation and management of living resources, as well as the conservation of marine mammals, for example. Parties are also obliged to co-operate in the field of marine scientific research, and in the development and transfer of marine technology.

Under the law of the sea, States are also required to co-operate in the development of rules, norms, practices and procedures to protect and preserve the marine environment, as well as in the application of the relevant rules. This is likely to mean that States have committed to developing the legal framework relevant to the protection of the marine environment with new hard- and soft-law instruments.[110] There is similarly an obligation to co-operate in scientific research on marine pollution as well as in the area of monitoring and evaluating marine pollution.[111] Alternatively, there is an obligation to provide technical aid and assistance under UNCLOS. This includes the duty to notify in the event of an accident or imminent danger, as well as joint action plans for dealing with emergencies.[112] It should also be noted that the Convention envisages different levels of obligation for developing countries as well as rendering special assistance to developing countries.[113]

As is well-known, UNCLOS provides for the 'International Seabed Area', which is often simply referred to as 'the Area'. This is the area beyond the limits of national jurisdiction and includes the seabed, the ocean floor and its subsoil. The Area and its resources are part of the common heritage of humankind,[114] and extractive activities in the Area are administered by the International Seabed Authority,[115] an autonomous legal person that is both independent from its

[106] *MOX Plant case (Ireland* v *United Kingdom)*, ITLOS Request for Provisional Measures, 1999, para 20.

[107] *Southern Bluefin Tuna cases (New Zealand* v *Japan; Australia* v *Japan)*, ITLOS Order of 27 August 1999; for an overview of these cases, see also Laurence Boisson de Chazournes, 'The International Tribunal for the Law of the Sea' in Chiara Giorgetti (ed), *The Rules, Practice, and Jurisprudence of International Courts and Tribunals* (Martinus Nijhoff, 2012) 111–32.

[108] *Case Concerning Land Reclamation by Singapore in and around the Straits of Johor (Malaysia* v *Singapore)*, ITLOS Order of 8 October 2003.

[109] *Request for an Advisory Opinion submitted by the Sub-Regional Fisheries Commission (SRFC)*, ITLOS Advisory Opinion of 2 April 2015.

[110] Mathias Forteau and Jean-Marc Thouvenin (eds), *Traité de droit international de la mer* (Pedone, 2018) 794.

[111] See Arts 200–6 of UNCLOS.

[112] ibid, Arts 198 and 199.

[113] ibid, Arts 202 and 203.

[114] ibid, Art 140.

[115] See ibid, Art 157.

Member States but also obliged to act in the interests of its Member States and on behalf of humankind as a whole. This regime is intended to ensure that resources extracted from the Area, which can include valuable minerals, are distributed fairly and equitably. Article 148 of UNCLOS provides that:

> [t]he effective participation of developing States in activities in the Area shall be promoted as specifically provided for in this Part, having due regard to their special interests and needs, and in particular to the special need of the land-locked and geographically disadvantaged among them to overcome obstacles arising from their disadvantaged location, including remoteness from the Area and difficulty of access to and from it.

When extractive activities are conducted, this must be by an organ of the International Seabed Authority, known as the 'Enterprise',[116] and potentially in collaboration with other actors authorised to do so under the Agreement Relating to the Implementation of Part XI of UNCLOS. Those who are authorised to exploit the common goods must share the benefits with those who might need them most.[117] The Secretariat of the International Seabed Authority also publishes information on, for example, marine environmental protection, for the purposes of public accountability. Similarly, marine scientific research conducted in the Area must be carried out for the benefit of humankind as a whole. This regime indicates a further trend in the realm of co-operation over natural resources, one towards a community-based approach.[118]

IV ANALYSIS

Co-operation is multifaceted and is manifested in a variety of ways. We have shown that international co-operation can be much broader than the pursuit of efforts at the diplomatic level. It can include a duty to notify, to take positive action and to commit resources. Moreover, it can imply specific action such as the offering of technological assistance, the adoption of international measures or sharing information, for example. It can occur within an institutional context or outside of one. These facets of international co-operation have gradually been developed over time, particularly since the Second World War. As a result, this principle has become broader and deeper, and will continue to develop.

It plays a fundamental role in the universal realisation of human rights.[119] In the context of development co-operation, it can imply reducing poverty by reshaping the international economic system as well as investment and financial systems, participatory trading, improving access to markets for developing countries, cancelling debt incurred by developing countries and creating a system for the transfer of resources to developing countries.[120] Furthermore, it can have a wide-ranging role in ensuring developed countries offer international co-operation and assistance in all aspects of their external action, including, for example, trade, security, military

[116] Established under Art 170 of UNCLOS, which provides that the Enterprise is '[t]he organ of the Authority which shall carry out activities in the Area directly as well as the transporting, processing and marketing of minerals recovered from the Area'.

[117] ibid. See also, Edward Brown, *Sea-Bed Energy and Minerals: The International Legal Regime* (Martinus Nijhoff, 2001) ch 7.

[118] Andrew Clapham, *Brierly's Law of Nations* (7th edn, Oxford University Press, 2012) 199.

[119] Margot Salomon, *Global Responsibility for Human Rights: World Poverty and the Development of International Law* (Oxford University Press, 2007).

[120] ibid 102–3.

assistance, development and cultural exchange.[121] In a different area again, it has informed the development of rules around environmental protection, with specific manifestations being found in information sharing or obligations to assist developing countries in meeting their environmental commitments. Under the law of the sea, States are expected to co-operate to prevent marine pollution and in activities concerning the deep seabed, in particular by sharing valuable resources that have been extracted and which are part of the common heritage of humankind.

One of the most expansive expressions of a positive duty to co-operate is to be found in the ICESCR, where it has a special role to play in the realisation of socio-economic rights. The character of the duty to co-operate and assist in the realisation of economic, social and cultural rights, as well as the special responsibility placed on developed countries in this context is evident in the statement of the CESCR in its General Comment No. 3 on the 'Nature of States Parties' Obligations (Art. 2, Para. 1, of the Covenant)' that '[i]t is particularly incumbent upon those States which are in a position to assist others in this regard'.[122] This statement appeals to the moral sensitivities of States and underlines that without international co-operation and assistance the full realisation of socio-economic rights will be hindered. Rather than attaching liability to a failure to pursue a programme of international assistance and co-operation, the prospect of non-fulfilment of rights in third countries is offered as a consequence.

While the obligation to co-operate and its many facets, such as the duties to consult and negotiate, can be found in many different international instruments, the legal contours of the obligation are not precisely defined. This has an impact on the implementation of co-operation, particularly in terms of what is required of States in discharging their obligation to co-operate.[123] Such requirements are dependent on the specifics of the relevant regime.[124] Greater precision around co-operation obligations has been achieved in contexts beyond international environmental law. In the implementation of economic, social and cultural rights, for example, the CESCR has illustrated the types of co-operative activities expected of States under the ICESCR.[125]

Similarly, the central role of good faith in co-operation must be better established. International co-operation is closely connected to reciprocity and good faith.[126] But good faith can have much wider application in co-operative activities. Good faith should, for example, guide States when they conduct EIAs, which are a manifestation of co-operation insofar as they are concerned with sharing information between States. Good faith is also important when States are requested to co-operate with recommendations from international bodies regarding the protection and preservation of the environment and natural resources. In light of a rapidly

[121] Sigrun Skogly, *Beyond National Borders: States' Human Rights Obligations in International Co-operation* (Intersentia, 2006); see also Sigrun Skogly and Mark Gibney, 'Economic Rights and Extraterritorial Obligations' in Shareen Hertel and Lanse Minkler (eds), *Economic Rights: Conceptual, Measurement and Policy Issues* (Cambridge University Press, 2007) 267; Alston and Quinn (n 22) 191; Arjun Sengupta, 'Poverty Eradication and Human Rights' in Thomas Pogge (ed), *Freedom from Poverty as a Human Right: Who Owes What to the Very Poor?* (Oxford University Press, 2007) 344.

[122] CESCR (n 62), para 14.

[123] See Malgosia Fitzmaurice, 'Legitimacy of International Environmental Law. The Sovereign States Overwhelmed by Obligations: Responsibility to React to Problems Beyond National Jurisdiction' (2017) 77 *Zeitschrift für ausländisches öffentliches Recht und Völkerrecht* 339–70, 347.

[124] See Robert Steenkamp, 'UNCLOS, CITES and the IWC – A Tailored International Duty to Co-operate', *EJIL: Talk!*, 26 November 2018.

[125] See eg CESCR (n 62), paras 9–12.

[126] Christina Leb, 'One Step at a Time: International Law and the Duty to Co-operate in the Management of Shared Water Resources' (2015) 40(1) *Water International* 21–32.

changing geopolitical landscape, it should also be emphasised that the legal framework around co-operation dictates that it must occur despite any political, economic or social differences that States may have.

Another open question is the extent to which the duty to co-operate is shaped by the principle of common but differentiated responsibilities. How these two concepts interact should be carefully spelt out in specific regimes. In a different context, the CESCR has underscored that co-operation for development and thus for the realisation of economic, social and cultural rights is an obligation of all States, but also that those States with plentiful resources bear a heavier commitment.[127] Inroads have already been made and financial mechanisms intended to facilitate co-operation between developing and developed countries do reflect the principle of common but differentiated responsibilities. This is the case, for example, with the Global Environment Facility (GEF) and the Forest Carbon Partnership Facility, which promote capacity-building and financial assistance.[128] Moreover, the recent approach of the Paris Agreement, emphasising that developed countries owe a special responsibility to developing countries in respect of financial and technical assistance, is a step in this direction.

Finally, there remains disagreement as to whether international co-operation leads to enforceable rights. The negotiating history of the ICESCR reveals that there was a division among the negotiating States on this point and, ultimately, the issue was avoided in the final text.[129] However, the issue had to be considered again when the Optional Protocol to the Covenant was under negotiation. Developed countries in those negotiations accepted there was a moral responsibility to co-operate internationally but did not accept the Covenant provided for a legally binding obligation to co-operate for the realisation of socio-economic rights.[130] However, General Assembly resolutions and other international agreements have suggested that stronger legal obligations do flow from international co-operation in certain contexts. Examples are the General Assembly resolution on the Right to Food[131] and the Sustainable Development Goal 17, which is concerned with strengthening of a global partnership for sustainable development.

Georges Abi-Saab has argued that increased institutional density is necessary where additional normative density pertains.[132] This is confirmed by the experience of international co-operation. Abi-Saab argues that co-operation is intended to tackle profoundly ambitious tasks and, as a result, the law of co-operation must be institutionalised. He explains that

> [t]his is in application of what could be termed a law or fundamental hypothesis of 'legal physics', which can be formulated as follows: 'each level of normative density requires a corresponding level of institutional density in order to enable the norms to be applied in a satisfactory manner'.[133]

International co-operation is particularly effective and can be manifested in more elaborate ways when it is found within an institutional context. This is evident, for example, through the

[127] CESCR (n 62), para 14.

[128] See Laurence Boisson de Chazournes, 'Is There Room for Coherence in Climate Financial Assistance' (2015) 4 *Laws* 541–58.

[129] Alston and Quinn (n 22) 188–90.

[130] Commission on Human Rights, Report of the Open-ended Working Group to Consider Options Regarding the Elaboration of an Optional Protocol to the International Covenant on Economic, Social and Cultural Rights on its Third Session, 14 March 2006, UN Doc E/CN.4/2006/47.

[131] The Right to Food, UNGA Res 59/202 (31 March 2005), UN Doc A/RES/59/202, paras 20 and 32.

[132] See eg Abi-Saab, 'Cours general de droit international public (Volume 207)' (n 2) 93; Abi-Saab, 'Whither the International Community?' (n 2) 256.

[133] Abi-Saab, 'Whither the International Community?' (n 2) 256.

protection and management of water resources through basin organisations. These institutions have been successful at ensuring and promoting co-operative activity. In a similar way, the climate-change regime is beginning to create institutional machinery around the appraisal of co-operative efforts made by developed countries in providing technological and financial assistance to developing countries so that they can mitigate and adapt to the effects of climate change. As a result, co-operation is operationalised in this particular context through transparency, reporting and accountability mechanisms. In contrast, stronger institutional mechanisms that take account of and evaluate co-operative efforts are necessary to properly operationalise co-operation for the realisation of human rights and development.

International institutions come into existence as a product of co-operation. International organisations can take many different shapes and sizes: they can be formal or informal, highly structured or flexible frameworks for co-operation. To show how loosely organised co-operation can be in an institutional context we may refer to the examples of the Quartet on the Middle East, the Group on Earth Observations, the BRICS, the G8 and the G20.[134] Over time, the institutional intensity of co-operation can change and, as a result, unstructured forms of international co-operation can evolve into more structured international organisations.[135] Depending on the functional necessity, States will delegate more or less of their sovereignty to international organisations in an attempt to resolve questions of international co-operation.[136] As Paul Reinsch observed in 1911:

> It is not so much the case that nations have given up certain parts of their sovereign powers to international administrative organs, as that they have, while fully reserving their independence, actually found it desirable, and in fact necessary, regularly and permanently to co-operate with other nations in the matter of administering certain economic and cultural interests.[137]

International organisations are hubs for functional co-operation and facilitate giving effect to a desire to co-operate. They allow for harmonisation, dialogue, accountability and the coagulation of epistemic communities, all of which give meaning to co-operation.[138]

V CONCLUSIONS

Through a consideration of different legal instruments that make provision for international co-operation, it has been possible to trace its multifaceted dimensions and evolution since its appearance in the UN Charter and the Friendly Relations Declaration. That said, it should also be noted that international co-operation can be found in much earlier expressions in the creation of the first international institutions on shared natural resources and administrative unions, for example. Today, there are many sites of co-operation and these have generally contributed new characteristics to the general conception of co-operation under the UN Charter and Friendly Relations Declaration.

General international law provides a basic expression of the duty to co-operate. But this duty is without much meaning. It has been the task of specialised regimes of international law to add

134 Henry Schermers and Niels Blokker, *International Institutional Law* (Brill, 2018) 35–36.

135 ibid 36.

136 David J Bederman, 'The Souls of International Organizations: Legal Personality and the Lighthouse at Cape Spartel' (1995–96) 36 *Virginia Journal of International Law* 275, 339.

137 Paul Reinsch, *Public International Unions, Their Work and Organization: A Study in International Administrative Law* (Ginn and Company, 1911) 14.

138 Bederman (n 136) 374.

shades of colour to the general obligation. Co-operation for the realisation of human rights – particularly economic, social and cultural rights – has provided content and scope to the duty. The law of development co-operation has provided nuance in the application of the duty, with a special responsibility incumbent on developed countries to provide financial and technical assistance to developing countries. Co-operation over shared natural resources, particularly in respect of fresh water or the deep seabed, has shown how institutions can play an important role in operationalising co-operation. Finally, environmental co-operation, such as in the context of climate change, evidences new attempts to compel co-operation through transparency and accountability mechanisms.

International co-operation finds application in many more areas of international law than those explored in this chapter. But we have endeavoured to highlight that, in order to operationalise co-operation, the general duty must be connected to some functional need and, in turn, that need will shape the way in which co-operation is manifested in practice. Our analysis shows that co-operation is most successful in specific contexts with a well-defined institutional structure. Transparency and accountability add new dimensions to international co-operation, though the extent to which such dimensions make co-operation more effective remains to be seen.

The Friendly Relations Declaration did little to advance the substance of international co-operation but it did cement this principle at the centre of the international legal order, building in this way on the work of the UN Charter before it, and providing a solid foundation for the many and varied manifestations of co-operation that we may find in so many areas of international law today.

7

Self-Determination

*Marcelo G. Kohen**

I INTRODUCTION

Alongside the prohibition of the use of force, self-determination constitutes the most important fundamental principle of contemporary international law. It can certainly be described as the most revolutionary of all existing fundamental principles. For the first time in the history of international law, one of its rules recognises the right of certain human communities, the 'peoples', to freely decide their international status, which includes the possibility of independence. In other words, the right to create their own State.[1] Before the emergence of such a right, all struggles for independence were considered to be internal conflicts or civil wars, for which international law had little to say. They were merely envisaged as 'domestic matters'.

The road to such a legal revolution has been long, even if the period in which the norm crystallised and deployed its effects was relatively short, speaking in historical terms. This assertion presupposes a specific stance on a number of issues; in particular, that self-determination as a *right of peoples* must not be conflated with other uses of the same term that were in vogue before its actual incorporation into the *corpus juris gentium*, and indeed with some uses of the term still in use today. What will be considered in this chapter is the right of peoples to self-determination as enshrined in the UN Charter, and the legal developments that occurred as a result of such inclusion. For the first time in history, a treaty – and indeed the very treaty creating an international organisation with a universal scope of action – incorporated self-determination among the principles governing the institution thus created. This does not mean that our analysis will begin in 1945. The struggle for its recognition began well before the end of the Second World War and other related political or legal principles played a role – with varying

* The author is grateful to Professor Jorge Viñuales, without his help it would have not been possible to finish this chapter in due time. He also thanks Mr Najib Messihi, PhD candidate at the Graduate Institute, Geneva, for his assistance and the drafting of the section on the *travaux préparatoires*.

[1] The ICJ expressly acknowledged that:'[d]uring the second half of the twentieth century, the international law of self-determination developed in such a way as to create a right to independence for the peoples of non-self-governing territories and peoples subject to alien subjugation, domination and exploitation'. *Accordance with International Law of the Unilateral Declaration of Independence in Respect of Kosovo*, Advisory Opinion, ICJ Reports 2010, 403, 436, para 79 (20 July) (referring to *Legal Consequences for States of the Continued Presence of South Africa in Namibia (South West Africa) notwithstanding Security Council Res 276 (1970)*, Advisory Opinion, ICJ Reports 1971, 16, 31–32, paras 52–53 (21 June); *East Timor (Portugal v Australia)*, Judgment, ICJ Reports 1995, 90, 102, para 29 (30 June); *Legal Consequences of the Construction of a Wall in the Occupied Palestinian Territory*, Advisory Opinion, ICJ Reports 2004, 136, 171–72, para 88 (9 July).

degrees – in the historical process that led to the emergence of the right to self-determination and its recognition as one of the fundamental principles of international law.

Given its revolutionary nature, conceptually and in practice, it is unsurprising that, until very recently, some colonial powers and authors have continued to deny its legal character, despite paying formal tribute to it as a – mere – 'aspirational' concept (i.e. not one that would possess concrete legal force). Neither is it surprising that the manner in which it is sometimes invoked by some powers is '*à géométrie variable*', fiercely defending its application in one case and completely disregarding it in another. Also, all political groups advancing secessionist claims will duly remember to claim that their community constitutes a 'people' and hence is entitled to the right to self-determination. And we should not overlook some demagogic presentations of the principle, which combine a generous recognition of a broad category of 'right-holders' with, at the same time, a substantial limitation of its content, which practically removes much of its substance. Even if today no one denies its existence as a legal right, self-determination apparently remains an obscure concept, with vague contours and possible right-holders. Highlighting these difficulties, contradictions and different practices is important to appraise the contribution of the Friendly Relations Declaration to the characterisation and operation of the principle of self-determination. It is probably the principle whose formulation in the Declaration contributed the most to the clarification of its content and scope, even if, unsurprisingly, contradictory approaches and claims remain.

In this context, this chapter first attempts to provide an archaeology of the principle, from its roots in the early stages of the science of international law up to the very introduction of the term 'self-determination' in the international political language and to its formal inclusion in the UN Charter. From that moment, the chapter surveys the discussions within and outside the United Nations about its legal character and content, with a particular focus on the *travaux préparatoires* of the Friendly Relations Declaration. The chapter then moves to the characterisation of the principle, first in the Friendly Relations Declaration, and then in the wider body of international law. The latter examination is intended to clarify key questions relating to the legal basis and nature of the principle, its recognition as a 'right', the contexts in which it has deployed its effects, the question of identifying the right-holder under international law and the relations between self-determination and other fundamental principles. The last two sections of the chapter refer to some common 'loose' uses or outright misuses of the principle in international practice, before concluding on the evolution and prospects of self-determination.

II AN ARCHAEOLOGY OF THE IDEA OF SELF-DETERMINATION

The idea that sovereignty resides in the people and not in the prince or king is certainly an important precedent for the idea of self-determination, although it remains distinct from it. The backdrop of popular sovereignty is the pre-existence of a State. This doctrine concerns indeed the identification of the ultimate holder of power within the State as a political organisation. By contrast, whereas the basic meaning of self-determination is the idea that the people decide their own status, its main content resides in the external capacity to decide, a matter that was not of concern for the doctrine of popular sovereignty. It is then for the 'people' to decide whether they will constitute an independent State or be part of on existing State or, still, otherwise determine their international status. As such, the principle was incorporated into international law in the twentieth century, but the idea, and even a parody of 'self-determination' by which some peoples 'decided' to lose their capacity to decide, was already present long before.

When Spain started its colonial expansion in the Americas, the Salamanca School considered that there were no *terrae nullius* and that the sovereignty over such territories was vested in their inhabitants.[2] The Spanish government disregarded this stance and invoked instead the Papal Bull *Inter Ceatera* and then the Treaty of Tordesillas as the basis to acquire sovereignty over the 'new continent'.[3] The practice of European powers to conclude treaties with local entities in order to acquire sovereignty in Asia and Africa demonstrates the recognition by such powers of the legal capacity of such entities to be holders of sovereignty over their territory. Paradoxically, those agreements both implied such recognition and, at the same time, subjected these peoples to the status of colonies or protectorates deprived of the possibility of deciding their destiny by themselves.[4]

In his most prominent work, Grotius examined the question of who is entitled to alienate sovereignty.[5] If sovereignty is vested in the king, only he has capacity to alienate it. If it is vested in the people, then the king could alienate sovereignty but only with the consent of the people. If only a part of the State's territory is alienated, the consent of that part would be necessary. A part of the State cannot secede from the rest, except in a situation of extreme necessity for its conservation. An uninhabited territory, on the contrary, can be alienated by a 'free people' or by the king with the consent of the people.

The French Revolution brought about two related but distinct political principles: popular sovereignty and the principle of nationalities. Condorcet's draft Constitution established a principle that still features in the contemporary French Constitution of the Fifth French Republic: '*Nulle cession, nul échange, nulle adjonction de territoire n'est valable sans le consentement des populations intéressées.*'[6] On this basis, plebiscites were organised in Savoy, Nice, Belgium and the Rhineland region in Germany.[7] This article did not preclude French colonialism all along the nineteenth century and later on and a rather contradictory practice by France in contemporary times.

According to the principle of nationalities, each nation is entitled to constitute its own State. Politically, it was one of the bases invoked in struggles for the emergence of nation-States in the European continent. It was also under this banner, together with that of human rights, that France attempted to conquer the whole continent, disregarding Robespierre's warning: 'Ce n'est pas à la pointe des baïonnettes qu'on porte aux peuples la Déclaration des Droits de l'Homme.'[8]

The first waves of what we would call 'decolonisation' today occurred at the end of the eighteenth and the beginning of the nineteenth centuries, with the independence of the United States of America in 1774, Haiti in 1804 and the Spanish American colonies starting in 1810. The

[2] Francisco de Vitoria, 'The First Reflection on the Indians Lately Discovered (Translation by John Pawley Bate)' in James Brown Scott (ed), *The Classics of International Law* (Carnegie Institution of Washington, 1917) 115–28.

[3] Pope Alexander VI, The Bull Inter Caetera, 4 May 1493 in Frances Davenport (ed), *European Treaties Bearing on the History of the United States and Its Dependencies to 1648* (Carnegie Institution of Washington, 1917) 61–63; Treaty between Spain and Portugal concluded at Tordesillas, 7 June 1494, ibid 93–100.

[4] See Mamadou Hébié, *Souveraineté territoriale par traité. Une étude des accords entre puissances coloniales et entités politiques locales* (PUF, 2015); and, by the same author, 'The Acquisition of Original Titles of Territorial Sovereignty in the Law and Practice of European Colonial Expansionism' in Marcelo G Kohen and Mamadou Hébié (eds), *Research Handbook on Territorial Disputes in International Law* (Edward Elgar, 2018) 36–86.

[5] Grotius, *De iure belli ac paci libri tres* (1625), bk 2, ch 6, V, VI and VII.

[6] Plan de Constitution présenté à la Convention nationale les 15 et 16 février 1793, Titre 13, Art 2; Constitution of the French Republic, 4 October 1958, Art 53.

[7] Over time, there was a degradation in the way in which such consultations took place, most of the times under the pressure and influence of the French authorities. See J Heimweh (probably a pseudonym), *Droit de conquête et plébiscite* (A Colin, 1896) 1–19.

[8] Cited in Jean Jaurès, *L'Armée nouvelle*, vol 1 (Impr Nationale, 1992 [1910]) 125.

bases underlying these independence claims were different. The British colonies based their independence on a matter of (lack of) representation. The Haitian revolution was essentially a matter of liberation from slavery. It was the Spanish American independence that was accomplished under the banner of national struggle inspired by the French revolutionary ideas and also based on local economic interests, which were curtailed by the Spanish monopoly of trade. All these struggles for independence were perceived from a legal perspective as a matter of civil war. The international law of the time did not grant any right to independence. On the contrary, since this was perceived as a pure matter of domestic concern, it entitled the colonial powers to suppress these aspirations by force and required other States not to lend support to the national liberation struggle. Only the success in their struggle allowed these newly independent States to become members of the still closed international legal system.

The idea that peoples, all of them, have a *right* to freely determine their destiny started to be developed as a political claim. On the international plane, it was the Congress of London of 1896 of the Second International which first asserted 'the rights of nations to self-determination'.[9] The matter was in the agenda of the socialist movement. They distinguished class struggle in what today would be called developed countries, including colonial powers, and national struggle in dependent territories or subjugated nationalities within multinational States. The debate was between those who considered that the independence of subjugated nations would favour the development of capitalism, thereby catalysing the advent of socialism, and those who argued that this issue should not be included in the socialist programme. Karl Kautsky was the main exponent of the former idea and Rosa Luxembourg of the latter. In his work *The Rights of Nations to Self-Determination*, Lenin strongly supported Kautsky and criticised Rosa Luxembourg. He provided the following definition:

> self-determination of nations means the political separation of these nations from alien national bodies, and the formation of an independent national state … it would be wrong to interpret the right to self-determination as meaning anything but the right to existence as a separate state.[10]

The Decree on Peace of the Soviet Provisional Government adopted the day following the Revolution (26 October 1917 according to the Julian calendar, equivalent to 8 November 1917) included a concrete manifestation of the principle of self-determination when defining what, in the view of the new government, would be a peace 'without annexations':

> In accordance with the sense of justice of democrats in general, and of the working class in particular, the government conceives the annexation of seizure of foreign lands to mean every incorporation of a small or weak nation into large or powerful state without the precisely, clearly, and voluntarily expressed consent and wish of that nation, irrespective of the time when such forcible incorporation took place, irrespective also of the degree of development or

[9] 'This Congress declares that it stands for the full right of all nations to self-determination [*Selbstbestimmungsrecht*] and expresses its sympathy for the workers of every country now suffering under the yoke of military, national or other absolutism. This Congress calls upon the workers of all these countries to join the ranks of the class-conscious [*Klassenbewusste* – those who understand their class interests] workers of the whole world in order jointly to fight for the defeat of international capitalism and for the achievement of the aims of international Social-Democracy.' See the official German report of the London Congress: *Verhandlungen und Beschlüsse des internationalen sozialistischen Arbeiter und Gewerkschafts-Kongresses zu London, vom 27. Juli bis 1. August 1896* (Berlin, 1896), S18. A Russian pamphlet has been published containing the decisions of international congresses in which the word 'self determination' is wrongly translated as 'autonomy'.

[10] Vladimir Ilych Lenin, 'The Right of Nations to Self-Determination (1914)', *Lenin's Collected Works*, vol 20 (Progress Publishers, 1972) 393–454, www.marxists.org/archive/lenin/works/1914/self-det/.

backwardness of the nation forcibly annexed to the given state, or forcibly retained within its borders, and irrespective, finally, of whether this nation is in Europe or in distant, overseas countries.

If any nation whatsoever is forcibly retained within the borders of a given state, if, in spite of its expressed desire – no matter whether expressed in the press, at public meetings, in the decisions of parties, or in protests and uprisings against national oppression – is not accorded the right to decide the forms of its state existence by a free vote, taken after the complete evacuation of the [aggressive] troops of the incorporating or, generally, of the stronger nation and without the least pressure being brought to bear, such incorporation is annexation, i.e., seizure and violence.[11]

The Decree granting independence to Finland specifically refers (as a ground) to the principle of the right of nations to self-determination.[12]

Another putative father of self-determination is the American President Woodrow Wilson. Much emphasis has been placed on his famous Fourteen Points.[13] However, his true direct references to self-determination can be found in three speeches delivered between 1917 and 1918. The first one, before the US Senate on 22 January 1917 is eloquent:

No peace can last, or ought to last, which does not recognize and accept the principle that governments derive all their just powers from the consent of the governed, and that no right anywhere exists to hand peoples about from sovereignty to sovereignty as if they were property.[14]

The second one, before a joint session of the US Congress on 11 February 1918, explicitly mentions the term 'self-determination':

There shall be no annexations, no contributions, no punitive damage. Peoples are not to be handed about from one sovereignty to another by an international conference or an understanding between rivals and antagonists. National aspirations must be respected; peoples may now be dominated and governed only by their own consent. 'Self-determination' is not a mere phrase. It is an imperative principle of actions which statesmen will henceforth ignore at their peril.[15]

President Wilson expounded these ideas for the peace that was to follow the First World War at his Mount Vernon's speech of 4 July 1918:

The settlement of every question, whether of territory, of sovereignty, of economic arrangement, or of political relationship, upon the basis of the free acceptance of that settlement by the people immediately concerned, and not upon the basis of the material interest or advantage of any other nation or people which may desire a different settlement for the sake of its own exterior influence or mastery.[16]

Wilson's well-known Fourteen Points did not specifically address the idea of self-determination of peoples. Although they deal with territorial issues, they consist rather of a mix of ethnic and

[11] Second All-Russian Congress of Soviet of Workers' and Soldiers' Deputies, www.marxists.org/archive/lenin/works/1917/oct/25–26/26b.htm.

[12] Decree on Finnish State Independence, 18 (31) December 1917, in Russian, www.law.edu.ru/norm/norm.asp?normID=1118681.

[13] Woodrow Wilson, Fourteen Points, 8 January 1918, https://avalon.law.yale.edu/20th_century/wilson14.asp.

[14] Woodrow Wilson, Address of the President of the United Stated to the Senate, 22 January 1917, www-personal.umd.umich.edu/~ppennock/doc-Wilsonpeace.htm.

[15] Woodrow Wilson, Address of the President of the United Stated to the Congress, 11 February 1918, www.gwpda.org/1918/wilpeace.html.

[16] www.mountvernon.org/preservation/mount-vernon-ladies-association/mount-vernon-through-time/mount-vernon-during-world-war-i/woodrow-wilsons-july-4-1918-mount-vernon-speech/.

convenience criteria for the emergence of new independent States, such as Poland, or the drawing of boundary lines, which are not applied in a systematic way. The idea of autonomy was also envisaged in the cases of the Austro-Hungarian and the Ottoman Empires.[17] The Point relating to colonial issues deserves to be cited in full, as it shows that it was out of the question to let the colonised peoples decide their own fate:

> A free, open-minded, and absolutely impartial adjustment of all colonial claims, based upon a strict observance of the principle that in determining all such questions of sovereignty the interests of the populations concerned must have equal weight with the equitable government whose title is to be determined.

The idea of 'the consent of the governed', which is traditionally linked to Woodrow Wilson's name, can be found in this exact formulation already in the 1774 American Declaration of Independence. Woodrow Wilson had in mind this notion for the settlement of territorial conflicts after the First World War. It did not amount to a recognition of a collective right of a given community to freely decide its destiny. The plebiscites organised (or not) in the inter-war period are very telling in this regard. They were not systematically employed for the decision of the Peace Conference on the fate of certain territories (i.e. there were no plebiscites for the determination of the status of Alsace-Lorraine, Danzig or the Sudeten).

The Covenant of the League of Nations did not contain any reference whatsoever to self-determination in any explicit or implicit form, in any interpretation thereof. The novelty was the establishment of the Mandate regime for territories detached from the defeated States (i.e. within the Ottoman Empire and the German colonies).[18] The alternatives discussed were conquest, as it was the prior practice, or internationalisation of those territories.[19] The compromise, proposed by the South African General Smuts, was the Mandate regime and the establishment of three different categories of Mandates to be applied on the basis of the degree of 'civilisation'. The 'sacred mission of civilisation', the fact that according to the Covenant, the peoples inhabiting those territories were 'not yet able to stand by themselves under the strenuous conditions of the modern world' and the reference to a need for their 'tutelage by advanced nations' all demonstrate that the basis of this regime was not at all self-determination in any recognisable form. General Smuts himself was of the idea that self-determination, understood as the need to have 'the consent of the governed', was exclusively applicable in Europe.[20] Consequently, independence was envisaged for some of the Mandates only (those of type 'A') and not as a right, but as a decision of the States parties to the Covenant and the Mandate agreements.

The debate within the League of Nations concerning the Aaland Islands is perhaps the most representative illustration of the meaning of self-determination and its (lack of) legal value in the inter-war period. The case has been mentioned during the advisory procedure concerning the unilateral declaration of independence of Kosovo, and it was even referred to by some participants as the *locus classicus* on self-determination.[21] The islands belong to Finland but their population is Swedish. A body of jurists was instituted within the League of Nations to study the

[17] See particularly Points VI to XIII.

[18] Covenant of the League of Nations, 29 June 1919, Art 22.

[19] Norman Bentwich, 'Le Système des mandats' (1929) 29 *Recueil des Cours* 121.

[20] Jan C Smuts, *The League of Nations: A Practical Suggestion* (Hodder & Stougthon, 1918) 12–20.

[21] *Accordance with International Law of the Unilateral Declaration of Independence by the Provisional Institutions of Self-Government of Kosovo*, Advisory Opinion, Verbatim Record, 8 December 2009, Ms Kaukoranta (Finland), CR 2009/30, 56, para 12.

issue and make recommendations. The second paragraph of the Committee's Report,[22] reaffirmed in the Commission's Report,[23] clearly stated that self-determination was not a positive rule of the Law of Nations.[24] In the words of the Committee, 'positive International Law does not recognise the right of national groups, as such, to separate themselves from the State to which they form part by the simple expression of a wish'.[25]

The Commission also examined the question from the angle of the right to minorities and explained its rejection of the applicability of the right to self-determination because:

> [t]o concede to minorities . . . or to any fractions of a population the right of withdrawing from the community to which they belong, because it is their wish or their good pleasure, would be to destroy order and stability within States and to inaugurate anarchy in international life.[26]

The Commission also questioned the very need for separation when minority rights are respected. It stated the following in this respect:

> what reasons would there be for allowing a minority to separate itself from the State to which it is united, if this State gives it the guarantees . . . for the preservation of its social, ethnical or religious character? Such indulgence, apart from every political consideration, would be supremely unjust to the State prepared to make these concessions.[27]

Indeed, if something characterises the impact of international law on collective rights during the inter-war period, this is the focus on the protection of the rights of national minorities in Europe through specific rules and procedures dealing with each of them.

The fight against Nazism during the Second World War was a trigger for the idea of self-determination. The 1941 Atlantic Charter signed by F. D. Roosevelt and Winston Churchill contained two related points carefully drafted to make only limited room for genuine self-determination. The second and third points read as follows:

> Second, they desire to see no territorial changes that do not accord with the freely expressed wishes of the peoples concerned;
>
> Third, they respect the right of all peoples to choose the form of government under which they will live; and they wish to see sovereign rights and self government restored to those who have been forcibly deprived of them.[28]

The 1942 Declaration by United Nations simply endorsed the points of the Atlantic Charter and did not contain any reference to self-determination. The Declarations adopted in the 1943 Moscow Conference did not mention the principle either. The Four Powers Dumbarton Oaks Proposals of 1944, which contained the embryo of the purposes and principles of the future Charter did not refer to self-determination. Article 1, paragraph 2, just mentioned the aim '[t]o develop friendly relations among nations, and to take other appropriate measures to strengthen universal peace'. It was only at the San Francisco Conference in 1945, on the proposal of the

[22] 'Report of the International Committee of Jurists entrusted by the Council of the League of Nations with the task of giving an advisory opinion upon the legal aspects of the Aaland Islands Question', League of Nations Official Journal, October 1920, Special Supp No 3, 5, para 2.

[23] 'The Aaland Islands Question', Report submitted to the Council of the League of Nations by the Commission of Rapporteurs, 16 April 1921, League of Nations Doc 21/68/106, 27.

[24] 'Report of the International Committee of Jurists' (n 22) 5, para 2.

[25] ibid.

[26] 'The Aaland Islands Question' (n 23) 28.

[27] ibid 28.

[28] Declaration of Principles issued by the President of the United States and the Prime Minister of the United Kingdom, 14 August 1941, www.nato.int/cps/en/natohq/official_texts_16912.htm.

USSR, that this article was revised to state that the friendly relations are 'based on respect for the principle of equal rights and self-determination of peoples'. Yet, the real question concerned the determination of the content of this formula as well as of its legal scope.

In a summary of the discussions within the Committee in charge of the preparation of a draft of the preamble, purposes and principles of the United Nations, the general view was that the principle of self-determination:

> corresponded closely to the will and desires of peoples everywhere and should be clearly enunciated in the Chapter; on the other side, it was stated that the principle conformed to the purposes of the Charter only insofar as it implied the right of self-government of peoples and not the right of secession.[29]

The Rapporteur of this Committee, M. Farid Zeineddine of Syria observed in this regard that:

> It was understood: That the principles of equal rights of people [*sic*] and that of self-determination are two component elements of one norm. That the respect of that norm is a basis for the development of friendly relations, and is in effect, one of the appropriate measures to strengthen universal peace. It was understood likewise that the principle in question, as a provision of the Charter, should be considered in function of other provisions. That an essential element of the principle in question, is a free and genuine expression of the will of the peoples; and thus to avoid cases like those alleged by Germany and Italy. That the principle as one whole extends as a general basic conception to a possible amalgamation of nationalities if they so freely chose.[30]

And, explaining the rejection of a proposal, and the link between self-determination and the principle of equality of rights, the rapporteur further noted that the latter principle 'extends in the Charter to states, nations, and peoples'.[31]

Another reference to self-determination in the UN Charter is found in Article 55, linking self-determination with economic and social progress and human rights.[32] Again, the idea repeated here is that this right means self-government and not secession. No mention of the principle appears in Chapter XI, dealing with Non-Self-Governing Territories,[33] and Chapter XII, dealing with the regime of Trusteeship, that replaced that of the Mandates of the League of Nations. However, Article 76 of the UN Charter established that the basic objectives of the latter regime were, in accordance with the purposes laid down in Article 1 (which include self-determination), to promote the progressive development of the inhabitants of the trust territories 'towards self-government or *independence* as may be appropriate to the particular circumstances of each territory and its peoples and the freely expressed wishes of the peoples concerned'. Unlike the

[29] Commission I, Committee 1, General Provisions, UNCIO, Doc 343 I/1/16, 16 May 1945, 1.

[30] Commission I, Committee 1, General Provisions, UNCIO, Doc 723, I/1/A/19, 1 June 1945, 8–9.

[31] ibid 9.

[32] 'With a view to the creation of conditions of stability and well-being which are necessary for peaceful and friendly relations among nations based on respect for the principle of equal rights and self-determination of peoples, the United Nations shall promote: a. higher standards of living, full employment, and conditions of economic and social progress and development; b. solutions of international economic, social, health, and related problems; and international cultural and educational co-operation; and c. universal respect for, and observance of, human rights and fundamental freedoms for all without distinction as to race, sex, language, or religion.'

[33] Nevertheless, in 1975, the Court made a link between Art 1, para 2 and Arts 55 and 56 with Chapter XI in the following manner: 'The Charter of the United Nations, in Art 1, para 2, indicates, as one of the purposes of the United Nations: "To develop friendly relations among nations based on respect for the principle of equal rights and self-determination of peoples . . ." This purpose is further developed in Arts 55 and 56 of the Charter. Those provisions have direct and particular relevance for non-self-governing territories, which are dealt with in Chapter XI of the Charter.' *Western Sahara*, Advisory Opinion, ICJ Reports 1975, 31, para 54.

mandates system, this objective applied to all territories and was not qualified by the type of mandate.

It can be concluded that, at the time of the adoption of the Charter, the principle of self-determination of peoples was recognised as such for the first time in a treaty of general character and constitutive of an international organisation of universal vocation. However, the text itself did not explicitly settle the divergence of views regarding its legal character and scope. For some Member States it was a right and included the right of colonial peoples to independence, whereas for others (the colonial powers), it had a limited scope and did not confer such a right. The only major area of consensus was that the principle did not apply to, and consequently did not favour, secession from existing States. Over the years, the evolution of practice following the application of the UN Charter through the work of the organisation, both in the field of human rights and on the application of Chapter XI, allowed the principle to consolidate, as discussed next.

III THE PRACTICE OF THE UNITED NATIONS: A 'CHAPTER XI *BIS*'

Soon after the entering into force of the Charter in 1945 the question of self-determination came to the forefront. The discussion leading to the adoption of the Universal Declaration of Human Rights saw the opposition between the Soviet Union and the Western countries in this regard. The insistence of the former to include the right of self-determination, with the understanding that it was applicable to colonial peoples, met the opposition of most of the members of the United Nations, leading the USSR to abstain from voting on the adoption of the Declaration.[34] Instead, a British proposal was accepted, emphasising individuals and their rights, irrespective of the status of the territory concerned.[35]

Another context where the scope of self-determination was raised concerned the information transmitted by Administering Powers of Non Self-Governing Territories under Article 73 of the UN Charter. Article 73 of the Charter sets out a number of goals to be achieved for these territories and obligations for the colonial States (administering powers) that have been extensively developed by the practice of the General Assembly. The International Court of Justice (ICJ) recognised this practice in its 1971, 1975 and 2019 advisory opinions.[36] It was with the strong participation of the United Nations in general and the General Assembly in particular that many current members of the organisation achieved their independence. More than eighty former colonies comprising some 750 million people have gained independence since the creation of the United Nations.[37] As early as 1950, the UN General Assembly recognised the 'right of peoples and nations to self-determination' as a fundamental human right.[38] Then it decided to include the right of peoples to self-determination in the future Covenant (or Covenants) on Human Rights and explicitly mentioned that self-determination was applicable to non-self-governing territories.[39] Thereafter, the General Assembly adopted, on a yearly basis, resolutions declaring that Member States 'shall recognize and promote the realization of the right to

[34] A/PV183, 926.

[35] The following text was added to Art 2: 'Furthermore, no distinction shall be made on the basis of the political, jurisdictional or international status of the country or territory to which a person belongs, whether it be independent, trust, non-self-governing or under any other limitation of sovereignty.'

[36] *Western Sahara*, Advisory Opinion (n 33) 32, para 56 (referring to its 1971 Namibia Advisory Opinion).

[37] www.un.org/en/decolonization/.

[38] UNGA Res 421 D (V) (4 December 1950).

[39] UNGA Res 545 (VI) (5 February 1952) (42–7–5).

self-determination of peoples of Non-Self-Governing and Trust Territories who are under their administration'.[40] This law of decolonisation developed not without resistance from some colonial powers. In some cases, they denied that particular territories fell within the classification of non-self-governing or colonial territory. The General Assembly considered that it was not for the administering power to unilaterally determine whether the territories fall under Chapter XI. Rather, it was for the General Assembly itself to make this ascertainment. That was for instance the case of the colonies held by Portugal, since the Portuguese government of that time denied that they had such status, claiming they were mere overseas provinces.[41] Through the analysis of the situation in the colonies, the General Assembly also established the general rules for the administration of the territory during the transitional period as well as the modalities for the decolonisation of different territories.

Following the adoption, on 14 December 1960, of the landmark General Assembly Resolution 1514 (XV), 'Declaration on the Granting of Independence to Colonial Countries and Peoples',[42] the monitoring of the decolonisation process was entrusted to the Special Committee on the Situation with regard to the Implementation of the Declaration on the Granting of Independence to Colonial Countries and Peoples. Known as the 'Decolonisation Committee', this body was created in 1961 as the subsidiary organ of the General Assembly exclusively devoted to the issue of decolonisation.[43] In addition to these important developments, other General Assembly resolutions also played an important role in the development of the law of decolonisation. Referring to this growing body of resolutions, the late French jurist Michel Virally spoke of a veritable rewriting of the UN Charter to include 'Chapter XI *bis*'.[44] Of particular significance are the following:

Resolution 1541 (XV) of 15 December 1960: Principles which should guide Members in determining whether or not an obligation exists to transmit the information called for under Article 73 e of the Charter.

Resolution 2621 (XXV) of 12 October 1970: Programme of action for the full implementation of the Declaration on the Granting of Independence to Colonial Countries and Peoples, which states inter alia that 'Members shall intensify their efforts to promote the implementation of the resolutions of the General Assembly and the Security Council relating to Territories under colonial domination', considers that 'military activities and arrangements by colonial Powers in Territories under their administration . . . constitute an obstacle to the full implementation of resolution 1514 (XV)' and states that the Decolonization Committee 'shall continue to examine the full compliance of all States with the Declaration and with other relevant resolutions on the question of decolonization' and '[w]here the resolution 1514 (XV) has not been fully implemented with regard to a given Territory, the General Assembly shall continue to bear responsibility for that Territory until such time as the

40 UNGA Res 637 (VII) (16 December 1952), 738 (VIII) (28 November 1953), 833 (IX) (4 December 1954), 1188 (XII) (11 December 1957).

41 See Transmission of information under Art 73 (e) of the Charter, UNGA Res 1542 (XV) (15 December 1960), para 1.

42 This resolution is a turning point, and its importance has been recognised by the ICJ in several occasions. See *Western Sahara* (n 33), para 57; *Accordance with International Law of the Unilateral Declaration of Independence in Respect of Kosovo*, Advisory Opinion (n 1) 436, para 79 and 438, para 82; *Legal Consequences of the Separation of the Chagos Archipelago from Mauritius in 1965*, ICJ, Advisory Opinion (25 February 2019), paras 150–53.

43 The Situation with Regard to the Implementation of the Declaration on the Granting of Independence to Colonial Countries and Peoples, UNGA Res 1654 (XVI) (27 November 1961).

44 Michel Virally, 'Droit international et décolonisation devant les Nations Unies' (1963) 9 *Annuaire français de droit international* 508, 526.

people concerned has had an opportunity to exercise freely its right to self-determination and independence in accordance with the Declaration'.

Resolution 2625 (XXV) of 24 October 1970: Declaration on Principles of International Law concerning Friendly Relations and Co-operation among States in accordance with the Charter of the United Nations.

Resolution 35/118 of 11 December 1980: Plan of the Action for the full implementation of the Declaration on the Granting of Independence to Colonial Countries and Peoples, adopted at the twentieth anniversary of Resolution 1514 (XV) and being a development of Resolution 2621 (XXII). For the purposes of this case, the condemnation of measures of disruption of the demographic composition of the colonial territories and the request for the immediate and unconditional withdrawal from colonial territories of military bases and installations of colonial powers are specifically relevant.

Resolution 65/119 of 10 December 2010: Third International Decade for the Eradication of Colonialism, which declared the period 2011–20 as the Third International Decade for the Eradication of Colonialism.[45]

In this regard, it can be said that resolutions of the General Assembly establishing which territories are subject to decolonisation, as well as the determination of the manner in which these territories must be decolonised, and when the process has come to an end and consequently the territory ceases to be a 'non-self-governing' one, are more than simple recommendations. Since the General Assembly has the competence to make these ascertainments, its resolutions are authoritative in this regard.

It is against this background and developments that the discussions on the scope of the principle of self-determination within the Committee in charge of the elaboration of what became the Friendly Relations Declaration occurred.

IV SELF-DETERMINATION IN THE FRIENDLY RELATIONS DECLARATION

1 *Introduction*

The process which, between 1963 and 1970, led to the debate, formulation and adoption by consensus of the Friendly Relations Declaration is of major significance for the principle of self-determination. Although the principle had already received in 1960 what became, over time, its canonical formulation, the Friendly Relations Declaration placed it at the heart of the post-war international legal order, alongside other fundamental principles of international law. The process that led to such an achievement was difficult and only completed at the very last session of the intersessional Special Committee established in December 1963, which took place in Geneva from 31 March to 1 May 1970. The purpose of the following sections is to situate self-determination within both the debates of the Special Committee and the broader context of the Friendly Relations Declaration.

2 *The* Travaux Préparatoires

The Special Committee on Principles of International Law concerning Friendly Relations and Co-operation among States was initially established in 1964 by the UN General Assembly to deal with the principles of the prohibition of the threat or use of force, the peaceful settlement of

[45] See *Chagos* (n 42), Written Statement of Argentina, para 19.

disputes, non-intervention and sovereign equality of States. It was reconstituted in 1966 and enlarged to thirty-one Member States for the purpose of completing the study of the above-mentioned principles and considering the remaining ones, notably, the principle of equal rights and self-determination of peoples.[46] The Special Committee considered this principle at its 1966, 1967, 1968, 1969 and 1970 sessions, issuing a yearly report that was later discussed within the UN General Assembly, especially its Sixth Committee.

From the very beginning of discussions, there was a general agreement on the fact that self-determination constituted a rule of international law and not a mere moral or political precept.[47] However, States differed on how to give expression to it. If the so-called socialist and non-aligned States formulated it as a right,[48] other States such as the United States of America and the United Kingdom preferred to frame it in terms of an obligation, resting upon States, to respect the principle of self-determination on territories under their jurisdiction, pointing out the difficulty of defining the beneficiaries of the right, namely the 'peoples'.[49] Ultimately, the Drafting Committee of the Special Committee decided to adopt both views by enunciating the principle of self-determination as a 'right of peoples' and a 'duty to respect' imposed on every State.[50]

Member States also disagreed on the scope of the principle of self-determination, including its beneficiaries. For some, the right to self-determination had to be limited to peoples under colonial rule while for others, it had to be either limited or at least extended to the population of already independent and sovereign States.[51] It had also been advanced that the term 'peoples' should correspond to the majority of the population of generally accepted political units or be extended to those living in a zone of military occupation.[52] The case of federal unions whose constitutional law explicitly refers to the principle of self-determination as well as that of territories in free association with the former administering power were mentioned.[53] Finally, the possibility of granting the right of self-determination to the distinct peoples of multinational States was also raised.[54]

The final text of the Declaration did not define the term 'peoples'. However, it stated that '*all* peoples have the right' to self-determination. The proposal by the representative of Nigeria to use the expression 'all *subject* peoples' instead of 'all peoples' was not followed.[55] In the same vein, the suggestion by the United States of America, later endorsed by the United Kingdom, to include an exhaustive list of territories to which the principle of self-determination applies was finally not retained by the Drafting Committee.[56]

The applicability of the principle to both colonial peoples and peoples already possessing a State is confirmed by the discussions related to the content of the right to self-determination. Since the first sessions of the Special Committee that were devoted to this principle, several representatives argued that the right to self-determination had two aspects, an external and a domestic one. It encompassed the right of peoples to freely determine their international

[46] UNGA, Res 2103 (XX).
[47] A/C.6/SR.926, para 9 (USA); Report of the Sixth Committee (1966), para 69.
[48] Report of the Special Committee (1966), paras 457 and 458.
[49] ibid, para 459; Report of the Special Committee (1967), paras 176 and 192.
[50] Report of the Special Committee (1970), para 83; UNGA Res 2625 (XXV) (24 October 1970).
[51] Report of the Special Committee (1967), para 195, A/C.6/SR.928, para 5 (Canada); A/C.6/SR.1002, para 33 (Central African Republic); A/C.6/SR.1160, para 38 (Burma).
[52] Report of the Special Committee (1968), para 163; Report of the Special Committee (1969), para 156 A/5725, p 28 (Cyprus); A/C.6/SR.1182, para 46 (Libya).
[53] Report of the Special Committee (1969), para 156.
[54] Report of the Sixth Committee (1969), para 26.
[55] A/C.6/SR.996, para 28.
[56] Report of the Special Committee (1966), para 459; Report of the Special Committee (1967), para 176.

political status, which includes the establishment of an independent State, but also their right to choose their political, economic and social systems without external interference.[57] This second aspect was understood as permanent in nature. After their independence, peoples remained entitled to internal self-determination, in conformity with other fundamental principles of international law such as the sovereign equality of States and non-intervention.[58]

With regard to the exercise by peoples of their internal self-determination within independent States, some representatives argued that the democratic dimension of the principle of self-determination had to be recognised, for it is based on the free will of peoples.[59] This was further strengthened by the development of human rights at the international level which prohibit discrimination and prescribe that the will of the people shall be the basis of the authority of government.[60] In this respect, the United States proposed to include in the Declaration, a paragraph which reads as follows: 'The existence of a sovereign and independent State possessing a representative Government, effectively functioning as such to all distinct peoples within its territory, is presumed to satisfy the principle of equal rights and self-determination as regards those peoples.'[61]

Some representatives welcomed this formulation. Others expressed their fear about the disruption of the territorial integrity and political unity of States and wanted to make clear that self-determination does not grant to ethnic, racial, national or religious minorities a legal ground for secession.[62] To overcome this difficulty and mitigate the risks, Italy suggested in 1970, drawing upon a previous draft prepared by the Drafting Committee, to add a saving clause right after the US based proposal: 'Nothing in the foregoing paragraphs shall be construed as authorizing any action which would impair, totally or in part, the territorial integrity, or political unity, of such States.'[63] As will be discussed below, the final text adopted by the UN General Assembly included that general safeguard or saving clause. The *a contrario* reading of this clause led some authors and States to invoke a 'remedial secession' exception. A close look at the *travaux préparatoires* of the Declaration discards such interpretation. Statements made by the representatives of States directly involved in the drafting of the saving clause clearly indicate that its object and purpose was to safeguard the territorial integrity and political unity of States. The representative of Italy declared that the inclusion of the saving clause ensured 'that the principle would not be interpreted in such a way as to undermine the territorial integrity of independent States, which was safeguarded as fundamental by the Charter'.[64] In the same vein, the representative of Canada – who assumed, within the Drafting Committee, the chairmanship of the working group on the implementation of self-determination by a State with respect to peoples within its jurisdiction – stated that, thanks to the adoption of the saving clause, there was 'no danger that some might be misled in attempting to invoke the principle to justify the dislocation of a State within which various communities had been cohabitating successfully and peacefully

57 Report of the Special Committee (1967), para 198; Report of the Sixth Committee (1968), para 47; A/5725, 47 (Romania); A/C.6/SR.998, para 9 (Congo, Brazzaville).

58 Report of the Special Committee (1966), paras 480–81.

59 ibid, paras 515 and 518; Report of the Special Committee (1969), para 176.

60 Report of the Special Committee (1967), para 222.

61 Report of the Special Committee (1966), para 459. The United Kingdom presented exactly the same proposal one year later: UN Doc A/AC.125/L.44, part VI, repr in Official Records of the General Assembly, Twenty-Second Session, annexes, agenda item 87, UN Doc A/6799 (19 July 1967), para 176.

62 Report of the Special Committee (1967), paras 221 and 223.

63 Report of the Special Committee (1970), para 63.

64 Report of the Special Committee (1969), para 187.

for a considerable period of time'.[65] This interpretation was backed by other States in the last debates preceding the adoption of the final text of the Declaration.[66] In fact, the *a contrario* reading of the saving clause was only evoked by the representative of South Africa, still under the apartheid regime, for the purpose of criticising the clause and expressing reservations.[67]

The interpretation of the saving clause as a provision aiming primarily at protecting the territorial integrity of States is further confirmed by the statements of many States, which considered explicitly during the whole process that the right to self-determination was not applicable to national, ethnic, tribal, racial or religious minority groups.[68] It is also further strengthened by the last paragraph of the Declaration which stipulates that 'Every State shall refrain from any action aimed at the partial or total disruption of the national unity and territorial integrity of any other State or country.'[69] This paragraph was adopted without much debate or difficulties, notably because it 'reassured those who feared that the universal application of the principle might favour secessionist movements inside independent States'.[70]

It is worth noting that the emphasis of the Declaration on the principle of territorial integrity does not undermine or weaken the right of peoples to self-determination, since the sixth paragraph of the text in question sets out that 'the territory of a colony or other Non-Self-Governing Territory has, under the Charter, a status separate and distinct from the territory of the State administering it'. This rule was initially advocated by the so-called Socialist and Non-aligned States and opposed by mainly colonial States which contended that it was in contradiction with the established doctrine of international law.[71] It has been nonetheless included in the final text thereby confirming that the accession of a colony to independence does not amount to a violation of the territorial integrity of the administering power.

The *travaux préparatoires* of the Declaration also reveal that States differed on the modes of implementation of the right to self-determination. Some of them were of the view that the principle could only be regarded as fully implemented when the people concerned had attained the status of a sovereign State. For these States, the prior access to independence was a necessary condition for a truly free choice of peoples regarding their future political, economic and social status.[72] However, drawing upon Resolution 1541 of the UN General Assembly and pointing out the differences that might exist in terms of resources, size and population between the different Non-Self-Governing Territories, other States considered that self-determination could also be achieved through free association or integration with an independent State.[73]

The work of the Special Committee on the principle of self-determination was marked by strong opposition over two further aspects: the legal assessment of colonialism and the question of the right of peoples to self-defence. From the very beginning of the process, several States advocated the inclusion of a clear statement that colonialism in all its forms, including racial discrimination, amounted to a violation of international law in general and the principle of self-

[65] Report of the Special Committee (1970), para 177.
[66] ibid, para 219 (India), A/C.6/SR.1183, para 11 (India) and 39 (Ecuador).
[67] A/C.6/SR.1184, para 15.
[68] A/C.6/SR.1002, para 33 (Central African Republic); A/C.6/SR.1003, para 55 (Ecuador); A/C.6/SR.1163, para 18 (Philippines).
[69] UNGA, Res 2625 (XXV).
[70] Report of the Special Committee (1968), para 190.
[71] Report of the Special Committee (1967), para 216.
[72] ibid, para 212; A/C.6/SR.1158, para 31 (Czechoslovakia).
[73] Report of the Special Committee (1967), para 213; A/C.6/SR.1181, para 8 (New Zealand).

determination in particular.[74] Other States, notably the United Kingdom, objected to this proposal, claiming that not all colonial relationships were illegal per se, and pointing out that the Charter did not outlaw colonialism but regulated it instead and provided for its orderly termination in Chapters XI, XII and XIII.[75] The final text of the Declaration borrowed the terms of Resolution 1514 of the UN General Assembly by stating that the 'subjection of peoples to alien subjugation, domination and exploitation constitutes a violation of the principle, as well as a denial of fundamental human rights, and is contrary to the Charter'. It also called for a 'speedy end to colonialism'.[76]

From the outset too, the so-called socialist and non-aligned countries stressed that self-determination entailed the right of peoples to self-defence against colonial oppression and their right to receive appropriate assistance in their struggle for liberation.[77] Other States considered that such position was incompatible with other fundamental principles of the UN Charter such as the prohibition of the threat or use of force or the principle of non-intervention.[78] The outcome of this debate was a compromise formula recognising the right of peoples to resistance against the forcible actions of the coloniser but limiting the assistance and support to which these peoples are entitled to those which are 'in accordance with the purposes and principles of the Charter'.[79]

3 *The Final Outcome*

The formulation of the self-determination principle in the Friendly Relations Declaration is, with the benefit of hindsight, a major achievement. Although it does not expressly refer to the 1960 Declaration on the Granting of Independence to Colonial Countries and Peoples, it largely relies on it, thus striking a compromise in the absence of which it would have been impossible to complete the work on the Friendly Relations Declaration. Unsurprisingly, the formulation of the principle was one of 'the most difficult tasks the Committee faced',[80] given the deep and various dividing lines across Committee members and the revolutionary character of this norm.

The final text, with its many nuances and compromises, owes much to the calibre of the international lawyers who took part in the negotiations and drafting. Its significance cannot be underestimated. Self-determination is not only recognised but also woven into the fabric of post-1945 international law and, more specifically, of its fundamental principles. Indeed, the 'principle of equal rights and self-determination of peoples' was now fleshed out in significant detail, including by reference to other principles of the Friendly Relations Declaration. In its eight paragraphs, the Declaration defines the content of the right, the possible outcomes of its exercise, the obligation to put an end to any situation contrary to that right and to promote its

[74] Report of the Special Committee (1966), paras 457, 458 (Written Proposal by Czechoslovakia, para 2), 458 (Joint Written Proposal by Algeria, Burma, Cameroon, Dahomey, Ghana, India, Kenya, Lebanon, Madagascar, Nigeria, Syria, the United Arab Republic and Yugoslavia, para 2(a)) and 482; A/C.6/SR.999, paras 63–65 (United Republic of Tanzania).

[75] A/C.6/SR.1000, para 32 (United Kingdom).

[76] UNGA, Res 2625 (XXV).

[77] Report of the Special Committee (1966), para 458 (Joint Written Proposal by Algeria, Burma, Cameroon, Dahomey, Ghana, India, Kenya, Lebanon, Madagascar, Nigeria, Syria, the United Arab Republic and Yugoslavia, para 2(b)); A/C.6/SR.997, para 17 (Poland); A/C.6/SR.999, paras 42–43 (Ukrainian Soviet Socialist Republics).

[78] Report of the Special Committee (1966), para 497; A/C.6/SR.1000, paras 32–33 (United Kingdom).

[79] UNGA Res 2625 (XXV).

[80] See the article by the US representative to the Special Committee, R Rosenstock, 'The Declaration of Principles of International Law Concerning Friendly Relations: A Survey' (1971) 65 *American Journal of International Law* 713, 730.

respect, the different legal status of colonial territories, the safeguard or saving clause against dismemberment and the obligation to respect the territorial integrity of States and other countries:

> [Paragraph 1] By virtue of the principle of equal rights and self-determination of peoples enshrined in the Charter of the United Nations, all peoples have the right freely to determine, without external interference, their political status and to pursue their economic, social and cultural development, and every State has the duty to respect this right in accordance with the provisions of the Charter.
>
> [Paragraph 2] Every State has the duty to promote, through joint and separate action, realization of the principle of equal rights and self-determination of peoples, in accordance with the provisions of the Charter, and to render assistance to the United Nations in carrying out the responsibilities entrusted to it by the Charter regarding the implementation of the principle, in order:
>
> (a) To promote friendly relations and co-operation among States; and
> (b) To bring a speedy end to colonialism, having due regard to the freely expressed will of the peoples concerned;
>
> and bearing in mind that subjection of peoples to alien subjugation, domination and exploitation constitutes a violation of the principle, as well as a denial of fundamental human rights, and is contrary to the Charter.
>
> [Paragraph 3] Every State has the duty to promote through joint and separate action universal respect for and observance of human rights and fundamental freedoms in accordance with the Charter.
>
> [Paragraph 4] The establishment of a sovereign and independent State, the free association or integration with an independent State or the emergence into any other political status freely determined by a people constitute modes of implementing the right of self-determination by that people.
>
> [Paragraph 5] Every State has the duty to refrain from any forcible action which deprives peoples referred to above in the elaboration of the present principle of their right to self-determination and freedom and independence. In their actions against, and resistance to, such forcible action in pursuit of the exercise of their right to self-determination, such peoples are entitled to seek and to receive support in accordance with the purposes and principles of the Charter.
>
> [Paragraph 6] The territory of a colony or other Non-Self-Governing Territory has, under the Charter, a status separate and distinct from the territory of the State administering it; and such separate and distinct status under the Charter shall exist until the people of the colony or Non-Self-Governing Territory have exercised their right of self-determination in accordance with the Charter, and particularly its purposes and principles.
>
> [Paragraph 7] Nothing in the foregoing paragraphs shall be construed as authorizing or encouraging any action which would dismember or impair, totally or in part, the territorial integrity or political unity of sovereign and independent States conducting themselves in compliance with the principle of equal rights and self-determination of peoples as described above and thus possessed of a government representing the whole people belonging to the territory without distinction as to race, creed or colour.
>
> [Paragraph 8] Every State shall refrain from any action aimed at the partial or total disruption of the national unity and territorial integrity of any other State or country.

The final text has eight paragraphs, identified between square brackets in the above quotation for ease of reference. The first paragraph expressly recognises a 'right' of 'all peoples' to self-determination, which includes, according to the paragraph 'the establishment of a sovereign and independent State' as one of the 'modes of implementing the right of self-determination by that people'. All States have a 'duty to respect this right in accordance with the provisions of the Charter' (paragraph 1) as well as other more specific duties, including 'to promote ... realization of the principle' and 'to render assistance to the United Nations in carrying out' its responsibilities inter alia 'to bring a speedy end to colonialism, having due regard to the freely expressed will of the peoples concerned' (paragraph 2), 'to promote ... universal respect for human rights' (paragraph 3), 'to refrain from any forcible action' against the exercise of such right (paragraph 5) but also from 'any action' against 'the partial or total disruption of the national unity and territorial integrity of any other State or country' (paragraph 8).

The recognition of a 'right' to self-determination in a text adopted by consensus was a major step in the codification process. Since the adoption of Resolution 2625 (XXV), there has been no challenge of the legal character of the principle. The ICJ has rightly considered that such right was already binding as a matter of general international law in the 1960s, as will be discussed below.[81] The Friendly Relations Declaration largely contributed to the determination of its content.

Two issues of particular importance concern the wider relations between, on the one hand, the right to self-determination and, on the other hand, the prohibition of the use of force and the principle of territorial integrity. The first issue (use of force) is addressed in paragraph 5, whereas the second is covered by paragraphs 6 and 7. Paragraph 8 is relevant for both issues. The issue of secession and, more generally, the relations between self-determination and territorial integrity will be discussed in some detail in sections V.2.3 and 2.4 below. Regarding the use of force, paragraph 5 recognises that forcible actions to prevent peoples exercising their right to self-determination are illegal. However, the final text does not recognise the doctrine of 'self-defence against colonialism', fiercely opposed by the West.[82] According to paragraph 5, peoples are 'entitled to seek and to receive support', and this support cannot be considered as a breach of the principle of non-intervention.[83] Western powers required the addition of the formula 'in accordance with the purposes and principles of the Charter', in order to prevent reliance on paragraph 5 to justify the 'export of revolution', a doctrine in vogue during the 1960s after the triumph of Castro's revolution in Cuba.[84] After the adoption of Resolution 2625 (XXV), it was uncontested that what were popularly called 'wars of national liberation' against colonialism and alien domination had an international character and were not mere internal conflicts. Seven years later, the Additional Protocol I to the four 1949 Geneva Conventions confirmed this categorisation, with an explicit reference to the Friendly Relations Declaration.[85]

V SELF-DETERMINATION IN INTERNATIONAL LAW

1 *Legal Basis and Hierarchy of the Norm*

After the inclusion of self-determination in the UN Charter, the position of some colonial powers and some authors was still to consider the principle a mere aspiration without implying

[81] *Chagos* (n 42), para 152.

[82] See the chapter by O Corten in this volume.

[83] See *Military and Paramilitary Activities in and against Nicaragua (Nicaragua v United States of America)*, Merits, Judgment, ICJ Reports 1986, 108, para 206.

[84] Rosenstock (n 80) 733.

[85] Art 1(4) reads: 'armed conflicts in which peoples are fighting against colonial domination and alien occupation and against racist regimes in the exercise of their right of self-determination, as enshrined in the Charter of the United Nations and the Declaration on Principles of International Law concerning Friendly Relations and Co-operation among States in accordance with the Charter of the United Nations'.

legal obligations.[86] This position has reached the present day in some more refined variations. During the proceedings relating to the advisory opinion in *Chagos* before the ICJ, the United Kingdom (the colonial power) and the United States (the beneficiary of the lease over the Chagos occupied territory) argued that decolonisation was a political rather than a legal process,[87] that the right to self-determination had not yet become a customary norm at the time of the separation of the Chagos island from the territory of the colony in 1965[88] and, for that reason, the UK was not bound to respect the territorial integrity of Mauritius.[89] Indeed, exactly the same arguments had been invoked by the UK during the Chagos Marine Protected Area Arbitration.[90] These arguments called for a clarification by the ICJ of the moment in time when the right to self-determination had entered general international law.

The Court began by recalling Article 1(2) and Chapter XI (particularly Article 73) of the UN Charter and premised its analysis on the observation that 'the Charter included provisions that would enable non-self-governing territories ultimately to govern themselves'. Such was the context in which 'the Court must ascertain when the right to self-determination crystallized as a customary rule binding on all States'.[91] Thereafter, in a few paragraphs that provide both a historical survey of the most relevant instruments and an analysis of their content, the Court observed that Resolution 1514 (XV) of 1960 was 'declaratory' as regards 'the right to self-determination as a customary norm'.[92] The relevant paragraphs read as follows:

> The adoption of resolution 1514 (XV) of 14 December 1960 represents a defining moment in the consolidation of State practice on decolonization. Prior to that resolution, the General Assembly had affirmed on several occasions the right to self-determination (resolutions 637 (VII) of 16 December 1952, 738 (VIII) of 28 November 1953 and 1188 (XII) of 11 December 1957) and a number of non-self-governing territories had acceded to independence. General Assembly resolution 1514 (XV) clarifies the content and scope of the right to self-determination. The Court notes that the decolonization process accelerated in 1960, with 18 countries, including 17 in Africa, gaining independence. During the 1960s, the peoples of an additional 28 non-self-governing-territories exercised their right to self-determination and achieved independence. In the Court's view, there is a clear relationship between resolution 1514 (XV) and the process of decolonization following its adoption … The Court considers that, although resolution 1514 (XV) is formally a recommendation, it has a declaratory character with regard to the right to self-determination as a customary norm, in view of its content and the conditions of its adoption.[93]

Thereafter, the Court observed that common Article 1 to the two 1966 Covenants on Human Rights 'reaffirm[ed]' this right and, importantly for present purposes, that 'the nature and scope of the right to self-determination of peoples … were reiterated' in the Friendly

86 Among the authors who did not consider self-determination as a legal right, see Boris Mirkine-Guetzevitch, 'Quelques problèmes de la mise en œuvre de la Déclaration Universelle des Droits de l'Homme' (1953-II) 83 *Recueil des Cours* 351; Ivor Jennings, *The Approach to Self-Government* (Cambridge University Press, 1956) 56; Gerald Fitzmaurice, 'The Future of the International Legal System in the Circumstances of Today' in Institut du droit international (ed), *Livre du Centenaire 1873–1973: Evolution et perspectives du droit international* (S Karger, 1973) 233; Wolfgang Friedmann, 'General Course in Public International Law' (1969–II) 127 *Recueil des Cours* 187.

87 UK, Written Observations, para 4.4.

88 US, Written Statement, paras 4.46, 4.61 and 4.64, Written Observations, para 3.27; UK, Written Statement, para 8.65, Written Observations, paras 4.18–4.28.

89 UK, Written Statement, paras 8.55–8.58, Written Observations, para 4.48.

90 Chagos Marine Protected Area Arbitration, UK, Counter-Memorial, paras 7.14, 7.17 and 7.25. The arbitral award did not discuss this issue. See https://pca-cpa.org/en/cases/11/.

91 *Chagos* (n 42), para 148.

92 ibid, para 152.

93 ibid, paras 150, 152.

Relations Declaration, which further recognised this right as one of the 'basic principles of international law'.[94]

Regarding the hierarchy of the right to self-determination, there is substantial authority to conclude that this right both generates correlative obligations that must be respected by all States (*erga omnes*) and is a peremptory norm of international law.[95] The terminology used for such recognition has varied, however. In the *East Timor* case, the ICJ famously observed that '[t]he assertion that the right of peoples to self-determination, as it evolved from the Charter and from United Nations practice, has an *erga omnes* character, is irreproachable' and that self-determination is 'one of the essential principles of contemporary international law'.[96] Also in connection with East Timor, both the UN General Assembly and the Security Council has recognised 'the inalienable right of the people of Portuguese Timor to self-determination', calling upon all States to respect it.[97] While in the *Chagos* advisory opinion the Court did not pronounce about the *jus cogens* character of self-determination, it made explicit the point of the legal interest of all States in the respect of this right and their obligation to co-operate to put it into effect:

> Since respect for the right to self-determination is an obligation *erga omnes*, all States have a legal interest in protecting that right (see *East Timor (Portugal* v. *Australia), Judgment, I.C.J. Reports* 1995, p. 102, para. 29; see also *Barcelona Traction, Light and Power Company, Limited (Belgium* v. *Spain), Second Phase, Judgment, I.C.J. Reports* 1970, p. 32, para. 33). The Court considers that, while it is for the General Assembly to pronounce on the modalities required to ensure the completion of the decolonization of Mauritius, all Member States must co-operate with the United Nations to put those modalities into effect.[98]

Of particular note, the Court referred to the Friendly Relations Declaration (specifically to paragraph 2 of the statement on the right to self-determination) to flesh out the obligations arising for all States.[99]

Today, there can be no doubt about the peremptory norm character of the right to self-determination.[100] The establishment of protectorates or colonial domination in today's world under the cover of the law is simply unthinkable.

2 *Scope of the Norm*

2.1 *A 'Principle' and a 'Right'*

As early as 1952, the UN General Assembly decided to include the 'right' of peoples to self-determination in the future Covenant (or Covenants) on Human Rights and explicitly mentioned that self-determination was applicable to non-self-governing territories.[101] Thereafter, the

[94] ibid, paras 154–55.

[95] Fourth Report of the Special Rapporteur on Peremptory Norms of General International Law (*Jus Cogens*), Dire Tladi, UN Doc A/CN.4/727, paras 108–15 (providing a comprehensive review of international and domestic practice).

[96] *East Timor* (n 1), para 29. See also *Legal Consequences of the Construction of a Wall in the Occupied Palestinian Territory*, Advisory Opinion (n 1), paras 88, 149 and 155.

[97] See eg UNGA Res 3485 (XXX) (12 December 1975), UNSC Res 384 (1975), preamble and para 1.

[98] *Chagos* (n 42), para 180. In their declarations and opinions joined to the advisory opinions, the following judges expressly recognised the *jus cogens* character of the right of peoples to self-determination: Cançado Trindade and Robinson (joint declaration, para 8; Sebutinde (separate opinion, para 31), Robinson (separate opinion, paras 70–82).

[99] ibid, para 180.

[100] See Fourth Report of the Special Rapporteur on Peremptory Norms of General International Law (*Jus Cogens*), Dire Tladi, UN Doc A/CN.4/727, 48–52, paras 108–15.

[101] UNGA Res 545 (VI) (5 February 1952) (42–7–5).

recognition of a 'right', not merely an 'aspirational principle', followed two parallel and interconnected pathways.

One culminated with the adoption in December 1960 of Resolution 1514 (XV). Paragraph 2 of the Declaration contains what has become the canonical formulation of the principle, both as regard the express recognition of a 'right' and the holders and contents of it: 'All peoples have the right to self-determination; by virtue of that right they freely determine their political status and freely pursue their economic, social and cultural development.' Paragraph 1 gives the context of such right, namely the outlawing of colonialism: 'The subjection of peoples to alien subjugation, domination and exploitation constitutes a denial of fundamental human rights, is contrary to the Charter of the United Nations and is an impediment to the promotion of world peace and co-operation.' As noted earlier, the ICJ has recognised that it is in this formulation that the customary norm was 'declared' by Resolution 1514 (XV).

The second pathway led to the adoption of the International Covenant on Civil and Political Rights (ICCPR) and the International Covenant on Economic, Social and Cultural Rights (ICESCR) in 1966.[102] Article 1 common of the two Covenants reads:

> 1. All peoples have the right of self-determination. By virtue of that right they freely determine their political status and freely pursue their economic, social and cultural development.
> 2. All peoples may, for their own ends, freely dispose of their natural wealth and resources without prejudice to any obligations arising out of international economic co-operation, based upon the principle of mutual benefit, and international law. In no case may a people be deprived of its own means of subsistence.
> 3. The States Parties to the present Covenant, including those having responsibility for the administration of Non-Self-Governing and Trust Territories, shall promote the realization of the right of self-determination, and shall respect that right, in conformity with the provisions of the Charter of the United Nations.

Two traditional colonial powers, the United Kingdom and France, made reservations to this provision on the implicit grounds that the recognition of such right was not necessarily in conformity with the UN Charter itself. According to these two States, in case of contradiction between what is stipulated in Article 1 of the Covenants and Articles 1(2) and 73 of the Charter, the obligations under the Charter would prevail.[103] That amounted to an attempt both to play down the extent to which self-determination was recognised in the Charter and to make such restrictive interpretation prevail over common Article 1 to the two 1966 Covenants. The argument resurfaced in the context of the advisory proceedings relating to the Chagos Archipelago, but the ICJ rejected both premises, reasserting that self-determination is indeed a 'right' and it has been so under customary international as declared by Resolution 1514 (XV).[104]

[102] ICCPR, UNGA Res 2200A (XXI) (16 December 1966); ICESCR, UNGA Res 2200A (XXI) (16 December 1966).

[103] British reservation: 'First the Government of the United Kingdom declare their understanding that, by virtue of Article 103 of the Charter of the United Nations, in the event of any conflict between their obligations under Article 1 of the Covenant and their obligations under the Charter (in particular, under Articles 1, 2 and 73 thereof) their obligations under the Charter shall prevail.' French reservation: 'The Government of the Republic considers that, in accordance with Article 103 of the Charter of the United Nations, in case of conflict between its obligations under the Covenant and its obligations under the Charter (esp Articles 1 and 2 thereof), its obligations under the Charter will prevail.' https://treaties.un.org/Pages/ViewDetails.aspx?src=TREATY&mtdsg_no=IV-4&chapter=4&clang=_en#EndDec.

[104] *Chagos* (n 42), paras 152–54 (for the argument, see the Written Statement of the United Kingdom, 15 February 2018, paras 8.71–8.75).

The fact that the two Human Rights Covenants of 1966 begin with a common article that enshrines the right of self-determination of peoples does not mean that such right is an individual right, as the Human Rights Committee has observed on different occasions, rejecting requests from individuals who claimed to be victims of a violation of the right to self-determination.[105] By definition, it is a 'collective' right. Individuals participate as such in the exercise of this right together with the other members of the community to which he or she belongs. At the same time, in its General Comment on the first Article of the ICCPR, the Human Rights Committee noted that the realisation of the right to self-determination:

> is an essential condition for the effective guarantee and observance of individual human rights and for the promotion and strengthening of those rights. It is for that reason that States set forth the right of self-determination in a provision of positive law in both Covenants and placed this provision as Articles 1 apart from and before all the other rights in the two Covenants.[106]

Thus, despite attempts by colonial powers to cast doubts on the recognition of a 'right',[107] such recognition is no longer in question today:

> The recognition of a right of 'peoples' to self-determination is, of course, not the end of the matter. Different views have been expounded regarding the content and the holders of this right, with some terminological confusion arising from the use of the term 'people' or 'peoples' to refer to different collective subjects with different rights.

2.2 *Content of the Right*

Opinion No. 2 of the Arbitration Commission established in the framework of the Peace Conference for Yugoslavia (the 'Badinter Commission') stated that 'international law as it currently stands does not spell out all the implications of the right to self-determination'.[108] It is a rather surprising statement coming from an organ whose function was to determine the applicable law to the different aspects of the collapse of the former Yugoslavia.

Despite its abstraction, the right of peoples to self-determination has a content and the interpreter can (and must, if it is a judge or arbitrator or someone performing similar functions) draw the current legal consequences. Of course, the legal scope of the principle as it exists today may or may not please the interpreter or the person who has to apply it, but this is a question of *lege ferendae*. Its salient features can be summarised by saying that (i) the holders of the right of self-determination are the 'peoples', (ii) that, as noted earlier, they can invoke it *erga omnes*, (iii) that the principle is a peremptory norm of international law (*jus cogens*), (iv) that it is applicable everywhere and not only in cases of colonial or foreign domination and (v) that it includes the right of the people concerned to determine their internal and external (or international) political status in complete freedom.

In its 'internal' aspect, the principle implies the freedom for the people to choose their form of government, their economic and social system and the way to freely pursue their economic, social and cultural development. In its 'external' aspect, it grants the freedom to decide their

[105] See *Kitok v Sweden* (CCPR/C/33/D/197/1985); *RL v Canada* (CCPR/C/43/D/358/1989).

[106] CCPR General Comment No 12 on the Right to Self-Determination (Article 1 of the Covenant), 13 March 1984, HRI/GEN/1/Rev.9 (vol I).

[107] The British position was summarised as follows: 'it was not before the 1970s, at the earliest, that the United Kingdom accepted that it could be said that the principle of self-determination had become a right under general international law' (Counter-Memorial of the United Kingdom, *Chagos Marine Protected Area Arbitration (Mauritius v UK)*, Perm Ct Arb, 15 July 2013, para 7.17.

[108] Conference on Yugoslavia, Arbitration Commission, Opinion No 2, 11 January 1992, (1992) 31 ILM 1488, 1498.

international political status, be it independence, free association, integration with another State or any other status. These two aspects are mere manifestations of one indivisible norm, and therefore they cannot be severed from one another. There is no legal basis, whether in treaty or customary law, as reflected by declaratory resolutions, to support the existence of two separate categories or 'rights' to self-determination, one broader than the other. Paragraph 4 of the statement of self-determination in the Friendly Relations Declaration leaves no ambiguity on this point:

> The establishment of a sovereign and independent State, the free association or integration with an independent State or the emergence into any other political status freely determined by a people constitute modes of implementing the right of self-determination by that people.

The same is true of earlier statements. Both paragraph 2 of the 1960 Declaration on the Granting of Independence to Colonial Countries and Peoples and common Article 1 of the two 1966 Covenants on Human Rights use the same wording to state that 'by virtue of that right [all peoples] freely determine their political status', without any qualification of the scope of the right, which is one and indivisible.

The following sections discuss in some detail the relations between the right to self-determination and territorial sovereignty and then move to the examination of the meanings of 'people'.

2.3 *Implications for Territorial Sovereignty*

The principle of self-determination produces two main legal effects on territorial sovereignty. First, it extinguishes territorial titles of colonial powers, if they possessed it. For example, if colonial powers possessed sovereignty over their colonies, it extinguishes their sovereignty, even if their titles were validly acquired in the past. By virtue of the second rule of intertemporal law, colonial powers are recognised as mere administering States of the colonial territories that they still maintain under their control. Second, given the establishment of self-determination as a fundamental principle of international law, peoples that have not yet achieved statehood are also holders of territorial sovereignty. Because, by virtue of their right to self-determination, colonial peoples and peoples under military occupation or under foreign domination possess the right to determine their own status; as a corollary, they also possess the right to dispose of their territory.

One important implication is that their territory cannot be dismembered by the colonial power. As noted earlier, that argument was advanced by the UK in the advisory proceedings relating to the Chagos islands. Because the right was allegedly not yet consecrated, the dismemberment was an admissible reorganisation of the territories and Mauritius would only emerge as a sovereign State within the redesigned boundaries of the colonial power. The ICJ rejected this argument on the grounds that Resolution 1514(XV) protects territories from dismemberment in its paragraph 6, as does the Friendly Relations Declaration in its sixth paragraph.

The UK also invoked the principle of *uti possidetis juris*, which would guarantee territorial integrity of the newly independent State only to the extent of its territory at the time of independence. The question is whether, under this principle, a dismemberment by the colonial power made before independence would be possible and binding as regards the scope of the territory of a newly independent State. The examples furnished by the UK concerned cases of creation of two different colonial units from a single one, or the transfer of territory from one colonial unit to another. The situation of Chagos was completely different. The archipelago was separated from Mauritius with the purpose of being maintained under colonial rule.

The sixth paragraph of the Declaration clarifies the implications of self-determination for territorial sovereignty on this point by stating that:

> The territory of a colony or other Non-Self-Governing Territory has, under the Charter, a status separate and distinct from the territory of the State administering it; and such separate and distinct status under the Charter shall exist until the people of the colony or Non-Self-Governing Territory have exercised their right of self-determination in accordance with the Charter, and particularly its purposes and principles.

In other words, the colonial power cannot claim that its sovereignty over its metropolitan territory extends to the territory of its colonies: the territorial status of the latter is different. This status is of international concern and its main purpose is to allow the exercise of the right to self-determination by the peoples concerned, with the aim of putting an end to colonialism in all its forms and manifestations as early as possible.

2.4 *Self-Determination and* Uti Possidetis Juris

In *Burkina Faso/Mali*, the ICJ envisaged the possibility of conflict between *uti possidetis* and self-determination but disregarded it in the following manner:

> At first sight this principle conflicts outright with another one, the right of peoples to self-determination. In fact, however, the maintenance of the territorial status quo in Africa is often seen as the wisest course, to preserve what has been achieved by peoples who have struggled for their independence, and to avoid a disruption which would deprive the continent of the gains achieved by much sacrifice. The essential requirement of stability in order to survive, to develop and gradually to consolidate their independence in all fields, has induced African States judiciously to consent to the respecting of colonial frontiers, and to take account of it in the interpretation of the principle of self-determination of peoples.[109]

For its part, the Badinter Commission categorically asserted that the right to self-determination must not involve changes to existing boundaries at the time of independence (*uti possidetis juris*), except where States concerned agreed otherwise.[110]

However, it was advanced at the doctrinal level that self-determination overrides *uti possidetis juris*. The primacy of self-determination would be due to the fact that it is a supervening peremptory norm, to which another rule not having this character cannot be validly opposed.[111] Indeed, there is no need to resort to this hierarchical approach. Self-determination addresses the right to create a State (or to freely choose a specific connection with an existing one), while *uti possidetis juris* defines the territorial extension of the new entity. If there are existing boundaries, these are the boundaries of the new State. If the boundaries are subject to dispute, this is the situation inherited by the newly independent State. Insofar as there are no prior established boundaries, because the new State is a completely new entity without any prior administrative antecedent, *uti possidetis juris* has no role to play. As will be seen below, if one follows a 'territorial approach' to the identification of the holders of the right to self-determination (the 'peoples'), there is, in fact, no room for any contradiction at all.

109 *Burkina Faso/Mali*, ICJ Reports 1986, para 25.
110 Self-Determination, Arbitration Commission of the Peace Conference on Yugoslavia, Opinion No 2, 11 January 1992.
111 G Naldi, 'The Case Concerning the Frontier Dispute (Burkina Faso/Republic of Mali): *Uti Possidetis* in an African Perspective' (1987) 36 *International & Comparative Law Quarterly* 900 and 902–3.

2.5 *Secession*

The inclusion of self-determination in international law raised the question of its link with secession. As seen above, when this right was incorporated in the Charter and in later deliberations, the common view was that self-determination did not include a right to secession.

The term secession refers to the creation of a new independent entity through the separation of part of the territory and population of an existing State, without the consent of the latter. Secession can also take the form of the separation of part of the territory of a State in order to be incorporated as part of another State, without the consent of the former.[112]

In the early nineteenth century, when the Spanish colonies in the American continent declared independence, there was neither a legal right to self-determination nor an international law of 'decolonisation'. Therefore, the process took the form of secession and the existence of the newly independent States was a matter of fact and of recognition by the other members of the more limited community of States of the time.

This legal approach drastically changed in the second half of the twentieth century, during the UN era. Decolonisation, the most important means of creation of new States during the second half of the twentieth century, was not viewed by the international legal order as a case of secession. One of the reasons for this is summarised in paragraph 6 of the Friendly Relations Declaration, namely the separate status of the territorial basis of the non-self-governing territory. Nevertheless, secession remained – actually or potentially – another factual possibility as a means of creating States in the contemporary world.

The end of the Cold War brought about new secessionist aspirations and the strengthening and re-awakening of existing or dormant separatist claims in nearly all regions of the world. These concerned mostly the territory of the former USSR and the Socialist Federal Republic of Yugoslavia in the 1990s, and have continued with varying degrees of success. Notably, when some of these attempts at creating new States were successful, they occurred with the consent of the parent State.

The separation of Eritrea from Ethiopia (1993) led to the emergence of important disputes and a bloody armed conflict. Unilateral declarations of independence were issued with respect to Kosovo in February 2008, and regarding Southern Ossetia and Abkhazia some months later. In January 2011, in a referendum held in South Sudan on the basis of the Peace Agreement of 2005 between the Sudanese government and the Sudan People's Liberation Movement/Army, the overwhelming majority of participants decided in favour of the creation of a new State,[113] which came into being on 9 July 2011, and was the last member to be admitted to the United Nations.[114] In the context of the Ukrainian crisis, Crimea and the city of Sebastopol were incorporated into Russia after having declared 'independence', and self-proclaimed independent entities appeared in the eastern part of the country in 2014. Referenda on independence were held in Quebec (1995) and Scotland (2014), with the participants having opted for keeping these territories within their respective States. Another referendum took place in New Caledonia at the end of 2018, in which the population decided to maintain the territory within the French

[112] When a new State is formed from part of the territory of another State with its consent, it is a situation of 'devolution' rather than 'secession'. This presupposes an agreement between both entities and, as such, is not a source of conflict, at least with regard to the existence of the new State itself.

[113] The Comprehensive Peace Agreement between the Government of the Republic of the Sudan and the Sudan's People's Liberation Movement/Sudan People's Liberation Army is available on the website of the United Nations Mission in Sudan at http://unmis.unmissions.org. The results of the referendum of 9 January 2011 are discussed in the Report of the Secretary-General on the Sudan, 12 April 2011, UN Doc D/2011/239.

[114] UNGA Res 65/308 (14 July 2011).

Republic. Other controversial referenda were organised unilaterally in Iraqi Kurdistan and in Catalonia (Spain) in 2017.

The question of secession was brought before the ICJ in connection with the unilateral declaration of independence of Kosovo. Yet, the advisory opinion rendered by the Court avoids the core issue and focuses, instead, on the aspirational character of declarations of independence and the fact that – in a controversial assertion contradicted by clear evidence – the authors of the Declaration of Independence were not the provisional institutions of self-government created on the basis of Resolution 1244 (1999) of the Security Council.[115]

The ambiguity of the Court has been exploited in other circumstances in which secession has been at stake. The Russian annexation of Crimea has been justified by Russia as a secession followed by integration with Russia on the grounds that international law does not prohibit unilateral declarations of independence.[116]

The question, of course, is not whether a specific rule prohibiting secession exists. The matter cannot be assessed in a vacuum and it remains governed by the fundamental principles of international law, including the prohibition of the use of force, respect for sovereign equality and territorial integrity, as well as the applicability or not of the right of peoples to self-determination. By focusing on declarations of independence as mere expressions of will not prohibited by international law, the *Kosovo* advisory opinion indirectly recognised that the right of peoples to self-determination was not applicable to the case.

2.6 *The Doctrine of Remedial Secession Based on the 'Saving Clause'*

The idea that a minority within a State that is victim of grave breaches of human rights is entitled to secede as a remedy of last resort has been discussed for a long while. It was officially invoked by some States and strongly rejected by others during the Kosovo advisory proceedings.[117]

To support the doctrine of 'remedial secession', an *a contrario* reading of paragraph 7 of the formulation in the Friendly Relations Declaration is advanced. The territorial integrity of States would be preserved insofar as the State concerned conducts itself 'in compliance with the principle of equal rights and self-determination' and thus possessing 'a government representing the whole people belonging to the territory without distinction as to race, creed or colour'. According to this doctrine, if the minority is oppressed and the government of the State does not include its representation, then the minority will be entitled to separate since the territorial integrity of the State would no longer be guaranteed.

As mentioned above, the *travaux préparatoires* do not allow such a conclusion to be reached. A careful reading of the seventh paragraph within its context and in the light of the object and purpose of the Declaration also leads to the disregarding of this doctrine. The object and purpose of paragraph 7 was to make clear that self-determination would not run against the

[115] *Kosovo*, Advisory Opinion (n 1), para 105. For a comment, see Marcelo Kohen and Katherine Del Mar, 'The Kosovo Advisory Opinion and UNSCR 1244 (1999): A Declaration of "Independence from International Law"?' (2011) 24(1) *Leiden Journal of International Law* 109, 114–18.

[116] Vladimir Putin, Address of the President of the Russian Federation to State Duma deputies, Federation Council members, heads of Russian regions and civil society representatives in the Kremlin, 18 March 2014, http://en.kremlin.ru/events/president/news/20603.

[117] Unilateral Declaration of Independence of Kosovo, Finland, Written Statement, 4–5, paras 9–10; Ireland, Written Statement, 2, 8–10, paras 27–32; Poland, Written Statement, 26, para 6.10; United Kingdom, Written Statement, 92 (however, in its Written Comments, 5–6, para 10, the United Kingdom considers that the Court should not apply this concept in this case); *Contra*: Serbia, Written Statement, 214–30, paras 589–625, Written Comments, 142–49, paras 339–59; Argentina, Written Statement, 34, paras 85–86; Cyprus, Written Statement, 36–38, paras 140–47; Spain, Written Comments, 5–6, para 8; Iran, Written Statement, 6–7, para 4.1; Romania, Written Statement, 42, para 147 and 44, para 156; Russia, Written Statement, 36–38, paras 97–103; Slovakia, Written Statement, para 28.

territorial integrity of existing States. It is for this reason that it is called the 'safeguard' or the 'saving clause'. The historical context in which the Declaration was adopted cannot be neglected either. In the decade that ended with its adoption, the United Nations actively opposed Katangese separatism in the Congo as well as Biafra's attempted secession from Nigeria. Just some months before the adoption of the Declaration, Secretary-General U Thant made his famous statement:

> As far as the question of secession of a particular section of a State is concerned, the United Nations attitude is unequivocable. As an International Organization, the United Nations has never accepted and does not accept and I do not believe will ever accept the principle of secession of a part of its member States.[118]

The text of the paragraph is indeed an interpretation of the six foregoing paragraphs, nothing in them 'must be understood as authorising or encouraging any action which would dismember or impair, totally or in part, the territorial integrity or political unity of sovereign and independent States'. The addressees of this paragraph are the actual or potential entities or groups claiming to exercise the right to self-determination. The end of the paragraph recalls nevertheless that States so protected must conduct themselves in compliance with the principle and consequently their government must represent the whole people belonging to the territory without distinction. This is a clear reference to States in which policies such as apartheid – a main concern at that time – were contrary to the principle of self-determination. It was not concerned with secession at all. This interpretation is also reinforced by the eighth and last paragraph, which is a repetition of paragraph 6 of Resolution 1514 (XV) and its addressees are States.

In the *Kosovo* advisory opinion the ICJ decided not to take an explicit stance on the matter, although it ascertained that there were 'radically different views' among those having participated in the proceedings about a right to 'remedial secession'.[119]

3 *Holders of the Right to Self-Determination*

3.1 *The Legal Definition of 'Peoples'*

At the end of the day, the crucial aspect of the entire question of self-determination lies in determining who holds this right or, in other words, what is meant by 'peoples' in the sense of international law. The legal notion of 'people' may or may not coincide with any sociological ones. As a matter of course, it cannot simply adopt the definition any specific group gives itself. No legal system gives to its subject the possibility to decide for themselves whether they are subjects or not and in which category. It is the legal system itself that determines whether or not one is a subject and what one's rights and obligations may be. Hence, 'peoples' as holders of the right to self-determination in international law are neither defined through self-qualification nor through exclusively socio-cultural criteria.

The first conclusion then is that not every population inhabiting a territory constitutes a 'people' from this perspective. The Court reflected this basic premise in its *Western Sahara* and *Chagos* advisory opinions:

> [t]he validity of the principle of self-determination, defined as the need to pay regard to the freely expressed will of peoples, is not affected by the fact that in certain cases the General Assembly

[118] (1970) 7 *UN Monthly Chronicle* 36.
[119] *Kosovo*, Advisory Opinion (n 1), para 82.

> has dispensed with the requirement of consulting the inhabitants of a given territory. *Those instances were based either on the consideration that a certain population did not constitute a 'people' entitled to self-determination* or on the conviction that a consultation was totally unnecessary, in view of special circumstances.[120]

International law distinguishes different types of human communities with different rights. 'Peoples', 'minorities'[121] and 'indigenous peoples'[122] are three legal categories whose existence in a given territory implies different consequences as to the possibility to decide about territorial sovereignty. Only 'peoples', in the international legal sense of the word, are holders of the right to self-determination. As an example, the ICJ's *Wall* advisory opinion, while discussing the applicability of the principle to the issue, noted that as regards the right of self-determination, 'the existence of a Palestinian "people" is no longer an issue'.[123]

National, religious, linguistic and other minorities enjoy their specific rights, which do not include the right to self-determination. If the opposite were true (i.e. if minorities were 'peoples' entitled to self-determination), there would be no need to make this legal distinction. It is worth mentioning the commentary to Article 27 of the ICCPR (related to individual belonging to minorities) made by the Human Rights Committee in this regard:

> 3.1. The Covenant draws a distinction between the right to self- determination and the rights protected under article 27. The former is expressed to be a right belonging to peoples and is dealt with in a separate part (Part 1) of the Covenant. Self-determination is not a right cognizable under the Optional Protocol. Article 27, on the other hand, relates to rights conferred on individuals as such and is included, like the articles relating to other personal rights conferred on individuals, in Part III of the Covenant and is cognizable under the Optional Protocol.
>
> 3.2. The enjoyment of the rights to which article 27 relates does not prejudice the sovereignty and territorial integrity of a State party.[124]

The fact that there is no explicit definition of 'peoples' in any international instrument must not detract the interpreter, both practitioners and scholars, from the identification of the holder of a recognised right in international law. A look at the relevant instruments and practice followed allows such right-holders to be identified. In order to determine who is the holder of the right to self-determination, international law follows a 'territorial approach'. Undoubtedly, the right of self-determination applies to peoples in non-self-governing territories, including colonies,[125] mandates or trust territories recognised as such by the relevant international organ.[126] Still in these cases, it is for the relevant supervisory organ to recognise the existence (or not) of a people or even a plurality of them in the territory concerned. Beyond the decolonisation context,

[120] *Western Sahara*, Advisory Opinion (n 36) 12, 33, para 59 (16 October); *Chagos* (n 42), Advisory Opinion, para 158 (emphasis added).

[121] See Declaration on the Rights of Persons Belonging to National or Ethnic, Religious and Linguistic Minorities; European Framework Convention for the Protection of National Minorities, Council of Europe, UNGA Res 47/135 (10 November 1994).

[122] See UN Declaration on the Rights of Indigenous Peoples, UNGA Res 61/295 (13 September 2007).

[123] *Construction of a Wall on Occupied Palestinian Territory*, Advisory opinion (n 1), para 118.

[124] CCPR General Comment No 23 on the Rights of Minorities (Article 27 of the Covenant) CCPR/C/21/Rev.1/Add.5 (1994).

[125] The definition of non-self-governing territories given in principle IV of UNGA Res 1541 (XV) (15 December 1960) is normally used to define peoples subject to colonial domination: 'a territory which is geographically separate and is distinct ethnically and/or culturally from the country administering it'. The primary criterion is of a territorial nature, but ethno-cultural considerations are also taken into account, particularly to avoid including in the definition the own populations exported by the colonial power to the colonial territory.

[126] For a consistent view see Bernt Elsner, *Die Bedeutung des Volkes im Völkerrecht. Unter besonderer Berücksichtigung der historischen Entwicklung und der Praxis des Selbstbestimmungsrechts der Völker* (Duncker & Humblot, 2000).

the notion of a people applies to the entire population inhabiting an independent State, even when there are minorities within it. The exception to this is when the State itself recognises that it is composed of several peoples entitled to exercise their right of self-determination. Some examples include the former Yugoslavia, Serbia-Montenegro, Saint-Kitts and Nevis, Ethiopia and Uzbekistan.[127] Such recognition entitles these peoples to exercise a right to self-determination.

In addition, there are also cases in which human communities that were not considered as holders of the right to self-determination succeeded in creating new States. This was the case in Bangladesh and South Sudan. It was then their factual capacity to create a sovereign State that transformed these communities in 'peoples'. It is to be noticed that in the former case the recognition of the parent State came later, whereas in the latter case it came earlier, allowing the community to decide upon the creation of a new State. In its *Kosovo* advisory opinion, the ICJ noticed that, if many States were created during the second half of the twentieth century as a result of the exercise of the right to self-determination, there were other 'declarations of independence' outside of this context.[128]

At first sight, the territorial approach may appear to put more emphasis on geography than on the human factor. In *Western Sahara*, Judge Dillard wrote that 'it is for the people to determine the destiny of the territory and not the territory the destiny of the people'.[129] This assertion sounds sympathetic. However, as Judge Rosalyn Higgins commented in her Hague lectures, the territorial question must come first since until it is determined where territorial sovereignty lies, it is impossible to see if the inhabitants have a right of self-determination.[130] Indeed, it is impossible to define a 'people' in the international legal sense without a prior specific determination of its spatial scope.

The definition of 'people' in international law then is a legal one and practice in the last half-century shows that the key criterion is the territorial basis. It is the territory which defines the 'people' in legal terms rather than the other way around. Neither objective conceptions of 'peoples' (based on ethnic, religious, linguistic and other considerations) nor subjective ones (based on the 'self-qualification' of a group as a people) or any combination thereof provide clear guidance as to the definition of peoples in international legal practice. These different elements can of course be taken into account, but they are not decisive. It is on the basis of the territorial approach that the inhabitants of Taiwan, Hong Kong or Macau have not been considered a separate people. All these populations are technically part of the Chinese people. Similarly, the population of Mayotte, an island which is part of the Comoros Islands, is only a component of the Comorian people, despite its declared will to be considered as French.[131] Similarly, self-determination has not been applied to the inhabitants of the Falkland/Malvinas Islands by the UN General Assembly and its Decolonization Committee.[132] The *Chagos* advisory opinion also

[127] Constitution of Ethiopia, Art 47; Constitution of Saint Kitts and Nevis, Art 113; Constitution of Uzbekistan, Art 74; Constitution of Serbia-Montenegro, Art 60. In the latter case, Montenegro effectively exercised its right to self-determination and became independent in 2006 following a referendum.

[128] *Kosovo*, Advisory Opinion (n 1), para 79.

[129] *Western Sahara*, Advisory Opinion (n 36) 122.

[130] Rosalyn Higgins, 'International Law and the Avoidance, Containment and Resolution of Disputes: General Course on Public International Law' (1991) 230 *Recueil des Cours* 174.

[131] See UNGA Res 3385 (XXX) (12 November 1975), in which the Comoros is admitted as a member of the United Nations and which explicitly states that the four islands are part of the archipelago, and Res 32/7 (1 November 1977), on the 'Question of the Comorian island of Mayotte'.

[132] See among others UNGA Resolutions 2065 (XX) (16 December 1965), 3160 (XXVIII) (14 December 1973), 31/49 (1 December 1976), 37/9 (4 November 1982) and 38/12 (16 November 1983). The UK amendment project of what became Res 40/21 (27 November 1985), which referred to the applicability of the right to self-determination to the

offers an important insight in this regard: the people entitled to self-determination considered for the ICJ analysis were the Mauritian people, which includes the inhabitants of the Chagos Archipelago, not the latter separately.[133]

In this regard, international recognition by the relevant organ is much more important, even decisive, than the recognition of new States by their peers. The UN practice on decolonisation is, indeed, decisive. An example is the position of the UN General Assembly on the creation of two different States in the former Palestine, due to the recognition of two different peoples.[134] By contrast, the absence of a recognised separate people in the Falkland/Malvinas has led the General Assembly to recommend an end to this colonial situation through the settlement of the sovereignty dispute between Argentina and the United Kingdom, just taking into account the 'interests' of the population but not their 'will'.[135] This analysis is confirmed by instances in which some States have authorised the holding of referenda in parts of their territory to determine whether this territory will become independent. The holding of these referenda is the product of the decision of the State concerned, and not the result of an obligation imposed by international law. It is a matter that international law leaves to the discretion of the domestic law of States.

3.2 *Other 'Peoples' and Other 'Rights'*

The fact that some human communities that are not recognised as peoples under international law do not possess a right to decide the fate of the territory they inhabit does not mean that they do not possess other important collective rights. Certain populations within existing States, such as 'indigenous peoples', 'tribal peoples' and 'first nations' are holders of collective rights recognised by instruments such as the African Charter of Human and Peoples' Rights,[136] the International Labour Organization (ILO) 1989 Convention No. 169 Concerning Indigenous and Tribal Peoples in Independent Countries,[137] or the 2007 UN Declaration on the Rights of Indigenous Peoples.[138]

Yet, none of these instruments clearly confer a right to self-determination with the same scope as the one discussed so far on these other groups. Article 1(3) of the ILO Convention No. 69 expressly states that 'The use of the term *peoples* in this Convention shall not be construed as having any implications as regards the rights which may attach to the term under international law.' Thus, the Convention preserves the understanding of the right to self-determination of peoples developed under the aegis of UN practice.

The situation of Article 20 of the African Charter, although more complex, does not question the conclusion reached in the previous section of this chapter. Article 20 of the African Charter states:

1. All peoples shall have the right to existence. They shall have the unquestionable and inalienable right to self-determination. They shall freely determine their political status

inhabitants of the islands, was rejected by the UN General Assembly (see Doc A/40/L.20 of 22 November 1985. See also (1985) 56 *British Yearbook of International Law* 402–6 and (1985) 31 *Annuaire Français de Droit International* 560). For the Decolonization Committee, see the resolution adopted on 21 June 2018: A/AC.109/2018/L.8.

[133] Only two judges expressed a different view: see the declaration by Judge Abraham and the separate opinion of Judge Gaja, para 6.

[134] UNGA Res 181 (II) (29 November 1947).

[135] See n 132.

[136] African Charter of Human and Peoples' Rights, OAU, 27 June 1981.

[137] Convention Concerning Indigenous and Tribal Peoples in Independent Countries, ILO C169, 27 June 1989.

[138] UN Declaration on the Rights of Indigenous Peoples, UNGA Res 61/295 (13 September 2007).

and shall pursue their economic and social development according to the policy they have freely chosen.

2. Colonized or oppressed peoples shall have the right to free themselves from the bonds of domination by resorting to any means recognized by the international community.
3. All peoples shall have the right to the assistance of the States parties to the present Charter in their liberation struggle against foreign domination, be it political, economic or cultural.

The specific content of the right to self-determination in this provision does not mention 'independence' as a possible outcome, although that possibility is implicit in the free determination of their political status (paragraph 1) and right to 'free themselves' or 'to assistance . . . in their liberation struggle' (paragraphs 2 and 3). What remains undefined is the term 'peoples'. One prominent commentator has noted, in this regard, that this term 'varies in nature according to the right which is to be implemented'.[139] In *Mgwanga Gunme* v. *Cameroon*, the African Commission observed that the term had been deliberately left open so as to afford flexibility in the subsequent implementation of the African Charter.[140] In this context, the complexity comes from the use of the term 'peoples' and the term 'rights' to refer to different realities as explained by the African Court in the *Ogiek* case, although with some lack of clarity:

> It is generally accepted that, in the context of the struggle against foreign domination in all its forms, the Charter primarily targets the peoples comprising the populations of the countries struggling to attain independence and national sovereignty . . .
>
> In the circumstances, the question is whether the notion 'peoples' used by the Charter covers not only the population as the constituent elements of the State, but also the ethnic groups or communities identified as forming part of the said population within a constituted State. In other words, the question that arises is whether the enjoyment of the rights unquestionably recognised for the constituent peoples of the population of a given State can be extended to include sub-state ethnic groups and communities that are part of that population . . .
>
> In the view of the Court, the answer to this question is in the affirmative, *provided such groups or communities do not call into question the sovereignty and territorial integrity of the State without the latter's consent*. It would in fact be difficult to understand that the States which are the authors of the Charter intended, for example, to automatically recognize for the ethnic groups and communities that constitute their population, the right to self-determination and independence guaranteed under Article 20(1) of the Charter, which in this case would amount to a veritable right to secession. On the other hand, nothing prevents other peoples' rights, such as the right to development (Article 22), the right to peace and security (Article 23) or the right to a healthy environment (Article 24) from being recognised, where necessary, specifically for the ethnic groups and communities that constitute the population of a State.[141]

Thus, the collective rights recognised in respect of 'other' peoples are also 'other' rights, not including the right to self-determination as understood in UN practice.

Similar considerations are applicable to the right to self-determination recognised in the preamble and Articles 3 and 4 of the 2007 UN Declaration on the Rights of Indigenous Peoples, which was perhaps the most controversial issue of the drafting process and possibly responsible for a

[139] Fatsah Ouguergouz, *The African Charter on Human and Peoples' Rights: A Comprehensive Agenda for Human Dignity and Sustainable Development* (Martinus Nijhoff, 2002) 211.

[140] Communication 266/03, *Kevin Mgwanga Gunme et al* v *Cameroon* (2009), para 169.

[141] *African Commission on Human and Peoples' Rights* v *Republic of Kenya (Ogiek case)*, ACtHPR App 006/2012, Judgment of 26 May 2017, paras 197–99 (emphasis added).

delay of ten years in its adoption.[142] Indeed, whereas Article 3 applies to 'indigenous peoples' the wording used in common Article 1 to the two 1966 Covenants on Human Rights, Article 4 immediately adds that:

> Indigenous peoples, in exercising their right to self-determination, have the right to autonomy or self-government in matters relating to their internal and local affairs, as well as ways and means for financing their autonomous functions.

Moreover, Article 46(1) of the Declaration clearly states that:

> Nothing in this Declaration may be interpreted as implying for any State, people, group or person any right to engage in any activity or to perform any act contrary to the Charter of the United Nations or *construed as authorizing or encouraging any action which would dismember or impair, totally or in part, the territorial integrity or political unity of sovereign and independent States*. [emphasis added]

This language is familiar. It is taken from the saving clause (paragraph 7) in the formulation of self-determination in the Friendly Relations Declaration. Since the adoption of this Declaration, one can conclude that, together with peoples and minorities, a third legal category has been delineated with specific rights: that of indigenous peoples. If one follows the Declaration, they are holders of the right to self-determination, but only in its internal dimension.

4 *The 'Human Factor' and 'Self-Determination' in Territorial Disputes*

Outside the principle of self-determination, the human factor still plays an important role in territorial disputes today, not with regard to the fate of the territory, but with respect to the rights and obligations that must be applied and respected with regard to the inhabitants. In the *El Salvador/Honduras* case, the ICJ held that:

> The effect of the Chamber's Judgment will however not be that certain areas will 'become' part of Honduras; the Chamber's task is to declare what areas are, and what are not, already part of the one State and the other. If Salvadorians have settled in areas of Honduras, neither that fact, nor the consequences of the application of Honduran law to their properties, can affect the matter.[143]

But the Chamber also recognised that:

> [T]he situation may arise in some areas whereby a number of the nationals of the one Party will, following the delimitation of the disputed sectors, find themselves living in the territory of the other, and property rights apparently established under the laws of the one Party will be found to have been granted over land which is part of the territory of the other. The Chamber has every confidence that such measures as may be necessary to take into account of this situation will be framed and carried out by both Parties, in full respect for acquired rights, and in a humane and orderly manner.[144]

[142] See Marc Weller, 'Self-Determination of Indigenous Peoples: Articles 3, 4, 5, 18, 23 and 46(1)' in Jessie Hohmann and Marc Weller (eds), *The UN Declaration on the Rights of Indigenous Peoples: A Commentary* (Oxford University Press, 2018) 116.

[143] *Land, Island and Maritime Frontier Dispute (El Salvador/Honduras: Nicaragua intervening)*, Judgment, ICJ Reports 1992 351, 419, para 97 (11 September).

[144] ibid at para 66. In *Croatia/Slovenia*, the tribunal also noted that 'in some limited areas (such as the situations described in paragraphs 565 and 630) the course of the boundary, as it results from an application of the law, may not be considered the most practical boundary, whether for reasons of physical or human geography. For the avoidance of

Similarly, in the *Cameroon* v. *Nigeria* case, the nationals of the parties had occupied villages located on the other side of the boundary. The Court reaffirmed in this context that:

> [I]t has no power to modify a delimited boundary line, even in a case where a village previously situated on one side of the boundary has spread beyond it. It is instead up to the Parties to find a solution to any resultant problems, with a view to respecting the rights and interests of the local population.[145]

In the same case, the Court dismissed the relevance of services that Nigeria had provided to the inhabitants of the disputed territory. Although they could be seen as *effectivités*, these Nigerian actions came up against the established title of Cameroon over the disputed territory. In such circumstances, preference is to be given to the title.[146]

The human factor can also play a role in territorial disputes when equity *infra legem* is applicable. Faced with its duty to make a decision in circumstances in which sovereignty does not appear in a clear manner from the available evidence, a tribunal can choose a solution that better reflects the human factor. For example, in *Burkina Faso/Mali*, the ICJ divided the pools in the disputed area in such a way as to allow equal access to water in these arid regions.[147] In the *Frontier Dispute (Burkina Faso/Niger)*, the Court was also guided by such considerations when deciding the point at which the boundary line reaches the 'River Sirba at Bossebangou'. The Court observed that it was unclear whether the boundary line stopped at one or the other of the banks of the river or that the river was attributed in its entirety to one of the parties. As a result, the Court held that:

> In this regard, the Court notes that the requirement concerning access to water resources of all the people living in the riparian villages is better met by a frontier situated in the river than on one bank or the other. Accordingly, the Court concludes that, on the basis of the Arrêté, the endpoint of the frontier line in the region of Bossébangou is located in the River Sirba. This endpoint is more specifically situated on the median line because, in a non-navigable river with the characteristics of the Sirba, that line best meets the requirements of legal security inherent in the determination of a boundary.[148]

When a decision on territorial sovereignty subjects a group or a private person to the sovereignty of another State, there is a rebuttable presumption that vested rights acquired in good faith in the area – or at least the narrower category of 'traditional rights' – are not affected. After reviewing the relevant case law, the arbitral tribunal in the *Abyei* case reached the following conclusion:

> The jurisprudence of international courts and tribunals as well as international treaty practice lend additional support to the principle that, in the absence of an explicit prohibition to the contrary, the transfer of sovereignty in the context of boundary delimitation should not be construed to extinguish traditional rights to the use of land (or maritime resources).[149]

doubt, the Tribunal reiterates that, while the present Award fixes the boundary in such areas with binding effect (as the Parties have requested), the Award does not preclude the Parties from subsequently reaching agreement between themselves on practical arrangements concerning the boundary.' *Croatia/Slovenia Arbitration*, Award, Perm Ct Arb, 29 June 2017, 1, 114, para 357.

145 *Land and Maritime Boundary between Cameroon and Nigeria (Cameroon v Nigeria: Equitorial Guinea intervening)*, Merits, ICJ Reports 2002, 303, 373–74, para 123 (10 October). See also 370, para 107.

146 ibid 415, paras 222–23.

147 *Frontier Dispute (Burkina Faso/Mali)*, Judgment (n 109) 554, para 150.

148 *Frontier Dispute (Benin/Niger)*, Judgment, ICJ Reports 2005, 90, 85, para 101 (12 July).

149 *Delimitation of the Abyei Area between the Government of Sudan and the Sudan People's Liberation Movement/Army*, Award, Perm Ct Arb, 22 July 2009, RIAA, vol XXX, 145, para 263. *Concerning maritime delimitation, reference may be*

VI SELF-DETERMINATION AS A REVOLUTIONARY PRINCIPLE

In what became his last written contribution, the former President of the ICJ, the late Sir Robert Jennings, questioned the legal character of the principle of self-determination due to its easy manipulation in territorial matters:

> International lawyers have tended not to look for better ways of making policy territorial decisions but have instead tried to extend the legal 'modes'; as for example by the transformation of 'self-determination' from being a useful political notion, into a 'right' of 'self-determination', apparently enjoyed by 'peoples'. This circular and question-begging 'right' still calls for a political decision about what is a 'people' for this purpose, as indeed also what status they self-determine on a scale varying between independence and dependence. How much better it would have been to recognize that wise or right policy sometimes makes certain changes desirable and that there should therefore be a regular legal machinery for making changes on grounds of policy, rather than a 'right' that actually by the 'self' element puts a premium on successful violence.[150]

The ostensible manipulations by some States of the right to self-determination are well known,[151] as is the fact that any separatist movement within States claims to be the representative of 'the people' and that 'the people' are entitled to self-determination. However, these situations must not lead to the denial of the legal existence of this right. This is not the first time that a right is misconstrued and will certainly not be the last.

Self-determination has become a fundamental principle of international law. All relevant texts affirm that 'all peoples have the right to self-determination'. This clear assertion contradicts the view that only peoples subject to colonial, racist or foreign domination are beneficiaries of the right to self-determination. Peoples who are not in these situations also hold the same right. Situations of colonial, racist or foreign domination are simply flagrant cases of violations of the right of peoples to self-determination. The fact of not being deprived of the exercise of one's right does not mean that one is not – or no longer – a holder of the right concerned. General Assembly Resolution 56/141 on the 'Universal realization of the right of peoples to self-determination' is correct when it reaffirms, on the one hand, the right of peoples 'under colonial, foreign or alien occupation' and, on the other hand, that foreign military intervention and occupation are threatening to suppress, or have already suppressed, the right to self-determination of sovereign peoples and nations'.[152] There are people who have already achieved statehood and others who have not. Both categories, however, hold the same right of peoples to self-determination.

The interpretation of self-determination followed here is the one that conciliates the right of peoples and the equality of human beings within existing States, no matter their origin, language, religion or other differences. Other alleged 'contemporary' interpretations of the principle are rather the expression of atavistic approaches based on ethnic considerations or on the simplistic idea that the way to solve ethnic, regional or cultural problems within States is by their division. For the time being, international law does not follow this dangerous path, while at the same time favours the liberation of those 'peoples' whose exercise of the right to self-determination continues to be denied. It is in this sense that it can be categorised as a revolutionary principle, not an anarchical one.

made, with certain reservations, to the award in Maritime Delimitation Procedure (Eritrea/Yemen) (Second Stage of the Proceedings), Award, 1999, RIAA, vol XXII, 335, 357–8, paras 92 and 95 (17 December).

[150] Robert Y Jennings, 'The Imbalance of the International Law System' (2004) 6 *Forum de droit international* 127–28.

[151] See Marcelo Kohen, 'Sur quelques vicissitudes du droit des peuples à disposer d'eux-mêmes' in N Angelet, O Corten and P Klein (eds), *Droit du pouvoir, pouvoir du droit, Mélanges offerts à Jean Salmon* (Bruylant, 2007) 961–82.

[152] UNGA Res 56/141 (11 February 2002).

8

Sovereign Equality

Martti Koskenniemi and Ville Kari

I INTRODUCTION

Why did the legal principle of sovereign equality of States need a restatement in 1970? After all, it was not only expressly declared in the UN Charter ('The Organization is based on the sovereign equality of its members', Article 2(1)) but also deeply embedded in the conceptual structure of international law. One could say (and some have said) that the restatement was simply a redundancy.[1] To be a 'State' was to possess sovereignty, and 'sovereignty' meant that one was not subordinated to another entity. All sovereigns would thus be equal in their non-subordination to each other. But whatever purists might say, the Friendly Relations Declaration was intended by its initiators neither as an exercise around the meaning or logic of the key concepts of the Charter nor as a formal celebration of their 25-year-old existence. It was instead part of the push by the decolonised world, the majority of the UN members that had not participated in the drafting of the Charter, to give its major provisions a meaning that would better include their objectives.[2]

The debate on the Friendly Relations Declaration in the various Special Committees during 1963–70 provides a good example of how international legal concepts are used as 'fighting words' in order to advance or oppose specific policies. Who could possibly have anything against 'Friendly Relations and Co-operation'? Is it not obvious that this is what all members of the United Nations – indeed all human beings – crave? And yet, some Western lawyers were dubious of the project from the start. In a long review of its preparatory work until 1966, George Haight from the United States, for example, regarded the title as a 'euphemism for "peaceful coexistence" and an old stalking horse in the Cold War', created to 'meet the propaganda challenge of the Soviet bloc'. A 'major objective', he wrote, was to 'foment wars of liberation in order to assist allegedly "enslaved peoples" in the struggles against allegedly "imperialist

[1] For Arangio-Ruiz, sovereign equality is 'too tautological for words'. Gaetano Arangio-Ruiz, *The UN Declaration on Friendly Relations and the System of Sources of International Law* (Sijthoff & Noordhoff, 1979) 144.

[2] There is a tendency in academic literature to diminish the programmatic aspect of the 1970 declaration and to take the principle of 'sovereign equality', as Brad Roth puts it, 'no[t] as a political slogan, but as a reference to a core set of legal entitlements that the legal order attributes equally to all states'. Brad Roth, *Sovereign Equality and Moral Disagreement* (Oxford University Press, 2011) 53. As such, it appears as a merely analytical devise which – while perhaps useful from a moral-jurisprudential perspective – fails to capture its role in the late-twentieth-century debates over the character of the international order.

oppressors"'.[3] We may (indeed we should) disagree with the tone of Haight's point, but not really with his perspective.

The project for a declaration was not just to spell out truisms that would leave the United Nations and the world as it was. True, that is how many Western representatives saw it during the preparatory process, when they were keen to stress that the Declaration would, above all, deal with the 'juridical equality of States' and 'respect' for their 'personality'.[4] But for the representatives of the formerly colonised countries – supported by the socialist bloc – it was instead part of the collective effort that had commenced by the passing of the Decolonization Declaration (UNGA Res 1514 (1960)) and would peak in the Charter of Economic Rights and Duties of States (UNGA Res 3281 (1974)). With all these instruments, the Third World countries, or the Group of 77, aimed at tweaking the Charter and the activities of the United Nations towards their political objectives, especially the push towards more than the merely *formal* equality that UN membership offered to them.[5] In the drafting process, this was most clearly visible in the failed effort by the representatives from developing States to include a reference to what was labelled '[t]he right of States to dispose freely of their national wealth and natural resources'. For these representatives, a declaration of 'sovereign equality' in 1970 would need to draw attention to the world's immense political, military and above all economic inequalities. Failing to go beyond 'juridical equality' would underline the hypocrisy of an institution that tolerated and, as history would show, helped to produce the massively unequal distribution of power and resources between what we have now learned to call the global South and the developed North. 'Sovereign equality' was a fighting expression, not a logical redundancy. Everyone understood that it was to be read as a call for transformation.

We now know that nothing came of that effort. According to the most recent Oxfam report, 'eighty two percent of the wealth generated [in 2018] went to the richest one percent of the global population, while the 3.7 billion people who make up the poorest half of the world saw no increase in their wealth'.[6] Such data could, of course, be produced endlessly. It has become part of the background noise that merges with the flow of global information which, instead of inciting to action, contributes to the melancholic consciousness around the world that acquiesces to the inevitability of what exists. What a difference half a century makes! In 1970 the United Nations had begun a number of reform projects to attack the injustices of the old world – from control of multinational companies to the sharing of space technology, from the distribution of marine resources to supporting national liberation movements. It was the point of the Declaration to bring such and many other projects under a single restatement that would show

[3] George Haight, 'Principles of International Law Concerning Friendly Relations and Cooperation among States' (1966) 1 *The International Lawyer* 96–97.

[4] See eg the proposal by the United Kingdom, UN Doc A/AC.119/L.8, included in Report of the Special Committee on Principles of International Law concerning Friendly Relations and Co-operation among States, UN Doc A/5746 (16 November 1964), 149 (para 296). The proposal listed four elements in the principles: (a) that States are juridically equal; (b) that each State enjoys the rights inherent in its sovereignty; (c) that the personality of the State is respected, as well as its territorial integrity and political independence; (d) that the State should, under international order, comply faithfully with its duties and obligations.

[5] This objective was well expressed in the emblematic work of a late phase in that era, Mohammed Bedjaoui, *Towards a New International Economic Order* (UNESCO, 1979). 'Sovereign equality', he wrote there, was to be 'formulated afresh so as to restore to each State the basic elements of its national independence on the economic level' (at 87). In the 'vast and prodigious battle against inequality', UN General Assembly resolutions would be the favoured instruments of the Third World (at 13 and 138–43).

[6] 'Richest 1 Percent Bagged 82 Percent of Wealth Created Last Year – Poorest Half of Humanity Got Nothing', Oxfam Press Release, 22 January 2018, www.oxfam.org/en/press-releases/richest-1-percent-bagged-82-percent-wealth-created-last-year-poorest-half-humanity.

the United Nations as not just a post-war institution set up to perpetuate the control of the victorious powers but as a mechanism for building a fairer world. Of course, the general and question-begging nature of many of its provisions shows the complexity of that task and how little agreement there was on where it should begin or what it might mean. 'Sovereign equality' concentrates all the ambivalences of that very effort. Its pure formalism tells us not to discriminate between the 'just' and the 'unjust'; and on those impatient with such formalism it puts the impossible burden of having to convert everyone else (including the unjust) to a faith that is at its weakest precisely when it has to explain itself.

Sovereign equality is both necessary and impossible. In the absence of a universal moral truth – or at least access to anything of the kind – it invites us to live with the special truths of different nations, as if saying: there is no world empire, so let's accept the world we have and try to make the best of it. Sovereign equality invites pluralism, tolerance and an effort to work in good faith and on fair terms with those with whom we disagree. But behind its façade of common-sense and practical advice, it holds the wish for transformation in abeyance. The tension between merely 'formal' and truly 'substantive' equality keeps pressing legal actors to move from words to deeds, their hypocrisy reminding them over again of the virtue of justice to which they pay endless compliment.

The inequality of sovereign nations is so ingrained in the fabric of the international system that a single chapter may hardly hope to properly unpack the reasons and stakes behind it. But one thing we can try is to stand back and behold the sheer immensity of the challenge that sovereign equality has always posed international lawyers. Accordingly, in the following we will walk alongside the discipline's long-term past and take stock of some of the attempts of our predecessors to deal (or avoid dealing) with this most controversial equation.

II SOVEREIGN EQUALITY: AN IDEA OF THE ENLIGHTENMENT

The European world of sovereign States with a law of nations between them was born out of the demise of the pretence of the Holy Roman Emperor of being a *dominus mundi*, Lord of the world. The monarchs of France, England and Spain had been claiming independence from the emperor and used the expression of 'sovereign' to distinguish their kingship from that of other feudal lords at least since the thirteenth century. Even as ruling families in Europe and elsewhere often asserted their special status by invoking divine institution or their role as protectors of the faith, by the eighteenth century it was largely accepted that one could think of Europe as a 'system' composed of several nations or 'States' that were in some respect equal to each other. This moved the focus away from the person of the ruler or the de facto power of the structure that was the object of rule – that is 'statehood' – and onto the recognition that, as a 'State', it was to be legally treated as equal to every other such (European) entity.

But qualitative distinctions between sovereigns had been already useful for the Roman Empire and careful distinctions were made in medieval times between the Empire and barbarians, or Christendom and infidels. Long after the Reformation and the Peace of Westphalia had introduced a new European family of sovereign States, the distinction between *those* sovereigns and all the rest remained central to the law of nations. Variations of this distinction would continue to be deployed to mark a rejection of non-European peoples as well as colonial insurgents, maroons and fugitive slaves beyond the pale of international law.

Whatever the treaty-makers in Münster and Osnabruck may have believed they were doing, mid-eighteenth-century jurists came to agree that 'Westphalia' marked the end of any legitimate pursuit of formal Europe-wide hegemony. The Peace of Utrecht (1713), which ended the War of

Spanish Succession and what contemporaries saw as the French pursuit of 'universal monarchy', affirmed this interpretation by consecrating the technique of balance of power at the heart of European diplomacy. It also served as the paradigm and the principal reference for the most important eighteenth-century work on European diplomacy and the law of nations, Emer de Vattel's *Droit des gens* (1758). According to Vattel, 'Europe forms a political system, an integral body, closely connected by the relations and different interests of the nations inhabiting this part of the world.'[7] Two 'general laws' formed the core of that 'system'. One was the duty of every nation, as Vattel put it, 'to contribute everything in her power to the happiness and perfection of all the others', and the second was the perfect 'liberty and independence' of each such nation, their ability to freely determine what they shall or shall not do in the pursuit of the 'natural rights' that each enjoyed.[8] 'Liberty and independence' meant that no other nation could compel another to act in particular ways; each was entitled to follow its own lights. Vattel strengthened that point by a domestic analogy: nations were 'composed of men' and could therefore be 'considered as so many free persons' who were 'naturally equal, and inherit from nature the same obligations and rights'.[9] True, diplomatic mores recognised all kinds of formal precedence and pre-eminence among the *representatives* of nations, but none of this deviated from the *legal* equality of their nations.[10] Vattel concluded with these famous lines: 'A dwarf is as much a man as a giant; a small republic is no less a sovereign state than the most powerful kingdom.'[11]

The idea of 'sovereign equality' was the product of enlightenment rationalism: if an entity was internally free and externally independent, then it was logically equal to every other such entity. The account was also limited in the same ways as enlightenment rationalism was. In the first place, it remained confined to the European world. Few eighteenth-century lawyers had much to say about the world outside. The commonplace lament about Spanish behaviour in the 'Indies' did not translate into arguments about equality. Vattel, for instance, mentioned China, Japan, Ceylon and the Ottoman Empire in several places, recognising the binding nature of the legal arrangements made with them. But he also labelled the Ottomans as a 'savage nation' that could be seen as an 'enemy to the human race' that could be subjected to punishment or even 'extermination'.[12] Although he put forward no general distinction between 'civilised' and 'uncivilised' nations, he did use 'civilisation' itself as a criterion for discriminatory treatment (including *within* Europe).

The second limitation of rationalism was, well – that it was *rationalism*. Perhaps the most important effort in the eighteenth century to make diplomatic reality of sovereign equality was the proposal of twenty-one articles, made by one of the great survivors of the French revolutionary period, the abbé Henri Grégoire in the National Convention in the spring of 1793. According to the proposed *Déclaration de droits des gens* (Declaration on the Rights of Nations), all peoples (*gens*) were 'independent and sovereign' and connected to each other by 'universal morality'. Each people was master of its territory while areas not subject to occupation (such as the seas) belonged to all. Foreigners were to abide by the laws of the country where they stayed, and a people had the right to refuse entry to foreigners it considered dangerous to their security.

7 Emer de Vattel, *The Law of Nations* (ed and intro B Kapossy and R Whatmore, Liberty Fund, 2008 [1758]), III 3.47 (496).
8 ibid, Preliminaries, 13–16 (73–74).
9 ibid 18 (75).
10 ibid II 3.36–40 (281–84).
11 ibid, Preliminaries, 18 (75).
12 ibid III 3.34 (487). For details, see Jennifer Pitts, 'Empire and Legal Universalisms in the Eighteenth Century' (2012) 117 *The American Historical Review* 92–121.

Any attack against the liberty of one people was an attack on all of them and offensive leagues were contrary to the 'human family'. There were to be no ranks among the representatives of peoples, and they enjoyed immunity from the laws of their receiving countries. Finally, even as Grégoire expressed the view that 'no other government [was] in conformity with the rights of peoples than ones that [were] based on equality and liberty', he also accepted that no people had the right to intervene in the government of another.[13]

The Declaration was never adopted. In view of the tense international situation in June 1793, the deputies held it sufficient to state that France declare its friendship with all peoples; there was reason to be 'political' and not to express futile philanthropic sentiments. The same fate befell Grégoire's second try two years later. Already at the time, German lawyers ridiculed Grégoire's idealism. Its submission gave reason for Georg-Friedrich von Martens at the University of Göttingen to write a new foreword to his widely read *Einleitung in das positive europäische Völkerrecht* (later repeated in the 1820 and 1864 French editions as a kind of methodological-political *credo* of its author). There were many aspects of international law, Martens wrote, where agreement between European powers would be desirable. But to believe that they would suddenly adopt a general code of this type was devoid of any realism. Moreover, to declare principles of morality was pointless: they can be realised only under conditions which, if they were present, would make their declaration unnecessary.[14] The Declaration consisted of principles that were self-evident, but empty as practical directives. Some of them were undoubtedly part of 'pure natural law' – such as the equality of State representatives – that, however, would never be actually adopted. The representative of San Marino would never be equal to the Ambassador of France.

Nineteenth-century diplomacy, the system of Concert of Europe, followed Martens rather than Grégoire. The great powers took upon themselves leadership of European affairs and would eventually carry out their colonial projects without the item of sovereign equality being seriously raised in any quarter. The Concert of Europe was thoroughly built upon an assumption that the old States were more legitimate than newcomers. Its hard core, Metternich's Holly Alliance, was to be remembered as a bastion of Christian monarchism against the rise of constitutionalism and all sorts of 'real cosmopolitans, securing their personal advantage at the expense of any order of things whatever – paid State officials, men of letters, lawyers, and the individuals charged with the public education'.[15] Later on in the century, it was the turn of the Germans to demand sovereign equality against France. In the same correspondence that motivated Johann Caspar Bluntschli and other European international jurists to establish the *Institut de droit international*, Francis Lieber defended German unification and Wilhelm's empire by insisting that France should 'give up her absurd and pretended leadership of civilization' and stop interfering with the German constitution.[16] The matter would not be solved until after the Franco-Prussian

[13] For the articles, see Pierre Fauchon, *L'abbé Grégoire. Le prêtre-citoyen* (Nouvelle-République, 1989) 87–88. For a critical commentary highlighting the 'chimerical' aspects of the articles, see Linda Frey and Marsha Frey, 'Grégoire and the Breath of Reason: The French Revolutionaries and the *Droit des gens*' (2010) 38 *Journal for the Western Society of French History* 163–77. The best discussion of the context and a full list of the twenty-one articles can be found in Marc Bélissa, 'La Déclaration du droit des gens de l'abbé Grégoire (juin 1793, 4 floréal an III)', https://revolution-francaise.net/2010/10/06/399–declaration-droit-des-gens-abbe-gregoire-juin-1793. The text has also been reprinted in Vladimir-Djuro Degan, 'L'Affirmation des principes du Droit naturel par la Révolution française. Le projet de Déclaration du Droit des Gens de l'abbé Grégoire' (1989) 35 *Annuaire français de droit international* 99–116.

[14] Georg-Friedrich Martens, *Einleitung in das positive europäische Völkerrecht* (1796) viii–ix.

[15] See Metternich's political confession of faith in *Memoirs of Prince Metternich 1815–1829*, vol 3 (Mrs Alexander Napier tr, Bentley & Son, 1881), No 488, at 454–76.

[16] Thomas S Perry (ed), *Life and Letters of Francis Lieber* (James R Osgood and Co, 1882) 365, 373.

war and the fall of the French Empire, when also the *Institut* was founded to seek and to develop a more civilised and liberal law of nations.[17]

Beyond Europe, on the other hand, the nineteenth-century maritime powers operated through the pragmatic lens of colonialism and inter-imperial relations, with their reactions ranging from intervention in the Greek rebellion to a persistent non-recognition of Haiti, and from an overall neutrality in Spanish American revolutions to their ruthless gunboat diplomacy in the Far East. The 1884–85 Berlin Africa Conference underlined the distinction, joining the great legal minds of Europe in a multilateral treaty-making enterprise designated to achieve the partitioning and colonial exploitation of Africa.

III SOVEREIGN EQUALITY AS A PROCESS 1869–1919

The *Institut de droit international* was established to act as 'the legal conscience of the civilized world'. In one of its very first studies, it asked whether the customary European law of nations could also apply to Oriental nations.[18] The issue had been in the air since 1856 when the Ottoman Empire had declared 'welcome to participate in the advantages of the public law and the concert of Europe'.[19] But the relationship between European powers and the Porte had hardly become one of sovereign equals; even the old Ottoman capitulations were not voided until the Treaty of Lausanne in 1923, and arguably the Turkish position remained peripheral for a long time afterwards, regardless of their vindication in the case of the *S.S. Lotus*.[20] The *Institut*'s study on the oriental question was framed in a keynote speech by Dudley Field, who thought that the separation between Christians and the Orientals was originally caused by the seclusive attitudes of the latter.[21] Field proposed that non-Christian nations should be admitted to all the rights and subjected to all the duties of the nations of the West under international law – with the single exception that 'until there is a greater assimilation between the nations of the East and the West with respect to judicial institutions, mixed courts and a special procedure should be established for the decision of all cases, public or private, in which Americans and Europeans are parties'.[22]

The study group of the Institute produced its report in 1879.[23] The results were inconclusive. Although there did not seem to be fundamental obstacles to a gradual rapprochement of the European and Oriental civilisations – the latter for example also accepted that nations could only be bound by obligations to which they had consented – considerable difficulties lay in the practical implementation of any sovereign equality. In particular, 'all the European experts' were of the opinion 'that the moment had not yet arrived when the European nations could dispose of

[17] On this confrontation, see Ville Kari, 'A Less Elevated Cosmopolitanism: Victor Hugo, Francis Lieber, and the Franco-Prussian War of 1870' in Jan Klabbers, Maria Varaki and Guilherme Vasconcelos Vilaça (eds), *Towards Responsible Global Governance* (University of Helsinki, 2018) 31–52.

[18] 1 *IDI Annuaire* 7–10. The topic was thus on par with the treatment of private property in maritime wars, the establishment of an international prize court, the development of the laws and customs of war, and the conflict of laws.

[19] General Peace Treaty of Paris (30 March 1856), 114 CTS 409, 46 BFSP 8, Art VII.

[20] Treaty of Peace signed at Lausanne (24 July 1923) 28 LNTS (1924) No 701, Art 28; SS *Lotus*, PCIJ Rep Series A–No 10 (7 September 1927) 4. On the capitulations, see Arnulf Becker Lorca, *Mestizo International Law* (Cambridge University Press, 2014) 79–85. See further Eliana Augusti, *Questioni D'Oriente. Europa e imperio Ottomano nel diritto internazionale dell'Ottocento* (Edizioni Scientifichi, 2013).

[21] AP Sprague (ed), *Speeches, Arguments and Miscellaneous Papers of David Dudley Field* (D Appleton and Company, 1884) 447–56, 450–51.

[22] ibid 456.

[23] 3–4 *IDI Annuaire* (1879–80) 301–5.

the protective guarantees on which the administration of justice are safeguarded by virtue of the capitulations'.[24] In the end, the commission found the question was too general and recommended it to be studied one Oriental power at a time.

In one respect, however, the study group did point a way forward. It restated and retrenched Europe's ancient 'civilising mission'. Citing notorious incidents such as the Opium War, professor Joseph Hornung scolded the Christian powers for treating the question of the Orient simply as a narrow matter of protecting their own interests. But instead of suggesting that the Orient be treated as equals, Hornung demanded that Europe step up its civilising efforts in the 'intelligent and disinterested tutelage of the feeble'. Europe was to intervene in violations of 'the laws of humanity' and to safeguard 'the grand interests of humanity'. The stakes were the highest possible: 'The *Völkerstaat* dreamt by Kant cannot begin to materialize until the civilized humanity comprehends the grander morality of its mission and begins to see other things besides its own self-interest or that of its nationals or its co-believers.'[25] The view that colonialism was not just a deeply entrenched economic and political reality, but that it was something which in fact the Orient *needed* and to which Europe was *obliged* under international law, helped the European jurists circumvent many uncomfortable questions about the ethics of their world order. But they made sure to back this view up with the increasing practice of written treaties between the colonisers and the natives, thus securing the (putative) consent of the indigenous populations to European domination.[26] Such views were not eccentric but rather the norm in European international legal scholarship. The civilising mission was then very much in vogue during the 1884–85 Berlin Conference.[27]

At the same time, plenty of inequality remained wrought within the internal fabric of the 'civilised' world as well. As the intensifying transatlantic economy operated mainly between formally equal and fully recognised sovereigns, new international rules and principles emerged to govern the protection of foreign property and interests in sovereign States. State responsibility in particular became something of 'a rite of passage for new States' regardless of the efforts of Latin American jurists such as Carlos Calvo to set its standards in terms favourable to their countries.[28] The League of Nations would become one of the arenas for Latin American resistance to this practice.[29] But retrospective critics such as Carl Schmitt saw in this nothing less than a transmutation of the civilised/non-civilised distinction into a new hierarchy between creditor and debtor States.[30]

[24] ibid 304.

[25] ibid, Note de M Hornung, 305–7.

[26] Martti Koskenniemi, *The Gentle Civilizer of Nations: The Rise and Fall of International law 1870–1960* (Cambridge University Press, 2001) 136–43.

[27] For a notorious example see James Lorimer, *The Institutes of the Law of Nations: A Treatise of the Jural Relations of Separate Political Communities*, vol 1 (William Blackwood and Sons, 1883–4) 93, 101–2, 156–62. See further Martti Koskenniemi, 'Race, Hierarchy and International law: Lorimer's Legal Science' (2016) 27 *European Journal of International Law* 415–29. Around the same time, Hornung had developed his initial thesis into a series of articles on the distinction of the civilised and barbarians, and his views were much in tune with Lorimer's. See Joseph Hornung, 'Civilisés et barbares' (Parts I–V) (1885) 17 *Revue de droit international* 1–18, 447–470, 539–560; 18(1886) *Revue de droit international* 188–206, 281–298.

[28] The expression is from Tzvika Alan Nissel, 'A History of State Responsibility: The Struggle for International Standards 1870–1960', Doctoral thesis, Helsinki, 2016, 192. See also 154–60 and 191–95.

[29] Kathryn Greenman, 'The History and Legacy of State Responsibility for Rebels 1839–1930', Doctoral thesis, Amsterdam, 2019, 189–206; Arnulf Becker Lorca, *Mestizo International Law* (Cambridge University Press, 2014) 317–26.

[30] Carl Schmitt, 'Forms of Modern Imperialism in International Law' in Stephen Legg (ed), *Spatiality, Sovereignty and Carl Schmitt: Geographies of the Nomos* (Matthew Hannah tr, Routledge, 2011) 29–45, esp 30–31.

IV SOVEREIGN EQUALITY AND THE LEAGUE OF NATIONS

The Paris Conference of 1919 began a thorough renovation of international relations. From the ashes of war rose not only the League of Nations, but also a much revised and redrawn map of the empires, States and dependencies of the world. The mandates system sought to define the boundary between sovereign and non-sovereign peoples, and through it, the hierarchy was openly written down into an international constitution of the civilised world. The League also exposed other deep-rooted shortcomings in terms of sovereign equality. Membership itself was restricted, and some aspects of the organisation – council membership, for instance – placed nations within the organisation in variable positions of power. Most famously, the drafting of the Covenant saw an express legal debate about – and a rejection of – the principle of racial equality among nations. As a consequence, it can hardly be said that sovereign equality was ever at the core of the League of Nations project. Rather, the League project included a restatement of the prevailing sovereign inequalities under its formal international framework.[31]

1 *Members and Mandates*

The League of Nations was not open to all. There would always be sovereign States in the world that were either not interested in, or not admitted to, the League. Delegates were sent to Paris by many hopeful nations and peoples inspired by Wilson's call for the self-determination of peoples, seeking to secure support or even recognition and statehood. These were not fringe groups but among them were ancient and often populous peoples such as Egyptians, Indians, Koreans and different African peoples supported by pan-Africanists. Some new nations managed to get themselves recognised and elevated among the civilised peoples, while others would be disappointed.[32] Many peoples had to simply acquiesce to the continuation of colonialism.

The mandates system emerged as a sort of compromise between British and French plans to simply keep the Ottoman territories and German colonies as old-fashioned conquests, and Woodrow Wilson's ideal of national self-determination which desired to open these areas for the open intercourse of all free nations.[33] Because the colonial peoples were 'not yet able to stand by themselves under the strenuous conditions of the modern world, there should be applied the principle that the well-being and development of such peoples form a sacred trust of civilisation', stated the League Covenant. Accordingly, the best method of giving practical effect to this principle was entrusting the 'tutelage' of such peoples to 'advanced nations' 'on behalf of

[31] Rose Parfitt, '*Empire des Nègres Blancs*: The Hybridity of International Personality and the Abyssinia Crisis of 1935–36' (2011) 24 *Leiden Journal of International Law* 849, 850–51.

[32] Arnulf Becker Lorca, *Mestizo International Law* (Cambridge University Press, 2014) 227–30, 237–39, 247, 270–74; Margaret MacMillan, *Paris 1919: Six Months that Changed the World* (Random House, 2001) 225–42. On the significance of the 'Wilsonian moment' in the colonised world, see Erez Manela, *The Wilsonian Moment: Self-Determination and the International Origins of Anticolonial Nationalism* (Oxford University Press, 2007).

[33] Susan Pedersen, *The Guardians: The League of Nations and the Crisis of Empire* (Oxford University Press, 2015) 17–35; Taina Tuori, 'From League of Nations Mandates to Decolonization: A History of the Language of Rights in International Law', Doctoral thesis, Helsinki, 2016, 31–36. See also the Sykes-Picot Agreement of 1916, 221 CTS 323. Even the American negotiators were not confident about the appropriateness of granting full independence to nations that were, in their eyes, likewise only partially civilised or even uncivilised. Their own experts in colonial affairs felt that the British model of colonial administration was nevertheless the best model to manage and develop the underprivileged populations. The mandates compromise was finally proposed by South African General Jan Smuts, an ardent pioneer of apartheidism. On the role of Smuts, see Thomas W Burkman, *Japan and the League of Nations: Empire and World Order, 1914–1938* (University of Hawai'i Press, 2008) 69; MacMillan (n 32) 88–90, 98–100. The Smuts plan is also discussed in David Hunter Miller, *Drafting of the Covenant*, vol 2 (GP Putnam's Sons, 1928) 34–39.

the League'.[34] In other words, the white man's burden was translated to the language of universal civilisation. However, by the time the actual mandates system kicked off, the United States had had a change of heart and rejected its membership in the League. The key non-European component of the equation thus removed, the reality of the colonial administration in many of the mandated territories differed little from that of the remaining 'proper' colonies. As Susan Pedersen observes, '[n]ot administration but rather the work of legitimation moved to Geneva'.[35] This is not to say that the mandates system was entirely irrelevant; it forced the colonisers to constantly explain themselves and created the prototypal body of international civil servants tasked with such oversight as it was able to exercise, but it certainly failed to satisfy the colonised peoples who were supposed to most benefit from the arrangement.

2 *Racial Equality between Nations*

Among the victorious powers, sovereign equality was not a fait accompli either. The most famous encounter in this respect involved the demand of Japan – now a major power – to include in the Covenant an express provision rejecting racial discrimination. Japan had come to Paris in part to rid itself of the residues of its second-class citizenship in the family of nations, and it intended to place this as a condition for its membership in the League.[36] Its delegate Makino Nobuaki therefore presented an amendment that sought to expand the Covenant's draft clause on 'religious liberty' to encompass also racial equality:

> The equality of nations being a basic principle of the League of Nations, the High Contracting Parties agree to accord, as soon as possible, to all alien nationals of States members of the League equal and just treatment in every respect, making no distinction, either in law or in fact, on account of their race or nationality.[37]

Although the Japanese themselves had intended the proposal to be understood as juridical equality between the signatory States and the rights of their nationals, their audience saw in it a proposal for a broader racial equality in the world. It was received with both interest and scepticism by the Western powers, but above all it was seen as problematic. In back-room negotiations, the Americans sought to ameliorate the proposal by rephrasing it to reflect their own constitutional maxim that 'all men are created equal', to which the British Foreign Secretary Lord Balfour allegedly responded that 'that was an eighteenth century proposition which he did not believe was true'.[38] On a more practical level, the proposal could not be accepted by countries such as Australia and the United States that were very concretely restricting the movement and property rights of Japanese immigrants.[39] In a telling note, the American drafter David Hunter Miller advised Wilson's advisor:

> The trouble with the Japanese proposition is this: ... This draft was not acceptable because it had, as you appreciated, no particular legal effect, because it was not intended to have any. Any draft which had a real effect would, of course, be impossible.[40]

34 League of Nations Covenant, Art 22.
35 Pedersen (n 33) 5.
36 Japan's three objectives were the Pacific islands, Shandong and the racial equality clause. Burkman (n 33) 60.
37 Hunter Miller (n 33) 183; Margaret MacMillan (n 32) 317–18.
38 Hunter Miller (n 33) 183–84.
39 Burkman (n 33) 81–86; MacMillan (n 32) 316, 318–19.
40 Hunter Miller (n 33) 184.

In the final meeting on the Covenant, the Japanese delegates proposed a watered-down compromise of the equality clause, one demoted to the preamble and merely calling for 'the endorsement of the principle of equality of nations and just treatment of their nationals'.[41] They spoke eloquently and gradually gained support from all quarters, but in the absence of unanimity the proposal was ultimately rejected.[42]

The League of Nations was never established on the basis of sovereign equality. Although the Paris Peace Conference and Wilson's project for the Covenant were envisioned as a new beginning for an ever more peaceful and civilised world, that world was still one where colonialism and discrimination were understood as established aspects of modern life. The debates and decisions taken then clearly reflect that reality. It is therefore remarkable to see how fundamentally unequal States and peoples were only fifty years before the Friendly Relations Declaration, not only in practice but in the letter of the law as well.

V SOVEREIGN EQUALITY AND THE UNITED NATIONS

Unlike the League of Nations, the United Nations Organization was established on the principle of sovereign equality. The principle emerged already in Allied wartime declarations which 'recognize(d) the necessity of establishing, at the earliest practicable date, a general international organization, based on the principle of the sovereign equality of all peace-loving States'.[43] This principle was subsequently enshrined in Article 2(1) of the Charter. But just as much, the United Nations has also been characterised as representing 'a deliberate retreat from the League's comparative egalitarianism back to the great power conclaves of the past'.[44] In the United Nations there are sovereigns and then there are Sovereigns. Insofar as sovereign equality of States was inserted into the Charter as the general and principal rule, then it meant that the exceptions and conditions to that main rule became increasingly visible and formal. From its very beginning, the United Nations was built on a division between the exclusive club of the Security Council with its veto-wielding permanent five, the General Assembly of all nations, the (now redundant) 'enemy States' and, beyond them all still, the Non-Self-Governing Territories (i.e. colonies) and trusteeships. What, if anything, did sovereign equality in such a reality really come to mean? The battle for sovereign equality would very much preoccupy the United Nations for its first three decades.

1 Charter Drafting and Security Council

During the preparations of the San Francisco conference, intense debates took place about the relations between the members of the future organisation. In many ways the Dumbarton Oaks draft plan looked like a continuation of the League, with a strengthened position for the great

[41] Burkman (n 33) 81–82.

[42] ibid 85; MacMillan (n 32) 320; Hunter Miller (n 33) 461–64. Japan was later propitiated with the disputed Chinese province of Shandong, which in turn marked a travesty and public scandal for the Chinese. See Treaty of Versailles (1919), Arts 156–58. On Wellington Koo's concerns on the 'Asiatic Monroe Doctrine', see Hunter Miller (n 33) 453–54, 457–61; MacMillan (n 32) 322–44.

[43] Declaration of Four Nations on General Security, para 4, in *United Nations Documents 1941–1945* (London: Royal Institute of International Affairs, 1947) 13. There were similar brief references to the need of a security organisation in the Atlantic Charter, the Declaration of the United Nations and other similar proclarations. The term 'peace-loving' was inserted at the initiative of the Soviet Union.

[44] Mark Mazower, *No Enchanted Palace: The End of Empire and the Ideological Origins of the United Nations* (Princeton University Press, 2009) 149.

powers over others. International experts decried particular rules and omissions, such as the optionality of peaceful settlement of disputes or the lack of appeal from the Security Council to the General Assembly.[45] Haiti proposed an amendment that echoed the old Japanese initiative in 1919: 'The Organization is based on the principle of the sovereign equality of all States that love peace and exclude from their relations any racial or religious discrimination.'[46] The most contentious issue was the privileged position of the permanent members of the Security Council. Smaller States raised concern over the compatibility of those privileges with the ideal of sovereign equality. Moreover, if they now signed the Charter these distinctions would be made permanent.[47] Some therefore proposed alterations to the Security Council's role. Turkey, for one, submitted that the principle of sovereign equality should lead to the concentration of all matters of peace and security in the hands of the General Assembly, at least in the last instance.[48] But there was no way to secure the accession of the leading powers without granting them their special status.[49] Ultimately, the resultant hierarchy was the price the signatories were willing to pay (albeit reluctantly) for a new security mechanism with a broad membership. But a hierarchy it was. In 1946, the Soviet jurist Eugene Korovin stated the situation candidly:

> It is nothing new in history for Great Powers to occupy a privileged position. What is new is that definite privileges are accorded the great democratic states not in their own interests but in the interests of all the states, of the whole international collectivity, by making their international rights correspond to their international obligations.[50]

2 *Trusteeships and Bretton Woods*

In the United Nations, the old mandates system was replaced by a new mechanism of trusteeships. The trusteeship system was quite consciously drafted to require little immediate change from the colonial powers, and came as an acquiescence by the United States and other non-European powers to the continuance of European colonial possessions (with a trade-off at

[45] Hans Kelsen argued that 'The only way to establish on the principle of "sovereign equality" an international organization able to "maintain international peace and security" more efficiently than the League of Nations did, is the establishment of an international community whose main organ is an international court endowed with compulsory jurisdiction.' Only an impartial and compulsory court could furnish the international community with authoritative interpretations of legal facts that would determine the applicable rules. 'If, however, this hope is, indeed, too optimistic', he warned, 'if it shall be impossible to realize this minimum of centralization because it will be considered as incompatible with the "sovereign equality of all peace loving States," there will, then, be no hope at all for a real improvement of international relations, and the peace organized by those States will prove to be nothing more than a short armistice between this and another world war.' Hans Kelsen, 'The Principle of Sovereign Equality of States as a Basis for International Organization' (1944) 53 *Yale Law Journal* 207–20, 214, 218, 220.

[46] Proposed Amendments to the Dumbarton Oaks Proposals Submitted by the Haitian Delegation: Amendment to Chapter II, *Documents of the UN Conference in San Francisco*, 1945, vol III, 52.

[47] The government of the Netherlands voiced this quite openly: 'The smaller powers, who are invited in the Dumbarton Oaks Plan to perpetuate and legalise an existing de-facto position of inferiority, may be permitted to point out that, if exorbitant special rights were granted virtually placing the great powers above the law, this Plan would be of little avail for the rest of the world, inasmuch as a return of the world to anarchy would not be excluded.' Suggestions presented by the Netherlands on the Dumbarton Oaks proposals, January 1945, *Documents of the UN Conference in San Francisco*, 1945, vol III, 306, 315.

[48] Turkish opinion, *Documents of the UN Conference in San Francisco*, 1945, vol III, 481.

[49] Daniel-Erasmus Khan, 'Drafting History' in Bruno Simma et al (eds), *The Charter of the United Nations: A Commentary*, vol 1 (3rd edn, Oxford University Press, 2012) 15–18, paras 41–51.

[50] Eugene Korovin, 'The Second World War and International Law' (1946) 40 *American Journal of International Law* 742, 746. Also cited in Mazower (n 44) 150.

Bretton Woods).[51] Many of the attending States were content with the insertion of a grandiose and visionary preamble in the Charter, and on the new principles of human rights, such as the goal of promoting and encouraging respect for human rights 'for all without distinction as to race, sex, language, or religion' in Article 1(3). Arguably, this new human equality was emphasised instead of old sovereign equality.

As formal colonialism itself proved unsustainable soon after the signing of the Charter, the trusteeship system gradually succeeded in making itself obsolete. But in 1945, this was not yet to be seen, and some trusteeships lingered on until the 1990s as the concerned nations gradually either gained independence or voluntarily joined existing States.[52] By that time, however, independence did not necessarily mean the attainment of full sovereign equality in the decolonising world. Already a year before the UN Charter was brought to San Francisco, the other half of the bargain between the old colonial Europe and the new ascendant United States had played out at Bretton Woods – and in those discussions, the word 'equals' was scarcely mentioned except in the domain of mathematical calculus. That conference was one of the starting points for a new restructuring of the international community, where sovereign equality was substituted for old colonial subordinations, but at the same time new legal foundations were laid for safeguarding the continuing economic interests and privileges between developed and developing countries.

During the Second World War, the major Allied powers had become acutely aware of their dependence on natural resources and raw materials from across the seas. Moreover, among them the exigencies of war meant that the balance of power was shifting to the Western side of the Atlantic. When designing the economic future for the post-war period, it was increasingly obvious that as a price for their involvement in the war, the Americans expected that the centuries of colonial monopolies would now come to an end.[53] In the 1941 Atlantic Charter the United States and the United Kingdom agreed, as part of their common policies 'for a better future for the world … to further the enjoyment by all States, great or small, victor or vanquished, of access, on equal terms, to the trade and to the raw materials of the world which are needed for their economic prosperity'.[54] In Article VII of the 1942 lend-lease agreement, Britain agreed to join the United States in like-minded action for the development of world trade, including 'the elimination of all forms of discriminatory treatment in international commerce, and to the reduction of tariffs and other trade barriers'.[55] This was the project of the Bretton Woods conference in July 1944, and the convenors of the event made no mistake about it.[56]

[51] Mazower (n 44) 60–65. On the Bretton Woods Conference and the emerging principles for the organisation of the world economy see the chapter by J Kurtz, JE Viñuales and M Waibel in this volume.

[52] For an overview of the termination of the trusteeships, see Andriy Y Melnyk, 'United Nations Trusteeship System' in *Max Planck Encyclopedia of Public International Law* (April, 2008), paras 23–27.

[53] Benn Steil, *The Battle of Bretton Woods* (Princeton University Press, 2013) 4, 13–15.

[54] Atlantic Charter (1 January 1942) 204 LNTS 381, preamble and fourth principle. On the hemispheric and transatlantic background of the Atlantic Charter, see Mark Seddon, 'The Origins and Limitations of the Atlantic Charter: Britain, the USA, Venezuela, and the Development of Free Trade, 1933–1944' (2016) 14 *Journal of Transatlantic Studies* 65–82.

[55] US–Britain Lend-Lease Agreement (23 February 1942), Art VII, in Charles I Bevans, *Treaties and Other International Agreements of the United States of America 1776–1949*, vol 12 (Department of State Publication 8761, 1974) 603, 605.

[56] In his welcoming statement, Franklin Roosevelt went straight to the point: 'Commerce is the life blood of a free society. We must see to it that the arteries which carry that blood stream are not clogged again, as they have been in the past, by artificial barriers created through senseless economic rivalries. Economic diseases are highly communicable. It follows, therefore, that the economic health of every country is a proper matter of concern to all its neighbors, near and distant. Only through a dynamic and a soundly expanding world economy can the living standards of individual nations be advanced to levels which will permit a full realization of our hopes for the future.' Secretary of

When the new post-war economic institutions were set up, the goal of the full use of the resources of the world was also included in the first articles of the foundational documents of the World Bank and the International Monetary Fund (IMF).[57] Unlike the UN Charter, the Articles of Agreement of the World Bank and the IMF did not mention sovereign equality. Instead, the voting power of each Member State was dependent on its contributions and shares.[58] The goal of 'developing the full use of the resources of the world and expanding the production and exchange of goods' was included then in the 1947 General Agreement on Tariffs and Trade (GATT).[59] The early activities of bodies such as the Economic and Social Council (ECOSOC) and the UN Food and Agriculture Organization (FAO) also included the surveying of natural resources and charting their distribution.[60] In the post-war years the sentiment among the leading powers was that there was a scarcity of resources and that the economic reconstruction of the world (and the disaggregation of their wartime economies back to private entrepreneurship) required unimpeded access to the raw materials wherever they were found. In practice, this meant often operating abroad in the less developed countries of the world.

3 *The 'Developing World'*

The United Nations was no longer predominated by European empires. Europe was becoming increasingly provincialised, and its foremost global powers – the British and French empires – were breaking up internally.[61] The colonies had helped save their war-torn metropolitan centres, and now saw independence as their due. Ethnic and colonial disputes flared up throughout the colonial world, from South Africa to India and the Far East, and, by the time India and Pakistan gained their independence, the members of the United Nations were well aware of the tide of history. In 1960, the General Assembly famously declared that 'the subjection of peoples to alien subjugation, domination and exploitation constitutes a denial of fundamental human rights, is contrary to the Charter of the United Nations and is an impediment to the promotion of world peace and co-operation', and that 'immediate steps shall be taken' in colonised areas 'to transfer all powers to the peoples of those territories'.[62] To put an end to talks about a lack of civilisation or the ability of nations to stand on their own feet, as had been the idioms in 1919, the Assembly

the Treasury Henry Morgenthau was equally eloquent: 'We are to concern ourselves here with essential steps in the creation of a dynamic world economy in which the people of every nation will be able to realize their potentialities in peace; will be able, through their industry, their inventiveness, their thrift, to raise their own standards of living and enjoy, increasingly, the fruits of material progress on an earth infinitely blessed with natural resources. This is the indispensable cornerstone of freedom and security. All else must be built upon this.' See *United Nations Monetary and Financial Conference Final Act and Related Documents* (US Government Printing Office, 1944) 1–4.

57 IMF Articles of Agreement (1944) 2 UNTS 39, Art I section ii; IBRD Articles of Agreement (1944), 2 UNTS 134, Art I, sections i–iii.

58 IBRD Articles of Agreement, Art II and Art V, section 5; IMF Articles of Agreement (n 57), Art III, Art XII, section 5.

59 General Agreement on Tariffs and Trade (1947), 55 UNTS 187, preamble.

60 See Nico Schrijver, *Sovereignty over Natural Resources: Balancing Rights and Duties* (Cambridge University Press, 1997) 38–39.

61 Great Britain let go of India and Pakistan (1947), Burma (1948), Palestine (1948), Ceylon (1948), followed by Sudan, Ghana and Malaysia in the 1950s, and the major wave of decolonisation beginning in 1960. France abandoned its colonial empire officially in its constitution of 1946, but lingered in control over several overseas territories. These territories experienced several uprisings and insurrections from the 1950s onwards, and the Algerian war of liberation (1954–62) was one of the major starting points of the decolonisation movement. On the legacy of that war, see generally Todd Shepard, *The Invention of Decolonization: The Algerian War and the Remaking of France* (Cornell University Press, 2006).

62 The Granting of Independence to Colonial Countries and Peoples, UNGA Declaration 1514(XV)/1960, paras 1 and 5. See also Principles, UNGA Res 1514 (XV) (14 December 1960); UNGA Res 1654 (XVI) (27 November 1961).

underlined that 'Inadequacy of political, economic, social or educational preparedness should never serve as a pretext for delaying independence.'[63] The conditional form 'should' and the initial reluctance of Europeans notwithstanding, the Declaration did mark the way towards the transformation of colonies and trusteeships into independent States or voluntary overseas territories.

The Decolonization Declaration heralded a transition from a distinction between empires and colonies to one between developed and developing countries. The post-war vision of international free trade and circulation of raw materials did not seem perfectly acceptable to many of the newly independent States, many of which had had no say in their drafting. Accordingly, their representatives increasingly began to express a concern that these States were allocated a passive role in the extraction of their natural resources for the benefit of the 'First World'. Questions arose about the extent of their self-determination and especially their rights to introduce their own autonomous economic policies that might differ from what the leading powers and the international economic institutions recommended. As the newly independent 'third world' countries reached superior numbers, they joined together in the non-aligned movement and the Group of 77, hoping to leverage the authority of the General Assembly, UN Conference on Trade and Development (UNCTAD) and other international fora to redesign the economic structures of the international system.[64]

The primary impact of the movement was felt in the context of the exploitation of raw materials enshrined in the Atlantic Charter and the GATT. Increasing need was felt for global access to natural resources in the developing world. As pointed out by Kurz, Viñuales and Waibel (chapter 14 of this volume), in the debates between 1949 and 1951 it was anything but clear how to set the balance between local and global interests. In the wake of the debacle that followed the nationalisation of the Anglo-Iranian Oil Company, the argument over natural resources was reignited by a draft resolution by Uruguay, which recommended that Member States recognise 'the right of each country to nationalize and freely exploit its natural wealth, as an essential factor of economic independence'.[65] The outcome was a compromise which omitted any direct reference to nationalisation but recognised that 'the right of peoples freely to use and exploit their natural wealth and resources is inherent in their sovereignty' and which 'recommended' the use of this right consistently with international economic co-operation among nations.[66] Accordingly, Resolution 626 (VII) would be remembered in history as the 'nationalization resolution'.[67] Similar aspirations also blended with the ongoing drafting work of the international covenants of human rights. In 1958 the then-current draft of the Covenants included in the right of self-determination a 'permanent sovereignty over . . . natural wealth and resources'.[68] The General Assembly constituted a specific commission to explore the permanent

[63] UNGA Declaration 1514(XV)/1960 para 3.

[64] eg Final Communiqué of The Asian-African Conference, Bandung, 24 April 1955, in Kweku Ampiah, *The Political and Moral Imperatives of the Bandung Conference of 1955* (Global Oriental, 2007), Annex I, 228; Joint Declaration of the 77 Developing Countries made at the conclusion of the UNCTAD, in *Proceedings of the UNCTAD Geneva, 23 March –16 June 1964*, vol 1 (UN, 1964) 66.

[65] UN Doc A/C.2/L.165, 5 November 1962 and Corr 1–3, as cited in Schrijver (n 60) 42–43.

[66] UNGA Res 626 (VII) (21 December 1952).

[67] Schrijver (n 60) 36, 41–49.

[68] Commission on Human Rights to ECOSOC Eighteenth Session, Supp No 7, Doc E/2573(SUPP), 7–8, 62. On the other hand, there had been proposed an article on the right of property as a human right, as well as an expropriation clause, but these had not been adopted. Neither the reference to permanent sovereignty over natural resources nor the property right and expropriation clause made it to the final wording of the CCPR.

sovereignty over natural resources,[69] which produced its report in 1961,[70] and the following year the Declaration on the permanent sovereignty over natural resources was adopted,[71] in the spirit of the 'mutual respect of States based on their sovereign equality'.[72]

And that is just about how far it went. In the final plenary debate before the vote, the Assembly had, on the insistence in particular of the United Kingdom and the United States, rejected a specific amendment proposed by the Soviet Union, which would have provided that the Assembly 'unreservedly supports measures taken by peoples and States to re-establish or strengthen their sovereignty over natural wealth and resources, and considers inadmissible acts aimed at obstructing the creation, defence and strengthening of that sovereignty'.[73] That wording was seen as leading into disequilibrium between property rights and sovereign authority. In the end, while the Declaration affirmed the sovereignty of States over their natural wealth, it also maintained that in cases of 'nationalization, expropriation or requisitioning ... the owner shall be paid appropriate compensation, in accordance with the rules in force in the State ... and in accordance with international law'.[74] It also included a general reference to the possibility of freely agreed arbitration as well as the specific notion that 'foreign investment agreements ... shall be observed in good faith'.[75] As a result, the Declaration did not substantially venture into the terrain of the international law of State responsibility, which would still apply in situations of investment disputes.

As pointed out by Kurz, Viñuales and Waibel,[76] this is not to say that the Third World push in the Friendly Relations Declaration would have been utterly without effect. The oil-exporting developing countries that joined the Organization of the Petroleum Exporting Countries (OPEC) cartel had by 1973 largely succeeded in gaining control of the vast majority of their fossil fuel reserves, had become important actors in the economic policy scene and, among other things, were able to establish an embargo against Western countries collaborating with Israel at the time of the Yom Kippur war. Western petroleum conglomerates had been transformed from imperial actors into something like service providers. Significant gains were also attained in respect of the law of the sea. The establishment of the Exclusive Economic Zone (EEZ) in the 1982 UN Convention on the Law of the Sea and the employment of the straight baselines method for the delimitation of the territorial waters of archipelagic States such as the Philippines and Indonesia helped in enclosing resources in large maritime areas under the jurisdiction of developing coastal States.[77] The development of deep seabed resources in the interests of the developing States did not commence as it was expected and the partial dilution of the provisions concerning the operation of the International Seabed Authority (ISA) after the entry into force of the Convention may have been disappointing to the developing States.[78] But the operations of

69 UNGA Res 1314(XIII) (12 December 1958).

70 Report of the Commission on Permanent Sovereignty over Natural Resources (26 May 1961) UN ESCOSOC 32nd Sessn, Agenda item 9, A/AC97/13.

71 UNGA Res 1720(XVI) (19 December 1961); UNGA Res 1803(XVII) (14 December 1962).

72 UNGA Res 1803(XVII), para 5.

73 Report of the Second Committee (12 December 1962) Doc A/5344/Add.1, UNGA plenary meeting Agenda item 39, 22; GAOR Verbatim Records of the 1193rd and 1194th Plenary Meetings, XVII Sessn (14 December 1962).

74 UNGA Res 1803(XVII), para 4.

75 ibid, paras 4 and 8.

76 See ch 14 in this volume.

77 See Arts 47 and 57 of the UN Law of the Sea Convention and comments eg in Francisco Orrego-Vicuña, *The Exclusive Economic Zone* (Cambridge University Press, 1999) and Tara Davenport, 'The Archipelagic Regime' in Donald Rothwell et al, *The Oxford Handbook of the Law of the Sea* (Oxford University Press, 2015) 138–142.

78 See eg Martti Koskenniemi and Marja Lehto, 'The Privilege of Universality. International Law, Economic Ideology and Seabed Resources' (1996) 65 *Nordic Journal of International Law* 533–55.

the ISA, limited as they are, are among the few remaining institutional results of the call for a New International Economic Order (NIEO), launched formally by the General Assembly in 1974.[79] At the heart of that call was the continuing insistence of a permanent right of States over their natural resources.

While States continued to disagree on whether the permanent right of States over their natural resources entailed the duty to pay 'full' or 'appropriate' compensation for expropriations (the many arbitral awards remained indeterminate in that regard), the developed States began their counter-offensive by endorsing, in 1958, the New York Convention on the Recognition and Enforcement of Foreign Arbitral Awards, in which they gave their blanket consent to the direct enforceability of awards of not only arbitrations appointed for each case but also those made by permanent arbitral bodies to which the parties had submitted.[80] In 1965 the International Centre for Settlement of Investment Disputes (ICSID) Convention brought into existence a dedicated investment arbitration framework under the auspices of the World Bank,[81] and after blanket consent to investor–State arbitration was introduced in bilateral investment treaties (BITs) since 1969, the structures undergirding the present-day practices of investor–State arbitration were in place and ready to be discovered by the claims industry in the 1990s.[82] Since then, as Kurtz, Viñuales and Waibel discuss at length in chapter 14, national sovereignty has often come under pressure owing to an arbitral practice that pays scarce regard to the principles underlying the 1962 UN Resolution on the Permanent Sovereignty over Natural Resources.[83]

VI SOVEREIGN EQUALITY IN THE DRAFTING OF RESOLUTION 2625

The Friendly Relations Declaration was officially intended to mark the twenty-fifth anniversary of the United Nations and to remind Member States of the aspirations on which the organisation was supposed to have been based. But in fact, it was understood by the majority of the members as an occasion to remind everyone of the distance between those aspirations and the reality of the international world. It became part of the push from the decolonised world to address the role of the United Nations in seeking a less unequal world. The attainment of formal independence and membership in the United Nations had not erased poverty and deprivation and the greatest part of Member States remained still massively dependent on the former colonial powers. The alliance between the G77 and the socialist bloc remained firm and the shared intention was not only to restate the principles of the Charter but to give them an interpretation that would, as far as possible, highlight the objective of eradicating the colonial heritage and the global economic inequality that was part of it. The use of a Special Committee instead of the International Law Commission (ILC) 'gave weight', according to Bedjaoui, 'to the modern process for the elaboration of law by means of the resolution'.[84]

[79] Declaration on the New International Economic Order, UNGA Res 3201 and 3202 (S-VI) (1 May 1974).

[80] Convention on the Recognition and Enforcement of Foreign Arbitral Awards, New York, 10 June 1958, 330 UNTS 38.

[81] Convention on the Settlement of Investment Disputes between States and Nationals of Other States, Washington, 18 March 1965, 575 UNTS 159.

[82] Rudolf Dolzer and Christoph Schreuer, *Principles of International Investment Law* (2nd edn, Oxford University Press, 2012) 6–11. According to Dolzer and Schreuer, the first BIT to offer investor–State arbitration was the Italy–Chad BIT of 1969.

[83] UNGA Res 1803 (XVII). Arguably, as the regulatory freeze caused by investment arbitrations increasingly concerns the 'developed' States as well as the 'developing' ones, the outcome may be an increase in sovereign equality as the planetary privatisation processes leave public institutions equally powerless in all quarters of the globe.

[84] Bedjaoui (n 5) 181.

'The principle of sovereign equality of States' was one of the seven principles that the UN General Assembly had requested the Special Committee set up in 1964 to 'study . . . so as to secure [its] more effective application'.[85] Although the debate on this principle turned out, perhaps surprisingly, to be the least problematic of the seven principles, the basic differences of approach were apparent from the outset. Three proposals lay on the table in 1964 – one from the socialist bloc (formally presented by Czechoslovakia), one from the developing countries (formally by Ghana, India, Mexico and Yugoslavia) and a Western proposal presented by the UK. Although the Special Committee was able to produce a consensus definition on 'sovereign equality' already at that first meeting, its report nevertheless was supplemented by a number of proposals that had fallen outside the consensus. There had been two principal points of contention. The first one had to do with the nature of the exercise. Was it intended merely to 'clarify' or 'highlight' the principles of sovereign equality as laid out in Article 2(1) of the Charter, perhaps, as it was suggested, by restating the San Francisco definition of it? Or was the intention also to 'develop' it 'in the light of the current needs of the world community, taking into account the progress achieved since 1945 in international law and in decolonization'?[86] The other principal point of contention had to do with the inclusion of economic aspects of equality in the Declaration. This was often formulated in terms of the familiar Third World claim on permanent sovereignty over natural resources, although in the course of the debate it was sometimes supplemented by the more widely expressed call for the right to 'dispose freely of their national wealth and natural resources'.[87] Reference was made in the debates to the UNCTAD as well as the General Assembly resolutions on permanent sovereignty of 1962 and 1966. On both issues, the developing countries failed to have their way. Some of their representatives expressed their disappointment at the final session in 1970 quite directly. In the end, the Committee had relied heavily on a draft produced at the San Francisco conference in 1945 – a draft to which reference was also made in Article 5 of the Draft Declaration on Rights and Duties of States prepared by the ILC in 1949 (but never adopted by the General Assembly).[88]

The consensus definition reached in 1964, which eventually became also the final text, was this:

> 1. All States enjoy sovereign equality. They have equal rights and duties and are equal members of the international community, notwithstanding differences of an economic, social, political or other nature.
> 2. In particular, sovereign equality includes the following elements:
>   (a) States are juridically equal.
>   (b) Each State enjoys the rights inherent in full sovereignty;
>   (c) Each State has the duty to respect the personality of other States;
>   (d) The territorial integrity and political independence of the State are inviolable;
>   (e) Each State has the right freely to choose and develop its political, social, economic and cultural systems;

[85] UNGA Res 1815 (XVII) (18 December 1962).

[86] Report of the Special Committee on Principles of International law concerning Friendly Relations and Co-operation among States, UN Doc A/5746 (16 November 1964), 151 (paras 301–2).

[87] Report of the Special Committee on Principles of International law concerning Friendly Relations and Co-operation among States, UN Doc A/6799 (26 September 1967), 191 (para 426).

[88] See esp UNCIO vol VI, Commission I, Committee 1 (preamble, Purposes and Principles), Report of Subcommittee A (1 June 1945), 717–18. Draft Declaration on Rights and Duties of States, UNGA Res 375 (IV) (6 December 1949); and commentary in Bardo Fassbender, 'Chapter I: Purposes and Principles, Art 2(1)' in Bruno Simma et al (eds), *The Charter of the United Nations: A Commentary*, vol 1 (3rd edn, Oxford University Press, 2012) 144–50.

(f) Each State has the duty to comply fully and in good faith with its international obligations and to live in peace with other States.[89]

The only substantive addition to the 1945 text was Cold War-inspired subparagraph (e) that underwrote the right of States to choose their 'political, social, economic, and cultural systems'. It came from the drafts of socialist and developing States and, according to the sponsors, was intended to implement ideas embedded in the 1955 Bandung and Belgrade Declarations.

In the course of the debate six proposals were presented that did not command consensus and never made it to the text of the Declaration. By far the most important of these was any formulation of the 'permanent sovereignty of natural resources'. This would have enshrined a key objective of the NIEO in the resolution – especially the principle that nationalisation of foreign property would have been permitted in accordance with domestic law.[90] While the proposal to include something on substantive equality did receive – at least in an abstract way – some support from the Western representatives as well, in the end finding a set of words that would not simply legislate the NIEO into existence proved impossible. The painfulness of the debates was expressed in the cryptic summary of the last substantive debate on the matter that 'Agreement in principle was reached on the desirability of including the concept of the right of every State freely to dispose of its national wealth and natural resources, but no agreement was reached on the text of such a provision.'[91]

As the Special Committee ended its work, many representatives noted that it had been reduced to 'barest essentials' and that it 'was not entirely satisfactory and needed to be completed'.[92] But it turned out to be impossible to proceed further. So, what the Committee did instead was to list the proposals that had not attained consensus and brought them to the notice of the General Assembly. In addition to the reference to freedom to use national wealth and domestic resources, these proposals included equality in participation in international institutions and multilateral treaties, prohibition of discrimination within the UN system, the right of each State to remove foreign military bases and the prohibition of 'experiments having harmful effects' on other countries.[93] Perhaps a little enigmatically, also the suggestion that the sovereignty of the State was limited by international law failed to find its way into the principle. While a US delegate such as Rosenstock suspected that this represented an absolutist Soviet conception of sovereignty, it was more likely that the (otherwise perhaps self-evident truism) did not get in because it was understood as a coded endorsement of the Western position that compensation for nationalised property had to be paid under the 'prompt, adequate and effective' rule (the notorious 'Hull formula').[94]

The Declaration was accepted unanimously at the twenty-fifth anniversary session of the United Nations. The speeches at the General Assembly were, generally speaking, celebratory, although some also lamented the lack of ambition in their formulation. The representative of Nigeria, speaking on behalf of the forty-one Organisation of African Unity Member States,

[89] Report of the Special Committee on Principles of International Law concerning Friendly Relations and Co-operation among States, UN Doc A/6799 (26 September 1967), 185 (para 409).

[90] That this was clearly understood at the time is revealed, for example, by the counter-proposal that such a right should be made 'subject to international law and to terms of agreements entered into by the State'. Report of the Special Committee on Principles of International Law concerning Friendly Relations and Co-operation among States, UN Doc A/5746 (16 November 1964), 160 (para 331).

[91] Report of the Special Committee on Principles of International Law concerning Friendly Relations and Co-operation among States, UN Doc A/6799 (26 September 1967), 197 (para 438).

[92] ibid 190 (para 421).

[93] Report of the Special Committee on Principles of International Law concerning Friendly Relations and Co-operation among States, UN Doc A/6230 (27 June 1966), 166–76 (paras 373–402).

[94] See Robert Rosenstock, 'The Declaration of Principles of International Law Concerning Friendly Relations: A Survey' (1971) 65 *American Journal of International Law* 713, 734 n49.

highlighted the importance of the United Nations for the newly decolonised countries and used the occasion to remind the members of the struggle against colonialism and apartheid. He was broadly supported by the representative of Poland on behalf of the socialist countries – the latter not failing to highlight peaceful co-existence 'of states with different political and social systems'.

VII SOVEREIGN EQUALITY SINCE 1970

Gradually, the Friendly Relations Declaration became a standard reference point for subsequent multilateral UN instruments having to do with international law. Yet, one may suspect that not many will remember, for example, the 1982 Manila Declaration on Peaceful Settlement of Disputes, the 1987 Declaration on the Enhancement of the Effectiveness of the Principle of Refraining from the Threat or Use of Force in International Relations or the 1988 Declaration on the Prevention and Removal Disputes and Situations which May Threaten International Peace and Security and on the Role of the United Nations in this Field.[95] The fact is that reiterations of UN principles by subsequent declarations has rarely translated into tangible action.

But the Friendly Relations Declaration also received life within the 'Helsinki process' and served as the example for the drafting of the Helsinki Final Act in 1975. Article I of that act was precisely on 'Sovereign equality, respect for the rights inherent in sovereignty', and while the first paragraph repeated the familiar wordings on 'juridical equality', 'territorial integrity and political independence' as well as respect for political, economic and cultural systems, they also added another paragraph with partly new content:

> Within the framework of international law, all the participating States have equal rights and duties. They will respect each other's right to define and conduct as it wishes its relations with other States in accordance with international law and in the spirit of the present Declaration. They consider that their frontiers can be changed, in accordance with international law, by peaceful means and by agreement. They also have the right to belong or not to belong to international organizations, to be or not to be a party to bilateral or multilateral treaties including the right to be or not to be a party to treaties of alliance; they also have the right to neutrality.[96]

Here now was some material that did not get into the UN Declaration, such as confirming their equal right to become members of international institutions and multilateral treaties – a provision underwriting their different security alliances (NATO and the Warsaw Pact) as well as the right to stay out of them. Attention is drawn to the intangibility of boundaries, a key aspect of the Helsinki process and a major achievement especially for the socialist bloc. Why this would be included under 'sovereign equality' is hard to say, apart from as an explication of the point about territorial integrity.

One might want to know more generally about the fate of the principle of sovereign equality in the international law field. Third World lawyers never fail to reference sovereign equality in their works or speeches. It is highlighted in various instruments dealing with international development, including, for example, the Declaration of Principles Governing the Seabed and the Ocean Floor and the Subsoil Thereof, beyond the Limits of National Jurisdiction, adopted also in 1970, that enshrined the principle that the areas outside domestic jurisdiction constituted a 'common heritage of mankind' and eventually led to the Third UN Conference on

[95] See UNGA Res 37/10 (15 November 1982), UNGA Res 42/22 (18 November 1987) and UNGA Res 43/51 (5 December 1988).

[96] Final Act of the Conference on Security and Co-operation in Europe (CSCE), 1 August 1975.

the Law of the Sea and the 1982 Montego Bay Convention.[97] In the 1984 UN report on the progressive development of international law relating to the NIEO, sovereign equality still stood elevated as a chief principle,[98] but after the demise of the NIEO in the late 1980s and 1990s its appearance has diminished together with the other Third World themes associated with it.

Principle 2 of the 1992 Rio Declaration on Environment and Development fails to expressly mention sovereign equality, instead including a slightly revised version of the famous 'Principle 21' of the Stockholm Declaration (1972), according to which all States have 'the sovereign right to exploit their own resources pursuant to their own environmental and developmental policies, and the responsibility to ensure that activities within their jurisdiction or control do not cause damage to the environment of other States or of areas beyond the limits of national jurisdiction', itself preceded by a reference to 'in accordance with the United Nations Charter and the principles of international law'. The practical implementation of that provision has involved some recognition by the developed world that the duties of States may vary (e.g. the reference to 'developmental policies' in Principle 2 and, more generally, Principles 6 and 7 of the Rio Declaration) and that developed States may have an obligation to assist the less developed ones technologically and financially on meeting the objectives laid out in such later environmental and sustainable development instruments as the UN Framework Convention on Climate Change 1992 or the subsequent Paris Agreement.

One of the key problems with respect to 'sovereign equality' has been that of positive discrimination. In a number of situations treaty partners have moved beyond a purely formal treatment of everyone 'similarly' so as to recognise historical differences in de facto capacity in determining the rights and duties of States, such as in the provisions on preferential treatment within the GATT/WTO regime. Whether this recognition would have crystallised into anything like a customary rule may be usefully approached from the perspective of the widely applicable anti-formal principles about equity, reasonableness, proportionality and the like into multilateral treaties – the principle of 'equitable utilisation' in the Convention on the Law of the Non-Navigational Uses of International Watercourses possibly serving as one example.[99] Much criminal or otherwise harmful activity in the natural environment or in cyberspace takes place by private actors, and there may be some agreement that the duty of control (whether 'overall' or 'effective') and of due diligence that applies to them varies in relation to the capacities of the State in question. But the statement of the International Court of Justice from the early 1980s still remains that economic considerations cannot affect party obligations:

> since they are variables which unpredictable national fortune or calamity, as the case may be, might at any time cause to tilt the scale one way or the other. A country might be poor today and become rich tomorrow as a result of an event such as the discovery of a valuable economic resource.[100]

A similar point has been made by the Seabed Chamber of the International Tribunal for the Law of Sea in connection with States sponsoring activities in the seabed and subsoil beyond national jurisdiction, the so-called 'Area'.[101]

97 UNGA Res 2749 (XXV) (16 December 1970).

98 Progressive Development of the Principles and Norms Of International Law Relating to the New International Economic Order, Report of the Secretary-General, UN Doc A/39/504/Add.1 (23 October 1984).

99 Convention on the Law of the Non-Navigational Uses of International Watercourses (New York, 21 May 1997), Art 5. Included in UNGA Res 51/229 (21 May 1997).

100 *Continental Shelf (Tunisia v Libya)*, ICJ Reports 1982, 63 (para 107).

101 *Responsibilities and Obligations of States sponsoring Persons and Entities with respect to Activities in the Area*, Advisory Opinion of 1 February 2011, ITLOS Reports 2011, paras 158–59.

In the years since the passing of the Friendly Relations Declaration, Western academic lawyers have often been sympathetic towards the claims of the G77 but suspicious of reading the sovereign equality principle as legally binding in its own right. Generally speaking, in their view, international law and the UN Charter had nothing to do with the past injustices, and the best way for the developing world to catch up was to join the system and seek to influence its content from the inside. In the 1979 edition of his widely read *How Nations Behave*, Louis Henkin noted that new States had not posed any great challenge to international law but had joined without great protest because '[a]cceptance into that society as an independent equal was the proof and crown of their successful struggle, and international law provided the indispensable framework for living in that society'.[102] For Henkin and for the majority of Western lawyers, to be addressed as sovereign equals cancelled whatever problems about colonialism and the rhetoric of 'civilisation' had existed earlier. No great structural impediments for attaining substantive equality existed any longer. Now it was simply the task of the Third World to use the UN and other international institutions to attain their policy objectives.

It is very uncertain whether that is still a correct assessment of the situation – and it probably never was. The most obvious and unobjectionable aspects of sovereign equality relate usually to its 'technical' uses in formalities or questions of protocol. Here there is less of a problem – Vattel's view of small and large States standing on the same line still applies – with the most significant exceptions having to do with the position of the five permanent members of the UN Security Council and weighted voting especially in international financial institutions where formal influence in decision-making is measured by reference to a country's contribution. But there is no reasonable effort to undermine the first of the elements of the 1970 definition, the 'juridical equality' between States, the equality of their standing in front of international law-applying bodies. Of course, even this matter is influenced by developments in the 'real' or political world, and one may enquire into the way in which the uneven jurisdiction of the International Criminal Court might be invoked as a counter-example. The effort of the United States to exempt its military personnel and its later action against the Court and its officials are part of the imperialist turn of its recent government that is happy to lead the country outside a world where protocols and formality are taken seriously.[103]

VIII SOVEREIGN EQUALITY AND JUSTICE

Equality is not a measurable thing like mass or temperature that can be described using precise units derived from universal constants of nature.[104] To be 'equal' refers to a relative system or standard – it refers to the question 'equal in what respect?' It involves a comparison and needs an external point of view, a standard and a comparator or at least a shared understanding from which two entities may or may not appear as sufficiently similar to be treated in the same way. Poor communities can be equal in respect to each other but unequal in respect to rich ones. Neither equality not sovereign equality exclude different treatment as such. On the contrary, equality does not only mean treating those that are similar in some respect in a similar way, but also treating differently those whose situation is de facto different – again, different in a *relevant*

[102] Louis Henkin, *How Nations Behave: Law and Foreign Policy* (2nd edn, Columbia University Press, 1979) 122.

[103] Anne Peters, 'Compensatory Constitutionalism: The Function and Potential of Fundamental International Norms and Structures' (2006) 19 *Leiden Journal of International Law* 579–610, 604–5; Robert C Johansen, 'The Impact of US Policy toward the International Criminal Court on the Prevention of Genocide, War Crimes, and Crimes against Humanity' (2006) 28 *Human Rights Quarterly* 301–31.

[104] See 'Metrologists Ditch Last Physical Standard Units' (2018) 563 *Nature* 451–52.

respect. While this principle is frequently accepted in domestic societies – people with different income levels pay different amounts of tax and people with disabilities are provided assistance not available to those who have no such disabilities – it has been much more difficult to accept anything of the kind on the international plane. Mechanisms of 'positive discrimination' of the kind involved in preferential treatment in international trade law or in contributions to international environmental regimes are weak and often contested. We may easily understand why this would be the case. In the domestic context, there is some rudimentary solidarity that allows citizens to recognise that their shared 'citizenship' entitles them to view each other from the perspective of some imagined idea of what binds them together – a shared religion, history, common ideas of nationhood and the like. These ideas constitute the 'point of comparison' – the basic criteria or values – that enable treating otherwise different individuals similarly (as 'citizens') but also taking account of *relevant* differences as bases for different treatment (e.g. by taxing richer citizens with a higher percentage or by creating quota to ensure the representation of formerly under-represented groups of citizens).

In the international world, there is no such 'third' – no shared criteria, understandings or values – that could justify deviation from the utterly formal standard of 'sovereign statehood'.[105] Of course, States could in principle try to agree on some relative classifications through mutual agreement or by relying on quantitative criteria and indexes. But all this would come uncomfortably close to seeking a 'standard of civilisation' anew and would be very hard to administer. In practice, it has been seen that it is hard to object to a State's self-qualification as a member of a special class of States in case benefits might accrue to such membership. In any case, such instances would be bound to remain rare and of marginal importance.

Thus, we are left with an indeterminate vision of equality, a seemingly common standard which still harks back to Vattel's intuitive Utopia: whether large or small, rich or poor, old or new, all States must be similarly treated. That is an easy standard to apply. It operates automatically and presupposes no evaluation on anybody's part. *'If you are a state, then this is how you will be treated.'* That is of great value in a society where there is a priori no solidarity and no trust that law-appliers would use their discretion in an acceptable way. So they are granted none. But like any bright-line rule, this, too, is both over- and under-inclusive. It is over-inclusive to the extent that it applies the *same* treatment also to those who *in actual fact would deserve being treated differently*. And it fails to apply that treatment to those 'non-States' who in a relevant respect would deserve to be treated just like States because there is no relevant difference between them and 'formal States' (Palestine, Western Sahara, Tibet . . .).

It is true of course, that people constantly complain about the injustice of formal equality – we have seen the repeated claim by the global South that historical injustices against them ought to be taken into account in assessing the contributions that those States would have to pay for participating in international co-operation on environmental protection, for example. The call for preferential treatment appeals to one type of solidarity across the world. But that is by no means the only basis on which deviation from formal equality is proposed. Others critique that:

> [t]he smallest and financially weakest states, representing a minority of the total population in the organization, possess a majority of the votes. Paying a fractional share of the assessments of the organization, they are able to outvote those paying the highest rates.[106]

[105] Martti Koskenniemi, *From Apology to Utopia* (Cambridge University Press, 2005 [1989]).
[106] Robert A Klein, *Sovereign Equality among States: The History of an Idea* (University of Toronto Press, 1974) 148.

An occasional Western complaint in the past against majorities in the UN General Assembly, this claim is bound to be resuscitated with the neo-right nationalism en vogue in the United States and parts of Europe. It, too, builds on a 'third' that enables treating different entities differently – only this time not building on solidarity but on white supremacism.

By and large, the Friendly Relations Declaration may well be understood as a vocal renunciation of any further formal structures de jure of distinction between sovereigns. Understood as such, it is a vow of humanity to never return to the rhetoric of Lorimer and his contemporaries. And for many observers, in particular those in affluent and influential countries of the past decades, this may well have been enough. But the question of ever-increasing inequality in the factual world, combined with the seemingly perpetual distinction between the 'developed' world and the 'developing' world, cannot but lead one to ask whether indeed a degree of factual equality is a prerequisite for true formal intercourse between equals. The boundary here is hard to determine, for in a world of formal equals but factual un-equals, most structural inequalities can be rephrased as matters of chance and circumstance, and vice versa. The wealthier States may always argue that their status as nuclear powers or their precedence in deep-sea mining or the conquest of the Antarctic is due to their hard-earned success, not structural inequality; but, in the same way, a brutal dictatorship may declare that its people are happy and more determined to live in surveillance, discipline and punishment, having no desire for standardised guarantees of basic human dignity. On the other hand, the same brutal dictator might on some other occasion explain that the hellish conditions of his or her citizens are forced upon them by the unfair balances with which the game of global economy and imperialism are rigged. But speaking of structural inequality, a powerful State may for its own part decide to veto any form of world-improvement, arguing that it is itself a victim of structural bias which threatens to undermine the fairness of the mutually agreed global institutions, therefore demanding that the advanced powers resign from multilateralism altogether.

Again, the great problem with 'sovereign equality' is that it cannot be applied without some criterion of justice that points to the relevant quality in accordance with which entities such as 'States' may appear either 'similar' or 'different'. The attainment of statehood is expected to endow every entity filling the requisite criteria with all the rights and privileges, as well as all the obligations, of statehood. It was this type of justice that was highlighted during decolonisation. But equality also requires that entities that are different are not forced in the same straight-jacket, that it would be wrong to impose obligations on those who, for whatever reason, are unable to bear them. Rules about 'reverse discrimination', special rights and preferential treatment are a commonplace in domestic legal systems, even if their application is always more or less contested. Such contestations reflect differing ideas about the type of justice that the domestic polity should stand for. But usually there is no disagreement that it should stand for *some* justice. By contrast, on the international plane, it is much harder to say not only what type of justice the international system should seek to advance, but whether it should advance any ideas of justice at all. The Cold War view of international law as a pure co-ordination between systems sharing no concept of justice at all has been thoroughly discredited. For a moment, in the 1990s, it may even have appeared that a broadly liberal, free trade and human-rights oriented justice was being institutionalised in international bodies. In the present world of nationalist conflict and Realpolitik, it would be much more daring to suggest that international law stands for some idea about a just world – beyond repeating the hypocritical mantra about 'friendly relations among nations'. It would be a tragedy if, looking back fifty years from 2020, we found that we have made no progress from where we were then.

9

Good Faith

Guillaume Futhazar and Anne Peters

I INTRODUCTION: SENSE IN ABSTRACTION

Good faith is the object of a surprising consensus. Most authors writing about good faith as a general principle of international law stress that it is an essential element for the very existence of the international legal order.[1] In other words, without good faith, it would be impossible to have international law. At the same time, they also agree that good faith escapes any precise definition.[2]

During the negotiations of the Friendly Relations Declaration, a seminal scholarly treatise on the protection of legitimate expectations and good faith was conceived. It was the book by the Swiss scholar Jörg Paul Müller, published in 1971.[3] His legacy has been carried on by Robert Kolb who is today one of the most prolific authors on good faith in international law. To quote Robert Kolb, 'it is impossible to grasp the principle in the immutable majesty of its abstraction'.[4] Its very nature as an abstract notion allows good faith to play a foundational role in international

[1] See eg Georg Schwarzenberger, 'The Fundamental Principles of International Law' (1955) 87 *Recueil des Cours* 195–385, 326: 'a fundamental principle which can be eradicated from international law only at the price of the destruction of international law itself forms necessarily part of the international public order. This consideration alone would suffice to qualify good faith as one of the fundamental principles of international law.' In the same vein, Manfred Lachs, 'The Development and General Trends of International Law in our Time' (1980) 169 *Recueil des Cours* 9–377, 198: 'Good faith is the rock upon which States should be able to build their legitimate hopes linked with each agreement entered into.' On the importance of good faith in international law, see also Alfred Verdross, 'La Bonne Foi comme fondement du droit international public' (1952) 5 *Revue Hellénique de Droit International* 17–21; Michel Virally, 'Review Essay: Good Faith in Public International Law' (1983) 77 *American Journal of International Law* 130–34; Gillian White, 'The Principle of Good Faith' in Vaughan Lowe and Colin Warbrick (eds), *The United Nations and the Principle of International Law* (Routledge, 1994) 230–55; Markus Kotzur, 'Good Faith' in *Max Planck Encyclopedia of Public International Law* (January 2009). The only notable exception to this trend is Elisabeth Zoller who gave a harsh account of the utility of good faith in international law. See Elisabeth Zoller, *La Bonne Foi en Droit International Public* (Pedone, 1977).

[2] Authors either do not attempt to define good faith, as if the meaning of the notion were self-evident, or reach the conclusion of the indeterminacy of good faith when they actually engage in an inquiry. For some, such as Elisabeth Zoller, this indeterminacy is harmful, while others, such as Robert Kolb, find it a strength. See Zoller (n 1) 335–54 and Robert Kolb, 'La Bonne Foi en droit international public' (1998) 43 *Revue Belge de Droit International* 661–732, 674. As an exception, John F O'Connor, *Good Faith in International Law* (Dartmouth, 1991) specifically tries to establish a precise definition of the principle in international law based on a study of its legal manifestations in the international legal order.

[3] Jörg Paul Müller, *Vertrauensschutz im Völkerrecht* (Carl Heymanns Verlag, 1971).

[4] Kolb (n 2) 674 (our translation from the French version). He recently summarised in English the entirety of his work on good faith, Robert Kolb, *Good Faith in International Law* (Hart, 2017). Our analysis of the legal effects of good faith relies on the work of Robert Kolb.

law. While trying to lay down a precise definition of the principle is bound to be unsatisfactory, the term does not escape all attempts of conceptual clarification.

The etymology of 'good faith' provides some indications as to the general meaning of the term. The word 'faith' derives from the Latin word '*fides*', itself originating in the Indo-European word '*beidh-*' which broadly relates to the current understanding of 'trust'. On its own, the word 'faith' generally relates to religious ideas. Accompanied by the adjective 'good', it sheds its religious meaning and refers to honesty and sincerity in human behaviour.

Set in a legal context, the notion of good faith gains additional meaning. Historically, this notion emanates from Roman law where the concept was used both in the public and the private sphere. In its relations with other nations, the Roman Empire applied the *fides publica romanorum*, or *fides publica inter populus* as elements of mutual trust and protection.[5] With regard to agreements between individuals, Cicero argued that 'the foundation of justice ... is good faith – that is, truth and fidelity to promises and agreements'.[6] In the Roman sphere of influence, good faith mainly played a role in contracts between individuals.[7] However, good faith was not the sole foundation of contractual obligations. The conformity of contracts with the law was also a prerequisite for their binding nature.[8] This idea is, however, not easy to apply at the international level due to the absence of a central law-making body.

Indeed, in the legal-positivistic paradigm, a treaty between States relies on their 'will' to enter into an agreement. It was Grotius who suggested that good faith on its own was the source of the obligatory character of agreements between persons, whoever they might be, individuals, princes or States.[9] By placing the necessity of holding one's promises at the very heart of the legal order, Grotius conceptualised good faith as the *alma mater* of law.[10] This might have facilitated, around the turn of the twentieth century, the emergence of the idea of a 'common will' as the ultimate basis of international law, an idea which sought to overcome the strictures of voluntarism.

In a broader and contemporary legal perspective, good faith can be understood in two different ways: 'subjectively' and 'objectively'.[11] 'Subjective' good faith is the reflection of the state of mind of an actor engaging in a legal act. A frequent legal example is that of a person buying a stolen good without knowing it was illegally acquired. In this situation, the person is acting in good faith as she believed that she was engaging in a legitimate legal transaction. That belief must be taken into account in adjudication in order to ensure legal security.

This 'subjective' understanding of good faith, as a state of mind, is difficult to directly transfer to the sphere of international law. States, international organisations and other transnational or

5 Zoller (n 1) 19. Good faith was perceived as being sufficiently universal to allow nations with different legal traditions to nevertheless co-operate legally. On this aspect see Arnaud Vergne, 'Observations liminaires, historiques et terminologiques sur la loyauté et le droit' in Sébastien Ferrari and Sébastien Hourson (eds), *La Loyauté en droit public* (Institut Universitaire Varenne, 2018) 11–19, 13.

6 Cicero, *De Officiis* (tr Walter Miller, Heinemann, 1913), bk I, 24. In Latin, '*Fundamentum autem est institiae fies, id est dictorum convetorumque constantia et veritas.*'

7 O'Connor (n 2) 23.

8 ibid.

9 As argued in Guy Augé, 'Le Contrat et l'évolution du consensualisme chez Grotius' (1968) 13 Archives de Philosophie du Droit 99–114, 108–9. Hugo Grotius, *De iure belli ac pacis* (Blaeu, 1663), bk II, ch XIII.

10 The Grotian legacy has therefore been heralded as a source of a more community- and individual-oriented understanding of international law. See Hersch Lauterpacht, 'The Grotian Tradition of International Law', first published in (1946) 23 *British Yearbook for International Law* 1–53, here as published in Elihu Lauterpacht (ed), *International Law: being the Collected Papers of Hersch Lauterpacht*, vol 2 (Cambridge University Press, 1970–78) 307–65. This idealist reading of Grotius is nowadays often considered a distortion.

11 We draw this typology from Kolb (n 2) 673–74 who, however, distinguishes *three* understandings (subjective good faith, standard, principle).

global actors do not have states of mind. They are complex aggregates of individuals and institutional networks. The difficulty is partly overcome by the fact that good faith, in the subjective sense, exists as a postulate, or an axiom. Good faith has to be presumed in most legal relations, because the opposite would make no sense. Two persons openly acting in bad faith could never fulfil, or even reach, an agreement because each of them would try to defeat the purpose of the agreement for the sake of their own interest. Of course, such *mala fide* behaviour can happen in reality. In international relations theory, realists would say that, more often than not, States conclude treaties or memoranda for motives which may have little to do with the facial objective of the agreement (for example appeasing domestic audiences, gaining international prestige or the like) or with the reservation not to comply fully anyway. But if the postulate of good faith were to be erased, there would be absolutely no reason to enter into a legal agreement with anyone. This explains why good faith is often presumed in litigation and, consequently, why bad faith has to be proven.

The second understanding of good faith is more 'objective'. In this reading, good faith is a standard or a principle. As a standard, good faith refers to what should be the normal or adequate behaviour.[12] In this sense, good faith is a rough synonym for 'reasonable'.[13] Importantly, this standard is highly abstract and does not entail specific legal consequences. Moreover, good faith, as a standard, does not in itself impose any obligation but is only a modality, a way of applying (making, interpreting, enforcing etc.) *other* legal norms. In legal language, broad normative standards are often called principles. As a principle, good faith manifests itself in or undergirds a number of legal rules and principles which flesh out this term and make it more concrete. For example, the prohibition of an abuse of rights seeks to ensure that an actor does not exercise its right or competence in order to cause harm to someone else or in a way that would defeat the right's object and purpose. The Latin idea of '*venire contra factum proprium*' prevents illegitimate contradictions in a legal dispute. The principle '*pacta sunt servanda*', gives a binding nature to agreement between parties. All these legal institutions ultimately stem from the principle of good faith.

We will address the legal manifestations of the principle of good faith later. For the purpose of this introduction, we retain that good faith, as a principle of international law, seeks to protect the following core ideas: *trust and predictability in legal relations of co-operation*. Among individuals, trust refers to their subjective state of mind, to their expectations and beliefs. When entering into an agreement with someone else, a person assumes that the other will comply with it. When a person trusts another, he or she assumes that an agreement between them will be followed by actions or omissions in compliance with what was agreed. 'Predictability' refers to this future state of the law or of the legal relationship. When entering into an agreement, not only does the contractor expect that the other will act (or refrain from acting), he or she can anticipate and predict exactly how the other party will act. Finally, the above-mentioned relations of co-operation express the idea that good faith (in this classical, contractual sense) operates outside of a relation of authority and rather in a relation between equal players. In contrast, a person responding to an authority which is competent to issue legally binding acts does not strictly need to act in good faith, because the normative basis of the obligation emanates from a vertical configuration. Paying a fine for a misdemeanour escapes the classic rationale of

[12] Kolb (n 4) 22.

[13] For a study of this notion, see Olivier Corten, 'The Notion of "Reasonable" in International Law: Legal Discourse, Reason and Contradictions' (1999) 48 *International & Comparative Law Quarterly* 613–25.

good faith previously exposed. However, it is not aberrant to demand good faith by both sides even in an 'asymmetrical' (hierarchical) setting, as will be shown later.[14]

In analogy to the contractual setting, good faith plays an obvious role in the relation between sovereign States. In this constellation, good faith can be linked to other foundational concepts of international law. For instance, the function of good faith as a guarantee for trust and predictability in legal relations makes it similar to the concept of rule of law which demands that political power is constrained and kept in check by law.[15] In international law, good faith tempers the potential excesses of sovereignty and voluntarism by strengthening the international rules that constrain them.[16]

In this chapter, we will discuss the role of the principle of good faith in international law, fifty years after its formal consecration in the Friendly Relations Declaration. To do so, we will first look at the place of good faith in the Declaration and how it has been stated (section II). We will highlight the process that led to its incorporation in the Declaration and will discuss its history in the legal framework of the United Nations. From here, we will engage in a detailed analysis of the legal effects of the principle of good faith in international law (section III). We will show that the principle exerts its influence in all the stages of the legal process: the creation of rules, their interpretation and implementation, and their termination. Based on this analysis, we will discuss the normative quality of good faith and determine whether it is an autonomous rule or not (section IV). The following section will address the contemporary functions of good faith (section V). We will discuss the different functions that the principle has in a thematically and structurally diversified international legal order. By doing so, we will demonstrate how the principle has accompanied the changes in the international legal order and how these changes might indicate a slight expansion of the traditional scope of good faith. Drawing on this analysis, we will debate whether the principle of good faith is still relevant to achieve the goals of the Friendly Relations Declaration fifty years on (section VI). We will suggest that the strengthened and upgraded legal status of individual human beings in the international legal order requires a conceptual enrichment of good faith in international law in order to properly take this upgraded status into account. We will conclude with a broader reflection on how to think of good faith in international law in times of instability (section VII).

II GOOD FAITH IN THE FRIENDLY RELATIONS DECLARATION AND IN THE UNITED NATIONS CHARTER

The seventh principle of the Friendly Relations Declaration provides that 'States shall fulfil in good faith the obligations assumed by them in accordance with the Charter.'[17] This general statement is complemented by four specifications with regard to the operation of good faith in the context of certain obligations:

[14] See section VII.

[15] For a recent brief discussion of this concept, see Philip Allott, 'The Rule of Law' in Jean D'Aspremont and Sahib Singh (eds), *Concepts for International Law. Contributions to Disciplinary Thought* (Edward Elgar, 2019) 804–14.

[16] Kolb (n 2) 732.

[17] UN Doc A/RES/2625(XXV) 24 October 1970, Declaration on Principles of International Law Concerning Friendly Relations and Co-operation among States in Accordance with the Charter of the United Nations. For a deeper analysis of the history of the Friendly Relations Declaration, see the chapters by J Kurtz, JE Viñuales and M Waibel, S Moyn and U Özsu in this volume. For a contemporary study of the Friendly Relations Declaration, see Gaetano Arangio-Ruiz, 'The Normative Role of the General Assembly of the United Nations and the Declaration of Principles of Friendly Relations' (1972) 137 *Recueil des Cours* 419–742.

> Every State has the duty to fulfil in good faith the obligations assumed by it in accordance with the Charter of the United Nations.
>
> Every State has the duty to fulfil in good faith its obligations under the generally recognized principles and rules of international law.
>
> Every State has the duty to fulfil in good faith its obligations under international agreements valid under the generally recognized principles and rules of international law.
>
> Where obligations arising under international agreements are in conflict with the obligations of Members of the United Nations under the Charter of the United Nations, the obligations under the Charter shall prevail.

Importantly, good faith is not limited to this principle in the Friendly Relations Declaration. It permeates the entire Declaration. Good faith is mentioned in the preamble as a prerequisite for the maintenance of international peace and security.[18] It is also present in other principles of the Declaration, such as the prohibition of the use of force[19] or the principle of sovereign equality of States.[20]

A closer look at the *travaux préparatoires* of the Friendly Relations Declaration highlights that incorporating the principle of good faith in the resolution was basically uncontroversial.[21] The main point of disagreement during the discussions on the seventh principle was the reference to 'international agreements valid under the generally recognized principles and rules of international law'.[22] At the time, several non-Western countries were concerned with the unfair or unequal character of several agreements concluded with Western powers at a time when the latter's hegemony was unchallenged.[23] Because of the unequal nature of these treaties, there was concern over the possibility of implementing them in good faith. However, the intergovernmental meetings for the preparation of the Friendly Relations Declaration were not the most relevant forum for such a debate, especially since the Vienna Convention on the Law of Treaties (VCLT) was being negotiated during the same period. Consequently, State representatives agreed to keep this reference in the Friendly Relations Declaration and to discuss the legal implications of 'international agreements valid under the generally recognized principles and rules of international law' within the framework of the Vienna Convention.[24]

To understand why good faith was so easily incorporated in the Friendly Relations Declaration, we have to look back at the initial incorporation of the principle in the UN Charter in 1945. The main reference to good faith in the Charter is in Article 2(2): 'All Members, in order to ensure to all of them the rights and benefits resulting from membership, *shall fulfil in good faith*

[18] UN Doc A/RES/2625(XXV). 'Considering that the faithful observance of the principles of international law concerning friendly relations and co-operation among States and the fulfillment in good faith of the obligations assumed by States, in accordance with the Charter, is of the greatest importance for the maintenance of international peace and security and for the implementation of the other purposes of the United Nations.'

[19] ibid. 'All States shall pursue in good faith negotiations for the early conclusion of a universal treaty on general and complete disarmament under effective international control and strive to adopt appropriate measures to reduce international tensions and strengthen confidence among States.'

[20] ibid. 'Each State has the duty to comply fully and in good faith with its international obligations and to live in peace with other States.'

[21] Report of the Special Committee on Principles of International Law concerning Friendly Relations and Co-operation among States, UN Doc A/6799 (26 September 1967), paras 258–60.

[22] ibid, paras 269–73.

[23] See Anne Peters, 'Treaties, Unequal' in *Max Planck Encyclopedia of Public International Law* (February 2018).

[24] Report of the Special Committee on Principles of International Law concerning Friendly Relations and Co-operation among States, UN Doc A/6799 (26 September 1967), para 272: 'It was important ... that the Special Committee should not do anything to prejudice either the future work of the Commission on the subject of succession of States, or the discussion on the law of treaties at the forthcoming Conference, both of which were more suitable places for considering the difficulties of the question than was the Special Committee.'

the obligations assumed by them in accordance with the present Charter.'[25] The incorporation of the notion of good faith in this provision proved more difficult than it would be in 1970, specifically due to the different legal traditions of the countries engaged in the negotiation of the Charter.

The addition of good faith to the Charter was initially a proposition of the Colombian representative, Jesús María Yepes, who sought to add elements of morality and justice to the Charter.[26] This was intended as a strong signal after the atrocities of the Second World War – atrocities that had remained covered by formal legality. This proposal had strong support from other Latin American countries, such as Uruguay, Venezuela and Panama, and from countries with a Roman law legacy.[27] This is not surprising considering that good faith is a common element in this broader legal tradition. In contrast, good faith is mostly absent from common law traditions, or at least not recognised as a pillar of legal relations.[28] Consequently, the addition of the good faith requirement was seen as unnecessary by common law countries, specifically the United States. They argued that the addition of good faith was redundant because obligations assumed by the members of the UN simply had to be implemented. Fulfilment in good faith made no sense as, in their understanding, an obligation could either be fulfilled or not.[29]

This misunderstanding was overcome thanks to the intervention of the Belgian representative, Henri Rolin, who clarified that the reference to good faith in the Charter was to be understood as an interpretative tool.[30] Good faith allows for more than a strictly textual interpretation of the Charter in order to better reach the Charter's goals.[31]

In 1970, good faith was already a well-established principle in the UN legal framework. This explains why its incorporation in the Friendly Relations Declaration was fairly uncontroversial, although it was one further step. Indeed, in the UN Charter, good faith only concerned the obligations foreseen in the Charter itself. With the Friendly Relations Declaration, members of the UN agreed to generalise the principle. Good faith was now a requirement applicable to all international treaties and other rules and principles of international law. Arguably, this was already the case before the term was incorporated in the UN Charter and in the Friendly Relations Declaration,[32] but the codification amounted to a significant confirmation of the principle.

[25] Emphasis added. For a general comment on this provision, see Jörg P Müller and Robert Kolb, 'Article 2(2)' in Bruno Simma et al (eds), *The Charter of the United Nations: A Commentary*, vol 1 (2nd edn, Oxford University Press, 2002).

[26] The general philosophy of international relations of Jesús María Yepes is detailed in his book: JM Yepes, *Philosophie du Panaméricanisme et Organisation de la Paix* (Editions de la Baconnière, 1945).

[27] Romain Yakemtchouk, *La Bonne Foi dans la conduite internationale des États* (Éditions Techniques et Economiques, 2002) 49–54.

[28] The compatibility of the concept of good faith with common law systems is still called into question today, see eg Maud Piers, 'Good Faith in English Law: Could a Rule Become a Principle?' (2011) 26 *Tulane European and Civil Law Forum* 123–70. On the tension that the notion of good faith can create between civil law systems and common law systems, see eg Michael Bridge, 'Good Faith, the Common Law and the CISG' (2017) 22 *Uniform Law Review* 98–115.

[29] Hans Kelsen held a similar opinion. See Hans Kelsen, *The Law of the United Nations* (Stevens, 1950) 89, 'The words "in good faith" in Article 2§2 are superfluous for it is impossible to "fulfil" an obligation in bad faith.'

[30] Conference on International Organization: Documents of the United Nations Conference on International Organization, vol VI, 95, '[La bonne foi] est un principe d'interprétation de droit romain qu'une obligation s'exécute de bonne foi et que si elle est susceptible de deux interprétations, dont l'une permet l'exécution littérale mais qui n'est pas conciliable avec la bonne foi, cette interprétation doit être écartée.' Yakemtchouk (n 27) 53.

[31] Yakemtchouk (n 27) 53.

[32] See n 1.

Having clarified the place and history of good faith in the Declaration, we now turn to the exact meaning of 'fulfilling in good faith international obligations'. What lies behind this statement? What are the legal effects of the principle of good faith?

III THE LEGAL EFFECTS OF GOOD FAITH

Good faith is an omnipresent principle. It has a bearing on all international law at all stages: its creation, its interpretation, its implementation and the cessation of its application. Good faith mostly appears in the different rules, or meta-rules, that are specifically designed to ensure trust and predictability in the international legal order. These rules mainly manifest themselves in the context of litigation where judges and arbitrators use them to settle disputes. These interpreters have progressively detailed how good faith shapes the different stages of international law. In this section, relying both on the international case law and the abundant literature,[33] we will highlight the importance of good faith in the different stages of the international legal process.

1 *Good Faith and the Creation of International Law*

Good faith impacts on the creation of international law in two constellations. First, the principle of good faith is essential in the genesis of international treaties (section III.1.1). This is not surprising considering the historical origins of this legal term. Good faith here bears on the process of treaty negotiation and on the rights and obligations that treaties may generate before their entry in force. Second, good faith is one explanation why unilateral conduct of States also can generate legal obligations (section III.1.2).

1.1 *Good Faith and the Genesis of International Agreements*

Pacta sunt servanda is the core principle of the international law of treaties.[34] As plainly stated in Article 26 VCLT, 'every treaty in force is binding upon the parties to it and must be performed by them in good faith'. The principle of *pacta sunt servanda* is nowadays recognised as being an expression of the requirements of good faith.[35]

But when it comes to international agreements, good faith does not only operate by conferring upon them a binding character once they are in force. It can also shape the process that leads to their creation, and ensure that their purpose is protected before they enter into force.

1.1.1 THE OBLIGATION TO NEGOTIATE IN GOOD FAITH The obligation to negotiate in good faith is not an absolute requirement that shapes all the possible processes of treaty negotiation. It has a bearing specifically in two situations. The first is the peaceful settlement of international disputes, when States have been requested to work on an agreement following a judicial sentence. This was highlighted in the Manila Declaration on the Peaceful Settlement of International Disputes, which refers to the principles of the Friendly Relations Declaration.[36]

[33] This section is particularly inspired by the work of Robert Kolb; see Kolb (n 2 and n 4). The references to the most recent case law go beyond Kolb.

[34] See, inter alia, Anthony Aust, 'Pacta Sunt Servanda' in *Max Planck Encyclopedia of Public International Law* (February 2007). See also Christian Tomuschat, 'Pacta Sunt Servanda' in Andreas Fischer-Lescano and Michael Bothe (eds), *Frieden in Freiheit: Festschrift für Michael Bothe zum 70. Geburtstag* (Nomos, 2008) 1047–65.

[35] The idea of *pacta sunt servanda* was intensely debated during the drafting of the VCLT. See W Paul Gormley, 'The Codification of Pacta Sunt Servanda by the International Law Commission: The Preservation of Classical Norms of Moral Force and Good Faith' (1970) 14 *Saint Louis University Law Journal* 367–428.

[36] Manila Declaration on the Peaceful Settlement of Disputes, UNGA Res 37/10 (15 November 1982).

The second constellation is where States have agreed to negotiate an agreement within the context of an existing treaty. For instance, Article VI of the Treaty on the Non-Proliferation of Nuclear Weapons requires its parties to negotiate in good faith in order to reach an agreement on effective disarmament.[37] In the absence of a dispute, when States spontaneously engage in negotiations in order to elaborate a treaty, the obligation to negotiate in good faith will apply, but not as strictly.

The obligation to negotiate in good faith has often been discussed in the case law of the International Court of Justice (ICJ).[38] In its judgment of 2019 in the *Obligation to Negotiate Access to the Pacific Ocean*,[39] the ICJ had the opportunity to recall what the obligation to negotiate in good faith entailed for the parties concerned. Bolivia had requested the ICJ to adjudicate its claim that Chile was not negotiating in good faith an agreement that would grant Bolivia sovereign access to the Pacific Ocean. The ICJ found that Chile had no obligation to negotiate such an agreement. It nevertheless provided a short analysis on the obligation to negotiate in good faith. It referred to its previous case law, the *North Sea Continental Shelf* case and the *Application of the Interim Accord of 13 September 1995* case, to stress that States 'are under an obligation so to conduct themselves that the negotiations are meaningful, which will not be the case when either of them insists upon its own position without contemplating any modification'[40] and also that '[e]ach of them "should pay reasonable regard to the interests of the other"'.[41] This means that States are not allowed to deprive the negotiation of its object and its purpose. For instance, in the *Pulp Mills* case, Uruguay disregarded its obligation to negotiate in good faith with Argentina by authorising the construction of the mills before the expiration of the period of negotiation.[42] Of course, the difficulty remains to identify at which point the obstruction reaches the point of illegality.

Some authors have suggested that the obligation to negotiate in good faith at the same time protects the legitimate expectations of the negotiating parties.[43] This is accurate to the extent that these expectations relate to the negotiation process, but not to its outcome. Indeed, in *Obligation to Negotiate Access to the Pacific Ocean*, the ICJ stressed that the obligation to negotiate in good faith implies several requirements regarding the process between the States but does not determine the result of the process.[44] On its own, the obligation to negotiate in good faith does not require to reach an agreement. For instance, Article VI of the Treaty on the Non-Proliferation of Nuclear Weapons specifies what the negotiations should lead to (a treaty on effective disarmament), but it is not an obligation to come to an agreement. If the negotiations are conducted in good faith, but do not result in the adoption of an agreement, this provision is not breached.[45] At most, good faith can indicate the envisioned outcome of the

[37] See Treaty on the Non-Proliferation of Nuclear Weapons, 1 July 1968, 729 UNTS 161.

[38] See eg *North Sea Continental Shelf cases (Federal Republic of Germany* v *Denmark; Federal Republic of Germany* v *Netherlands)*, Judgment, ICJ Reports 1969, 3, para 85; *Fisheries Jurisdiction case (United Kingdom of Great Britain and Northern Ireland* v *Iceland)*, Judgment, ICJ Reports 1974, 3, paras 73–78; *Interpretation of the Agreement of 25 March 1951 between the WHO and Egypt*, Advisory Opinion, ICJ Reports 1980, 73, paras 49–50; *Applicability of the Obligation to Arbitrate under Section 21 of the United Nations Headquarters Agreement of 26 June 1947*, Advisory Opinion, ICJ Reports 1988, 12, paras 51–57; *Application of the Interim Accord of 13 September 1995 (The Former Yugoslav Republic of Macedonia* v *Greece)*, Judgment, ICJ Reports 2011, 644, paras 127–38.

[39] *Obligation to Negotiate Access to the Pacific Ocean (Bolivia* v *Chile)*, Judgment, ICJ General List No 153.

[40] ibid, para 86.

[41] ibid.

[42] *Case Concerning Pulp Mills on the River Uruguay (Argentina* v *Uruguay)*, Judgment, ICJ Reports 2010, 14, para 149.

[43] Kolb (n 4) 201–3.

[44] *Obligation to Negotiate Access to the Pacific Ocean* (n 39), paras 160–62.

[45] *Application of the Interim Accord of 13 September 1995* (n 38), para 134.

negotiations.[46] Even if a State may legitimately expect that an agreement will be reached, as was the case for Bolivia in the dispute with Chile, these expectations do not give rise to an international obligation to effectively attain one.[47]

1.1.2 PRE-CONVENTIONAL OBLIGATIONS Besides its influence on inter-State negotiation, the principle of good faith shapes and protects the creation of international agreements in several ways. For example, good faith influences the conditions under which a treaty signed in violation of municipal law may nevertheless produce legal effects at the international level.[48] Good faith also creates the possibility to tacitly conclude an international agreement through conduct, although this situation is rare.[49] This was the case for a loan agreement signed between Costa Rica and Italy in 1985 which Costa Rica had not formally ratified, yet acted as if it had.[50] Another constellation are the obligations entailed by a treaty signed but not yet entered into force. On this issue, Article 18 VCLT provides:

> A State is obliged to refrain from acts which would defeat the object and purpose of a treaty when:
>
> (a) It has signed the treaty or has exchanged instruments constituting the treaty subject to ratification, acceptance or approval, until it shall have made its intention clear not to become a party to the treaty; or
> (b) It has expressed its consent to be bound by the treaty, pending the entry into force of the treaty and provided that such entry into force is not unduly delayed.

This provision is meant to protect the core elements of good faith: trust and predictability. Indeed, when signing a treaty, States create legitimate expectations between themselves, expectations that refer to the object and purpose of the treaty that has been signed.

But the object and purpose are not always obvious, and identifying them might require subtle interpretation.[51] Generally speaking, the 'object' is what the treaty does. For instance, the Convention on International Trade in Endangered Species of Wild Fauna and Flora (CITES)[52] establishes a legal and administrative system for the management of international trade of endangered species. The 'purpose' of the treaty is the finality of that object. The purpose of the CITES is the conservation of endangered species. Treaties with identical objects but different purposes have to be interpreted differently. For example, if the CITES were intended not to preserve endangered species but to maximise the profit generated by their international

46 Treaty on the Non-Proliferation of Nuclear Weapons (n 37).

47 *Obligation to Negotiate Access to the Pacific Ocean* (n 39), para 162. On this point the ICJ states that 'The Court notes that references to legitimate expectations may be found in arbitral awards concerning disputes between a foreign investor and the host State that apply treaty clauses providing for fair and equitable treatment. It does not follow from such references that there exists in general international law a principle that would give rise to an obligation on the basis of what could be considered a legitimate expectation. Bolivia's argument based on legitimate expectations thus cannot be sustained.' The importance of legitimate expectation in international investment will be discussed further in section V of this chapter.

48 See Art 46 VCLT: Provisions of international law regarding competence to conclude treaties. For a brief analysis of this topic see Michael Bothe, 'Article 46 (1969)' in Olivier Corten and Pierre Klein (eds), *The Vienna Conventions on the Law of Treaties: A Commentary*, vol II (Oxford University Press, 2011) 1090–99.

49 Kolb (n 4) 49–52.

50 See *Loan Agreement between Italy and Costa Rica*, Perm Ct Arb, Sentence of 26 June 1988, RIAA, vol XXV, 21–82, 41–46 and 53.

51 See eg Isabelle Buffard and Karl Zemanek, 'The "Object and Purpose" of a Treaty: An Enigma?' (1998) 3 *Austrian Review of International and European Law* 311–43.

52 Convention on International Trade in Endangered Species of Wild Fauna and Flora, 3 March 1973, 993 UNTS 271.

trade, the result of its interpretation would be fundamentally different.[53] Of course, the distinction is not always clear cut and object and purpose may sometimes overlap, thus becoming indistinguishable. It nevertheless provides a useful starting point to assess the pre-conventional obligations States may have to follow.

Robert Kolb provides the following example of a situation that would lead to a pre-conventional obligation.[54] A State agrees, through a bilateral treaty, to cede a part of its territory to another State. The purpose of this agreement is the possibility of exploiting the natural resources of the ceded part. If before the entry into force of the treaty, the State ceding the territory depletes it from its natural resources, then it would be a situation where Article 18 VCLT is breached.

To summarise, Article 18 VCLT illustrates that the scope of good faith is not limited to agreements which are formally valid and in force. The principle aims more broadly at the protection of the spirit of the agreement.

1.2 *Good Faith and Unilateral Acts of States*

Although good faith conceptually originates in a contractual setting, it is not limited to this constellation. In international law, the conduct of a State can, under certain conditions, create commitments. The ultimate reason for the binding character of unilateral acts is good faith, as other participants in the international process may legitimately trust such behaviour.

We will discuss two scenarios: States remaining silent in the face of certain legal acts, and States issuing public promises in the form of unilateral declarations.

1.2.1 ACQUIESCENCE In international law, acquiescence is a 'qualified silence'.[55] Acquiescence means doing nothing in the face of other legal acts that could or should have called for a specific reaction. For instance, the exercise of sovereign prerogatives by a State over a disputed area may amount, in the absence of public reaction by the other State concerned, to the acquisition or consolidation of title by the State displaying such powers. In such a situation, the silence of a State expresses its legal view and can therefore become the foundation for the trust and expectations of others.

Several ICJ cases illustrate the binding nature of acquiescence. In the *Norwegian Fisheries* case,[56] the ICJ stated that the United Kingdom could not claim the illegality of the maritime boundaries established by Norway because it had tolerated these boundaries for more than sixty years. During this period, the UK did not express any reservation concerning the legality of these boundaries. Since the UK could not have overlooked the Norwegian decree establishing these boundaries,[57] the ICJ concluded that the silence of the UK amounted to its acquiescence to the legal acts of Norway. Consequently, the UK was bound not to contest the legality of the Norwegian maritime boundaries.

In the first *Temple of Preah Vihear* case,[58] the ICJ followed this logic and decided that Thailand had tacitly accepted the boundary established with Cambodia for more than fifty years.

[53] On this understanding of the object and the purpose, see eg Mustafa Kamil Yasseen, 'L'Interprétation des traités d'après la Convention de Vienne sur le droit des traités' (1976) 151 *Recueil des Cours* 1–114, 55.

[54] Kolb (n 4) 43–44.

[55] ibid 92. See also Paulina Starski, 'Silence within the Process of Normative Change and Evolution of the Prohibition on the Use of Force: Normative Volatility and Legislative Responsibility' (2017) 4 *Journal on the Use of Force and International Law* 14–65.

[56] *Fisheries case (United Kingdom v Norway)*, Judgment, ICJ Reports 1951, 116, 138–39.

[57] ibid.

[58] *Case Concerning the Temple of Preah Vihear (Cambodia v Thailand)*, Judgment, ICJ Reports 1962, 6, 27–29.

Even though the boundaries between the countries were the result of negotiations between former colonial powers, Thailand did not express any reservation to their validity. It even acted as if it had accepted them. Here again, the acquiescence of Thailand barred it from contesting the boundaries.[59]

From the case law, we can extract three elements that make acquiescence binding: the duration of the silence, the silent State's knowledge of the other's behaviour, and the silent State's opportunity to react. The factual elements of the dispute remain decisive for finding acquiescence.

Both the ICJ[60] and scholarship[61] generally stress that acquiescence produces its legal effects because of good faith. By opting for silence in reaction to other States' behaviours which potentially have legal consequences, silent States create trust and expectations. These elements have to be protected in order to preserve the integrity of the legal order.

1.2.2 UNILATERAL DECLARATIONS Unilateral declarations of States, for instance promises, are nowadays unanimously considered as a source of international obligations. This was not always the case. Early twentieth-century literature on international law tended to deny the binding nature of these acts.[62] The doctrinal position slowly evolved over time. The insight grew that unilateral acts needed to be acknowledged as a source of international obligations.[63] This position was consecrated by the ICJ in the *Nuclear Tests* case.[64] Here, the Court acknowledged the binding character of the French unilateral declarations to discontinue atmospheric nuclear tests:

> *One of the basic principles governing the creation and performance of legal obligations, whatever their source, is the principle of good faith.* Trust and confidence are inherent in international cooperation, in particular in an age when this cooperation in many fields is becoming increasingly essential. Just as the very rule of *pacta sunt servanda* in the law of treaties is based on good faith, so also is the binding character of an international obligation assumed by unilateral declaration. Thus interested States may take cognisance of unilateral declarations and place confidence in them, and are entitled to require that the obligation thus created be respected.[65]

Two factors explain the binding nature of unilateral declarations. The first factor is good faith: such declarations generate trust and give rise to expectations. The denial of a declaration's potential to generate a legal obligation would disappoint these expectations and would consequently create legal instability. The second factor (more implicit in the reasoning of the Court) is voluntarism: these acts should be recognised as binding because the State has *decided* to make them so by having specific authorities issuing them.[66]

[59] Further examples of acquiescence in boundary disputes are *Case Concerning Delimitation of the Maritime Boundary in the Gulf of Maine Area (Canada* v *United States of America)*, Judgment, ICJ Reports 1984, 246, paras 126–54. *Case Concerning the Territorial and Maritime Dispute (Nicaragua* v *Colombia)*, Preliminary Objections, Judgment, ICJ Reports 2007, 832, paras 79–80.

[60] *Case Concerning Delimitation of the Maritime Boundary in the Gulf of Maine Area* (n 59), para 130.

[61] Seminally, Jörg Paul Müller, *Vertrauensschutz im Völkerrecht* (Carl Heymanns Verlag, 1971). See for a recent contribution Nuno Sérgio Marques Antunes, 'Acquiescence' in *Max Planck Encyclopedia of Public International Law* (September 2006), para 19.

[62] On this doctrinal tendency, see Vladimir Duro Degan, 'Unilateral Act as a Source of Particular International Law' (1994) 5 *Finnish Yearbook of International Law* 149–266.

[63] ibid. Also Víctor Rodríguez Cedeño and María Isabel Torres Cazorla, 'Unilateral Acts of States in International Law' in *Max Planck Encyclopedia of Public International Law* (January 2019), para 7.

[64] *Nuclear Test case (Australia* v *France)*, Judgment, ICJ Reports 1974, 253.

[65] ibid, para 46 (emphasis added).

[66] See on voluntarism and good faith as explaining the binding nature of unilateral acts the conclusions of the ILC on the matter, ILC, 'Guiding Principles to Unilateral Declarations of States Capable of Creating Legal Obligations' (2006).

Acquiescence and unilateral declarations follow the same rationale and are both unilateral acts. However, in a dispute, both are examined in different ways. A finding of acquiescence relies on a factual analysis (elements of time, knowledge and opportunity to react). In contrast, the analysis of unilateral declarations is more formalist. They must be issued by specifically authorised individuals and institutions that can convey the expression of the State's sovereignty at the international level.[67] The competences required to perform a unilateral legally relevant act are the same as those required to sign a treaty on behalf of a State.

The legal effects of unilateral acts highlight that good faith in international law is far from being confined to the realm of international treaties. Good faith protects trust, secures predictability and seeks to honour legitimate expectations more broadly.

2 *Good Faith and the Interpretation and Application of International Law*

Interpretation and application of international law are overlapping activities as any implementation of a norm requires its prior interpretation. This section explains how the duty to interpret and implement international rules in good faith is associated with the prohibition of the abuse of rights and with the teleological interpretation of legal rules. We will then turn to the principle of estoppel, whose rationale relates to the ideas that justify the legal power of unilateral acts. The last subsection will be dedicated to the modification of treaties through practice.

2.1 *Good Faith and Reasonable Interpretation and Application*

The call for an interpretation of international rules in good faith seeks to contain the possibly perverse effects that a strict textual interpretation might produce.[68]

Good faith is apt to contain the discretionary power of States parties under treaty provisions which grant them some leeway. As concurring Judge Xue wrote in the *Whaling* case, 'discretion under Article VIII, paragraph 1 [of the International Convention on the regulation of Whaling] as a corollary, also means a duty on every authorizing party to exercise the power properly and reasonably by virtue of the principle of good faith under the law of treaties. For these reasons, it cannot be said that Article VIII has bestowed a self-defined right on the Contracting Parties.'[69]

Instances of bad faith in applying treaties date from antiquity up to recent investments case law. In his account of the Peloponnesian war, Thucydides relates how a promise to repatriate prisoners at the end of the conflict was indeed fulfilled, but only after having killed said prisoners.[70] In 1713, France agreed to destroy the port of Dunkirk following the signature of the Treaty of Utrecht. However, after having done so, it initiated the construction of another port only a few miles away from the former one.[71] These extravagant cases are not

[67] ICJ, *Nuclear Test* case (n 64), para 49, 'Of the statements by the French Government now before the Court, the most essential are clearly those made by the President of the Republic. There can be no doubt, in view of his functions, that his public communications or statements, oral or written, as Head of State, are in international relations acts of the French State.' Similarly, the guiding principles of the ILC on unilateral acts clearly mirror Art 7 VCLT on the question of the author of unilateral acts. See ILC (n 66), para 4.

[68] On the role of good faith in interpretation, see Ulf Linderfalk, 'What Are the Functions of the General Principles? Good Faith and International Legal Pragmatics' (2018) 78 *Zeitschrift für ausländisches öffentliches Recht und Völkerrecht* 1–31.

[69] See *Whaling in the Antarctic (Australia v Japan)*, Judgment, 31 March 2014, separate opinion Judge Xue, para 9, on the ICRW of 2 December 1946, UNTS 161, No 72.

[70] Thucydides, *The History of the Peloponnesian War* (431–404 BC), English translation by Benjamin Jowett (Ashendene Press, 1930), bk II, ch VI, para V–VII.

[71] Zoller (n 1) 81.

necessarily examples of an abuse of rights. They illustrate that a rigid textual reading of a rule can prevent its implementation if its spirit is ignored completely. In these cases, the agreements were simply not complied with because of a bad-faith interpretation of their provisions.

An abuse of rights is a subtler notion. To quote Alexandre Kiss, 'abuse of rights refers to a State exercising a right either in a way which impedes the enjoyment by other States of their own rights or for an end different from that for which the right was created, to the injury of another State'.[72]

In inter-States disputes, the prohibition of the abuse of rights has occasionally been mentioned by courts or invoked by plaintiffs[73] but, to our knowledge, has never been explicitly upheld by judges and arbitrators.[74] The latest example is the *Jadhav* case at the ICJ.[75] This dispute between India and Pakistan stemmed from a death sentence handed out by a Pakistani court to an Indian citizen, Mr Jadhav, accused of espionage. In the proceedings leading to this sentence, India requested consular access to Mr Jadhav, access that was never granted by Pakistan. Consequently, India seized the ICJ on the basis of Article 1 of the Optional Protocol to the Vienna Convention on Consular Relations concerning the Compulsory Settlement of Disputes.[76] Before the ICJ, Pakistan alleged that India had abused its conventional right[77] to request 'consular assistance' because it was violating other international obligations at the same time.[78] As noted by the Court, Pakistan failed to explain precisely the link between the two allegations.[79] After a brief examination of the claims, the ICJ found that India's actions could not be seen as an abuse of rights.[80]

The prohibition of an abuse of rights finds more concrete applications in other fields of international law, such as international human rights[81] and international economic law.[82] In human rights litigation, negative behaviour of the individual plaintiff can qualify as an abuse of procedural rights (see e.g. Article 35(3)(a) of the European Convention on Human Rights (ECHR). This was the case in July 2019, when the European Court of Human Rights (ECtHR) held that a plaintiff, Mr Alekseyev, a Russian LGBT activist, had abused his right of application because of his repeated and serious insults to the court on public social networks.[83] This

[72] Alexandre Kiss, 'Abuse of Rights' in *Max Planck Encyclopedia of Public International Law* (December 2006), para 1.

[73] eg *Case Concerning Certain German Interests in Polish Upper Silesia*, Judgment of 25 May 1926, PCIJ Series A, No 27, 1, 30; *Case Concerning Certain Phosphate Lands in Nauru (Nauru v Australia)*, Judgment, ICJ Reports 1992, 240. For a general overview of the notion and its use in inter-State litigation, see Michael Byers, 'Abuse of Rights: An Old Principle, A New Age' (2002) 47 *McGill Law Journal* 389–431.

[74] A possible exception could be the *Trail Smelter* case. *Trail Smelter case (United States v Canada)*, Sentence of 11 April 1941, RSA vol III, 1938. Although the term 'abuse of rights' was not mentioned, limiting the way in which a sovereign state can make use of its territory operates on the same logic as the prohibition of the abuse of rights.

[75] *Jadhav (India v Pakistan)*, Judgment of 19 July 2019, ICJ General List No 168, 1.

[76] Optional Protocol to the Vienna Convention on Consular Relations concerning the Compulsory Settlement of Disputes, 24 April 1963, 596 UNTS 487.

[77] As provided in article 36 of the Vienna Convention on Consular Relations, 24 April 1963, 596 UNTS 261.

[78] *Jadhav* (n 75), paras 121–24.

[79] ibid, para 57: 'Pakistan has not clearly explained the link between these allegations and the rights invoked by India on the merits'.

[80] ibid, para 124.

[81] See Ludovic Hennebel and Hélène Tigroudja, *Traité de Droit International des Droits de l'Homme* (Pedone, 2016) 491–94.

[82] For a brief overview of the case law in the field of commercial and investment law, see Charles T Kotuby and Luke A Sobota, *General Principles of Law and International Due Process* (Oxford University Press, 2017) 107–19.

[83] Quote from the press release issued by the Registrar of the Court (ECHR 267 (2019)). See *Case of Zhdanov and Others v Russia*, ECtHR, App No 12200/08, Judgment of 16 July 2019 (publication pending), paras 82–86.

approach is in line with the prior case law in which repeated insults were taken into account to establish an abuse of procedural rights.[84]

A prominent example in the field of international investments is the *Philip Morris* case.[85] At a time when Australia was on the verge of adopting a series of regulations that would impose strict conditions on the packaging of tobacco products, Philip Morris International initiated a restructuring of its group so as to transfer its Australian subsidiaries to Philip Morris Asia, in Hong Kong, and thereby benefit from the protection of the investment treaty between Hong Kong and Australia. Relying on this treaty, Philip Morris Asia, now the owner of Philip Morris Australia, initiated an arbitration procedure against Australia. The Permanent Court of Arbitration (PCA) considered that 'it may amount to an abuse of process to restructure an investment to obtain [bilateral investment treaty] benefits in respect of a foreseeable dispute'.[86] Because Philip Morris was aware that Australia was going to adopt stricter tobacco regulation, and because the restructuration was made primarily in order to exploit the dispute settlement mechanism in the treaty, it constituted an abuse of rights. Therefore, the claim was declared inadmissible.[87]

These examples illustrate that the prohibition of the abuse of rights, whether substantial or procedural, is aimed at protecting the object and purpose of these rights upon which legitimate expectations of other participants in the legal systems are founded.

Following the same logic, good faith encourages a teleological interpretation of rules. Teleological interpretation mirrors the prohibition of abuse of rights. Both ideas seek to ensure an appropriate link between rules and their objective (telos). However, while abuse of rights is concerned with sanctioning certain behaviours, teleogical interpretation, inter alia, has an investigative function. This function is laid down explicitly in the VCLT, which provides in Article 31(1) that a 'treaty shall be interpreted in good faith in accordance with the ordinary meaning to be given to the terms of the treaty in their context and *in the light of its object and purpose*'.[88] International judges and arbitrators have relied on teleological interpretation on numerous occasions, although never as an exclusive technique. For instance, in 1922, the Permanent Court of International Justice (PCIJ), when asked whether the International Labour Organization (ILO) had competence over 'the regulation of the conditions of persons employed in agriculture',[89] relied on both the object and purpose of the organisation's founding treaty and on the general context in which the rules on competence were set. The Court highlighted that the purpose of Part XIII of the Treaty of Versailles was to establish a 'permanent labour organisation' and that it would be nonsensical to imagine that agriculture, which is the most ancient form of labour, would fall outside of the scope of such an institution.[90] The Court additionally stressed that the general context of the treaty was crucial to determine the extent of the competences of the ILO.[91] The ICJ, in the *LaGrand* case,[92] was led to interpret Article 41 of the ICJ Statute on provisional measures to determine whether these measures were binding or

[84] *Rehak* v *Czech Republic*, ECtHR, Appl No 67208/01, Decision of Inadmissibility of 18 May 2004; *Mirolubovs and Others* v *Latvia*, ECtHR, Appl No 798/05, Judgment of 15 September 2009, para 64.

[85] *Philip Morris Asia Ltd* v *Australia*, Case No 2012–12, Award on Jurisdiction and Admissibility, Perm Ct Arb, 17 December 2015. For a comment on this case, see Ulf Linderfalk, '*Philip Morris Asia Ltd.* v. *Australia* – Abuse of Rights in Investor–State Arbitration' (2017) 86 *Nordic Journal of International Law* 403–19.

[86] *Philip Morris Asia Ltd* v *Australia* (n 85), para 545.

[87] ibid, para 591.

[88] Emphasis added. See for the concepts of object and purpose above text with nn 52 and 53.

[89] *Competence of the ILO in Regard to International Regulation of the Conditions of the Labour of Persons Employed in Agriculture*, Advisory Opinion of 12 August 1922, PCIJ Series B, No 02, 1.

[90] ibid 23–25.

[91] ibid 35.

[92] *LaGrand (Germany* v *United States of America)*, Judgment, ICJ Reports 2001, 466.

not. Its answer was positive, and it reached this conclusion by pointing, inter alia, to the object and purpose of the Statute, which lays down a judicial power based on 'the necessity, when the circumstances call for it, to safeguard, and to avoid prejudice to, the rights of the parties as determined by the final judgment of the Court'.[93]

To conclude, teleological interpretation can be said to manifest the idea of good faith because it seeks to safeguard the spirit of legal rules by referring to their purpose rather than a strict reading of their letter.

2.2 *Estoppel*

Estoppel is frequently mentioned as a principle deriving from good faith.[94] It is commonly understood as the prohibition, within a dispute, against contradicting a previously held position or behaviour upon which others had founded their legitimate expectations.[95] Robert Kolb describes it as a 'doctrine of qualified non-contradiction'.[96] The finding of estoppel by a judge or arbitrator will lead to the rejection of a claim on the merits. The claimant will be 'estopped' from making a claim. This result, of course, is decisive for the outcome of an international dispute. Consequently, estoppel cannot be lightly affirmed. A court will find it only if strict cumulative conditions are met.[97]

First, the initial conduct or declaration must have been clear and unequivocal. Second, this behaviour must have generated legitimate expectations in the other party (or parties) which led it to take actions. Finally, the change in the former party's behaviour must have nullified these actions so that the trusting party suffers damage because of its detrimental reliance on the initial representation.[98]

Estoppel has been often discussed in disputes brought before the ICJ, but it has so far not been explicitly applied.[99] A remarkable illustration of the effect of estoppel can be found in the arbitration between the United Kingdom and Mauritius concerning the Chagos Archipelagos in 2015.[100] In this case, the arbitral tribunal, after having examined that all the conditions for the acceptance of estoppel were met, declared that:

> after its independence in 1968, Mauritius was entitled to and did rely upon the Lancaster House Undertakings to (a) return the Chagos Archipelago to Mauritius when no longer needed for defence purposes; (b) preserve the benefit of any minerals or oil discovered in or near the Chagos Archipelago for the Mauritius Government; and (c) ensure that fishing rights in the Chagos Archipelago would remain available to the Mauritius Government as far as practicable. *The Tribunal, therefore, holds that the United Kingdom is estopped from denying the binding effect of these commitments, which the Tribunal will treat as binding on the United Kingdom in view of their repeated reaffirmation after 1968.*[101]

93 ibid, para 102.
94 For recent studies, see Kaijun Pan, 'A Re-Examination of Estoppel in International Jurisprudence' (2017) 16 *Chinese Journal of International Law* 751–86; Jack Wass, 'Jurisdiction by Estoppel and Acquiescence in International Courts and Tribunals' (2016) 86 *British Yearbook of International Law* 155–95.
95 Hermann Mosler, 'The International Society as a Legal Community' (1974) 140 *Recueil des Cours* 1–320, 147.
96 Kolb (n 4) 101.
97 eg *North Sea Continental Shelf* cases (n 38), para 30: 'by reason of past conduct, declarations, etc., which not only clearly and consistently evinced acceptance of that régime, but also had caused Denmark or the Netherlands, in reliance on such conduct, detrimentally to change position or suffer some prejudice'.
98 Kolb (n 4) 100–18.
99 The *Temple of Preah Vihear* case is arguably an implicit use of estoppel. Pan (n 94) 756.
100 *Chagos Marine Protected Area Arbitration (Mauritius v United Kingdom)*, Case No 2011–03, Perm Ct Arb, 18 March 2015.
101 ibid, para 448.

The effect of estoppel in this case seems to be to confer a binding force to the *Lancaster House Undertakings* made between the UK and Mauritius before its independence. Because Mauritius effectively relied on these undertakings to make concessions during the negotiation of its independence and as both parties had repeatedly reaffirmed their binding character after 1968, the UK could not renege on them and claim before the arbitral tribunal that the undertakings were not binding. This outcome shows that, under specific conditions, the principle of good faith can serve as a basis for the binding character of an agreement even if that agreement does not appear to be a formal source of international law.

Estoppel combines the logic of the abuse of rights, as it bars a participant to a dispute from making certain claims, and the logic of unilateral acts, as it takes into account how a State may have unilaterally shaped the expectation of another. Some authors have indeed linked acquiescence or unilateral acts of States to the principle of estoppel.[102] This is partly accurate. For instance, a State might be estopped from claiming that its unilateral act did not bind it in any way. However, estoppel has a distinctly procedural nature: it exists within the confines of a legal dispute. By contrast, unilateral acts are a source of international law, and their scope of operation is much wider. The connection between estoppel and acquiescence is less clear. While some authors have suggested that acquiescence and estoppel are equivalent, the judicial practice dealing with acquiescence has not established a clear link between the concepts. In conclusion, unilateral declarations and acquiescence can produce legal effects irrespective of a dispute, while estoppel can protect these legal effects by preventing a State from claiming that its prior behaviour is devoid of such effects.

2.3 *The 'Modification' of Treaties through Dynamic Interpretation and Tacit Amendment*

Article 31(3)(a)–(b) VCLT provides that subsequent agreements and practice shall be taken into account when interpreting a treaty. So the VCLT acknowledges that the subsequent application and implementation of a treaty by its parties provide indications as to the meaning of the provisions of the treaty.[103]

Subsequent practice may help to better identify the object and purpose of an agreement. An illustration is the *Land and Maritime Boundary between Cameroon and Nigeria* case, where the ICJ relied on the practice of the parties to the dispute to conclude that the Lake Chad Basin Commission was not intended to have competence over matters relating to the maintenance of international peace and security.[104]

Subsequent agreements and subsequent practice can be convenient ways of developing a treaty. They eschew the formal requirements of amendments and allow for more flexibility. Both the case law and treaty texts postulate that the interpretation and the outright change, modification or amendment of legal rules are two conceptually and legally distinct operations.[105] Also, doctrinal international legal scholarship postulates a conceptual dividing line between

[102] Wass (n 94); Thomas Cottier and Jörg Paul Müller, 'Estoppel' in *Max Planck Encyclopedia of Public International Law* (April 2007).

[103] On this matter, see Georg Nolte (ed), *Treaties and Subsequent Practice* (Oxford University Press, 2013).

[104] *Case Concerning the Land and Maritime Boundary between Cameroon and Nigeria (Cameroon v Nigeria)*, Preliminary Objections, Judgment, ICJ Reports 1998, 275, paras 66–68.

[105] The leading case is an ICJ Advisory Opinion on treaty interpretation of 1950 in which the Court stated that '[i]t is the duty of the Court to interpret the Treaties, not to revise them'. *Interpretation of Peace Treaties*, Second Phase, Advisory Opinion, ICJ Reports 1950, 221, 229. See in that sense already *Acquisition of Polish Nationality*, Advisory Opinion of 15 September 1923, PCIJ, Series B No 7, 6–21, 20.

interpretation 'proper' and silent modification 'effected under the pretext of interpretation'.[106] However, this line is blurry. That blurriness between interpretation and silent modification of a legal text does not pose a normative problem when it is performed by the same actors, and when no third parties are affected by the development of the law. Then, it is not necessary to determine whether the members to a given treaty only interpret that treaty or silently modify (change) it.[107]

The 'reinterpretation' or 'modification' of treaties by subsequent practice requires that all parties to the agreement act in a converging manner over a certain period of time.[108] Moreover, subsequent practice may not defeat the object and purpose of the agreement or contradict a norm of *jus cogens*.[109] When the practice becomes settled, it provides the basis for the legitimate expectations of all the parties to the agreement.

There is a parallel between this development of treaties by State practice and the birth of a customary norm. A treaty can be modified de facto by the practice of the parties if they act in the belief that they are merely interpreting and applying the treaty or that the practice reflects their understanding of the treaty. This process is akin to the idea of State practice and *opinio juris* as the cumulative elements of international custom.[110] In the same way that good faith undergirds the legal possibility of developing a treaty, it also undergirds the emergence and modification of customary rules. In both cases, State expectations, trust and confidence are upheld by a uniform practice and beliefs in a community of States.[111]

3 *Good Faith and the Termination of International Norms*

Finally, good faith plays a role when treaties are repealed or other international norms are brought to an end. First, it prevents abusive denunciations of treaties and, second, it provides a justification of the doctrine of *rebus sic stantibus*.

[106] Reports of the Commission to the General Assembly, *Yearbook of the International Law Commission*, vol 2 (UN, 1966) 236; Wolfram Karl, *Vertrag und spätere Praxis im Völkerrecht* (Springer, 1983) 21–46, 43 on the fluid boundary; Ian M Sinclair, *The Vienna Convention on the Law of Treaties* (2nd edn, Manchester University Press, 1984) 138; Georg Nolte, 'Report 1 – Jurisprudence of the International Court of Justice and Arbitral Tribunals of Ad Hoc Jurisdiction Relating to Subsequent Agreements and Subsequent Practice' in Nolte (ed) (n 103) 169–209, 200. Simplistically speaking, the interpretation of a legal rule is considered to be somehow bounded (although it is not fully clear by what), whereas the modification of a rule is potentially unlimited. Also, an interpretation happens, first of all, for one single case (and lives on only through precedent) while a modification of a treaty provision governs all future cases.

[107] See on a modification of Art 2 ECHR through Member State practice *Al-Saadoon and Mufdhi* v *The United Kingdom*, ECtHR, Appl No 61498/08, Judgment of 2 March 2010. The Court found the state practice on the death penalty as 'strongly indicative that Article 2 [ECHR] has been *amended* so as to prohibit the death penalty in all circumstances. Against this background, the Court does not consider that the wording of the second sentence of Article 2 § 1 continues to act as a bar to its *interpreting* the words "inhuman or degrading treatment or punishment" in Article 3 as including the death penalty' (para 120, emphases added). The Court here confused interpretation and amendment through practice.

[108] This will be assessed on a case-by-case basis, ILC, Second Report on Subsequent Agreements and Subsequent Practice in Relation to the Interpretation of Treaties, UN Doc A/CN.4/671, 26 March 2014, paras 44–48.

[109] Gerhard Hafner, 'Subsequent Agreements and Practice: Between Interpretation, Informal Modification, and Formal Amendment' in Nolte (n 103) 105–22, 118–20.

[110] Draft Conclusions with Commentary, *Yearbook of the International Law Commission*, vol II(2) (2016), Report International Law Commission, Eighty-Sixth Session, UN Doc A/71/10 (2 May–10 June and 4 July–12 August 2016), ch V: Identification of customary international law.

[111] On the relation between good faith and custom, see Kolb (n 4) 81–84.

3.1 *Prohibition of Abusive Termination*

It is frequent for international agreements to contain clauses of withdrawal. For instance, in 2017, President Trump declared that the United States intended to exercise its right to withdraw from the Paris Agreement on Climate Change[112] as soon as the State is eligible to do so and '[u]nless the United States identifies suitable terms for reengagement'.[113] This communication was in accordance with its Article 28 of the Agreement.[114]

Even in the absence of a withdrawal or termination clause, Article 56 VCLT provides that the parties to a treaty can withdraw from it unless it is explicitly forbidden by the treaty. However, the right to withdraw is demarcated by several parameters arising from good faith. Any withdrawal has to follow a notification procedure and cannot take effect immediately (unless otherwise provided for in the treaty). The opposite would create an unstable legal landscape where States could unilaterally retract from their treaty commitments. That, in turn, would undermine the trust and predictability necessary for agreements to order international relations.

This logic can be applied to unilateral acts too, such as optional declarations of jurisdiction, as noted by the ICJ in the *Military and Paramilitary Activities In and Against Nicaragua* case.[115] In this case, the United States tried to avoid the competence of the Court by suspending its optional declaration of jurisdiction at short notice before the Court could consider the preliminary questions of jurisdiction and admissibility. The Court concluded that such withdrawal with immediate effect went against the requirement of good faith. In its reasoning, the Court drew an analogy with the law of treaties and the application of the requirements of good faith governing the modalities of withdrawal from treaties.[116]

This analogy was taken up in the work of the UN International Law Commission (ILC) on unilateral acts. In its 'Guiding Principles Applicable to Unilateral Declarations of States Capable of Creating Legal Obligations', the Commission specified that '[a] unilateral declaration that has created legal obligations for the State making the declaration cannot be revoked arbitrarily'.[117] The guiding principles further specify the relevant factors in assessing whether a unilateral act has been revoked arbitrarily. These include, inter alia, a reference to a fundamental change of circumstances, which could potentially justify a revocation, as it could also provide a basis for the termination of a treaty.

3.2 *Fundamental Change of Circumstances*

Article 62 VCLT gives expression to the doctrine of *rebus sic stantibus* in the international law of treaties. It states the conditions under which a treaty may be validly terminated due to a fundamental change of circumstances.

First, the change has to affect conditions that constituted the essential basis for the consent of the parties to be bound by the treaty, and, second, the change of these conditions must radically

[112] Paris Agreement, 12 December 2015, (2016) 55 ILM 743.

[113] UN, Depositary Notification, Communication of the United States, 4 August 2017, UN Doc C.N.464.2017.TREATIES-XXVII.7.d (Depositary Notification).

[114] Under Art 28 of the Paris Agreement, withdrawal is possible only three years after the entry into force of the Agreement. For the United States (which was 4 November 2016), that is on 4 November 2019. Nevertheless the domestic and international legality of this announcement has been questioned. See eg David Hubinger, 'Can He Do That: A Constitutional Analysis of President Trump's Withdrawal from the Paris Agreement' (2018) 20 *San Diego International Law Journal* 127–60.

[115] *Case Concerning Military and Paramilitary Activities In and Against Nicaragua (Nicaragua v United States of America)*, Jurisdiction of the Court and Admissibility of the Application, Judgment, ICJ Reports 1984, 392.

[116] ibid, para 63.

[117] ILC (n 66).

transform the extent of the obligations to be performed. For instance, if two States enter into an international agreement to protect a specific ecosystem at their respective borders, and this ecosystem collapses, then the conditions that motivated the existence of the treaty in the first place can be considered to have fundamentally changed. The very reason for the international agreement has disappeared, thus leaving no need to uphold its requirements.

Additionally, Article 62 specifies that the fundamental change of circumstances cannot be invoked to withdraw or terminate a treaty if the treaty establishes a boundary or if the fundamental change invoked has been caused by the party invoking it. In our previous example, if the collapse of the protected ecosystem has been caused by the activities of one party, such party will be barred from invoking the fundamental change of circumstances for terminating or withdrawing from the treaty.

Fundamental changes of circumstances have rarely been invoked in international disputes nor have they received much attention in recent scholarly work in international law.[118] Mention must be made of the *Gabčíkovo Nagymaros* case, where the ICJ discussed the conditions allowing to invoke fundamental changes of circumstances. Hungary claimed that the evolution of its political system, economic benefits and environmental knowledge and law constituted fundamental changes to the circumstances in which the agreement with Czechoslovakia was concluded. This claim was rejected by the ICJ as the 'changed circumstances advanced by Hungary are ... not of such a nature, either individually or collectively, that their effect would radically transform the extent of the obligations still to be performed in order to accomplish the Project'.[119]

The logic of good faith is obvious with regard to fundamental changes as a legitimate reason to terminate or withdraw from a treaty. The actors' trust and the predictability of the norms both rely on the existence of a legal relationship and on the factual conditions that have prompted the creation of that relationship. If those very conditions disappear or fundamentally change, then considerations of good faith would prevent a party from seeking enforcement of the obligations arising from the treaty.

IV THE NORMATIVE QUALITY OF GOOD FAITH

Our analysis of the legal effects of good faith illustrated the diverse and important functions of this principle in international law. Despite its conceptual indeterminacy, good faith has been mobilised as a tool that can generate significant outcomes. However, the very plasticity of the concept, with its many manifestations and applications, raises a difficult question that must now be addressed: is the principle of good faith an autonomous legal norm, and what is its legal quality? Specifically, can a State or non-State actor such as an investor be held responsible for having violated the principle of good faith?

On this topic, the opinions are divided. The first and most radical stance is that of Elisabeth Zoller, who considers that good faith is simply a moral requirement devoid of any legal existence.[120] In her 1977 study on this topic, she goes even further and argues that the way in which judges and arbitrators rely on good faith is a threat to legal security as it makes the outcome of the legal process largely indeterminate.[121] On the other side of the spectrum, Robert

118 The leading case is *Fisheries Jurisdiction case (UK v Iceland), Jurisdiction of the Court*, Judgment, ICJ Reports 1973, 3, paras 30–45.
119 *Case Concerning the Gabčíkovo-Nagymaros Project (Hungary v Slovakia)*, Judgment, ICJ Reports 1997, 7, para 104.
120 Zoller (n 1) 350.
121 ibid 354.

Kolb argues that good faith is an autonomous legal norm and that the numerous legal concepts, rules and meta-rules discussed in the previous section are direct expressions or manifestations of good faith.[122] An intermediate position can be distilled from several decisions of the ICJ, which emphasised that good faith provides a reason for the binding nature of international obligations, but is not in itself an obligation. In the *Case Concerning Border and Transborder Armed Actions*, the ICJ recalled that good faith was indeed 'one of the basic principles governing the creation and performance of legal obligations' but immediately stressed that good faith 'is *not in itself* a source of obligation where none would otherwise exist'.[123] This understanding is now broadly accepted and has also been upheld in investment arbitration.[124]

We subscribe to this understanding of good faith. Good faith is neither a merely moral requirement nor an autonomous rule. In the words of Michel Virally, good faith should be seen as a legal catalyst,[125] a principle that allows for the international legal order to develop and produce its effects. In a similar vein, the idea of 'interstitial norms', put forward by Vaughan Lowe for explaining the legal effects of sustainable development,[126] is pertinent. Interstitial norms do not operate on their own, nor do they require actors to observe a specific conduct. Rather, these norms exist in between other autonomous rules, and they allow one to interpret them in a certain way. They are 'interstitial' because they form the cement that brings other rules together as 'bricks'. Interstitial norms foster coherence in legal structures, and they prompt the creation of rules. As the previous section showed, good faith does exactly this: motivating the emergence and development of new rules, and pushing the realisation of extant rules' objects and purposes through interpretation and overall thereby fostering legal coherence. Thus, good faith could be called an interstitial norm.

In conclusion, it appears that the way good faith is put in the Friendly Relations Declaration appropriately reflects its normative nature. The Declaration calls indeed for States to 'fulfil in good faith the obligations assumed by them in accordance with the Charter'. It does not ask States to act in good faith. Good faith is a 'modality' in which States shall fulfil other obligations.

V THE CONTEMPORARY FUNCTIONS OF THE PRINCIPLE OF GOOD FAITH

1 *Introduction*

Since the creation of the United Nations, international law underwent significant transformations. The sheer quantative increase of rules and the qualitative unfolding of special regimes dealing with specific topics have led commentators to complain,[127] perhaps

[122] Kolb (n 4) 29–31.

[123] *Case Concerning Border and Transborder Armed Actions (Nicaragua v Honduras)*, Judgment, ICJ Reports 1988, 69, para 98 (emphasis added).

[124] *Mobil Investments Canada Inc v Canada*, ICSID/ARB/15/6, 13 July 2018, para 168.

[125] This concept was invented by Michel Virally in a critical review of Elisabeth Zoller's work. Michel Virally, 'Review Essay: Good Faith in Public International Law' (1983) 77 *American Journal of International Law* 130–34.

[126] Vaughan Lowe, 'The Politics of Law-Making: Are the Method and Character of Norm Creation Changing?' in Michael Byers (ed), *The Role of International Law in Politics: Essays in International Relations and International Law* (Oxford University Press, 2000) 207–26.

[127] The emblematic complaint is the speech of Gilbert Guillaume before the General Assembly of the UN at a time when he was president of the ICJ: HE Judge Gilbert Guillaume, President of the International Court of Justice, Speech to the General Assembly of the United Nations (30 October 2001).

excessively so,[128] about risks posed by the so-called fragmentation of the international legal order.[129] In parallel to this process, we believe that international law has continued its development into different structural branches. While the entire body of international law was thought of as being 'private law writ large' around the turn of the twentieth century,[130] various subfields now can be said to possess distinct structures and features, such as constitutional, administrative and criminal law.[131] The different logics surfaced at different times. Notably, the UN Charter added a 'constitutional' element to the international legal order that was missing before. International administrative law was already emerging with the activities of international organisations starting in the 1920s. The criminal law logic was embryonic before 1945 but became positive international law with the Nuremberg trials. Since 1970, when the Friendly Relations Declaration was adopted, this structure has not radically changed, but the intensification of international legal activities has contributed to reinforcing it.

As a result, today's international legal landscape is different from the one that saw the inclusion of the principle of good faith in the UN Charter and in the Friendly Relations Declaration. At that time, good faith was embedded into a less dense, and less thematically and less structurally diverse international legal order. Considering this evolution, the question is whether the principle of good faith still serves its original functions or whether it has acquired new ones in this current landscape. To answer this question, we will try to flesh out the uses of good faith in two respects.

First, we will highlight that good faith, in the context of the specialisation of international law, can work both in the direction of a dissociation and of an integration of regimes (section 2.1). Second, we will show how the underlying logic of good faith can be seen at play in the different structures of international law (private, constitutional, public and criminal) (section 2.2).

This analysis will demonstrate that the functions of good faith have not changed with the transformation of international law. Rather, thanks to its malleability and foundational nature, good faith has accompanied these changes.

2 *Good Faith as a Janus-Faced Tool for Dissociation and Integration in a Thematically Diverse International Legal Order*

2.1 *Good Faith as a Reinforcer of the Telos of the Various Thematic International Legal Regimes*

Global problems can only be tackled through transnational co-operation based, inter alia, on legal norms. The emergence of numerous international regimes during the second half of the

[128] As suggested by Martti Koskenniemi and Païvi Leino, 'Fragmentation of International Law? Postmodern Anxieties' (2002) 15 *Leiden Journal of International Law* 553–79.

[129] Though nowadays, there is a consensus in legal scholarship that the international legal order is equipped with the appropriate tools to deal with the threats of fragmentation. See eg Mireille Delmas-Marty, *Les Forces imaginantes du droit le pluralisme ordonné* (Editions du Seuil, 2006); Mads Tønnesson Andenæs and Eirik Bjorge, *A Farewell to Fragmentation* (Cambridge University Press, 2015); Anne Peters, 'The Refinement of International Law: From Fragmentation to Regime Interaction and Politicization' (2017) 15 *International Journal of Constitutional Law* 671–704.

[130] Thomas Erskine Holland, *Studies in International Law* (Clarendon Press, 1898) 152.

[131] Anne Peters, 'Transnational Law Comprises Constitutional, Administrative, Criminal and Quasi-private Law' in Peter HF Bekker, Rudolf Dolzer and Michael Waibel (eds), *Making Transnational Law Work in the Global Economy: Essays in Honour of Detlev Vagts* (Cambridge University Press, 2010) 154–73.

twentieth century responds to this need. International economic law has sought to increase wealth by progressively liberalising trade worldwide. International environmental law has endeavoured to mitigate the impact of human activities on the biosphere. The international law of the sea was meant to strike a balance between the different uses of a globally shared space. This list could go on and on.

All of these now familiar branches of international law evolved through interpretation, through the application of law by international and domestic authorities and courts, and through the creation of further international institutions which have often adopted new primary and secondary international rules. In these operations, notably in the process of interpretation, we witness that the principle of good faith has been used to strengthen the various regimes' purposes. The community of interpreters participating in the process of consolidation and expansion of the purposes of international regimes is diverse. Not only judges and arbitrators but also scholars contribute to creating a common understanding of international law and its operation.

2.1.1 INTERNATIONAL TRADE AND INVESTMENT LAW The principle of good faith has been frequently invoked in disputes within the World Trade Organization (WTO).[132] Its case law on good faith has been abundantly commented upon.[133] One recent example is a Dispute Settlement Body (DSB) report of April 2019 on Ukraine and the Russian Federation.[134] Ukraine argued that Russia had established unlawful 'restrictions on traffic in transit from Ukraine through the Russian Federation to third countries'. In particular, Ukraine claimed that Russia had not made use of the security exception of Article XXI(b) of the 1994 General Agreement on Tariffs and Trade (GATT) in good faith.[135] The panel proceeded to examine the legal implication of the principle of good faith[136] and assessed whether Russia had made use of Article XXI(b) in a way that would not contradict the requirements of the principle. The provision foresees that the GATT 'shall not be construed … to prevent any contracting party from taking any action which it considers necessary for the protection of its essential security interests'. Considering the crisis that was ongoing between Russia and Ukraine at the time of the restriction of traffic – a crisis which was explicitly acknowledged by the UN General Assembly as involving armed

[132] eg Appellate Body Report, *United States – Transitional Safeguard Measure on Combed Cotton Yarn from Pakistan*, WT/DS192/AB/R, 8 October 2001; Appellate Body Report, *United States – Safeguard Measure on Imports of Fresh, Chilled or Frozen Lamb from New Zealand*, WT/DS177/AB/R, 1 May 2001. The WTO lists twenty different cases dealing specifically with the principle of good faith. See www.wto.org/english/tratop_e/dispu_e/repertory_e/p3_e.htm.

[133] See eg Andrew D Mitchell, M Sornarajah and Tania Voon (eds), *Good Faith and International Economic Law* (Oxford University Press, 2015); Andrew D Mitchell, 'Good Faith in WTO Dispute Settlement' (2006) 7 *Melbourne Journal of International Law* 339–71; Marion Panizzon, *Good Faith in the Jurisprudence of the WTO: The Protection of Legitimate Expectations, Good Faith Interpretation and Fair Dispute Settlement* (Hart, 2006); Helge Elisabeth Zeitler, 'Good Faith in WTO Jurisprudence: Necessary Balancing Element or an Open Door to Judicial Activism?' (2005) 8 *Journal of International Economic Law* 721–58; Jing Kang, 'The Presumption of Good Faith in the WTO "as such" Cases: A Reformulation of the Mandatory/Discretionary Distinction as an Analytical Tool' (2012) 46 *Journal of World Trade* 879–912.

[134] Panel Report, *Russia – Measures Concerning Traffic in Transit (Complaint by Ukraine)*, WT/DS512/R, 5 April 2019.

[135] ibid, para 7.33.

[136] ibid, para 7.133: 'The *obligation of good faith* requires that Members not use the exceptions in Article XXI as a means to circumvent their obligations under the GATT 1994. A glaring example of this would be where a Member sought to release itself from the structure of "reciprocal and mutually advantageous arrangements" that constitutes the multilateral trading system simply by re-labelling trade interests that it had agreed to protect and promote within the system, as "essential security interests", falling outside the reach of that system' (emphasis added).

conflict[137] – and the margin of appreciation left to the members,[138] the Panel concluded that Russia acted in good faith when it established the traffic restrictions for security interests.[139]

Robert Kolb has argued that the dispute settlement mechanism of the WTO led to a legal refinement of the principle of good faith, but that good faith does not operate distinctly here.[140] In contrast, Marion Panizzon considered that in the context of the WTO, the principle of good faith is specifically used in order to promote the liberalisation of trade.[141] It thus fulfils a specific objective in line with the overall purpose of the regime. Commentators agree that in the field of WTO law, the most important and tangible manifestation of the principle of good faith is the doctrine of the protection of legitimate expectations.[142] These expectations are the prerequisite for any commercial and economic partnership at the international level.[143] In conclusion, it seems that good faith has mainly been instrumental in stressing the goals of the regime, thus contributing to setting it apart from general international law.

Good faith is also a fundamental component of international investment law,[144] as illustrated by its frequent appearance in investment-related disputes.[145] On this point, Robert Kolb has argued that international investment law has developed a specific understanding of the principle of good faith in order to further the fundamental purposes of international investment law: fair and equitable treatment, the protection of legitimate expectation and the prohibition of abuse of procedure.[146] Matthias Goldmann has suggested that the recent legal and policy developments in the field of international investment law showed a shift in the general purpose of this regime.[147] What was initially based on a private model had now incorporated elements of public law, namely a 'common global interest in sovereign debt sustainability'.[148] In this respect, he has argued that the principle of good faith can be used to promote sovereign debt sustainability and smooth sovereign debt workout. The assertion that good faith can contribute to achieve novel purposes – be they broadly acknowledged or not – is telling of the flexibility of the principle.

Good faith is so important for international trade and investment that States have sought to ensure its applicability in international contractual relations between individuals. This is apparent in the numerous conventions adopted within the framework of the UN Commission on International Trade Law. Its 1980 Convention on Contracts for the International Sale of

137 ibid, para 7.137.
138 ibid, para 7.147.
139 ibid, para 7.148. The panel report was not appealed.
140 Kolb (n 4) 178.
141 Panizzon (n 133) 371: '[The WTO Panels and the Appellate Body] will only substantiate good faith if it serves the multilateral system's principle goal of trade liberalization.' However, the case we just provided as an example may go against this assessment.
142 See eg Panel Report, *India – Patent Protection for Pharmaceutical and Agricultural Chemical Products (Complaint by US)*, WT/DS/50/R, 5 September 1997, para 7.18: 'good faith interpretation requires the protection of legitimate expectations derived from the protection of intellectual property rights provided in the Agreement'.
143 Thomas Cottier and Krista Nadakavukaren Schefer, 'Good Faith and the Protection of Legitimate Expectations in the WTO' in Marco Bronckers and John Howard Jackson (eds), *New Directions in International Law: Essays in Honor of JH Jackson* (Kluwer Law International, 2000) 47–68.
144 For a recent study of the notion, see Teerawat Wongkaew, *Protection of Legitimate Expectations in Investment Treaty Arbitration: A Theory of Detrimental Reliance* (Cambridge University Press, 2018).
145 See eg *Mobil Investments Canada Inc* v *Canada*, ICSID/ARB/15/6, 13 July 2018; *Malicorp Ltd* v *The Arab Republic of Egypt*, ICSID/ARB/08/18, 7 February 2011; *Inceysa Vallisoletana SL* v *Republic of El Salvador*, ICSID/ARB/03/26, 2 August 2006; *Sempra Energy International* v *Argentine Republic*, ICSID/ARB/02/16, 28 September 2007.
146 Kolb (n 4) 243–50.
147 Matthias Goldmann, 'Putting your Faith in Good Faith: A Principled Strategy for Smoother Sovereign Debt Workouts' (2016) 41 *The Yale Journal of International Law* 117–40.
148 ibid 127.

Goods[149] (CISG) is intended to generate a uniform law governing international sales of goods between individuals based in States parties. Article 7 of the CISG specifically mentions good faith as a guiding principle for the interpretation of the Convention.[150] By recalling that good faith is applicable to every private contract that deals with international sales of goods, the parties to the convention have 'transnationalised' the domestic principle of good faith as an essential element for the liberalisation of trade.[151]

2.1.2 OTHER THEMATIC REGIMES In the field of human rights, Article 2 of the American Convention of Human Rights[152] is considered a manifestation of the principle of good faith.[153] The Inter-American Court of Human Rights (IACtHR) implicitly references the principle of *pacta sunt servanda* as the reason why States have the obligation of bringing their legal order in conformity with the Convention.[154] The IACtHR also relied on an extensive interpretation of this provision to elaborate its theory of the '*control de convencionalidad*'.[155]

Of course, the obligation to implement and, if necessary, transpose international law into domestic law is not limited to international human rights law.[156] However, this branch of law has the specific objective to benefit and empower individuals. It therefore allows for individual complaints to the regional human rights courts and for communications to some of the universal human rights committees. Those bodies' decisions have a peculiar quality and their proper implementation is arguably even more urgent than in other fields of international law.

Good faith also impacts on the output of the UN Human Rights Committee (HRC), established under Article 28 of the International Covenant on Civil and Political Rights (ICCPR). The Committee may receive and consider communications from individuals who

149 United Nations Convention on Contracts for the International Sale of Goods, 11 April 1980, 1489 UNTS 3.

150 ibid Art 7.1: 'In the interpretation of this Convention, regard is to be had to its international character and to the need to promote uniformity in its application and the observance of good faith in international trade.'

151 On this aspect of the CISG see, François Diesse, 'La Bonne Foi, la coopération et le raisonnable dans la Convention des Nations Unies Relative à la Vente Internationale de Marchandises (CVIM)' (2002) 129 *Journal du Droit International (Clunet)* 55–112. Other authors are sceptical as to the concrete use of the principle. See Steven D Walt, 'The Modest Role of Good Faith in Uniform Sales Law' (2015) 33 *Boston University International Law Journal* 37–71.

152 Art 2 ACHR reads: 'Where the exercise of any of the rights or freedoms referred to in Article 1 is not already ensured by legislative or other provisions, the States Parties undertake to adopt, in accordance with their constitutional processes and the provisions of this Convention, such legislative or other measures as may be necessary to give effect to those rights or freedoms.'

153 Hennebel and Tigroudja (n 81) 119.

154 *Case of Garrido and Baigorria* v *Argentina*, IACtHR, Judgment of 27 August 1998, Series C No 39, para 68: 'Under the law of nations, a customary law prescribes that a State that has concluded an international agreement must introduce into its domestic laws whatever changes are needed to ensure execution of the obligations it has undertaken. This principle is universally valid and has been characterized in case law as an evident principle.' This statement was repeated in other cases, eg *Case of Heliodoro Portugal* v *Panama*, Preliminary Objections, Merits, Reparations and Costs, IACtHR, Judgment of 12 August 2008, Series C No 186, para 179; and *Case of Fornerón and Daughter* v *Argentina*, IACtHR, Judgment of 27 April 2012, Series C No 242, para 130.

155 *Almonacid Arellano y otros* v *Chile*, IACtHR, Judgment of 26 September 2006, Series C No 154, para 124: 'The Court is aware that domestic judges and courts are bound to respect the rule of law, and therefore, they are bound to apply the provisions in force within the legal system. But when a State has ratified an international treaty such as the American Convention, its judges, as part of the State, are also bound by such Convention. This forces them to see that all the effects of the provisions embodied in the Convention are not adversely affected by the enforcement of laws which are contrary to its purpose and that have not had any legal effects since their inception. In other words, the Judiciary must exercise a sort of "conventionality control" between the domestic legal provisions which are applied to specific cases and the American Convention on Human Rights. To perform this task, the Judiciary has to take into account not only the treaty, but also the interpretation thereof made by the Inter-American Court, which is the ultimate interpreter of the American Convention.'

156 Evelyne Lagrange, 'L'Efficacité des normes internationales concernant la situation des personnes privées dans les ordres juridiques internes' (2012) 356 *Recueil des Cours* 239–552.

claim to be victims of a violation by that State party of any of the rights set forth in the Covenant.[157] Article 5(4) of the First Optional Protocol to the ICCPR describes the decisions of the Committee as 'views'. These views of the HRC do not have the same quality as judgments; they are therefore not formally binding. However, the legal effect of the views has been described as follows: 'States Parties cannot simply ignore them, but have to consider them in good faith (bona fide). On the other hand, they are not debarred from dismissing them, after careful consideration, as not reflecting the true legal position with regard to the case concerned. Not to react at all to a finding by the HRC, however, would appear to amount to a violation of the obligations under the ICCPR.'[158] The legal consequence is that Member States are under the obligation to take the HRC's final views into consideration in good faith.

Manifestations of the principle of good faith can be found in other regimes. Here too, the principle can be used to reinforce the regime's purposes. For instance, in the 2015 *Award in the Arbitration regarding the Chagos Marine Protected Area between Mauritius and the United Kingdom of Great Britain and Northern Ireland*,[159] the arbitral tribunal constituted under Annex VII of the United Nations Convention on the Law of the Sea (UNCLOS) referred to the notion of good faith in order to highlight the general purpose of the UNCLOS to balance competing rights and interests relating to the sea.[160] In doing so, it came to the conclusion that the UK breached several provisions of the UNCLOS by establishing a marine protected area in the Chagos.[161] Anastasia Telesetsky has argued that the good faith requirement contained in Article 300 UNCLOS[162] is an element strengthening certain aspects of the UNCLOS, most notably its call for the sustainability of fishing activities.[163] She has opined that the presence of good faith within the UNCLOS means that States must not only refrain from certain actions but also proactively engage in others that will allow reaching the purposes of the UNCLOS, such as taking part in regional fisheries management organisations and ensuring their effectiveness.

With regard to the law of armed conflict, Robert Kolb has suggested that the principle of good faith is the source of the prohibition of perfidy in the conduct of hostilities.[164] Perfidy is a feigned use of the law of armed conflict in order to gain strategic advantage; for instance, using regulated emblems to gain the trust of an enemy. Perfidy, therefore, undermines the whole function of humanitarian law as it undermines the trust and confidence in its rules. Consequently, through the prohibition of perfidy, good faith bolsters the main purposes of humanitarian law as a whole.

[157] Only against those States parties that have ratified the First Optional Protocol (OP I) The procedure of the Committee for individual communications is laid out in Art 5 OP I to ICCPR.

[158] Christian Tomuschat, 'Human Rights Committee' in *Max Planck Encyclopedia of Public International Law* (April 2019), para 14.

[159] *Chagos Marine Protected Area Arbitration* (n 100).

[160] ibid, paras 520–43.

[161] For comments on this case, see Jérémy Drisch, 'L'Affaire de l'Aire Marine Protégée des Chagos ou de l'usage de la bonne foi dans la mise en place d'un "Ordre Juridique International des Mers et des Océans"' (2014) 19 *Annuaire du Droit de la Mer* 221–50; Stefan Talmon, 'The Chagos Marine Protected Area Arbitration: Expansion of the Jurisdiction of UNCLOS Part XV Courts and Tribunals' (2016) 65 *International and Comparative Law Quarterly* 927–51.

[162] 'States Parties shall fulfil in good faith the obligations assumed under this Convention and shall exercise the rights, jurisdiction and freedoms recognized in this Convention in a manner which would not constitute an abuse of rights.'

[163] Anastasia Telesetsky, '"Good Faith" Obligations to Protect and Preserve the Marine Environment: A Proposal on Uniform High Seas Fisheries Management' in Clive Schofield, Seokwoo Lee and Moon-Sang Kwon (eds), *The Limits of Maritime Jurisdiction* (Martinus Nijhoff, 2014) 449–71.

[164] Kolb (n 4) 251–54. For a recent analysis of perfidy, see Matthew J Greer, 'Redefining Perfidy' (2015) 47 *Georgetown Journal of International Law* 241–77.

2.1.3 INTERIM CONCLUSIONS Since the principle of good faith allows for the teleological interpretation of rules in international law, it can be used in order to set apart, individuate and characterise the diverse regimes based on their specific overall purpose. But identifying the object and purpose of a treaty or a broader regime is not a straightforward endeavour and the outcome of such an effort is hardly predictable. Indeed, interpretation is a discursive process in which meaning is not 'discovered' but created, so that the outcome of the enterprise depends on the *Vorverständnis* of the interpreter and the response of the interpretive community.[165] Of course the pronouncements of interpreters endowed with institutional authority, such as international judges and arbitrators, carry more weight in the political evolution of the diversification of legal regimes than scholarly writings. This partly explains why specialised regimes with higher judicial activity are the ones where the principle of good faith is more likely to play its differentiating role. If, for example, international environmental law had a system of specialised courts, good faith would likely operate as a reinforcer of the *finalité* of this legal branch.

But this regime-reinforcing function of good faith leads to a double-edged result. If good faith underlines and promotes the various distinct purposes of international regimes, then good faith could at the same time create regime conflicts and fragmentation. This is the case when the global liberalisation of trade clashes with sustainable development.[166] Conflicts of norms, if mismanaged, could undermine trust and confidence between States in international law and therefore erode good faith. The effects of the principle at a 'micro' level (specialised regimes) could weaken it at the macro level (the international legal order as a whole). Yet – as a testimony of the versatility of good faith – the principle can also prevent such negative outcomes.

2.2 *Good Faith as a Tool for Global Coherence*

The principle of good faith not only helps to strengthen the *telos* of particular regimes, it also serves the same purpose with regard to the international legal order in its entirety. The UN Charter and the Friendly Relations Declaration contain authoritative statements about the objectives of international law as a whole, notably the preservation of world peace for the benefit of humankind. However, critical scholars have highlighted that the declared purpose might be fundamentally different from true motives of law-making actors and their lobbyists who mainly seek to pursue self-interested political and economic goals merely cloaked in the language of universality and the common good.[167] In any case, independently of the substantive objectives (real or just feigned) of the international legal norms, a number of formal features must be present to speak meaningfully of an international legal order (as opposed to a mere set of rules), and of an international 'rule of law'. A minimum clarity of rules and the predictability of their

[165] See for the interpretation of international legal norms notably Ingo Venzke, *How Interpretation Makes International Law* (Oxford University Press, 2012); François Ost and Michel Van De Kerchove, *De la Pyramide au Réseau ? Pour une Théorie Dialectique du Droit* (Faculté Universitaire de Saint Louis, 2002) 421–31.

[166] As illustrated in numerous WTO cases. See eg Appellate Body Report, *Canada – Certain Measures Affecting the Renewable Energy Generating Sector; Canada – Measures relating to the Feed-in Tariff Program*, WTO Doc WT/DS412/AB/R; WTO Doc WT/DS426/AB/R (adopted 6 May 2013). The Canadian province of Ontario sought to encourage the use of renewable energy through a pricing scheme. The measures were held to be inconsistent with Art 2(1) of the Agreement on Trade-Related Investment Measures April 15, 1994, Marrakesh Agreement Establishing the World Trade Organization, Annex 1A, 1868 UNTS 186 and Art III(4) GATT 1994: General Agreement on Tariffs and Trade 1994, April 15, 1994, Marrakesh Agreement Establishing the World Trade Organization, Annex 1A, 1867 UNTS 187, 33 ILM 1153 (1994). Or, a State's entitlement or even obligation to restrict imports based on an environmental treaty or the Convention on International Trade in Endangered Species of Wild Fauna and Flora (CITES) may conflict with that same State's obligation to open up its markets for products under trade agreements.

[167] For an overview of critical theories in international law, see Andrea Bianchi, *International Law Theories: An Inquiry in Different Ways of Thinking* (Oxford University Press, 2016) 135–62.

application are two salient features which both contribute to legal security, which is in turn a core feature of 'justice through law'.[168] As demonstrated throughout this chapter, good faith should minimally aim at safeguarding these elements of clarity and predictability.

The clash of inconsistent or even conflicting international norms creates situations where predictability and clarity are weakened. To manage and resolve such conflicts, it is necessary to use the legal techniques of interpretation, as provided for in the VCLT. Article 31 VCLT states that treaties must be interpreted in 'good faith'. Besides wording, context, and object and purpose, '[t]here shall be taken into account: ... (c) any relevant rules of international law applicable in the relations between the parties' (Article 31(3)(c) VCLT). The references to 'context' and 'any relevant rules' have guided the practice of harmonising or 'systemic' interpretation of treaties (and other legal acts). Systemic interpretation of the norms of a specialised regime requires one to interpret them both in the light of a different regime's special rules, and in conformity with general international law. Since the prominent discussion on Article 31(3)(c) as the 'master-key' to the house of international law[169] in the ILC fragmentation report of 2006, parties to disputes more often rely on that provision.

If an ambiguous term of a treaty is to be interpreted in good faith, the object and purpose of the treaty will be taken into account to ascribe a more precise meaning to that term. This can then lead to a higher differentiation between regimes, as previously described. If two conflicting yet equally valid international norms are simultaneously applicable, the good faith requirement of Article 31(1) VCLT will lead the interpreter to try to preserve the overall coherence of the legal system in which these norms co-exist. Doing so requires a reinterpretation of one or both of the conflicting norms.

This was the case for instance in the *Oil Platform* cases where Article XX(1) of the Treaty of Amity between the Islamic Republic of Iran and the United States was interpreted in light of the international customary norms on the use of force.[170] The judges restricted the potential meanings of Article XX(1) in order to acknowledge the evolution of international law since the adoption of the Treaty of Amity. In doing so, they highlighted that this provision could not be understood as allowing the use of force outside of a situation of self-defence.[171] Ignoring the customary developments on the use of force would have breached the requirement of predictability of the international legal order, and therefore not be a good faith interpretation.

Similarly, the WTO Appellate Body famously stated that the GATT 'is not to be read in clinical isolation from public international law'.[172] The Appellate Body has been known to refer to general development in other fields of international law. It made explicit reference to international environmental law in the 1998 *Shrimp-Turtle* case[173] when it declared that the

[168] As argued by Lon Fuller, *The Morality of Law* (rev edn, Yale University Press, 1963) 33–94. For a study of the relevance of Fuller's theory in our contemporary understanding of the international legal system, see Jutta Brunnée and Stephen Toope, *Legitimacy and Legality in International Law: An Interactional Account* (Cambridge University Press, 2010).

[169] This term was coined by ICJ Judge Hanqin Xue when she still was an International Law Commission member in debates in the ILC. ILC, Fragmentation of International Law: Difficulties Arising from the Diversification and Expansion of International Law, UN Doc A/CN.4/L.682, para 420.

[170] *Case Concerning Oil Platforms (Islamic Republic of Iran v United States of America)*, Judgment, ICJ Reports 2003, 161, paras 41–42.

[171] ibid, para 78.

[172] Appellate Body Report, *United States – Standards for Reformulated and Conventional Gasoline*, WT/DS2/9, 20 May 20 1996, 17.

[173] Appellate Body Report, *United States – Import Prohibition of Certain Shrimp and Shrimp Products*, WT/DS58/AB/R, 12 October 1998.

notion of 'exhaustible natural resources' comprised living species.[174] While a panel had, in the *EC-Biotech* report,[175] drastically restricted the reach of Article 31(3)(c) VCLT, the WTO Appellate Body later moved away from this narrow approach.

International human rights courts have also taken into account general legal developments in order to interpret the key terms of their regimes.[176] For instance, in the *Zolotukhin* case,[177] the ECtHR had to interpret the term 'offence' contained in Article 4 of Additional Protocol 7 which codifies the *non bis in idem* principle.[178] To do so, it relied on a multitude of other international instruments, such as the ICCPR, the Charter of Fundamental Rights of the European Union, and the Inter-American Convention on Human Rights.[179] Similarly, the IACtHR in the *Artavia Murillo*[180] case interpreted Article 4.1 of the American Convention on Human Rights by taking into account other international instruments. In order to determine what was exactly meant by 'the right to life shall be protected by law and, in general, *from the moment of conception*',[181] the judges referred to several other international agreements[182] and came to the conclusion that there was no trend towards the protection of the embryo in international law.[183]

Although good faith was not explicitly referred to in these cases, it was a powerful driving force. The explicit or implicit use of Article 31(3)(c) VCLT aimed at establishing greater predictability about the applicable law in a context of overlapping regimes. In other words, these cases attempted to protect one of the core elements of good faith in the international legal order. Systemic interpretation promoted coherence within international law. This said, one should bear in mind that coherence is, as pointed out in the report of the ILC Group on Fragmentation, only 'a formal and abstract virtue. For a legal system that is regarded in some respects as unjust or unworkable, no added value is brought by the fact of its being coherently so.'[184] On the other hand, a loss of coherence implies the loss of international law's quality as a

[174] ibid, paras 130–34. However, while conducting its analysis, the Appellate Body never cited Art 31(3)(c) VCLT.

[175] Panel Report, *European Communities – Measures Affecting the Approval and Marketing of Biotech Products*, WT/DS291/R; WT/DS292/R; WT/DS293/R, 29 September 2006, para 7.70. The *Biotech* panel required a parallelism: a treaty norm can only be taken into account as an interpretative guideline in a WTO-related dispute when *all* parties to that dispute – or even all parties to the WTO Agreement which must be interpreted – have ratified that other treaty. This would render Art 31(3) VCLT largely meaningless. Such an approach would make other treaties non-usable for the interpretation of treaties with a broad membership, such as the WTO-Agreement (which moreover has also non-state members which cannot accede to most other international treaties). The narrow reading would in addition have the paradoxical result that the more universal a treaty is, the smaller the chance that it could 'meet' other treaties. The strict *Biotech* approach has been mitigated in later disputes (Appellate Body Report, *European Communities and Certain member States – Measures Affecting Trade in Large Civil Aircraft*, WT/DS316/AB/R, 18 May 2011, para 845).

[176] For a recent overview, see, Adamantia Rachovitsa, 'The Principle of Systemic Integration in Human Rights Law' (2017) 66 *International & Comparative Law Quarterly* 557–88, arguing that the principle of systemic integration might not be the most appropriate tool to mitigate the potential negative effects of legal proliferation in international law.

[177] *Case of Sergey Zolotukhin* v *Russia*, ECtHR, Appl No 14939/03, Judgment of 10 February 2009.

[178] Art 4.1: 'No one shall be liable to be tried or punished again in criminal proceedings under the jurisdiction of the same state for an offence for which he has already been finally acquitted or convicted in accordance with the law and penal procedure of that state'.

[179] *Case of Sergey Zolotukhin* v *Russia* (n 177), paras 78–84.

[180] *Artavia Murillo et al* v *Costa Rica*, IACtHR, Judgment of November 2012, Series C No 257.

[181] Emphasis added.

[182] Such as the Convention on the Elimination of All Forms of Discrimination Against Women or the Convention on the Rights of the Child. IACtHR, *Artavia Murillo et al* v *Costa Rica* (n 180), paras 224–44.

[183] ibid, para 253: 'Accordingly, the Court observes that the regulatory trends in international law do not lead to the conclusion that the embryo should be treated in the same way as a person, or that it has a right to life.'

[184] Study Group of the ILC, Draft Conclusion of the Work of the Study Group, UN Doc A/CN.4/L.682/Add.1, 2 May 2006, para 491.

legal order (or system). An agglomeration of isolated and diverse norms does not amount to a legal order. Along this line, H. L. A. Hart had notoriously described international law as only being 'rules which constitute not a system but a simple set'.[185] A legal order is present only when norms refer to each other (ordered norms). But legal order means not only ordered law but also order through law. These two dimensions are mutually reinforcing: the normative pull of law is fortified by its stringency and consistency.[186] Understanding this interrelationship means understanding why consistency is particularly important for international law (more than for domestic law): because its normative power is more precarious.

Therefore, what is at stake in fragmentation is unity, harmony, cohesion, order and – concomitantly – the quality of international law as a truly normative order. Without some glue holding together the 'special regimes' and 'institutional components', writes Georges Abi-Saab, 'the special regime becomes a legal order unto itself – a kind of legal Frankenstein' that 'no longer partakes in the same basis of legitimacy and formal standards of pertinence'.[187] So ultimately, at the bottom of the fragmentation debate lies a concern for a loss of legitimacy of international law, a loss which will ultimately threaten that law's very existence. Good faith, thanks to its high abstraction, versatility and axiological nature, is a principle suited to play this role of 'glue' between the regimes.

3 *Manifestations of the Principle of Good Faith in a Structurally Differentiated International Legal Order*

In this section, we will discuss how patterns of good faith are apparent in each of the different structures of the international legal order. While the presence of good faith is obvious in the private law-like structures of international law (section V.3.1) and within the subset of constitutional law (section V.3.2), the principle's influence is less clear in the administrative law-type (section V.3.3) and criminal law contexts (section V.3.4).

Nevertheless, the underlying rationale of good faith, namely trust and predictability, are clearly shaping the legal developments in the latter two areas. Considering the importance of good faith in an administrative setting, we suggest that the principle is no longer strictly limited to symmetric, 'horizontal' relations between global actors such as States, international organisations or transnational businesses.

3.1 *An Obvious Role in the Private Law-Like Structures of International Law*

As previously mentioned, the principle of good faith originates from Roman civil law systems, where it was an essential element for the conduct of legal relations between individuals. Simply put, good faith was the cornerstone of any contract.

Thomas Erskine Holland has insisted on the fact that international law, the 'Law of Nations', was the application to States of concepts initially applied to the relations between individuals.[188] In its earlier forms, international law was mainly made of agreements between sovereign entities considered formally as equals. Their legal relationship is, on a strictly conceptual level, identical to contracts between individuals in domestic settings. Holland's already-cited expression 'private

[185] Herbert LA Hart, *The Concept of Law* (2nd edn, Clarendon Press, 1994) 234.

[186] Jacques Chevallier, 'L'Ordre juridique' in Jacques Chevallier (ed), *Le Droit en procès* (Presse Universitaire de France, 1983) 7–49, 7–8.

[187] Georges Abi-Saab, 'Fragmentation or Unification: Some Concluding Remarks' (1999) 31 *New York University Journal of International Law & Politics* 919–34, 926.

[188] Holland (n 130) 152.

law writ large' accurately describes this. And, since good faith is the cornerstone of contractual relations between individuals in a horizontal setting, it naturally plays an equivalent role between sovereign States. This is visible, as mentioned, in the importance ascribed to the idea of *pacta sunt servanda*. This maxim is existential for treaties in international law.

However, international law today is far from simply being a transposition of the domestic and private law-based contractual model to the international level. Since at least 1945, the structure of international law displays further characteristics, among them some constitution-like features.

3.2 *Good Faith in International Constitutional Law*

The foundational importance of good faith in the 'privatist' reading of international law naturally leads to consideration of its function as a constitutional element of the international legal order.

The usual functions of constitutional law are to establish, organise, integrate and stabilise a political community, to contain political power, to provide normative guidance and to regulate the governance activities of law-making, law application and law enforcement. International norms fulfilling those tasks for the international legal system at large, for specific international organisations or regimes, and for the interaction of international law with domestic law might therefore, from a functional perspective, be qualified as 'constitutional' norms as well. In addition, international norms taking over or reinforcing the said constitutional functions of domestic law also belong to the overarching and multi-level body of global constitutional law.[189]

In this reading, good faith holds an obvious prime place. It upholds the operation of the entire international legal order. Its corollary, *pacta sunt servanda*, is regarded as one of the most basic norms of international law.

The principle of proportionality,[190] a typical constitutional norm, can be seen as a manifestation of good faith. It applies in the international law of countermeasures (sanctions), the law of international responsibility, the law of self-defence, the law of natural resources, the law of armed conflict, international and regional human rights protection, world trade law (WTO and the North American Free Trade Agreement) and in international investment protection law. In all these contexts, proportionality requires that the means applied must stand in a proper relationship to the ends. For example, the use of force in self-defence may not lead to the total destruction of the belligerent State. Proportionality is closely linked to trust and predictability, because the principle assures the participants in the legal system that rights or competences will not be exercised in a way that defeats their objective. Thus, the principle of proportionality and the prohibition of the abuse of rights, also an emanation of the principle of good faith, overlap.

To conclude, the role of the principle of good faith can easily be conceptualised both in the purely private law-like structures of international law and in those structures which are akin to constitutional law. In contrast, its operation in international ('global') administrative law and international criminal law is more ambiguous.

[189] See most recently Takao Suami et al (eds), *Global Constitutionalism from European and East Asian Perspectives* (Cambridge University Press, 2018). For a literature overview on the topic, see Thomas Kleinlein and Anne Peters, 'International Constitutional Law' in *Oxford Bibliographies in International Law*. The legal and political process in which parts of international law has come to perform these constitutional functions has been called the 'constitutionalisation' of international law. See most recently Anne Peters, 'Constitutionalization' in Jean D'Aspremont and Sahib Singh (eds), *Concepts for International Law: Contributions to Disciplinary Thought* (Edward Elgar, 2019) 141–53.

[190] Anne Peters, 'Proportionality as a Global Constitutional Principle' in Anthony Lang and Antje Wiener (eds), *Handbook on Global Constitutionalism* (Edward Elgar, 2017) 248–64.

3.3 *Good Faith in the Administrative Structures of International Law*

The administrative dimension of international law has been analysed notably in the paradigm of Global Administrative Law (GAL).[191] Noting the multiplication of international institutions and transnational regulatory networks endowed with the powers to make and enforce law vis-à-vis individuals, the proponents of GAL have identified the common principles governing these activities such as transparency, participation, reasoned decision, legality and effective review of rules and decisions.[192] Additionally, the GAL framework seeks to improve the accountability of the administrative activity. Among the administrative principles already in place and potentially worthy to be strengthened to that end, transparency stands out.

Like good faith, transparency is an opaque and multifaceted term.[193] It generally relates to both the absence of secrecy and access to information. In relation to good faith, transparency is paradoxical, because it both potentially undermines and reinforces good faith. By demanding maximum access to information and by limiting the realm of secrecy, transparency as a standard creates conditions that can potentially reinforce trust and predictability (the 'objective' dimension of good faith).[194] The decision of being transparent in the conduct of one's activity can be interpreted as a declaration of good faith. But at the same time, transparency might undermine trust because of the change of expectations and attitudes, and the risk of misinformation and information overflow.[195] However, this reservation against transparency policies seems one-sided because lack of transparency is also apt to generate distrust. Secrecy is often understood to indicate bad intentions and disclosure is perceived as a sign of trustworthiness.[196] Moreover, in order to judge whether to place our trust in a given entity, for example an international organisation, we must first have sufficient information. Even if we consider that, overall, transparency fosters trust, it inevitably affects the role of 'subjective' good faith as a postulate for the functioning of the legal order. The requirements of transparency push participants to show that they are acting in good faith, by giving access to information. Their good faith is no longer simply assumed, but it is – as far as possible – materially ensured through transparency. At the very least, the possibilities for acting in bad faith are reduced. For instance, in international environmental law, the requirement of transparency allows for a better monitoring of the implementation of multilateral agreements.[197] This is often done through reporting requirements placed on States, completed by the possibility of taking into account the information

191 See seminally Benedict Kingsbury, Nico Krisch and Richard Stewart, 'The Emergence of Global Administrative Law' (2005) 68 *Law and Contemporary Problems* 15–61; Sabino Cassese, 'Administrative Law without the State? The Challenge of Global Regulation' (2005) 37 *New York University Journal of International Law and Politics* 663–94; Sabino Cassese, 'Global Administrative Law: The State of the Art' (2015) 13 *International Journal of Constitutional Law* 465–68.

192 Kingsbury, Krisch and Stewart (n 191).

193 Andrea Bianchi, 'On Power and Illusion: The Concept of Transparency in International Law' in Andrea Bianchi and Anne Peters (eds), *Transparency in International Law* (Cambridge University Press, 2013) 1–19.

194 Anne Peters, 'Towards Transparency as a Global Norm' in Andrea Bianchi and Anne Peters (eds), *Transparency in International Law* (Cambridge University Press, 2013) 534–607. See, for the distinction between 'objective' and 'subjective' good faith, section I of this chapter.

195 Onora O'Neill, A *Question of Trust*, The BBC Reith Lectures 2002 (Cambridge University Press, 2002) esp 70: '[i]f we want to restore trust we need to reduce deception and lies rather than secrecy. Some sorts of secrecy indeed support deception, others do not. Transparency and openness may not be the unconditional goods that they are fashionably supposed to be. By the same token, secrecy and lack of transparency may not be the enemies of trust.'

196 Ann Florini, 'Conclusions' in Ann Florini (ed), *The Right to Know: Transparency for an Open World* (Columbia University Press, 2007) 348.

197 On this topic, see Tom Sparks and Anne Peters, 'Transparency in International Environmental Law' in Jacqueline Peel and Lavanyia Rajamani (eds), *Oxford Handbook of International Environmental Law* (forthcoming).

provided by non-governmental organisations and international institutions.[198] With the double scrutiny of other States parties and further international stakeholders, the possibilities for States to cheat when implementing their international obligations are considerably reduced.

The requirement of transparency also benefits non-State participants in the international legal order. It allows civil society actors who take part in international governance and individuals who might be affected by international legal measures to see, and indeed foresee, the legal developments and the application of the law. This is, for example, the rationale of the Aarhus Convention which mandates States parties to furnish information on the environment to members of the public.[199] Thus, transparency promotes the main elements of the principle of good faith between States and also between States and their citizens.

3.4 *Good Faith in International Criminal Law*

This subfield of international law is formed by specific norms whose violation triggers the criminal responsibility of individuals and which organise and operationalise prosecution, judgment and sentencing. This body of law has an inherently 'vertical' structure in the sense that it is set in a relation between public actors (States and international criminal courts and tribunals) on the one end, and individuals on the other end, with the individuals seen as subordinated or subjected to the institutions.

The creation trust and the assurance that the application of the law is predictable for those under its authority is very important for international criminal law. This idea is manifest in its core principle *nulla poena sine lege* which is a particularly strict version of the principle of legality. The principle demands that legal obligations imposed on individuals, especially those saddled with criminal sanctions, must be fixed beforehand so that individuals know what is expected from them and can adjust their behaviour. The principle of legality is classically expressed in Article 4 of the French Declaration of the Rights of Man and of the Citizen, from a human rights perspective: the limits of freedom 'can only be determined by law'.[200] In this tradition, the law appears as an expression of the *volonté générale* and as a guarantor for the equal treatment of citizens. The principle of legality is a public law principle. It is a key achievement of liberal constitutionalism, arising from the idea that citizens owe obedience to the State only on the basis of clearly established rules, and are otherwise free.

Although the principle originates from national legal settings, Kenneth Gallant has argued that it is now a general principle of law as referred to in Article 38(1)(c) of the ICJ Statute and hence also an international legal norm.[201] As an international legal norm, the rationale of the principle is to some extent analogous to the idea of legitimate expectations inherent to good faith. Individuals, wherever they may be, can legitimately expect that they will not be punished for a behaviour that is not specifically prohibited by law.

198 See, eg, the importance of the NGO TRAFFIC for the work of CITES.

199 Aarhus Convention on the Access to Information, Public Participation in Decision-Making and Access to Justice in Environmental Matters, 25 June 1998, 2161 UNTS 447.

200 'La liberté consiste à pouvoir faire tout ce qui ne nuit pas à autrui: ainsi l'exercice des droits naturels de chaque homme n'a de bornes que celles qui assurent aux autres Membres de la Société, la jouissance de ces mêmes droits. Ces bornes ne peuvent être déterminées que par la Loi' (Déclaration des droits de l'homme et du citoyen of 26 August 1789, Art 4).

201 Kenneth S Gallant, *The Principle of Legality in International and Comparative Criminal Law* (Cambridge University Press, 2009) 241.

VI GOOD FAITH AND THE OBJECTIVES OF THE FRIENDLY RELATIONS DECLARATION FIFTY YEARS ON

Is the principle of good faith, in its current form, suited to achieve the purposes of the Friendly Relations Declaration? For the sake of peace and security and the development of friendly relations between nations, the Friendly Relations Declaration stresses the importance of fundamental human rights and acknowledges the principle of equal rights and self-determination of peoples. The Declaration recognises that individuals are beneficiaries of protection by the international legal order. This approach manifests a patriarchal conception of international law in which States are charged with guaranteeing the safety and well-being of their population.[202] This paradigm also shines up in the debates around the responsibility to protect – where sovereignty is linked to the duty to protect the population[203] – or in recent theories of the fiduciary State – where the State is entrusted by people with the discretionary powers to act on their behalf for their best interest.[204]

Yet, there is a discrepancy between the arguable consideration of the Friendly Relations Declaration for individuals, and the main operation of the principle of good faith in international law. Individuals are practically absent from the numerous legal applications of the principle of good faith studied in this chapter. Except for human rights treaties, good faith in international law seems to only concern actors that co-operate on the same level: mainly States, international organisations and powerful transnational businesses. The absence of individuals makes sense if good faith is understood primarily as a concept governing contractual and 'symmetric' legal relationships between actors on the same plane. As said, good faith originates from such a legal setting, namely contracts between individuals. It works in international law on the basis of a rigid fiction of States as sovereign equals, acting as individuals in horizontal relations.

However, this picture leaves aside the numerous ways in which contemporary international law affects individuals.[205] For example, international environmental agreements influence the physical life conditions of countless individuals. International financial institutions can both threaten or safeguard economic and social rights. In both cases, the impact – or lack of impact– of international law menaces the security of individuals.[206] In many ways, the ultimate stakeholders of any international agreement are individuals.[207] Yet, they do not benefit from the principle of good faith in its traditional inception.

It is a truism today that international law is not the exclusive domain of States, and that one of its key objectives is to secure conditions in which individual human beings can flourish.[208]

[202] Anne Peters, *Beyond Human Rights: The Legal Status of the Individual in International Law* (Cambridge University Press, 2016) 541.

[203] For an overview of the notion, see Ingo Winkelmann, 'Responsibility to Protect' in *Max Planck Encyclopedia of Public International Law* (October 2010). A comprehensive study can be found in Alex Bellamy and Tim Dunne (eds), *The Oxford Handbook of the Responsibility to Protect* (Oxford University Press, 2016).

[204] See Evan Criddle and Evan Fox-Decent, *Sovereignty's Promise: The State as Fiduciary* (Oxford University Press, 2011).

[205] See Tilmann Altwicker, 'Transnationalizing Rights: International Human Rights Law in Cross-Border Contexts' (2018) 29 *European Journal of International Law* 581–606.

[206] Security threats linked to environmental changes are frequently highlighted at the international level. For a recent example, see World Economic Forum, *The Global Risks Report* (14th edn, World Economic Forum, 2019).

[207] This was already an idea held by Georges Scelle in the first half of the twentieth century. See, inter alia, Georges Scelle, *Manuel de droit international public* (Domat-Monchrestien, 1934) 17–24.

[208] Christian Tomuschat, 'International Law: Ensuring the Survival of Mankind on the Eve of a New Century: General Course on Public International Law' (1999) 281 *Recueil des Cours* 13–438; Anne Peters, 'Humanity as the A and Ω of Sovereignty' (2009) 20 *European Journal of International Law* 513–44; Rafael Domingo, *The New Global Law* (Cambridge University Press, 2010); Augusto Cançado Trindade, 'International Law for Humankind: Towards a

Despite contemporary antagonistic trends such as the recurring emphasis of State sovereignty, the increased protection of State borders and critique against human rights overreach,[209] international law continues to be concerned with the well-being of individuals. Therefore, we need to think of ways in which the principle of good faith can take into account the individual in international law. The rise of transparency in international law which clearly echoes the requirements of the principle of good faith and at the same time benefits individuals is a case in point.

Beyond this aspect, the principle of good faith in international law should be further developed in order to become more relevant for individuals. Good faith needs to be applied in legal relationships characterised by an unequal distribution of power, typically in the State–individual relation. That means that when a State enters into an international agreement, it would not only have to implement it in good faith with regard to the other parties to the agreements, but also with regard to all individuals that might be affected by this agreement.

Similar manifestations of an 'asymmetric' application of good faith exist in the administrative law of numerous domestic legal orders, at least in Europe. At this point, we need not engage in a meticulous survey in order to identify a 'general principle of law recognized by civilized nations' in the sense of Article 38(1)(c) of the ICJ Statute.[210] A rough survey shows that it is plausible to imagine a novel understanding of the principle of good faith in international law, an understanding that gives due consideration to the legitimate expectations of individuals.

The most prominent example of administrative duties of good faith towards citizens is found in the Swiss Federal Constitution of 1999.[211] It stipulates that both the State and individuals must act in conformity with the 'rules of good faith' (Article 5).[212] Moreover, every person has the fundamental right not to be treated arbitrarily, but in accordance with the rules of good faith by the organs of the State (Article 9).[213] Put differently, Article 5 requires that States organs display a loyal behaviour towards citizens; a behaviour that is free from contradictions and deceptions.[214] Article 9 protects the legitimate trust that citizens may place in the administration, relying on the latter's prior behaviour.[215] This protection of trust can even trump the formal requirement of legality. If a promise has been made incorrectly to the citizen (without a proper legal basis) Article 9 of the Constitution requires that this promise must nevertheless be fulfilled. For instance, a construction initiated upon approval by the administration was protected by the principle of good faith although the project was in breach of a federal law on forests.[216]

New Jus Gentium: General Course on Public International Law' (2005) 316 *Recueil des Cours* 1–439; Ruti Teitel, *Humanity's Law* (Oxford University Press, 2013); Peters (n 202).

209 On a potential backlash against the 'proliferation' of human rights and the individualisation of international law, see Makau Mutua, 'Is the Age of Human Rights Over?' in Sophia A. McClennen and Alexandra Schultheis Moore (eds), *The Routledge Companion to Literature and Human Rights* (Routledge, 2016) 450–58; Ingrid Wuerth, 'International Law in the Post-Human Rights Era' (2017) 96 *Texas Law Review* 279–349.

210 See for the various understandings of 'general principles', ILC, First Report on General Principles of Law, UN Doc A/CN.4/732, 5 April 2019.

211 Constitution fédérale de la Confédération suisse of 18 April 1999, Recueil Officiel (official gazette) 1999, 2556.

212 Art 5(3): 'Les organes de l'Etat et les particuliers doivent agir de manière conforme aux règles de la bonne foi.'

213 Art 9: 'Toute personne a le droit d'être traitée par les organes de l'Etat sans arbitraire et conformément aux règles de la bonne foi.'

214 Jean-François Aubert and Pascal Mahon, *Petit Commentaire de la Constitution Fédérale de la Confédération Suisse du 18 Avril 1999* (Schulthess, 2003) 46; Pascal Mahon, *Droit constitutionnel, vol II: Droit fondamentaux* (3rd edn, Faculté de droit de l'Université de Neuchâtel, 2015) 276–82; Paul-Henri Steinauer, 'La Bonne Foi en droit public et en droit privé' in Guido Corti and Marco Borghi (eds), *Diritto Senza Devianza* (Helbing & Lichtenhahn, 2006) 775–89; Alexander Misic and Nicole Töpperwien, *Constitutional Law in Switzerland* (2nd edn, Kluwer Law, 2018) 202–3.

215 Aubert and Mahon (n 214) 96–98.

216 See *Posewitz*, Swiss Federal Tribunal (ATF) 108 Ib 377, Judgment of 21 April 1982.

We see similar logics in the German, French and UK systems where the citizens are protected against unfair and unforeseen change of behaviour of the administration.[217] This protection is often referred to as the protection of legitimate trust or legitimate expectations, and echoes the objective elements of good faith analysed throughout this chapter.

'*Vertrauensschutz*' is a general principle of German public law.[218] It protects the trust of individuals in the continuity of the legal system and is seen by the German Federal Constitutional Court (*Bundesverfassungsgericht*; BVerfG) as a fundamental condition for the effective exercise of the individual rights guaranteed under the German Constitution (Basic Law, *Grundgesetz* (GG)). It is considered to emanate from the principle of the rule of law as codified in Article 20(3) GG. Additionally, the maxim '*nulla poena sine lege praevia*' is understood to be a special manifestation of *Vertrauensschutz*, and is codified in Article 103(2) GG. The exact scope of *Vertrauensschutz* varies, depending on the branch of government concerned. It does not apply to decisions of the judiciary. Laws may, with limited exceptions, be amended with effect for the future.[219] The application of new statutes to continuing situations that existed before the legislative change may violate *Vertrauensschutz* under certain conditions. One constellation is notably that an individual has actually relied on the prior laws (for example by making an investment) and when his or her interest in the protection of his or her legitimate expectation outweighs the public interest in applying the new statute. Then, transitional arrangements are required. *Vertrauensschutz* also applies to acts of the executive branch. When an administrative agency adopts an administrative act, it may only undo it in conformity with the provisions of §§ 48–52 of the *Länders*' parallel laws on administrative procedure (*Verwaltungsverfahrensgesetz*, VwVfG). The revocation of unlawful administrative acts that are favourable to the individual is generally permitted but gives rise to an obligation to compensate for any damage suffered due to the citizen's reliance on said act (§ 48(3) VwVfG). If the unlawful administrative act concerned provides for payment of money, then it may even not be revoked at all if certain conditions are met (§ 48(2) VwVfG).[220] The withdrawal of lawful administrative acts favourable to the individual is only allowed under limited circumstances (§ 49(2) and (3) VwVfG).

In contrast to the German system, French administrative law does not contain formal general rules on good faith. However, its case law protects the citizens' trust and seeks to guarantee the predictability of State action.[221] This tendency has been described as a fundamental shift in rationale of this body of law,[222] which had before been primarily concerned with the formal legality of acts of the administration rather than with the expectations of the administered

[217] For a detailed comparative analysis, see Paraskevi Mouzouraki, *Le Principe de confiance légitime en droit allemand, français et anglais. Un exemple de convergence des droits administratifs des pays européens?* (Bruylant, 2011).

[218] See Kyrill-Alexander Schwarz, *Vertrauensschutz als Verfassungsprinzip: Eine Analyse des nationalen Rechts, des Gemeinschaftsrechts und der Beziehungen zwischen beiden Rechtskreisen* (Nomos, 2002); Anna Leisner-Egensperger, *Kontinuität als Verfassungsprinzip Unter besonderer Berücksichtigung des Steuerrechts* (Mohr Siebeck, 2002); Hermann-Josef Blanke, *Vertrauensschutz im deutschen und europäischen Verwaltungsrecht* (Mohr Siebeck, 2000).

[219] See most recently German Federal Constitutional Court (*BVerfG*), Judgment of 10 April 2018 – 1 BvR 1236/11, para 134.

[220] See for a key case on the revocation of a subsidy infringing EU law: German Federal Administrative Court (BVerwG), Judgment of 17 February 1993 – 11 C 47/92.

[221] Sébastien Ferrari and Sébastien Hourson (eds), *La Loyauté en droit public* (Institut Universitaire de Varenne, 2018); Ana Beduschi-Ortiz, 'La Notion de loyauté en droit administratif' (2011) 17 *Actualité Juridique du Droit Administratif* 944–51. For a specific discussion on good faith and French administrative law, see Eric Carpano, 'Le Droit administratif français est-il perméable à la bonne foi?', *Lexis-Nexis Droit Administratif*, January 2005, Study 2; Benoît Plessix, 'Sécurité juridique et confiance légitime' (2016) 3 *Revue du Droit Public* 799–807; Léa Il, 'Le Principe de confiance légitime serait-il entré en droit public interne?' (2017) 3 *Petites Affiches* 6–11.

[222] ibid, specifically Carpano.

citizens. French administrative judges have been reluctant to formally consecrate a general principle of the protection of legitimate expectations.[223] Yet, administrative law has developed towards safeguarding them.[224] For instance, with regard to contractual relations between public and private actors, French administrative law has slowly been influenced by the logic of private law. This has led to the recognition of a general duty of loyalty of the administration in its contractual relations.[225] More broadly, French administrative law contains several rules and principles that protect the expectations of the citizen, irrespective of contractual relations. For instance, the theory of 'de facto civil servant'[226] protects the expectations of citizens who rightfully believed they had dealt with the administration.[227] Similarly, administrative judges have regularly taken into consideration the legitimate expectations of citizens who had been made an irregular promise by the administration.[228] Generally, good faith, loyalty or the protection of legitimate expectations imply that the administration shall refrain from behaviour that could mislead the citizen or any private actors it has contracted with.

Common law systems also possess refined regimes for the protection of legitimate expectations. This is striking, considering the explicit aversion of these systems toward the notion of good faith.[229] This seeming discrepancy can be explained by the fact that the opposition to good faith is limited to the domain of contracts in which adversarial attitudes between the contracting parties are deemed legitimate. Subjective good faith has therefore little utility in such a setting.[230] In contrast, trust and predictability are needed in the relationships between the British administration and the citizen. Similar to the French example, case law has developed protections for the trust that citizens may have due to assurances, promises or other behaviour of the administration.[231] UK national courts have, however, been reluctant to consider that the ratification of an international agreement could create legitimate expectations for citizens.[232]

Other jurisdictions such as Spain,[233] Italy[234] and Belgium[235] also protect citizens' legitimate expectations. The Europe-wide protection of legitimate expectations towards administrative bodies was likely influenced by the European Union[236] – whose administration complies with

[223] The judge declared that the principle of legitimate trust was valid only for matters covered by European Union law. *Société KPMG et Société Ernst & Young et autres*, Conseil d'Etat, 24 March 2006, Req No 288460: 'Considérant que le principe de confiance légitime, qui fait partie des principes généraux du droit communautaire, ne trouve à s'appliquer dans l'ordre juridique national que dans le cas où la situation juridique dont a à connaître le juge administratif français est régie par le droit Communautaire.'

[224] Plessix (n 221); Il (n 221).

[225] *Commune de Béziers*, Conseil d'État, 28 December 2009, Req No 304802.

[226] 'Fonctionnaires de fait' (our translation).

[227] Jean Waline, *Droit Administratif* (27th edn, Dalloz, 2018) 460.

[228] Plessix (n 221).

[229] See eg Gunther Teubner, 'Legal Irritants: Good Faith in British Law or How Unifying Law Ends Up in New Divergences' (1998) 61 *The Modern Law Review* 11–32.

[230] See section I of this chapter for the distinction between objective and subjective good faith.

[231] Timothy Endicott, *Administrative Law* (3rd edn, Oxford University Press, 2015) 293–308.

[232] For instance, *R v Secretary of State for the Home Department, Ex parte Ahmed (Mohammed Hussain) and Patel (Idris Ibrahim)*, United Kingdom: High Court (England and Wales), decision CO/3476/97, 27 April 1998.

[233] Jesús González Pérez, *El principio general de la buena fe en el derecho administrativo* (Thomas Civitas, 2004).

[234] See Livia Lorenzoni, *I principi di diritto comune nell'attività amministrativa* (Jovene, 2018) 130–95 on the administrative law principles of good faith and correctness ('correttezza').

[235] Renaud Simar and Pauline Abba, 'Sécurité juridique, légitime confiance, *patere legem quam ipse fecisti*. Transparence administrative ou principes transparents?' in Sarah Ben Messaoud and François Viseur (eds), *Les Principes généraux de droit administratif: Actualités et applications pratiques* (Larcier, 2017) 91–131, 103–23.

[236] Mouzouraki (n 217) 751.

the principle of legitimate expectations[237] – and by the Council of Europe and the ECtHR which promote good administration practises.[238]

These examples show that numerous national systems acknowledge an 'asymmetric' conception of good faith in the relationship between State and citizen. But how could this approach be transposed to the international level and what would be the tangible legal consequences of such an evolution?

A first option for the internationalisation of this approach would be through litigation. For instance, a judge or arbitrator could be invited to determine whether the protection of legitimate expectations of individuals is now a distinctive element of the principle of good faith. A (judicial) investigation of major national systems could lead to the identification of a general principle of international law in the sense of Article 38(1)(c) ICJ Statute. Of course, such an outcome could be reached only when a case presented itself and when a competent judge would indeed find the asymmetric conception of good faith in the relevant national administrative systems in the world.

A second option for bringing to bear an 'asymmetrical' conception of good faith benefiting individuals in their relations with international actors could be the soft-law approach. In the same way that the Friendly Relations Declaration recognised good faith as a principle permeating the entirety of international law, a new declaration by a global political body could push for an understanding of good faith that also benefits individuals. This strategy would, of course, not give birth to a new principle of international law, but only contribute to the sedimentation of such an understanding, possibly leading to a coherent and constant practice among States. The two options mainly differ in terms of speed and in terms of the norm entrepreneurs. The first approach (litigation) would imply that the dimension of the principle is a latent normative element in the existing international system which can be uncovered by judicial interpretation, while the other one (soft law-making) would push for its explicit acceptance by the international actors other than courts.

Giving due consideration to individuals in applying the principle of good faith could have several effects. First of all, it could contribute to strengthening the interaction between domestic legal orders with international law. Systems that already protect the legitimate expectations of individuals could see this protection enhanced for matters related to international law. This could be particularly relevant for the ongoing climate litigation which seeks to establish State responsibility at the domestic level for the failure to act appropriately.[239] The principle of citizens' good faith could bolster the substantive claims made against States. Second, the extended conception of good faith could bear on the interpretation of international law in inter-State disputes. However, one should keep in mind that a principle which is as general as good faith will often only play a supplementary role in disputes relating to more concrete legal questions. Therefore, even if good faith, as we know it, were to be reconceptualised, the direct

[237] See eg Marie-Christine Pujol-Reversat, 'La Bonne Foi, principe général du droit dans la jurisprudence communautaire' (2009) 45 *Revue Trimestrielle de Droit Européen* 201–29.

[238] Mouzouraki (n 217) 751. See eg *Case of Moskal* v *Poland*, ECtHR, Appl No 10373/05, Judgment of 15 September 2009, para 51: 'the principle of "good governance" requires that where an issue in the general interest is at stake it is incumbent on the public authorities to act in good time, in an appropriate manner and with utmost consistency'. See also the decision of the Committee of Ministers of the Council of Europe, 'Strategy on Innovation and Good Governance at Local Level' taken during the fifteenth session of the Conference of European Ministers responsible for local and regional government (Valencia, 15–16 October 2007) – Report by the Secretary-General (CM(2008)14, CM(2008)14-add, GR-DEM(2008)CB4-rev).

[239] The iconic case in climate litigation so far is Supreme Court of the Netherlands, *State of the Netherlands* v *Stitching Urgenda*, No 19/00135, Judgment of 20 December 2019 (ECLI:NL:HR:2019:2007). For an overview, see KJ de Graaf and JH Jans, 'The Urgenda Decision: Netherlands Liable for Role in Causing Dangerous Global Climate Change' (2015) 27 *Journal of Environmental Law* 517–27.

legal impact of such a reconceptualisation would not necessarily be obvious. It would probably take very specific cases to actually see new legal effects.

On the other hand, the impact of a new understanding would not necessarily be purely a legal one. At this point, a parallel can be drawn with the current debates on the recognition of legal personality for non-human natural entities (animals, ecosystems or the environment in general). Such a recognition does not only create legal effects. It can also shape, through discourse, our overall understanding of the new legal subjects.[240] If the principle of good faith included a duty towards individuals, it could contribute to our whole picture of international law as a legal space concerned not merely with States and transnational actors.

VII CONCLUSIONS

A glance at the current state of world affairs does not give the impression that good faith plays a decisive role in how States behave. Internal and international armed conflicts abound, despite the existence of the United Nations and numerous other organisations and institutions seeking to guarantee world peace and containing military violence. The global environmental impact of human activities has not been sufficiently mitigated by international environmental law and institutions. Inequalities are soaring despite the proclaimed goals of the international financial and economic institutions to alleviate poverty and contribute to wealth and growth. The rise of populism in numerous countries threatens multilateralism and compliance with international judgments. Fifty years after the adoption of the Friendly Relations Declaration, it would be an exaggeration to say that we have achieved friendly relations between States.

Does this mean, however, that good faith is missing? This diagnosis would hold if we understood good faith simply as a synonym for 'morality', 'decency' or 'virtue'. We have explained that the legal principle of good faith plays a more clear-cut role in international law. To grasp this role, we must first acknowledge that good faith, as a principle, is not in itself more specific than the trust and predictability it seeks to protect. It does not have the same normative structure as international law's substantive basic principles such as sovereign equality of States, self-determination of peoples, prohibition of the use of force and human rights. Rather, good faith is a vehicle for the realisation of the principles embodying values of the legal system in which it operates. As a vehicle, good faith is more neutral than its name might suggest. It is a tool in the hands of interpreters to defend a legal system's purpose and a guideline for the elaboration of rules that will foster trust and predictability in certain fields (for instance, the prohibition of perfidy, the protection of investors, the prohibition of the threat of military force and so on).

This means that good faith, as a principle, can be employed to combat cynical uses of international law only up to a certain point. For example, the prohibition of an abuse of rights (a manifestation of good faith) can justify the non-recognition of excessive conferrals of extraterritorial nationality as practiced by Russia in neighbouring regions prone to Russian meddling and invasion.[241] However, when States adopt international rules that appear to be fundamentally unfair or immoral – for example in a situation of massive power disparities and unequal bargaining power – good faith loses some of its influence. The injustice of such norms can only be tempered by referring to other rules, through systemic interpretation. Norms of *jus*

[240] Anne Peters, 'Liberté, Egalité, Animalité: Human–Animal Comparisons in Law' (2016) 5 *Transnational Environmental Law* 25–53, 48.

[241] Anne Peters, 'Extraterritorial Naturalizations: Between the Human Right to Nationality, State Sovereignty and Fair Principles of Jurisdiction' (2010) 53 *German Yearbook of International Law* 623–725.

cogens may also prevent the creation of patently unjust international treaties, but the reach of peremptory norms is very limited. For instance, nothing would prevent States from agreeing on the destruction of a rare ecosystem if it is not already protected under international law. In conclusion, good faith can help to achieve the purposes of the Friendly Relations Declaration, but only if international law contains the necessary substantive rules to do so.

But even if good faith is only a vehicle for realising the purposes of legal systems, this does not necessarily mean that the principle is confined to a passive and interstitial function. Because of its high degree of abstraction, good faith allows interpreters to shape the teleology of international rules. That means that once good faith is understood in novel, potentially expanded, ways, the overall dynamic of international law would change, too. If – as we argue – good faith is becoming a guarantor of trust for international actors among themselves, and for individuals towards those international actors, this could contribute to giving human beings the place they deserve in the international legal system.

Writing in the era of the Friendly Relations Declaration, Jörg Paul Müller posited legitimate expectations squarely as the centrepiece of the international legal order. That understanding of the legal order is, of course, irreconcilable with voluntarism – that is, the idea that international law exists as a legitimate framework because this is the sovereign states' 'will'.[242] Müller deemed voluntarism to be obsolete anyway.[243] Instead, his vision grounds international law on the *effects* of one State's behaviour on other participants in the legal order and on consideration (*Rücksichtnahme*). This means that the interests of, for instance, treaty partners (other States and international organisations) and the common (public) interest needs to be accommodated when taking action on the international plane.[244] The binding nature of international legal acts (both treaties and unilateral declarations) thus flows from the 'objective' legal order rather than from the 'subjective' will of international legal persons. Thus, trust is arguably the foundation of international law in its entirety.[245] Trust and consideration acquire an ever-increasing importance in a constellation of interdependence.[246] Ultimately, the effectiveness and legitimacy of a legal order does not lie in its terms and sanctions but in the willingness of its members and participants to form part of a community. This is an attitude or mindset which is ultimately 'unsecured or unguarded', as Müller puts it.[247] If this attitude is lacking, then a vital basis of any legal order (including the international legal order) breaks away – even if its formal legality is maintained (but rather becomes an empty shell then). Put differently, the existential foundations of international law lie beyond its own reach. To paraphrase the German constitutional scholar Ernst-Wolfgang Böckenförde, international law feeds on preconditions which it cannot guarantee itself.[248] It is therefore always precarious. Good faith marks exactly this point: a legal order can never be safeguarded or preserved entirely with juridic means, through purely legal instruments and procedures. Good faith – although a legal concept – at the same time transcends the sphere of the law by appealing to the actors' social, political, and moral

242 See above text with nn 9 and 10 and with n 66.
243 Müller (n 3) 260.
244 ibid 255.
245 ibid 260.
246 ibid 264.
247 ibid 265.
248 See for the State Ernst-Wolfgang Böckenförde, 'Die Entstehung des Staates als Vorgang der Säkularisation' in *Säkularisation und Utopie: Erbacher Studien, Ernst Forsthoff zum 65. Geburtstag* (Kohlhammer, 1967) 75, 93. English translation in Mirjam Künkler and Tine Stein (eds), *Religion, Law, and Democracy: Selected Writings of Ernst-Wolfgang Böckenförde* (Oxford University Press, 2020).

responsibility. Müller, writing in 1970, recalled that the international legal order will never be secured by legal norms but will always rely on the international actors' constantly renewed willingness to co-operate and compromise. Otherwise, international law would fall into a 'most serious existential crisis'.[249] These insights on the role of good faith for international law could not be more relevant nowadays.

[249] Müller (n 3) 265.

PART II

Fundamental Principles of International Law beyond the Friendly Relations Declaration

10

Human Rights Protection as a Principle

Eibe Riedel

I THE ABSENCE OF A HUMAN RIGHTS PRINCIPLE IN THE FRIENDLY RELATIONS DECLARATION

The Friendly Relations Declaration of 1970 marks a most significant step in the development of international relations and international law, and it seeks to contribute to the progressive development and codification of fundamental principles in the sense of Article 13(1) UN Charter. The fact of its being adopted by consensus stressed its importance in the relations amongst Member States of the United Nations. The Declaration addresses seven fundamental principles that other participants in this volume have analysed and evaluated. It picks up principles derived from the text of the UN Charter itself, namely the prohibition of the threat or use of force against the territorial integrity or political independence of any State,[1] the principle of peaceful settlement of disputes,[2] the duty not to intervene in matters essentially within the domestic jurisdiction of any State,[3] the duty of States to co-operate,[4] the principle of equal rights and self-determination of peoples,[5] the principle of sovereign equality of States[6] and the principle that States shall fulfil the obligations assumed by them in good faith.[7] All these principles spell out in detail obligations derived from the UN Charter itself, yet surprisingly, no mention is made of human rights as a self-standing principle.

However, the Friendly Relations Declaration is not devoid of human rights references altogether. Thus, early on in the preamble of the Declaration, human rights figure prominently:

> Bearing in mind the importance of maintaining and strengthening international peace founded upon freedom, equality, justice and *respect for fundamental human rights* and of developing friendly relations among nations irrespective of their political, economic and social systems or the level of their development. [Emphasis added]

And in the fourth principle of the Declaration – the duty to co-operate with one another in accordance with the Charter – it is mentioned that States 'shall co-operate in the promotion of universal respect for, and observance of, human rights and fundamental freedoms for all, and in

[1] See the chapter by O Corten in this volume.
[2] See the chapter by S Hamamoto in this volume.
[3] See the chapter by D Tladi in this volume.
[4] See the chapter by L Boisson de Chazournes and J Rudall in this volume.
[5] See the chapter by MG Kohen in this volume.
[6] See the chapter by M Koskenniemi and V Kari in this volume.
[7] See the chapter by G Futhazar and A Peters in this volume.

the elimination of all forms of racial discrimination and all forms of religious intolerance'. Also, in the fifth principle of the Declaration – the principle of equal rights and self-determination of peoples – fundamental human rights are spelt out as a subcategory of that principle, with the focus on combating 'subjection of peoples to alien subjugation, domination and exploitation' representing a denial of fundamental human rights contrary to the Charter. Moreover, right at the end of the Friendly Relations Declaration it is pointed out that the principles of the Declaration embody principles of the UN Charter and constitute basic principles of international law.

Taken together, the Friendly Relations Declaration refers to human rights only *en passant*. The express mention in the preamble, important as it is to set the contextual background of the Declaration, from a strictly legal point of view does not amount to a binding obligation. The references to human rights in some principles serve to elucidate the scope and content of those specific principles and tend to lower the emphasis and strength of the human rights arguments, as compared with the more assertive human rights references flowing from the UN Charter itself.

Nowhere in the Declaration are human rights formulated as a principle in itself. But then, the text of the UN Charter also does not mention human rights as a 'principle', and instead sees them as one of the three main purposes and aims of the organisation.

II THE NOTION OF PRINCIPLES IN INTERNATIONAL LAW

Before addressing in more detail the role and function of human rights under the UN Charter, possibly as a 'principle' analogous to the principles of the Friendly Relations Declaration, a few words about the notion of principles in international law seem called for.

Legal doctrine usually distinguishes between rules and principles. *Rules* are concrete normative prescriptions which can be applied directly and immediately to particular problem situations, without further ado. Thus, the rule in German traffic law that overtaking can only take place on the left-hand side of the road, or on the right hand side in the United Kingdom, is so concrete and explicit that it needs no further analysis and evaluation, beyond measuring it against the facts of the case, unless exceptions are specifically spelled out in the legal norm provided. By contrast, *principles* embody abstract obligations, regularly at a fairly high level of abstraction, needing further concretisation to be applicable to a particular situation under review. Moreover, principles often have to compete against other principles, requiring a balancing exercise to determine which principle ultimately takes precedence. Principles can either formulate legally binding obligations or refer to moral or political norms without legally binding effect.[8] Principles as fully binding norms in international law (so-called 'formal sources') usually start out from Article 38(1)(c) of the Statute of the International Court of Justice (ICJ). There, principles are highlighted as those recognised by civilised nations at the domestic law level, alongside treaty provisions and rules of customary international law. Thus, if a treaty provision does not offer a specific answer to a legal question, either because it does not cover the conflict situation at all, or only in part, and no specific customary international law rule exists, then a general principle under Article 38(1)(c) of the ICJ Statute may offer a solution. Typically, the general principles consist of norms found at the national law level, capable of being applied at

[8] See R Alexy, *Theorie der Grundrechte* (1st edn, Nomos, 1985) 85 et seq; E Riedel, 'Rechtliche Optimierungsgebote oder Rahmensetzungen für das Verwaltungshandeln' (1999) 58 *Vereinigung der Deutschen Staatsrechtslehrer* 180–220, esp 183 et seq.

the international level as well, such as procedural rules of prescription, *pacta sunt servanda*, proportionality, reasonableness or principles of legal logic, such as that specific norms trump general norms, or later norms trump earlier ones about the same issues. Generally, these principles follow a 'bottom-up' approach, from specific national norms to generalised international norms, showing that they are capable of being applied at that level, too. There are, however, also general principles created at the international level in a 'top-down' fashion. Such principles of international law comprise, inter alia, the principle of consent, equality of States, or the prohibition of intervention. In fact, such 'top-down' principles are to be found in the UN Charter itself, as for example, outlined in its Article 2.

The UN Charter text does not, however, spell out clearly and consistently the notion of principles: in the preamble, it mentions them only in relation to the use of force, while highlighting there three fundamental 'aims' and 'purposes' of the UN – namely the maintenance of international peace and security, human rights and the promotion of social progress – as the founding pillars of the UN. In Article 1, which deals with UN purposes, the term 'principle' is only used in relation to equal rights and self-determination of peoples, but the respect for human rights and for fundamental freedoms for all is singled out as one of the three pillars or fundamental purposes of the UN, and thus given equal prominence with the other purposes. In Article 2, one finds the specific Charter principles which were taken up by the Friendly Relations Declaration. One remarkable difference in the structure of the principles as formulated in the Friendly Relations Declaration and in the UN Charter is the fact that Article 2 starts out by saying that the organisation and its members will act 'in pursuit of the Purposes stated in Article 1' in following the subsequent seven Charter principles, thus according human rights a much higher status vis-à-vis the other principles.

This raises the question of the relationship between the UN Charter as a fundamental treaty and the Friendly Relations Declaration as an instrument that takes up the Charter principles and adds detail to and expands upon the Article 2 UN Charter provisions. Most commentators will agree that the Charter provisions in this respect take precedence over the principles of the Friendly Relations Declaration, even though the formulations in the latter have gained legal force through subsequent State and UN practice.

As the UN Charter text itself does not speak of human rights as a principle, it remains to be assessed whether the human rights references in the preamble, Articles 1, 13(1)(b), 55(c), 56, 68 and 76(c) of the UN Charter, read together, may be regarded as a 'conglomeration principle', flowing from the fundamental three pillars of the United Nations. Such a conglomeration principle may be seen as a roof or umbrella principle, embracing a number of human rights norms of different legal quality and different levels of abstraction which, read together, make up one of the fundamental 'aims' and 'purposes' on which the UN is based. The conglomeration principle might also be termed 'foundational principle', as one of the main UN Charter aims and purposes. A foundational principle, however, focuses more on the role that it plays in underlining the notion of the United Nations as a community of States rather than merely as a co-existence of Member States[9]. The notion of a conglomeration principle, by contrast, specifically addresses the human rights protection purposes of the organisation, and could be utilised both under the notions of community of States and mere co-existence of States. The term conglomeration principle therefore is to be preferred in this context. As the topic of this chapter focuses on human rights as a principle rather than using the description of human rights as one

[9] On foundational principles in international law see the recent study by J Rauber, *Strukturwandel als Prinzipienwandel* (Springer, 2018).

of the three 'pillars' or 'aims' and 'purposes' on which the United Nations is based, the following sections will utilise the word 'principle' in that generic fashion.

III EVOLUTION AND LEGAL CHARACTER OF THE HUMAN RIGHTS 'PRINCIPLE' IN THE UN CHARTER

1 *Overview*

By giving human rights such prominence in the UN Charter it becomes clear that the human rights 'principle' from the very beginning of the UN organisation developed in a new and quite unprecedented fashion.[10] Two World Wars within twenty years, the failure of the Versailles peace arrangements, and the cruelties, brutality and inhumanity of modern warfare, sparked off by fascism and totalitarianism, plus the devastating economic and social crises like the hyper-inflation in Germany in 1923 and the Great Depression of the 1930s, had proved that the international system, based as it was on the sovereign State, had failed in maintaining peace and security at the international level.[11] So it did not come as a surprise that the world leaders united in the new United Nations decided to ground their future intergovernmental relations on new parameters, alongside the existing ones, and amongst the main novelties was the universal protection of a set of fundamental rights, particularly to protect the life and dignity of every individual, to be known as human rights.[12] But the dogma of national sovereignty and non-intervention still prevailed, as evidenced by the principles in Article 2 of the UN Charter, which focus on Member State rights. This dogma also served as a shield for preventing international concern with issues deemed to be internal matters, with Article 2(7) of the Charter explicitly prohibiting intervention 'in matters which are essentially within the domestic jurisdiction of any State'. Furthermore, while Chapters VI–VIII of the Charter specifically spelt out in some detail the organisation's scope of action in the maintenance of international peace and security, the second of the three main Charter purposes, human rights, only received mention in a few articles that mostly addressed institutional and procedural questions.[13]

It was not possible in 1945 to include a full chapter on human rights in the text of the Charter,[14] and it was decided to leave the task of elaborating a 'Universal Bill of Rights' to the newly created Commission on Human Rights. The Commission then elaborated a

[10] For the following, see E Riedel, 'Rethinking Human Rights – Real Reforms in Procedure and Substance' in J Delbrük et al (eds), *Aus Kiel in die Welt. Kiel's Contribution to International Law* (Duncker and Humblot, 2014) 421–45.

[11] ibid 421; E Riedel, G Giacca and C Golay (eds), *Economic, Social and Cultural Rights in International Law, Contemporary Issues and Challenges* (Oxford University Press, 2014) 4 et seq.

[12] E Riedel and J Arend, 'Article 55c' in B Simma et al (eds), *The Charter of the United Nations: A Commentary*, vol II (3rd edn, Oxford University Press, 2012) 1565–602; C Tomuschat, *Human Rights: Between Idealism and Realism* (2nd edn, Oxford University Press, 2009) 7; W Kälin and J Künzli, *The Law of International Human Rights Protection* (Oxford University Press, 2009) 3–26; T J Farer and F Gaer, 'The UN and Human Rights. At the End of the Beginning' in A Roberts and B Kingsbury (eds), *United Nations, Divided World, the UN's Roles in International Relations* (2nd edn, Oxford University Press, 1993) 240–44; MA Baderin and M Ssenyonjo, *International Human Rights Law: Six Decades after the UDHR and Beyond* (Ashgate, 2010) 3–27; H Hannum, 'United Nations and Human Rights Law' in C Krause and M Scheinin (eds), *Internationl Protection of Human Rights: A Textbook* (2nd edn, Abo, 2012) 61–78; P Alston and R Goodman, *International Human Rights* (Oxford University Press, 2013) 33 and 58.

[13] See Riedel and Arend (n 12); E Riedel and G Giacca, 'Article 68' in B Simma et al (eds), *The Charter of the United Nations: A Commentary*, vol II (3rd edn, Oxford University Press, 2012), Art 68.

[14] R Russell and JE Muther, *A History of the United Nations Charter* (Brookings Institution, 1958) 303; see also E Riedel, G Giacca and C Golay, 'The Development of Economic, Social and Cultural Rights in International Law' in E Riedel, G Giacca and C Golay (eds), *ESC Rights in International Law, Contemporary Issues and Challenges* (Oxford University Press, 2014) 3–48.

comprehensive human rights catalogue, based on the results of a United Nations Educational, Scientific and Cultural Organization (UNESCO) symposium in 1947,[15] which led to the adoption of the Universal Declaration of Human Rights by the General Assembly in 1948.[16] It stressed the fact that human rights apply in all legal systems and cultural contexts.[17] The Universal Declaration embraced both civil and political rights, as well as economic, social and cultural rights in one single document, and in remarkably concise language. Apart from rights of the first generation – better termed dimension[18] – understood as freedom rights or negative rights, it also included rights of the second dimension which referred to minimum claim rights affecting working life, health protection, social security, education systems and institutional cultural guarantees, without which an adequate standard of living, ultimately flowing from human dignity as the fundamental basis of all human rights, could not be secured. It refers to the guarantee of a survival kit that is required to ensure a life in dignity, a minimum existence level as a precondition for living. Without such a protection standard, most required for the support of the neediest, in particular the marginalised and disadvantaged individuals and groups of individuals, human rights protection would not be met.[19] Freedom of speech alone may matter little to a starving person. The preamble of the UN Charter had made this abundantly clear when stating the three main purposes and functions of the organisation, namely the maintenance of international peace and security, guaranteeing the rule of law (embracing the protection of human rights and the dignity and worth of the human person)[20] and furthering social progress.[21]

The Universal Declaration therefore proclaims a comprehensive human rights catalogue, joining economic, social and cultural rights with civil, political, liberal, equality and participation rights on an equal basis as a 'common standard of achievement for all peoples and all nations'. The approach mirrored the famous Four Freedoms speech of F. D. Roosevelt of 1941, highlighting freedom of speech and opinion, religious freedom, freedom from want and need, as well as freedom from fear.

2 *The Universal Declaration of Human Rights (1948)*

In its thirty articles, the Declaration contains some general provisions (Articles 1 and 2), then a catalogue of freedom rights (Articles 3–20) and political rights (Article 21), followed by equality rights in the sphere of economic, social and cultural activity (Articles 22–28). In Article 17 a guarantee of the right to property was also formulated. Article 29(2) then addresses legitimate limitations enacted by statute. Also, rights of others must be respected and – in fairly vague formulation – 'meeting the just requirements of morality, public order and the general welfare in a democratic society'. Article 30 then concludes by stating clearly that 'nothing in this Universal Declaration may be interpreted as implying for any State, group or person any right to engage in any activity or to perform any act aimed at the destruction of any of the rights and freedoms set forth herein'. Possibilities of limitation of rights thus are limited themselves. The

[15] UNESCO Symposium, Human Rights, Comments and Interpretations with introduction by J Maritain, Paris 1948.

[16] UNGA Res 217 A III (10 December 1948).

[17] See Riedel (n 10) 422.

[18] E Riedel, 'Menschenrechte der dritten Dimension' [Human Rights of the Third Dimension] [1989] *Europäische Grundrechte Zeitschrift* 9–21, on replacing 'generations' by 'dimensions', as human rights do not die away.

[19] On this see generally E Riedel, 'Monitoring the 1966 ICESCR' in G Politakis (ed), *Protecting Labour Rights as Human Rights* (International Labour Office, 2007) 3–13.

[20] Preamble UN Charter, second pillar, para 2.

[21] ibid, third pillar, para 4.

Universal Declaration was adopted by forty-eight States participating in the process, with none against, and only eight States abstaining,[22] but failed to be accepted as a fully binding treaty. Instead, it recognised the human rights claims as political and moral precepts, on the understanding that a universal treaty would subsequently spell out in detail the norms formulated in the Declaration, but then in legally binding form.

3 *The UN Covenants 1966/76*

The Human Rights Commission was then empowered to elaborate such a human rights treaty.[23] By 1952, though, it became evident that, due to the growing ideological conflicts in the wake of the Korean crisis and the ensuing deepening of the Cold War, adopting a single unified treaty which would comprise all the human rights of the Universal Declaration would not be possible. The Commission therefore split up these rights into two sets and drafted separate treaties. Negotiations over these two drafts lasted until 1966.[24] Both treaties were adopted unanimously and entered into force in 1976.

The two Human Rights Covenants showed marked differences of implementation:[25] while the International Covenant on Civil and Political Rights (ICCPR) foresaw three monitoring devices at the global level, namely State reporting at regular intervals, individual communications spelt out in Optional Protocol 1, and a State complaint procedure, the International Covenant on Economic, Social and Cultural Rights (ICESCR) merely foresaw a State reporting obligation. Furthermore, the ICESCR did not even establish a separate supervisory committee in the treaty text but left that to be determined by the Economic and Social Council (ECOSOC). The Committee on Economic, Social and Cultural Rights (CESCR) was only set up by ECOSOC resolution in 1985 and took up its work in 1987.[26] Unlike under the ICCPR, the CESCR could theoretically be abolished by simple resolution of ECOSOC. But in the practice of the treaty bodies under both Covenants, these formal distinctions have not played a significant role.[27] In fact, both committees since then have worked along the same lines procedurally. Moreover, the adoption of an Optional Protocol to the ICESCR, entered into force in 2014,[28] which also contained the institution of a State complaint mechanism and an enquiry procedure like under the ICCPR,[29] consolidating the parallelism of both Covenant procedures, as foreseen by the Universal Declaration.

Substantively, both Covenants contained the full list of rights of the Universal Declaration, with the exception of the right to property under Article 17 of the latter, and each Covenant broadly follows the same pattern: like a chapeau, both Covenants contain an identical Part

22 Instead of many see J Rehman, *International Human Rights Law: A Practical Approach* (Longman, 2003) 53 et seq.
23 See Riedel and Giacca (n 13) 1753 et seq.
24 See UNGA Res A/RES/2200 XXI (16 December 1966).
25 For the following see Riedel (n 10) 423 et seq.
26 ECOSOC initially instituted a Sessional Working Group on the Implementation of the ICESCR by ECOSOC decision 1978/10 of 3 May 1978. The Sessional Working Group was later renamed CESCR by ECOSOC decision 1985/17 of 28 May 1987 and started work in 1987.
27 The most prominent difference lies in the election procedures: the HRCee members are elected by all the States party, the CESCR members by the ECOSOC.
28 For the *travaux préparatoires* see C Mahon, 'Progress at the Front. The Draft Optional Protocol to the ICESCR' (2008) 8 *Human Rights Law Review* 617; E Riedel, 'New Bearings in Social Rights?' in U Fastenrath et al (eds), *From Bilateralism to Community Interest, Essays in Honour of Judge Bruno Simma* (Oxford University Press, 2011) 574–89.
29 In the Committee practice of both Covenants, not a single instance of an inter-State procedure – unlike under the ECHR system – can be found, but it remains a possibility and may act as a warning to States that violate human rights to a larger degree.

I (common Article 1), dealing with the right to self-determination, and the free disposal of natural resources, picking up the principle of self-determination referred to in Article 1(2) UN Charter. In Part II overarching principles of non-discrimination and equality are to be found, applicable to all ensuing specific rights, and provisions on limitations as cross-cutting State obligations of a general nature. In Part III, the Covenant-specific rights are outlined. Part IV lays down certain institutional provisions and, finally, Part V (ICESCR) and Parts V and VI (ICCPR) contain ordinary final provisions. The Social Covenant contains four different groups of substantive rights in its Part III: work-related and social security rights (Articles 6–9); family protection, marriage rights, motherhood and protection of minors (Article 10); an adequate standard of living and health (Articles 11–12); the rights to education and culture, to one's cultural identity and to freely participate in cultural life, to enjoy the benefits of scientific progress, authors' rights and to conduct scientific research freely (Articles 13–15). The Civil Covenant in its Part III starts out with the right to life and personal inviolability (Articles 6–7), then addresses prohibition of torture and degrading treatment or punishment, slavery and forced labour, and personal security, habeas corpus or justice rights (Articles 8–11); and the full range of freedom rights, and embracing personal liberty, freedom of movement, thought, conscience, religion, peaceful assembly, family protection and privacy (Articles 12–24) and political participation rights (Article 25). While the Social Covenant dealt with issues of non-discrimination and equality in Part II, the Civil Covenant only dealt with equality issues in Part II, leaving the broader question of non-discrimination as a stand-alone right to Article 26 in Part III. This looks unsystematic, but the subsequent treaty practice shows that both Covenant Committees treat these issues in a similar fashion.[30] Part III of the Civil Covenant concludes with a provision on minority rights for ethnic, religious or linguistic minorities (Article 27), entitling members of such groups, jointly with other members of their minority, to enjoy their own cultural life, religion and language.

During the Cold War climate of the 1950s and 1960s, the view prevailed that economic, social and cultural rights (esc-rights) were fundamentally different from civil and political rights (cp-rights). Since the Vienna World Conference on Human Rights in 1993 that debate has subsided, if not died down.[31] Yet some States, foremost amongst them the United States of America, and many common law countries at the domestic law level, including the United Kingdom, continue to stress the differences of esc-rights and cp-rights. But while the United States, not having ratified the Social Covenant, can uphold its position of denying equal status to both sets of rights, the other States cannot do so: having ratified the Social Covenant, they are bound by the legal quality of the Covenant rights as fully binding norms that need to be implemented at the domestic law level, either as self-executing norms, or as non-self-executing treaty obligations still needing transformation into domestic law before becoming directly applicable.[32] Such interpretation clearly reflects the *travaux préparatoires* and the opinions voiced in the 1950s and 1960s, but the subsequent Social Covenant State practice reveals a different picture: the conclusions of the sceptics of esc-rights have been contested vigorously in the literature,[33] and since the demise of the Soviet Union in 1990 also by the CESCR itself.

[30] See E Riedel, 'Reflections on the UN Human Rights at Fifty' (2016) 54 *Archiv des Völkerrechts* 132–52, 135 et seq.

[31] E Riedel, 'Core Obligations in Social Rights and Human Dignity' in ME Geis (ed), *Festschrift für Friedhelm Hufen* (C H Beck, 2014) 79–91.

[32] Riedel (n 10) 423 et seq.

[33] See also Vienna World Conference 1993, UN Doc A/CONF.157/23; also E Riedel, 'Global Human Rights Protection at the Crossroads: Strengthening or Reforming the System' in M Breuer et al (eds), *Der Staat im Recht, Festschrift für Eckart Klein* (Duncker & Humblot, 2013) 1289–306, 1291.

Basically, four arguments are raised for why esc-rights should not be treated the same way as cp-rights: it is alleged that esc-rights are not human rights at all, but merely reflect notions of charity which can be supplied, but do not have to be granted. They would reflect no more than policy options for administrative or legislative acts, and they would always remain subject to availability of resources. The counter-arguments start out from the notion of human dignity as the source of all human rights, as pin-pointed in the Vienna Declaration and Programme of Action of 1993.[34] Without the right to an adequate standard of living and equal access to health services, education facilities and available work, civil and political rights would also suffer, if not be rendered meaningless.

The second argument alleges that esc- and cp-rights vary fundamentally, because esc-rights require costly positive State action and allocation of resources that should rather be left to the discretion of the democratic process in parliaments. By contrast, cp-rights are assumed to be cost-free or cost-neutral. Furthermore, rights such as a right to work, would presuppose a planned socialist straightjacket, promising something that in times of crisis is unaffordable and unfulfillable. Esc-rights thus would cost a great deal more than cp-rights. However, that argument seems flawed: cp-rights are by no means cost-free, they also presuppose positive and sometimes very costly action. To secure the functioning of the rule of law, and to protect peaceful demonstrations as a freedom right, sometimes very substantial resources may have to be spent for putting police forces on the alert, and to guarantee the seemingly cost-free right to a fair hearing involves considerable costs for maintaining a properly functioning judicial and penitentiary system. No one ever contests that. Put more generally, all human rights involve costs, a price paid for having the rule of law and thus protection of human rights.

The third argument is that esc-rights are vague and lack specificity, while cp-rights are clear, following the tradition of fundamental rights at the domestic law level. The counter-position argues that all human rights are formulated in the abstract, needing concretisation through court decisions or other measures, just as happens at the constitutional law level, and applies to all human rights. Accordingly, abstract formulation is not a disadvantage, but rather opens the way for 'evolutive interpretation' by decision-makers, taking into account changing societal values.[35]

The fourth contention is that esc-rights are not legal rights at all, and are not capable of being assessed judicially, at least not at the universal level. The counter-view stresses that justiciability is a matter of policy, as a result of political choices made by States, not as a result of international law precepts. All in all, the position that cp- and esc-rights are fundamentally different is no longer held now, even by esc-rights sceptics.[36]

In the light of the interpretation disputes, a closer glance at the central provision of Article 2(1) ICESCR – which has no corresponding provision in the ICCPR – is needed. That article states that:

> (each) State to the present Covenant undertakes to take steps, individually or through international assistance and co-operation, especially economic and technical, to the maximum of its

[34] E Riedel, 'International Law Shaping Constitutional Law' in E Riedel (ed), *Constitutionalism – Old Concepts, New Worlds* (Berliner Wissenschafts-Verlag, 2005) 105–21.

[35] Riedel (n 31) 80.

[36] For a fuller discussion, see C Tomuschat, *Human Rights Between Idealism and Realism* (2nd edn, Oxford University Press, 2008) 29 et seq, arguing that the issue is not esc-rights as rights, but the form of rights in comparison, with reference to M Freeman, 'Human Rights: Asia and the West' in JTH Tang (ed), *Human Rights and International Relations in the Asia Pacific Region* (Pinter Publishers, 1995) 13, 14.

available resources, with a view to achieving progressively the full realization of the rights recognized in the present Covenant by all appropriate means, including particularly the adoption of legislative measures.

If one compares that provision with guarantees under the ICCPR, one notes that the Civil Covenant obligations regularly refer directly to individual rights, namely 'everyone has the right to ...', while the Social Covenant by contrast uses indirect language, such as 'the States parties recognize the right to ...' or 'undertake to ensure the right', or 'recognizing that ... the widest possible protection and assistance should be accorded to ...'. Such language entices one to accept the misleading conclusion that cp-rights are self-executing, directly applicable norms, while the esc-rights only formulate indirect non-self-executing obligations that require implementation steps at the national level, before individuals can rely on their Social Covenant rights. Since 1990, the Committee on esc-rights has rejected the view that esc-rights merely represent programmatic goals or promotional obligations, left to the discretion of Member States, whether they want to accept them or not. Since General Comment[37] No. 3 of 1990,[38] the CESCR has held that, under Article 2(1) ICESCR, States have to prove that they have actually taken steps in the direction of fulfilment of the rights under the Covenant. Developed States have to meet higher standards of rights realisation, as they already are at a higher level of rights realisation and have the resources to better fulfil the rights guaranteed. Developing States start from a much lower level of rights realisation. Yet those States at least have to show that they have done their utmost to fulfil the rights, to the best of their ability under prevailing difficult economic conditions. And then they are obliged under Article 2(1) to seek international co-operation and assistance. Sometimes, such States refuse to seek such assistance for misguided 'prestige' reasons, because they do not wish to show their inability to meet basic human rights, as promised by the Covenant. But then the CESCR will criticise them in the concluding observations to that State's report. The developed States, as a corollary, have the obligation to provide such co-operation and assistance, even if that obligation is not specified in any detail by way of concrete amounts. They usually do grant such assistance as development aid, but allegedly do so as a charitable, purely voluntary exercise, not as part of their international treaty obligation.[39] In its General Comment 3, the CESCR emphasised that 'to take steps by all appropriate means' involves progressive, long-term realisation of promised rights, without burdening States parties with immediate obligations of result. But the core areas of each Covenant right take immediate effect and must be safeguarded by all States, rich or poor, without delay. Importantly, the principle of non-discrimination in Article 2(2) ICESCR does not admit differentiations in performance, because every State is capable of implementing it immediately, as it is not dependent on resource allocation but on political choice. To do nothing or taking a different view would contradict the very *raison d'être* of the Social Covenant as a binding international law treaty which States, when adopting the text of both interrelated Covenants, would not have accepted.[40]

[37] On General Comments, see E Riedel, 'Allgemeine Bemerkungen zu Bestimmungen des Internationalen Paktes über Wirtschaftliche, Soziale und Kulturelle Rechte der Vereinten Nationen' [General Comments to provisions about esc-rights of the UN] in *Deutsches Institut für Menschenrechte, Die 'General Comments' zu den VN-Menschenrechtsverträgen* (Nomos, 2005) 160–71, 164–66.

[38] UN Doc E/1991/23 (13 December 1990).

[39] See ibid, paras 13 and 14.

[40] See Riedel (n 30) 138.

4 *The Sources of Human Rights (HR) in International Law*

Against this background, the legal character of the human rights 'principle' needs clearer analysis. To start with, the legal authority of the human rights principle is based on the traditional sources triad developed in international law, namely treaties, customary international law and general principles of law, as declared in Article 38(1) of the ICJ Statute.

4.1 *Treaties*

The treaty avenue follows the approach as carefully outlined in the Vienna Convention on the Law of Treaties (VCLT),[41] which by now seems generally accepted. One difficulty does arise, however: most international law treaties, whether bilateral or multilateral in nature, rely on reciprocity of rights and duties. Yet human rights treaties do not easily fit that classical construct, because the traditional treaties heavily rely on the idea of horizontal inter-State relations. By contrast, human rights treaties primarily affect the vertical relationship between a State and its own population. But that difference is accepted because the States as such also have obligations vis-à-vis each other, particularly when it comes to monitoring treaty interpretation. Human rights treaties usually also contain a provision about inter-State monitoring, as a mode of dispute settlement, but in the practice under the two Covenants not a single case of such a procedure can be found. Usually only State reporting, individual communication procedures ('complaints'), and occasionally on-site enquiry procedures are utilised.

The difficulties encountered when dealing with human rights treaties can be illustrated by looking at the reservations regime. When it comes to human rights treaties, Articles 19–23 VCLT do not properly fit: the distinction between invalid reservations going to the core, the object and purpose of the treaty, and those that merely address non-essential or ancillary matters, makes little sense in human rights treaties.[42] Every reservation to a human rights provision of a treaty invariably touches upon the core area of the treaty, and thus invalidates the reservation. This applies in particular to the two UN Covenants that do not contain express reservation clauses.[43] States frequently try to by-pass that difficulty with diplomatic action, by formulating interpretive declarations, postulating the subjective view of the State of how a particular norm of the treaty ought to be interpreted. But Article 2(1)(d) VCLT clearly puts a stop to that attempt; whether or not such a unilateral declaration will objectively amount to a valid reservation, is not dependent on the wording of the document. In case of dispute it would be up to a dispute settlement procedure, like the ICJ, to determine whether such declaration is merely a reservation in disguise or not.

The human rights treaties foresee political monitoring, and quasi-judicial monitoring in the case of individual 'complaints' or communication procedures, which represent quasi-judicial monitoring, based on a person's individual complaint of a human rights violation. But the outcome of such treaty body monitoring strictly speaking is not a judicial decision with immediate effect, but a suggestion or recommendation to the State party involved, to provide redress for a grievance. These quasi-judicial procedures, in fact, remain at the level of political

[41] E Riedel, 'Standards and Sources: Farewell to the Exclusivity of the Sources Triad in International Law?' (1991) 2 *European Journal of International Law* 58–84; see also E Riedel, *Theorie der Menschenrechtsstandards* (Duncker & Humblot, 1986) 260 et seq.

[42] On reservations to HR treaties see generally Kälin and Künzli (n 12) 125–28.

[43] For an in-depth discussion of the effects off reservations to HR treaties, see N Ando, 'Reservations to the ICCPR and the Human Rights Committee. Personal Experience of its former Member' in Breuer et al (eds) (n 33) 977–84, 981; see also Riedel (n 10) 428 et seq.

monitoring of State action. However, the practice of States under such monitoring has generally been to follow recommendations made, sometimes with the proviso that the State does not feel legally obliged to do so, but will apply the recommendation as a policy choice.

The major human rights treaties as such may be regarded as regime treaties or integral treaties, where the obligations are set in motion by ratification, and then take on their own life.[44] They may also be qualified as '*traités cadres*' as against '*traités lois*', supplying additional considerations in application. This newer approach has led to broader and dynamic interpretation of the human rights treaties, giving some space to 'evolutive interpretation' as against the normal word-by-word or static literal interpretation. Moreover, State practice in the last fifty years has broadened the application of the human rights treaties and increased the applicability and visibility of human rights in international relations generally and in shaping relations between States parties to the treaties.

A side-effect of the central role that human rights played in the UN activities, particularly since the adoption of the two UN Covenants in 1966, has been the ever-increasing number of human rights treaties with not infrequent overlapping provisions. The operation of those treaties consequently has become quite complicated and often unwieldy. Philip Alston early on commented that what we need is not new norms, but better implementation of the existing human rights treaties.[45] Yet this advice has not been followed. Nearly every few years, a new project for a new human rights treaty tends to be proposed, focusing on one of the rights mentioned in the Universal Declaration or one of the Covenants. The latest examples are access to water and sanitation, the rights of older persons and issues relating to business and human rights.[46]

4.2 *Customary International Law*

The question of how international human rights can be shaped by customary international law was much discussed in the 1960s and 1970s, but has become much less relevant in recent years, as the number of ratifications of human rights treaties has increased very substantially, particularly since the Vienna World Conference on Human Rights in 1993. Only some two dozen States, out of 193 Member States of the United Nations now, have not ratified one or both of the two Covenants.[47] In general, though, there is substantial evidence of State practice or *opinio juris* components of customary human rights rules, but fewer acceptances of fully binding customary law rules. Regarding resolutions and declarations when adopted unanimously or at least by large representative majorities, or even as 'instant customary law',[48] this has to be taken to be sufficient proof for the existence of a customary law rule. But this has often also met with opposition: even if an ambassador votes in favour of a resolution or declaration in the UN General Assembly that denotes organisation practice, not automatically State practice *strictu sensu*, namely acceptance in the inter-State sphere. The better view would appear to be that only

[44] See E Klein, *Statusverträge im Völkerrecht* (Springer, 1980) 234 et seq; R Wolfrum, *Internationalisierung staatsfreier Räume* (Springer, 1984) 688, with references.

[45] P Alston, 'Conjuring up New Human Rights: A Proposal for Quality Control' (1984) 78 *American Journal of International Law* 607–21.

[46] On this, see E Riedel, 'The Right to Health under the ICESCR Existing Scope, New Challenges, and How to Deal with It' in A von Arnauld, K von der Decken and M Susi (eds), *New Human Rights. Recognition, Novelty, Rhetoric* (Cambridge University Press, 2020); Riedel (n 10) 438–40.

[47] ICESCR: 169, OP ICESCR: 24; ICCPR: 172, OP I: 116, OP II: 86, status as of 6 March 2019.

[48] Riedel, *Theorie der Menschenrechtsstandards* (n 41); OY Asamoah, *The Legal Significance of the Declarations of the General Assembly of the United Nations* (Martinus Nijhoff, 1966); B Cheng, 'International Law in the United Nations' (1954) 8 *Yearbook of World Affairs* 170 et seq.

if a State in its international relations subsequently follows that resolution or declaration, can one speak of a customary human rights norm.

New customary rules may, however, be created when interpreting treaty rules. With the huge increase in human rights treaty norms, the development of customary law extensions has become quite a prominent feature of human rights sources. This often happens by strengthening the arguments with recourse to general principles of law.

In addition, a significant amount of customary human rights law has developed regarding the 'minimum standards of human rights protection' comprising, inter alia, acquired rights of aliens; protection against expropriation and nationalisation, which is only permissible under certain conditions; access to justice of aliens; habeas corpus rights, in particular legal hearing; and the protection of life, liberty, property and dignity of aliens. Although initially only guaranteed to foreigners legally residing in the host State, by now there seems to exist general acceptance that these minimum standards apply to all persons,[49] as most of them find their grounding in the Universal Declaration.

4.3 *General Principles of Law and of International Law*

In recent decades, following extensive debates in the literature, the treaty category has been supplemented by *jus cogens* and *erga omnes* obligations as peremptory norms under Articles 53 and 64 VCLT, and has also been introduced into the reasoning of textual interpretations in the human rights sphere, usually to strengthen the persuasiveness and interpretation of treaty or customary international law rules. As Bruno Simma and Philip Alston have convincingly argued,[50] some of the core obligations of rights under both Covenants gain added prominence and persuasion having been accepted widely by most States, such as the prohibition of aggression, genocide, slavery, racial discrimination, crimes against humanity, torture, freedom of religion, self-determination of peoples, to mention the most frequently cited examples. Ian Brownlie, however, had assessed succinctly that while there is general approval of a handful of such *jus cogens* norms, and of the category as such,[51] many newer candidates usually meet with fierce opposition from particular States, either generally, or as specific *jus cogens* norm proposals. The most notable opposition comes from States that have not ratified the Covenants. The prevailing view maintains that such peremptory norms by now can be regarded as part of customary international law, or as general principles of law which apply universally, even for States not party to the Covenants. These principles can be deduced from extensive State practice, such as the adoption of the Universal Declaration or parts of it in national constitutions, which many States have done on gaining independence in the post-colonial period.

Most of the accepted general principles of law affect procedural guarantees, such as estoppel, limitation clauses, proportionality or the standard of reasonableness, if not already accepted as part of customary international law. In recent times, however, general principles also tend to be applied to questions of substance, not just procedural guarantees. Examples of that can be 'PANTHER' issues, an acronym standing for the principles of participation, accountability, non-discrimination, transparency, human dignity, empowerment of discriminated persons, plus the

[49] See E Riedel, 'Universeller Menschenrechtsschutz, Vom Anspruch zur Durchsetzung' in G Baum, E Riedel and M Schaefer (eds), *Menschenrechtsschutz in der Praxis der Vereinten Nationen* (Nomos, 1998) 25–55, 28 et seq.

[50] B Simma and P Alston, 'The Sources of Human Rights Law: Custom, Jus Cogens, and General Principles' (1992) 12 *Australian Yearbook of International Law* 82 et seq. The authors generally take the view that in the human rights area, the arguments in favour of general principles of law instead of customary international law should prevail, not least because of easier proof of principles than State practice and *opinio juris*.

[51] I Brownlie, *Principles of Public International Law* (6th edn, Oxford University Press, 2003) 490.

rule of law and redress of grievances. All these newer principles do not necessarily start out from domestic law being applied in an international setting (bottom-up approach), but instead these general principles of international law start out at the international level, triggering implementation at the national level (top-down approach). Some such PANTHER principles can also be regarded as flowing directly from the UN Charter goals and principles, particularly in the human rights sphere. Read together with existing treaty obligations, such general principles of international law bolster up specific human rights norms, and concretise them.[52]

4.4 *Subsidiary Sources of International Law*

An increasing number of ICJ decisions have enhanced the human rights protection system. Cases most frequently cited in that connection are *Reparations for Injuries*, *Reservations to the Genocide Convention*, *Nottebohm*, *Barcelona Traction*, *LaGrand*, the *Wall* advisory opinion, and the *Chagos* advisory opinion, to name but a few.[53] While the main focus in all these cases is on State responsibility, they increasingly touch upon rights of individuals, coming close to recognition of individuals as subjects of international law in their own right. It marks a profound change of the nation State and of individuals inside those States. But many States still maintain a reserved position in that respect, insisting that they alone remain the key actors in the international arena. By redefining State sovereignty as a responsibility-bound empowerment to serve public interests,[54] and thus also interests of individuals, the role of the modern State is undergoing fundamental changes: its main function in international relations now is to act as trustee for the realisation of fundamental rights of its citizens, mirroring life, liberty and property in the Lockean sense, as the true justification of recognition in international relations.[55] The State thus is no longer an end in itself. Anne Peters goes one step further: according to her view, the individual is the primary legal personality in international law, capable of being a holder of rights and duties that traditionally only applied to States. This, of course, redefines and widens the notion of subjectivity in international law. Anne Peters illustrates this with examples from humanitarian law and assistance, international criminal law, international environmental law, international investment law, but also consular and diplomatic law, and international labour law and refugee law. If generally accepted, this will have a profound effect also on the realisation of human rights.[56] Needless to say, presently many States vigorously reject this approach, insisting on their *domaine réservé*, but at least there is a trend the other way.

[52] For a fuller discussion, see A Clapham, *Brierly's Law of Nations* (7th edn, Oxford University Press, 2012) 62 et seq.

[53] *Reparations for Injuries suffered in the Service of the UN*, ICJ Reports 1949, 174; *Reservations to the Convention on the Crime of Genocide*, ICJ Reports 1951, 15; *Nottebohm case (Liechtenstein v Guatemala)*, ICJ Reports 1955, 4; *Barcelona Traction, Light and Power Company Ltd (Belgium v Spain)*, ICJ Reports 1967, 9; *LaGrand (Germany v USA)*, ICJ Reports 2001, 466; *Legal Consequences of the Construction of a Wall in the Occupied Palestinian Territory*, Advisory Opinion, ICJ Reports 2004; *Legal Consequences of the Separation of the Chagos Archipelago from Mauritius in 1965*, ICJ Reports 2019, 25 February 2019, General List No 169.

[54] On public interests, see E Riedel, 'Wir, die Völker der Vereinten Nationen . . .' in S Hobe et al (eds), *Die Präambel der UN Charta im Lichte der aktuellen Völkerrechtsentwicklung* (Duncker & Humblot, 1997) 34–46, 44; see also J Delbrück, 'Die Adäquanz völkerrechtlicher Kriegsverhütungs- und Friedenssicherungsinstrumente im Lichte der Kriegsursachenforschung' in K Dicke et al (eds), *Die Konstitution des Friedens als Rechtsordnung* (Duncker & Humblot, 1996) 201 et seq.

[55] E Riedel, 'Die Eigentumsgarantie als Problem der allgemeinen Staatslehre und des Verfassungsrechts am Beispiel Großbritanniens' [The Guarantee of Property as a Problem of the Theory of the State and of Constitutional Law with Reference to the United Kingdom] in J Schwartländer and D Willoweit (eds), *Das Recht des Menschen auf Eigentum* (Engel Verlag, 1983) 129–150.

[56] See A Peters, *Jenseits der Menschenrechte. Die Rechtsstellung des Individuums im Völkerrecht* [Beyond Human Rights. The Legal Status of the Individual in International Law] Jus Internationale et Europaeum (Mohr Siebeck, 2014) 387–400.

4.5 *Standards*

In the practice of the CESCR under the Social Covenant, increasing use has been made of legal standards which *may* be applied, but do not *have* to be applied.[57] As Alfred Verdross and Bruno Simma have argued: 'Norm creation . . . is not limited to particular kinds of sources, but finds itself in a state of liquid aggregation',[58] whereby States, rather than purely relying on Article 38(1) of the ICJ Statute, also employ more direct means of norm creation, such as recognition, toleration, simple acceptance and the dispute of claims and situations by means of a 'process of continuous interaction, of continuous demand and response'.[59]

Most writers on international law and international relations will agree and concede that something new has emerged from within the United Nations, but dissent persists in evaluating these new phenomena.[60] While the discipline of international law concerns itself with the normative framework of the international community as a legal order, the discipline of international relations looks at the modes of action and the practice of actors in a political context. A juxtaposition of these two disciplines, irrespective of marked differences of approach, suffers from a fundamental flaw: norms do not merely belong to the realm of oughtness, but may also be analysed as facts. Legal positivists tried to reduce legal discourse to the pure discussion of relations between norms and to questions of legal validity, to a pure exercise in systematisation of ought-propositions by means of syllogistic analysis.[61] The traditional national approach to legal norms to this very day follows the positivistic legal pattern of subsumption of conditional programme, consequence and conclusion, supplemented by a sanction or at least the threat of sanctions for breach of those legal obligations. This pattern fits many developments in international law as well, particularly in the law of treaties, because there the analogy to national private law is obvious. By contrast, a wider conception of law will embrace relevant factual bases or norms as an empirical basis of a social and political nature, bringing into focus the reality of the international community. When one looks at the international legal process, one soon finds that the stage of final decisions binding on the disputing parties is only reached in relatively few instances. Usually the application of the law stops far short of that and remains at the stage of more or less divergent self-assessments of rights and duties under international law.[62] It is suggested here that some of the newer parameters of international relations can best be labelled as 'standards'. For there are many instances where States do not wish to bind themselves by treaty, for example because of internal legal reasons. Instead, other political modes of action are sought and applied.

When looking at standards, one realises that many different usages of that term are possible. In Anglo-American law and civil law jurisdictions, standards frequently are synonymous with legal rules. But of course, standards may also be used to highlight ethical, moral, religious or political norms outside the sphere of legally binding norms. The reason for utilising standards in a wider context may originate in States which for one reason or another do not wish to bind themselves

[57] On the following see Riedel, 'Standards' (n 41) 58–84.

[58] A Verdross and B Simma, *Universelles Völkerrecht* (3rd edn, Duncker & Humblot, 1984), para 518 (translation), with further references.

[59] M McDougal, 'The Hydrogen Bomb Tests and the International Law of the Sea' (1955) 49 *American Journal of International Law* 356; see also R Falk, 'New Approaches to the Study of International Law' (1967) 61 *American Journal of International Law* 477 et seq; JP Müller, *Vertrauensschutz im Völkerrecht* (Carl Heymanns, 1971) 35 et seq.

[60] B Simma, 'Völkerrechtswissenschaft und Lehre von den internationalen Beziehungen. Erste Überlegungen zur Interdependenz zweier Disziplinen' (1972) 23 *Österreichische Zeitschrift für öffentliches Recht* 293 et seq.

[61] See H Kelsen, *Reine Rechtslehre* (2nd edn, Franz Deuticke, 1960) 78; same author, 'The Pure Theory of Law and Analytical Jurisprudence' (1941) 55 *Harvard Law Review* 44–70.

[62] Simma (n 60) 303.

by treaty, sometimes only to avoid the need to involve parliamentary ratification procedures, as had frequently been the case with the power to conduct foreign affairs in the United States. Instead, other forms of international political modes of action along the diplomacy channel are sought and applied.

After 1945 international law developed several categories of degrees of norm density. Basically, two broad categories can be made out: rules of 'hard' law and transpositive norm programmes of 'soft' law.[63] Apart from the treaty-based rules of hard law, a whole range of international norms have evolved which are derived from legally non-binding instruments that undoubtedly express normative claims, such as 'norms of imperfect obligation'. There the norm programme is clearly spelled out, but no mode of implementation or sanction in case of breach is to be found. An example is the international prescription of a right to work, as found in Articles 6 and 7 ICESCR. Such a right is even accepted by Western States that often feel unable to treat esc-rights the same way as cp-rights, owing to the fear that they might be unable to fulfil such a right in times of economic crisis, unless one opted for a socialist planned economy.[64] Such norms about a right to work may, however, be accepted as norms of imperfect obligation, as yardsticks or standards, meant to serve as incentives for better implementation steps at the national level.

Apart from this type of standard, there are those that formulate promotional obligations, such as enabling seminars, expert meetings, workshops or educational programmes, in the hope of attracting special attention to particular norm programmes, in order to arouse clearer awareness for esc-rights and to create stronger moral and political pressure at the national level to implement international parameters, in the hope of inducing national legislative or executive agencies to translate these standards into nationally binding rules.

Another type of standard, aiming at goals or targets that are considered to be desirable *de lege ferenda*, can be described as 'norms of aspiration', serving as landmarks for the direction of programmatic aims in longer-term projection. Such aspirational norms are frequently to be found in human rights discourse and politics.[65] The right to work formulated in Articles 6 and 7 ICESCR, based on the Universal Declaration is an example of this. Irrespective of the disputes surrounding esc-rights as such, that standard of aspiration has been underpinned and concretised in over 100 International Labour Organization (ILO) Conventions.[66] And these conventions openly utilise the 'standard-setting' procedures, whereby norm formulation at the universal level is joined with national modes of implementation, and parallel regular references and controls in ILO expert fora.[67] At least seventy ILO Conventions cover aspects of the right to work or rights *in* work or employment, even embracing the possibility of on-site inspection. In fact, many States parties to the ILO conventions have subsequently even altered their substantive national law, upon ratification of those treaties. Such standards may even function as reminders for the legislators when debating new bills, or when the essentials of such international human rights standards are in danger of being overlooked or neglected.

The transpositive norm programmes may also include standards that are completely non-legal, rooted in religious, natural law, anthropological, contractualist or consent-based concepts.

[63] This categorisation is reminiscent of John Austen's limiting definition of strict positivism, 'laws properly so-called' and 'laws improperly so-called'. See J Austin, *The Province of Jurisprudence Determined* (Weidenfeld and Nicolson, 1954), ch 1.

[64] The merits of that argument will not be pursued here, see generally Riedel, *Theorie der Menschenrechtsstandards* (n 41), chs 1 and 2.

[65] Riedel, 'Standards' (n 41) 68 et seq.

[66] ibid 70 et seq.

[67] Riedel, *Theorie der Menschenrechtsstandards* (n 41), ch 7.

Amongst those standards as 'norms of non-legal societal influence' may also be found usages and practices falling short of legal norms, but showing psychological and sociological preferences, or simply general usages or habits of obedience. Yet, non-legal as these standards may be, they often influence State behaviour, as if non-compliance with such usage or practice might entail sanctions.[68]

Such standards also may be used as interpretation aids when decision-makers or judges are faced with binding, but very abstract and vague norms. The reasoning for the decision to be taken in a concrete case can utilise the non-legal standard as outlined above, as prefabricated model reasons for the actual decision to be taken, usually to strengthen the interpretation task of the decision-maker. The decision will ultimately rest on the hard-law norm but may incorporate a standard of reasoning that strengthens the arguments advanced for the decision taken. Such standards and also combination standards or 'zebras' – bringing together binding norms and concrete standards (for example, codes of conduct and guidelines) – have influenced human rights interpretation under the ICESCR.[69] The standard may be a declaration of the General Assembly adopted with near-universal acceptance, like the Universal Declaration, or legally non-binding conference documents like the Vienna Declaration of Human Rights of 1993 which, read together with particular human rights treaty provisions, produce convincing reasoning for dynamic or evolutive treaty interpretation. The strictly speaking non-binding Anti-Apartheid Code of Conduct, that European Union ministers developed to ensure that European firms operating in South Africa at the time did not support the Apartheid regime through their practices, effectively led to a liberalisation of employment conditions of non-white people in those firms.[70] The reason why many of those firms ultimately complied with the legally non-binding code of conduct was that if they contravened this code, they subsequently would, for example, be excluded from discretionary export risk guarantees under German law. 'Zebras' play an increasing role to take on board newer developments in human rights situations, especially when many decades have passed since the adoption of the treaty provisions, and when the societal values and views have changed as, for example, in relation to the acceptance of single-sex partnerships or even marriages and adoption rights in those situations.

IV THE IMPLEMENTATION OF THE UN HUMAN RIGHTS 'PRINCIPLE'

1 *The Role of the Human Rights Council (HRC)*

Apart from the human rights treaty approach to achieve protection of rights at the international level, gradually the UN system has developed a monitoring system with a non-treaty approach, based entirely on the provisions of the UN Charter ('Charter-based system of monitoring'). Particularly at a time after 1976 when many States still had not ratified the major human rights treaties, the Commission on Human Rights started to deal with human rights petitions that were sent to the UN Secretary-General. With no existing monitoring procedure available, for a long

[68] ibid ch 7.
[69] Riedel, 'Standards' (n 41) 82.
[70] See Code of Conduct for European Community Companies with Subsidiaries, Branches or Representation in South Africa, 19 November 1985, in 24 ILM (1985) 1477. For other types of Codes of Conduct established by UN organs, see eg the Restrictive Business Practices Code (1980), the International Code of Marketing of Breast-milk Substitutes (Infant Formula Code) (1981), and see also the OECD Guidelines for Multinational Enterprises (1976), OECD Paris 2011, updates 2017 and 2018; and generally on codes of conduct see C Heidenreich, 'The OECD Guidelines for Multinational Enterprises' in M Windfuhr (ed), *Beyond the Nation State, Human Rights in times of Globalization* (Global Publications Foundation, 2005) 242–54.

time these were not attended to. Starting with the so-called 1253- and 1503-procedures, the Commission, and from 2006 onwards the Human Rights Council, dealt with a multitude of petitions alleging gross and massive human rights violations, displaying a reliably attested pattern of violation, and this led to recommendations by the Commission on a purely political level, with no legal sanctions attached. However, global public discussion and clear pronunciation of massive rights violations had quite some effect, as States generally do not like to be criticised for their human rights record, even if they continue to insist on their *domaine reservé* as regards those human rights issues.

The Human Rights Council has continued most of the procedures developed by the Commission on Human Rights, amongst them the new Universal Periodic Review (UPR), and the special procedures of independent and special rapporteurs on general and specific human rights questions.[71] On a positive note, the activities of the Council have led to increased problem awareness, inspired by much media attention devoted to the political and diplomatic activities of the intergovernmental Council – unlike with independent expert treaty bodies which unfortunately receive much less attention from the mass media, both internationally and nationally. It also led to voluntary political measures to improve national implementation. However, States under review of the Council remain free to accept, reject or reserve judgment on the very large number of recommendations made in the UPR, and very little concrete redress of grievances is achieved for the individuals affected. On the positive side, however, it can be mentioned that States often voluntarily accept some of the recommendations, but the possibility of full rejection of recommendations – usually on the most burning human rights grievances – is a real backward step at the universal implementation level. The possibility of reserving judgment is often no more than a diplomatic means to indicate that little or nothing is going to be done in the foreseeable future to remedy the human rights violations attested.[72] On the positive side, again, is the fact that all 193 Member States of the United Nations now have to appear before the Human Rights Council at four-year intervals, irrespective of whether or not they have ratified the human rights treaties. But to create a new human rights monitoring mechanism at considerable cost, giving States the power to reject out of hand recommendations made, seems another backward step in the quest for better human rights protection at the universal level, but clearly reflects the 'Realpolitik'-approach of maintaining full governmental control of the processes of human rights protection.[73] However, the human rights treaty bodies have emphasised the human rights positions in their recommendations to States parties to the treaties, and this has been given greater attention in the Council, particularly when States under Council review are parties to the Covenants and other human rights treaties. In that case, the rejection of Council recommendations would amount to treaty violations. Presently, a full review of the political human rights protection system under the Council, and especially its UPR procedure, is to be evaluated in 2020/2021.

[71] See A Clapham, 'United Nations Charter-Based Protection of HR' in C Krause and M Scheinin (eds), *International Protection of Human Rights* (2nd edn, Åbo Akademi University, 2012) 79–103, 88 et seq; see also RKH Smith, 'The UN Human Rights System' in MA Baderin and M Ssenyonjo (eds), *International Human Rights, Six Decades after the UDHR and Beyond* (Routledge, 2010) 215–34, 220–24; C Tomuschat, 'Universal Periodic Review: A New System of International Law with Special Ground Rules?' in U Fastenrath et al (eds), *From Bilateralism to Community Interest, Essays in Honour of Bruno Simma* (Oxford University Press, 2011) 574–89.

[72] For further details see Riedel (n 33) 1293; Riedel (n 30).

[73] Riedel (n 10) 436.

2 *The Interaction of Human Rights Policies, Strategies and Plans of Action with Human Rights Treaty Obligations*

At the same time, maybe unintentionally, the primarily political-diplomatic approach under the Human Rights Council's procedures has a potentially negative effect on the work of the treaty bodies: a notable number of treaty body recommendations in concluding observations tend to copy the policy orientation of the UPR, lessening the thrust of the legally fully binding treaty norms, replacing them by vague and general policy recommendations, which leave ample discretion to States as to what they intend to do regarding violations of the rights of their population. This tendency is increased by the fact that each treaty body has amongst its members a large number of former diplomats or sometimes even former members of government, who quite naturally keep close relations with their governments or permanent missions in Geneva, and quite often prefer the policy orientation rather than the violations approach of the treaty bodies. In recent years this has led to an increasing number of policy-oriented suggestions and recommendations rather than concentration on the binding specific treaty provisions. However, the conjunction of political and legal monitoring of human rights violations has its merits, too. Encouraging the development of progressive realisation of human rights by way of strategies, policies and plans of action as preparatory steps for fuller realisation of specific human rights is a value in itself, as long as that does not lead to diminishing the effects of the full and legally binding, directly applicable human rights treaty provisions.

On balance, even if misgivings about the working and working modalities of the Human Rights Council remain, quite a number of positive effects are emerging: the UPR now is on the permanent and visible political agenda worldwide, which is quite remarkable, even in States that have a poor record in human rights-related matters. Also, the visibility of the UPR is quite notable, exceeding that of the monitoring by the independent expert treaty bodies by far. The greatest positive point no doubt is the huge media attention and debates triggered off at the national political and legal levels, for example in parliaments, and in civil society awareness-raising activities, taken up by the media. The Human Rights Council thus clearly shows that human rights protection can be pursued both by the legally binding human rights treaty system avenue, as well as by means of political, non-legal policies, strategies or plans of action in a parallel, often interacting, non-contradictory fashion. In fact, taken together, norms laid down in human rights treaties and non-legal recommendations, resolutions and declarations of the organs of the United Nations can support each other at the political and also at the legal levels. Increasingly, declarations and recommendations developed in the Human Rights Council, in ECOSOC and in the General Assembly can play an important role in dynamically developing human rights treaty parameters by way of combination standards, zebras and other types of standards, as outlined above.

V THE INTERACTION OF THE HUMAN RIGHTS 'PRINCIPLE' AND THE FRD PRINCIPLES

1 *The Limited Space Devoted to Human Rights in the Friendly Relations Declaration*

As was shown at the outset, human rights did not play a prominent role in the formulation of the Friendly Relations Declaration. There are a couple of reasons why that happened. To start with, the focus of the Friendly Relations Declaration is on the UN Charter principles of Article 2, whereas human rights serving as Charter goals and one of the Charter purposes are not mentioned as principles in the UN Charter at all. The preambular paragraph in the Friendly Relations Declaration seems to address that, mentioning respect for fundamental human rights clearly, but the entire Declaration focuses on rights and duties of nations, meaning States as members of the UN rather than on individuals and groups inside those States. It still reflects the traditional view of States as the primary subjects of international law. The preamble also does not by itself create legal obligations of States, but merely recalls the context in which the Friendly Relations Declaration finds itself and shows the direction of future developments. Another reason for leaving out human rights from the Friendly Relations Declaration as an equal principle is that when the negotiations on the Declaration took place, the General Assembly was working in parallel on the elaboration of the two UN Human Rights Covenants, based on the Universal Declaration. Drafting of the Covenants was finished in 1966 in the middle of the negotiations of the Friendly Relations Declaration, and those treaties entered into force in 1976. Another reason is the fact that the Friendly Relations Declaration came at a time when many former colonies and dependent territories achieved independence and on joining the world organisation showed a keen interest to see to it that the progressive development of international law should no longer be shaped only by their former rulers and the founding members of the United Nations. Newly independent and development States also had a keen interest to demonstrate that the rules of international law in the future should be interpreted, shaped and applied in such a way that their own interests would be adequately represented, and particularly when the application of rules was at stake where these States had not been part of the law-creating processes. As Sir Ian Sinclair emphasised:

> the work of the Special Committee on Friendly Relations provided an ideal opportunity for the representatives of some newly independent States to flex their muscles in the international arena, and to pursue their quest for a 'new' international law which would be responsive to their needs and which would be freed from the constraints of what they perceived to be outmoded, Eurocentric and inevitably 'colonialist' concepts.[74]

The text of the Charter principles in Article 2 of the UN Charter could be used to strengthen their argument, stressing sovereignty, territorial integrity, non-intervention and equality for States large and small. Their views were strongly reflected in the Decolonization Declaration of 1960.[75] During the following decade the position of the newly independent States was vigorously propagated, yet agreement on the specific contents of the decolonisation principle was not achieved, not least because of the Cold War situation and the socialist States' attempts to draw the newly independent States to their ideological position of 'peaceful co-existence'.

2 *The Human Rights Reference in the Principle of Self-Determination in the Friendly Relations Declaration*

The newly independent States insisted on the right to self-determination (SD) serving as the legal ground for achieving independence from colonial power, and this was firmly established as a human rights position in the common Articles 1 of the two UN Human Rights Covenants of 1966/76.[76] In the Friendly Relations Declaration, self-determination was focused on

[74] I Sinclair, 'The Significance of the Friendly Relations Declaration' in V Lowe and C Warbrick (eds), *The United Nations and the Principles of International Law, Essays in Memory of Michael Akehurst* (Routledge, 1994) 1–32, 28.

[75] Declaration on the Granting of Independence to Colonial Countries and Peoples, UNGA Res 1514 (XV) (14 December 1960).

[76] UNGA Res 2200 A (XXI) (16 December 1966).

decolonisation situations and as a right of peoples to achieve their independence. However, while supporting that position, the Covenants' treaty bodies have widened its scope of application, to cover more than just decolonisation situations.

The Friendly Relations Declaration thus puts the position of the traditional nation State at the centre of its provisions. The newer developments of international law, particularly in the field of human rights and of enhancing the role of individuals and groups were not dealt with prominently and at any length in the Friendly Relations Declaration. The linkage to the text of Article 2 of the UN Charter with its focus on Member States rather than on individuals, groups, minorities and peoples were in the forefront of discussion during the negotiation phase of the Friendly Relations Declaration. Thus, in the double preamble to the Resolution and to the Declaration scant reference is made to human rights: in paragraph 3 of Resolution 2625 (XXV) at least the promotion of the rule of law among nations is mentioned which could be interpreted as embracing the protection of human rights as one of the major constituent elements of the rule of law. In the very long preamble to the Declaration, human rights are only referred to in a very general and oblique fashion in preambular paragraph 3, reiterating the vague formulations of the UN Charter in its preamble and in Articles 1(3), 13(1)(b), 55(c), 56(2) and 68 of the Charter, and utilising in part the formulation of Article 76(c) on trusteeship territories. In the operative paragraphs of the Friendly Relations Declaration, human rights only appear in paragraph (b) of the fourth principle on the duty to co-operate and in paragraph (b) of the fifth principle on equal rights and self-determination of peoples. The only addition to the short and vague human rights provisions in the Charter involves the focus on bringing colonialism to a speedy end, 'bearing in mind that the subjection of peoples to alien subjugation, domination and exploitation constitutes a violation of the principle [of self-determination], *as well as a denial of fundamental human rights*' (emphasis added). But then follows another sentence on the 'duty to promote through joint and separate action universal respect for and observance of human rights and fundamental freedoms in accordance with the Charter'. While the first mention fits the emphasis of self-determination of peoples as the dominant feature of the fifth principle of the Declaration, the second reference has a universal, unlimited scope and acknowledges that human rights protection applies to every State. It looks as though the full scope of human rights protection was sneaked into the text of the Friendly Relations Declaration in this manner, but from a systematic point of view that position cannot be upheld: the reference to human rights remains limited to the principle of self-determination, as far as it goes, and in relation to the principle of co-operation in ensuring 'international peace and security, international economic stability and progress', and the 'general welfare of nations', free from discrimination.[77] As Gaetano Arangio-Ruiz aptly has said, it is regrettable that the Friendly Relations Declaration merely reiterates the vague Charter provisions, and 'it seems odd to put so much emphasis on Statehood and so little emphasis on the full enjoyment of those benefits of representative government and civil, economic and social rights'.[78] As mentioned before, the UN Covenants of 1966 were not mentioned specifically in the Friendly Relations Declaration, perhaps also on the ground that those treaties were still at the drafting stage, being adopted in 1966, and not yet ratified by 1970.

In the literature on the topic, the right to self-determination of peoples is now almost unanimously regarded as binding international law, either as a treaty obligation under the UN

[77] Friendly Relations Declaration, fourth principle, para 1.

[78] G Arangio-Ruiz, *The UN Declaration on Friendly Relations and the System of the Sources of International Law* (Sijthoff & Noordhoff, 1979) 175.

Charter, or as a rule of customary international law, as a binding Charter principle or even as part of *jus cogens*, disputes only remaining as to the concrete contents of this and other *jus cogens* candidates.[79] In the 1960s, however, debates still raged as regards the precise content of the principle of self-determination, but the Decolonization Declaration (1960) clearly set the trend of development.[80] The language of that Declaration was most emphatic: 'Recognizing the passionate yearning for freedom in all dependent peoples'[81] and 'Recognizing that the peoples of the world ardently desire the end of colonialism in all its manifestations'. It culminated in the repetitive assertion that 'an end must be put to colonialism' and solemnly proclaimed 'the necessity of bringing to a speedy and unconditional end colonialism in all its forms and manifestations'.[82] The Decolonization Declaration in its operative paragraphs then starts out by saying that '(the) subjection of peoples to alien subjugation, domination and exploitation constitutes a denial of fundamental human rights, is contrary to the Charter... and an impediment to the promotion of world peace and cooperation'. The fifth principle of the Friendly Relations Declaration on equal rights and self-determination in its paragraph 2(b) picks up the points already raised in the Decolonization Declaration and reiterates the human rights basis for that principle, saying that 'subjection of peoples to alien subjugation, domination and exploitation constitutes a violation of the principle, as well as a denial of fundamental human rights'. But it then adds a new dimension by postulating every State's duty to promote through joint and separate action universal respect for and observance of human rights ... in accordance with the Charter'.[83] While the Decolonization Declaration merely stated the obligation of self-determination as flowing from the UN Charter, the Friendly Relations Declaration here goes one step further by declaring that three modalities of realising self-determination exist: (a) establishing an independent State (the external dimension of self-determination), (b) association or integration with another independent State, or (c) by achieving another status within an existing State, usually the internal dimension of self-determination, in the form of federalist or other sub-national structures, autonomy rules or other modes of achieving non-discriminatory treatment of individuals, groups of individuals, minorities or peoples.[84]

It was clear, though, that no consensus could be attained on the specific modalities of that principle, particularly as regards who could exercise SD, and on the questions of SD, the use of force and the issue of territorial integrity.[85] The net result, therefore, of dealing with HR issues in the fifth principle on SD of the Friendly Relations Declaration does not produce practically usable details on human rights, except in relation to the one-time issue of decolonisation.

3 *The Reference to Human Rights in the Principle of Co-Operation*

As can be seen in the chapter on the principle of co-operation[86] the reference to human rights in principle 4(2) again is relatively short but, in comparison with principle 5(2)(b) on self-

[79] I Brownlie, *Principles of Public International Law* (4th edn, Oxford University Press, 1990) 509 et seq, particularly 515: 'more authority exists for the category of ius cogens than exists for its particular content'. That still applies today.

[80] The ICJ in its Advisory Opinion (25 February 2019) on *Legal Consequences of the Separation of the Chagos Archipelago from Mauritius in 1965*, ICJ Reports 2019, General List No 169, strongly argues in favour of self-determination as part of customary international law. See esp paras 142, 145–50, 155, 174, 177 and 183.

[81] Decolonization Declaration, preambular paras 3 and 6.

[82] ibid, preambular, paras 9 and 12.

[83] ibid, fifth principle, para 2b and 3.

[84] ibid, fifth principle, para 4. See further the chapter by MG Kohen in this volume.

[85] See on this VS Mani, *Basic Principles of Modern International Law* (Lancers Books, 1994) 272–77.

[86] See Arangio-Ruiz (n 78) 142; and also the chapter by L Boisson de Chazournes and J Rudall in this volume.

determination, much broader: 'States shall co-operate in the promotion of universal respect for, and observance of, human rights and fundamental freedoms for all, and in the elimination of all forms of racial discrimination and all forms of religious intolerance.' The addition of the duty to eliminate racial discrimination and religious intolerance is an important concretisation of the principle of co-operation. The whole principle may be regarded as a roof or umbrella principle above all other principles of the Declaration, which can be deduced from the very title of the Declaration: Declaration on the Principles of International Law Concerning Friendly Relations *and Co-operation among States* (emphasis added). The four elements of that principle outlining the objectives of co-operation highlight, in turn, (a) the maintenance of peace and security; (b) human rights; (c) co-operation in the economic, social, cultural, technical and trade fields, based on sovereign equality and non-intervention; and (d) taking joint and separate action. By using the term 'shall' a clear obligation to co-operate factually and legally is stressed. But little is said about modalities of implementation of these four sub-categories.[87] To then state that States should co-operate in the economic, social and cultural fields, as well as in science and technology, plus seeking cultural and educational progress, really promises a lot, but without adding concrete consequences, actually achieves little. In fact, the principle as stated in 1970 remains a highly abstract general statement with which no one will disagree, but entails no concrete implementation steps. And yet, as discussed elsewhere in this volume,[88] the principle of co-operation subsequently developed in the practice of States and of international organisations in a quite unprecedented manner.

4 *Principles 4 and 5 of the Friendly Relations Declaration in Human Rights Practice*

When discussing co-operation and self-determination from the human rights perspective one has to remember that, after the First World War, international law underwent four distinct phases: first, minority rights protection under the League of Nations system, understood as a primarily territorial group protection scheme; second, the retraction of the autonomous minority rights protection system after the Second World War and integration of the group protection dimension within the human rights system under the UN Charter with an essentially personalistic, individualistic orientation; third, the conjunction of minority rights protection with self-determination of peoples since the Decolonization Declaration of 1960; and fourth, the rediscovery of minority rights protection and self-determination as an independent topic of international human rights protection since the middle of the 1970s.[89]

The UN Covenants spelt out clearly the principle of self-determination in common Article 1, as laid down in a separate part, as an overriding general principle that should always be borne in mind when discussing specific human rights in a later part of the Covenants. Thus, under the ICCPR and its First Optional Protocol (OP I) the issue of self-determination is briefly raised as a group right or collective right, but dissent remains about whether all civil and political rights have a collective dimension. The Human Rights Committee in its practice has generally insisted

[87] Arangio-Ruiz (n 78) 143.

[88] See the chapters by L Boisson de Chazournes and J Rudall; L-A Duvic-Paoli and JE Viñuales; and J Kurtz, JE Viñuales and M Waibel in this volume.

[89] See E Riedel, 'Gruppenrechte und kollektive Aspekte individueller Menschenrechte' [Group Rights and Collective Aspects of Individualistic Human Rights] in *Aktuelle Probleme des Menschenrechtsschutzes* [Current Problems of Human Rights Protection] Berichte der Deeutschen Gesellschaft für Völkerrecht, vol 33 (1994), 49–82, 50 et seq, with English summary, 80–81.

on the approach of rights of individuals and groups of individuals, rejecting a purely collective right,[90] mainly because of Article 27 ICCPR on minority rights, which is formulated differently from most other Civil Covenant rights.[91] Article 27 at least opens the door slightly by stating: 'In those States in which ethnic, religious or linguistic minorities exist, *persons belonging to such minorities* shall not be denied the right, *in community with the other members of their group . . .'* (emphasis added). In the over forty years of Committee practice, self-determination as a self-standing collective right has not played a major role, even though in the State reporting procedure under OP I questions in that regard are frequently raised and occasionally find their way into suggestions and recommendations of Concluding Observations. This also applies to the individual communications procedure under OP I. Under the ICESCR, similarly, no recommendations are made generally regarding alleged violations of Article 1 ICESCR about self-determination of peoples, unless *en passant* when dealing with specific allegations of violations of other Covenant rights in Part III of the Covenant. The Optional Protocol to the ICESCR has not altered that practice,[92] but since this instrument has only been in force since 2014, no cases on that issue have yet been examined. However, self-determination has played a more significant role as a self-standing collective right in a regional context, particularly under Article 20 of the African Charter on Human and Peoples' Rights of 1981, as applied by the African Commission and the African Court of Human and Peoples' Rights.[93]

Looking at the Committee practice under the ICCPR in over forty years, a number of concrete cases nevertheless have been discussed under its OP I. A few examples can illustrate this: thus, in the case of *Lovelace* v. *Canada*[94] the Canadian citizen and born Maliseet Indian Sandra Lovelace had lost her status as an Indian under Canadian law on Indians after leaving the Indian Reservation, marrying a non-Indian Canadian citizen, thereby losing the right of residence in the Reservation. A couple of years later, after her marriage failed and she was divorced, she wished to return to the Reservation with a child. The Maliseet tribe refused to accept her. The Committee decided that her rights under Article 27 ICCPR were violated. Canada consequently was under an obligation to change its Law on Indians.

In the case of *Kitok* v. *Sweden* (1985)[95] a member of the Sami indigenous group had alleged a breach of his rights as a member of that group. The Committee stressed, however, that Ivan Kitok as such was not entitled to base his communication solely on Article 1 ICCPR, since that article affected only a collective right, not covered by OP I, which is restricted to violation claims of individuals and groups of individuals. Kitok had lost his right to breed elks, because he had been occupied in another profession for three years, thus losing his membership of the Sami village community. However, he continually had kept his relations with the tribe, and still lived on Sami territory. The Committee did not find that the Swedish law that has taken away his elk-breeding rights had contravened Article 27 ICCPR because that law had the intention of protecting the lifestyle of the Sami people. Just like in the *Lovelace* case the communication,

[90] B Saul, D Kinley and J Mowbray, *The International Convention on Economic, Social and Cultural Rights: Commentary, Cases, and Materials* (Oxford University Press, 2014) 22 et seq.

[91] The ICCPR usually speaks of 'all persons', 'every citizen', 'everyone' or 'no-one'.

[92] See Riedel (n 28) 574–89.

[93] See eg *Kevin Mgwanga Gunme et al* v *Cameroon*, Communication 266/03 (2009); *African Commission on Human and Peoples' Rights* v *Republic of Kenya (Ogiek case)*, ACtHPR, App 006/2012, Judgment of 26 May 2017; *Sir Dawda K Jawera* v *The Gambia*, Communications No 147/95 and 149/96 (2000); *Democratic Republic of Congo* v *Burundi, Rwanda and Uganda*, Communication No 227/99 (2003); *Constitutional Rights Project* v *Nigeria*, Communication No 102/93 (1998).

[94] *Lovelace* v *Canada*, Communication No 24/1977, UN Doc A/36/ 40 (1981) 166.

[95] *Kitok* v *Sweden*, Communication No 197/1985, (1990) 11 *Human Rights Law Journal* 148.

however, did raise the question of which position ultimately would be preferred if a conflict between the rights of the group and the rights of an individual or as member of the group arose.

In the complaint of *Mikmaq Tribal Society* (1984)[96] only a violation of a right of the group as such was at issue, namely the direct application of Article 1 of the Covenants. The 'Grand Captain' of the Tribal Society claimed that he based his complaint purely on behalf of the tribe as such. He categorically rejected the applicability of Article 27 ICCPR on minority rights, as the tribal society in his view represented a people ('first nation') and not just a Canadian minority group. The question whether Article 1 of the Covenants covered the group rights dimension at all remained open, as the legal standing for the tribal leader could not be proved sufficiently. Thus the complaint failed on formal grounds.

In the case of *EP* v. *Colombia* (1988) four years later,[97] the Committee added that no individual or group of individuals could bring a case based on an *actio popularis*. They could only claim to be a victim under Article 1 OP I if they are actually affected personally.

In the case of *Lubikon Lake Band* (1990)[98] the leader of the Cree Indians in Alberta, Canada, Bernard Ominayak, alleged a breach based on Article 1 in conjunction with Article 27 ICCPR, because the traditional lifestyle of the Cree Indians would be destroyed if expropriations for the purpose of industrially exploiting oil and gas finds were allowed. The Committee refused to answer the question of whether the Lubikon Lake Indians represented a people in the sense of Article 1 ICCPR and decided that under the Optional Protocol to the ICCPR no claim could be maintained, based solely on the group as such. Only the individually based rights under Articles 6–27 ICCPR could be relied upon. The arguments put forward by the tribal chief were then, however, interpreted benevolently by the Committee, stating that ultimately the Cree Indians represented a group of individuals who based their individual claims on Article 27, and only pleaded a violation of their rights as individuals which they brought forward jointly as members of the group, as Article 27 requires. The result was that the Committee confirmed a violation of the rights of the tribe to conduct its lifestyle according to traditional modes of living and culture, according to the will of the group. Consequently, the tribe's land rights were restored and even damages were awarded.[99] Manfred Nowak and Christian Tomuschat pointed out that in this way, a group protection direction had gradually become visible in the interpretation of Article 27: the legal claim remains based on the rights of individuals but, as far as contents of the rights are affected, the group as such would be privileged.[100] That position has been confirmed in the complaint *Diergaard et al.* v. *Namibia*, where the Committee stated that the provisions of Article 1 may be relevant in the interpretation of other rights protected by the Covenant, in particular Articles 25, 26 and 27.[101] Ultimately, therefore, the Committee has gradually used Article 27 ICCPR in a broad manner, to cover group rights as such to a certain extent, albeit only in an indirect manner.

A similar approach has been developed by the CESCR. So far, no group-right complaint has been brought to the CESCR under its Optional Protocol based solely on common Article 1 of the Covenants. However, Article 1 has been discussed repeatedly in the State reporting

96 *The Mikmaq Tribal Society* v *Canada*, HRC Communication No 78/1980, 29 July 1984.
97 *EP* v *Colombia*, HRC Communication No 318/1988, 10 June 1988.
98 *Lubikon Lake Band* v *Canada*, Communication No 167/1984, (1990) 11 *Human Rights Law Journal* 305 et seq.
99 See Riedel (n 89) 66–68, 67.
100 M Nowak, *CCPR Commentary* (1st edn, Engel Verlag, 1989) 525 et seq.; same author, 'The Evolution of Minority Rights in International Law' in C Brölmann et al (eds), *Peoples and Minorities in International Law* (Kluwer, 1993) 103 et seq; see also C Tomuschat, 'Protection of Minorities under Article 27 of the ICCPR' in *Festschrift für Hermann Mosler* (Springer, 1983) 949 et seq.
101 *Diergaard et al* v *Namibia*, Communication No 760/1997, 25 July 2000, points 2.3–2.5, 10.3 and 10.8.

procedure, in conjunction with other Covenant provisions, particularly when indigenous and tribal communities are affected.[102] The CESCR has also quoted ILO Convention 169 on Indigenous Peoples and also the UN Declaration on the Rights of Indigenous Peoples (1992) in its General Comment No. 21,[103] intended to strengthen the argumentative force of the legally binding Article 15(1)(a) ICESCR, by mingling the hard-law norm with legally non-binding, but strongly persuasive, norms in the form of a combination standard, or zebra, as described above.[104] More could be said about other aspects of the right to self-determination, but a full chapter is devoted to it in this volume.[105]

In relation to the fourth principle of the Friendly Relations Declaration on co-operation the reference to human rights is brief and abstract, but emphasises its link to the elimination of all forms of racial discrimination and all forms of religious intolerance. The human rights dimension has subsequently been developed in other specialist human rights treaties[106] and in the work of human rights treaty bodies,[107] but also in a number of other UN documents which do not focus specifically on the human rights dimension.[108] The most detailed contribution to the issue of co-operation and human rights is to be found in the ICESCR, Part II, particularly Article 2(1) and 2(2), as was shown above.[109] The importance of international co-operation and of rendering assistance to countries in need has figured prominently in the State reporting procedure, and nowadays is raised with every State, whether developed or developing. If the State is unable to fulfil its treaty obligations, owing to lack of resources, then other States that find themselves in a better economic position are obliged to render assistance – not as a matter of charity, but as a clear Covenant obligation. The less-developed States must, however, show that they have done everything in their power to meet the most essential human needs as a human rights obligation, to the best of their ability.[110] Since not all issues are resource-dependent, such as non-discrimination matters, those States have to demonstrate what they are doing presently to abolish discriminatory practices, as the CESCR has pointed out in its General Comment No. 20 on Non-Discrimination[111] raised under Article 2(2) of the Covenant in its Concluding Observations

[102] See Saul, Kinley and Mowbray (n 90) 41, giving examples of the first decade of the twenty-first century: Concluding Observations on Cambodia, E/C.12/KHM/CO/1, 12 June 2009, paras 15 and 16; Colombia, E/C.12/COL/CO/5, 7 June 2010; Democratic Republic of Congo, E/C.12/COD/CO/4, 16 December 2009, paras 12 and 35; Ecuador, E/C.12/1/Add.100, 4 June 2004, paras 12 and 35; Philippines, E/C.12/PHIL/CO/4, 4 December 2008, paras 6 and 16; Russian Federation, E/C.12/1/Add.94, 12 December 2003, paras 11 and 39; Sweden, E/C.12/SWE/CO/5, 1 December 2008, para 15; Brazil, E/C.12/BRA/CO/2, 12 June 2009, para 9.

[103] CESCR, General Comment No 21 on the Right of Everyone to Take Part in Cultural Life (Art 15, para 1(a) of the Covenant), UN Doc E/2010/22–E/C.12/2009/3, annex VII, paras 7 and 9b.

[104] See above section III.4.5.

[105] See the chapter by MG Kohen in this volume.

[106] Such as the Convention on the Rights of the Child, UN Doc Res 44/25, 20 November 1989, particularly preamble, last paragraph and Art 4 regarding specifically economic, social and cultural rights of the child.

[107] Foremost amongst them the CESCR.

[108] See eg the Universal Declaration on the Eradication of Hunger and Malnutrition, UNGA Res 3180 (XXVIII) (17 December 1973), endorsed by UNGA Res 3348 (XXIX) (17 December 1974), which followed the Declaration on Social Progress and Development, UNGA Res 2542 (XXIV) (11 December 1969); see also the Declaration on the Establishment of a New International Economic Order, UN Doc A/RES/S-6/3201, 1 May 1974; and also Declaration on the Right to Development, UNGA Res 41/128 (4 December 1986), esp preambular, para 5 and Art 3(3).

[109] See section III.4.5.

[110] See also CESCR Statement No 16 on the obligation to take steps to the 'maximum of available resources' under an optional protocol to the Covenant, UN Doc E/2008/22–E/C.12/2007, annex VIII.

[111] General Comment No 20 (2009) on Non-Discrimination in Economic, Social and Cultural Rights (Art 2, para 2 of the Covenant), UN Doc E/2010/22–E/C.12/ 2009/3, annex VI.

on most States.[112] It has also been developed in the application of Article 11, paragraph 1 ICESCR on the right to food.[113] All this elaborates the duty of States to co-operate as spelt out in the fourth principle of the Friendly Relations Declaration.

VI CONCLUSION

The human rights dimensions delineated in principles 4 and 5 of the Friendly Relations Declaration have been elaborated in an unprecedented manner since 1970. After the UN Covenants entered into force in 1976, the newly established treaty bodies actively dealt with the issues raised in the Friendly Relations Declaration, but in their practice concentrated on many other human rights issues not mentioned in the text of the Friendly Relations Declaration. But the principle of co-operation, in particular, has played a key role in all matters of realising economic, social and cultural rights. After the Vienna World Conference on Human Rights in 1993 this tendency has increased tremendously.[114] States have been reminded frequently that their human rights obligations under the duty to co-operate ultimately rests on UN Charter purposes, aims and principles, as reflected in the Friendly Relations Declaration, as was shown above.

In general, the human rights approaches in international law became more focused on international co-operation during the 1990s and beyond, as illustrated by the Vienna Declaration and Programme of Action of 1993. In paragraph 4 of the preamble of that Declaration, it is stated that proper emphasis be placed 'on developing effective international co-operation for the realization of the purposes set out in article 55 (UN Charter), including universal respect for, and observance of, human rights and fundamental freedoms for all'. This is emphasised again in paragraph 16, where achieving substantial progress in human rights endeavours is called for, and demanding 'increased and sustained efforts of international co-operation and solidarity . . .'. This then is spelled out in several paragraphs of the Declaration,[115] and the Friendly Relations Declaration is specifically addressed in paragraph 2(3), and the purposes of fulfilling the right to development[116] and alleviating extreme poverty[117] are emphasised. The Declaration thus enhances the human rights links with the Friendly Relations Declaration, and the subsequent practice of the CESCR under Article 2(1) bears witness to that.

With the Charter-based approach of the Human Rights Council putting special emphasis on policies, programmes, strategies and plans of action, co-operation as under the Friendly Relations Declaration and the general provisions under the ICESCR, the human rights track has been broadened and provided with a new dynamism, linking the traditional treaty-based human rights approach with the more policy-oriented approach of intergovernmental activities. Dogmatically, this is justified by using human rights standards and combination standards when interpreting ICESCR and ICCPR provisions. Thus, recourse to the principles of the Friendly Relations Declaration can serve to bolster up and emphasise the legally binding provisions of the Covenants. The continuing disagreements about the binding character of components of

[112] At the regional level, this issue is spelled out in the African Charter on Human and Peoples' Rights (Banjul Charter), adopted at Nairobi on 26 June 1981.

[113] On this see also CESCR General Comment No 12 on the Right to Adequate Food (Art 11 of the Covenant), UN Doc E/C.12/ 1999/5, 12 May 1999.

[114] Vienna World Conference on Human Rights, Vienna Declaration and Programme of Action, adopted on 25 June 1993.

[115] ibid, paras 1(2), 2(3), 6, 9 and 10(4).

[116] ibid, paras 11 and 12.

[117] ibid, para 14.

Friendly Relations principles thereby lose much of their impact and persuasion. Thus, for example, the principle of co-operation can be utilised to provide additional reasons when interpreting specific human rights norms. The decision ultimately rests on the usually vague and general human rights norm, but the more progressive components of the standard, based on the Friendly Relations Declaration and other UN declarations, serve as human rights standards, or 'zebras', as shown above.[118]

In sum, it is submitted that the Friendly Relations Declaration's limited recourse to human rights and the subsequent practice of the UN organisation has not produced negative results: the interrelationship of Charter principles, purposes and aims, principles in the Friendly Relations Declaration and human rights standards in their inseparable connectivity and co-existence, can be appreciated as a strong pillar of the developing international law of co-operation and development.

118 See section III.4.5.

11

The Fundamental Principles of International Humanitarian Law

*Bing Bing Jia**

I INTRODUCTION

On the eve of the fiftieth anniversary of the 1970 Friendly Relations Declaration, it is time to reflect upon its enduring influence upon post-1970 international relations, which have to a considerable extent been built on its interpretation of the principles of the UN Charter. What is to be examined in this chapter is not only what fundamental principles of international humanitarian law the Friendly Relations Declaration has neglected, but also whether this instrument must, for sake of continuing vitality and authority, reflect these basic tenets of international humanitarian law.

In the discipline of pre-1970 international law, the category of fundamental principles had been less well studied.[1] There is, in addition, the jurisprudential tangle that the dividing line between these fundamental principles, 'general principles of law recognized by civilized countries' under Article 38(1)(c) of the International Court of Justice (ICJ) Statute, and custom may be less than clear-cut, except that principles, and fundamental principles *a fortiori* may have a degree of abstraction from actual practice constituting custom.[2] The advent of the Friendly Relations Declaration has largely settled all such arguments, by distilling seven principles that are as truly fundamental to the discipline as generally accepted by States.[3] The importance of this set of commands is beyond dispute, as other authors of this volume will eloquently demonstrate. Indeed, the Friendly Relations Declaration was negotiated and drafted by eminent lawyers who represented different national approaches to international law that were existing at a

* In the course of writing this chapter, the author has benefited from the research assistance provided by Ms Charlotte Verdun, a JD candidate at NYU School of Law.

[1] The emergence of newly independent countries since 1960 would seem to be the catalyst for the move for identifying and declaring fundamental principles of international law: M Sahovic, 'Influence des états nouveaux sur la conception du droit international. Inventaire des positions et des problèmes' (1966) 12 *Annuaire français de droit international* 30, 35–37.

[2] H Waldock, 'General Course on Public International Law'(1962–II) 106 *Recueil des Cours* 62–64; I Brownlie, *Principles of Public International Law* (7th edn, Oxford University Press, 2008) 19. On the third source of international law, see B Cheng, *General Principles of Law as applied by International Courts and Tribunals* (Cambridge University Press, 1993) 24.

[3] The lingering query may remain with the search for a nuanced view of the relations between customary rules of great importance and general principles of the discipline: P-M Dupuy, *Droit international public* (5th edn, Dalloz, 2000) ss 333–39. This would be reflected in the ICJ practice to be discussed below.

time when co-existence was necessary for East and West.[4] As a sign of change in the then international relations, self-determination movements were widely accepted as legitimate in spite of stern opposition by a few powerful countries.[5] It was a moment when the United Nations found its voice, amidst and above the intense confrontation between geopolitical blocs,[6] to express the wish of the international community for a stable world based on common (and yet minimum) values, and to reshape the post-Second World War world order according to the lofty ideals of the UN Charter.[7] The seven principles enshrined in the Friendly Relations Declaration embodied the faith of States in the pivotal role of international law in keeping the order of the world, and political forces were for once harnessed to adopt those juridical principles in the UN forum.[8] Whether the principles could be implemented effectively or otherwise,[9] that world order, subject to international law, was all that the normally bickering nation States could support in regulating and managing their fraught relations. There was no alternative normative system. The heptad of principles, however, raises one particular problem that gives rise to this chapter's musings.

That problem is whether the Friendly Relations Declaration principles would be adequate for ordering the world where there are clearly places and times that transcend peaceful co-existence. During those periods, the world exists according to particular rules of international law to which the principles in the Declaration do not relate. This problem is obviously acute with, for instance, the lack of provision in the Declaration for fundamental principles of international humanitarian law. These latter principles, it may be added, had already been established as customary law prior to the 1970s. This omission may be due to the fact that international humanitarian law at the time could perhaps be seen in a state of flux, and not ripe for codification in the Friendly Relations Declaration. For soon after the issuance of the Declaration, the international community began revising the so-called 'Geneva Law' embodied in the four conventions of 1949,[10] resulting in the adoption, in 1977, of two protocols additional to the Geneva Conventions (API and APII). It is known, however, that the 1977 protocols did not

4 See the chapter by S Moyn and U Özsu in this volume. Also see I Sinclair, 'The Significance of the Friendly Relations Declaration' in C Warbrick and V Lowe (eds), *The United Nations and the Principles of International Law: Essays in Memory of Michael Akehurst* (Routledge, 1994) 8, 10.

5 As attested by the Advisory Opinion (25 February 2019) of the ICJ in *Legal Consequences of the Separation of the Chagos Archipelago from Mauritius in 1965*, ICJ Reports 2019, General List No 169, paras 142, 151–61, www.icj-cij.org/files/case-related/169/169-20190225-01-00-EN.pdf. The Court stated, in para 161, that '[i]n the Court's view, the law on self-determination constitutes the applicable international law during the period under consideration, namely between 1965 and 1968'.

6 A possible explanation for this change seems to be that the aspirations of the newly independent States coincided with what the existing geopolitical blocs saw as their own interests, resulting in concerted efforts at laying out the fundamental principles of international law: PH Houben, 'Principles of International Law concerning Friendly Relations and Co-Operation among States' (1967) 61 *American Journal of International Law* 703–4. Also see E McWhinney, 'The New Countries and the New International Law: The United Nations' Special Conference on Friendly Relations and Co-Operation among States' (1966) 60 *American Journal of International Law* 1–33, 1–2 and 4 (the time was marked by a *détente* between the East and West).

7 For instance, the principle of equal rights and self-determination was already part of the UN Charter before the Friendly Relations Declaration was proclaimed: Advisory Opinion (n 5), para 148. Also see P-M Dupuy, 'L'Unité de l'ordre juridique international: cours général de droit international public' (2002) 297 *Recueil des Cours* 215–17, 222–24.

8 The principles were, however, elaborated in 'a series of political compromises': S Riesenfeld, book review of *Principles of International Law concerning Friendly Relations and Co-Operation* (ed. M Sahovic, 1973) (1973) 71 *American Political Science Review* 424.

9 The drafting of the Friendly Relations Declaration came to fruition in spite of the distrust of *a priori* principles by 'Western common lawyers': McWhinney (n 6) 30.

10 *Legality of the Use or Threat of Nuclear Weapons*, Advisory Opinion, ICJ Reports 1996, 226 [*Legality Opinion*], at para 75. As for the conventions, Convention (I) for the Amelioration of the Condition of the Wounded and Sick in Armed Forces in the Field (GCI); Convention (II) for the Amelioration of the Condition of Wounded, Sick and Shipwrecked

produce new principles of a fundamental nature, as the basic tenets of international humanitarian law at the time remained those derived from existing practice as codified in the Geneva Conventions of 1949.[11] It is also possible that as the seven principles, first set forth by the UN General Assembly after debates in 1962,[12] were those that concerned the foundation of the international legal order, which included the branches of international law such as the law of armed conflict, they were supposed to underpin all those branches; whereas general principles specific to each branch do not necessarily impact upon the legal order in similarly significant ways.

Be that as it may, fifty years on, can the Friendly Relations Declaration still be seen as the full embodiment of the fundamental principles that underpin the legal system for today's world? Three thoughts will be explored in making a case for inclusion of certain international humanitarian law principles in the framework of the Friendly Relations Declaration, or perhaps in one or more new declarations to complement the latter, in order to provide an updated bundle of principles for the contemporary and future world.[13]

First, the Friendly Relations Declaration was crafted to regulate inter-State relations in time of peace, and did not cover the time of armed conflict.[14] There is room for the view that Charter law differs from international humanitarian law.[15] Yet, the concurrence and succession of periods of armed conflict and peace – including the duration of a national liberation movement fighting for self-determination, is emblematic of the post-1945 times,[16] for which the principles of the Friendly Relations Declaration remain influential and yet clearly inadequate. Many armed conflicts of today's world last more than just a few days, and cannot be characterised as the exception to the norm of peaceful times. In fact, their existence is part of international life, affecting both neighbouring countries and distant continents for protracted periods.[17] Where life

Members of Armed Forces at Sea (GCII); Convention (III) relative to the Treatment of Prisoners of War (GCIII); and Convention (IV) relative to the Protection of Civilian Persons in Time of War (GCIV), were together adopted in Geneva on 12 August 1949, all entering in force in 1950. The four conventions are called 'Geneva Conventions' in this chapter. As of 2 April 2014, the four conventions became universally adopted by States, with each attracting 196 States parties: www.icrc.org/en/war-and-law/treaties-customary-law/geneva-conventions. In comparison, the 'Hague Law' comprises conventions adopted in 1899 and 1907: Y Dinstein, *The Conduct of Hostilities under the Law of International Armed Conflict* (3rd edn, Cambridge University Press, 2016) 21–24. It may be added that the tags of 'Geneva Law' and 'Hague Law' are only used in this chapter for sake of convenience.

[11] The 1977 protocols complement the 1949 Geneva Conventions by adding detailed and in some instances, new, rules to existing provisions of the conventions: W Solf, 'Development of the Protection of the Wounded, Sick and Shipwrecked under the Protocols Additional to the 1949 Geneva Conventions' in C Swinarski (ed), *Etudes et essais sur le droit international humanitaire et sur les principes de la Croix-Rouge en l'honneur de Jean Pictet* (Martinus Nijhoff, 1984) 237, 238–39.

[12] UNGA Res 1815 (XVII) (18 December 1962), operative para 1. cf 'Report of the 1966 Special Committee on Principles of International Law concerning Friendly Relations and Co-operation among States', A/6230, 27 June 1966, Rapporteur Mr W Riphagen, paras 3–23.

[13] At the beginning of the work of the Special Committee, established by UNGA Res 1966 (XVIII) in 1964 and reconstituted in 1966 by UNGA Res 2103 A (XX), to study the seven principles, it was unclear whether one declaration or a number of separate declarations would be the end product: R Rosenstock, 'The Declaration of Principles of International Law concerning Friendly Relations: A Survey' (1971) 65 *American Journal of International Law* 713, 715.

[14] Like the UN Charter, the fundamental purposes of the Friendly Relations Declaration also include that of maintenance of international peace and security: first preambular paragraph. The first principle of the Friendly Relations Declaration is aimed at preventing threat or use of force in violation of international law.

[15] *Legality Opinion* (n 10), paras 34 and 36 (the Court seemed to place these two bodies of law on an equal footing).

[16] The origin of the permanency of recurrent periods of great armed conflict in modern history could be traced to the nineteenth century: S Neff, *War and the Law of Nations: A General History* (Cambridge University Press, 2005) 177–91, 357–58. Self-determination as a mature concept has become prominent only in the UN era.

[17] The First Gulf War, between Iraq and Iran, lasted from 1980 to 1988, and the break-up of the former Yugoslavia resulted in a series of mixed-natured armed conflicts between 1992 and 1995 and the conflict over Kosovo in 1999. The

goes on in the form of an armed conflict, can fighters claim a status above international law by pleading the Friendly Relations Declaration, as long as they pursue, in the midst of armed violence, self-determination as an end? Or leaving aside any attempt at moral characterisation by reference to the doctrine of self-determination, should international humanitarian law continue its non-judgemental application in all situations of conflict regardless of their cause?

In retrospect, an account for any century of human history would be incomplete if no record were to be made of instances of armed conflict. The normal pattern of State behaviour is both peaceful and warring.[18] The complexity of forms of peaceful co-existence is matched by that of the innumerable types of conflict and civil strife that bookend or fragment peaceful times.[19] Insomuch as armed conflict subsists as a state of inter-State relations, international law is often the only guarantee that the occurrence of the worst atrocities does not become inevitable, for fear of, among other things, post-conflict trials. But the fundamental principles of international humanitarian law serve more than just as a warning. Together with rules, they impose constraints upon States at loggerheads to behave in a humane way after they resort to armed violence. If fighting cannot be eradicated, it can be subject to limitations of international law, which are clearly not exhausted by the Friendly Relations Declaration.

Second, there has emerged, after the Friendly Relations Declaration was proclaimed, a trend in practice to apply both international humanitarian law and international human rights law in a situation of armed conflict or occupation, and the Friendly Relations Declaration clearly endorses human rights law under the 'Principle of Equal Rights and Self-Determination of Peoples'.[20] The two branches of international law complement each other, strengthening the protection of individuals and property in all circumstances. This merger of two bodies of international law is required by a reality where there is no clear distinction between armed violence and instable peace, unless the international community is happy to live with a vacuum of law in respect of situations of constant transition from one state of affairs to another and vice versa. Could it be argued that, in those situations, the principle of equal rights and self-determination, as proclaimed by the Friendly Relations Declaration, is sufficient to cover them, thus obviating the need for addition of new principles? It will be shown later that the contrary is the better answer.

Third, even within the limited scope of the Friendly Relations Declaration, confined to the time of peace, there is the question as to the way and manner in UN Charter recognised situations in which force may be legally used. The Friendly Relations Declaration does not readily apply in this type of situation, and the door is opened for international humanitarian law to claim a residual role. Some thought may be given to the question of non-intervention during a non-international armed conflict. International humanitarian law certainly does not stop application at the border of a country embroiled in civil war, if the consequences spill over

consequences of both conflicts were felt far beyond the territories of the warring parties. The continuing, complicated situations in Iraq and Syria that have emerged since the early twenty-first century are also eloquent in illustrating the continuum between conflict and peace. cf V Bernard, 'Editorial: Conflict in Syria: Finding Hope amid the Ruins' (2017) 99 *International Review of the Red Cross* 865–73 (an overview of a field trip to Syria in 2018 with an account of live actions and problems on the ground, with the conflict claiming close to half a million deaths between 2011 and 2018).

[18] Neff (n 16) 177: he notes that, in the nineteenth century, war became an institution of international law and 'a thoroughly ordinary and expected feature of everyday international relations'.

[19] ICRC, *Commentary on the Additional Protocols of 1977 to the Geneva Conventions of 1949* (Martinus Nijhoff, 1987) 1325–26; L Moir, *The Law of Internal Armed Conflict* (Cambridge University Press, 2002), ch 1.

[20] 'Every State has the duty to promote through joint and separate action universal respect for an observance of human rights and fundamental freedoms in accordance with the Charter.'

into other countries.[21] Moreover, for a State party to the 1949 Geneva Conventions, which finds itself in such a situation, other parties to the treaties may invoke Article 3, common to the Conventions, in cases of violation by the country in question. Would that constitute a violation of the principle of non-intervention even if the other parties claim a breach of obligations under those treaties? This question depends on how internal affairs are to be understood. In the text of the Friendly Relations Declaration, there is nothing that prevents the preceding question from arising, and from becoming trenchant after the ICJ judgment in *Senegal* v. *Belgium* (2012).[22]

Hence the need for the category of fundamental principles of international humanitarian law to be included in a future declaration alongside the Friendly Relations Declaration. This chapter will examine the typology and meaning of those principles. Oddly enough, there is a degree of uncertainty surrounding both issues in practice and in literature, even though all writers on international humanitarian law are agreed that this body of law is underpinned by certain principles of customary nature. Substantive rules of international humanitarian law reflect, conceptually, one or several of the principles. Efforts or, as is the case sometimes, a lack of them, in categorising and defining these principles has, however, managed to confound their meanings and, accordingly, clarification would be quite welcome.

After setting forth the typology and connotation of those principles, it is intended to show that relations between States will be more fully addressed by adherence to international humanitarian law principles in time of armed conflict, as (1) the law of peace (and human rights law in particular) and international humanitarian law share space and time in application, with the latter being a clear instance of *lex specialis*; and (2) a time of armed conflict always morphs into a time of peace with accountability often high on the post-conflict agenda of political settlement, and accountability is invariably related to violations of international humanitarian law. The intention is to show that international humanitarian law is a veritable system of rules, self-contained in large measure, and yet closely meshed into human rights law to the extent that both complement each other in situations that may be neither peaceful nor warring.

II TYPOLOGY OF THE FUNDAMENTAL PRINCIPLES OF INTERNATIONAL HUMANITARIAN LAW

1 *The Notion of a Principle*

Legal principles, formulated in general terms, are of capital importance as they define the nature of a legal system composed of certain categories of rules of law. With them at hand, the international lawyer among others will not face a situation of *non liquet* because of the lack of relevant rules in known sources of the law.[23]

Normally, principles may be relied on to extrapolate a rule, but they themselves are not always capable of solving a dispute. As Bin Cheng cites in his treatise,

> A rule ... is essentially practical and, moreover, binding; there are rules of art as there are rules of government, while a principle expresses a general truth, which guides our action, serves as a

[21] *Prosecutor* v *Tadić*, Case No IT-94-1-AR72, Decision on the Defence Motion for Interlocutory Appeal on Jurisdiction, ICTY Appeals Chamber, 2 October 1995, paras 98 and 127.

[22] As the Court stated, 'The common interest in compliance with the relevant obligations under the Convention against Torture implies the entitlement of each State party to the Convention to make a claim concerning the cessation of an alleged breach by another State party': *Questions relating to the Obligation to Prosecute or Extradite (Belgium* v *Senegal)*, Judgment, ICJ Reports 2012, 422, para 69.

[23] Brownlie (n 2) 16.

theoretical basis for the various acts of our life, and the application of which to reality produces a given consequence.[24]

He continues that this part of international law does not consist in specific rules formulated for practical purposes, but in general propositions underlying rules of law which express the essential qualities of juridical truth itself, though short of law.[25] But, it may be cautioned, there is no denial that even principles may afford the reasons for decisions by courts and tribunals.[26]

The seven principles of the Friendly Relations Declaration partake of the features described above. One feature is especially noteworthy at this juncture, namely they do not necessarily serve as the thread that runs through each and every one of the various branches of international law, such as the law of the sea, statehood, international responsibility, treatment of aliens, dispute settlement, international organisations and the law of armed conflict. To place this in historical context, a comparison may be drawn between, for instance, these principles and those related to the new international economic order.[27] In a branch of international law, basic principles tend to be specific to the aims and goals of the branch, and of a correspondingly substantive nature. In the light of this point, the seven principles are more defined by the trait of fundamentality than by that of omnipresence within the system of international law. They are fundamental and probably *a priori* (when looked at in hindsight), in that the international community must have them in place *before* it can build a legal order in concrete conditions of the world, and that their significance lies in their singular function to guarantee the stability of such a legal order. In a way, the central aim and combined effect of all seven principles is to achieve peace in international relations.[28]

However, the function of those principles being one of foundation, there is no denial that they may dominate one branch of international law more than another, to the extent that rules comprising the former are valid because of their consistence with the dominating principles. They may thus serve as principles fundamental to the legal order of international law and/or to the branch of international law from whose cumulative practice they chiefly emerge. Their importance to other branches of international law may vary, but their existence is indispensable for the *whole* system of international law. For instance, while not limiting the relevance of sovereign equality to the law of international organisations and the making of multilateral treaties, that principle may not be directly related to the principle of non-use of force in violation of the UN Charter and associated rules and practices. But the principle of sovereign equality is fundamental to the system of international law[29] because it is part of the constitutional basis on which that system, with the United Nations sitting in a central position, has been developed. In other words, today's international society consists primarily of sovereign States. International organisations in the mould of the United Nations, paradigmatic of a society of sovereign States

[24] Cheng (n 2) 24, citing the award of the Italian–Venezuelan Mixed Claims Commission in the *Gentini* case of 1903.

[25] Identification of principles, to be successful, would require the establishment of criteria, which could be rather controversial: HLA Hart, *The Concept of Law* (3rd edn, Oxford University Press, 2012) 263–68.

[26] eg ibid 265. Also see FA Mann, 'Reflections on a Commercial Law of Nations' (1957) 33 *British Yearbook of International Law* 20, 36.

[27] Progressive Development of the Principles and Norms of International Law relating to the New International Economic Order, *Report of the Secretary-General, Addendum*, A/39/504/Add.1 (23 October 1984), presenting the analytical report produced by UNITAR (United Nations Institute for Training and Research), esp paras 4–5.

[28] The differentiation between the principles of the Friendly Relations Declaration, in terms of significance, is not unknown: P Cahier, 'Changements et continuité du droit international: cours général de droit international public' (1985) 195 *Recueil des Cours* 9, at p 31.

[29] The principle is paralleled by the new norm of 'international community': Dupuy (n 7) 248, 263–64.

organised into groups, account for a large proportion of international relations and events. The principle on which they are formed and operated is, accordingly, fundamental.

In comparison, the principle of equal rights and self-determination would be hard pressed to include international humanitarian law principles, without some mental gymnastics in order to get around the fact that the Friendly Relations Declaration, first above all, deals with non-use of force in international relations, and thus serves to *prevent* armed conflict.

2 *Identification of Fundamental Principles*

General principles under Article 38(1)(c) of the ICJ Statute are not necessarily identical to principles of international law, which are derived from a historical mass of practices and rules in existence, and have been so long and so generally accepted as to be no longer directly attached to a particular practice or rule.[30] The processes leading to the identification of these principles are perceptibly different.

The general principles under Article 38(1)(c) of the ICJ Statute are derived from practices of major legal systems of the world, and principles of international law are grounded in customary rules and practices.[31] The methodology for arriving at general principles of law is that of comparative study;[32] whereas, for the determination of the latter type of principles, an examination of State practice is essential.[33] In a way, finding the latter type of principles is not always useful a practical exercise, since practical issues can be dealt with by rules, derived from practice, of sufficient clarity. Where, however, rules of a similar nature and function are many and congested, knowing a principle simplifies them by pointing to a golden thread that sums them all up. A principle of international law is that thread that captures the gist of those rules.

If this is the way to identify a principle of international law, the way to identify a fundamental principle could well differ, in that this latter principle must be fundamental to the system of international law as a whole, beyond and above recognition that it is part of customary law, having been repeatedly given solemn expression in international instruments of generality. It becomes first of all a principle of customary law before assuming the elevated status of a fundamental principle of the international legal order. Its disappearance, *ex hypothesi*, will definitely render the order unstable and destined for extinction.

A fundamental principle, in other words, is existential in nature, much like the indispensability of the principle of non-use of force in international relations to the existence of the international community as well as the attendant legal order based in the UN Charter. Such principles, which include all the principles of the Friendly Relations Declaration, could be both abstract and concrete in content. They are abstract because of their distance from particular practice;[34] they are also concrete, in that they originate initially from customary law specific to an area of activity, a fact or a legal relation.

This is the standard that this chapter will apply in identifying fundamental principles of international humanitarian law.

[30] Each branch of international law or any international organisations may find it possible to gather its basic principles of operation in a single document; eg J Pictet, *The Fundamental Principles of the Red Cross: Commentary* (Henry Dunant Institute, 1979) (with regard to certain principles declared by the Twentieth International Red Cross Conference in 1965).

[31] cf H Thirlway, *The Sources of International Law* (Oxford University Press, 2014) 94–96.

[32] Mann (n 26) 36.

[33] F Seyersted, *United Nations Forces in the Law of Peace and War* (Sijthoff, 1966) 187.

[34] Extreme abstractness may sometimes be discerned in principles of this kind, depending on perspective: J Pictet, 'Les Principes du droit international humanitaire' (1966) 48(573) *Revue Internationale de la Croix-Rouge* 411, 419.

3 *Instances of the Fundamental Principles of International Humanitarian Law*

In *Legality of the Threat or Use of Nuclear Weapons* (*Legality Opinion*), the ICJ stated in its advisory opinion that:

> The cardinal principles contained in the texts constituting the fabric of humanitarian law are the following. The first is aimed at the protection of the civilian population and civilian objects and establishes the distinction between combatants and non-combatants; states must never make civilians the object of attack and must consequently never use weapons that are incapable of distinguishing between civilian and military targets. According to the second principle, it is prohibited to cause unnecessary suffering to combatants; it is accordingly prohibited to use weapons causing them such harm or uselessly aggravating their suffering. In application of that second principle, states do not have unlimited freedom of choice of means in the weapons they use.[35]

This statement of the ICJ does not elaborate on whether these, one of distinction and the other of humanity, are the only cardinal principles of international humanitarian law.

As will be shown below, there are other principles of similar stature that underpin this branch of international law. Are they cardinal or fundamental too? Without answering that question for now, it is proposed to collate what have been known as the fundamental principles of international humanitarian law. It is noteworthy that all of them may seem to have originated in the St Petersburg Declaration, of 29 November 1868.[36]

3.1 *Principle of Military Necessity*

This principle, not mentioned in the *Legality Opinion*, should perhaps be logically placed at the top of any list of fundamental principles of international humanitarian law. While not endorsing use of force, it permits a party engaged in an armed conflict to use a certain degree and kind of force, not otherwise prohibited by international humanitarian law, in order to achieve the legitimate purpose of the conflict, namely the complete or partial submission of the enemy at the earliest possible moment with the minimum expenditure of life and resources.[37] With that content,[38] it is a principle that seeks to excuse armed hostilities by tempering them through laying down certain restraining factors. It is said that international humanitarian law is based on the balance between military necessity and humanitarian considerations.[39]

At operational level, the principle is said to consist of four basic elements:[40] (i) the force used *can be* and is being controlled; (ii) since military necessity permits the use of force only if it is 'not otherwise prohibited by the law of armed conflict', necessity cannot excuse a departure from

[35] ICJ Reports 1996, 226, para 78.

[36] See St Petersburg Declaration, 29 November 1868: 'That the only legitimate object which States should endeavour to accomplish during war is to weaken the military forges of the enemy; that for this purpose it is sufficient to disable the greatest possible number of men; that this object would be exceeded by the employment of arms which uselessly aggravate the sufferings of disabled men, or render their death inevitable; that the employment of such arms would, therefore, be contrary to the laws of humanity.' The text may be found in D Schindler and J Toman (eds), *The Laws of Armed Conflicts: A Collection of Conventions, Resolutions and Other Documents* (4th rev and completed edn, Martinus Nijhoff, 2004). The texts of conventions and other official documents, with the exception of UNGA resolutions, can all be found in this valuable collection.

[37] cf St Petersburg Declaration, ibid: 'That the only legitimate object which States should endeavour to accomplish during war is to weaken the military forges of the enemy; that for this purpose it is sufficient to disable the greatest possible number of men ...'.

[38] It paraphrases what has been stated in the *Hostages Trial*: see below.

[39] Dinstein (n 10) 8–9. Also see I Detter, *The Law of War* (2nd edn, Cambridge University Press, 2000) 395–96.

[40] UK Ministry of Defence, *The Manual of the Law of Armed Conflict* (Oxford University Press, 2004) 22.

that law; (iii) the use of force in ways which are not otherwise prohibited is legitimate if it is necessary to achieve, as quickly as possible, the complete or partial submission of the enemy; (iv) conversely, the use of force which is not necessary is unlawful, since it involves wanton killing or destruction.

Since it appeared in Article 14 of the 1860 Lieber Code,[41] the principle has occupied a prominent place in practice. One may be struck by the existence of this principle in international humanitarian law which serves as an exception to the application of this body of law in certain situations.[42] For instance, Article 53 of the Fourth Geneva Convention states that 'any destruction by the occupying power of real or personal property belonging individually or collectively to private persons, or to the State, or to other public authorities, or to social or cooperative organizations, is prohibited, except where such destruction is rendered absolutely necessary by military operations'. In respect of objects indispensable to the survival of the civilian population, such as foodstuffs, crops, livestock etc., Article 54(5) API, provides that 'in recognition of the vital requirements of any Party to the conflict in the defence of its national territory against invasion, derogation from the prohibitions contained in paragraph 2 may be made by a Party to the conflict within such territory under its own control where required by imperative military necessity'.

In armed conflicts, the principle features prominently in cases of reprisals waged against civilians. In *US* v. *Wilhelm von List et al.*, also known as 'the Hostages Trial',[43] the US military tribunal stated:

> Military necessity permits a belligerent, subject to the laws of war, to apply any amount and kind of force to compel the complete submission of the enemy with the least possible expenditure of time, life and money. In general, it sanctions measures by an occupant necessary to protect the safety of his forces and to facilitate the success of his operation. It permits the destruction of life of armed enemies and other persons whose destruction is incidentally unavoidable by the armed conflicts of the war [this view seems to be an early version of the concept of collateral damage]; it allows the capturing of armed enemies and others of peculiar danger, but it does not permit the killing of innocent inhabitants for purposes of revenge or the satisfaction of a lust to kill. The destruction of property to be lawful must be imperatively demanded by the necessities of war. Destruction as an end in itself is a violation of international law . . . It is lawful to destroy railways, lines of communication, or any other property that might be utilized by the enemy. Private homes and churches even may be destroyed if necessary for military operations.[44]

The passage included three elements that would become standards for later expressions of this principle: law-restrained use of maximum force and means; its applicability in times of occupation; recognition of collateral damage to civilian and civilian properties (through the reference to 'other persons').

[41] *Instructions for the Government of Armies of the United States in the Field*, prepared by Francis Lieber, promulgated as General Orders No 100 by US President Lincoln, 24 April 1863. Art 14 states: 'Military necessity, as understood by modern civilized nations, consists in the necessity of those measures which are indispensable for securing the ends of the war, and which are lawful according to the modern law and usages of war.'

[42] But derogation from certain human rights is not unknown to human rights law: ICCPR, Art 4.

[43] The trial was conducted from July 1947 to February 1948. The accused were all former high-ranking German army officers and charged with responsibility for war crimes committed by troops under their command during the occupation of Greece, Yugoslavia, Albania and Norway, in the form of so-called 'reprisal killings' – purportedly committed in an attempt to maintain order in the occupied territories in the face of guerrilla warfare, as well as wanton destruction of property *not justified by military necessity*. See *Trials of War Criminals before the Nuremberg Military Tribunals under Control Council Law No 10* (TWC) (US Government Printing Office, 1949–53), vol XI.

[44] ibid 1253–54.

The difficulty in applying the preceding principle is illustrated in another case. In *US v. Wilhelm von Leeb et al.*, also known as the 'German High Command Trial', the tribunal stated as follows:

> The devastation prohibited by the Hague Rules and the usages of war is devastation not warranted by military necessity. This rule is clear enough but the factual determination as to what constitutes military necessity is difficult ... What constitutes devastation beyond military necessity in these situations requires detailed proof of an operational and tactical nature.[45]

However, necessity cannot justify actions prohibited by international humanitarian law. In *Prosecutor* v. *Galić*,[46] an International Criminal Tribunal for the Former Yugoslavia (ICTY) Trial Chamber states that 'This provision [Art. 51(2) of API] states in clear language that civilians and the civilian population as such should not be the object of attack. It does not mention any exceptions. In particular, it does not contemplate derogating from this rule by invoking military necessity.'[47] It further explains that:

> the principle of military necessity acknowledges the potential for unavoidable civilian death and injury ancillary to the conduct of legitimate military operations. However, this principle requires that destroying a particular military objective will provide some type of advantage in weakening the enemy military forces. Under no circumstance are civilians to be considered legitimate military targets. Consequently, attacking civilians or the civilian population as such cannot be justified by invoking military necessity.[48]

The difficulty in weighing military necessity and protection of innocent civilians was revealed in the *Kordić* Appeal Judgment,[49] which seemingly ran counter to the terms of Article 51(2) that provide that 'the civilian population as such, as well as individual civilians, shall not be the object of attack'. Indeed, the ICJ in the *Legality Opinion* stated that States must *never* make civilians the object of attack and must never use weapons that are incapable of distinguishing between civilian and military targets.[50]

In short, the applicability of the principle of military necessity is limited mainly to attacks on civilian objects, but not on individual civilians or civilian population taking no part in hostilities.

3.2 *Principle of Distinction*

This principle, mentioned by the ICJ in the *Legality Opinion* as one of the two cardinal principles of international humanitarian law, is sometimes referred to as the principle of discrimination. It requires that a clear distinction be drawn between armed forces and civilians, or between combatants and non-combatants, and between objects that might legitimately be attacked and those that are protected from all attacks.[51] The conventional origin of the principle could be traced to the St Petersburg Declaration, the preamble of which stated that 'the only legitimate object which States should endeavour to accomplish during war is to weaken the

[45] ibid 541. The trial was conducted from late 1947 to late 1948, with fourteen accused all being former high-ranking officers of the German Army and Navy working in the German High Command. They were charged with crimes against peace and humanity and war crimes. The underlying acts included the implementation and execution of criminal orders against enemy soldiers and civilians.

[46] This case was mainly concerned with the sniping campaign around Sarajevo.

[47] ICTY, Case No IT-98–29–T, Trial Judgment, 5 December 2003, para 44.

[48] ibid, n. 76.

[49] *Prosecutor* v *Kordić and Čerkez*, ICTY, Case No IT-95–14/2–A, Appeal Judgment, 17 December 2004, para 54.

[50] *Legality Opinion* (n 10), para 78.

[51] JM Henckaerts and L Doswald-Beck, *Customary International Humanitarian Law*, vol 1: *Rules* (ICRC and Cambridge University Press, 2005), rules 1 and 7.

military forces of the enemy'. It may seem that the core of this principle somewhat overlaps that of the principle of military necessity, in that both emphasise military forces as the object of attacks. But the principle of military necessity is also concerned with the circumstances and purpose of military operations.

The current version of the principle is set out in Article 48 API, as follows:

> In order to ensure respect for and protection of the civilian population and civilian objects, the Parties to the conflict shall at all times distinguish between the civilian population and combatants and between civilian objects and military objectives and accordingly shall direct their operations only against military objectives.

Article 52(1) API defines civilian objects as 'all objects which are not military objectives'. Military objectives are defined by Article 52(2) as 'those objects which by their nature, location, purpose or use make an effective contribution to military action and whose total or partial destruction, capture or neutralization, in the circumstances ruling at the time, offers a definite military advantage.'[52] Article 52(2) further states that '[a]ttacks shall be limited strictly to military objectives'. These civilian objectives include undefended localities,[53] buildings dedicated to science or charity, historic monuments, works of art or places of worship which constitute the cultural or spiritual heritage of peoples, works and installations containing dangerous forces, or objects indispensable to the survival of the population.

The natural environment should also be protected under this principle and associated rules, but probably to a limited extent.[54] While the ICJ states that '[s]tates must take environmental considerations into account when assessing what is necessary and proportionate in the pursuit of legitimate military objectives',[55] it seems that, in this context, the environment was considered in relation to both legitimate military targets and, more pertinently, the *jus ad bellum* of self-defence.[56] Not much else can be read into this statement, as far as its importance to international humanitarian law is concerned.

The principle has certain aspects that need to be further examined. Indiscriminate attacks, for instance, are prohibited under this principle.[57] Here it is only intended to look at the condition of taking a direct part in hostilities, which, more narrowly construed than that of making a contribution to the war, may excuse attackers from otherwise breaching this principle by directing their attacks on one type of civilians: those participating directly in hostilities.[58] Thus a munitions factory is a legitimate military target, as it meets the conditions of Article 52(2) API.

[52] As for a detailed analysis of the notion of military objectives, including the meaning of military advantage, see A Jachec-Neale, *The Concept of Military Objective in International Law and Targeting Practice* (Routledge, 2015), chs 2–5.

[53] Art 25, Regulations respecting the Laws and Customs of War on Land (Hague Regulations), annexed to the IV Hague Convention respecting the Laws and Customs of War on Land (Hague Convention IV), 18 October 1907; Art 59(1) API.

[54] Arts 35(3) and 55(1) API, are both concerned with restricting means of warfare that may affect the environment, and Art 55(2) forbids attacks on the environment in one situation: reprisal.

[55] *Legality Opinion* (n 10), para 30.

[56] The first principle of the Friendly Relations Declaration on the prohibition of the threat or the use of force and the criminalisation of a war of aggression in international relations does not delve into the law of self-defence, and is irrelevant to international humanitarian law.

[57] Art 51(4) API.

[58] A threshold of harm has been suggested for an individual act to reach the level of direct participation in hostilities: ICRC, *Interpretative Guidance on the Notion of Direct Participation in Hostilities* (ICRC, 2009) 46.

But the civilian workers employed there should not be targeted as they are not participating directly in hostilities.[59] But this view could be too simplistic to be meaningful in practice.

For one, distinction to be made by the attacker is normally based on the information he receives. If he makes reasonable efforts to gather intelligence, reviews the intelligence carefully and concludes in good faith that he is attacking a military objective, he does not violate the principle of distinction if the target turns out to be a civilian object after all. Variants involved in this evaluation process could be many, though, given the complexity of circumstances attending each conflict.[60]

It seems, therefore, only natural that the principle has been proved difficult to apply in practice,[61] and no more so than in the case of objects of dual use.[62]

During NATO's bombing campaign in 1999, certain events prompted the Prosecutor of the ICTY to set up a committee to inquire into whether violations of international humanitarian law had been committed on the part of NATO. A report was issued on 13 June 2000 by the Prosecutor's Office. In respect of an incident where a passenger train was hit by two missiles fired by a NATO war plane on the Leskovac railway bridge on 12 April 1999, resulting in the death of ten passengers and fifteen injured, the report stated in paragraph 58 that 'the designated target was the railway bridge, which was claimed to be part of a re-supply route being used for Serb forces in Kosovo'.[63] The report then stated that:

> It is the opinion of the committee that the bridge was a legitimate military objective. The passenger train was not deliberately targeted. The person controlling the bombs, pilot or WSO, targeted the bridge and, over a very short period of time, failed to recognize the arrival of the train while the first bomb was in flight . . . It is the opinion of the committee that the information in relation to the attack with the first bomb does not provide a sufficient basis to initiate an investigation. The committee has divided views concerning the attack with the second bomb in relation to whether there was an element of recklessness in the conduct of the pilot or WSO . . . Despite this, the committee is in agreement that, based on the criteria for initiating an investigation (see para. 5 above), this incident should not be investigated.[64]

The criteria for investigation were set out in paragraph 5 of the report that:

> In the course of its review, the committee has applied the same criteria to NATO activities that the Office of the Prosecutor (OTP) has applied to the activities of other actors in the territory of the former Yugoslavia. The committee paid particular heed to the following questions:
>
> (a) Are the prohibitions alleged sufficiently well-established as violations of international humanitarian law to form the basis of a prosecution, and does the application of the law to the particular facts reasonably suggest that a violation of these prohibitions may have occurred? and

[59] ICRC has listed some other examples: ibid 48 and 50.

[60] E David, 'Respect for the Principle of Distinction in the Kosovo War' (2000) 3 *Yearbook of International Humanitarian Law* 81, 93–96 (citing, among others, a Yugoslav publication listing objects targeted during the Kosovo bombing campaign).

[61] See F Kalshoven, 'Prohibitions or restrictions on the use of methods and means of warfare' in I Dekker and H Post (eds), *The Gulf War of 1980–1988* (Martinus Nijhoff, 1992) 97, 102–6.

[62] See *Western Front, Aerial Bombardment and Related Claims, Eritrea's Claims 1, 3, 5, 9–13, 14, 21, 25 & 26 (State of Eritrea* v *The Federal Democratic Republic of Ethiopia)*, Eritrea–Ethiopia Claims Commission, Partial Award, 19 December 2005, paras 117–21 (on the Hirgigo power plant), https://pcacases.com/web/sendAttach/757.

[63] Final Report to the Prosecutor by the Committee Established to Review the NATO Bombing Campaign against the Federal Republic of Yugoslavia, dated 13 June 2000, and attached to the press release issued that day. The text can be found in the archives of the (now defunct) tribunal, or in (2000) 39 *International Legal Materials* 1257–83.

[64] ibid, para 62.

(b) upon the reasoned evaluation of the information by the committee, is the information credible and does it tend to show that crimes within the jurisdiction of the Tribunal may have been committed by individuals during the NATO bombing campaign?

The negative findings of the committee indicated that the mental element of recklessness was difficult to prove from available evidence, thus thwarting any further attempt at launching a full investigation. Recklessness, unless specifically provided for under treaties, does not form a main type of mental element that accompanies a crime under international humanitarian law. In the situation instanced above, Article 8(2)(b)(i) of the Rome Statute of the International Criminal Court (Rome Statute) would only be applicable as a war crime if evidence shows that the bomber was *intentionally* targeting the civilian population or a civilian individual not participating in combat.

The inceptive nature of the principle of distinction is therefore laid bare. An apparent breach of the principle may not necessarily result in individual responsibility in the absence of an instrument recognising its illegality, or due to a lack of evidence proving material elements of an unlawful attack set out in such an instrument. For international humanitarian law, however, this principle is of first importance, since it precedes and largely defines the juridical nature of military actions. An attack without regard to the principle is *prima facie* illegal, until it is exonerated by mitigating circumstances recognised under international humanitarian law.

Another remark is that there may be cases where combatants infiltrate a civilian population, which are common in today's armed conflicts. In these cases, a decision to attack or not may be extremely difficult to take. The practice seems to be that attack must be halted if the nature of the population is not changed by the presence in its midst of combatants.[65] Further queries concern such things as the threshold number of soldiers and whether the soldiers are on leave,[66] which go beyond the scope of this chapter.

3.3 *Principle of Proportionality*

This principle, not mentioned in the *Legality Opinion*, follows the principle of distinction in application. Once the military objectives are selected, the attacks must still be launched subject to this principle, which requires that the losses resulting from a military action should not be excessive in relation to the expected military advantage. The losses referred to are those of civilians, including injury or death to civilians, damage to civilian objects, or a combination thereof.[67] Article 57(2)(b) API, stipulates that

> an attack shall be cancelled or suspended if it becomes apparent that the objective is not a military one or is subject to special protection or that the attack may be expected to cause incidental loss of civilian life, injury to civilians, damage to civilian objects, or a combination thereof, which would be excessive in relation to the concrete and direct military advantage anticipated.

[65] *Prosecutor* v *Stanislav Galić*, ICTY, Case No IT-98–29–A, Appeal Judgment, 30 November 2006, para 136 ('The Appeals Chamber finds that the jurisprudence of the International Tribunal in this regard is clear: the presence of individual combatants within the population attacked does not necessarily change the fact that the ultimate character of the population remains, for legal purposes, a civilian one').

[66] *Prosecutor* v *Tihomir Blaškić*, ICTY, Case No IT-95–14–A, Appeal Judgment, 29 July 2004, paras 114–15.

[67] Art 51(5) API, provides that: 'Among others, the following types of attacks are to be considered as indiscriminate: . . . (b) an attack which may be expected to cause incidental loss of civilian life, injury to civilians, damage to civilian objects, or a combination thereof, which would be excessive in relation to the concrete and direct military advantage anticipated.' Art 51(4) provides that 'indiscriminate attacks are prohibited'.

This principle has also been reflected in Article 3(3) APII, as well as in Article 8(2)(b)(iv) of the Rome Statute. There is a general acceptance of this principle in State practice.[68] Proportionality is therefore between the losses and the anticipated military advantages.[69] The advantages are referred to relevant and proportional contributions to the objective of the military attack involved.[70] As to the measurement of a concrete and direct military advantage, the International Committee of the Red Cross (ICRC) considers that such advantage must be 'substantial and relatively close', and an imperceptible and future advantage does not count.[71]

In practice, incidental or collateral damage is a difficult issue, for proportionality is a difficult standard to measure. The assessment is compounded by the presumption that a proportionate loss to civilians or civilian property may fall within the four corners of international humanitarian law. Civilian immunity does not make unlawful the unavoidable incidental civilian casualties and damage which may result from legitimate attacks upon military objectives, provided that the incidental casualties and damage are not excessive in relation to the concrete and direct military advantage anticipated.[72] The crucial mark of legitimacy in relation to civilian casualties is thus the absence of a direct attack on civilians or civilian objects or at least the absence of such an intention.[73] Relevant factors, such as the number of incidental casualties and the scale of property damage caused among civilians living near, for instance a power plant supplying the military that is located in a populated area, should also be considered. Although modern weaponry has increased the options available to the military planner, he must select methods of conducting operations and exercise feasible precautions in minimising incidental loss.[74] One reminder is that collateral damage does not necessarily violate the principle of distinction, if the attack causing it is not directed at civilians or civilian property.

There are other elements which have also been considered in connection with the principle. Thus, it is held that the test for proportionality includes 'a rational fit between goal and means' and requires that the claimant of proportionality has chosen the 'least harmful means' to achieve its ends by resorting to a certain method of war.[75]

There may be room to consider if this principle overlaps the namesake principle applicable in the law of self-defence. This question, if answered in the affirmative, may strengthen the view that the fundamental principles of international humanitarian law are not cleanly compartmentalised, but expansive enough to reach out into other branches of international law. However, without delving into this question, it is proposed to end this section by the observation that given the basics of the law of self-defence,[76] the two principles do not carry the same content.

[68] Henckaerts and Doswald-Beck (n 51) 47–48.

[69] S Oeter, 'Methods and Means of Combat' in D Fleck (ed), *The Handbook of International Humanitarian Law* (2nd edn, Oxford University Press, 2008) 119, section 444.

[70] Art 52(2) API. Also see J Gardam, *Necessity, Proportionality and the Use of Force by States* (Cambridge Uuniversity Press, 2004) 100–2.

[71] ICRC (n 19) 684, section 2209.

[72] US Department of Defence, Final Report to Congress: Conduct of the Persian Gulf War (Pursuant to Title V of the Persian Gulf Conflict Supplemental Authorization and Personnel Benefits Act of 1991 (Public Law 102–25)) (1992) 615, www.globalsecurity.org/military/library/report/1992/cpgw.pdf.

[73] See the 2000 Report (n 63).

[74] See W Boothby, *Weapons and the Law of Armed Conflict* (Oxford University Press, 2009), ch 2.

[75] *Mara'abe* v *Prime Minister of Israel*, Case No HCJ 7957/04, Judgment, Israeli Supreme Court, 15 September 2005, para 30, http://elyon1.court.gov.il/eng/home/index.html.

[76] *Military and Paramilitary Activities in and against Nicaragua (Nicaragua* v *USA)*, Merits, ICJ Reports 1986, 14, para 176 ('self-defence would warrant only measures which are proportional to the armed attack and necessary to respond to it, a rule well established in customary international law').

3.4 *Principle of Humanity*

This principle overarches the whole body of international humanitarian law,[77] and it comes into play whether or not the preceding principles are observed. In a way, it gives international humanitarian law its unique identity as a separate branch of public international law, the latter being a system of *lex generalis*.[78]

The principle forbids the infliction of suffering, injury or destruction not actually necessary for the accomplishment of legitimate military purposes, which are to destroy or weaken the military might of the enemy.[79] It is based on the notion that once the military purpose has been served, further infliction of suffering is unnecessary.[80] Thus, wounded or sick enemy soldiers should no longer be attacked.[81] Rather, they shall be treated humanely and respected. Furthermore, during combat, 'the right of belligerents to adopt means of injuring the enemy is not unlimited'.[82] The thrust of this principle is opposed to that of the principle of military necessity.[83] Although the principle was originally intended to limit the suffering of persons involved in armed conflict, it has taken on other, broader dimensions since it appeared first in the Hague Regulations of 1907.[84]

Under the Geneva Law, as supplemented by API and APII, this principle forbids starvation of civilians as a means of warfare.[85] It also includes a number of prohibitions or rights to protect human dignity, such as the provisions of Article 3 common to the Geneva Conventions[86] and Article 75 API.[87] The broader scope of Article 75,[88] in comparison with human rights law, is shown in the feature that:

[77] See R Liivoja, 'Technological Change and the Evolution of the Law of War' (2015) 97(900) *International Review of the Red Cross* 1157, 1165–66.

[78] *Legality Opinion* (n 10), para 25. It features prominently with the Convention on Prohibitions or Restrictions on the Use of Certain Conventional Weapons which may be Deemed to be Excessively Injurious or to have Indiscriminate Effects, adopted on 10 October 1980 and entering into force on 2 December 1983, in *United Nations Treaty Series*, vol 1342, 137. As of June 2019, there had been 125 States parties: https://treaties.un.org/Pages/ViewDetails.aspx?src=TREATY&mtdsg_no=XXVI-2&chapter=26&clang=_en.

[79] See St Petersburg Declaration, 29 November 1868: 'That the only legitimate object which States should endeavour to accomplish during war is to weaken the military forges of the enemy; that for this purpose it is sufficient to disable the greatest possible number of men; that this object would be exceeded by the employment of arms which uselessly aggravate the sufferings of disabled men, or render their death inevitable; that the employment of such arms would, therefore, be contrary to the laws of humanity.' Also see ICRC (n 19) section 1411.

[80] Art 23(e), Hague Regulations; Art 35(2) API.

[81] See Art 3 common to the Geneva Conventions.

[82] Art 22, Hague Regulations.

[83] Dinstein (n 10) at 9–10.

[84] The most obvious example would be that of Art 3 common to the Geneva Conventions.

[85] Art 54(1) API.

[86] As the ICJ stated, 'Article 3 which is common to all four Geneva Conventions of 12 August 1949 defines certain rules to be applied in the armed conflicts of a non-international character. There is no doubt that, in the event of international armed conflicts, these rules also constitute a minimum yardstick, in addition to the more elaborate rules which are also to apply to international conflicts; and they are rules which, in the Court's opinion, reflect what the Court in 1949 called "elementary considerations of humanity"' (citing the Court's judgment in the *Corfu Channel* case, ICJ Reports 1949, 4, 22): ICJ, *Military and Paramilitary Activities in and against Nicaragua (Nicaragua* v *USA)*, Merits, ICJ Reports 1986, 14, para 218.

[87] As the ICRC comments, 'Article 75 … represents an important step forward in humanitarian law by laying down several minimum rules of protection for the benefit of all those who find themselves in time of armed conflict in the power of a Party to the conflict, whereas in such circumstances provisions of human rights law are subject to possible derogations. This article must therefore be seen as a victory for humanitarian law…': ICRC (n 19) section 3006.

[88] The scope of application of the provision extends to 'persons' who 'shall be treated humanely in all circumstances': Art 75(1) API.

> Most of the guarantees listed in sub-paragraphs (a)–(j) are contained in the Conventions and the Covenant on Human Rights, but in each of these treaties there is a clause permitting derogations from the articles in question in time of war. Article 75 is not subject to any possibility of derogation or suspension and consequently it is these provisions which will play a decisive role in the case of armed conflict. Besides, the provisions in all these instruments are more or less equivalent.[89]

A more expanded form of this principle can be found in the *Corfu Channel* case as underlying an obligation for Albania to notify foreign shipping passing through its territorial waters of the existence therein of a minefield.[90] The impact of the view of the ICJ upon international humanitarian law may be limited, due to the fact that the Court deliberately avoided to pass on the issue in the context of armed conflict.

Given its overarching nature, it is no surprise that the principle is also represented as part of the 'Martens Clause', to which we should return later.

III INTERPLAY OF INTERNATIONAL HUMANITARIAN LAW AND HUMAN RIGHTS LAW

In a general way, human rights norms and norms of international humanitarian law overlap to the extent that both seek to protect individual rights,[91] albeit often in different contexts. One of the fundamental principles of international humanitarian law, that of humanity, aptly highlights this overlapping relationship between these two sets of norms.[92] In the present context, it is the fact that both sets of rules can apply to one and the same situation that is to be examined. The question is not whether human rights law applies to situations which traditionally call for application of international humanitarian law, which is no longer in dispute,[93] but whether human rights law can include international humanitarian law in those situations. If not, human rights law is not all embracing, and gaps may call for international humanitarian law to fill in. Consequently, full protection of the rights of the individual requires both human rights law and international humanitarian law to apply jointly or successively. To address all this, attention should first be turned to the basics of human rights law.

The philosophy of human rights is concerned with the protection of the individual from the arbitrary exercise of power by the state. While the law of human rights has developed mainly after the Second World War, it was not unknown before that time. Treatment of the sick and wounded and prisoners of war had been subject to international regulations in the earlier editions of the Geneva Conventions of 1864 and 1929. Further, the 1919 Treaty of Versailles also included in the Covenant of the League of Nations the regime of mandates on the basis of the principle that the well-being and development of such peoples form a sacred trust of

[89] ICRC (n 19) section 3092. 'The Covenant on Human Rights' was referred to the International Covenant on Political and Civil Rights of 1966 (ICCPR), and esp Art 14 of the covenant. On the applicability of Art 75 to unlawful combatants, see K Dörmann, 'The Legal Situation of "Unlawful/Unprivileged Combatants"' (2003) 85(849) *International Review of the Red Cross* 45, 67–70.

[90] ICJ, *Corfu Channel* case, Judgment, ICJ Reports 1949, 4, 22: 'Such obligations are based, not on the Hague Convention of 1907, No VIII, which is applicable in time of war, but on certain general and well-recognized principles, namely: elementary considerations of humanity, even more exacting in peace than in war...'. While this statement was confined to the time of peace, Art 75 API seems to suggest that it might apply beyond international armed conflict by using the words 'at any time and in any place' in the chapeau of Art 75(2): ICRC (n 19) section 3039.

[91] *Prosecutor v Anto Furundžija*, ICTY, Case No IT-95–17/1–T, 10 December 1998, para 183.

[92] I Blinshchenko, 'Les Principes du droit international humanitaire' in Swinarski (ed), *Etudes* (n 11) 293.

[93] See the text accompanying nn 107–115.

civilisation and that the securities of performance of this trust should be embodied in the Covenant. The 1919 peace treaties with Eastern European and Balkan States included provisions relating to the protection of minorities.[94]

Three generations of rights have been in existence: the first generation of civil and political rights, the second generation of economic, social and cultural rights and, in later times, the 'third generation' of human rights.[95] Examples of this last batch of rights include the right to peace, the right to development and the right to the enjoyment of a healthy environment.

The UN Charter leads the field in setting the standard. In the preamble to the Charter, it is said that the United Nations is determined 'to reaffirm faith in fundamental human rights, in the dignity and worth of the human person, in the equal rights of men and women and of nations large and small'. It was thus one of the fundamental values that underlay the establishment of the UN organisation. Article 1 also includes as a purpose of the United Nations 'to achieve international cooperation in solving international problems of an economic, social, cultural, or humanitarian character, and in promoting and encouraging respect for human rights and for fundamental freedoms for all without distinction as to race, sex, language, or religion'. Further, Article 55 requires the United Nations to promote universal respect for, and observance of, human rights and fundamental freedoms for all without distinction as to race, sex, language or religion. All this has been enhanced by the relevant principle of the Friendly Relations Declaration.[96]

As already conceded, human rights instruments have had profound influence upon the development of international humanitarian law.[97] The Universal Declaration of Human Rights of 10 December 1948, while not a legal instrument, contains provisions that either constitute general principles of international law or represent elementary considerations of humanity.[98] Great value has been attached to this document as an authoritative guide to the interpretation of related provisions of the UN Charter,[99] and the Declaration has been referred to by both the ICJ and the European Court of Human Rights in their jurisprudence.[100] More pertinently, the Declaration influences the development of international humanitarian law in our times. Conversely, it is plain that human rights law has increasingly shown an inclination towards criminalisation, often by way of treaty, of certain offences of international concern. This is a compliment to the impact of post-Second World War military trials and the Geneva Conventions.[101] In *Reservations to the Genocide Convention*, the ICJ stated in its advisory opinion that the crime of genocide, as the subject-matter of the convention, 'shocks the conscience of mankind, results in great losses to humanity ... and is contrary to moral law and to the spirit and aims of the United Nations'.[102] The rights and obligations contained in the convention are

94 See N Berman, '"But the Alternative Is Despair": European Nationalism and the Modernist Renewal of International Law' (1993) 106 *Harvard Law Review* 1792, 1834–42.

95 Brownlie (n 2) 567.

96 See the chapter by E Riedel in this volume.

97 ICRC (n 19) section 3092: most of the guarantees included under Art 75 API are borrowed from Art 14 ICCPR.

98 A Cassese, *International Law* (2nd edn, Oxford University Press, 2005) 381–82; Brownlie (n 2) 559–60.

99 Principle VII of the Declaration on Principles Guiding Relations between Participating States, Conference on Security and Co-operation in Europe, Final Act, Helsinki, 1 August 1975, www.osce.org/helsinki-final-act. On the argument over Principle VII's legal consequences, A Kiss and M Dominick, 'The International Legal Significance of the Human Rights Provisions of the Helsinki Final Act' (1980) 13 *Vanderbilt Journal of Transnational Law* 293, 302–3.

100 *Case Concerning United States Diplomatic and Consular Staff in Tehran*, ICJ Reports 1980, 3, para 91; *Golder* case, ECHR, (1975) 57 International Law Report 201, 216–17.

101 See H Steiner, P Alston and R Goodman, *International Human Rights in Context: Law, Politics, Morals (Text and Materials)* (3rd edn, Oxford University Press, 2008) 133.

102 ICJ Reports 1953, 15, 23.

of the *erga omnes* nature in a later case.[103] When the ICTY was granted jurisdiction over genocide, the crime was considered to exist in both time of peace and time of war.[104]

One more word should be said of the tendency that the two bodies of law are increasingly complementary.[105] This tendency has been nurtured in three ways. First, the fundamentals of the two branches of laws are largely the same, all derived from the principle of humanity.[106] It may be recalled that, in 1968, the UN General Assembly adopted, by a vote of 111:0, Resolution 2444 (XXIII), entitled 'Respect for Human Rights in time of Armed Conflict'. The resolution affirmed certain principles of international humanitarian law, being at the same time human rights, including that (a) the right of the parties to a conflict to adopt means of injuring the enemy is not unlimited; (b) it is prohibited to launch attacks against the civilian populations as such; (c) distinction must be made at all times between persons taking part in the hostilities and members of the civilian population to the effect that the latter be spared as much as possible.

Second, thanks to recent developments in judicial practice, international humanitarian law has borrowed from rules of human rights law in dealing with situations of both armed conflict and occupation.[107] The ICJ stated in the *Legality Opinion* to the effect that the International Covenant on Civil and Political Rights (ICCPR) did not cease to apply in times of war, subject to conditions laid down in Article 4 of the treaty.[108] The ICJ subsequently confirmed that the ICCPR applied to the benefit of the population of the Israel-occupied territories, for all conduct by Israel officials or agents that would affect the rights enshrined in the covenant,[109] and that:

> the territories occupied by Israel have for 37 years been subject to its territorial jurisdiction as the occupying power. In the exercise of the powers available to it on this basis, Israel is bound by the provisions of the International Covenant on Economic, Social and Cultural Rights.[110]

Third, the two bodies of law complement each other in international criminal proceedings that enforce international humanitarian law against individuals. In the proceedings at the ICTY, references to human rights law were frequent, both procedurally and substantively. For example, in the oft-quoted *Prosecutor* v. *Anto Furundžija*, the Trial Chamber stated, in relation to the issue of rape as a form of torture, that 'the prohibition of torture laid down in international humanitarian law with regard to situations of armed conflict is reinforced by the body of international treaty rules on human rights'.[111] It also noted that the prohibition of torture was an absolute right in human rights law, and could not be derogated from, not even in time of emergency.[112] To define torture for trial purposes, it referred to the Convention against Torture of 1984, and justified this reference on the ground that the definition reflected customary law regarding

[103] *Case Concerning Application of the Convention on the Prevention and Punishment of the Crime of Genocide (Bosnia and Herzegovina* v *Serbia and Montenegro)*, Preliminary Objections, ICJ Reports 1996, 595, 615.

[104] Report of the Secretary-General pursuant to Paragraph 2 of Security Council Resolution 808 (1993), S/25704, 3 May 1993, para 45.

[105] See T Hadden and C Harvey, 'The Law of Internal Crisis and Conflict' (1999) 81 (833) *International Review of the Red Cross* 119; D Thürer, *International Humanitarian Law: Theory, Practice, Context* (Pocket Book) (Hague Academy of International Law, 2011), ch 3, and 138–42.

[106] *Prosecutor* v *Furundžija*, Case No IT-95-17-1/T, Trial Judgment, 10 December 1998, para 106. Also see R Provost, *International Human Rights and Humanitarian Law* (Cambridge University Press, 2002) 26–27; Thürer (n 105) 200.

[107] See D Momtaz, 'Le Droit international humanitaire applicable aux conflits armés non internationaux' (2001) 292 *Recueil des Cours* 9, 34–37.

[108] ICJ Reports 1996, 226, para 25.

[109] *Legal Consequences of the Construction of a Wall in the Occupied Palestinian Territory*, Advisory Opinion, ICJ Reports 2004, 136, paras 107–11.

[110] ibid, para 112.

[111] IT-95-17/1-T, Trial Judgment, 10 December 1998, para 143.

[112] ibid, para 144.

torture and should be applied to the practice of both the ICTY and International Criminal Tribunal for Rwanda (ICTR).[113] There was no distinction drawn between the time of peace and the time of armed conflict. Regarding the expression 'inhumane acts' as contained in the ICTY Statute, which was very much related to the notion of humanity, another ICTY Trial Chamber stated, in *Prosecutor* v. *Kupreskić et al.*, that:

> Less broad parameters for the interpretation of 'other inhumane acts' can instead be identified in international standards on human rights such as those laid down in the Universal Declaration on Human Rights of 1948 and the two United Nations Covenants on Human Rights of 1966. Drawing upon the various provisions of these texts, it is possible to identify a set of basic rights appertaining to human beings, the infringement of which may amount, depending on the accompanying circumstances, to a crime against humanity.[114]

The transition from human rights law to international humanitarian law was seamless. The vacuum, in terms of the content of crimes against humanity, was an open invitation for the ICTY to fill in with assistance of its judges possessing expertise in human rights law.

In *Prosecutor* v. *Blaškić*, the ICTY AC stated that 'it is not the case that any type of act, if committed with the requisite intent, amounts to persecutions as a crime against humanity', and that 'this test will only be met by gross or blatant denials of fundamental human rights'.[115]

Procedurally, international humanitarian law is enforced by international criminal tribunals which have to follow human rights standards. Article 21 of the ICTY Statute, for instance, reflects closely Article 14 of the ICCPR.

However, as international humanitarian law is regarded as *lex specialis*, it not only applies in armed conflict in preference to human rights law, but contains rules that are nowhere to be found in human rights law. This latter difference is easily demonstrated by reference to the 'Hague Law' and relevant rules of API.[116] There is, in matters such as these, no role for human rights law to play. There may be other presumed differences between human rights law and international humanitarian law, but generalisations or propositions such as these may not always be in line with practice. For instance, it is presumed that human rights law and international humanitarian law each applies to a distinct period of time – of war or of peace[117] – but this has become less pronounced due to recent developments. The ICJ rejected this view in the *Legality Opinion* in 1996.[118] In its advisory opinion in *Legal Consequences of the Construction of a Wall*, the ICJ states that '[a]s regards the relationship between international humanitarian law and human rights law, there are thus three possible situations: some rights may be exclusively matters of international humanitarian law; others

[113] ibid, para 159.

[114] IT-95-16-T, Trial Judgment, 14 January 2000, para 566.

[115] Case No IT-95-14-A, Appeal Judgment, 29 July 2004, para 139.

[116] *Armed Activities on the Territory of the Congo (Democratic Republic of the Congo* v *Uganda)*, Judgment, ICJ Reports 2005, 168, para 172: 'The Court observes that, under customary international law, as reflected in Article 42 of the Hague Regulations of 1907, territory is considered to be occupied when it is actually placed under the authority of the hostile army, and the occupation extends only to the territory where such authority has been established and can be exercised.' Also see ibid, paras 173–74. Thus, when deciding on whether Uganda was an occupying power, the Court only looked at the Hague Regulations of 1907.

[117] The temporal difference may be less pronounced than those in terms of values and interests: G Mettraux, *International Crimes and the Ad Hoc Tribunals* (Oxford University Press, 2005) 51–52.

[118] ICJ Reports 1996, 226, para 25.

may be exclusively matters of human rights law; yet others may be matters of both these branches of international law'.[119]

On a different note, the institutional difference between the two branches of international law seems to hold firm.[120] International humanitarian law has mechanisms of enforcement through national implementation of treaties or in international judicial bodies specially designed to enforce international humanitarian law, whereas human rights law relies for enforcement on national implementation, supervisory bodies on the international level and regional courts of human rights. While the emergence of the ad hoc tribunals in the 1990s, and the International Criminal Court (ICC) in 1998, seems to blend together the two bodies of law as part of applicable law, the institutions have maintained separate identities.

IV INTERNATIONAL HUMANITARIAN LAW IN PEACEKEEPING OR ENFORCEMENT OPERATIONS

The desirability of a list of fundamental principles of international humanitarian law is also bolstered by the long existence of the institution of UN Forces. These forces may be established for peacekeeping missions organised and directed by the United Nations, or authorised to enter into open hostilities by the UN Security Council as enforcement measures under Chapter VII of the Charter.[121] In either case, international humanitarian law is directly relevant and likely comprises the main part of relevant international law. The Friendly Relations Declaration has little substantial to offer in these types of operation.

Since 1948, seventy operations have been mounted, including fourteen currently in operation involving some 110,000 military, police and civilian staff.[122] The approved budget for UN Peacekeeping operations for the fiscal year 1 July 2018–30 June 2019 is $ 6.7 billion, and this is less than half of 1 per cent of world military expenditures (estimated at $1,747 billion in 2013), with the top three providers of assessed contributions to UN Peacekeeping operations for 2018 being the United States (28.47 per cent), China (10.25 per cent) and Japan (9.68 per cent).[123] Under this model, the UN Security Council authorises peacekeeping operations by resolution, and the UN General Assembly approves budget and resources.

The UN peacekeeping forces are often employed to maintain or re-establish peace in an area of armed conflict. The United Nations acts as an impartial third party in order to prepare the ground for a settlement of the issues that have provoked armed conflict. If it proves impossible to achieve a peaceful settlement, the presence of UN forces may contribute to reducing the level of conflict. The UN forces may only be employed when both parties to a conflict accept their presence, and they are subordinate to the leadership of the United Nations. Operational control belongs to the Secretary-General and the Secretariat. Typically, two kinds of peacekeeping operation are commonly employed – unarmed observer groups and lightly armed military forces which later become augmented by civilian police. The latter are only allowed to employ their weapons for self-defence. Given that the basic principles for peacekeeping operations are those of consent of the parties, impartiality, non-use of force except in self-defence and defence of the

[119] ICJ Reports 2004, 136, para 106. In the 2005 *Congo* Judgment (n 116), the Court found that the occupying power, Uganda, was responsible for securing respect for both human rights law and international humanitarian law in the occupied territory (see para 178).

[120] Other differences, such as the ways for protection of rights, may exist: Provost (n 106), ch 1.

[121] D Schindler, 'United Nations Forces and International Humanitarian Law' in Swinarski (ed), *Etudes* (n 11) 522–23.

[122] See https://peacekeeping.un.org/en/our-history.

[123] ibid.

mandate,[124] it goes without saying that such operations are subject to the UN Charter, the specific Security Council resolutions establishing them and their mandates, relevant memoranda of understanding, and relevant treaties protecting UN personnel and regulating their privileges and immunities. But outside the provision of Article 51 of the UN Charter, is there room for international humanitarian law to play a role when there is fighting between UN peacekeepers and their attackers?

International humanitarian law surely applies in such situations, where other related treaties may no longer be applicable.[125] A different view is that the forces are not instantly subject to international humanitarian law if they are not involved in genuine armed conflicts. This is said with regard to the possibility that the threshold of armed conflict is not crossed.[126] However, it may be said that such a right might only exist if the peacekeeping forces are under armed attack. This interpretation has been recognised by the Institute of International Law in a 1971 resolution with the title 'Conditions of Application of Humanitarian Rules of Armed Conflict to Hostilities in which United Nations Forces may be Engaged'.[127]

If, as part of enforcement operations authorised by the UN Security Council under Chapter VII of the UN Charter, UN forces are engaged in armed conflicts, they are bound by international humanitarian law. This has been recognised under the Convention on the Safety of United Nations and Associate Personnel 1994 (1994 Safety Convention).[128] Article 2(2) provides that '[t]his Convention shall not apply to a United Nations operation authorized by the Security Council as an enforcement action under Chapter VII of the Charter of the United Nations in which any of the personnel are engaged as combatants against organized armed forces and to which the law of international armed conflict applies'.

The rules of international humanitarian law applicable to the UN forces have by now been conveniently gathered in the document entitled 'Observance by United Nations Forces of International Humanitarian Law', promulgated by the UN Secretary-General on 6 August 1999.[129] The bulletin entered into force on 12 August 1999. Section 1.1 of the document expresses that the principles and rules of international humanitarian law set out therein are applicable to enforcement actions, or peacekeeping operations 'when the use of force is permitted in self-defence'. Section 4 of the 1999 Bulletin provides that the responsibility for violation of international humanitarian law by the military personnel of UN forces remains that of national authorities. Sections 5–9 reflect such fundamental principles of international humanitarian law as those of distinction and humanity.

Besides the principles and rules reflected in the 1999 Bulletin, the UN forces enjoy protection of international humanitarian law, if they are not party to an armed conflict. They are not, first of all, military objectives. Any attack on them in such circumstances will be illegal. Indeed the 1994 Safety Convention outlaws, under Article 9, a series of actions against the UN personnel or

124 See https://peacekeeping.un.org/en/principles-of-peacekeeping.

125 See the following discussion on the 1994 Safety Convention.

126 *Tadić* Decision (n 21), para 70 ('an armed conflict exists whenever there is a resort to armed force between States or protracted armed violence between governmental authorities and organized armed groups or between such groups within a State').

127 (1971) 54(2) *Annuaire de l'Institut de Droit International* at 465–70. The resolution stated that the entire body of international humanitarian law would apply to UN forces. Under Art 1, the term 'United Nations Forces' signifies, in this series of articles, 'all armed units under the control of the United Nations'. The preamble specifically indicated that these forces, 'whatever their mission', might be involved in hostilities.

128 UNGA Res 49/59, 49 UN GAOR Supp No 49, 299, UN Doc A/49/49 (1994), and *United Nations Treaty Series*, vol 2051, 363.

129 ST/SBG/1999/13 (1999 Bulletin). On the early situation, see Schindler (n 121) 526–30.

those associated with UN operations, who (or whose equipment and premises), according to Article 7(1), 'shall not be made the object of attack or of any action that prevents them from discharging their mandate'.

V ACCOUNTABILITY AS A PRELUDE TO PEACE

International humanitarian law has long been enforceable. Rules of this system are frequently couched in obligatory terms, and lead to individual responsibility as determined by customary law.[130] The first principle of the Friendly Relations Declaration, prohibiting the threat or use of force in violation of international law and the UN Charter, does address the criminality of a particular type of illegal use of force: war of aggression. Responsibility arises for it, and there is no distinction drawn between the responsibility of an aggressor State and that of individuals. The limited scope of the principles of the Friendly Relations Declaration is again confirmed. Breaches of international humanitarian law that give rise to criminal responsibility may span the whole duration of an armed conflict, and may continue to hamper efforts in reaching a final settlement when fighting dies down. Accountability for such breaches of international humanitarian law is therefore a vital factor in changing the condition of a territory engulfed in hostilities from conflict to rebuilt peace. Modern international criminal law, as it has turned out, develops its substantive rules mainly from the mid-twentieth-century military trials of violations of international humanitarian law. Those trials attest to the long maturity of international humanitarian law rules and the intrinsic link between violations of such rules and major categories of international crimes. As will be shown, that mature body of law was firmly established long before the idea of the Friendly Relations Declaration was hatched among the UN Member States.

In 1946, the International Military Tribunal at Nuremberg stated that the Nuremberg Charter,[131] with all the principles embodied in it, must be seen as 'the expression of international law existing at the time of its creation; and to that extent is itself a contribution to international law',[132] and that 'crimes against international law are committed by men, not by abstract entities, and only by punishing individuals who commit such crimes can the provisions of international law be enforced'.[133]

The regime of grave breaches under the Geneva Conventions of 1949 is also illustrative.[134] As the treaties provide, the States parties undertake to make violations of this type the subject of effective penal sanction. Since the provisions in question have become part of customary law, the rules they carry also exist independently of the treaties.[135]

After the trial of major war criminals, the UN General Assembly adopted Resolution 95(I) on 11 December 1946 to 'affirm' the principles of international law recognised by the Nuremberg Charter and the Nuremberg judgment. By Resolution 177(II) of 21 November 1947, the UN General Assembly, having established the International Law Commission (ILC) by Resolution 174(II) of the same date, requested the ILC to formulate such principles and to start work on a

[130] eg Art 228 of the Versailles Treaty, 28 June 1919, https://avalon.law.yale.edu/subject_menus/versailles_menu.asp.

[131] The Agreement for the Prosecution and Punishment of the Major War Criminals of the European Axis, 8 August 1945, *United Nations Treaty Series*, vol 82, No 251.

[132] International Military Tribunal (Nuremberg) [IMT], Judgment, 1 October 1946, 41 *American Journal of International Law* (1947) 172, 216. Also see H Donnedieu de Vabres, *Les Principes modernes du droit pénal international* (Editions Panthéon-Assas, Collection Les Introuvables, 2004) 500.

[133] IMT (n 132) 221.

[134] cf Art 50 GCI; Art 51 GCII; Art 130 GCIII; Art 147 GCIV; and Art 85 API.

[135] Report of the Secretary-General, S/25704 (n 104), para 35.

Draft Code on Offences against the Peace and Security of Mankind. At its second session in 1950, the Nuremberg Principles were adopted by the ILC.

For present purposes, some of the principles are set out. Principle I provides that any person who commits an act which constitutes a crime under international law is responsible for it and liable to punishment. It establishes individual responsibility. Principle III states that the fact that a person who committed an act which constitutes a crime under international law acted as Head of State or responsible government official does not relieve him from responsibility under international law. It ushers in the era of denial of impunity to officials. Principle IV provides that the fact that a person acted pursuant to order of his government or of a superior does not relieve him from responsibility under international law, provided a moral choice was in fact possible to him. It excludes superior orders as an excuse for crimes. Principle V allows any person charged with a crime under international law the right to a fair trial on the facts and law. Principle VI declares three types of international crime, being (a) crimes against peace; (b) war crimes; and (c) crimes against humanity.

The Principles were affirmed by the UN General Assembly as part of international law.[136] This view was supported by, for instance, the Israeli Supreme Court in the *Eichmann* judgment of 29 May 1962.[137] The impact of the principles was plain to see even at the time, and this was particularly the case with the recognition of individual responsibility for violations of international law, even though the prevalent precepts and injunctions of international law were not yet addressed to individuals.[138]

With the adoption of statutes for ad hoc tribunals by the UN Security Council in the 1990s,[139] international jurisdiction, based in customary law, including the Nuremberg Principles, has since become, in a general way, concurrent with national jurisdiction. Another notable legacy of the 1990s was the general reaffirmation that, under customary law, individual responsibility arises from serious violations of international humanitarian law.[140]

All this reflects, at the beginning of the 1990s, the conviction of the UN Security Council that the establishment of ad hoc international tribunals 'would bring about the achievement of the aim of putting an end to' serious violations of international humanitarian law as international crimes, 'and would contribute to the restoration and maintenance of peace'.[141] That sentiment was echoed in 1998 when the Rome Statute was adopted at a UN-convened diplomatic conference. The Statute recognises that international crimes, including serious violations of international humanitarian law, 'threaten peace, security and well-being of the world', and the

[136] F Sloan, 'The Binding Force of a Recommendation of the General Assembly of the United Nations' (1948) 25 *British Yearbook of International Law* 1, 24–25. (UNGA 'has already adopted resolutions declaring what it finds to be an existing rule of international law. Perhaps the most important of such resolutions have been the affirmation of the Nuremberg principles ... If fifty-eight nations unanimously agree on a statement of existing law it would seem that such a declaration would be all but conclusive evidence of such a rule.')

[137] *Attorney-General of the Government of Israel* v A *Eichmann*, Judgment of the Supreme Court, 29 May 1962, 36 ILR 277, 296. Also see ibid 311: the Nuremberg Principles 'have become part of the law of nations and must be regarded as having been rooted in it also in the past'.

[138] E Zoller, 'The Status of Individuals under International Law' in G Ginsburgs and V Kuriadtsev (eds), *The Nuremberg Trial and International Law* (Martinus Nijhoff, 1990) 101, cited by M Kelly and T McCormack, 'Contributions of the Nuremberg Trial to the Subsequent Development of International Law' in D Blumenthal and T McCormack (eds), *The Legacy of Nuremberg: Civilising Influence or Institutionalised Vengeance?* (Martinus Nijhoff, 2008) 101, 102.

[139] UNSC Res 808 and 827 (1993) (ICTY); UNSC Res 955 (1994) (ICTR).

[140] *Tadić* Decision (n 21), para 129.

[141] UNSC Res 808 (1993).

States parties to the treaty resolve 'to guarantee lasting respect for and the enforcement of international justice'.[142]

VI CONCLUSION

The fundamental principles identified in the preceding pages may not be exhaustive, and they of course underlie other, secondary principles and rules of international humanitarian law.[143] The selection of such principles is a matter of opinion. Others may be of a different arrangement and more detailed.[144]

The advantage in having these principles is that they concisely set forth the basic prohibitions of international humanitarian law, providing military planners with easy reference to the limits of hostile actions in armed conflict. Being skeletal, the four principles identified in this chapter may be able to account for the conceptual foundation of the great majority of international humanitarian law rules known to be in existence. It is, however, noteworthy that the forces driving the development of this body of law anticipated, at the inception of the 'Hague Law', that allowance had to be made for changes and revisions, as they identified what is known as the 'Martens Clause'.[145]

It reads, in the modern version as contained in Article 1(2) API, as follows:

> In cases not covered by this Protocol or by other international agreements, civilians and combatants remain under the protection and authority of the principles of international law derived from established custom, from the principles of humanity and from the dictates of public conscience.

Principles of international humanitarian law, fundamental or otherwise, are already part of customary law, and will continue to apply where treaties or custom are silent in a specific situation. But the clause seems to include even those principles not derived from custom (in this field), but nonetheless appropriate to the object and purpose of international humanitarian law, so that they can be relied on by, among others, a court or tribunal in finding applicable law. This residual function of the clause is confirmed by the comments of the ICRC on the continuing usefulness of the clause.[146]

Judge Shahabuddeen once said that the clause provided authority for treating the principles of humanity and the dictates of public conscience as principles of international law or principles of international humanitarian law, leaving the precise content of the standards implied by these principles of international law to be ascertained in the light of changing conditions, including changes in the means and methods of warfare and the outlook and tolerance levels of the international community.[147] He also considered that the clause had the basic function of putting beyond challenge the existence of principles of international law which residually serve, with current effect, to govern military conduct by reference to the principles.[148] He regarded the clause itself as the *source* of the principles in question.

[142] Preamble, Rome Statute.

[143] N Melzer, *International Humanitarian Law: A Comprehensive Introduction* (ICRC, 2016) 17–20.

[144] J Pictet, *Development and Principles of International Humanitarian Law* (Martinus Nijhoff, 1985), ch 3.

[145] The original version of the clause was to be found in the preambles to the 1899 Hague Convention II and the 1907 Hague Convention IV.

[146] ICRC (n 19) section 55: that codification of international humanitarian law could not possibly be complete, and that principles reign even though circumstances may later change due to technological development.

[147] *Legality Opinion* (n 10) 226, Dissenting Opinion of J Shahabuddeen at 406.

[148] ibid 408.

What the learned judge had predicted would align with the views expressed in this chapter. The principle of humanity is already one of the fundamental principles identified here. The other principles – distinction, proportionality, and military necessity – are neatly summed up in terms of 'principles of international law derived from established custom'. But the potential of the clause is clearly not exhausted after fitting the four principles into its ample scope. Custom is still evolving in many aspects, and it is fertile ground for germinating new principles. Then there is the panacea of public conscience, which seems to be a limitless source for inspiration, given its intrinsic link to morality and ethics. These latter two extra-legal sources of ideas mark international humanitarian law out as a separate branch of international law,[149] and a very special one indeed.

A word of caution is needed here. The four principles identified for their fundamental importance to the system of international humanitarian law, or the international law of armed conflict, are not exhaustive. A more optimistic vision would be for a similar committee to be set up by the UN General Assembly to work out, hopefully, *all* fundamental principles of international humanitarian law, much in the same way the Special Committee drafted and presented the report on the Friendly Relations Declaration in the 1960s. This is said with the statement of the ICJ ringing in one's ear:

> [A] great many rules of humanitarian law applicable in armed conflict are so fundamental to the respect of the human person and 'elementary considerations of humanity' as the Court put it in its Judgment of 9 April 1949 in the Corfu Channel case (note omitted), that the Hague and Geneva Conventions have enjoyed a broad accession. Further these fundamental rules are to be observed by all States whether or not they have ratified the conventions that contain them, because they constitute intransgressible principles of international customary law.[150]

Much can be said of this statement. What is relevant to our discussion is the Court's vision of 'a great many rules' of international humanitarian law that are 'intransgressible'. Are these therefore non-derogable? To answer this question, one has to examine the view of the Court that equated the rules with 'principles' of customary law. The problem is that principles of that nature may not be applicable to persistent objectors. How, then, could the principles be intransgressible? Or is it only in reference to a desired effect of customary law? The further question would be whether fundamental principles, if understood to mean those that underpin a legal order, could really be a 'great many' – say, more than the seven principles of the Friendly Relations Declaration and the four principles suggested in this chapter? Without attempting to answer all these questions, it suffices to say that many principles may indeed exist in international humanitarian law, and that, if so, they are in need of codification.

On the whole, international humanitarian law extends the scope of the principles of the Friendly Relations Declaration to cover a recurrent stage in human history when peace is replaced by sustained periods of hostilities. Yet, from the ashes of armed conflict, new world orders may arise, and history will have to be continually rewritten. Waxing and waning over time, international humanitarian law has almost single-handedly regulated the pre- and post-conflict inter-state relations that revolve around armed conflict, and, more importantly, rightly claims its supremacy during such conflict. No other normative system can provide an alternative to it in armed conflict.[151] For that indispensable role alone, the fundamental principles of this body of law deserve to be written into *lex scripta*, or as a compromise, a declaration.

[149] R Kolb and R Hyde, *An Introduction to the International Law of Armed Conflicts* (Hart, 2008) 7–8.

[150] *Legality Opinion* (n 10), para 79.

[151] In comparison with para 79 of the *Legality Opinion* (n 10) cited above, lack of alternatives may better explain the universality of international humanitarian law, and especially of the Geneva Conventions.

12

Prevention of Environmental Harm

Leslie-Anne Duvic-Paoli and Jorge E. Viñuales

I INTRODUCTION

The prevention principle, in its accepted formulation of Principle 21 of the Stockholm Declaration[1] and, later, of Principle 2 of the Rio Declaration[2] (hereafter 'Principle 21/2') is an extension of an older norm aimed at ensuring respect of the rights of other States which could be hampered as a result of activities conducted in the territory of a State. The activities which called for such an extension concerned inter alia the exploitation of natural resources. Before the emergence of an environmental consciousness in the 1960s, the 'environment' was perceived through the lenses of 'natural resources' and, to a far lesser extent, of 'conservation'.[3] What today is called 'environmental' harm was only a concern inasmuch as the exploitation of natural resources would have damaging consequences on a neighbouring State. The international legal response to such damage rested on the rules of State responsibility for internationally wrongful acts. The focus on reparation and compensation in case of environmental harm was an application of the traditional legal concepts protecting State sovereignty – these included in particular the *sic utere tuo ut alienum non laedas* rule ('use your own property so as not to harm that of another'), the prohibition of *abus de droit* and the rules on good neighbourliness.[4] These concepts translated the idea that, in an interdependent world, sovereignty can only be relative and is limited by the obligation to respect the sovereignty of other States. Such recognition crystallised in the 'no harm' rule, the obligation of States not to cause transboundary environmental harm.

Yet, the 1960s witnessed a fundamental change in human perceptions of life on Earth and the ensuing necessity to protect nature, which, in turn, provided the socio-political foundations for a shift in the legal paradigm. Reparation of environmental damage appeared as an ancillary approach whilst its prevention became the *raison d'être* of international environmental law.

[1] Declaration of the United Nations Conference on the Human Environment, Stockholm, 16 June 1972, UN Doc A/CONF.48/14/Rev.1.

[2] Rio Declaration on Environment and Development, 13 June 1992, 31 ILM 874 (1992).

[3] On the evolution of international efforts to protect the environment and its different approaches see JE Viñuales, 'The Rise and Fall of Sustainable Development' (2013) 22 *Review of European, Comparative and International Environmental Law* 3.

[4] See J Andrassy, 'Les Relations internationales de voisinage' (1951) 79 *Recueil des Cours* 73; A Kiss, *L'Abus de droit en droit international* (LGDJ, 1952); I Pop, *Voisinage et bon voisinage en droit international* (Pedone, 1980).

As a result, the understanding of the 'no harm' rule evolved towards the more comprehensive principle of 'prevention'.[5]

As noted earlier, the prevention principle in its contemporary form was formulated at the Stockholm Conference on the Human Environment, in Principle 21 of the Stockholm Declaration:

> States have, in accordance with the Charter of the United Nations and the principles of international law, the sovereign right to exploit their own resources pursuant to their own environmental policies, and the responsibility to ensure that activities within their jurisdiction or control do not cause damage to the environment of other States or of areas beyond the limits of national jurisdiction.

The Stockholm Conference placed environmental problems within the remit of the United Nations and framed co-operation in this area through the lenses of prevention and not of reparation. It did so in a political context marked by Cold War tensions and, no less importantly, also by the rise of developing and newly independent countries, who opened several normative 'battlefronts' to redefine the international legal order. In the early days of global environmental governance, environmental protection was seen as the problem of developed countries, whereas the priority of developing countries was clearly on the use of their natural resources for their own economic development. Even today, such tension has not vanished. What could be called the environment–development 'equation', which in the early 1970s was diplomatically called a 'dialogue', has not been solved,[6] most probably because answers can be found only at a much more granular level, on an issue-by-issue basis.

Seen from this broader perspective, Principle 21/2 is based on two potentially competing imperatives, namely the right to exploit natural resources, itself a key achievement of the so-called 'Permanent Sovereignty' movement, and the duty (formulated as the 'responsibility') to protect the environment of other States and the global commons. Since its formulation in the Stockholm Declaration, the prevention principle has been widely taken up in both treaties and soft-law instruments, concerning different areas of international environmental law, all reaffirming the principle explicitly[7]

[5] On prevention see generally L-A Duvic-Paoli, *The Prevention Principle in International Environmental Law* (Cambridge University Press, 2018); and L-A Duvic-Paoli and JE Viñuales, 'Principle 2: Prevention' in JE Viñuales (ed), *The Rio Declaration on Environment and Development: A Commentary* (Oxford University Press, 2015) 107–38. This chapter relies upon, distils and expands the material in these and other works conducted by the authors in the last few years, which are identified here for ease of reference: JE Viñuales, 'Due Diligence in International Environmental Law: A Fine-grained Cartography' in H Krieger, A Peters and L Kreuzer (eds), *Due Diligence and Structural Change in the International Legal Order* (Oxford University Press, 2020); P-M Dupuy, G Le Moli and JE Viñuales, 'Customary International Law and the Environment' in L Rajamani and J Peel (eds), *Oxford Handbook of International Environmental Law* (2nd edn, Oxford University Press, 2020), ch 23; JE Viñuales, 'La Protección Ambiental en el Derecho Consuetudinario Internacional' (2017) 69 *Revista Española de Derecho Internacional* 71; JE Viñuales, 'The Contribution of the International Court of Justice to the Development of International Environmental Law' (2008) 32 *Fordham International Law Journal* 232.

[6] See Development and Environment: Report and Working Papers of Experts Convened by the Secretary-General of the United Nations Conference on the Human Environment, Founex, Switzerland, 4–12 June 1972 [Founex Report 1971], at iii (in the preface, Maurice Strong, the Secretary-General of Stockholm Conference on the Human Environment, noted that he regarded the report, which was one of the first attempts to reconciliate development and environmental protection, as 'a major contribution to the preparation for the Conference, and a historic turning point in the "development-environment" dialogue').

[7] See, inter alia, texts reaffirming almost *verbatim* Principle 21: Convention on the Prevention of Marine Pollution by Dumping of Wastes and Other Matter, London, 29 December 1972, in force 30 August 1975, (1972) 11 ILM 1294, preamble; Charter of Economic Rights and Duties of States, UNGA Res 3281 (XXVII) (1974), Art 30; Final Act of the Helsinki Conference on Security and Co-operation in Europe, Helsinki, 1 August 1975, (1975) 14 ILM 1292, section 5; Convention on Long-Range Transboundary Air Pollution, Geneva, 13 November 1979, in force 16 March 1983, (1979)

or implicitly.[8] However, the focus of the present chapter is not on how prevention has influenced environmental instruments but rather on its history, components, interconnections and place in the wider corpus of general international law.

Part II of this chapter discusses the processes through which the Friendly Relations Declaration and the Stockholm Declaration were drafted and the reasons why the latter played no significant role in the former. Part III examines the precedents, components and current legal recognition of the prevention principle, with reference to a growing body of jurisprudence. Part IV analyses the interconnections between prevention and a wider cluster of environmental principles and concepts. Part V offers a concluding assessment, situating prevention of environmental harm within the broader body of principles enshrined in the Friendly Relations Declaration.

II TWO SEPARATE PROCESSES

1 *Absence of the Principle from the Friendly Relations Declaration*

Environmental concerns are absent from the UN Charter. This is most likely due to the fact that they were not yet part of the international agenda in 1945. This absence and the limited attention payed to them in international circles in the 1960s explains why the prevention principle was not considered for inclusion in the Friendly Relations Declaration. The latter was conceived as a text that would contribute to the progressive development and codification of the fundamental principles found in the UN Charter.[9]

Yet, environmental issues were not completely absent from the discussions held during the drafting of the Friendly Relations Declaration. Some proposals put forward to develop the seven principles formulated therein touched upon aspects of prevention. Most prominently, the right of the State to freely dispose of its natural wealth and resources, which is the starting point of the prevention principle, was discussed under several of the core principles – non-intervention,[10] self-determination[11] and sovereign equality.[12] Some connections were quickly dismissed, such as referencing the right under the principle of non-intervention,[13] as it was considered difficult to establish when an act hinders 'the free disposition of wealth and resources and cease[s] to be merely a move in the process of free bargaining by which sovereign States endeavoured to

18 ILM 1442, preamble; Principles on Conservation and Harmonious Utilisation of Natural Resources Shared by Two or More States, UNEP Governing Council Decision, UNEP/IG12/2 (1978), Principle 3, para 1; World Charter for Nature, UNGA Res 37/7 (XXXVII) (30 October 1980), para 21(d); United Nations Convention on the Law of the Sea, Montego Bay, 10 December 1982, in force 16 November 1994, 1833 UNTS 3 [UNCLOS], Arts 192–94.

[8] The rationale of prevention can be identified in the majority of multilateral environmental agreements, such as: Convention on International Trade in Endangered Species of Wild Fauna and Flora, Washington, 3 March 1973, in force 1 July 1975, 993 UNTS 243; UNESCO Convention for the Protection of the World Cultural and Natural Heritage, Paris, 16 November 1972, in force 17 December 1975, (1972) 11 ILM 1358; Convention for the Conservation of Antarctic Seals, London, 1 June 1972, in force 11 March 1978, (1972) 11 ILM 251; Convention on the Conservation of European Wildlife and Natural Habitats, Berne, 19 September 1979, in force 1 June 1982, (1982) UKTS 56 Cmnd 8738; Convention on the Conservation of Migratory Species of Wild Animals, Bonn, 23 June 1979, in force 1 November 1983, (1980) 19 ILM 15; Convention on the Conservation of Antarctic Marine Living Resources, Canberra, 20 May 1980, in force 7 April 1982, (1980) 19 ILM 841.

[9] UNGA Res 1815 (XVII) (1962), para 1.

[10] On this principle see generally the chapter by D Tladi in this volume.

[11] On this principle see generally the chapter by MG Kohen in this volume.

[12] On this principle see generally the chapter by M Koskenniemi and V Kari in this volume.

[13] 'Report of the Special Committee on Principles of International Law concerning Friendly Relations and Co-operation among States' (16 November 1964), UN Doc A/5746, paras 278–80.

accommodate their mutual interests'.[14] But the context of discussion is telling: the main concern was to avoid any hindrance of the right to freely exploit natural resources for the sole national interest.

Free disposition of natural resources was also discussed under the right of peoples to self-determination, on the basis that 'the right to choose their political, economic and social systems include the right to develop and dispose of their natural resources'.[15] The connection between political independence (self-determination) and economic independence (permanent sovereignty) was a major issue in the international agenda of the 1960s. Yet, the effort to formulate the principle of self-determination in its political dimension was already such a challenge that little time was given to discuss the right to dispose of natural resources.

This right to freely exploit natural resources found more resonance in the discussions on the principle of sovereign equality.[16] Some representatives highlighted that it was one of the 'great achievements of the post-Charter era' and, as a result, it should be included in the Friendly Relations Declaration.[17] Yet, whereas there was a general agreement on the desirability of including such right, there was little consensus over how the provision should be worded.[18] Given that Resolution 1803 (XVII) on 'Permanent Sovereignty over Natural Resources' already 'contained a carefully worded and reasonably balanced treatment of the subject', it was eventually not considered necessary to include this right in the formulation of the Friendly Relations Declaration.[19]

Another principle with an environmental rationale that was discussed during the drafting of the Declaration was the prohibition of actions having harmful effects on other States, which was initially put forward by Ghana[20] and the then United Arab Republic.[21] Although the exact meaning of the principle remained unspecified, similar proposals also insisted on the prohibition to conduct potentially harmful 'experiments', possibly a reference to nuclear testing which was a prominent concern at the time. There was however no agreement on this proposal, which was eventually dismissed.[22] As a result, the Friendly Relations Declaration makes no explicit reference to the protection of the environment under international law and its contribution to it is only indirect (see below section IV).

2 *A Parallel Process of Consolidation*

Although the lack of explicit reference to environmental protection in the UN Charter goes a long way in explaining the absence of such references in the Friendly Relations Declaration, it is not the only reason. Other norms developed after the adoption of the Charter were mentioned either in the debates (e.g. principle of sovereignty over natural resources, as noted earlier) or in the text of the Declaration itself. Notably, principles applicable to Outer Space, which only

[14] ibid, para 280.

[15] 'Report of the Special Committee on Principles of International Law concerning Friendly Relations and Co-operation among States' (October 1969), UN Doc A/7619, para 159.

[16] Report A/5746 (n 13), paras 328–31.

[17] ibid, para 329.

[18] 'Report of the Special Committee on Principles of International Law concerning Friendly Relations and Co-operation among States' (26 September 1967), UN Doc A/6799, paras 425–29.

[19] Report A/5746 (n 13), para 280.

[20] Report A/6799 (n 18), para 415.

[21] ibid, para 413.

[22] ibid, para 438.

emerged in the 1960s,[23] are referenced in the preamble of the Friendly Relations Declaration. The absence of environmental considerations therefore results from other reasons too, including a combination of lack of sufficient interest or familiarity or perceived importance and, possibly, also the fact that, by the time the Special Committee last met in 1970, the separate process that would lead to the 1972 Stockholm Conference was only starting.[24]

At the time, awareness of the risks arising from environmental degradation was growing, fuelled by influential publications such as Rachel Carson's *Silent Spring*,[25] which unmasked the pernicious side-effects of pesticides, and the much-cited report of the Club of Rome, *The Limits to Growth*,[26] which highlighted that the Earth's supply of natural resources was limited and at risk due to economic and demographic growth. The advisors of US President Richard Nixon saw the environment as a possible platform both for domestic political purposes and for co-operation with the USSR[27] and, more generally, as a way to deflect the negative image of the United States resulting from the Viet-Nam war.[28] All these factors contributed to the realisation that an international conference was needed, whose main purpose would be:

> to serve as a practical means to encourage, and to provide guidelines for, action by Governments and international organizations designed to protect and improve the human environment and to remedy and prevent its impairment, by means of international cooperation, bearing in mind the particular importance of enabling the developing countries to forestall the occurrence of such problems.[29]

But it was too late in the day to bring such emerging considerations into a restatement of fundamental principles largely prompted by the quest of developing and newly independent States to reshape the international legal order to reflect their needs.

In fact, the Stockholm process was clearly led by the West and largely resisted by developing and newly independent countries, who saw it as a hindrance for their assertion of powers over natural resources and their claim to development. Such resistance found expression in a meeting held in Founex, near Geneva, the year preceding the Stockholm Conference[30] and, subsequently, in a highly symbolic resolution adopted by the UN General Assembly in December 1971, on the initiative of Brazil, according to which the overriding goal of international co-operation should be development.[31] In this context, it is unsurprising that the matter received no

23 See, in particular, Declaration of Legal Principles Governing the Activities of States in the Exploration and Use of Outer Space, UNGA Res 1962 (XVIII) (13 December 1963); Treaty on Principles Governing the Activities of States in the Exploration and Use of Outer Space, including the Moon and Other Celestial Bodies, New York, 19 December 1966, in force 10 October 1967, 610 UNTS 205.

24 The proposal was made on 20 May 1968 by the Swedish government to convene an 'international conference on the problems of the human environment'. The UN General Assembly adopted that same year Problems of the Human Environment, UNGA Res 2398 (XXIII) (3 December 1968). The preparatory process was spearheaded by Sweden in what came to be known in UN circles as the 'Swedish matter'.

25 R Carson, *Silent Spring* (Houghton Mifflin, 1962).

26 DH Meadows et al, *The Limits to Growth* (Universe Books, 1972).

27 K Hünemörder, 'Environmental Crisis and Soft Politics: Détente and the Global Environment, 1968–1975' in JR McNeill and C Unger (eds), *Environmental Histories of the Cold War* (Cambridge University Press, 2010) 257–76.

28 See S Macekura, *Of Limits and Growth: The Rise of Global Sustainable Development in the Twentieth Century* (Cambridge University Press, 2015) 94–133 (explaining, however, that this strategy was ill-conceived because it did not anticipate the explosive nature of the issue in the eyes of developing and newly independent countries).

29 See United Nations Conference on the Human Environment, UNGA Res 2581(XXIV) (15 December 1969), para 2.

30 Founex Report 1971 (n 6) (the opening sentence of chapter 1 of this report states '[t]he current concern with the Human Environment has arisen at a time when the energies and efforts of the developing countries are being increasingly devoted to the goal of development').

31 Development and Environment, UNGA Res 2849 (XXVI) (20 December 1971).

serious consideration within the Special Committee which drafted the Friendly Relations Declaration.

The emphasis on development matters remained a priority of developing countries. With the end of the Cold War in the early 1990s, a new window of opportunity seemed open to anchor development considerations within the fabric of international law. In the run-up to the 1992 UN Conference on Environment and Development, the 'Stockholm principle' underwent a minor but symbolically significant change. The atmosphere of the negotiations on the prevention principle in the first days is well captured by the Earth Summit Bulletin, which reported that:

> Many governments were of the view that [Principle 21 of the Stockholm Declaration] would be best suited for inclusion in the preamble. Some thought it should be restated verbatim, while others argued for greater elaboration which would take into account the important fact that UNCED, unlike Stockholm, is charged with the mandate to consider development as well as environmental problems.[32]

The prevention principle featured prominently in the different drafts.[33] Whereas some formulations introduced significant variations with respect to the language of the Stockholm formulation, others – including the one that eventually prevailed – followed such language closely with only minor variations. The negotiations of what became the Rio Declaration were largely influenced by a draft submitted by the G77+China (the 'L.20'). In this draft, the sovereign right to exploit natural resources was to be exercised pursuant to a State's environmental 'and developmental policies'. Other drafts, such as those proposed by the United States and by Nordic countries omitted any qualification of such 'right', even the one appearing in Principle 21 of the Stockholm Declaration. Eventually, the L.20 formulation prevailed and what became Principle 2 of the Rio Declaration stated that States have 'the sovereign right to exploit their own resources pursuant to their own environmental *and developmental policies*'.

The difference between Principle 21 of the Stockholm Declaration and Principle 2 of the Rio Declaration is subtle but nevertheless revealing. On the one hand, Principle 21 was reaffirmed as the cornerstone of international environmental law and was not replaced by another concept. As expressed in the preamble of the Declaration, the Rio Declaration is to be seen as a continuation of the Stockholm Declaration, and the reaffirmation of Principle 21 stresses such continuity. Yet, its inclusion in the Declaration and the focus on developmental policies strengthens the position of the first component of the principle (sovereignty over natural resources) as compared to the environmental protection components. These components are discussed in detail in section III.2.

III PREVENTION OF ENVIRONMENTAL HARM IN INTERNATIONAL LAW

1 *A Tale of Two Precedents*

1.1 *An Unexpected Source: The* Alabama *Claims Arbitration*

The 1872 *Alabama* claims arbitration has been known for providing an authoritative statement of several rules of international law and also a prominent illustration of the benefits of international

[32] 'Earth Summit Bulletin', vol 1–6, from UNCED-Prep Com IV, 8 March 1992.

[33] See 'Rio de Janeiro Charter/Declaration on Environment and Development', UN Doc A/CONF.151/PC/WG.III/L.20/Rev.1, Principle 2; Draft presented by: the United States, UN Doc A/CONF.151/PC/WG.III/L.21, Principle 5; Japan, 'Rights and Obligations', UN Doc A/CONF.151/PC/WG.III/L.22, Principle 5; Canada, UN Doc A/CONF.151/PC/WG.III/L.23, Principle 4; Australia, UN Doc A/CONF.151/PC/WG.III/L.24, Principle 5; Nordic countries, 'Earth Charter. Elements for Consideration', UN Doc A/CONF.151/PC/WG.III/L.27, Principle 7.

arbitration, even in a highly political dispute between major powers.[34] Arbitrators were called to decide, in essence, the lawfulness of the neutral conduct of the hegemon of the time (i.e. the United Kingdom), in the most destructive war of the nineteenth century, the American Civil War. But the place of this arbitration in discussions of due diligence in international environmental law has been overshadowed by references to the *Trail Smelter* arbitration, despite the attention that this question received before, during and also in the aftermath of the 1872 decision.

Overlooking the contribution of the *Alabama* arbitration to the clarification of due diligence would be a mistake, particularly in a study that aims to connect the prevention principle to its wider legal context. The question was so central in this dispute that the provision on applicable law (Article VI) stated in the Treaty of Washington (the *compromis*)[35] was one of the most contentious points in the debates between the representatives of the two countries,[36] and it expressly referred to 'due diligence' in two of the three rules explicitly formulated therein. Moreover, the three rules were taken up and debated in great detail in a variety of circles, including two sessions (Geneva 1874 and The Hague 1875) of the *Institut de Droit International*.[37] Furthermore, placed in its historical context, the symbolic relevance of the *Alabama* arbitration is higher[38] than that of the *Trail Smelter* case,[39] not least because of the political context (a possible interference by a foreign power in a civil war creating an existential threat for another), the parties (the United Kingdom and the United States), and the monetary award (one of the largest in history). Thus, the role of the *Trail Smelter* case as a precedent in discussions about the duty of due diligence must be nuanced. It is true that it specifically addressed issues that today would be seen as part and parcel of international environmental law, and that the award was much more detailed and closer to the drafting style that we nowadays use. Yet, the fact remains that the concept of due diligence as a duty of States precedes the *Trail Smelter* case, and its formulation in the *Alabama* arbitration, although there was concise, catalysed lengthy and detailed discussions by the most prominent international lawyers of the time.[40]

The definition of the duty of 'due diligence' found in Article VI of the Treaty of Washington was the result of a compromise between the more encompassing American formulation, which spoke of 'active diligence' and regarded such duty as part of international law, and the narrower British formulation, which spoke of 'reasonable care' and only assented to the expression 'due diligence' as a rule arising from treaty, not general international law. The final formulation stated that:

> A neutral Government is bound –
>
> First, to use due diligence to prevent the fitting out, arming, or equipping, within its jurisdiction, of any vessel which it has a reasonable ground to believe is intended to cruise or to carry on war against a Power with which it is at peace; and also to use like diligence to prevent the departure from its jurisdiction of any vessel intended to cruise or carry on war as above, such vessel having been specially adapted, in whole or in part, within such jurisdiction, to warlike use.

[34] This section follows and expands Viñuales, 'Due Diligence in International Environmental Law' (n 5).
[35] Reproduced in JB Moore, *History and Digest of the International Arbitrations to which the United States has been a Party*, vol 1 (Government Printing Office, 1898) 547–53.
[36] ibid 541–44.
[37] *Annuaire de l'Institut de Droit International*, vol 1 (Durand & Pedone-Lauriel, 1877), further discussed in Moore, *History and Digest* (n 35) 671 et seq.
[38] Moore, *History and Digest*, vol I, 652–3.
[39] *Trail Smelter Arbitration*, RIAA, vol III, 1905–82.
[40] See Moore, *History and Digest* (n 35) 672–74.

> Secondly, not to permit or suffer either belligerent to make use of its ports or waters as the base of naval operations against the other, or for the purpose of the renewal or augmentation of military supplies or arms, or the recruitment of men.
>
> Thirdly, to exercise due diligence in its own ports and waters, and, as to all persons within its jurisdiction, to prevent any violation of the foregoing obligations and duties.

The provision expressly mentioned the United Kingdom's position that such rules could not be said to be the principles of international law in force at the time the disputed acts/omissions had taken place. But both parties 'agree[d] to observe these rules as between themselves in the future, and to bring them to the knowledge of other maritime powers, and to invite them to accede to them'.[41] The latter point would raise significant – and analytically useful – controversy in subsequent years.

During the debates, counsel for the United States argued, by reference to the opinions of Hautefeuille, Bluntschli, Rolyn-Jacquemin, Ortolan, Pierantoni, Martens, De Cussy, Phillimore and Heffter, that such rules were indeed a reflection of positive international law and, interestingly, he interpreted the degree of diligence as:

> a diligence proportioned to the magnitude of the subject and to the dignity and strength of the power which is to exercise it . . . a diligence that shall in like manner deter designing men from committing acts of war upon the soil of the neutral against its will . . . No diligence short of this would be 'due'; that is, *commensurate with the emergency or with the magnitude of the results of negligence*.[42]

In his counter-argument, counsel for the United Kingdom advanced a narrower conception of due diligence, less dependent on the risk and more on a sort of national treatment or, in other words, diligence measured by the standards applied by a State for its own affairs:

> It would commonly, however, be unreasonable and impracticable to require that it [the level of due diligence] should exceed that which the governments of civilized states are accustomed to employ in matters concerning their own security or that of their own citizens.[43]

The United Kingdom also argued that the burden of proof of lack of due diligence was borne by the United States, and that the standard could only be satisfied if 'sustained on strong and solid grounds' because '[t]he general assumption that such powers were exercised with good faith and reasonable care ought to subsist until it had been displaced by proof to the contrary'.[44] The United States had the burden of showing, according to this line of argument, 'a failure to use, for the prevention of an act which the government was bound to endeavour to prevent, such care as governments ordinarily employ in their domestic concerns, and may reasonably be expected to exert in matters of international interest and obligation'.[45]

The Arbitration Court found, with different majorities depending on the vessels at stake, that the United Kingdom had breached these duties in most, but not all, cases.[46] In its reasoning, the Court made a number of important considerations that are still relevant today, including for action/inaction relating to environmental protection. The first consideration was that:

[41] ibid 550.
[42] ibid 572–73 (italics in original).
[43] ibid 600.
[44] ibid 610.
[45] ibid.
[46] See *Alabama claims of the United States of America against Great Britain*, RIAA, vol. XXIX, 125–34 [*Alabama*].

> the 'due diligence' referred to in the first and third of the said rules [Article VI of the *compromis*] ought to be exercised by neutral governments in exact proportion to the risks to which either of the belligerents may be exposed, from a failure to fulfil the obligations of neutrality on their part.[47]

In casu, the Court noted that the circumstances, namely the eventuality that the vessels constructed in the United Kingdom be used by the Confederates in their fight against the Union, were such that the United Kingdom was held to the highest level of diligence or, in the words of the Court, 'all possible solicitude for the observance of the rights and duties involved in the proclamation of neutrality'.[48] This observation is important for at least three reasons. First, it links due diligence to 'risk', which is different from actual damage. Second, the degree of diligence is not static; it may be higher or lower depending on the level of risk (no sliding scale of diligence is yet envisaged on the basis of a State's capabilities and resources, although this was argued by counsel for the United States). Third, the duty of due diligence, however demanding (in this case the Court set the bar at the highest 'possible solicitude'), does not amount to strict liability. In fact, the Court found that in some specific cases, the United Kingdom had met the requirements of due diligence, despite the occurrence of undesirable results. None of these points is obvious, even today, and they are all significant for international environmental law as it presently operates.

A second consideration is the significance of representations by the aggrieved State (the United States representative had informed the government of the United Kingdom that vessels were being built for possible use in the civil war), which should have triggered 'in due time' at least some 'effective' measures of prevention. Thus, action by a possibly aggrieved State (a State at risk), although not a requirement, may catalyse the duty of due diligence or, more specifically, it may be instrumental in setting at the very least the time for action.

A third consideration is the fact that subsequent measures could have cured the initial negligence, although the United Kingdom failed to take such subsequent action or did so in a manner 'so imperfect as to lead to no result, and therefore cannot be considered sufficient to release Great Britain from the responsibility already incurred'.[49] The latter point suggests that the duty of due diligence is a continuous rather than a discreet one. Due diligence must be constantly exercised. This is important, for example, in the requirement for what we would call today continuous 'monitoring' of the situation.[50]

As a fourth and final consideration, the formulation of the due-diligence rule in Article VI makes it clear that failure to effectively control the acts of 'all persons within its jurisdiction' may be a breach of the duty. This simple point is significant because it clearly covers the actions of private persons, and it makes due diligence relevant for extraterritorial situations, much like in today's discussions of human rights extraterritoriality and their link to environmental principles.[51]

[47] ibid 129.

[48] ibid 130.

[49] ibid 130.

[50] Draft Articles on the Prevention of Transboundary Harm from Hazardous Activities, 12 December 2001, UNGA Res 56/82, UN Doc A/RES/56/82 [ILC Prevention Articles], commentary to Art 12, para 2; *Gabčíkovo-Nagymaros Project (Hungary v Slovakia)*, Judgment, ICJ Reports 1997, 7, paras 112, 140; *Pulp Mills on the River Uruguay (Argentina v Uruguay)*, Judgment, ICJ Reports 2010, 14, paras 197 and 204.

[51] See the account of extraterritoriality in JE Viñuales, 'A Human Rights Approach to Extraterritorial Environmental Protection? An Assessment' in N Bhuta (ed), *The Frontiers of Human Rights: Extraterritoriality and its Challenges* (Oxford University Press, 2016) 177–221, 218–19, followed by the Inter-American Court of Human Rights in *Advisory Opinion OC-23/17 of 15 November 2017, requested by the Republic of Colombia: Environment and Human Rights (State*

The duty of due diligence therefore finds a solid basis in the *Alabama* claims arbitration. The contribution of the latter to the clarification of this duty thus merits a place in the storyline and warrants comparison with the *Trail Smelter* case.

1.2 *From the* Alabama *to the* Trail Smelter

The *Alabama* precedent was invoked before the *Trail Smelter* tribunal and duly noted by it.[52] The latter recognised the *Alabama* decision as the starting point of the relevant line of precedents, although it eventually relied on the domestic practice of Switzerland and the United States, as federal systems having faced disputes among 'quasi-sovereign' entities. This was possible because Article VI of the *compromis* specifically required the tribunal to decide the dispute on the basis of 'the law and practice followed in dealing with cognate questions in the United States of America as well as international law and practice' and to 'give consideration to the desire of the high contracting parties to reach a solution just to all parties concerned'.

The tribunal premised its entire analysis of the latter point on the proposition that there was no need to decide whether the solution to the dispute would be governed by US law or by international law because 'the law followed in the United States in dealing with the quasi-sovereign rights of the States of the Union, in the matter of air pollution, whilst more definite, is in conformity with the general rules of international law'.[53] This assertion remained, however, largely unproven as the tribunal itself acknowledged that no international tribunal had, to its knowledge, decided matters cognate to the dispute at hand.[54] The famous and oft-quoted statement of the rule to be applied rests, hence, on an unclear basis:

> The Tribunal, therefore, finds that the *above decisions, taken as a whole*, constitute an adequate basis for its conclusions, namely, that, under the principles of international law, as well as of the law of the United States, no State has the right to use or permit the use of its territory in such a manner as to cause injury by fumes in or to the territory of another or the properties or persons therein, when the case is of serious consequence and the injury is established by clear and convincing evidence.[55]

If, among 'the above decisions, taken as a whole', one is to include international decisions, the only explicitly identified precedent of unquestionable authority is indeed the *Alabama* decision. On this point, there is clear convergence between the two decisions.

Further convergence can be found in that States may be responsible for allowing private parties to use their territory in harmful ways, irrespective of any attribution inquiry. The relevant conduct of the State is indeed its own inaction, not the action of the private person. Two other points of convergence are the reference to the notifications by the aggrieved State, although the *Trail Smelter* decision does not attach any significant relevance to this point, and, much more importantly, the continuous character of the due-diligence duty, which is formulated in the *Trail Smelter* decision in terms that are so advanced[56] that they would be progressive even for an

obligations in relation to the environment within the framework of the protection and guarantee of the rights to life and to personal integrity – interpretation and scope of Articles 4.1 and 5.1 in relation with Articles 1.1 and 2 of the American Convention on Human Rights) [*ICtHR Advisory Opinion*], para 102.

[52] *Trail Smelter* (n 39) 1963.

[53] ibid.

[54] ibid.

[55] ibid 1965 (italics added).

[56] The tribunal indeed set up a provisional regulatory regime and then a permanent one to be implemented by Canada, with the explicit possibility of adjusting the system if the circumstances (or their scientific understanding) changes. See ibid, part IV, 1966 et seq.

international tribunal deciding a dispute today. The drawback is that the content of due diligence is not spelt out in general terms and remains embedded in, indeed consubstantial to, the technical specifications provided by the tribunal and cannot be detached from them.

But there is also some divergence between the two decisions and, in that, the *Trail Smelter* award, despite its much greater length and detail, provides a more limited statement of the due-diligence duty. First, unlike the *Alabama* decision, the *Trail Smelter* award makes no explicit reference to the possibility of curing a breach through subsequent action. The attempts of the smelter to manage the initial complaints from farmers in Washington are mentioned as part of the factual record, but the award does not derive any legal principle from them. Second, and more significantly, the rule stated in *Trail Smelter* concerns injury that has actually materialised in the form of damage, and not any damage but 'material' damage.[57] Thus, the regime set out in the award, which is the embodiment of the diligence due by Canada in this case, is aimed only at preventing 'material' damage, not any damage. By contrast, the *Alabama* rule is not confined to damage and encompasses 'risk'. That was a result of the circumstances of the case, which were so serious as to require 'all possible solicitude' from the UK. But a similar argument can be made for ultra-hazardous activities such as the generation of nuclear energy or the production of highly toxic substances, in that due diligence is not only 'required' from the State where the operations take place but it is also 'actionable' – that is, it can be legally and specifically demanded, by potentially affected States, irrespective of the occurrence of damage. Such is the rule in Article 3 of the 2001 Articles on Prevention drafted by the International Law Commission (ILC): 'the State of origin shall take all appropriate measures to prevent significant transboundary harm or at any event to minimize the risk thereof'. The commentary of this provision expressly relies on the *Alabama* case.[58]

The basic conclusion to be drawn from the foregoing paragraphs is that both the *Alabama* arbitration and the *Trail Smelter* case must be taken into account to understand the foundations of the prevention principle in relation to environmental harm.

2 *The Components of Principle 21/2*

2.1 *Overview*

The discussion of the main components of the prevention principle[59] can take, as a starting point, the formulation in Principle 2 of the Rio Declaration, which restates Principle 21 of the Stockholm Declaration, with the variation flagged earlier in this chapter:

> States have, in accordance with the Charter of the United Nations and the principles of international law, the sovereign right to exploit their own resources pursuant to their own environmental and developmental policies, and the responsibility to ensure that activities within their jurisdiction or control do not cause damage to the environment of other States or of areas beyond the limits of national jurisdiction.

This formulation includes three main components of Principle 21/2, namely the *sovereign right of States* to exploit their natural resources for their own purposes, the duty not to cause harm to the environment of other States ('no harm') and the duty not to cause harm to the *environment*

[57] ibid 1980 (italics added).

[58] ILC Prevention Articles (n 50), commentary to Art 3, para 9.

[59] This section follows and expands Duvic-Paoli and Viñuales, 'Principle 2: Prevention' (n 5); Duvic-Paoli, *The Prevention Principle in International Environmental Law* (n 5); and Dupuy, Le Moli and Viñuales, 'Customary International Law and the Environment' (n 5).

beyond national jurisdiction. Importantly, these three components are preceded by a sub-sentence ('in accordance with the Charter of the United Nations and the principles of international law'), which qualifies the three components. This sub-sentence is of particular significance for present purposes because it connects the prevention principle, in its 1972 formulation, to the 'principles of international law' which had been restated shortly before, with the adoption in 1970 of the Friendly Relations Declaration.

However, these four components are insufficient to characterise the scope and operation of the prevention principle. Two additional components of the customary norm are indeed omitted, namely the characterisation of the harm as 'significant' and the requirement to minimise 'risk' of significant harm, which implies that the principle may be breached even in the absence of harm. These two components are found in the Draft Articles on Prevention adopted in 2001 by the ILC.[60] Yet, the Draft Articles have their own shortcomings, including a narrow spatial scope limited to 'transboundary' harm,[61] which confines them to the 'no harm' logic, and a potentially confusing sequence between prevention and two of its procedural expressions, namely the duty to conduct an environmental impact assessment (EIA) and the duty to co-operate in a transboundary context, specifically to notify and consult.[62]

Even when combined, Principle 21/2 and the Draft Articles remain unclear regarding three key aspects of the prevention principle in customary international law, which have been fleshed out in the case law. One is its *spatial scope of application* irrespective of the powers exercised by a State over a given area, which could include, in addition to the environment in other States and the environment beyond national jurisdiction, also a State's own territory or areas where it exercises sovereign powers over the exploitation of natural resources.[63] The second is the *level of diligence* that must be displayed by the State of origin. Such level depends on three main criteria, namely the gravity of the outcome that may result from negligence,[64] the capabilities of the State of origin[65] and the historical moment at which diligence is assessed.[66] The latter is noteworthy because it is a proxy for what can reasonably be required under the scientific and technological knowledge prevailing at a given point in time. That, in turn, provides a direct entry point into the content of the customary norm to a range of technical regulations, often of a

[60] ILC Prevention Articles (n 50), Arts 2(a) and 3.

[61] ibid, Art 2(c).

[62] ibid, Arts 7 and 8, applied in *Certain Activities Carried Out by Nicaragua in the Border Area (Costa Rica v Nicaragua) and Construction of a Road in Costa Rica along the San Juan River (Nicaragua v Costa Rica)*, Judgment, ICJ Reports 2015, 665, para 104.

[63] See *Dispute Concerning Delimitation of the Maritime Boundary between Ghana and Côte d'Ivoire in the Atlantic Ocean*, Provisional Measures, ITLOS Case No 23, Order of 25 April 2015, paras 68–73; *Request for an Advisory Opinion Submitted by the Sub-Regional Fisheries Commission (SRFC)*, Advisory Opinion of 2 April 2015, ITLOS Case No 21, paras 111, 120; *In the matter of the South China Sea Arbitration before and Arbitral Tribunal constituted under Annex VII of the United Nations Convention on the Law of the Sea*, Case No 2013–19, Award, Perm Ct Arb, 12 July 2016, para 927; *Dispute Concerning Coastal State Rights in the Black Sea, Sea of Azov, and Kerch Strait (Ukraine v Russian Federation)*, PCA Case No 2017-06, Award concerning the preliminary objections of the Russian Federation (21 February 2020), para 295.

[64] See *Alabama* (n 46) 129; *Responsibilities and obligations of States sponsoring persons and entities with respect to activities in the Area*, Advisory Opinion of 1 February 2011, ITLOS Case No 17 [*Responsibilities in the Area*], para 117. This is acknowledged in the commentary to the ILC Prevention Articles, when it is stated that 'degree of care required is proportional to the degree of risk involved in the business', ILC Prevention Articles (n 50), commentary to Art 3, para 18.

[65] This is only partially admitted in order to avoid important loopholes in the due-diligence system. See *Responsibilities in the Area* (n 64), paras 158–9 (where the Chamber only admitted the possibility that the requirement to adopt precautionary measures may be graduated according to the capabilities of States). The commentary to the ILC Articles also reflects this criterion, ILC Prevention Articles (n 50), commentary to Art 3, para 13.

[66] *Responsibilities in the Area* (n 64), para 117.

soft-law nature, that are generally referred to as 'standards'. The third aspect highlights the requirement to exercise due diligence not only when adopting suitable regulations to prevent environmental harm but also to ensure that they are *effectively implemented*.[67] However, diligence in ensuring implementation does not mean that the mere occurrence of harm is sufficient for the prevention principle to be breached. In the absence of fault, there is no breach. This conclusion was reached in the *Alabama* arbitration in connection with some specific vessels[68] as well as, in 2016, in the *South China Sea Arbitration*, with respect to some specific instances of environmental damage.[69]

All these components and aspects of prevention of environmental harm make it a complex principle. In what follows, the examination of the principle is organised around the four main components, but the analysis integrates the other aspects introduced here.

2.2 *The Prevention of Environmental Harm 'in Accordance with The Charter of the United Nations and the Principles of International Law'*

In discussions of the prevention principle, the sub-sentence 'in accordance with the Charter of the United Nations and the principles of international law' has been neglected. This sub-sentence qualifies both the right and the duty (the 'responsibility') formulated in Principle 21/2. Looking at the history of the drafting of Stockholm Principle 21, the inclusion of the sub-sentence can be traced back to an initial proposal made by UN Secretary-General U Thant. As part of the preparatory work of the Stockholm Conference, the Secretary-General sent a questionnaire to Member States to seek their views about the potential format and content of a Declaration to be adopted at the Conference.[70]

In this questionnaire, which was accompanied by an explanatory note, the UN Charter is mentioned twice. First, the Secretary-General suggested that the following reference could be included in the preamble:

> *in accordance with the Charter of the United Nations*, all Member States have pledged themselves to take joint and separate action for the achievement of solutions, inter alia, of international economic, social health and related problems.[71]

Second, and more directly related to the final wording of what became known as the 'Stockholm Principle', the report proposed a list of principles that would be applicable with regard to other States and which read as follows:

> States should be guided by the principle of co-operation and mutual assistance and should conduct all their activities related to environmental problems with due regard to the corresponding interests of other States, *in accordance with international law, including the Charter of the United Nations*, with particular reference to ... the principle that States are internationally responsible for harm caused by them or their citizens to environmental resources shared with

[67] *Pulp Mills* (n 50), para 197; *Responsibilities in the Area* (n 64), paras 115 and 239; ILC Prevention Articles (n 50), commentary to Art 3, para 10.
[68] *Alabama* (n 46) 132 (discussion relating to the vessel 'Retribution').
[69] *South China Sea Arbitration* (n 63), paras 972–75; see further *Pulp Mills* (n 50), para 187; *Responsibilities in the Area* (n 64), para 110; ILC Prevention Articles (n 50), commentary to Art 3, para 7.
[70] 'Replies to questionnaire of 21 December 1970 circulated by the Secretary-General of the Conference in Connexion with the Preparation of a Draft Declaration on the Human Environment', [Replies to questionnaire], Annex I, A/CONF.48/PC/WG.1/CRP.4 (1 April 1971) [Replies to questionnaire, Annex I].
[71] Replies to questionnaire, Annex I (n 70) 8 (emphasis added).

> other States and for ensuring that national activities are carried out in conformity with the principles set forth in the present Declaration.[72]

This proposal comes close, in its broad components, to the final formulation of Principle 21.

The fact that a reference to international law and the UN Charter was kept in the final formulation is noteworthy because the proposals subsequently made by States during the drafting of the Stockholm Declaration did not refer to international law and/or the UN Charter. Instead, they concentrated on the core message of sovereignty over natural resources and responsibility to avoid environmental harm. Yet, the Intergovernmental Working Group (IWG) set up by the Preparatory Committee to draft the Declaration built on the Secretary-General's proposal and initially suggested the inclusion of a Principle 6 that would read as follows:

> Each State has the responsibility, *in accordance with the Charter of the United Nations and consistent with the principles of international law*, to conduct its activities so as not to cause damage to the environment of other States, or to the environment of areas beyond the limits of national jurisdiction.[73]

The formulations of the principles proposed by the IWG were contested during the first substantive session of the Group. With regard to prevention, the main bone of contention was about how to include and formulate the concept of sovereignty over natural resources. However, little disagreement was expressed in relation to Principle 6[74] and no comments were made in relation to the sub-sentences. At a second working session, the major change in Principle 6 (which subsequently became Principle 21) was to combine the concept of sovereignty over natural resources with the responsibility of the State not to cause transboundary harm. The reference to the UN Charter and the principles of international law was retained. Notably, proposals made by States thereafter kept the reference to the Charter and the principles of international law,[75] which thus made its way to the final wording of Principle 21.

The addition of the sub-sentence is significant. It embeds the Stockholm principle into the wider general international law framework and avoids the risk that prevention may be framed as a *lex specialis* principle, which might collide with general international rules. Instead, the prevention principle needs to be interpreted systemically in light of the UN Charter and 'principles of international law'. Although there may be some uncertainty as to which norms would fall under the category of 'principles of international law', the seven core principles formulated in the Friendly Relations Declaration are certainly part of it, as emphasised in the last paragraph of the 'General Part' of this Declaration.

[72] Replies to questionnaire, Annex I (n 70), 14 (emphasis added).

[73] Report of the Preparatory Committee, Third Session' (14 June 1971) UN Doc A/CONF.48/PC.12 (emphasis added).

[74] See 'Annex II: Report of the Rapporteur on reservations and observations on the draft preamble and fundamental principles expressed by members of the Intergovernmental Working Group' A/CONF.48/PC.12, at 8 on comments on Principle 6.

[75] See PC, IWG, second session, A/CONF.48/PC/WG.1(II)/CRP.4 (5 January 1972), 'Draft principles for inclusion in the Declaration on the Human Environment submitted by the delegation of Canada', para 1; PC, IWG, second session, A/CONF.48/PC/WG.1(II)/CRP.5 (5 January 1972), 'Working Paper submitted by the Netherlands Delegation to the Intergovernmental Working Group on the Declaration on the Human Environment', A/CONF.48/PC/WG.1 (II)/CRP.5 (5 January 1972), para 14; PC, IWG, second session, A/CONF.48/PC/WG.1(II)/CRP.6 (5 January 1972), para 8; PC, IWG, A/CONF.48/PC/WG.1(II)/CRP.9 (10 January 1972), 'Australia: Working paper', para 9.

2.3 *Sovereign Right to Exploit Their Own Resources*

The principle of permanent sovereignty over natural resources is not an environmental concept at its core but it provides the backdrop of prevention because it affirms legal powers over natural resources. As noted earlier in this chapter, during the negotiations of the text of the Friendly Relations Declaration, this principle was the main environment-related concern raised, in particular in connection with the principle of sovereign equality of States.[76] Its subsequent adaptation to the environmental sphere has shaped the prevention principle in such a way as to create a dynamic balance between sovereignty and environmental protection.

The principle itself emerged from the affirmation of the rights to self-determination of colonial peoples and to economic development of newly independent States. For peoples under colonial rule, the main objective was to protect and preserve their natural resources from the colonial power. Once a right to self-determination leading to independence had been recognised, newly independent States further sought to ensure their economic emancipation against encroachments by foreign companies exploiting their resources. The concept of permanent sovereignty over natural resources emerged to secure both claims. Resolution 523 (VI) was the first resolution mentioning the States' 'right to determine freely the use of their natural resources'. It did not refer to permanent sovereignty over natural resources, nor did it characterise the principle as permanent and inalienable.[77] Resolution 626 (VII) confirmed that 'the right of peoples freely to use and exploit their natural wealth and resources is inherent in their sovereignty'.[78] Resolution 1314 (XIII) recognised that the concept was a 'basic constituent of the right to self-determination'.[79] Finally, the work culminated in the adoption of Resolution 1803 (XVII) on 'Permanent Sovereignty over Natural Resources'.[80]

Although the emphasis of this resolution is on the use of 'natural resources' (not on the protection of the 'environment'), the exercise of sovereignty is not unbridled, because it 'must be exercised in the interest of their national development and of the well-being of the people of the state concerned'.[81] Such limitations were further specified by the inclusion of a reference to sovereignty over natural resources in Principle 21 of the Stockholm Declaration with the explicit qualification that it must not be exercised to the detriment of the environment. At the same moment, however, the UN General Assembly further strengthened the first component of the principle by emphasising, in Resolution 3281 (XXVII), the right of States to use their natural resources as they see fit.[82]

The principle of sovereignty over natural resources is at the centre of Principle 2, perhaps to a greater extent than it was for Principle 21, since it is the developmental dimension of the principle that received further support at the Rio Summit. Developing countries, fearing that environmental protection would be used as an argument to curtail their development efforts, sought to ensure that environmental 'and developmental' policies remain in the hands of States.[83] They felt that if the classical concept of sovereignty was 'no longer beneficial to

[76] Report A/5746 (n 13), paras 328–31.
[77] UNGA Res 523 (VI) (12 January 1952).
[78] UNGA Res 626 (VII) (21 December 1952).
[79] UNGA Res 1314 (XIII) (12 December 1958).
[80] UNGA Res 1803 (XVII) (14 December 1962).
[81] UNGA Res 1803 (XVII), para 1.
[82] Charter of Economic Rights and Duties of States (n 7), Art 2(1).
[83] MA Bekhechi, 'Le Droit international à l'épreuve du développement durable. Quelques réflexions à propos de la Déclaration de Rio sur l'environnement et le développement' (1993) *Hague Yearbook of International Law* 59, 68.

developed countries it must now be beneficial to [developing countries]'[84] to justify why environmental protection should not be prioritised over economic development.

Today, the principle of sovereignty over natural resources remains at the heart of the prevention principle. Most often, it is invoked to limit the demands of environmental protection 'when states wish to resist international pressure to protect their natural resources from overuse and depletion'.[85] Yet, sovereignty and environmental protection are not necessarily competing considerations. In recent years, attempts have been made to reconceptualise sovereignty in 'functional' terms or as powers held in trust for the benefit of present and future generations.[86]

2.4 No Harm

The prohibition against causing harm to the environment of other States is widely recognised in international law. It pre-dates the Stockholm Conference and is based on the recognition of the limits of territorial sovereignty: a State can enjoy sovereignty over natural resources only inasmuch as it does not restrict the sovereignty of other States by causing transboundary harm.

Particularly well developed in early watercourse law,[87] the 'no harm' rule was recognised in 1941 in the *Trail Smelter* arbitration,[88] as discussed earlier. This approach was later confirmed by the International Court of Justice (ICJ) in the *Corfu Channel* case, where the Court noted that States have the 'obligation not to allow knowingly its territory to be used for acts contrary to the rights of other states'.[89] Such approach, focusing on an obligation of good neighbourliness, was further confirmed in the *Lac Lanoux* arbitration in which the arbitral tribunal affirmed that a State is entitled to exercise its rights so long as it does not 'ignore' the interests of the neighbouring State.[90]

Although the existence of an obligation not to cause harm to the territory of another State is not a matter of controversy, the definition of 'transboundary damage' and the 'threshold' that triggers the violation of the obligation of prevention is disputed. It is generally considered that not any environmental damage is prohibited, but only 'significant' environmental harm, a threshold recognised in treaty law,[91] case law[92] and in the ILC Draft Articles on

[84] I Porras, 'The Rio Declaration: A New Basis for International Co-Operation' (1992) 1 *Review of European Community & International Environmental Law* 245–53, 251.

[85] FX Perrez, *Cooperative Sovereignty: From Independence to Interdependence in the Structure of International Environmental Law* (Kluwer, 2000) 95.

[86] See in particular ibid 28 (on 'positive sovereignty'); F Francioni, 'The Private Sector and the Challenge of Implementation' in P-M Dupuy and JE Viñuales (eds), *Harnessing Foreign Investment to Promote Environmental Protection: Incentives and Safeguards* (Cambridge University Press, 2013) 30 (on 'functional sovereignty').

[87] See in particular the resolution of the Institut de Droit International, 'International Regulation regarding the Use of International Watercourses for Purposes other than Navigation', Session of Madrid, 1911.

[88] *Trail Smelter* (n 39) 1965.

[89] *Corfu Channel (United Kingdom/Albania)*, ICJ Reports 1949, 4, 22.

[90] *Lac Lanoux Arbitration (France v Spain)* (1957) 24 ILR 101, 140.

[91] See, inter alia, Convention for the Protection of the Ozone Layer, Vienna, 22 March 1985, in force 22 September 1988, (1985) 26 ILM 1529, Art 1(2); Convention on the Regulation of Antarctic Mineral Resource Activities, Wellington, 2 June 1988, not in force, (1988) 27 ILM 868, Art 4(2); Convention on Environmental Impact Assessment in a Transboundary Context, Espoo, 25 February 1991, in force 10 September 1997, (1991) 30 ILM 802, Art 2(1)–(2); Convention on the Protection and Use of Transboundary Watercourses and International Lakes, Helsinki, 17 March 1992, in force 6 October 1996, (1992) 31 ILM 1312, Art 1(2); United Nations Framework Convention on Climate Change, New York, 9 May 1992, in force 24 March 1994, 1771 UNTS 107, Art 1(1); Convention on Biological Diversity, Nairobi, 22 May 1992, in force 29 December 1993, (1992) 31 ILM 822, Art 14(1)(a); and Convention on the Law of the Non-navigational Uses of International Watercourses, New York, 21 May 1997, in force 17 August 2014, (1997) 36 ILM 700 [1997 New York Convention], Art 7.

[92] See esp *Iron Rhine Railway (Belgium v Netherlands)*, Permanent Court of Arbitration, (2005) 27 RIAA 35, para 222; *Pulp Mills* (n 50), para 101; *Indus Waters Kishenganga Arbitration (Pakistan v India)*, Partial Award, Perm Ct Arb,

Prevention.[93] The latter define the 'risk of causing significant transboundary harm' as including 'risks taking the form of a high probability of causing significant transboundary harm and a low probability of causing disastrous transboundary harm'.[94] The commentaries to the ILC Articles additionally note that:

> [t]he term 'significant' is not without ambiguity and a determination has to be made in each specific case. It involves more factual considerations than legal determination. It is to be understood that 'significant' is something more than 'detectable' but need not be at the level of 'serious' or 'substantial'.[95]

It remains that the determination of whether the prohibition applies is very much dependent on the circumstances. In addition, the significant harm threshold must address the important issue of cumulative harm, namely low-impact damage that accumulates over time and creates significant harm, which is particularly relevant in the climate change context.

The significance of harm is also defined in relation to its probability. This means that prevention can apply at different temporal stages, depending on when the magnitude–likelihood matrix is triggered. The ILC Prevention Articles are therefore concerned with long-term and short-term risks, including environmental emergencies,[96] as well as with mitigating harm that has already occurred.[97] They acknowledge that prevention is not 'a one-time effort but requires continuous effort' of harm avoidance, reduction and elimination.[98] Yet, they do not go as far as adopting a principle of rectification at source[99] that would express the anticipatory and environmental rationales of prevention in full by recognising that harm should be avoided as close as possible to the source of creation. The 'no harm' rule is concerned with the end result (harm avoidance) and gives States enough policy space to decide at which stage in the process of harm creation preventive action should take place.

Aside from the 'significance' of the harm, another important point concerns its 'nature'. Article 2(b) of the ILC Prevention Articles define 'harm' as 'harm caused to persons, property or the environment'. This definition must be read in the light of Article 1, which limits the scope of the prevention duty in the ILC Prevention Articles to 'physical consequences'. It therefore does not cover 'transboundary harm which may be caused by State policies in monetary, socio-economic or similar fields'.[100] This limitation of the nature of harm is explained in the commentary as an attempt to keep the codification work within manageable bounds.[101] This clarification suggests that the customary prevention principle is not equally limited. The distinction is not a purely academic point, as it is relevant to assess whether policies that restrict access to low-carbon technology in other countries or sanctions that force affected communities to behave in an environmentally adverse manner may come under the remit of the prevention principle.

18 February 2013, para 451, and Final Award (20 December 2013), para 112. Although there is currently a consensus on the 'significant' threshold, the earlier jurisprudence had dealt with other thresholds: see *Trail Smelter* (n 39), which used the words 'serious consequence[s]' (at 716); and *Lac Lanoux* (n 90), in which the tribunal highlighted the prohibition to 'seriously' prejudice a neighbouring State (at 129).

93 ILC Prevention Articles (n 50), Art 1.

94 ibid, Art 2(a).

95 ibid, commentary to Art 2, para 4.

96 ILC, 'Draft Articles on Prevention of Transboundary Harm', commentary to Art 17, para 2.

97 *Iron Rhine* (n 92), para 59; *Indus Waters Kishenganga* (n 92), Final Award, para 112.

98 ILC Prevention Articles (n 50), commentary to Art 12, para 2.

99 Treaty on the Functioning of the European Union, Lisbon, 13 December 2007, OJ C 83 (30 March 2010), Art 191(2).

100 ILC Prevention Articles (n 50), commentary to Art 1, para 16.

101 ibid, commentary to Art 1, para 16.

2.5 *Protection of the Environment beyond National Jurisdiction*

The third component of Principle 21/2 is the prohibition against causing damage to the environment beyond national jurisdiction. By moving beyond the transboundary approach, Principle 21/2 calls for a redefinition of international law as it was originally conceived; that is, with a focus on the 'State' and its territorial sovereignty. Indeed, the obligation not to cause harm to the environment beyond national jurisdiction changes the perspective of the entire prevention principle: the State is not only required to prevent transboundary harm in order to respect the sovereignty of other States but is also obliged to protect the environment as such, including those areas such as the global commons which have no connection to State sovereignty. This last component distinguishes prevention from 'no harm' by adopting a non-spatial approach to environmental protection.

The third component of prevention finds expression in provisions creating an obligation of environmental protection applicable to areas beyond the national jurisdiction of States, such as the high seas,[102] international air space[103] or the Antarctic.[104] Implementation and enforcement challenges arising from such non-reciprocal obligations have led some commentators to express scepticism regarding the applicability of prevention in areas beyond national jurisdiction.[105] Yet, judicial pronouncements have confirmed such extension[106] and ongoing initiatives aim to specify and strengthen due-diligence duties in areas beyond national jurisdiction.[107] The third component of Principle 21/2 envisages the global commons by contrast to areas under State jurisdiction. However, certain references to prevention have been formulated from an a-territorial perspective. For instance, Article 192 of the 1982 United Nations Convention on the Law of the Sea (UNCLOS) creates a general obligation of environmental protection by providing that 'States have the obligation to protect and preserve the marine environment.'[108] A similar obligation is found in the 1997 United Nations Convention on the Law of the Non-Navigational Uses of International Watercourses, which not only refers to an obligation not to cause harm[109] but also to a broader obligation to protect the ecosystems of international watercourses: '[w]atercourse States shall, individually and, where appropriate, jointly, protect and preserve the ecosystems of international watercourses'.[110] Such provisions, and others referring to the protection of ecosystems or nature in general,[111] can be seen as an extension of

[102] Arts 116–18 UNCLOS (on conservation and management of the living resources of the high seas) and Art 192 (on a general obligation to protect and preserve the marine environment).

[103] The right to take environmental measures to protect the international air space was recognised in *Air Transport Association of America and Others* v *Secretary of State for Energy and Climate Change, Judgment of the Court*, C-366/10, Court of Justice of the European Union, Grand Chamber (21 December 2011).

[104] Protocol on Environmental Protection to the Antarctic Treaty, Madrid, 4 October 1991, in force 14 January 1998, (1991) 30 ILM 1461, Art 2.

[105] See eg A Zahar, 'Mediated versus Cumulative Environmental Damage and the International Law Association's Legal Principles on Climate Change' (2014) 4 *Climate Law* 217.

[106] *Legality of the Threat or Use of Nuclear Weapons*, Advisory Opinion, ICJ Reports 1996, 226, para 29; *Responsibilities in the Area* (n 64), paras 145–48.

[107] ILC, 'Texts and titles of draft guidelines and preamble adopted by the Drafting Committee on first reading' (2018) UN Doc A/CN.4/L.909, guideline 3; 'Draft text of an agreement under the United Nations Convention on the Law of the Sea on the conservation and sustainable use of marine biological diversity of areas beyond national jurisdiction: Note by the President', A/CONF.232/2019/6 (17 May 2019), Part IV.

[108] *Ghana/Côte d'Ivoire* (n 63), paras 68–73; *Sub-Regional Fisheries Commission* (n 63), paras 111, 120; *South China Sea Arbitration* (n 63), para 927; *Ukraine/Russia* (n 63), para 295.

[109] 1997 New York Convention (n 91), Art 7.

[110] ibid, Art 20.

[111] See eg Principle 1 of the World Charter for Nature (n 7), which reads as follows: 'Nature shall be respected and its essential processes shall not be impaired.'

the third component of Principle 21/2. They move beyond Principle 21/2 as an anchor point for the preservation of sovereignty and create a duty to prevent damage to the environment per se.

2.6 *The Environment within the Jurisdiction of the State of Origin*

One important question is whether customary international law requires States to prevent harm to the environment within their territory or jurisdiction even when no external impact can be reasonably foreseen. Aside from the obligations that may arise from treaty law, there are four main considerations suggesting that such obligation exists.

The first has been already discussed in connection with the distinction between 'no harm' and prevention. The focus of the prevention principle on environmental protection per se irrespective of spatial considerations provides a strong indication that States must protect their own environment. In the *South China Sea Arbitration*, the arbitral tribunal asserted jurisdiction over, inter alia, a claim brought by the Philippines seeking a declaration that China had 'violated its obligations under the Convention to protect and preserve the marine environment' in connection with activities in some marine features.[112] The tribunal noted that the dispute regarding sovereignty and delimitation of the area (which remains disputed) was outside its jurisdiction but that such conclusion posed no impediment for the determination of the environmental claim because 'the environmental obligations in Part XII apply to States irrespective of where the alleged harmful activities took place'.[113] Thereafter, the tribunal relied on Article 192 of the UNCLOS together with the prevention principle in customary international law[114] as the basis for 'a positive "duty to prevent, or at least mitigate" significant harm to the environment when pursuing large-scale construction activities'.[115] The authorities relied upon to assert this duty, including the ICJ case law and the awards of two ad hoc arbitral tribunals,[116] suggest that prevention of environmental harm irrespective of the location of the harm is a requirement also beyond the context of the UNCLOS. Thus, it is prevention of harm to the environment per se, irrespective of spatial considerations, which is required by the customary norm.

The second and related consideration concerns the existence of a sophisticated framework for environmental protection in many States and the emphasis placed, during the negotiation of the Rio Declaration, on the need to adopt domestic environmental policies. Canada's proposal during PrepCom IV illustrates this point to the extent it framed 'external' prevention as a reflection of 'internal' prevention, through a sort of national treatment rule requiring States to protect the environment abroad to the same degree as their own environment.[117] If considered from an external point of view, there are limitations in this logic, because a State could provide no protection to the environment under its jurisdiction. But seen from a reverse perspective, to the extent that States have an express duty not to cause significant environmental harm beyond their jurisdiction, that same external level would apply internally. This is, of course, only a policy

[112] *South China Sea Arbitration* (n 63), paras 925–26.

[113] ibid, para 927, referring to the Award on Jurisdiction, para 408.

[114] *South China Sea Arbitration* (n 63), para 941 ('The corpus of international law relating to the environment, which informs the content of the general obligation in Article 192, requires that States "ensure that activities within their jurisdiction and control respect the environment of other States or of areas beyond national control."'). The tribunal referred here, in footnote 1094, to para 29 of the *Legality of Nuclear Weapons* advisory opinion (n 106), which is the first recognition of the customary character of the prevention principle.

[115] *South China Sea Arbitration* (n 63), para 941.

[116] *Indus Waters Kishenganga* (n 92), Partial Award, para 451, quoting *Iron Rhine* (n 92), para 59.

[117] See L.23 (n 33).

consideration, but it becomes legal when domestic environmental policies are connected to the undertakings of States under the environmental treaties to which they are parties.

The third consideration is also of a legal nature. The principle of sovereignty over natural resources is qualified by the requirement that sovereignty 'must be exercised in the interest of their national development and of the well-being of the people of the state concerned'.[118] Although this requirement is difficult to implement in practice, it clearly imposes on States a duty to use resources in a way which is not harmful to its own population.

Fourth, the indeterminacy of the foregoing requirement is offset by the existence of specific human rights obligations with environmental components. Irrespective of whether or not provisions such as Article 24 (peoples' right to a generally satisfactory environment) of the African Charter on Human and Peoples' Rights[119] have customary grounding, even basic human rights, the customary grounding of which is less controversial,[120] such as the human rights to life, health or private and family life or individual and collective cultural rights entail a proactive duty for the State to protect individuals from deprivation by activities conducted by third parties or even natural disasters.[121] The requirement to protect the domestic environment is now clearly recognised in the case law of regional human rights bodies as well as in that of the UN Human Rights Committee.[122]

3 *Legal Status of the Principle*

The prevention principle was considered, at the time of its formulation, as one of the 'fundamental principles' of the Stockholm Declaration.[123] Yet, although its grounding on general international law is widely recognised, its specific scope and operation requires some additional comments.[124]

The customary status of prevention raises some controversies not necessarily due to the status of the norm itself but rather related to the general difficulties arising from the identification of custom under general international law. The recognition of the customary status of prevention rests, essentially, on the jurisprudential determination of custom.[125] It generally relies on a line

[118] See ibid, Principle 4.

[119] African Charter on Human and Peoples' Rights, Banjul, 27 June 1981, in force 21 October 1986, 21 ILM 58 (1982).

[120] On human rights threatened by environmental harm, see the 'Report of the Independent Expert on the issue of human rights obligations relating to the enjoyment of a safe, clean, healthy and sustainable environment, John H Knox: Preliminary report', A/HRC/22/43, 24 December 2012, paras 18–24.

[121] The obligations to be respected in order to fulfil this proactive duty are detailed in the 'Report of the Independent Expert on the issue of human rights obligations relating to the enjoyment of a safe, clean, healthy and sustainable environment, John H Knox: Mapping Report', A/HRC/25/53, 30 December 2013, paras 26–68.

[122] On four recent decisions making this link see *Portillo Cáceres* v *Paraguay*, HRC, 9 August 2019, CCPR/C/126/D/2751/2016; *ICtHR Advisory Opinion* (n 51); *African Commission on Human and Peoples' Rights* v *Republic of Kenya*, ACtHPR App 006/2012, Judgment of 26 May 2017; *Cordella and Others* v *Italy*, ECtHR, Appl Nos 54414/13 and 54264/15, Judgment of 24 January 2019. See also, *ICtHR Advisory Opinion* (n 51), para 140. For a general overview of the link between environmental degradation and the protection of human rights see P-M Dupuy and JE Viñuales, *International Environmental Law* (2nd edn, Cambridge University Press, 2018), ch 10.

[123] Report of the Rapporteur, WG.1/CRP.5, 1.

[124] This section follows Duvic-Paoli and Viñuales, 'Principle 2: Prevention' (n 5); Duvic-Paoli, *The Prevention Principle in International Environmental Law* (n 5); Viñuales, 'La Protección Ambiental en el Derecho Consuetudinario Internacional' (n 5); Viñuales, 'Due Diligence in International Environmental Law' (n 5); and Dupuy, Le Moli and Viñuales, 'Customary International Law and the Environment' (n 5).

[125] On environmental protection in general international law see: P-M Dupuy, 'Overview of Existing Customary Legal Regime Regarding International Pollution' in D Magraw (ed), *International Law and Pollution* (University of Pennsylvania Press, 1991) 61–89; P-M Dupuy, 'Où en est le droit international de l'environnement à la fin du siècle?'

connecting the *Trail Smelter* award,[126] followed by a reference to the *Corfu Channel* case,[127] which confirmed the duty of States to exercise control over potentially harmful activities under their jurisdiction, and to the ICJ's advisory opinion on the *Legality of Nuclear Weapons*,[128] which for the first time recognised the customary character of Stockholm Principle 21. Since the mid-1990s, the customary status of the principle has been consolidated in the case law of the ICJ, most notably in the 2015 decision in *Costa Rica/Nicaragua*,[129] as well as in that of other adjudicative bodies, such as the International Tribunal for the Law of the Sea (ITLOS) Seabed Chamber,[130] the ITLOS itself,[131] ad hoc arbitral tribunals[132] and the Inter-American Court of Human Rights.[133]

As noted earlier in this chapter, prevention has also been at the centre of the work of the ILC on international liability for injurious consequences arising out of acts not prohibited by international law. After years of hesitation as to the proper angle for the topic, the ILC set two separate tracks, one focusing on the definition of prevention of environmental harm as a duty of States (ILC Prevention Articles adopted in 2001) and another setting parameters for the allocation of loss in the event harm occurs (ILC Principles on the allocation of loss adopted in 2006[134]). The first reads as an elaboration of the primary norm or duty of prevention, as stated in Principle 21 of the Stockholm Declaration and Principle 2 of the Rio Declaration, although with a narrower focus confined to a transboundary context. The second provides guidance on how to organise the consequences of damage to the environment at the national and international level, much as a civil liability treaty would.

The preamble of the ILC Prevention Articles makes clear that they are intended as an elaboration of the Rio Principles, particularly of the balance between sovereignty over natural resources and its limits.[135] To assess the scope of this normative development, two main questions must be addressed, namely the content of the obligation of prevention as defined in

[1997] *Revue Générale de Droit International Public* 873; Viñuales, 'The Contribution of the International Court of Justice to the Development of International Environmental Law' (n 5); P-M Dupuy, 'Formation of Customary International Law and General Principles' in D Bodansky et al (eds), *The Oxford Handbook of International Environmental Law* (Oxford University Press, 2008) 449–66; L Boisson de Chazournes and S Maljean-Dubois, 'Principes du droit international de l'environnement' (2011) *Jurisclasseur Environnement et Développement Durable* 1–20; M Fitzmaurice, 'The International Court of Justice and International Environmental Law' in C Tams and J Sloane (eds), *The Development of International Law by the International Court of Justice* (Oxford University Press, 2013) 354–74; J Juste-Ruiz, 'The International Court of Justice and International Environmental Law' in N Boschiero et al (eds), *International Courts and the Development of International Law. Essays in honour of Tullio Treves* (TMC Asser Press, 2013) 383–401; JE Viñuales (ed), *The Rio Declaration on Environment and Development* (Oxford University Press, 2015); T Stephens, 'The Development of International Environmental Law by the International Court of Justice' in D Fisher (ed), *Research Handbook on Fundamental Concepts of Environmental Law* (Edward Elgar, 2016) 221–47; Viñuales, 'La Protección Ambiental en el Derecho Consuetudinario Internacional' (n 5); and Dupuy, Le Moli and Viñuales, 'Customary International Law and the Environment' (n 5).

126 *Trail Smelter* (n 39) 1965.

127 *Corfu Channel* (n 89) 22.

128 *Legality of Nuclear Weapons* (n 106), para 29.

129 *Costa Rica/Nicaragua* (n 62), para 104. See also *Gabčíkovo-Nagymaros Project* (n 50), para 140; *Pulp Mills* (n 50), para 101.

130 *Responsibilities in the Area* (n 64), paras 131–35.

131 *Ghana/Côte d'Ivoire* (n 63), para 71.

132 *Iron Rhine* (n 92), paras 59, 222; *Indus Waters Kishenganga* (n 92), Partial Award, paras 448–51; *South China Sea Arbitration* (n 63), paras 940–48.

133 *ICtHR Advisory Opinion* (n 51), paras 97–99.

134 ILC, 'Draft Principles on the Allocation of Loss in the Case of Transboundary Harm Arising out of Hazardous Activities (with Commentaries)' (2006), UN Doc A/63/10.

135 The commentary to the ILC Prevention Articles (n 50) refers explicitly to Principle 2 of the Rio Declaration (general commentary, paras 3 and 4).

the ILC Prevention Articles and the relationship between this instrument and the customary rules of prevention embodied in, inter alia, Principle 21/2. The two are of course intertwined.

Regarding the contents of the ILC Prevention Articles, the focus is narrower than Principle 2 of the Rio Declaration, as the ILC carefully circumscribed the scope of its work according to several parameters.[136] Compared to Principle 2, the main differences are the transboundary scope of the ILC Prevention Articles (thus excluding areas beyond national jurisdiction and its application to purely domestic environmental harm) and the pragmatic recognition that in some cases harm may be admissible if it is minimised.[137] The risk of significant transboundary harm is defined in a non-limitative manner, as 'includ[ing] risks taking the form of a high probability of causing significant transboundary harm and a low probability of causing disastrous transboundary harm'.[138] Within these bounds, the duty of prevention is characterised by reference to several interrelated obligations, much in the same way as (and by reference to) the Rio Declaration. Inter-State or 'horizontal' obligations include: prevention (Article 3), co-operation in prevention and response (Articles 4, 8, 9, 11, 12, 16 and 17), and information to and protection of the public concerned (Articles 13 and 15). Intra-State or 'vertical' obligations include adopting domestic legislation (Article 5) and, more specifically, a system of authorisation of potentially harmful activities (Article 6) involving an environmental impact assessment (Article 7). These obligations give expression to the prevention principle but they also have a more specific grounding in other well-established principles, such as the duty to co-operate (Principles 18 and 19 of the Rio Declaration), the requirement to conduct environmental impact assessments (Principle 17 of the Rio Declaration) or public participation requirements (Principle 10). The articles also include a provision on the settlement of disputes (Article 19) and another one on the relations with other rules of international law (Article 18).

The latter provision raises the question of the relationship between the ILC Prevention Articles and the customary duty of prevention. The question has sometimes been asked from a different perspective, namely that of the customary status of the ILC Prevention Articles. Clearly, the core system (prevention, co-operation and environmental impact assessment) of this instrument rests on customary law, as recognised in the jurisprudential line mentioned earlier. It is also clear that some provisions of the ILC Prevention Articles, particularly the detail of the procedures set out in Articles 11 and 19 do not rest on a customary basis. As for the requirements of public participation, there is increasing support for the proposition that some measure of non-discriminatory participation is required by customary international law, as a result of environmental and human rights law.[139]

Beyond the specific status of different provisions of the ILC Prevention Articles, which in many ways convey the transboundary 'no harm' rule, it is important to note that the customary prevention principle operates in parallel (as regards transboundary matters) and has a broader scope, not only spatial but also substantive. Specifically, the customary prevention principle applies to environmental harm irrespective of spatial considerations, as discussed above. Moreover, its focus is not specifically on 'activities' with 'physical consequences' and may encompass 'policies' with other types of consequences (e.g. socio-economic). Furthermore, the prevention principle and, indeed, the customary international law of environmental protection are not

[136] See ILC Prevention Articles (n 50), commentary to Arts 1 and 2.

[137] See ibid, commentary to Art 3, para 7, and to Art 10(b), para 4.

[138] ibid, Art 2(a).

[139] See L-A Duvic-Paoli, 'The Status of the Right to Public Participation in International Environmental Law: An Analysis of the Jurisprudence' (2012) 23 *Yearbook of International Environmental Law* 80.

subject, unlike what a certain reading of the ILC Prevention Articles could suggest,[140] to any rigid sequence in the operation of each obligation.[141] In particular, the duty to co-operate (in its specific expression through the obligations to notify and consult) is not conditioned by a unilaterally defined and unilaterally conducted environmental impact assessment in the State of origin. Article 18 of the ILC Prevention Articles ('relationship to other rules of international law') is therefore important to underscore the significant differences between this codification effort and other rules of international law.

IV EXTENSIONS OF THE PREVENTION PRINCIPLE

In addition to its substantive manifestations in the form of Stockholm Principle 21 and more specific treaty obligations, the prevention principle manifests itself in a variety of related environmental principles, including the duty of due diligence, the duty to co-operate, the duty to undertake an environmental impact assessment, the precautionary principle/approach and the concept of sustainable development.[142]

1 *Prevention and the Duty of Due Diligence*

Due diligence creates a balance between two competing realities: most activities harmful to the environment are undertaken by private actors whose actions cannot always engage the responsibility of the State, but environmental harm might be left completely unregulated if the actions of private actors are uncontrolled. The State is therefore required to take proactive measures to ensure that third-party activities do not cause harm to the environment but will not be held responsible for each occurrence of harm. As a result, prevention is widely recognised as a due-diligence obligation. Treaty law,[143] codification works,[144] case law[145] and legal commentary[146] all converge in this sense.

Yet, the relationship between prevention and due diligence is unclear because, given their proximity, they are often used interchangeably. The commentary to the ILC Prevention Articles, for instance, uses the two terms together, mentioning that States have to discharge their 'duty of

[140] ILC Prevention Articles (n 50), Arts 7 and 8.

[141] See the discussion of *Costa Rica/Nicaragua* in Viñuales, 'La Protección Ambiental en el Derecho Consuetudinario Internacional' (n 5); and Dupuy, Le Moli and Viñuales, 'Customary International Law and the Environment' (n 5).

[142] This section follows Duvic-Paoli and Viñuales, 'Principle 2: Prevention' (n 5); Viñuales, 'La Protección Ambiental en el Derecho Consuetudinario Internacional' (n 5); Duvic-Paoli, *The Prevention Principle in International Environmental Law* (n 5); Viñuales, 'Due Diligence in International Environmental Law' (n 5); and Dupuy, Le Moli and Viñuales, 'Customary International Law and the Environment' (n 5).

[143] The expression used to express due diligence varies from one treaty to another and includes expressions such as 'take all measures', 'all appropriate measures', 'all necessary measures', 'to ensure'. The term 'due diligence' per se is rarely used in treaty law, often on the basis that the mentioned references are less technical and lead to less confusion regarding what is expected of the State.

[144] ILC Prevention Articles (n 50), commentary to Art 3, para 7, 154: 'The obligation of the State of origin to take preventive or minimization measures is one of due diligence.'

[145] *Responsibilities in the Area* (n 64), para 113; *Sub-Regional Fisheries Commission* (n 63), para 129; *Costa Rica/Nicaragua* (n 62), paras 104 and 153; *South China Sea Arbitration* (n 63), para 944.

[146] See eg H Xue, *Transboundary Damage in International Law* (Cambridge University Press, 2009), ch 5; T Braz Jardim Oliveira, 'La Diligence due dans la prévention des dommages à l'environnement' (2012) 2 *Brazilian Yearbook of International Law* 205; E Hey, *Advanced Introduction to International Environmental Law* (Edward Elgar, 2016) 71; J Kulesza, *Due Diligence in International Law* (Martinus Nijhoff, 2016); N Craik, *The International Law of Environmental Impact Assessment: Process, Substance and Integration* (Cambridge University Press, 2008) 62–63.

prevention or due diligence',[147] in an expression that leaves uncertain whether the ILC considers them as synonymous or as two different norms. As for the ICJ, it has approached the relationship between prevention and due diligence as a historical one stating that prevention had 'its origins in the due diligence that is required of a state in its territory'.[148]

There are, however, two noticeable differences between these two norms. The first stems from the broader scope of the duty of due diligence, which applies to several types of harm and risk other than environmental ones. In the *Alabama* claims, due diligence was applied to the duties of a neutral power. In the *Corfu Channel* case, Albania was negligent in allowing its territory to be used in such a manner as to cause harm to the British vessels transiting the channel. In contemporary human rights litigation, States have been held responsible for not having offered sufficient protection to the individuals under their jurisdiction against threats from third parties or even natural phenomena.[149] These examples, which have been discussed earlier in this chapter, all suggest that the scope of the duty of due diligence does not fully overlap with prevention of environmental harm.

The second difference is that the prevention principle concerns, as recognised since the *Trail Smelter* arbitration, only harm of a certain magnitude ('material' harm[150] or 'significant' harm[151]) or risk of thereof.[152] By contrast, the duty of due diligence is not similarly limited and, for this reason, action/inaction which results in harm or risk to the environment but which is below the threshold of significance required to trigger a breach of the prevention principle remains governed by the duty of due diligence. That much can be learnt from the *Alabama* arbitration, where due diligence was not limited by either upper or lower bounds in the magnitude of harm or risk.[153] This point has practical implications. A State may be required or entitled, under the duty of due diligence, to take precautionary measures even in the absence of scientific certainty as to the existence of risk of significant harm.[154] Such a requirement/justification would not flow from the prevention principle, which only operates when there is risk. Nor would it flow, in the absence of an applicable treaty, from the precautionary approach/principle, whose customary grounding is still debated.[155] It would derive instead from the duty of due diligence, which is unquestionably grounded in general international law since at least the period of the *Alabama* arbitration and has a scope which is not limited to the risk of 'significant' environmental harm. This conclusion does not mean that any harm or risk thereof may be subject to the duty of due diligence (this sort of 'absolute integrity' theory was early on discarded by international tribunals[156]) but only that this duty is not necessarily subject to the same definition of 'significance' or of 'risk' as the prevention principle.

Aside from these two differences, the operation of due diligence and prevention in an environmental context overlap. They do so to a point that the duty of due diligence must be considered as defining the 'responsibility to ensure', as stated in Principle 21/2.

[147] ILC Prevention Articles (n 50), general commentary, para 2, 148.
[148] *Pulp Mills* (n 50), para 1.
[149] *Velásquez Rodríguez* v *Honduras*, Merits, ICtHR Series C No 4 (29 July 1988), para 172 (referring specific to the duty of due diligence).
[150] *Trail Smelter* (n 39) 1980.
[151] See ILC Prevention Articles (n 50), Art 2(a); *Pulp Mills* (n 50), para 101.
[152] ILC Prevention Articles (n 50), Art 3.
[153] *Alabama* (n 46) 129.
[154] See *Responsibilities in the Area* (n 64), paras 125–35, esp paras 131 and 135.
[155] See Dupuy and Viñuales (n 122) 70–73.
[156] See *Lac Lanoux* (n 90) 281–317.

2 Prevention and the Duty to Co-Operate

Prevention and co-operation are closely linked given their common origin in good neighbourliness considerations. Their connection pre-dates the recognition of prevention as a principle of international environmental law. As the 'no harm' rule emerged to preserve the territorial integrity of a neighbouring State, a duty to co-operate also emerged to facilitate the management of shared natural resources.

The close link between prevention and co-operation is made clear in the ILC Prevention Articles. The prevention obligation stated in Article 3 is subsequently implemented by Article 4, which requires States to 'cooperate in good faith ... in preventing significant transboundary harm or at any event in minimizing the risk thereof'. This close relationship was highlighted in the ITLOS *MOX Plant* case in which the Tribunal held that 'the duty to co-operate is a fundamental principle in the prevention of pollution of the marine environment under Part XII of the Convention and general international law'[157] as well as in the *Pulp Mills* case where the Court held that the parties had an obligation to inform[158] and notify[159] in order to co-operate in a successful manner to 'jointly manage the risks of damage to the environment'.[160]

To flesh out the relations between prevention and co-operation, a partial analogy is possible with the relations between prevention and due diligence. Much like in the latter pair, inter-State co-operation is a wider concept recognised as a 'purpose' in Article 1(3) of the UN Charter and as a principle in the Friendly Relations Declaration, with general application to several specific contexts.[161] Even before such statements, the general duty to co-operate had featured in the law of international watercourses. As early as 1929, the Permanent Court of International Justice (PCIJ) reasoned in the *River Oder* case that a 'community of interest' in navigation among all riparian States existed, based on equality of rights over the whole navigable course of the river and without 'any preferential privilege of any one ... State in relation to the others'.[162] The concept of 'community of interest' entails that co-operation is required in order to take into account the interest of all the States concerned. An obligation to consult riparian States when exploiting the shared resources is one expression of such understanding. In the *Lac Lanoux* case, the tribunal recognised that while France could carry out diversion works entirely within its own territory, it had an obligation to consult Spain and to safeguard its rights in the watercourse.[163] In the case law of the ICJ, co-operation has played a significant role in matters such as maritime delimitation,[164] nuclear disarmament[165] and territorial disputes.[166] Thus, much like due diligence, co-operation cannot be fully subsumed under the prevention principle.

At the same time, much like due diligence, the duty to co-operate arises from the prevention principle as a procedural extension of it. As part of their duty to prevent environmental harm, States have to co-operate with each other, particularly through the notification of activities that

157 *MOX Plant case (Ireland v United Kingdom)*, Provisional Measures, ITLOS No 10 (3 December 2001), para 84.
158 *Pulp Mills* (n 50), para 102.
159 ibid, para 113.
160 ibid, para 77.
161 See the chapter by L Boisson de Chazournes and J Rudall in this volume.
162 *Territorial Jurisdiction of the International Commission of the River Oder* (Czechoslovakia, Denmark, France, Germany, Great Britain, Sweden/Poland) (1929) PCIJ Series A, No 23, 27.
163 *Lac Lanoux* (n 90) 140.
164 *North Sea Continental Shelf*, Judgment, ICJ Reports 1969, 3, paras 83–87.
165 *Legality of Nuclear Weapons* ((n 106), paras 98–103.
166 *Obligation to Negotiate Access to the Pacific Ocean (Bolivia v Chile)*, Judgment of 1 October 2018, ICJ General List No 153, paras 86–87, 91, 146–47, 152, 158–59, 162, 165–67.

may be detrimental to other States and the holding of consultations among them. This conclusion can be derived from Principles 18 and 19 of the Rio Declaration. However, the trigger of the duty to co-operate remains unsettled. This is not immediately apparent in the English formulation of Principle 19, which uses the term 'significant', much like the prevention principle. Yet, the French formulation uses terminology (*'effets transfrontières sérieusement nocifs sur l'environnement'*) which is closer to the *'effets nocifs importants'* required under Principle 17 (environmental impact assessment or EIA). In *Costa Rica/Nicaragua*, the ICJ seemed to condition the duty of notification and consultation to the ascertainment of the risk by means of an EIA unilaterally defined and conducted by the State of origin of the activity. In the French version of its judgment, the ICJ used a slightly reformulated version of the terminology of Principle 17 as the trigger of the duties to notify and consult (referring to *'risque de dommage transfrontière important'*).[167] Reliance on the trigger of Principle 17 does not necessarily mean that the duty to co-operate, including notification and consultation, may not be triggered earlier when there are other elements suggesting the existence of risk, even if not yet ascertained through an EIA. Neither the prevention principle nor its extensions (including co-operation) are conditioned upon the prior completion of a specific procedural step. The key issue is substantive, namely the existence of risk, even if the State of origin has not done enough to ascertain it. This is expressly contemplated in Articles 4, 9 and 12 of the ILC Prevention Articles. The commentary to Article 4 observes that the State affected 'may know better than anybody else' about the possible impacts.[168] And it has indeed been long held that the assessment of transboundary impact of an activity cannot be under the exclusive remit of the State of origin.[169]

3 *Prevention and the Requirement to Conduct an Environmental Impact Assessment*

Principle 17 of the Rio Declaration concerning the requirement to conduct an EIA makes a direct reference to the obligation to prevent significant damage to the environment. Despite some scepticism in legal commentary as to the specificity of the obligations arising from the prevention principle,[170] it is now well-established that, at the very least, prevention requires the conduct of a prior EIA. The connection between prevention and its expression through the EIA requirement is acknowledged in the codification work conducted by the ILC[171] and the International Law Association (ILA).[172] In the *Pulp Mills* case, after noting that the requirement to carry out an EIA in a transboundary context had become part of customary law, the ICJ noted that:

> due diligence, and the duty of vigilance and prevention which it implies, would not be considered to have been exercised, if a party planning works liable to affect the régime of the river or the quality of its waters did not undertake an environmental impact assessment on the potential effects of such works.[173]

167 *Costa Rica/Nicaragua* (n 62), paras 104, 108, 168.
168 ILC Prevention Articles (n 50), commentary to Art 4, para 1.
169 *Lac Lanoux* (n 90), para 21.
170 eg J Vessey, 'The Principle of Prevention in International Law' (1998) 3 *Austrian Review of International and European Law* 181, 183 (noting that the 'abstract principle of prevention is seemingly well-settled but the issue of translating that principle into specific obligations is not').
171 ILC Prevention Articles (n 50), Art 7.
172 ILA, Committee on International Law on Sustainable Development, Sofia Resolution No 7/2012, guiding statement 10.
173 *Pulp Mills* (n 50), para 204.

Subsequently, the ITLOS Seabed Chamber broadened the application of the EIA requirement to the global commons on the basis of the ICJ's comment on the relationship between prevention and EIA.[174]

As noted in relation to co-operation, the ICJ's 2015 decision in *Costa Rica/Nicaragua* has introduced some unnecessary rigidity in the interconnections between prevention, EIA and co-operation. According to the Court, the duties to notify and consult would only be triggered once the risk of significant transboundary harm has been confirmed – unilaterally – by an EIA in the State of origin, the contents of which are also defined unilaterally. Such an understanding gives too much power to the State of origin, which has an interest in developing the activity. Such State would have the unilateral power to decide whether to conduct the EIA, to define the EIA's content, to conduct it and even to interpret its results and consequences. By necessity, such unilateral powers are inconsistent with the existence of a right, correlative to the duty to conduct the EIA, for the State affected to require this procedure on the basis of its own assessment of the risk. Moreover, it is difficult to see how the procedural step of notification could be conditioned upon the unilateral conduct of an EIA given that Article 4 of the ILC Prevention Articles generally requires concerned States to co-operate. How could such co-operation take place in good faith if the affected State is not made aware, by notification, of the proposed activity, before the EIA has been conducted. Furthermore, Article 9 of the ILC Articles, which relates to 'consultations', is broad and encompasses situations where no EIA and/or notification has taken place. The commentary refers to consultations following notification as one among several other situations where consultations may take place[175] and, like Article 4, it emphasises the customary duty to co-operate in good faith.[176] Finally, certain shared resources such as international watercourses specifically require co-operation among the watercourse States as an integral part of the equitable and reasonable utilisation principle.[177] It is only within this broader context that the relations between prevention, EIA and co-operation must be read.[178]

4 Prevention and Precaution

The relationship between prevention and precaution is perhaps the most difficult to articulate at present under international environmental law. There is no doubt that prevention and precaution share the same objective of harm avoidance,[179] but the extent to which prevention is expressed in precaution has been interpreted in different ways.

The ITLOS Seabed Chamber has observed that both prevention and precaution are expressions of the States' due-diligence duty. According to the Chamber, like prevention, precaution:

> is also an integral part of the general obligation of due diligence of sponsoring States, which is applicable even outside the scope of the [Nodules] Regulations. The due diligence obligation of the sponsoring States requires them to take all appropriate measures to prevent damage that might result from the activities of contractors that they sponsor. This obligation applies in

[174] *Responsibilities in the Area* (n 64), para 148.
[175] ILC Prevention Articles (n 50), commentary to Art 9, para 4.
[176] ibid, commentary to Art 9, para 4.
[177] 1997 New York Convention (n 91), Arts 5(2), 8 and 9.
[178] ibid, Art 12.
[179] The precautionary approach was presented as a continuum to prevention during the oral proceedings of the *Gabčíkovo-Nagymaros Project* (n 50), as Hungary argued that 'le principe de précaution a émergé comme la forme la plus développée de la règle générale qui impose la prévention' (Oral Proceedings, CR/1997/2, 3 March 1997, 42, para 23).

> situations where scientific evidence concerning the scope and potential negative impact of the activity in question is insufficient but where there are plausible indications of potential risks.[180]

A less nuanced position considers that precaution, as a more advanced norm in relation to harm avoidance, means a direct endorsement of prevention but also has replaced it.[181] Whereas such a view may have some grounding in EU law, it is highly problematic from the perspective of international law. Given the unsettled status of precaution under international law, that view would amount to replacing a widely acknowledged and tested customary norm with a controversial and untested one. More fundamentally, such a view falls prey to a common mistake which has blurred, for years, the contours of the principles of international environmental law, namely the conflation between conceptual implication (the argument that a consequence can be logically derived from a premise) and legally recognised conceptual implication (the recognition of such logical step in a legal authority). Conceptual implication is very different from legal recognition and actual application.

As a general matter, prevention and precaution operate in distinct spheres.[182] On the one hand, prevention is a legal principle that aims to better respond to the notion of 'risk' (a negative outcome the probability of which can be reliably estimated). On the other hand, precaution emerged out of the realisation that it is not always possible to assess the consequences of some activities in advance (particularly whether an activity entails even a small probability of serious or irreversible damage) and that such uncertainty cannot be an excuse for inaction. The fact that scientific knowledge, and its social acceptance and consolidation, may not be easily subsumed under a strict certainty–uncertainty dichotomy places prevention and precaution alongside a spectrum from risk to uncertainty, with a grey (casuistic) area of transition between the two.

For this reason, the preventive rationale expounded by the ITLOS Seabed Chamber – expressed in the form of prevention and precaution, both as due-diligence obligations – defuses a major difficulty relative to the implementation of prevention, which is to assess whether the level of scientific knowledge is high enough to trigger a preventive obligation. In addition, it highlights the fact that some activities that justified a precautionary approach will move towards prevention as knowledge improves over time, such as in the case of climate change.[183]

5 *Prevention and Sustainable Development*

The main difficulty concerning the relations between prevention of environmental harm and the concept of sustainable development stems from the wide indeterminacy of the latter.[184] On this specific point, perhaps more than in any other one discussed so far, arguments of a policy, conceptual or merely aspirational nature are routinely amalgamated with legal claims and argumentations. For this reason, rather than a survey of instruments,[185]

180 *Responsibilities in the Area* (n 64), para 131.

181 A Trouwborst, 'Prevention, Precaution, Logic and Law: The Relationship between the Precautionary Principle and the Preventative Principle in International Law and Associated Questions' (2009) 2 *Erasmus Law Review* 105.

182 See JE Viñuales, 'Legal Techniques for Dealing with Scientific Uncertainty in Environmental Law' (2010) 43 *Vanderbilt Journal of Transnational Law* 43; *Pulp Mills* (n 50), Separate Opinion of Judge Cançado Trindade.

183 ILA, Committee on Legal Principles Relating to Climate Change, 'Declaration of Principles Relating to Climate Change', Washington, DC, Seventy-Sixth Session, 2014, Art 7B(3).

184 See JE Viñuales, 'Sustainable Development' in L Rajamani and J Peel (eds), *The Oxford Handbook of International Environmental Law* (Oxford University Press, 2020), ch 17.

185 Rio Declaration (n 2); Report of the United Nations Conference on Environment and Development, A/CONF.151/26/Rev.1 (vol 1), Res 1, Annex 2: Agenda 21; Res 1: 'Political declaration', 4 September 2002, Report of World Summit on Sustainable Development in Johannesburg (South Africa), 26 August to 4 September 2002, UN Doc

treaties[186] and judicial decisions[187] referring to sustainable development, the distinction must be stated concisely and as clearly as possible. It holds in two main propositions.

First, sustainable development is not a legal principle but a normative concept.[188] Specifically, unlike the prevention principle, sustainable development cannot operate as a primary rule of obligation (or 'primary norm') which could potentially be breached and trigger State responsibility. It can perform other normative functions such as influencing the content of an instrument or its interpretation.

Second, sustainable development as a legal norm (a normative concept) means, specifically, (i) development which, as a necessary procedural step, 'takes into account' environmental protection (integration) and (ii) which does so in a way that is consistent with the environmental treaty obligations undertaken by a country or, at the very least, with the core content of customary international environmental law applicable to all countries (i.e. the prevention principle, integrating the duty of due diligence in the context of environmental protection, as further expressed in procedural form by the duty to co-operate and the duty to conduct an EIA).[189] This understanding is suggested by the first judicial recognition, in explicit terms, of the 'concept of sustainable development' by the ICJ in the case concerning the *Gabčíkovo-Nagymaros Project*.[190]

Once the concept of sustainable development has been ascertained, its relations with the prevention principle can be clearly identified. In essence, development is sustainable if, at a minimum, it is consistent with the prevention principle and its expressions in both customary international law and treaty law. Conversely, prevention of environmental harm as a principle is a condition for the existence of sustainable development as a normative concept. Prevention both pre-dates and enables such normative concept.

V ASSESSMENT: PREVENTION OF ENVIRONMENTAL HARM AND THE FRIENDLY RELATIONS DECLARATION

The 1970 Friendly Relations Declaration is not only a synthesis but a culmination of a reappropriation process of the principles enshrined in the UN Charter by the three main blocs of the time, the West, the socialist countries, and the so-called 'Third World' countries. As

A/CONF.199/20, 1, 2002; Report of the World Summit on Sustainable Development at Johannesburg (South Africa), 26 August–4 September 2002, UN Doc A/CONF.199/20 (Implementation Plan); The Future We Want, 11 September 2012, UN Doc A/RES/66/288; Transforming our World: The 2030 Agenda for Sustainable Development, 21 October 2015, UN Doc A/RES/70/1.

[186] See nn 7 and 8.

[187] See, in chronological order, *Gabčíkovo-Nagymaros Project* (n 50), para 140; WTO Appellate Body Report on *US – Import Prohibition of Certain Shrimp and Shrimp Products*, WT/DS58/AB/R (October 12, 1998), paras 131 and 153; African Commission on Human and Peoples' Rights, *Social and Economic Rights Action Center (SERAC) and the Center for Economic and Social Rights (CESR)* v *Nigeria*, Communication No 155/96, 2001, para 52; *Hatton* v *UK*, Grand Chamber, ECtHR Appl No 36022/97, Judgment of 8 July 2003, Joint Dissenting Opinion of Judges Costa, Ress, Turmen, Zupancic and Steiner, para 1; *Iron Rhine* (n 92), paras 57–59; *Pulp Mills*, Provisional Measures, Order of 13 July 2006, ICJ Reports 2006, 133, para 80, Judgment, paras 75–77 and 177; *Indus Waters Kishenganga* (n 92), Partial Award, paras 448–52; *China – Measures Related to the Exportation of Various Raw Materials, Appellate Body Report*, WT/DS 394/AB/R (13 January 2012), para 306; *China – Measures Related to the Exportation of Rare Earths, Tungsten, and Molybdenum*, Panel Report (26 March 2014), para 7.263; *ICtHR Advisory Opinion* (n 51), paras 52–55.

[188] See Dupuy, Le Moli and Viñuales, 'Customary International Law and the Environment' (n 5).

[189] See Viñuales (n 184).

[190] *Gabčíkovo-Nagymaros Project* (n 50), para 140 (italics added).

discussed in other chapters of this volume,[191] the latter did not reject the principles of the Charter altogether; rather, they realised that many of them, such as sovereign equality and non-intervention, were very important to defend their position. They also managed to introduce a detailed formulation of the principle of and 'right' to self-determination. In such a context of reappropriation, there was no room for any innovation that would hamper the right to political and economic emancipation for which newly independent and developing countries had so strongly advocated.

By contrast, the 1972 Stockholm Declaration, with its 'Stockholm principle', was a beginning. It certainly acknowledges the 'sovereign right' of States to exploit their natural resources, but its essence was about placing bounds on the exercise of such right. Between 1968 and 1972 there was, in the values underpinning international law, a deep movement of tectonic plates which, while consolidating the previous order, paved the way for a new one which would become clear years later, with the end of the Cold War and the synthesis achieved at the 1992 Rio Conference between 'development' and 'environment'. The formulation of Principle 2 of the Rio Declaration, even more than that of Principle 21 of the Stockholm Declaration, consecrates this delicate balance between the sovereign right to exploit natural resources in accordance with environmental and 'developmental' policies and the duty to protect the environment from significant harm arising from the exercise of such right.

And yet, concluding that, between 1968 and 1970, a door was closed and another was open would be inaccurate. The fundamental character of the principles enshrined in the Friendly Relations Declaration is given not only by their importance but also by their ability to encompass both the old and the new. The fourth principle of the Declaration, the duty of States to co-operate with one another in accordance with the Charter, was an invitation for States to do more than to peacefully co-exist but to actively co-operate in matters of mutual concern. The Friendly Relations Declaration mentioned several areas of co-operation, including of course human rights but also 'the field of science and technology'. What at the time may have meant, essentially, development co-operation or technology transfer, today suggests a much wider set of problems, global environmental problems which urgently require genuine co-operation. Moreover, the last paragraph of the Friendly Relations Declaration recalls that the seven principles formulated therein 'constitute basic principles of international law' not 'the' basic principles.[192] The Declaration is not a closed instrument. Not only does it refer, in its preamble, to the situation of Outer Space, whose main principles had been laid down throughout the 1960s,[193] but the several 'principles of international law relating to friendly relations and co-operation among States' came to be interpreted in an environmental light. One clear illustration is the duty to co-operate itself, which, as discussed earlier in this chapter, is part of the core of environmental protection in general international law. Similarly, the sovereign equality of States and the right to self-determination, both foundations of the right to exploit natural resources, have been subject to limitations by the operation of the prevention principle. Also, the protection of the environment has been expressly recognised as a limit – through the necessity and proportionality requirements of the right to self-defence and of reprisals – to the resort to and conduct of hostilities.[194] The development of international environmental law has also reduced the scope of the 'matters within the jurisdiction' of States. Even the principles of peaceful

[191] See the chapters by S Moyn and U Özsu and by M Koskenniemi and V Kari in this volume.
[192] See the chapter by P-M Dupuy in this volume.
[193] See the chapter by T Treves in this volume.
[194] *Legality of Nuclear Weapons* (n 106), paras 30–32.

settlement of disputes and of good faith have been reinterpreted so as to provide adequate procedures to settle highly technical environmental disputes[195] or to interpret, in good faith, the purpose of a purported environmental measure.[196]

The two moments of international law represented by the Friendly Relations Declaration and by the Stockholm and Rio Declarations are therefore not antithetic. In the current, and we may add, in the future state of the world, both foundations are needed.

195 See A Boyle and J Harrison, 'Judicial Settlement of International Environmental Disputes: Current Problems' (2013) 4 *Journal of International Dispute Settlement* 245.

196 See eg *Chagos Marine Protected Area Arbitration (Mauritius v United Kingdom)*, Case No 2011–03, Award, Perm Ct Arb, 18 March 2015.

13

Freedoms in Common Areas

Tullio Treves

I INTRODUCTION

The Friendly Relations Declaration of 1970[1] may be seen as the culmination of a process of reassessment of international law in the time of the Cold War. It was the most advanced product of agreement between East and West in the field of international law since the UN Charter.

The Declaration was not born in isolation. Suffice it to recall that, prior to its adoption in 1970, important results in the effort to codify international law had been achieved by the UN International Law Commission. In particular, the Vienna Conventions of Diplomatic and Consular Relations,[2] the Geneva Conventions on the Law of the Sea[3] and, last but not least, the 1969 Vienna Convention on the Law of Treaties[4] were all issued from International Law Commission (ILC) codification efforts. It is especially necessary to mention that, by 1970, States had begun to grapple with the legal implications of the expansion, due to technological advances and economic and strategic needs, of human activities in areas over which no State claimed sovereignty: the high seas, Antarctica and Outer Space.[5] Of these, the Friendly Relations Declaration only mentions Outer Space in a provision of the preamble, not followed by any of the operative provisions.

The legal regime of areas described as 'common' or as 'belonging to no State' ('*res communes omnium*' or '*res nullius*') was envisaged in the customary international law rules codified in the 1958 Geneva Convention on the High Seas and in the notion of the 'freedom of the high seas'. However, already at the time of the Friendly Relations Declaration a notable expansion and a complex nuancing and development of the international law rules concerning common areas had started.

[1] Declaration on Principles of International Law concerning Friendly Relations and Co-operation between States in accordance with the Charter of the United Nations, UNGA Res 2625 (XXV) (24 October 1970).

[2] Vienna Convention on Diplomatic Relations, 18 April 1961, 500 UNTS 95; Vienna Convention on Consular Relations, 22 April 1963, 596 UNTS 261.

[3] Convention on the High Seas, 29 April 1958, 450 UNTS 11); Convention on the Continental Shelf, 29 April 1958, 499 UNTS 311; Convention on the Territorial Sea and Contiguous Zone, 29 April 1958, 516 UNTS 205; Convention on Fishing and Conservation of the Living Resources of the High Seas, 29 April 1958, 559 UNTS 285.

[4] Vienna Convention on the Law of Treaties, 23 May 1969, 1155 UNTS 331.

[5] An early comprehensive study is R Wolfrum, *Die Internationalisierung staatsfreier Räume, Die Entwicklung einer internationaler Verwaltung für Antarktis, Weltraum, Hohe See und Meeresboden* (Springer, 1984).

First, as regards the areas concerned: not only the high seas were envisaged, but also a whole continent, Antarctica, and the immense expanse of Outer Space. Moreover, concerns for a notion that covers both areas within and outside national jurisdiction, but whose protection and preservation is of common interest for all States, namely the environment, was emerging and found a multilateral consecration in the 1972 Stockholm Conference on the Human Environment, with the adoption of the Stockholm Declaration.[6]

Second, the notion of freedom in the common areas, although maintained as a point of departure, was beginning to become not as broad and uncontroversial as it had hitherto been. The idea that in the common areas freedom had to be reconciled with co-operation and exploitation of resources for the common interest of all States was beginning to emerge: the concept of the 'common heritage of mankind', although limited to certain mineral resources of the bed of the high seas, had been discussed at the UN General Assembly since 1967 and in 1970 was incorporated in a Declaration of the UN General Assembly[7] adopted at the same session of the Friendly Relations Declaration.

In this chapter, the evolution of the freedoms of common areas in the decades following the Friendly Relations Declaration will be traced looking at the common maritime spaces (section II), the regime of Antarctica (section III) and the regime of Outer Space (section IV). The focus will be on the tensions between the States' claims to appropriation and exclusivity and the appeal of the notion of the common interest and of the co-operative efforts needed to implement this notion. The continuing role of 'freedom' and of 'due regard' will be assessed.

II THE COMMON MARITIME AREAS

1 *The Regime of the High Seas*

The basic ideas, set out in the customary international rules on the high seas codified at Geneva, were: (i) that the high seas areas cannot be appropriated and (ii) that access to and use of them is open to all States (the freedoms of the high seas) with the only limitation that these freedoms must be exercised with due regard to the interest of other States in their exercise of those freedoms. These ideas were and remain fundamental and, with the variants we will see, apply also to Antarctica and Outer Space.

These ideas are restated in Part VII of the 1982 UN Convention on the Law of the Sea (UNCLOS)[8] devoted to the high seas. Article 89 prohibits subjecting any part of the high seas to State sovereignty, and Article 87 affirms the freedom of the high seas, specifying that it 'shall be exercised with due regard to the interests of other States in their exercise of the freedom of the high seas'.

While the Third UN Conference on the Law of the Sea made the text of these articles almost literally coincident with that of the corresponding provisions of the Geneva Convention on the

[6] Declaration of the United Nations Conference on the Human Environment, Stockholm, 16 June 1972, UN Doc A/CONF.48/14/Rev.1, 2 et seq.

[7] Declaration of Principles governing the Sea-Bed and the Ocean Floor, and the Subsoil Thereof, beyond the Limits of Nations Jurisdiction, UNGA Res 2749 (XXV) (17 December 1970).

[8] UN Convention on the Law of the Sea, Montego Bay, 10 December 1982, 1833 UNTS 33.

High Seas,[9] between 1958 and 1982, when the UNCLOS was adopted, the context changed. Substantial parts of the high seas became the object of a process of appropriation by States, through the notions of the continental shelf, exclusive economic zone and archipelagic waters. Sovereign rights and, in the case of archipelagic waters, sovereignty were claimed and recognised on areas hitherto belonging to the high seas. The spatial scope of the freedom of the high seas was, consequently, substantially curtailed. The new definition of the continental shelf, set out in Article 76, establishes the coastal States' sovereign rights up to a minimum distance of 200 nautical miles from the baseline and a possibility of further extension if certain conditions are verified by the Commission on the Limits of the Continental Shelf, an expert body established under UNCLOS.[10] The seabed beyond the limits of national jurisdiction has become smaller than what it was before the emergence of the customary rule granting the coastal State sovereign rights on the continental shelf under the admittedly imprecise definition of the continental shelf in the Geneva Convention of 1958.[11] Moreover, as will be seen in more detail below, the seabed beyond the expanded limits of the continental shelf is now the 'Area' proclaimed as the common heritage of mankind.

The high seas to which the freedoms of the high seas apply fully are now limited to the water column of the sea beyond the outer limit of the exclusive economic zone. Within the stretch of sea that extends beyond the external limit of the territorial sea and up to 200 miles from the baselines, these freedoms apply only in part, as they are limited to a specific list of activities set out in Article 58. This is a consequence of the fact that the newly established regime of the exclusive economic zone grants the coastal State 'sovereign rights' and jurisdiction on resource-oriented activities as well as on scientific research and the protection of the environment up to 200 nautical miles from the baselines.

2 *Is the Seabed beyond National Jurisdiction Part of the High Seas?*

A debated question is whether the seabed beyond the limits of national jurisdiction, notwithstanding its being the Area proclaimed as the common heritage of mankind, may still be considered as the bottom of the high seas, entailing, when this part of the seabed is utilised for other purposes, the applicability of the freedoms and obligations of due regard.[12] In discussions entertained upon the initiative of the International Seabed Authority (ISA) between consortia engaged in deep seabed mining and cable-owners and utilisers in order to determine the legal regime applicable to the relationship between these two activities, it is considered as an accepted starting point that the obligation of 'due regard' applies.[13] This indicates that a positive response to the question is preferable, namely that the seabed beyond national jurisdiction is part of the high seas and the regime of the Area is limited to exploration for and exploitation of mineral resources. The current negotiations held at the Intergovernmental Conference

[9] See Convention on the High Seas (n 3), Art 2, which contains language equivalent to Arts 87 and 89 UNCLOS. On the rule prohibiting claims to sovereignty on any part of the high seas, see D Guyfoyle, 'Article 89, Invalidity of Claims of Sovereignty over the High Sea' in A Proelss (ed), *United Nations Convention on the High Seas: A Commentary* (Beck-Hart-Nomos, 2017) 687.

[10] Art 76(8) UNCLOS and Annex 2.

[11] Convention on the Continental Shelf, Geneva, 29 April 1958, 499 UNTS 312, Art 1.

[12] T Treves, 'High Seas', *Max Planck Encyclopedia of Public International Law* (April 2008), para 9.

[13] See the reports of the two workshops convened by the International Seabed Authority and by the International Cable Protection Committee (ICPC) ISA Technical Study Nr 14, Kingston, 2015 and ISA Technical Study Nr 24, Kingston 2019, as well as T Treves, '"Due Regard" Obligations under the 1982 UN Convention on the Law of the Sea: The Laying of Cables and Activities in the Area' (2019) 34 *The International Journal of Marine and Coastal Law* 167.

convened by the United Nations aiming at adopting an 'international legally binding instrument for the conservation and sustainable use of marine biological diversity of areas beyond the limits of national jurisdiction' (known with the acronym BBNJ) also indicate that States consider possible the establishment of another international regime applicable to the seabed which constitutes the Area, in addition to the appurtenant water column. This widely accepted possibility confirms that the seabed beyond national jurisdiction remains the bed of the high seas. The residual rule being that of freedom, States can agree to establish different regimes over it. The rules of 'due regard' should apply to the interaction between these regimes, as it does to the interaction between deep seabed mining and the laying of submarine cables.

3 *Deep Seabed Mining: The 'Common Heritage'*

The most important development in the decades after the Friendly Relations Declaration was adopted is the establishment of a regime, completed by a 'machinery', namely the ISA, a new international organisation, for the exploration and exploitation of the mineral resources of the Area.

Article 136 UNCLOS states that: 'The Area and its resources are the common heritage of mankind.' This provision may be read in two different ways: as a label referring to existing rules or as having a normative content. In other words, it may be read, on the one hand, as referring to all the rules setting out the 'regime' and the 'machinery' for the exploration and exploitation of mineral resources in the Area (i.e. for conducting 'activities in the Area' under the definition of Article 1(3) UNCLOS). These rules are set out in Part XI of UNCLOS and the relevant annexes, as amended by the 1994 Agreement Relating to the Implementation of Part XI of the UN Convention on the Law of the Sea of 10 December 1982 (the Implementation Agreement[14]), and completed by the ISA's Rules and Regulations.[15] Article 136 UNCLOS would thus have no other content or function than a reference to such rules. This view is supported by the fact that Article 140 UNCLOS specifies that activities in the Area shall be conducted for the benefit of mankind as a whole 'as specifically provided for in this Part'. The alternative reading would not exclude the rules governing the Area, but it would also recognise in Article 136 the expression of a more fundamental 'principle', whose content is not confined to those rules and, therefore, which can serve as a basis to extract further normative content.

It seems fair to observe that the first reading[16] is preferred by those wishing to limit the expansive potential of the common heritage of mankind, while the second is preferred by those wishing to resort to this idea as a normative principle on which specific rules or approaches may be built. It is interesting to observe that the 2011 advisory opinion of the Seabed Disputes Chamber of the International Tribunal for the Law of the Sea in the paragraphs referring to the common heritage tries not to endorse either one of the above-mentioned competing approaches.[17]

[14] New York, 29 July 1994, 1836 UNTS 42.

[15] The most important are published in International Seabed Authority, *Consolidated Regulations and Recommendations on Prospection and Exploration* (rev edn, ISA, 2015).

[16] To which the present writer has subscribed in a scholarly contribution: T Treves, 'Judicial Action for the Common Heritage' in H Hestermeyer et al (eds), *Law of the Sea in Dialogue* (Springer, 2010) 113, 114–15.

[17] *Responsibilities and obligations of States with respect to activities in the Area*, Advisory Opinion of 1 February 2011, ITLOS Reports, 2011, 10, paras 76 and 226 (close to the descriptive reading of the 'common heritage') and 159 (close to the normative reading).

4 *Deep Seabed Mining: The 'Regime'*

The 'regime' and the 'machinery' for deep seabed mining established by UNCLOS are set out in a complex set of provisions that seek to strike a balance between equality of rights for all States and the recognition of the fact that only a minority of them have the financial and technological capability to engage in this risky and expensive activity.

The mineral resources of the Area are 'vested in mankind as a whole on whose behalf the Authority shall act' (Article 137(2) UNCLOS). Claims to rights to minerals recovered from the Area shall not be recognised except when acquired or exercised 'in accordance with' Part XI of UNCLOS (Article 137(3) UNCLOS). The prohibition of claims or exercise of sovereignty or appropriation is repeated for 'any part' of the Area in Article 137(1). The principle of due regard is also confirmed providing that the exercise of the freedoms of the high seas shall be exercised with due regard 'for the rights under this Convention with respect to activities in the Area' (Article 87(2) UNCLOS) and stated clearly as follows, in Article 147(1) and (3):

1. Activities in the Area shall be carried out with reasonable regard for other activities in the marine environment . . .
3. Other activities in the marine environment shall be conducted with reasonable regard for activities in the Area.[18]

The rules on the 'regime' provide access to deep seabed mining to States that can show that they, or entities sponsored by them, have the necessary means and capabilities. Such access is obtained on the basis of contracts with the ISA.[19] The prospecting work, conducted in order to collect the data necessary for the granting of a contract, is utilised also to facilitate the obtaining of such contracts by developing States.[20] The mechanism has worked. Contracts for exploration of polymetallic nodules and other mineral resources of the Area have been awarded not only to enterprises from industrially advanced countries (including some, as India and China, that are often classified as 'developing') but also to enterprises sponsored by developing States, such as Fiji and Tonga, which utilise mining sites identified by consortia from industrialised countries. It must, however, be remarked that enterprises from developing States and sponsored by them may be suspected of being the cover for interests of enterprises of developed States. The aforementioned advisory opinion of 2011 of the Seabed Disputes Chamber raised this issue when it observed that:

> the spread of sponsoring States 'of convenience' would jeopardize uniform application of the highest standards of protection of the marine environment, the safe development of activities in the Area and protection of the common heritage of mankind.[21]

5 *Deep Seabed Mining: The 'Machinery'*

As regards the 'machinery', the structure and decision-making of the ISA also reflects the compromise between the equality of Member States and special interests, not limited to those of the

[18] The expression 'reasonable regard' in Art 147 is equivalent to the expression 'due regard' contained in Art 87 and in other articles of UNCLOS. See with references Treves (n 13) 4.

[19] Art 153 UNCLOS and Annex III, esp Arts 3 and 4, Implementation Agreement, esp section 1, paras 6–9.

[20] UNCLOS, Annex III, Art 8, Implementation Agreement, section 1, Art 10.

[21] *Responsibilities and obligations of States with respect to activities in the Area* (n 17) 10, para 159. Sponsoring States 'of convenience' are defined in the same paragraph of the Opinion as 'commercial enterprises based in developed States . . . setting up companies in developing States, acquiring their nationality and obtaining their sponsorship, in the hope of being subjected to less burdensome regulations and controls'.

industrialised States engaged in deep seabed mining, but including also those of land-based producers and of the main importers of the minerals to be derived from the Area.

The structure of the ISA[22] includes a plenary body, the Assembly, whose wide powers do not include decisions on awarding contracts for the exploration and exploitation of the resources of the Area. These powers are entrusted to the Council, a thirty-six-member body in which special interests are represented in 'chambers', each of which may, by the vote of a majority of its members, veto a decision on matters of substance, even though this decision may have been approved by the prescribed majority of two-thirds of the members of the Council present and voting.[23] In fact the key role in reviewing and in recommending the adoption of requests for contracts for exploration and exploitation of deep seabed mineral resources is granted to a subsidiary body of the Council, the Legal and Technical Commission, composed of experts nominated by the States parties and elected by the Council, thus including the interests represented therein and in particular the interest of the industrialised States. Recommendations by the Legal and Technical Commission for the award of contracts are, in practice, automatically approved by the Council, as the Council has only the power to disapprove the contract by a two-thirds majority including the majority of the members present and voting in each of the chambers representing special interests. With this mechanism industrialised States achieve their objective to subtract to the main political bodies, the Assembly and the Council, as much as possible, the process and decisions concerning the award of contracts.

6 *The Substantial Adjustments in Favour of Developed States: The 1994 Implementation Agreement*

The balance between the interests of the industrialised States and the other States claiming to represent the interest of mankind as set out in UNCLOS as adopted in 1982 was the subject of a substantial adjustment negotiated after 1982 when it appeared very likely that the Convention would enter into force without any of the developed industrialised States becoming a party. This adjustment, in fact a substantial amendment to Part XI of UNCLOS and of the annexes thereto, was negotiated between 1990 and 1994 and took the form of the Implementation Agreement adopted on 28 July 1994.[24] This agreement is to be applied 'as a single instrument' together with Part XI of UNCLOS. The amendments address such key matters as the costs of the Authority, decision-making in its organs, the transfer of technology and production policy. The Implementation Agreement also postpones for an indefinite period of time the establishment of the industrial body of the Authority, the 'Enterprise', as a functional entity, which was envisioned in 1982 as a symbol of the internationalisation of the deep seabed.

The Implementation Agreement reflects requests by the industrialised countries, in particular of the United States who argued that the regime of deep seabed mining as set out in UNCLOS as adopted in 1982 did not take their interests sufficiently into consideration. Its adoption led to the decision of all the main industrialised States to ratify the Convention or to accede to it. Only the United States, notwithstanding the favourable opinion of most of its governments after 1994,

[22] The structure of the ISA is described on the basis of UNCLOS Part XI, section 4, as amended by the 1995 Implementation Agreement, esp section 3. The main changes introduced by the Implementation Agreement are examined below.

[23] Implementation Agreement, section 3, Art 5.

[24] For a more detailed analysis of the Implementation Agreement and of the negotiations preceding it, see T Treves, 'Entry into Force of the Law of the Sea Convention: The Road Towards Universality' in N Al Nauimi and R Meese (eds), *International Legal Issues Arising under the United Nations Decade for International Law* (Kluwer, 1995) 443–80.

has not joined the now 168 parties bound by UNCLOS as amended by the Implementation Agreement. The compromise reached with the 1994 Agreement shows that the overwhelming majority of States were convinced of the necessity that UNCLOS as a whole, including the reaffirmation of the basic principles on the high seas and recognition of the newly established sovereign rights on the exclusive economic zone, was a priority for all, and that it was necessary to avoid divergences on deep seabed mining imperilling the great achievement of the United Nations and of the diplomacies of all States represented by UNCLOS.

III ANTARCTICA: A RESTRICTED 'CLUB' FOR THE PROTECTION OF COMMON INTERESTS

1 *The Antarctic Treaty System*

Antarctica is a continent mostly covered by ice that includes the South Pole. A regime regulating its legal status and activities is set out in the Antarctic Treaty, adopted at Washington on 1 December 1959 and entered in force on 25 July 1961,[25] a decade before the Friendly Relations Declaration. The Treaty is complemented by recommendations adopted by the States parties at Antarctic Treaty Consultative meetings and by three international instruments: the Convention on the Conservation of Antarctic Seals adopted in 1972 and entered into force in 1978,[26] the Convention for the Conservation of Antarctic Marine Living Resources signed in 1980 and entered into force in 1982[27] and the Protocol on the Environmental Protection of the Antarctic Treaty ('Environmental Protocol'), signed in 1991 and entered into force in 1998.[28] The Antarctic Treaty, its Environmental Protocol and the above-mentioned Conventions form what is commonly referred to as the 'Antarctic System'.[29]

For the purposes of the present chapter it seems useful to focus on two aspects. The first is the mechanism through which the Antarctic System protects interests that are common to all States and avoids conflicts. The second concerns membership in the system and the way in which what was originally a restricted club of powerful and advanced countries has expanded to include a broad number of States, while resisting claims to make the system universal by involving the United Nations.

2 *The Protection of Common Interests and the Avoidance of Sovereignty Conflicts*

The Antarctic Treaty was concluded in the wake of the successful co-operation concerning Antarctica between scientists of many States in the framework of the International Geophysical Year (1 July 1957 to 31 December 1958). Freedom of scientific research in Antarctica was from the beginning the driving idea of the Treaty, as set out in the preamble and in Article 2. In the preamble, the contracting parties acknowledge 'the substantial contribution to scientific knowledge resulting from international cooperation in scientific investigation in Antarctica' and state that they are:

[25] 402 UNTS 71.
[26] 1080 UNTS 176.
[27] 1329 UNTS 47.
[28] 30 ILM 1455.
[29] For a detailed and concise treatment, see S Voneky and S Addison-Agyei, 'Antarctica' in *Max Planck Encyclopedia of Public International Law* (April 2008).

> Convinced that the establishment of a firm foundation to the continuation and development of such cooperation on the basis of freedom of scientific investigation in Antarctica as applied during the International Geophysical Year accords with the interests of science and the progress of all mankind

Article 2 states that:

> Freedom of scientific investigation in Antarctica and cooperation toward that end, as applied during the International Geophysical Year, shall continue, subject to the provisions of the present Treaty.

The Ministerial Declaration adopted on the fiftieth anniversary of the Antarctic Treaty, on 6 April 2009, confirms in the preamble that the Consultative Parties are '[m]indful that freedom of scientific investigation is and continues to be a cornerstone of the Treaty'.[30]

A necessary premise for the exercise of freedom of scientific research and co-operation for that purpose was that scientific research would not be entangled with territorial sovereignty claims or suspected of having non-peaceful and military purposes.

Territorial sovereignty claims on certain portions of Antarctica had been advanced by various States (the 'claimant States') since the beginning of the twentieth century. As these claims overlapped and were not recognised by the biggest powers involved in activities in Antarctica (the United States and the Soviet Union), the risk that scientific investigation would provoke political difficulties was real. The Antarctic Treaty prevented such difficulties by 'freezing' the existing territorial claims and prohibiting new such claims. Article IV, while stating in paragraph 1 that nothing in the Treaty can be interpreted as renunciation of territorial sovereignty claims or possible future claims or recognition or non-recognition thereof, states in paragraph 2 that:

> No acts or activities taking place while the present Treaty is in force shall constitute a basis for asserting, supporting or denying a claim to territorial sovereignty in Antarctica or create any rights of sovereignty in Antarctica. No new claim, or enlargement of an existing claim, to territorial sovereignty in Antarctica shall be asserted while the present Treaty is in force.

The sixty years of practice since the adoption of the Antarctic Treaty show that the freezing of claims was successful. This is confirmed by the follow-up of the inclusion by Australia and Argentina, both claimant States, of areas corresponding to the continental shelf appurtenant to the coasts of Antarctica upon which they claim sovereignty in their submissions to the Commission for the Limits of the Continental Shelf established under UNCLOS.[31] The submissions of Australia and of Argentina raised protests, in which Article IV of the Antarctic Treaty was invoked, by seven consultative parties. However, Australia explicitly requested the Commission 'not to take any action for the time being with regard to the information … that relates to the continental shelf appurtenant to Antarctica'.[32] Argentina, made an equivalent statement through its representative before the Commission for the Limits of the Continental Shelf.[33] While these submissions had the effect of showing that the territorial sovereignty claims, although 'frozen',

[30] Antarctic Treaty Consultative Meeting XXIII, Washington Ministerial Declaration on the Fiftieth Anniversary of the Antarctic Treaty, fifth para of the preamble.

[31] Art 176(8) UNCLOS and Annex II.

[32] Note by Australia directed to the UN Secretary-General Nr 89/2004 of November 2004, Attachment to the Continental Shelf Submission of Australia, Executive Summary, AU-DOC-ES.

[33] Commission on the Limits of the Continental Shelf, Summary of Recommendations of the Commission on the Limits of the Continental Shelf in Regard to the Submission Made by Argentina on 21 April 2009, para 4.

were still alive, the fact that they had no consequence shows that the involved States recognise that they are bound by Article IV.

3 *Prohibition of Military Activities*

Scientific research may be used for military purposes and may interfere with military activities. The incompatibility between the exercise of freedom of research and military activities is specifically recognised in the Antarctic Treaty. In the preamble the contracting parties recognise 'that it is in the interest of all mankind that Antarctica shall continue for ever to be used exclusively for peaceful purposes'.

Article I, after stating that 'Antarctica shall be used for peaceful purposes only', specifies that:

> There shall be prohibited, *inter alia*, any measures of military nature, such as the establishment of military bases and fortifications, the carrying out of military manoeuvres, as well as the testing of any type of weapons.

This provision is complemented by Article V, which prohibits 'any nuclear explosions in Antarctica and the disposal therein of radioactive wastes'.

It is noteworthy that the Antarctic Treaty does not limit itself to the 'peaceful purposes only' rule, as was to be done, for instance, in the UNCLOS (Articles 88 and 141). Military activities are prohibited whether or not they are consistent with the States' obligations under the Charter.

4 *The Protection of the Environment and the Opposition to Mineral Resource Activities in Antarctica*

An aspect of the interest of mankind as a whole not explicitly recognised in the Antarctic Treaty is the need to protect the environment of Antarctica, in particular in light of the importance, for the very purposes of scientific research, of preserving its pristine characteristics. This lack of mention of environmental protection is understandable in a Treaty adopted in 1959, when the legal aspects of environmental protection were yet to be widely recognised.

The connection between the freedom of scientific research in Antarctica and the protection of the environment was made in the practical application of the Treaty and in the recognition that knowledge concerning important global environmental questions could be obtained through research in Antarctica, and that such research was dependent on preserving Antarctica's pristine environment. Clear examples concern research on the Ozone Layer and on climate change. The first hole in the Ozone Layer was discovered in the 1980s over Antarctica. In the Ministerial Declaration for the fiftieth anniversary of the Antarctic Treaty the contracting parties acknowledge 'the key role that Antarctic science plays in understanding the world's climate system' and express their concern 'about the implications of global environmental change, in particular climate change, for the Antarctic environment and dependent and associated ecosystems'.

The turning point in making environmental protection a central issue of the Antarctic system came when the States parties concluded in 1988 the Convention on the Regulation of Antarctic Mineral Resource Activities (CRAMRA). This Convention provided for the possibility of exploration and exploitation of the mineral resources of Antarctica. Although such possibility was made conditional on very strict requirements, including environmental protection requirements, the CRAMRA met with strong opposition by environmental protection oriented non-governmental organisations. As a consequence, Australia and France, two of the Consultative

Parties most involved in the negotiation of the Convention, announced their decision not to ratify it. As ratification by all Consultative Parties was necessary for entry into force, this meant that the CRAMRA would never become law. The backlash against the mining of mineral resources led to a strong engagement of the parties to the Antarctic Treaty to protect the Antarctic environment. They quickly agreed on the Environmental Protocol that prohibits all activities relating to mineral resources other than scientific research (Article 7). A change in the provision containing such prohibition may be proposed fifty years from entry into force of the Environmental Protocol, although under very strict conditions (Article 25(5)).

The sinking of the CRAMRA and the adoption of the Environmental Protocol show that a perceived deviation by the States parties to the Antarctic Treaty from what may be seen as the common interest of all States is not tolerated by the international community. The Environmental Protocol not only prohibits mineral resource activities. Its contracting parties express in the preamble the conviction that 'the development of a comprehensive regime for the protection of the Antarctic environment and dependent and associated ecosystems is in the interest of mankind as a whole'. They moreover 'designate Antarctica as a natural reserve, devoted to peace and science' (Article 2).

How this designation may (if at all) be reconciled with regulation of tourism in Antarctica, a subject presently under active consideration, is still to be seen. Tourism may be considered as an activity aimed at broadening human experience and, as such, of general interest. However, it may also be seen as an industry based in the developed world that caters for people coming mostly from that world so that it may be argued that the negative impact on the environment should be seen as the decisive factor.[34]

5 *The Limited Membership of the Antarctic Treaty*

The rules and practice on participation in the Antarctic Treaty show that the Antarctic Treaty established a 'club' of a limited number of States engaged in research activity in Antarctica. This club is potentially an open one, as all States which are Members of the United Nations are entitled to become parties. In fact, since 1959, it has expanded to take into account that research in Antarctica had become of interest for a broadening group of States and that it had become politically expedient to include certain States whose engagement in Antarctic research is far from evident.

At the beginning, the parties were the twelve original signatory States. They are the 'Consultative Parties' which enjoy all rights under the Treaty. Access by a State to this category of parties requires it to have conducted 'substantial scientific research activity [in Antarctica] such as establishing a scientific station or the dispatch of a scientific expedition' (Article IX, paragraph 2). Compliance with this requirement is verified by the Consultative Parties. There have been seventeen acceding States which have met this requirement and have become Consultative Parties, which now total twenty-nine. In addition to the Consultative Parties, twenty-five other States have acceded to the Treaty, with the status of Non-Consultative Parties. They sit as observers, without the right of vote, in the Antarctic Treaty Consultative Meetings, the main decision-making body.

[34] R Wolfrum, S Vonecky and J Friedrich, 'The Admissibility of Land-Based Tourism in Antarctica under International Law' (2005) 65 *Zeitschrift für ausländische Öffentliche Recht und Völkerrecht* 735–40; S Vonecky and S Addison-Agyei, 'Antarctica' in *Max Planck Encyclopedia of Public International Law* (April 2008), paras 91–96.

The total number of parties is currently fifty-four. Even including the Non-Consultative parties, this number is just above one-quarter of the Member States of the United Nations. The Consultative Parties are less than one-sixth of the Members of the UN. Antarctic Treaty Parties include, nonetheless, all the most powerful and wealthiest States of the world and a majority of the most populous ones (with the exception of Indonesia and Bangladesh). Among the Consultative Parties are all the five permanent members of the Security Council, twelve of the members of the European Union, many developed States and some important developing States such as India, Argentina, Peru, Ecuador, Brazil and South Africa. It must be added that all the Consultative Parties are parties to the Environmental Protocol, as they must be according to its provisions, while this is the case for only eleven out of twenty-five Non-Consultative Parties.

6 *The Third World Attempt to Universalise the Antarctic System and Its Decay and Failure*

A Treaty through which a minority of the States of the world, including all the former colonial powers, claim to regulate 'in the interest of mankind' (Antarctic Treaty, second preambular paragraph) activities in an uninhabited continent with a great potential for scientific research as well as for mining, could not escape being questioned in the post-colonial world. In fact, during the 1980s, it came under heavy criticism, and even virulent attacks. It is noteworthy, however, that such criticism and attacks were overcome through a process of discussion and adaptation which did not jeopardise the dominant role of the Consultative Parties.

The criticism of the Antarctic Treaty system came from Third World countries led by Malaysia, whose then Prime Minister, Dr Mahatir Bin Mohamed, played a key role. It is significant that Malaysia connected Antarctica with the regime for deep seabed mining adopted at the Third UN Conference on the Law of the Sea. The Malaysian delegate concluded his address to the closing session of the Third United Nations Conference on the Law of the Sea stating: 'It is now time to focus on another area of common interest ... I refer to Antarctica where immense potentialities exist for the benefit of all mankind.'[35] Together with other Third World States, Malaysia secured in 1983 that the 'Question of Antarctica' be placed on the Agenda of the UN General Assembly. The question was actively debated, especially in the early years following its placing on the Assembly's Agenda,[36] up to 2005 when the consideration of the item was suspended.

The main criticism concerned the decision-making mechanism set out in the Antarctic Treaty and, in particular, the dominant role of the Consultative Parties. The idea of proclaiming Antarctica as the common heritage of mankind and of adopting an international mechanism for the management of the Antarctic continent entrusting such mechanism to the United Nations was evoked by Malaysia and other Third World States. Malaysia argued that the distinction between Consultative and Non-Consultative Parties went 'against the grain of current international reality'.[37]

[35] Third United Nations Conference on the Law of the Sea, Official Records, vol XVII, 118, para 34 (Intervention of Mr Gazali Shafie at the 192nd meeting of the Plenary, 9 December 1992).

[36] For a detailed analysis of the discussion at the thirty-eighth and thirty-ninth sessions on the UN General Assembly, M Hayashi, 'The Antarctica Question in the United Nations' (1986) 19 *Cornell International Law Journal* 275–90.

[37] UN General Assembly, First Committe, UN Doc A/C.1/38/42d meeting, 1.

The Third World criticism of the Antarctic system and the basic ideas for its reform were well synthetised in Malaysia's response, dated 31 May 1984, to inquiries of the UN Secretary-General:[38]

> [T]he international community, through the United Nations system, should be more directly involved in the decision-making process concerning Antarctica ... The present machinery for Antarctica has not kept pace with current international realities. The Antarctic system with its two-tiered membership is unacceptable because of its exclusivity, its unaccountability, and its secrecy. Membership as Consultative Parties requires the ability to meet stringent qualifications established by the original Consultative Parties themselves, which can only be met by rich and scientifically developed countries. The Consultative Parties are not, and do not regard themselves as accountable to the international community. Their deliberations are conducted in secrecy although their decisions are subsequently and necessarily made public. While the Consultative Parties assert that they have managed Antarctica in the interest of mankind, it is obvious that the interest of mankind can only be defined and managed by mankind itself, through a process or machinery which it establishes or finds acceptable, and not by any country or group of countries, however well-intentioned. The coincidence of the interest of mankind and the interest of the Consultative Parties is not inevitable or preordained ... [Malaysia] is firmly of the view that Antarctica as the common heritage of mankind requires a regime that is truly universal in character and committed to serving the interest of the entire international community.[39]

The initiative of Malaysia and its Third World allies at the UN General Assembly succeeded in making Antarctica a subject-matter for debate in the Assembly for two decades. It was also successful in that it led to the adoption of more transparent practices in the meetings of the Consultative Parties, including granting, as early as 1983, Non-Consultative Parties a role as observers in the meetings, establishing a permanent secretariat and making knowledge about the activities connected to the Antarctic System more easily accessible, including though the establishment of a website. Most importantly, the debates at the General Assembly stimulated participation in the Antarctic Treaty and in scientific activities in Antarctica, as many States were encouraged to fulfil the conditions for becoming Consultative Parties. The shelving of the CRAMRA eliminated one of the subjects of contention and reoriented the debate towards the protection of the environment.

Remarkably, a large majority of the present parties to the Antarctic Treaty have acceded after, or at the time of, the Malaysian initiative. Since then, fifteen States have been admitted as Consultative Parties, more than doubling the number of States in this category. Moreover, since 1984, twenty-two States have acceded to the Antarctic Treaty and are now Non-Consultative Parties.

The factors that may be seen as indications of the success of the Malaysian initiative were also drivers of its decline and failure. The debates brought to light the positive aspects of the Antarctic Treaty so that many States moved from the ranks of the criticisers to those of the Parties to the Treaty. The culmination of this process was the decision in 2005 not to continue the discussion of the 'Question of Antarctica' at the UN General Assembly, followed by the accession of Malaysia to the Antarctic Treaty, on 31 October 2011.[40]

38 UN Doc A/39/583 (Part II) of 9 November 1984, section 27, 107.

39 ibid, paras 6(1), 6(2) and 6(5).

40 A detailed description of the Malaysian initiative and of the factors that led to its abandonment and to Malaysia's accession to the Treaty, is in BA Hamzah, 'Malaysia and the Southern Ocean: Revisiting the Question of Antarctica'

IV OUTER SPACE: AN INTERNATIONAL SPACE RESISTING TO CLAIMS OF APPROPRIATION

1 *A New Law of Outer Space*

In the immediate aftermath of the first orbital flight of the Soviet artificial satellite *Sputnik* in 1957, and of the first manned flight into space by the Soviet astronaut Yuri Gagarin in 1961, it appeared clear to States that this was an area over which expansion of international law was necessary, especially in light of the risk of Outer Space being monopolised by the few States – in the early years only two, the USSR and the United States – having the ability to conduct activities there.

Very quickly, States addressed the issue in the framework of the UN General Assembly. Already in 1961, the same year of Gagarin's flight, they adopted unanimously a resolution[41] setting out as 'principles' that '[i]nternational law, including the Charter of the United Nations, applies to Outer Space and celestial bodies' and that '[o]uter space and celestial bodies are free to exploration and use by all States in conformity with international law and are not subject to national appropriation'.[42]

A more elaborate resolution setting out a 'Declaration of Legal Principles Governing the Activities of States in the Exploration and Use of Outer Space' was adopted in 1963,[43] followed in 1966 by the Treaty on Principles Governing the Activities of States in the Exploration and Use of Outer Space, including the Moon and Other Celestial Bodies (the Outer Space Treaty).[44] In light of the unanimous adoption of the 1963 Declaration and of the fact that it counts ninety-six States parties plus twenty-three signatory States, this treaty may be seen as a reflection of the current customary regime of Outer Space.

2 *Similarities with the High Seas, the Area, and Antarctica*

The provisions of the Outer Space Treaty present similarities with the regime of Antarctica and with that of the high seas.[45] The Treaty recognises in the preamble 'the common interests of all mankind in the progress of the exploration and use of Outer Space for peaceful purposes' and expresses the belief 'that the exploration and use of Outer Space should be carried on for the benefit of all peoples irrespective of the degree of their economic or scientific development'. In Article 1 the Treaty states that:

> The exploration and use of Outer Space, including the moon and other celestial bodies, shall be carried out for the benefit and in the interests of all countries, irrespective of their degree of economic or scientific development, and shall be the province of all mankind.

The Treaty also provides, in Article II, for an obligation of non-appropriation which was later repeated in the preamble of the Friendly Relations Declaration, and, in Article I, second and

(2010) 41 *Ocean Development and International Law* 186–95. Malaysia also acceded to the Environmental Protocol on 14 September 2016.

[41] UNGA Res 1721 (XVI) (20 December 1960).

[42] ibid, para 1(a) and (b).

[43] UNGA Res 1962 (XVIII) (13 December 1963).

[44] Treaty on Principles Governing the Activities of States in the Exploration and Use of Outer Space, including the Moon and Other Celestial Bodies, 27 January 1967, 610 UNTS 205, adopted by UNGA Res 2222 (19 December 1966), opened for signature in London, Moscow and Washington on 27 January 1967, 610 UNTS 205.

[45] As observed by J Crawford, *Brownlie's Principles on Public International Law* (8th edn, Oxford University Press, 2012) 348–49.

third paragraphs, for freedom of 'exploration and use' and of 'scientific research'. Like the Antarctic Treaty, the Outer Space Treaty further provides for the demilitarisation and denuclearisation of Outer Space (Article IV). Similar to the rule applicable to the high seas, it also provides that activities in Outer Space shall be conducted 'with due regard to the corresponding interests of the other States Parties to the Treaty' (Article IX). Concern for the protection of the environment is present in the Treaty. The relevant provision (Article IX) envisages however such concerns not for the purpose of protecting the environment of Outer Space but for protecting 'the environment of the Earth resulting from the introduction of extraterrestrial materials'.

Like Antarctica and the Area, but unlike the high seas, Outer Space is an area in which only a small number of States have the economic and technological possibility of conducting activities. The universal access and freedom of exploration and use thus apply, in practice, to a limited number of States, even though the door is open to new entrants. The interest of the international community, beyond the proclamation of Outer Space as the 'province of all mankind' and the reference to the 'common interest of all mankind', does not lead to the establishment of an organised regime as happened for Antarctica and for the seabed beyond the limits of national jurisdiction. The regime of Outer Space is closer to that of the high seas.

3 *Third World Criticism: The Claim to Sovereignty over the Geo-Stationary Orbit and Its Failure*

The regime of Outer Space as defined in the Outer Space Treaty was not, however, exempt from objections from Third World States. It was noted, for example, that:

> the international community is questioning all the terms of international law which were elaborated when the developing countries could not count on adequate scientific advice and were thus not able to observe and evaluate the omissions, contradictions and consequences of the proposals which were prepared with great ability by the industrialized powers for their benefit.

This argument is put forward in the 'Bogotá Declaration' adopted on 3 December 1976 by Brazil, Colombia, Congo, Ecuador, Indonesia, Kenya, Uganda and Zaire.[46] Notwithstanding the rhetoric invoking the UN General Assembly Resolution 1803 (XVII) on 'Permanent Sovereignty over Natural Resources'[47] and the 'Charter of economic rights and duties of States',[48] the proclamation pursued aims of appropriation, which make a comparison with the Malaysian criticism of the Antarctic Treaty system improper. The eight signatory States are all equatorial States, so that portions of the geostationary orbit[49] lie above their territories. In the Bogotá Declaration, these States proclaimed their sovereignty over the geostationary orbit 'as a limited natural resource'. They alleged, among other reasons, that the geostationary orbit does not belong to Outer Space because its characteristics depend on the effect of gravity. They claimed that the use of the geostationary orbit overlaying their territories (including maritime areas under their jurisdiction) required their authorisation, while the portions of the geostationary orbit overlaying the open seas beyond the national jurisdiction of States were the common heritage of mankind and should be regulated by 'the competent international agencies'.

46 Declaration of the first meeting of Equatorial Countries, adopted on 3 December 1976, www.jaxa.jp/library/space_law/chapter_2/2-2-1-2_e.html.
47 Permanent Sovereignty over Natural Resources, UNGA Res 1803 (XVII) (14 December 1962).
48 Charter of Economic Rights and Duties of States, UNGA Res 3281 (XXIX) (12 December 1974).
49 S Hobe, 'Geostationary Orbit', *Max Planck Encyclopedia of Public International Law* (April 2008).

The equatorial States' arguments were rejected by the industrialised States and found only lukewarm appreciation of most of the Third World States. The geostationary orbit was inscribed in the agenda of the UN General Assembly's Committee of the Peaceful Uses of Outer Space in vague terms in 1977,[50] and its formulation has remained so until now:

> Matters relating to:
>
> (a) The definition and delimitation of Outer Space;
> (b) The character and utilization of the geostationary orbit, including consideration of ways and means to ensure the rational and equitable use of the geostationary orbit without prejudice to the role of the International Telecommunications Union.[51]

No genuine progress has been made, however, in the decades-long consideration of the subject by the Legal Subcommittee and a special working group. The linkage between the geostationary orbit and the definition of Outer Space was in its terms reasonable, as the claims of the equatorial States were based on their view (strongly denied by other States) that the geostationary orbit is not part of Outer Space. In practice, it had the effect of justifying stalemate. The discussions on the definition of Outer Space were inconclusive but sufficient for the Subcommittee to avoid addressing the geostationary orbit part of the item. This was formalised in 2000 when it was agreed that 'no Working Group shall be convened on the issue of equitable access to the geostationary orbit'.[52] When the Working Group which had previously dealt, although inconclusively, with the geostationary orbit was reconvened in 2018, its mandate and title were limited to the 'Definition and Delimitation of Outer Space', in conformity with the agreement reached in 2000.[53] This meant that delegations may continue repeating in the Legal Subcommittee the opposing arguments on the geostationary orbit but that no progress is likely to be made. This finds corroboration in the report of the most recent meeting of the Legal Subcommittee.[54]

V DISPUTE-SETTLEMENT: A DIFFERENT LEVEL OF ENGAGEMENT

While the different regimes concerning common spaces have, as it has been shown, many common elements of substance, they diverge as regards the settlement of disputes. The regime of the high seas as well as the particular regime of deep seabed mining are provided by UNCLOS with an elaborate dispute settlement mechanism, based on the principle of compulsory jurisdiction of two permanent bodies, the International Court of Justice and the International Tribunal for the Law of the Sea, with its Seabed Disputes Chamber, and of ad hoc arbitration tribunals.[55] The BBNJ negotiations have not yet given clear indications of the direction taken as regards dispute settlement. It is nonetheless clear that the negotiating States are considering the possibility of adopting, as regards disputes concerning the interpretation or application of the agreement under negotiation, the mechanism of Part XV of UNCLOS. In

[50] UNGA Res 32/196 (XXXII) (20 December 1977), Art 6b.
[51] UNGA Res 72/77.
[52] The agreement is set out in a recommendation adopted by the Legal Subcommittee and published in the Report of the Subcommittee in UN Doc A/AC.105/738, of 20 April 2000, annex III, para 8c. The report was approved by the Committee on the Peaceful uses of Outer Space whose report was, in turn, approved by a General Assembly Resolution.
[53] UN Doc A/AC.105/1177, para 82.
[54] ibid, esp paras 86, 87, 102–7.
[55] UNCLOS, Part XV, and Part XI, section 5.

fact, a proposal to this effect has been included by the President of the Conference in the draft text submitted for discussion on 17 May 2019.[56]

The provisions concerning Antarctica and Outer Space are far less elaborate. The Antarctic Treaty Environment Protocol contains limited possibilities for the compulsory settlement of disputes,[57] while the Antarctic Treaty's provision on the settlement of disputes does not ensure submission to a court or arbitral tribunal in case of disagreement, although, even in this case, the parties are not absolved 'from the responsibility of continuing to seek to resolve' the dispute by peaceful means.[58] The Outer Space Treaty has no provision on the settlement of disputes.

The difference shows a different level of engagement of States. While the complex rules adopted in the matters covered by UNCLOS, as well as in the Antarctic Environmental Protocol, imposed the need to complement these detailed provisions with the possibility of submitting unilaterally disputes concerning their interpretation or application to a judge or arbitrator, this was not the case for the far less detailed rules established for Antarctica in general and for Outer Space.

VI CONCLUSION

During the decades since the Friendly Relations Declaration was adopted the areas beyond national jurisdiction have attracted the attention of the international community. States have confirmed the basic rules applying to the high seas and built upon them the regimes of Antarctica and Outer Space, as well as the special regime for deep seabed mining. The basic principles of non-appropriation, of freedom of access and research, and of due regard have been adopted in treaties applying to these areas.

The very regime of the high seas has nevertheless changed. The freedom of the high seas applies now to a smaller part of the seabed and of the water column. Moreover, an organised regime for the exploitation of the mineral resources of the bed of the high seas has been established on the basis of UNCLOS, a convention binding a very high number of States. The fact that this regime could be established shows that co-operation and the pursuit of common aims – synthetised in the idea of the common heritage of mankind – is seen as the only broadly acceptable approach to activities in common areas. This is confirmed by current negotiation on BBNJ.

The resistance to the attempt to appropriate the geostationary orbit is a further confirmation that a key element of the regime of common areas, namely the principle of non-appropriation, is strongly supported. On the other hand, the lack of success in the attempt to universalise the Antarctic system by eliminating the dominant position of the Consultative Parties shows that the establishment and functioning of an organised regime for common areas require that the interests of the most important States be taken into consideration. This is further confirmed by the shelving of the proposals concerning the geostationary orbit, and, even more so, by the role granted to special interests in the structure and decision-making process of the ISA, as well as by the fact that the regime for deep seabed mining originally designed in UNCLOS (as adopted in 1982) had to be substantially amended, even before the Convention entered into

[56] Draft text of an agreement under the United Nations Convention on the Law of the Sea on the conservation and sustainable use of marine biological diversity of areas beyond national jurisdiction, UN Doc A/CONF.232/2019/6, Art 55.

[57] Arts 19 and 29. T Treves, 'Compulsory Settlement of Disputes: A New Element in the Antarctic System' in F Francioni, T Scovazzi (eds), *International Law for Antarctica* (Kluwer, 1996) 603–12.

[58] Antarctic Treaty, Art XI.

force, in order to take into consideration the concerns of the most powerful and industrially advanced States.

Concern for the protection of the environment in common areas has progressively become a part of the regimes concerning these areas. UNCLOS has a whole part, Part XII, concerning the protection of the environment.[59] Some specific provisions of this Part and of Part XI apply to the high seas and to the Area.[60] The negotiations on BBNJ are in great part inspired by environmental concerns. The Antarctic regime has been substantially changed to include an elaborate set of provisions for the protection of the environment in the Environmental Protocol. The consideration of environmental concerns in Outer Space has made little progress beyond Article IX of the Outer Space Treaty,[61] even though discussions on space debris, while not exclusively inspired by environmental concerns, in fact envisages one of the main sources of man-made contamination of the Outer Space.

[59] See generally the chapter by L-A Duvic-Paoli and JE Viñuales in this volume.

[60] Arts 145 and 209 refer to pollution from activities in the Area; Art 218 states that the Port State may take measures concerning discharges from vessels outside its internal waters, territorial sea, exclusive economic zone: this space includes the high seas. More importantly, many of the general provisions set out in section 1 of Part XII apply in all maritime areas, including the high seas.

[61] P Chung, 'Emergence of Environmental Proection Clauses in the Outer Space Treaty: A Lesson from the Rio Principles' in A Froelich (ed), *A Fresh View of the Outer Space Treaty: Studies in Space Policy*, vol 13 (Springer, 2018) 1–13.

14

Principles Governing the Global Economy

Jürgen Kurtz, Jorge E. Viñuales and Michael Waibel

I INTRODUCTION

The main principles underlying the organisation of the global economy pre-date the Second World War, but mostly as ideas or policies, enshrined in domestic law, in international instruments of limited scope[1] or in aborted attempts at designing far-reaching ones.[2] The Second World War reset the approach to the global economy, either by taking such principles from a bilateral to a global level or by formulating new ones.

On 14 August 1941, when the odds of the war were unknown, Franklin D. Roosevelt and Winston Churchill meeting 'somewhere in the sea' issued a famous statement, the Atlantic Charter, in which they laid down, as a way of garnering support for their camp, some of the principles on which they hoped to establish the post-war order.[3] These were presented as 'certain common principles in the national policies of their respective countries on which they base their hopes for a better future for the world'.[4] Of the eight principles in the Atlantic Charter, two specifically concerned the organisation of the global economy. Under the fourth principle, both countries undertook (in American English) to:

> endeavor, with due respect for their existing obligations, to further the enjoyment by all States, great or small, victor or vanquished, of access, on equal terms, to the trade and to the raw materials of the world which are needed for their economic prosperity.

[1] For a survey see B Nolde, 'Le Clause de la nation la plus favorisée et les tarifs préférentiels' (1932) 39 *Recueil des Cours* 1; B Nolde, 'Droit et technique des traités de commerce' (1924) 3 *Recueil des Cours* 241.

[2] See eg the Convention for the Abolition of Import and Export Prohibitions and Restrictions, 8 November 1927, 97 LNTS 391 (1927 Convention). This Convention, although it is largely seen as the first multilateral trade convention, was very limited in its scope. As noted by a contemporary commentator, it only focused on 'embargoes, licensing systems, the fixing of quotas and other super-protective devices' (Percy W Bidwell, 'Trade, Tariffs, the Depression' (April 1932) *Foreign Affairs*). Moreover, with the growing protectionism, not the least in the US (with the infamous Smoot-Hawley Tariff Act of 1930), it was quickly abandoned. Another unsuccessful attempt was made at the 1933 London Monetary and Economic Conference. For an analysis see Rodney J Morrisson, 'The London Monetary and Economic Conference of 1933: A Public Goods Analysis' (1993) 52 *American Journal of Economics and Sociology* 307.

[3] Joint Declaration of President FD Roosevelt and Prime Minister W Churchill, 14 August 1941, known as 'The Atlantic Charter'. For background on the Atlantic Charter see Douglas Brinkley and David R Facey-Crowther (eds), *The Atlantic Charter* (St Martin's Press, 1994). On its relevance from the perspective of international law see Mohamed Bennouna, 'Atlantic Charter (1941)' in *Max Planck Encyclopedia of Public International Law* (April 2008). For a contemporary assessment see W Arnold-Forster, *Charters of the Peace: A Commentary on the Atlantic Charter and the Declarations of Moscow, Cairo and Teheran* (Victor Gollancz, 1944).

[4] Atlantic Charter, chapeau.

The fifth principle further stated their 'desire to bring about the fullest collaboration between all nations in the economic field with the object of securing, for all, improved labor standards, economic advancement and social security'.

These principles require, of course, more than a mere textual reading to be understood by an observer today. There were significant differences between Roosevelt and Churchill, not least on the question of self-determination,[5] and Josef Stalin saw the Charter as an 'anti-Soviet tract'.[6] Importantly, the understanding of the economic principles cannot be detached from that of other principles of the Charter. This is not only because currency devaluations and tariff increases embodying the so-called 'beggar thy neighbour' policies of the 1930s were seen as having contributed to the war, but also, no less importantly, because the principles of market access, non-discrimination and currency convertibility were seen in the United States as a 'sledgehammer to break the carapace of British Imperial Preference'.[7] Economic liberalisation, enabled by the envisioned end of empires, benefited the United States. The US Treasury Secretary at the time of the Bretton Woods Conference, Henry Morgenthau, and the lead US negotiator, Assistant Treasury Secretary Harry Dexter White, were conscious of this advantage. Morgenthau reportedly observed to his Assistant '[n]ow the advantage is ours here, and I personally think we should take it', to which White replied: '[i]f the advantage were theirs, they would take it'.[8]

The uncompromising position of the US on trade liberalisation and its prevailing position in the negotiations shifted the gravity centre of the 1944 Bretton Woods Conferences from the 'whether' to the 'how' question – that is, the monetary and financial conditions for liberalisation.[9] But trade liberalisation was not the only goal in the minds of the negotiators. The reconstruction of the global economic system had to tackle the mechanisms through which the Great Depression of the inter-war period had spread across countries. The economists of the League of Nations had emphasised, in this regard, the destabilising effects of 'mass movements of nervous flight capital', which, given their magnitude, could not be adequately offset by the use of international currency reserves held by central banks.[10] Capital controls were thus considered necessary in the post-war reorganisation. That, in turn, raised the question of investment. British economist J. M. Keynes, a leading figure in the conception of the scheme underpinning the Bretton Woods institutions, was sympathetic to capital controls as a permanent feature of the post-war system. But he cautioned against the potential of such controls to bring an end to the 'era of international investment'.[11] It would be up to States to decide, in their domestic policies and through international agreements, which forms of investment were welcome and which ones were unwanted.[12] Such investment was particularly important for

[5] On self-determination see the chapter by MG Kohen in this volume.

[6] Brenda G Plummer, *Rising Wind: Black Americans and US Foreign Affairs, 1935–1960* (University of North Carolina Press, 1996) 64.

[7] Harold James, 'The Multiple Contexts of Bretton Woods' (2012) 28 *Oxford Review of Economic Policy* 411, 415. James observes that these principles had been inserted in Art VII of the US-UK Lend-Lease agreement, and had been bitterly regarded by JM Keynes.

[8] Armand van Dormael, *Bretton Woods: Birth of a Monetary System* (Holmes and Meier, 1978) 211, reproduced in James (n 7) 414; Benn Steil, *The Battle of Bretton Woods : John Maynard Keynes, Harry Dexter White, and the Making of a New World Order* (Princeton University Press, 2013) 208 (US blocked Keynes' initiatives to spread the burden of adjustment between surplus and debtor countries).

[9] James (n 7) 416.

[10] Ragnar Nurkse, *International Currency Experience: Lessons of the Interwar Period* (League of Nations, 1944) 188, referred to in James (n 7) 419.

[11] James (n 7) 419.

[12] ibid 419.

the exploitation of natural resources for the benefit of the 'world economy' – that is, for the benefit of all, not just for the State and, often, the non-self-governing territory where they were plentiful.[13]

Thus, trade, monetary and investment relations were connected historically, conceptually, politically, and, of course, in economic reality. But not legally. Their curious disconnection from a legal perspective results from specialisation and its expression in separate sets of instruments, both old[14] and new, namely the agreements under the aegis of the World Trade Organization,[15] the constitutive instruments of the Bretton Woods institutions, as subsequently amended and expanded,[16] and a network of thousands of bilateral investment treaties.[17] Nonetheless, the principles underpinning the organisation of the global economy were and are closely interrelated. As a prominent economic historian noted:

> [t]he implications of free or multilateral trade for both the domestic and international economy differed depending on its relationship with other policy choices concerning exchange rates, capital controls, and domestic monetary policy.[18]

By focusing only on one term, he pursues, 'there is a serious danger of misunderstanding the processes that shape policy outcomes'. That interconnection was perceived at the moment of the 'resetting' of the system at the end of the Second World War, and the web of interconnected principles did not stop at the level of economic affairs but also involved other enabling principles, such as the self-determination of peoples.

Trade liberalisation required a managed monetary system, capable of providing stability without hampering the movement of desired investment. Access to new markets, both for goods and capitals, was premised on the end of colonial empires. Yet, the decolonisation process and the related development movement brought new challenges to the liberalisation effort, including renewed calls for resource and regulatory sovereignty in newly independent and developing countries, as well as the reshaping of the international economic order arising from the war, in a manner that would reflect the special situation of such countries. The legal principles designed by the end of the Second World War thus came to be fundamentally challenged by the very process – decolonisation and development – that, initially, had been seen as a condition for their full operation.

[13] See the discussion in Nico Schrijver, *Sovereignty over Natural Resources* (Cambridge University Press, 1997) 37 et seq.

[14] James refers to the separate treatment of trade and monetary issues in the run-up to the 1933 London Monetary and Economic Conference. The preparatory work was organised in two separate Sub-Committees, one dealing with financial issues and currency stabilisation, and the other with trade. And each Sub-Committee reached the conclusion that the other should solve things first. James observes, in this regard, that '[t]his was patently a perfect recipe for a deadlock, in which trade and currency experts thought that the other side should be the one to take the first move'. James (n 7) 414, referring to League of Nations archive, Geneva (United Nations), R2672, 1 xi 1932 Second Meeting of Monetary Sub-Committee; R2671, 7 xi 1932 Third Meeting of Preparatory Committee.

[15] Final Act Embodying the Results of the Uruguay Round of Multilateral Trade Negotiations, 1867 UNTS 14.

[16] Articles of agreement of the International Monetary Fund: adopted at the United Nations Monetary and Financial Conference, Bretton Woods, New Hampshire, 22 July 1944, as lastly amended effective 26 January 2016 by the modifications approved by the Board of Governors in Res No 66–2, adopted 15 December 2010.

[17] The compilation in UNCTAD's Investment Policy Hub include 2913 Bilateral Investment Treaties (BITs) (out of which 2,354 are in force) and 388 treaties with investment provisions or chapters (out of which 313 are in force).

[18] Martin Daunton, 'The Inconsistent Quartet: Free Trade versus Competing Goals' in M Daunton, A Narlikar and RM Stern (eds), *The Oxford Handbook of the World Trade Organization* (Oxford University Press, 2012) 40–60, 40–41. cf also Dani Rodrik, *The Globalization Paradox: Why Global Markets, States, and Democracy Can't Coexist* (Oxford University Press, 2011).

In this broad context, this chapter analyses the three separate legal regimes (trade, monetary and financial relations, foreign direct investment) and their evolution from the 'embedded liberalism'[19] (1945–80) over the Washington consensus (1980–2008) to the present. This examination provides the basis for a concise contemporary assessment and outlook offered by way of conclusion.

II THE LEGAL EXPRESSION OF THE PRINCIPLES UNDERLYING THE GLOBAL ECONOMY

1 *The International Law of Trade Transactions*

1.1 *Brief Historical Introduction*

The genesis of modern international trade law can be traced to the grand international project to transform political and economic co-operation among States in the aftermath of the Second World War. In 1948, the Charter for an International Trade Organization (ITO) was presented to a meeting of fifty-six States in Havana.[20] The ITO was to have been the third pillar of post-war economic reconstruction together with the International Monetary Fund (IMF) and the World Bank. The General Agreement on Tariffs and Trade (GATT) was signed as an interim tariff reduction agreement in 1947 and intended to operate only until the ITO was formally established. In the aftermath of the ITO's defeat (in the face of American refusal to ratify the Charter), the GATT famously was the only legal instrument left standing.

The efforts at imposing some form of discipline on the ability of States to protect their own producers and markets were underpinned by powerful political motivations influential in shaping the perspectives of the framers of the GATT. The inter-war period had been characterised by a widespread departure from policies of economic liberalism. Despite its position as the world's leading creditor nation in the immediate post-First World War period, the United States raised tariff levels with trigger effects on devastated debtor nations in Europe.[21] This increase made it difficult for those countries to earn the dollars in which to make required interest payments. The result was the so-called 'beggar thy neighbour' policies of progressively extreme and ruinous forms of trade protection. Although there was an attempt to ameliorate this tendency at the World Economic Conferences of 1927, these efforts ended without result by the onset of the Great Depression in 1929.[22] By the time of the stock market crash in the United States, international considerations became even more subordinate to national demands in fostering internal economic recovery. The infamous 1930 American Smoot-Hawley increase in tariffs as a response to the Depression saw retaliation by other governments leading to devastating levels of economic balkanisation.[23] From 1931 to 1932, Great Britain – the political champion of economic liberalism in the nineteenth century – shifted tack and turned inwards by negotiating

[19] John Ruggie, 'International Regimes, Transactions, and Change: Embedded Liberalism in the Postwar Economic Order' (1982) 36 *International Organization* 379.

[20] Final Act and Related Documents of the United Nations Conference on Trade and Employment, Havana, Cuba, 21 November 1947 to 24 March 1948, UN Doc ICITO/1/4 (1948).

[21] Andrew Brown, *Reluctant Partners: A History of Multilateral Trade Cooperation 1850–2000* (University of Michigan Press, 2003) 69.

[22] AG Kenwood and AL Lougheed, *The Growth of the International Economy 1820–1860* (Routledge, 1971) 186.

[23] Brown (n 21) 73.

the Ottawa agreements to set up a system of tariff preferences amongst the Commonwealth countries.[24] The impact of these protectionist policies on the international economy in the inter-war years was severe: from 1929 to 1934, world trade levels declined by 66 per cent.[25]

These disastrous outcomes affirmed the fundamental Kantian belief of policy-makers that economic discrimination engenders adverse political consequences such as instability in trade policies and resulting political irritation.[26] Indeed, it is clear that the framers of the modern international economic architecture saw trade discrimination practiced in the inter-war period as one of the proximate causes of the Second World War.[27] Most favoured nation (MFN) status within the GATT in turn was to play a central remedial role in international efforts to *both* reconstruct the world economy and embed political co-operation.

1.2 *The GATT System and Post-War Balance between Sovereignty and International Constraints*

The GATT's primary focus was to ensure market access for foreign goods in an importing State. It did so by liberalising border barriers that would directly restrict the flow of international trade. With some important exceptions, quantitative restrictions on the import (or export) of goods are prohibited.[28] Tariffs – taxes on foreign goods imposed at the border – were bound in schedules with members prevented from increasing these bound tariff rates.[29] The quantifiable and divisible nature of tariffs made their reduction relatively easy over time given the political importance of achieving a base level of reciprocity of concessions among the membership.[30] A reciprocal exchange of concessions is often fundamental to convincing domestic interests of the overall benefits of trade liberalisation.[31] In successive and periodic negotiating rounds,[32] members would agree to reduce their tariff rates and any such reduction would then be required to be extended to all other Member States via the MFN principle.[33] In addition, to ensure that the protection afforded by tariffs to domestic producers is not indirectly increased through internal measures, the GATT also provided for the national treatment principle, which requires importer States to treat foreign and domestic producers on an equal footing (other than the burden imposed on foreign producers by tariffs).[34]

In addition to the historical motivations for establishing the GATT, there is also a strong economic case for these constraints on sovereignty, especially MFN treatment towards tariffs on trade in goods. The economic consequences of tariffs as a form of discriminatory border tax levied only on imported goods are well understood. Tariffs distort the working of the price mechanism with both global and domestic efficiency implications. Different tariff

[24] Gilbert Winham, *The Evolution of International Trade Agreements* (University of Toronto Press, 1992) 30; Mitsuo Matsushita et al, *The World Trade Organization: Law, Practice and Policy* (3rd edn, Oxford University Press, 2015) 6.

[25] Gilbert Winham, *The Evolution of International Trade Agreements* (University of Toronto Press, 1992) 30.

[26] Immanuel Kant, *Perpetual Peace: A Philosophical Essay* (1795) (tr by M Campbell Smith, 3rd edn, George Allen and Unwin Ltd, 1917) 157.

[27] Richard Gardner, *Sterling–Dollar Diplomacy* (Columbia University Press, 1956) 4.

[28] General Agreement on Tariffs and Trade, 30 October 1947, TIAS No 1700, 55 UNTS 194, Art XI.

[29] ibid, Art II.

[30] Bernard Hoekman and Michel Kostecki, *The Political Economy of the World Trading System: The WTO and Beyond* (2nd edn, Oxford University Press, 2001) 25–33.

[31] Robert Hudec, '"Like Product": The Differences in Meaning in GATT Articles I and III' in Thomas Cottier, Petros Mavroidis and Patrick Blatter (eds), *Regulatory Barriers and the Principle of Non-Discrimination in World Trade Law* (University of Michigan Press, 2000) 108–9.

[32] Hoekman and Kostecki (n 30) 101–2.

[33] GATT, Art I.

[34] GATT, Art III.

discrimination amongst countries causes a shift in resources contrary to principles of comparative advantage. Demand for a given good dependant on the pricing mechanism shifts from efficient producers in a country subject to a high tariff rate to less efficient producers who are favoured by a low tariff rate. An MFN principle of equal tariffs for every foreign country provides for a more efficient allocation of resources than would be the case if discrimination is practiced. On an individual country level, the distortive effects of tariff discrimination are likely to lead to higher cost imports. An MFN policy allows a country to buy from the lowest cost and most efficient supplier with consequent welfare-enhancing effects for individual consumers. Of course, pure trade theory acknowledges that trade will yield losers. Import competition may displace domestic industries and, if so, some workers will lose their livelihoods. The manner and extent to which those who suffer loss from free trade are compensated is an important prism through which to assess whether free trade maximises overall social welfare.[35] Even with those distributional consequences in mind, a welfare-based case has provided an important degree of substantive legitimacy to multilateral trade rules that focus on the explicit, price-distorting effect of tariffs and comparable regulations.[36]

By comparison with its extensive regulation of border restrictions (such as quotas and tariffs), the GATT adopts a remarkably light-handed approach to domestic (or what is sometimes called 'behind the border') regulation. This principled modesty is on display in the obligation of national treatment in GATT Article III which operates *only* so as to protect the integrity of the bargain on tariff reduction. Specifically, it prevents a State from circumventing its tariff reduction commitments by substituting protectionist domestic tax[37] or regulatory[38] restrictions which discriminate against foreign goods. It is important to tease out the conservatism inherent in the GATT's oversight of domestic regulatory autonomy. Conceptually, the GATT is best understood as an instrument of negative rather than positive integration between States. It does not posit a minimum (positive) level of regulatory harmonisation amongst the membership. Domestic taxes and regulations are fully permitted under national treatment subject only to the (negative) condition that they are not protectionist devices that would distort the bargain on tariff reductions. This then is a system that allows for significant heterogeneity in regulatory and redistributive conditions and experimentation.

Moreover, under the insightful compromise of 'embedded liberalism'[39] that had been heavily influenced by the experience of the US negotiators with New Deal policies,[40] various GATT provisions actively contemplate the priority of domestic politics and intervention in certain situations to safeguard domestic values and stability. These extensive flexibilities include the right of GATT members to take short-term emergency action departing from their GATT commitments where unforeseen developments coupled with the effect of their GATT

[35] Economics alone cannot offer a rigorous justification of whether and how to compensate those actors that suffer losses from moves to freer trade. We are instead in the realm of normative perspectives or theories that would guide governments on what policies they should adopt in this context under some conception of right or wrong. On this, see Oisin Shuttle, *Distributive Justice and World Trade Law* (Cambridge University Press, 2018) 37–48 (outlining different theories).

[36] Robert Howse, 'The Legitimacy of the World Trade Organization' in Jean-Marc Coicaud and Veijo Heiskanen (eds), *The Legitimacy of International Organizations* (United Nations University Press, 2001) 355, 365.

[37] GATT, Art III(2).

[38] ibid, Art III(4).

[39] John Ruggie, 'Embedded Liberalism and Postwar Economic Regimes' in John Ruggie (ed), *Constructing the World Polity: Essays on International Institutionalization* (Routledge, 1998) 62–84.

[40] Anne-Marie Burley, 'Regulating the World: Multilateralism, International Law, and the Projection of the New Deal Regulatory State' in John Ruggie (ed), *Multilateralism Matters: The Theory and Praxis of an Institutional Form* (Columbia University Press, 1993) 125–56.

commitments cause or threaten serious injury to domestic producers.[41] Safeguard measures of this sort are an inherent recognition of the enormous political challenges faced by States when liberalising trade barriers, which may require short-term breathing space (as a matter of shoring up political support for liberalisation) and/or the ability to implement redistributive mechanisms to enable transition of affected industry and workers to more competitive sectors of the domestic economy. Even one of the most direct sovereignty constraints – the per se prohibition on quantitative restrictions – is subject to appropriate exceptions, most notably the freedom to impose temporary export limitations to safeguard food security.[42] There is a concession afforded to developing countries to enable them to directly depart from the strictures of economic liberalism in pursuit of developmental goals. Those States are explicitly permitted flexibility under the GATT to increase tariff barriers (to effect import substitution) for the purposes of 'the establishment of a particular industry'.[43] Lastly, and perhaps most famously of all, the GATT elevated certain core public values over and above the immediate project of trade liberalisation. Member States have the continuing right under GATT Article XX to directly depart from their commitments to facilitate trade in goods where, for instance, it is 'necessary to protect human, animal, plant life or health'.[44]

In contrast to these detailed substantive provisions, the institutional architecture of the GATT is sparse. This comes down to the GATT's status as an interim agreement with the framers intending that it would eventually be folded back into the ITO. Yet, over time, the GATT would transform itself, incrementally, into a type of de facto international organisation. Eight negotiating rounds conducted between 1947 and 1994 led to sizeable reductions in average tariff levels. Yet the incompleteness of the GATT was especially evident in its early dispute settlement mechanisms. In order to form an ad hoc panel to hear a dispute, a consensus decision of all GATT members was required.[45] Thus, any party, including the respondent, could block the panel's formation. Even adoption of the panel ruling required consensus so that any GATT member, including the losing party, could veto the ruling. The GATT's dispute settlement process has thus been aptly described as effecting 'diplomacy through other means'.[46] These ad hoc panels were composed largely of trade diplomats who understood their task as the investigation and recommendation of a proper solution to the disputants.[47] In these first few decades, GATT members had usually settled the underlying dispute by the time those recommendations had even been developed.[48]

1.3 *A New Grand Bargain: From the GATT to the WTO*

By the late 1970s, a number of GATT members had begun to advocate for greater discipline on non-tariff barriers to international trade. The United States in particular had become concerned about decreasing benefits from the GATT in light of the economic resurgence of Western Europe and Japan and the concomitant erosion of American comparative advantage in some

41 GATT, Art XIX.
42 ibid, Art XI(2)(a).
43 ibid, Art XVII(2).
44 ibid, Art XX(b).
45 John Jackson, *The Jurisprudence of the GATT and the WTO* (Cambridge University Press, 2000) 123.
46 Joseph Weiler, 'The Rule of Lawyers and the Ethos of Diplomats: Reflections on the Internal and External Legitimacy of WTO Dispute Settlement' (2001) 35(2) *Journal of World Trade* 191, 194.
47 Michael K Young, 'Dispute Resolution in the Uruguay Round: Lawyers Triumph over Diplomats' (1995) 29 *International Lawyer* 389.
48 John Jackson, 'GATT as an Instrument for the Settlement of Trade Disputes' (1967) 61 *American Society of International Law Proceedings* 144.

mass production and technology-intensive sectors. In this context, the Uruguay Round of GATT negotiations concluded in December 1993 and led to the formation of the World Trade Organization (WTO) in 1994. At a substantive level, the Member States had agreed to a significant expansion of the scope of the international trading system with new substantive disciplines on agriculture, textiles, services and intellectual property among others.

The scoping of some of these new provisions was conservative in orientation, often reflecting the sort of balance between constraint and flexibility struck in the GATT. Under the new General Agreement on Trade in Services (GATS) for instance, WTO members can opt in to legal coverage by either making horizontal commitments (across all services sectors) or sector-specific commitments (which cover a particular economic sector) to both the market access[49] and national treatment[50] obligations in the GATS.[51] This structure provides WTO members with significant latitude in determining when and in what manner to open up their service sectors to foreign competition. Indeed, analysis of commitment schedules under the GATS show that developing countries have utilised this structure to significantly control the extent of their liberalisation efforts in the services area,[52] which has included scheduling sectoral commitments by reference either to domestic laws on foreign direct investment and/or their bilateral investment treaty obligations.[53] Flexibility to pursue domestic prerogatives is given further impetus through exceptions where the GATS continues and deepens the embedded liberalism orientation of the original GATT. The GATS drafters notably expanded the list of bases upon which to exempt an otherwise inconsistent measure including new freedoms to regulate for 'public morals' and 'public order'.[54]

Yet other parts of the WTO push in a very different normative direction. Within the broader calculus of substantive trade-offs to result from the Uruguay Round, the Agreement on Trade-Related Aspects of Intellectual Property Rights (TRIPS) deserves particular attention as it reveals an especially stark departure from the conservative negative integration model that had underpinned the GATT. Certain forms of intellectual property protection (especially patents) are an inherent trade-off between incentives for innovation on the one hand and economic efficiency plus distribution of income on the other.[55] Yet the TRIPS Agreement requires intellectual protection at a high level for all WTO member countries regardless of their needs and the abilities of their citizenry to pay for the affected products.[56] This is obviously problematic for most developing countries where innovation is not a major source of economic activity. On the whole, developing countries are more likely to benefit in terms of consumer welfare in

49 General Agreement on Trade in Services, Annex 1B, Marrakesh Agreement Establishing the World Trade Organization, 15 April 1994, Final Act Embodying the Results of the Uruguay Round of Multilateral Trade Negotiations, Art XVI.

50 ibid, Art XVII.

51 ibid, Arts XX; WTO, *Revision of Scheduling Guidelines* (SC/CSC/W/19, 5 March 1999).

52 Bernard Hoekman, 'Assessing the General Agreement on Trade in Services' in Will Martin and L Alan Winters (eds), *The Uruguay Round and the Developing Countries* (Cambridge University Press, 1996) 88–124.

53 Rudolf Adlung, Peter Morrison, Martin Roy and Weiwei Zang, 'FOG in GATS Commitments: Boon or Bane', World Trade Organization: Staff Working Paper, ERSD-2011–04 (March, 2011) 10–11.

54 GATS, Art XIV(a).

55 Alan Deardorff and Robert Stern, 'Enhancing the Benefits for Developing Countries in the Doha Development Agenda Negotiations' (Policy Brief No 1, William Davidson Institute, University of Michigan Business School, 2003), pp 5–6.

56 As a targeted example of this base level of harmonization on patents, consider the fact that TRIPS mandates that '[t]he term of protection available shall not end before the expiration of a period of twenty years counted from the filing date'. Agreement on Trade-Related Aspects of Intellectual Property Rights, Annex 1C, Marrakesh Agreement Establishing the World Trade Organization, 15 April 1994, Final Act Embodying the Results of the Uruguay Round of Multilateral Trade Negotiations, Art 33.

permitting cheap domestic imitations of innovations created elsewhere.[57] While there are targeted flexibilities that ameliorate this trade-off scattered throughout the TRIPS Agreement, dissatisfaction with its overall impact would later prompt the WTO membership to seek amendment of key components. The TRIPS is not the only outcome of the Uruguay Round to require a level of regulatory harmonisation among the WTO membership. Both the Agreement on Technical Barriers to Trade[58] (TBT) and the Agreement on the Application of Sanitary and Phytosanitary Measures[59] (SPS) usher in a harder positive integration edge to WTO commitments. In the latter for instance, even non-discriminatory laws directed at human, animal or plant life or health can be challenged because they impose greater burdens on producers in an exporting State.[60]

Finally, the Uruguay Round ushered in institutional transformation to the manner in which disputes would be resolved under the WTO. The new Dispute Settlement Understanding (DSU) creates a reverse consensus rule so that adoption of a panel ruling can only be blocked if no WTO member objects.[61] This includes, obviously, the winning party such that WTO dispute settlement is made effectively automatic. Compulsory adjudication and binding outcomes were also supplemented and counter-balanced by a new layer of institutional review. The DSU establishes an Appellate Body with an explicit mandate to correct legal error.[62] Since the completion of the Uruguay Round, dispute settlement has comprised the most active part of the WTO. In its first decade of operation, WTO members brought 314 disputes to the WTO for resolution, which is more than in almost half a century of GATT dispute settlement.[63] In that same period, panels and the Appellate Body circulated 103 and 63 reports respectively.[64]

The pace and quality of judicial law-making in the WTO has contrasted sharply with the scarce output of its legislative branch. At the 2001 Doha Ministerial, the WTO members agreed to launch a new negotiation round[65] which triggered the first attempt to push back the ideological constraints imposed during the Uruguay Round. The TRIPS Agreement became an understandable flashpoint for developing countries both at Doha and the later 2003 Cancún Ministerial. The TRIPS Agreement attracted public scrutiny at the Doha Ministerial due to the human suffering and deaths connected with the HIV/AIDS pandemic, particularly in Sub-Saharan Africa. The strong patent protections mandated by the TRIPS Agreement had served to drive up drug prices, putting medicines out of reach of the poor citizenry of developing countries.[66] The public nature of this issue led to a political statement supportive of public

[57] Michael Trebilcock and Robert Howse, 'Trade Liberalisation and Regulatory Diversity: Reconciling Competitive Markets with Competitive Politics' (1998) 6 *European Journal of Law and Economics* 5, 18–21.

[58] Agreement on Technical Barriers to Trade, Annex 1A, Marrakesh Agreement Establishing the World Trade Organization, 15 April 1994, Final Act Embodying the Results of the Uruguay Round of Multilateral Trade Negotiations.

[59] Agreement on Sanitary and Phytosanitary Measures, Annex 1A, Marrakesh Agreement Establishing the World Trade Organization, 15 April 1994, Final Act Embodying the Results of the Uruguay Round of Multilateral Trade Negotiations.

[60] ibid, Art 2.2.

[61] Understanding on Rules and Procedures Governing the Settlement of Disputes, Annex 2, Marrakesh Agreement Establishing the World Trade Organization, 15 April 1994, Final Act Embodying the Results of the Uruguay Round of Multilateral Trade Negotiations, Art 16(4).

[62] ibid, Art 17(6).

[63] Peter Van den Bossche, *The Law and Policy of the World Trade Organization: Text, Cases and Materials* (Cambridge University Press, 2005) 284.

[64] ibid 287.

[65] Ministerial Declaration, WTO Doc WT/MIN(01)/DEC/1 (14 November 2001).

[66] On the high cost of medication to treat HIV/AIDS in developing countries, see Scott Hensley, 'Pfizer Makes Aid Pledge, Breaks Aid Pact', *The Wall Street Journal* (12 November 2003), B1.

health as part of the Doha Ministerial Declaration.[67] Not surprisingly, the issue did not disappear after Doha. In the weeks leading up to Cancún, WTO members agreed to a landmark relaxation of the stringent patent protection mandated by the TRIPS Agreement, despite the opposition of the pharmaceutical lobby.[68] Under this agreement, small countries that have insufficient manufacturing capacity in the pharmaceutical sector are allowed, in cases of public health emergency, to import low-cost generics produced under compulsory licence in other WTO member countries.

The opposition posed to TRIPS is not the only contemporary challenge faced by the WTO. At a macro level, WTO members are beginning to bifurcate their trade policy by negotiating bilateral and regional free trade agreements (FTAs) due to the difficulties of concluding the multilateral round of Doha negotiations in 2001. Those difficulties lie partly in the greater complexity of the subject-matter of the new negotiating round. But they are also indicative of a greater assertiveness by those WTO members that had felt sidelined by the final stages of the Uruguay Round. There is, to put it simply, a trade-off at play between input and output gains in these types of complex negotiations.[69] Smaller WTO members are insisting on greater transparency and participation in the negotiations which, given the need to reach consensus among the large membership of the WTO, added to the difficulty of completing the round. The reality then is that bilateral and regional outcomes comprise a key feature of the future trade landscape as developed States, frustrated with the glacial pace of law-making in the WTO, leverage their economic and political power in bilateral and regional fora. Even the WTO, which has inherent incentives to champion the cause of multilateralism, has conceded that preferential trade agreements are critical mechanisms to achieve deep levels of economic integration.[70]

1.4 *Global Value Chains: A Double-Edged Sword*

The development of FTAs is given powerful momentum by a key economic vector. In the hyper-globalised economic landscape of today, global value chains have reinforced the organic links between trade and foreign investment. Economic actors – especially multinational enterprises – splice production choices (particularly in sectors such as car manufacturing) to locate them in jurisdictions that offer the greatest prospect for efficiency gains. This has strategic importance for developing countries, which naturally seek to extract developmental benefits by joining these chains through specialisation in the labour components of manufacturing in which they have a natural comparative advantage.

Paradoxically, those very supply chains sit at the nucleus of the rapid outbreak of protectionism particularly in contemporary United States trade policy. Supply chains, especially as developed under the North American Free Trade Agreement, have been heavily criticised by the Trump Administration as mere mechanisms to outsource American jobs. Trade has even been framed as a security issue by the Trump Administration. This frame has been powerfully deployed not only against China but also for aluminium and steel imports from a range of long-standing American allies like Australia, Canada and Member States of NATO. Strikingly, the

[67] Declaration on the TRIPS Agreement and Public Health, WTO Doc WT/MIN(01)/DEC/2 (20 November 2001).

[68] Implementation of Paragraph 6 of the Doha Declaration on the TRIPS Agreement and Public Health – Decision of 30 August 2003, WTO Doc WT/L/540 (2003); 'WTO Countries in Deadlock on TRIPS' (2001) 1(43) *Inside US Trade* 1, 22–3.

[69] Robert Keohane and Joseph Nye, 'Redefining Accountability for Global Governance' in Miles Kahler and David Lake (eds), *Governance in a Global Economy: Political Authority in Transition* (Princeton University Press, 2003) 409–10.

[70] WTO, *World Trade Report 2011 – The WTO and Preferential Trade Agreements: From Co-Existence to Coherence* (WTO, 2011).

Trump Administration has even threatened to impose tariffs against car imports from the European Union suggesting that these threaten national security. From a legal perspective, these claims rest on remarkably weak grounds especially given recent WTO Panel rulings on the scope of State autonomy to invoke security exceptions under the law of the WTO.[71] But the legal position – hobbled in any event by the time delay in WTO dispute settlement coupled with the prospective nature of remedies in the WTO[72] – is no counter to the turbulent manner in which the security claim distorts trade policy dialogue and preference. Security is a forceful frame for shaping preferences, and it can provoke immediate loss aversion in behavioural psychology terms.[73]

The turbulent shift to protectionism in parts of the world should spark an assessment of the contours of globalisation and its legal manifestations and limits, both globally and domestically. It is important here to be mindful of the heterogeneity of the harm occasioned by trade-induced dislocation, and how it can slowly but inevitably acculturate over time into political demands. Generally speaking, adjustment of this sort has asymmetric effects based on age with younger workers experiencing relatively smaller costs vis-à-vis older workers. Aside from direct economic costs (including income/consumption foregone due to unemployment and adjustment costs of retraining to enable transition), there are hidden psychological costs of unemployment that must be borne in mind. A protracted period of unemployment can trigger physical and mental illness, family dissolution, anti-social behaviour (including through alcohol and drug dependence). In the absence of targeted or general support through a functioning social safety net, newly unemployed may seek employment at lower wage levels and in occupations of lower skill and labour productivity.[74] This phenomenon then bleeds into growing patterns of income inequality across much of the developed world and political concerns of the social costs associated with economic globalisation.[75] Economists argue that technological change is a more important source of decline of manufacturing employment and dislocation effects than trade and trade agreements.[76] Yet the political traction of this principled empirical claim is weakened by the recency and visibility of the so-called 'China shock'. Autor, Dorn and Hanson have documented the large, persistent and highly localised labour-market disruption in the United States from patterns of international trade flows from China over the period 1990 to 2007.[77] Globalisation (particularly trade from China) is a phenomenon that is far more visible than patterns of technological change and thus much easier to blame for transition challenges. In turn, the costs ascribed to economic globalisation can be easily turned into political fodder by anti-market, anti-elite political movements that span the political spectrum.

We encounter at this point a sharp difference with public discourse in the United States vis-à-vis the European Union. Populism too has permeated European policy discussions. Yet,

[71] Russia – Measures Concerning Traffic in Transit, Report of the Panel (WT/DS512/R), 5 April 2019, para 7.82 (finding that action must be 'objectively' found to fall within the security exception in GATT Art XXI).

[72] Joseph HH Weiler, 'Editorial: Black Lies, White Lies and Some Uncomfortable Truths in and of the International Trading System' (2018) 29 *European Journal of International Law* 339, 342.

[73] Martin Ardanaz, Victoria Murillo and Pablo Pinto, 'Sensitivity to Issue Framing on Trade Policy Preferences: Evidence from a Survey Experiment' (2013) 67 *International Organization* 411.

[74] Michael Trebilcock, *Dealing with Losers: The Political Economy of Policy Transitions* (Oxford University Press, 2014) 67.

[75] Christoph Lakner and Branko Milanovic, 'Global Income Distribution: From the Fall of the Berlin Wall to the Great Recession' (2016) 30 *The World Bank Economic Review* 203.

[76] Bernard Hoekman and Douglas Nelson, 'Reflecting on Populism and the Economics of Globalization' (2018) *Journal of International Business Policy* 1, 2.

[77] David Autor, David Dorn and Gordon Hanson, 'The China Syndrome: Local Labor Market Effects of Import Competition in the United States' (2013) 103(6) *American Economic Review* 2121–68.

European populism does not seem to be crudely anti-trade of the sort so visible in the United States nor does it target select countries like China. Of course, certain aspects of economic globalisation and their legal manifestations – especially austerity policies within the Eurozone and investor–State dispute settlement in bilateral investment treaties – are highly controversial in European discourse. But few European populist politicians and their political parties openly advocate trade barriers as seen in the United States context. In fact, the advocates of Brexit offer free trade as one of the claimed benefits of exit from the EU, arguing that it would allow them to pursue deeper levels of liberalisation through FTAs with third countries. Pointedly, some have suggested that this variance in populist discourse is attributable to the far stronger social protections and welfare provisions in Europe.[78] Openness to trade in the European setting has always been directly accompanied by far greater redistribution and social insurance. Somewhat ironically, the European opposition to immigration and refugees is driven, in part, by concern of erosion in greater access to those social benefits. But it offers social security benefits to workers affected by job displacement, whether induced by trade or other causal factors like technology.

2 *The International Law of Monetary and Financial Relations*

2.1 *Historical Roots of the Global Monetary and Financial Architecture*

The global architecture of international monetary and financial relations developed within the broader context of the evolution of the global economic architecture throughout the twentieth and twenty-first centuries. In this broad narrative, the 1960s and 1970s deserve special attention, as events during that period influenced the birth and development of the Friendly Relations Declaration.

Prior to the First World War, there was a significant degree of monetary stability among the major international currencies. As Lowenfeld observes, in the '35 years prior to the outbreak of World War I, the major Western countries – the UK, France, Germany, and the USA – all tied their currencies to gold', which had the effect of fixing their exchange rates.[79] The gold standard fell apart with the outbreak of the First World War. European countries intervened in trade matters with high tariffs, quotas and exchange controls.[80] Currencies 'went on and off a link to gold, and countries imposed a variety of subsidies, regulations and controls designed to increase their holdings of gold'.[81] Attempts to reign in the chaos in trade policy were largely unsuccessful. Point III of President Woodrow Wilson's 'Fourteen Points' called for trade liberalisation.[82] The League of Nations Covenant asked members to provide 'equitable treatment for the commerce of all Members', but only in accordance with existing or future international agreements.[83] The 1927 Convention on the Abolition of Import and Export Prohibitions and Restrictions, required signatories to remove certain trade barriers[84] and refrain from discrimination in maintaining

[78] Rodrik (n 18) 6.

[79] Andreas Lowenfeld, 'The International Monetary System: A Look Back Over Seven Decades' (2010) 13(3) *Journal of International Economic Law* 575, 576.

[80] Matsushita et al (n 24) 5.

[81] Lowenfeld (n 79) 576.

[82] President Woodrow Wilson's Fourteen Points, 8 January 1918, Yale Law School 'Avalon Project', http://avalon.law.yale.edu/20th_century/wilson14.asp.

[83] Covenant of the League of Nations, 28 April 1919, 225 Parry 195, Art 23(e).

[84] 1927 Convention (n 2), Art 2 provided: 'Subject to the exceptions provided for in the following articles, the High Contracting Parties undertake to abolish within a period of six months from the date of the coming into force of the present Convention, in so far as the respective territories of each of them are concerned, all import and export prohibitions or restrictions, and not thereafter to impose any such prohibitions or restrictions.'

allowable restrictions.[85] Those efforts were largely aborted in the context of the economic depression, starting in the United States in 1929. As is well documented, the United States raised tariffs through the Smoot-Hawley Tariff Act, which is widely believed to have prompted a chain-reaction of protectionist retaliation.[86] The United Kingdom, for instance, reintroduced its imperial preference system for its dominions and colonies.[87] Autarky prevailed and States aggressively pursued 'beggar thy neighbour' policies. Nazi Germany was 'particularly skillful and ruthless in using tariffs, quotas, barter, and discriminatory exchange controls to its advantage'.[88]

Following the Allied victory in the Second World War, the United States and the United Kingdom led the establishment of the contemporary global economic order. John Maynard Keynes and Henry Dexter White respectively led the United Kingdom and the United States delegations at Bretton Woods, in July 1944, to establish the post-war international monetary and finance system. As has been noted earlier in this chapter, two key institutions were established: the IMF and the World Bank. The IMF was established as an alternative to the 'desperate tactics of the past',[89] including competitive devaluations, to help stabilise international exchanges but without 'sacrificing the freedom of action necessary to meet' a State's 'internal economic problems'.[90] The IMF was to oversee a system of exchange rates based on agreed par values that could only be adjusted with the IMF's agreement to correct a 'fundamental disequilibrium' in a State's balance of payments.[91] The par value was to be expressed in terms of the US dollar, which was, in turn, backed by gold.[92] The key obligation of members under the original Articles of Agreement of the IMF was to establish exchange stability and avoid 'competitive exchange alterations'.[93] The original IMF system remained in place and operated more or less effectively until 1971.

In addition to the IMF, the Bretton Woods institutions led to the establishment of what could be seen as a foreign investment and development promotion component of the new architecture, namely the International Bank for Reconstruction and Development, better known as the 'World Bank'.[94] In subsequent years, the activities of the World Bank were devolved to a range of affiliated organisations, which together with the Bank make up the 'World Bank Group': the International Finance Corporation (IFC), established in 1956 to provide loans and investments to the private sector; the International Development Association (IDA), established in 1960 to provide interest-free credits and grants to its poorest members; the International Centre for Settlement of Investment Disputes (ICSID), established in 1966 to provide arbitration and conciliation facilities for international investment disputes; and the Multilateral Investment

[85] ibid, Art 4.

[86] See Douglas A Irwin, *Peddling Protectionism: Smoot-Hawley and the Great Depression* (Princeton, 2011) 144–83.

[87] Robert Schütze, 'From the "Closed" to the "Open" Commercial State: A Very Brief History of International Economic Law' (2017) 19 *Journal of the History of International Law* 495, 514.

[88] Lowenfeld (n 79) 576.

[89] ibid 576.

[90] Closing statements of the American Secretary of the Treasury Henry Morgenthau, Jr, in Proceedings and Documents of the United Nations Monetary and Financial Conference, vol I (US GPO, 1947) 117, 118.

[91] IMF Articles of Agreement (n 57), Art IV.

[92] ibid, Art IV(1)(a).

[93] ibid, Art IV(4)(a).

[94] International Bank for Reconstruction and Development, Articles of Agreement, adopted at the United Nations Monetary and Financial Conference, Bretton Woods, New Hampshire, 22 July 1944, as amended effective 27 June 2012.

Guarantee Agency (MIGA), established in 1988 to provide guarantees against non-commercial risk to foreign investors.[95]

The institutions and sets of rules emerging from (or after) Bretton Woods, were designed to contribute jointly to the post-war economic and political goals through the promotion of global economic growth and prosperity and thereby secure long-term peace and prevent a return to conflict. The IMF was to facilitate a stable international exchange rate system, in turn a 'key facilitator for international trade transactions',[96] whereas the 'GATT operated to introduce free trade among contracting parties whose capital facilities were reconstructed and developed for trading purposes by the [World Bank]'.[97] Nevertheless, US policy-makers considered the Bretton Woods institutions alone would be financially ill-equipped to bring Europe out of its post-war economic crisis. The IMF and World Bank received less than USD 20 billion to revive the international monetary system.[98] Britain's 'virtual bankruptcy in 1945 undermined the foundation' of the institutions. The US answer to this funding gap was the Marshall Plan, which saw the disbursement of USD 13 billion,[99] typically on condition that a bilateral agreement with the United States was signed to stabilise currency and reduce trade barriers.[100] Certain motivations for the Marshall Plan resembled those underlying Bretton Woods, while others differed. Secretary Marshall was warned of the 'awful implications' for the US domestic economy from European disintegration should the United States fail to provide aid.[101] Politically, the United States was concerned by the spread of communism and the left-ward turn in European politics.[102]

2.2 *The Quest for a New International Economic Order*

Over time, new realities led to changes in the overall objectives of the global economic architecture designed in Bretton Woods and its aftermath. This included tensions and diverging interests between, on the one hand, newly independent and developing countries and, on the other hand, capital-exporting countries, which were rendered even more complex by Cold War ideologies and alliances. This was the context in which the Friendly Relations Declaration came to be. Whilst economic governance concerns of developing countries were not agreed in that Declaration, those contemporaneous claims relating to the redefinition of the post-war economic order found expression in the search for a 'New International Economic Order' (NIEO).

Decolonisation saw the ranks of UN membership swell from 51 States in 1945 to 152 in 1975.[103] A powerful bloc sharing common interests formed,[104] and it found voice in the Group of 77 which 'advocated reform', such as increased participation in global economic governance,

95 Maurizio Ragazzi, 'World Bank Group' in *Max Planck Encyclopedia of Public International Law* (April 2008), para 1.

96 Dan Sarooshi, 'International Economic Law' in Peter Cane and Joanne Conaghan (eds), *The New Oxford Companion to Law* (online) (Oxford University Press, 2008).

97 Sabine Schlemmer-Schulte, 'International Bank for Reconstruction and Development' in *Max Planck Encyclopedia of Public International Law* (April 2008), para 4.

98 Diane B Kunz, 'The Marshall Plan Reconsidered: A Complex of Motives' (1997) 76(3) *Foreign Affairs* 162, 164.

99 Benn Steil, *Marshall Plan: Dawn of the Cold War* (Simon & Schuster, 2019).

100 Section 115, Economic Cooperation Act 1948 (United States), www.cia.gov/library/readingroom/docs/1948-04-03b.pdf.

101 Memorandum of WL Clayton 27 May 1947, cited in William L Clayton, 'GATT, The Marshall Plan, and OECD' (1963) 74(4) *Political Science Quarterly* 493, 496.

102 Kunz (n 98) 165.

103 Julio Faundez, 'Between Bandung and Doha: International Economic Law and Developing Countries', *Warwick Law School Research Paper* No 2015/10 (May 2015) 3.

104 ibid 6.

and 'fair access to ... finance'.[105] However, geographic security pacts controlled by either the United States or the USSR prevented trade and co-operation between members of opposing camps.[106] Integral to understanding the Friendly Relations Declaration are these politico-economic differences.[107] The impetus for the Declaration was a combination of Soviet efforts to promote 'peaceful co-existence', a 'real or supposed rejection' of capitalist international law,[108] and for developing countries, not present at San Francisco in 1945, to articulate a 'new' international law.[109] The United States and the USSR engaged in political posturing over the nomenclature,[110] with scant substantive impact.

Developing countries had two key economic objectives during this period: first, challenging the objective of prosperity in favour of redistribution of wealth;[111] and second, ensuring formal and substantive equality in the economic sphere between developed and developing countries. They pursued these objectives by: (i) seeking equal participation in multilateral economic bodies through the principle of sovereign equality; and (ii) seeking control over their economic systems through the principles of sovereign equality, permanent sovereignty over natural resources and non-intervention. Several issues proved too complex or controversial for the text of the Friendly Relations Declaration, although they underlie the interpretations of developing countries of the relevant principles. Nevertheless, as noted earlier, these ideas found more cogent expression in what came to be known as the NIEO. The NIEO addressed a 'major area in North–South economic relations' with 'strong implications' for South–South relations, including redirecting 'monetary and financial flows in a manner more compatible with the imperative of development'.[112] The sources of the NIEO are a number of key UN General Assembly resolutions, including: (i) Resolution 1803 (XVII) of 1962 entitled 'Permanent sovereignty over natural resources';[113] (ii) the Declaration on the Establishment of a New International Economic Order of 1974;[114] and (iii) the Charter of Economic Rights and Duties of States of 1974.[115] Unlike the Friendly Relations Declaration, developed capital-exporting States did not agree with many of the NIEO principles. The United States, for example, criticised the Charter of Economic Rights and Duties as 'imbalanced' and discouraging capital flow.[116] However, NIEO principles and philosophies informed the developing countries' negotiating

[105] Margot E Salomon, 'From NIEO to Now and the Unfinishable Story of Economic Justice' (2013) 62(1) *International and Comparative Law Quarterly* 31, 36.
[106] Faundez (n 103) 8.
[107] Milan Sahovic, 'Codification des principes du droit international des relations amicales et de la coopération entre les Etats' (1972) 137 *Recueil des Cours* 243, 255; Ian Sinclair, 'The Significance of the Friendly Relations Declaration' in Colin Warbrick and Vaughan Lowe (eds), *The UN and the Principles of International Law: Essays in Memory of Michael Akehurst* (Routledge, 1994) 1, 28; Gaetano Arangio-Ruiz, 'The Normative Role of the General Assembly of the United Nations and the Declaration of Principles of Friendly Relations' (1972) 137 *Recueil des Cours* 419, 599 fn 47.
[108] Arangio-Ruiz (n 107) 580; for an overview of the doctrine, see further 580–3.
[109] Robert Rosenstock, 'The Declaration of Principles of International Law Concerning Friendly Relations: A Survey' (1971) 65(5) *American Journal of International Law* 713, 716; Sinclair (n 107) 2.
[110] Sixth Committee of the General Assembly, Summary record of meeting No 1180, 24 September 1970 (A/C.6/SR.1180) 19, para 21; 30, para 36.
[111] Sarooshi (n 96).
[112] Progressive Development of the Principles and Norms of International Law Relating to the New International Economic Order, Report of the Secretary-General (23 October 1984) UN Doc A/39/504/Add/1, Annex III, UNITAR Analytical Study, 31, para 2 [UNITAR Report].
[113] UNGA Res 1803 (14 December 1962) UN Doc A/RES/1803(XVII).
[114] UNGA Res 3201 (1 May 1974) UN Doc A/RES/3201.
[115] UNGA Res 3281 (12 December 1974) UN Doc A/RES/3281.
[116] Charles N Brower and John B Tepe, 'The Charter of Economic Rights and Duties of States: A Reflection or Rejection of International Law?' (1975) 9(2) *The International Lawyer* 295, 299.

positions in the ensuing decades. The NIEO has been closely linked to calls for a 'right to development', which seeks a commitment from 'economically strong States to support developing countries'.[117]

2.3 *The Rise and Fall of the 'Washington Consensus'*

When, in August 1971, the United States announced the suspension of the US dollar's convertibility to gold, the system of pegged exchange rates on which the IMF system was based collapsed. By March 1973, despite an attempt to re-establish a fixed exchange rate, the peg system gave way to one of floating exchange rates among all major currencies. In this new 'non-system',[118] the role of the IMF shifted towards macro-economic matters. That and failures to rectify it, prompted an amendment to the IMF's Articles of Agreement in 1976 (coming into effect in 1978), which allowed members to freely choose their exchange arrangement (new Article IV(2)(b)), and leaving members with few substantive legal obligations, with the exception of requiring them to avoid manipulating exchange rates (Article IV(1)(iii)).[119]

Since the 1970s, the IMF's role has become that of a (i) surveillance organisation, issuing reports on States' economic and balance of payments situation;[120] (ii) a provider of financial assistance to support members experiencing temporary balance of payments problems,[121] and (iii) a provider of technical assistance in areas such as banking and monetary policy, foreign exchange and fiscal policy.[122] However, the provision of financial assistance gives the IMF a degree of control over developing countries.[123] Through the conditionality on using its resources: the approval or continuation of financing is linked to 'the implementation of specified elements of economic policy'.[124] These elements of economic policy came to be specified in a particular context. Indeed, the demise of communism at the end of the Cold War led to an ideational emphasis on 'free and competitive markets, combined with strong private property rights, as the surest road to wealth creation'.[125] This was reflected in the so-called 'Washington Consensus', a set of economic development ideas, promulgated by international financial institutions, focusing on market-liberalising reforms.[126]

In the twenty-first century, major debt crises impacting developed countries prompted a major rethink of approaches to economic governance. A sub-prime mortgage crisis in the United States in 2007 led to a global financial crisis when credits, disseminated (through securitisation and credit swaps) to banks and other financial intermediaries around the world, became virtually

[117] Matthias Herdegen, 'International Economic Law' in *Max Planck Encyclopedia of Public International Law* (April 2008), para 32; René Jean Dupuy, *Le Droit au développement au plan international: colloque, La Haye, 16–18 octobre 1979* (The Right to Development at the International Level: Workshop, The Hague, 16–18 October 1979) (Sijthoff & Noordhoff, 1980).

[118] The expression is often attributed to economist John Williamson, in 'The Benefits and Costs of an International Monetary Nonsystem' in Edward M Bernstein et al (eds), *Reflections on Jamaica* (International Finance Section, 1976) 54–59.

[119] Rosa Maria Lastra, *International Financial and Monetary Law* (2nd edn, Oxford University Press, 2015) 423.

[120] IMF Articles of Agreement (n 57), Art IV.

[121] ibid, Art V(3).

[122] ibid, Art V(2)(b).

[123] Richard N Gardner, 'Sterling–Dollar Diplomacy in Current Perspective' (1985–86) 62(1) *International Affairs* 21, 27–28.

[124] Lastra (n 119) 468.

[125] Andrew Lang, *World Trade Law after Neoliberalism: Reimagining the Global Economic Order* (Oxford University Press, 2011) 1.

[126] John Williamson, 'What Washington Means by Policy Reform' in John Williamson (ed), *Latin American Adjustment: How Much Has Happened?* (Institute for International Economics, 1990).

worthless, causing the 'quasi-disappearance of the interbank money market'.[127] In addition, since 2010 some EU members have faced sovereign debt crises due to imbalanced monetary integration, competitiveness crises, and fiscal imbalances in certain States (particularly Greece).[128] These crises prompted a serious re-evaluation of the existing global economic architecture guaranteeing financial stability in an increasingly globalised world with highly integrated markets. The global financial crisis led to additional global financial regulation, including increased responsibilities for the IMF and the establishment of the Financial Stability Board (FSB).[129] Further, the IMF benefited from a substantial increase in financial resources ($200 billion immediately, rising to $500 billion) as well as from a doubling of its concessional lending capacity for low-income countries.[130] The FSB oversees bodies that produce and implement international financial standards (including the Basel Committee on Banking Supervision), originally developed in 1975 to 'prevent system risk'.[131] The FSB is the 'successor to the Financial Stability Forum' with twenty-four countries, co-ordinating the standard-setting process and overseeing standard-setting bodies.[132] Eurozone members sought to restore financial stability, including through a funding facility: the European Stability Mechanism (ESM). Operating under strict conditionality, the ESM 'operate[s] as a liquidity provision and bank recapitalization mechanism'.[133]

The financial crises have also prompted a rethink of the dominant free-market paradigm. Increasingly, it has been realised that intervention may be needed by national governments to prevent failures and protect citizens.[134] More recently, from the ongoing economic woes in developed countries in Europe, the United States and elsewhere – growing inequality, high unemployment, low wage growth – populist agendas have emerged. Whilst not necessarily anti-internationalist, they are deeply sceptical of the effects of globalisation and multilateral economic governance.[135] This is most notably manifested in the hostility of the current Republican administration to multilateral free trade agreements and concern over currency manipulation.[136]

2.4 *Sovereign Prerogatives and International Constraints*

In the overall context discussed in the previous sections, one important question concerns the relevance of the principles enshrined in the Friendly Relations Declaration, particularly sovereign equality, non-intervention and co-operation, for monetary and financial matters. To the extent that such principles have assumed relevance in monetary and financial matters, this

[127] Mario Giovanoli, 'The Reform of the International Financial Architecture After the Global Crisis' (2009) 42 *NYU Journal of International Law & Politics* 81, 86.

[128] Emilios Avgouleas and Douglas W Arner, 'The Broken Glass of European Integration: Origins and Remedies of the Eurozone Crisis and Implications for Global Markets' in CL Lim and Bryan Mercurio (eds), *International Economic Law after the Global Crisis: A Tale of Fragmented Disciplines* (Cambridge University Press, 2015) 72, 90.

[129] G20, 'The Global Plan for Recovery and Reform' (2 April 2009), www.g20.utoronto.ca/2009/2009communique0402.pdf.

[130] G20, 'Declaration on Delivering Resources through the International Financial Institutions' (2 April 2009), www.g20.utoronto.ca/2009/2009delivery.pdf.

[131] Giovanoli (n 127) 84.

[132] ibid 99.

[133] Avgouleas and Arner (n 128) 97–98.

[134] eg Report of the Commission of Experts of the President of the United Nations General Assembly on Reforms of the International Monetary and Financial System (21 September 2009) 24.

[135] See, generally, James Crawford, 'The Current Political Discourse Concerning International Law' (2018) 81(1) *Modern Law Review* 1.

[136] Address by President Trump to the United Nations General Assembly (25 September 2018), www.theatlantic.com/international/archive/2018/09/trump-unga-transcript-2018/571264/.

section offers comment on how these norms protect sovereign prerogatives and/or impose international constraints, and how this balance may have shifted over time.

The Friendly Relations Declaration addresses the principle of sovereign equality,[137] which is enshrined in Article 2(1) of the UN Charter, providing that States 'have equal rights and duties and are equal members of the international community, notwithstanding differences of an economic, social, political or other nature'. One of the elements of sovereign equality listed in the Declaration is the right of each State to 'freely choose and develop its political, social, economic and cultural systems'. Sovereign equality has both internal and external elements. The internal element is set by the nature and extent of a State's international legal obligations, otherwise it is something of an empty shell.[138] To understand the internal element, '[a]t the least, one would need to consider related legal principles', such as jurisdiction and self-determination.[139] The external element is a State's 'capacity to engage in international legal relations with other States'.[140] Two of the manifestations of this principle that the prominent Egyptian lawyer, Georges Abi-Saab, has identified bear on financial and monetary matters: (1) the principle of participatory equality of developing countries in international economic relations; and (2) the right of States to freely choose their economic system.[141] These will each be considered in turn.

A procedural manifestation of sovereign equality is the equal participation by States (irrespective of their economic size) in the international economic organisations to which they are subject. Whilst this did not emerge in the Friendly Relations Declaration process, it was a feature of the NIEO.[142] The NIEO was chosen as the forum, due to dissatisfaction with the weighted voting procedures of the World Bank and IMF, which 'gave preference to the interests of developed states'.[143] Article 10 of the Charter of Economic Rights and Duties of States provides that States 'as equal members of the international community, have the right to participate fully and effectively in the international decision-making process in the solution of world economic, financial and monetary problems'. The governance rules and practices of the IMF and World Bank have been frequently targeted as a part of this debate. Voting power is not 'one country, one vote'. Instead it is based on the size of members' quotas in the IMF or capital stock in the Bank. These are in turn calculated based on a number of variables, including GDP, openness and currency reserves.[144] Quota reviews are conducted at regular intervals at the IMF. The Fifteenth Review fell short of the required majority. It would have involved a shift of more than 6 per cent of quota shares to 'dynamic emerging markets and developing countries'.[145] Given the failure of the Fifteenth Review, the IMF launched the Sixteenth Quota Review in October 2019, to be completed no later than end 2023. The stated objective is to achieve 'increases in the quota shares of dynamic economies in line with their relative positions in the world economy ... while protecting the voice and representation of the poorest members.'[146]

[137] See the chapter by M Koskenniemi and V Kari in this volume.

[138] Vaughan Lowe, 'Sovereignty and International Economic Law' in Wenhua Shan, Penelope Simons and Dalvinder Singh (eds), *Redefining Sovereignty in International Economic Law* (Hart, 2008) 77, 82.

[139] ibid.

[140] Colin Warbrick, 'The Principle of Sovereign Equality' in Warbrick and Lowe (eds) (n 107) 204.

[141] UNITAR Report (n 112) 12, para 3.

[142] Philippe Cahier, 'Changements et continuité du droit international' (1985) 195 *Recueil des Cours* 9, 36.

[143] Kate Miles, *Origins of International Investment Law* (Cambridge University Press, 2013) 94.

[144] Ariel Buria, 'The Bretton Woods Institutions: Governance without Legitimacy?' in Ariel Buria (ed), *Reforming the Governance of the IMF and the World Bank* (Cambridge University Press, 2012) 7, 10–11.

[145] IMF, Quotas Factsheet, IMF Communications Department, Washington DC (October 2017) 3, www.imf.org/external/np/exr/facts/quotas.htm.

[146] IMF Executive Board Approves Decisions to Implement a Package on Resources and Governance Reform, 17 January 2020, available at www.imf.org/en/News/Articles/2020/01/17/pr2010-nab-and-quota-imf-executive-board-approves-package-

For the time being, the disparity between voting power and economic strength at the IMF continues.[147]

The right of States to freely choose their economic system is elaborated on in the Charter of Economic Rights and Duties. This can be seen, for example, in Article 4 (right to choose form of foreign economic relations), Article 5 (right to associate in organisations of primary commodity producers), and Article 12 (right to participate in different co-operative arrangements). However, the right is challenged by conditional lending and assistance. As discussed earlier, conditionality is present in the IMF, but also World Bank development loans. Generally, the World Bank 'sought adjustment policies concerned with restructuring the economy to increase its long-term efficiency'.[148] The effect on a State's internal affairs is debated.[149] Recipients agree to such conditionality when requesting financial assistance. Framed from this perspective, such financial assistance, including when subject to market reform conditions, would be a manifestation of the duty to co-operate in economic matters. From another view, the exercise of conditionality amounts to economic coercion indirectly exercised – through the voting powers of country donors in the IMF and the World Bank – on recipients of financial resources. From this angle, the fact that recipient States seek funding in extraordinary and strenuous economic circumstances makes the request a need and not necessarily a choice, which may change the nature of the conditions placed on recipients from a negotiated term into an imposition, at least when such conditions encroach on matters normally within sovereign remit. That, in turn, could amount to a breach of the non-intervention principle[150] because it would concern matters (e.g. monetary and fiscal policy and, more generally, economic organisation) which remain within sovereign remit.

3 *The International Law of Foreign Investment Transactions*

3.1 *Brief Historical Background*

The transition from the broad conceptions of sovereignty[151] and, specifically, territorial sovereignty to the legal concepts formalising powers over resources in international law has been aptly characterised by Ian Brownlie in his 1979 Hague lectures: '[i]n classical international law natural resources had no place. The disposition of resources was assumed to follow the delimitation of sovereignty in spatial terms between States.'[152] There was no need, except with respect to some potentially unclear cases such as fisheries, to make specific provision for natural resources. Brownlie then adds that questions of natural resources were handled under the legal categories of the time, such as the acquisition of territory, the making of agreements, the freedoms in the high seas and, also, the recognition of foreign intervention. These two observations require some

resources-governance-reform; Fifteenth and Sixteenth General Reviews of Quotas—Report of the Executive Board to the Board of Governors, IMF Policy Paper No. 20/007, 13 February 2020.

147 Lowenfeld (n 79) 577. Vijay L Kelkar et al, 'Reforming the International Monetary Fund: Towards Enhanced Accountability and Legitimacy' in Buria (ed) (n 144) 45, 50.

148 Isabella D Bunn, *The Right to Development and International Economic Law: Legal and Moral Dimensions* (Hart, 2012) 237–8.

149 Sabine Schlemmer-Schulte, 'International Bank for Reconstruction and Development' in *Max Planck Encyclopedia of Public International Law* (April 2008), para 105.

150 See the chapter by D Tladi in this volume.

151 See the chapter by M Koskenniemi and V Kari in this volume.

152 Ian Brownlie, 'Legal Status of Natural Resources in International Law (Some Aspects)' (1979) 162 *Recueil des Cours* 245–318, 253.

clarification, which is also useful to grasp the novelty of the post-1945 law relating to natural resources.

In an international context where some States mutually recognised themselves as fully sovereign, their powers over natural resources were naturally assumed to flow from sovereignty. At the same time, other norms governing powers over natural resources beyond this selective circle of States would have curtailed the free acquisition and disposition of the resources located in the colonies or in other subjugated territories. It was only with the wave of decolonisation of the early nineteenth century in Latin America that such equation came to be challenged. Yet, as noted by Brownlie, the challenge was not framed in terms of new legal concepts relating to natural resources but, rather, through claims concerning the application of domestic law to foreigners ('national treatment'), the submission of disputes to the domestic courts of the host State, the recalibration of relations with foreign investors through contractual arrangements, and a general contestation of 'gunboat diplomacy'.[153] Underlying this legal framing, however, was the attempt to transition away from a state of affairs where the legal powers of dominant States over colonial (and formerly colonial) resources were well established.

After the end of the Second World War, the decolonisation script was replayed but, this time, in a different theatre (mainly the UN General Assembly), with different players (with the bulk of decolonisation taking place in Africa, Asia and the Middle East) and in different circumstances (with natural resources, particularly oil, becoming of extreme geopolitical importance). The legal framing was also different. The fears over inequality among States and the continued ownership and control of natural resources by foreign interests were challenged through an emphasis on 'sovereign equality' and the development, through normative resolutions adopted by the UN General Assembly, of explicit rules relating to powers over natural resources.[154]

It may be difficult to appreciate, for today's observers, what these rules effectively added. We have grown so familiar with the current conception of territorial sovereignty, which includes largely discretionary powers over energy resources and policy, that we fail to see what the rules developed between the 1950s and the 1970s aimed to achieve. But for the then called 'under-developed' countries or the colonies and non-self-governing territories that were then striving to become independent, sovereign 'equality', 'permanent' ownership and control over their resources irrespective of prior colonial arrangements, or the 'right to freely determine' their natural resources policy[155] were far from empty words; they were important perspectives which

[153] Following the blockade of Venezuelan ports by the UK, Germany and Italy, a major initiative from American (including the US) States led to the so-called Drago-Porter Convention (Convention between the United States and Other Powers Respecting the Limitation of the Employment of Force for the Recovery of Contract Debts, 18 October 1907, 36 *Statutes at Large* 2241). On the rationale of this instrument, see the article of the then Argentine Minister of Foreign Affairs L M Drago published in the very first volume of the *American Journal of International Law*: L M Drago, 'State Loans in their Relations to International Policy' (1907) 1 *American Journal of International Law* 692. For a retrospective account see Matthias Maass, 'Catalyst for the Roosevelt Corollary: Arbitrating the 1902–1903 Venezuela Crisis and Its Impact on the Development of the Roosevelt Corollary to the Monroe Doctrine' (2009) 20 *Diplomacy & Statecraft* 383; Michael Waibel, *Sovereign Defaults before International Courts and Tribunals* (Cambridge University Press, 2011) 30–35.

[154] See generally Nico Schrijver, *Sovereignty over Natural Resources* (Cambridge University Press, 1997).

[155] Schrijver refers to a curious episode. In 1947, a non-governmental organisation based in Brussels, submitted to ECOSOC a proposal tending to develop an international convention on oil resources (particularly those of the Middle East) granting equal access to all States as well as to create a UN Petroleum Commission to administer them. Although this proposal did not trigger any action in UN circles, it clearly reflects the tension between the needs (in oil) of the world economy, particularly in a post-war reconstruction context with growing fears of communism expansion, and the right of countries to freely determine the use of their natural resources. See ibid 37 et seq.

they sought to explicitly enshrine in the form of authoritative resolutions from the UN General Assembly, where they outnumbered capital exporting countries.

In briefly referring to this process, our intention is to provide some background regarding the emergence of the main principles relating to powers over natural resources as well as to the constraints placed on such powers by international law. It is often forgotten that the contemporary law of foreign investment was historically a loophole in a system reset after the Second World War and, particularly, from the 1960s onwards, to reflect the aspirations of developing and newly independent countries, where a large part of the globe's natural resources was located. Such loophole has grown out of proportion giving the impression, to an observer today, that the standards arising from the dense network of bilateral investment treaties and other similar agreements are, in fact, the rule, the default position in international law, rather than a historical exception.[156] That misperception has, in turn, led to significant practical consequences in the misapplication of customary international law in foreign investment disputes.[157] The following discussion is an attempt to place the relations between the principles expressing powers over natural resources and the now standardised limitations to such powers in a wider perspective.

3.2 *Powers over Natural Resources*

In the early 1950s, the assertion of a right to exploit natural resources in the national interest was not as obvious as it may appear today. Schrijver provides an illuminating example concerning the drafting history of what became UN General Assembly Resolution 523 (VI).[158] The draft proposed by Poland stated that 'under-developed countries' have the full right to determine freely the use of their natural resources. The United States opposed this formulation and proposed an amendment adding a reference to 'the interests of an expanding world economy'. The final compromise text, brokered by Egypt, India and Indonesia, referred to both the national interest and that of the world economy. Schrijver notes that, quite remarkably, this resolution states for the first time the 'right' of under-developed countries to freely determine the use of their natural resources and for the first *and last* time the obligation to use such resources not only in their national interest but also to further the expansion of the world economy.[159]

Today, this sovereign right to exploit natural resources for the national interest is neither confined in its formulation and understanding to certain ('under-developed') countries nor controversial. It is, in fact, an expressly recognised corollary of sovereignty. As noted by a WTO Panel in *China – Raw Materials*:

> An important element of the principle of state sovereignty is the principle of sovereignty over natural resources, recognized as a principle of international law, and allowing states to 'freely use and exploit their natural wealth and resources wherever deemed desirable by them for their own progress and economic development'.[160]

[156] On this thesis see Jorge E Viñuales, 'Sovereignty in Foreign Investment Law' in Zachary Douglas, Joost Pauwelyn and Jorge E Viñuales (eds), *The Foundations of International Investment Law* (Oxford University Press, 2014) 318–62.
[157] See Jorge E Viñuales, 'Customary Law in Investment Regulation' (2014) 23 *Italian Yearbook of International Law* 23.
[158] Integrated Economic Development and Commercial Agreements, 12 January 1952, UN Doc A/RES/523(VI).
[159] See Schrijver (n 154) 37 et seq.
[160] *China – Measures Related to the Exportation of Various Raw Materials*, DS394 Panel Report (5 July 2011) [*China – Raw Materials*], para 7.380 (referring to Resolutions 626 (VII) and 1803 (XVII) but, significantly, relying on the former, not the latter, to formulate the content of the principle).

This principle (including the right) has been formulated in a stream of UN General Assembly resolutions since 1952[161] as well as in some international instruments,[162] and it has been expressly acknowledged to be a principle of customary international law by several international courts and tribunals.[163] Its close connection with the principle of permanent sovereignty over natural resources, discussed next, arises both from the historical development of both principles and from the more recent recognition of their convergence.

The principle of permanent sovereignty over natural resources is very closely related to the right of States to exploit their natural resources, but these norms are not identical. From a historical perspective, two conceptual pursuits can be identified. One concerned the assertion of a right of the State where the resources are located to use such resources for its own benefit, rather than for the benefit of all States.[164] The other focused on a precondition for the exercise of the latter right, namely the assertion of ownership of and control over the resources by the people of the aspiring State, particularly against the attempts of colonial powers to detach and annex or otherwise keep control over resource-rich parts of the colonial territory.[165] Only through such an assertion could a people, once it had become a State, exercise its right to freely exploit and use its natural wealth. This second pursuit was therefore an expression of the broader quest for self-determination. Hence the formulation retained in the influential UN General Assembly Resolution 1803 (XVII), which is widely considered to reflect customary

161 See Right to Exploit Freely Natural Wealth and Resources, 21 December 1952, UN Doc A/RES/626/VII, operative part, para 1; Concerted Action for Economic Development of Economically Less Developed Countries, 15 December 1960, UN Doc A/RES/1515/XV, operative part, para 5; Permanent Sovereignty over Natural Resources, 14 December 1962, UN Doc A/RES/1803/XVII [Res 1803]; Permanent Sovereignty over Natural Resources, 25 November 1966, UN/RES/2158/XXI, operative part, para 1; Declaration on the Establishment of a New International Economic Order, 1 May 1974, UN Doc A/RES/S-6/3201, operative part, para 4(e); Charter of Economic Rights and Duties of States, 12 December 1974, UN Doc A/RES/3281/XXIX, Charter, chapter II, Art 2(1).

162 See Declaration of the United Nations Conference on the Human Environment, Stockholm, 16 June 1972, UN Doc A/CONF.48/14/Rev.1, 2 et seq, principle 21; Rio Declaration on Environment and Development, 13 June 1992, UN Doc A/CONF.151/26. Rev.1, principle 2.

163 The principle has been widely recognised in the case law. See eg *Texaco Overseas Petroleum Company and California Asiatic Oil Company* v *The Government of the Libyan Arab Republic*, Arbitral Award (19 January 1977), 17 ILM 1978, para 87; *Libyan American Oil Company (LIAMCO)* v *The Government of the Libyan Arab Republic*, Arbitral Award (12 April 1977), 20 ILM 1981, 99–103; *Kuwait* v *American Independent Oil Company (AMINOIL)*, Arbitral Award (24 March 1982), 21 ILM 1982, para 143; *Armed Activities on the Territory of the Congo (Democratic Republic of the Congo* v *Uganda)*, Judgment, ICJ Reports 2005, 168, paras 244–45. In other cases, the normative context relied upon is different and focuses on the obligation of prevention, which assumes, as its starting point the right of States to exploit their natural resources: *Gabčíkovo-Nagymaros Project (Hungary* v *Slovakia)*, Judgment, ICJ Reports 1997, 7, 152; *In the matter of the Indus Waters Kishenganga Arbitration before the Court of Arbitration constituted in accordance with the Indus Waters Treaty 1960 between the Government of India and the Government of Pakistan signed on 19 September 1960 (Islamic Republic of Pakistan* v *Republic of India)*, Partial Award, Perm Ct Arb, 18 February 2013, paras 448 and 451; *Dispute Concerning Delimitation of the Maritime Boundary between Ghana and Côte d'Ivoire in the Atlantic Ocean (Ghana/Côte d'Ivoire)*, ITLOS Case No 23, Order of 25 April 2015, para 61. Yet another strand of cases recognises the State's regulatory powers but also their constraints. See eg *Crystallex International Corporation* v *Bolivarian Republic of Venezuela*, ICSID Case No ARB(AF)/11/2, Award (4 April 2016), para 581; *Rusoro Mining Ltd* v *Bolivarian Republic of Venezuela*, ICSID Case No ARB(AF)/12/5, Award, 22 August 2016, para 531.

164 As noted by one historian, the promise, in the August 1941 Atlantic Charter, to grant equal access to raw materials for all nations, was seen by some (in this example the African National Congress) as 'likely to bring about a continuation of the exploitation of African resources to the detriment of her indigenous inhabitants and the enrichment of foreigners': Africans' claims in South Africa, 16 December 1943, cited in Brad Simpson, 'Self-Determination and Decolonization' in Martin Thomas and Andrew Thomson (eds), *The Oxford Handbook of the Ends of Empire* (Oxford University Press, 2017) 417–30, 419.

165 Declaration on the Granting of Independence to Colonial Countries and Peoples, 14 December 1960, UN Doc A/RES/1514(XV), para 6. For a recent application see *Legal Consequences of the Separation of the Chagos Archipelago from Mauritius in 1965*, Advisory Opinion, 25 February 2019, para 153.

international law.[166] The frequent assimilation of both norms is reasonable today. There is indeed convergence between the two norms insofar as a people, now organised in the form of an independent State, exercises the right to permanent sovereignty over natural resources through the very exercise of the new State's right to exploit its natural resources. Even then, tensions remain because the State, specifically a ruling class, may abuse the right of a State to exploit its natural resources leading to a 'resource curse'.[167] For present purposes, it may suffice to state the following basic tenets relating to permanent sovereignty: (i) the principle, including a right, was primarily aimed to serve as an instrument of economic emancipation against the existing (but not against the subsequently agreed) asymmetries in the ownership and control of natural resources by foreign interests, hence the need to stress the 'permanence'; (ii) in this nuanced formulation the principle has been deemed to enjoy customary grounding; (iii) in normal situations, it overlaps with the right of States to exploit their natural resources in the national interest; (iv) but in some exceptional cases this overlap may hide a tension between legal entitlements.

In the years that followed the adoption of Resolution 1803 (XVII), the normative channel provided by UN General Assembly resolutions was continuously relied upon by developing and newly independent countries. One important dimension of this extension was the emphasis on a State's sovereign prerogative to freely determine how its natural resources were put to use. The broader context of this extension is twofold. First, the Cold War ideological battles within the UN and elsewhere drew great attention to the choice of the economic system followed by each State. From a legal standpoint, that choice was at the crossroads of the principles of sovereignty[168] and non-intervention,[169] as well as of the doctrine of *domaine réservé*.[170] Second, and perhaps more importantly, the principle of permanent sovereignty over natural resources, as formulated in Resolution 1803 (XVII), clearly admitted the possibility that foreign investors may be allowed to develop the natural resources of a country as long as this was *freely* agreed between the foreign party (the investor or its home State) and the host State.[171] The economic emancipation embodied in the principle of 'permanent sovereignty' was therefore sought with respect to past asymmetries. For future relations with foreign interests, which many developing and newly independent countries very actively sought to attract, the emphasis was on 'free' determination of

[166] See *Texaco Overseas Petroleum Company and California Asiatic Oil Company* v *The Government of the Libyan Arab Republic*, Arbitral Award (19 January 1977), 17 ILM 1978, para 87; *Libyan American Oil Company (LIAMCO)* v *The Government of the Libyan Arab Republic*, Arbitral Award (12 April 1977), 20 ILM 1981, 99–103; *Kuwait* v *American Independent Oil Company (AMINOIL)*, Arbitral Award (24 March 1982), 21 ILM 1982, para 143; *Armed Activities on the Territory of the Congo (Democratic Republic of the Congo* v *Uganda)*, Judgment, ICJ Reports 2005, 168, paras 244–45; *China – Raw Materials* (n 160), para 7.380.

[167] See Richard A Auty, *Sustaining Development in Mineral Economies: the Resource Curse Thesis* (Routledge, 1993); Michael Ross, *The Oil Curse : How Petroleum Wealth Shapes the Development of Nations* (Princeton University Press, 2012); Frederick van der Ploeg, 'Natural Resources: Curse or Blessing?' 49 (2011) *Journal of Economic Literature* 366–420.

[168] See the chapter by M Koskenniemi and V Kari in this volume.

[169] See the chapter by D Tladi in this volume.

[170] These principles and concepts received an authoritative statement and clarification with the adoption of the Declaration on Principles of International Law concerning Friendly Relations and Co-operation among States in Accordance with the Charter of the United Nations, 24 October 1970, UN Doc A/RES/2625(XXV) and, later, with the detailed interpretation of some of these principles provided by the ICJ in *Military and Paramilitary Activities in and against Nicaragua (Nicaragua* v *United States of America)*, Merits, Judgment, ICJ Reports 1986, 14.

[171] Res 1803 (n 161), operative part, paras 3 ('profits derived [from foreign investment] must be shared in proportions *freely* agreed upon'), 4 ('[t]he *free* and beneficial exercise of the sovereignty of peoples and nations over their natural resources must be furthered by the mutual respect of States based on their sovereign equality') and, most importantly, 8 ('[f]oreign investment agreements *freely* entered into by or between sovereign States shall be observed in good faith') (italics added).

contractual arrangements. Starting in 1972, in the aftermath of the adoption of the important Friendly Relations Declaration, the assertion of 'freedom' was complemented by an emphasis on the prohibition of economic or other forms of coercion. Schrijver notes that UN General Assembly Resolution 3016 (XXVII) was the first instrument to stress this point in the specific context of natural resources.[172]

This characterisation of sovereign prerogatives to set national policies remains relevant today, with two important caveats arising from subsequent developments. First, the assertion of this sovereign prerogative is no longer confined to developing or newly independent States. It has also been widely recognised in the context of foreign investment disputes, where arbitral tribunals have consistently considered that the doctrine of the police powers of the State is a customary norm of general application.[173] Second, the normative context within which this prerogative can be exercised has undergone major changes since the 1970s,[174] in part due to the surge in both investment treaties and investment arbitration. States' sovereign prerogatives have often been subordinated, without clear legal grounds, to another expression of sovereignty, introduced as an exception or caveat in Resolution 1803 (XVII), namely the power to enter into agreements to regulate investment relations.[175] As discussed next, the exception has grown out of proportion and has become the rule,[176] to such an extent that a group of developed and developing countries and the EU are taking steps to tame the most salient aspects (particularly investor–State dispute settlement) of the system that they contributed to create.[177]

[172] Permanent Sovereignty over Natural Resources of Developing Countries, 18 December 1972, UN Doc A/RES/3016 (XXVII); see Schrijver (n 154). This emphasis was kept in subsequent resolutions. See eg Declaration on the Establishment of a New International Economic Order, 1 May 1974, UN Doc A/RES/S-6/3201, operative part, paras 4(d) and 4(e) in fine; Charter of Economic Rights and Duties of States, 12 December 1974, UN Doc A/RES/3281/XXIX, Charter, chapter II, Arts 1, 2(1).

[173] See eg *CME Czech Republic BV* v *Czech Republic*, UNCITRAL, Partial Award (13 September 2001), para 603; *Marvin Roy Feldman Karpa* v *United Mexican States*, ICSID Case No ARB(AF)/99/1, Award (16 December 2002), paras 103, 112; *Saluka Investments BV* v *The Czech Republic*, UNCITRAL, Partial Award (17 March 2006); *BG Group plc* v *Republic of Argentina*, UNCITRAL, Award (24 December 2007), para 268; *AWG Group Ltd* v *Argentine Republic*, UNCITRAL, Decision on Liability (30 July 2010), paras 149–50; *Total SA* v *Argentine Republic*, ICSID Case No ARB/04/01, Decision on Liability (27 December 2010), para 197; *Tza Yap Shum* v *Republic of Peru*, ICSID Case No ARB/07/6, Award (7 July 2011), para 145; *El Paso Energy International Company* v *Argentine Republic*, ICSID Case No ARB/03/15, Award (31 October 2011), paras 236–41, 243; *Les Laboratoires Servier, SAS, Biofarma, SAS, Arts et Techniques du Progres SAS* v *Republic of Poland*, UNCITRAL, Award (Redacted) (14 February 2012), paras 569–70, 584; *SAUR International SA* v *Argentine Republic*, ICSID Case No ARB/04/4, Decision on Jurisdiction and Liability (6 June 2012), paras 396–401; *TECO Guatemala Holdings, LLC* v *Republic of Guatemala*, ICSID Case No ARB/10/23, Award (19 December 2013), paras 490–93.

[174] Such is the key thesis of Schrijver's book, which looks at the increasing limitations arising from international environmental law, the law of the sea and international investment law.

[175] For some illustrations out of a vast body of case law see: *Yuri Bogdanov and Yulia Bogdanov* v *Republic of Moldova*, SCC Case No V091/2012, Final Award (16 April 2013), para 186; *British Caribbean Bank Ltd* v *Government of Belize*, Case No 2010–18/BCB-BZ, Award, Perm Ct Arb, 19 December 2014, para 236; *Quiborax SA and Non Metallic Minerals SA* v *Plurinational State of Bolivia*, ICSID Case No ARB/06/2, Award (16 September 2015), para 89; *Crystallex International Corporation* v *Bolivarian Republic of Venezuela*, ICSID Case No ARB(AF)/11/2, Award (4 April 2016), para 581; *Rusoro Mining Ltd* v *Bolivarian Republic of Venezuela*, ICSID Case No ARB(AF)/12/5, Award (22 August 2016), para 531; *Blusun SA, Jean-Pierre Lecorcier and Michael Stein* v *Italian Republic*, ICSID Case No ARB/14/3, Award (27 December 2016), paras 319, 372.

[176] On this phenomenon see Viñuales (n 156).

[177] Much has been written on the reform of investor–State dispute settlement. The question is currently being addressed by Working Group III of the UN Commission for International Trade Law (UNCITRAL). Concept papers providing an overview of a range of key issues have been prepared by the Centre for International Dispute Settlement. They are available at: www.cids.ch/academic-forum-concept-papers.

3.3 *From Exception to Rule*

The protection of foreign investors operating abroad has a long history in international law, with at least two centuries of debate and practice initially spurred by the independence of Spanish colonies in the Americas.[178] The decolonisation process in the aftermath of the Second World War, particularly in the late 1950s and early 1960s, reignited the debate between capital exporting countries and capital importing as well as newly independent countries.

Resolution 1803 (XVII) was one of the most notable achievements of this process. As noted earlier, this resolution was primarily aimed at correcting past asymmetries, and it expressly provided for the possibility that future investment from capital-exporting countries could be subject to special agreements. Paragraphs 4 and 8 are apposite for present purposes:

> 4. Nationalization, expropriation or requisitioning shall be based on grounds or reasons of public utility, security or the national interest which are recognised as overriding purely individual or private interests, both domestic and foreign. In such cases, the owner shall be paid appropriate compensation, in accordance with the rules in force in the State taking such measures in the exercise of its sovereignty and in accordance with international law. In any case where the question of compensation gives rise to a controversy, the national jurisdiction of the State taking such measures shall be exhausted. *However, upon agreement by sovereign States and other parties concerned, settlement of the dispute should be made through arbitration or international adjudication.*
>
> ...
>
> 8. *Foreign investment agreements freely entered into by or between sovereign States shall be observed in good faith ...*[179]

Read in context, it seems clear that foreign investment agreements and international arbitration were seen as exceptions to the principle of permanent sovereignty over natural resources. In retrospect, it is also clear that such exception has grown out of proportion. Although the first modern investment agreement is widely considered to be the BIT between Germany and Pakistan, concluded in 1959, the main wave of modern investment agreements came much later, starting in the 1990s.[180] Thus, from a historical standpoint, the instruments that allowed for the expansion of the foreign investment regime are relatively recent.

3.4 *The Three Pillars of the Investment Regime*

To understand the expansion process identified in the previous section, it is necessary to look more closely into the trajectory followed by the three pillars of international investment law – namely the object, the law and the judge – over time.

Regarding the object, historically, the paradigmatic example of a foreign investment transaction was either the exploitation of natural resources or investment in infrastructure. The distinction between 'foreign direct investment' and 'portfolio investment'[181] reflects the long-term nature of the former relative to the latter, which was a key consideration in the debates regarding the post-war global economic system, as noted in the introduction to this chapter. The reason why capital

[178] The following discussion relies on Jorge E Viñuales, 'Foreign Direct Investment: International Investment Law and Natural Resource Governance' in Elisa Morgera and Kati Kulovesi (eds), *Research Handbook on International Law and Natural Resources* (Edward Elgar, 2016) 26–45, and Jorge E Viñuales, 'L'Etat face à la protection internationale de l'entreprise: Regards sur le droit international des investissements contemporain' in Alain Supiot (ed), *L'Etat de l'entreprise dans un monde sans frontiers. Perspectives economiques et juridiques* (Dalloz, 2015) 103–14.

[179] Res 1803 (n 161), paras 4 and 8 (italics added).

[180] Jonathan Bonnitcha, Lauge Poulsen and Michael Waibel, *The Political Economy of the Investment Treaty Regime* (Oxford University Press, 2017) 20, Fig 1.5.

[181] See *OECD Benchmark Definition of Foreign Direct Investment* (2008), para 11, www.oecd.org/daf/inv/investmentstatisticsandanalysis/40193734.pdf.

importing countries accepted to grant enhanced protection to foreign direct investment was, in part, the expectation that such investment would contribute to their economic and social development.[182] Over time, and particularly in the last two decades, this understanding has been progressively eroded through the operation of two processes. First, States have included broader definitions of what constitutes an 'investment' held by a 'foreign investor' in their investment agreements. By way of illustration, assets such as 'shares, stocks or other forms of equity', 'bonds ... other debt instruments, and loans' or 'intellectual property rights' feature frequently in the definition of investment included in recent agreements.[183] Second, and perhaps more controversially, investment arbitration tribunals have interpreted expansively this term, encompassing portfolio investment or assets such as commercial loans[184] or sovereign bonds.[185] In some cases, the need for the investment to contribute to the development of the host country has been deemed an unnecessary component of the definition of investment, leading to significant controversy.[186] At present, it is possible to discern a reverse trend, at least in the practice of some States, which seeks to define the term investment more strictly, explicitly excluding transactions that lack the requisite permanence or duration or that do not clearly contribute to the prosperity of the host country.[187] Yet, this trend does not reflect the views of a majority of States and some alternative trends are also noticeable in some recent investment agreements.[188]

Regarding the standards of investment protection, historically, the main concern was the protection against uncompensated expropriation as well as – often relatedly – against potential denials of justice.[189] Such protection had been sought in competing approaches regarding the applicable standards, ranging from the extraterritorial application of the laws of the colonial powers during the nineteenth century, challenged by its precise opposite, namely the application of the laws of the host State and, eventually, a compromise solution which crystallised around the concept of an 'international minimum standard of treatment', still widely in operation today.[190]

182 See the preamble of the Convention on the Settlement of Investment Disputes Between States and Nationals of Other States, 18 March 1965, 575 UNTS 159, para 1, considering: 'the need for international cooperation for economic development, and the role of private international investment therein'.

183 See eg US Model BIT (2012), Art 1.

184 See eg *Ceskoslovenska Obchodni Banka, AS* v *The Slovak Republic*, ICSID Case No ARB/97/4, Award (24 May 1999), paras 76–89 (linking a loan to a broader transaction to consider it an investment).

185 See *Abaclat and Others* v *Argentine Republic*, ICSID Case No ARB/07/5, Decision on Jurisdiction and Admissibility (4 August 2011), paras 373–80, with an important dissent of arbitrator Abi-Saab, who concluded as follows on the territoriality link 'the present case is, to my knowledge, the first one to come before an ICSID tribunal in which the alleged investment is totally free-standing and unhinged, without any anchorage, however remote, into an underlying economic project, enterprise or activity in the territory of the host State. None of the logical short-cuts put forward by the majority award to palliate this absence, holds water' (para 118). In a similar, more recent, case against Greece, the tribunal followed declined jurisdiction on the basis of the different wording of the applicable treaty. See *Poštová banka, a.s. and Istrokapital s.e.* v *Hellenic Republic*, ICSID Case No ARB/13/8, Award (9 April 2015), paras 308, 331. Importantly, however, the award contains an obiter dictum endorsed by the majority to the effect that the bonds at stake would not constitute investments under Art 25 of the ICSID Convention (see para 371, concluding to the absence of contribution to development and of operational risk).

186 This debate is illustrated by the case *Malaysian Historical Salvors* v *Malaysia*, ICSID Case No ARB/05/10, Award (17 May 2007), where the sole arbitrator declined jurisdiction because the transaction did not contribute to the development of the host State. The award was subsequently annulled, albeit not unanimously, by an ad hoc committee: *Malaysian Historical Salvors* v *Malaysia*, ICSID Case No ARB/05/10, Decision on the application for annulment (16 April 2009), paras 62–63, 69, 71–72.

187 See eg the Model text for the Indian Bilateral Investment Treaty, 2015, Arts 1.6 and 1.2.1. The text is available at: https://mygov.in.

188 On the different trends see UNCTAD, *World Investment Report (2014)* 126–30.

189 Jan Paulsson, *Denial of Justice in International Law* (Cambridge University Press, 2005).

190 Martins Paparinskis, *The International Minimum Standard and Fair and Equitable Treatment* (Oxford University Press, 2013).

Over time, a wider variety of investment disciplines or standards were included in investment agreements covering impairments of foreign investments that fell short of expropriation or did not involve a denial of justice. Among these, three deserve particular mention here. First, the ambiguity as to the nature of investment contracts entered between a State and a foreign investor led some capital-exporting States, such as the United Kingdom, to introduce the so-called 'umbrella clauses' in its treaties.[191] The purpose of such clauses was to give an international dimension to the commitments, including contractual commitments, given by a host State to a foreign investor. In the last two decades, the extent to which such clauses 'elevate' or 'transform' contracts into international obligations has been widely discussed.[192] The question is not clearly settled in the case law, although it is generally considered that the solution lies somewhere midway between the two extreme possibilities – that is, that no term can be elevated or that all terms can be elevated to treaty level.[193] Second, and perhaps more importantly, virtually any type of State regulatory action is now subject to potential challenges under the broad 'fair and equitable treatment' (FET) standard. FET clauses merely declare that States shall accord fair and equitable treatment, leaving the specific implications of such treatment for arbitral tribunals to interpret. In many ways, the inclusion of FET amounts to a definitional delegation, which, unsurprisingly, has led over time to a wide range of interpretations and much controversy.[194] State action that is not a formal expropriation and that does not amount to an indirect expropriation (because it does not amount to a 'substantial deprivation' of the value of the investment) may breach the FET standard and, significantly, the rules and methodologies used for the assessment of compensation in case of expropriation have been extended by some tribunals to breaches of FET.[195] The growing reach and implications of FET, particularly in connection with the investor's 'legitimate expectations', has come under much criticism, prompting the International Court of Justice (ICJ) to make an *obiter dictum* stating that:

> references to legitimate expectations may be found in arbitral awards concerning disputes between a foreign investor and the host State that apply treaty clauses providing for fair and equitable treatment. It does not follow from such references that there exists in general international law a principle that would give rise to an obligation on the basis of what could be considered a legitimate expectation.[196]

Third, investment agreements specifically provide for non-discrimination standards, namely the national treatment and MFN clauses. Despite their similarities with the non-discrimination

[191] See H Abs and H Shawcross, 'The Proposed Convention to Protect Private Foreign Investment: A Round Table' (1960) 1 *Journal of Public Law* [now *Emory Law Journal*] 115–18.

[192] See eg J Antony, 'Umbrella Clauses Since *SGS* v. *Pakistan* and *SGS* v. *Philippines* – A Developing Consensus' (2013) 29 *Arbitration International* 607.

[193] See *El Paso Energy International Company* v *The Argentine Republic*, ICSID Case No ARB/03/15, Decision on Jurisdiction (27 April 2006), para 81. The tribunal supported its conclusion by reference to three other decisions, namely *SGS Société Générale de Surveillance SA* v *Islamic Republic of Pakistan*, ICSID Case No ARB/01/13, Decision on Jurisdiction (27 August 2003), paras 166, 168, 173; *Salini Costruttori Sp.A & Italstrade Sp.A* v *Hashemite Kingdom of Jordan*, ICSID Case No ARB/02/13, Decision on Jurisdiction (29 November 2004), para 126; *Joy Machinery Limited* v *Arab Republic of Egypt*, ICSID Case No ARB/02/11, Award (6 August 2004), para 81.

[194] On the range of interpretations see, among many other contributions, Ioana Tudor, *The Fair and Equitable Treatment Standard in the International Law of Foreign Investment* (Oxford University Press, 2008); Roland Kläger, *'Fair and Equitable Treatment' in International Investment Law* (Cambridge University Press, 2011).

[195] On this extension see P-Y Tschanz and Jorge E Viñuales, 'Compensation for Non-Expropriatory Breaches of International Investment Law: The Contribution of the Argentine Awards' (2009) 26 *Journal of International Arbitration* 729.

[196] *Obligation to Negotiate Access to the Pacific Ocean (Bolivia* v *Chile)*, Judgment of 1 October 2018, para 162.

standards applicable in international trade, the actual operation of these standards in investment proceedings presents important peculiarities,[197] one of which is discussed next.

Regarding the judge of foreign investment disputes, the main historical development that led to the current state of affairs was the possibility, recognised by the arbitral tribunal in *AAPL* v. *Sri Lanka*,[198] for a foreign investor to bring a claim based solely on an arbitration clause appearing in an investment agreement, irrespective of any privity of contract between the investor and the host State.[199] Since then, the number of investment claims has grown exponentially, driven by the realisation by investors and their lawyers of the significant possibilities offered by the system. For better or for worse, tribunals have expanded the legal grounds underpinning such claims through a variety of means, including an expansive interpretation of the MFN clause for jurisdictional purposes[200] as well as a dismissal of the rule – widely acknowledged in inter-State adjudication – that consent to jurisdiction, as other limitations to sovereignty, cannot be presumed and must be interpreted restrictively.[201] In recent years, the substantial grasp of adjudicative power resulting from the operation of investor–State arbitration has become under heavy criticism, even more so than the expansion experienced by the two other pillars of the system. There is currently a reverse trend tending to impose strict controls on the operation of such proceedings or even exclude them altogether from new investment treaties.[202]

3.5 *A Swinging Pendulum*

The balance between sovereign powers and international constraints with respect to foreign investment transactions has oscillated significantly since the end of the Second World War. From an early emphasis on investment and reconstruction, over to the permanent sovereignty movement, to the expansion of the investment agreement exception and, again, the more recent 'backlash' against investment arbitration, the oscillation between liberalisation and sovereignty persists. Across this oscillation, however, two trends can be discerned, each having led to different views.

The first trend concerns what could be called the 'judicialisation' of foreign investment disputes. International law of foreign investment has, to some extent, defused the political dimension of foreign investment disputes to a level which, however controversial, remains manageable through certain legal techniques. The main question in this regard concerns the appropriate comparator and, more specifically, whether such judicialisation process has yielded a positive balance overall or only when compared to a now vanished world. It is unquestionable that much has changed in international law since the early twentieth century, and among such changes the routine resort to international arbitration rather than to the more intrusive and forceful techniques of the nineteenth and early twentieth century are a clear sign of progress. From a system where arbitration acknowledged inequality and use of force to a point

[197] For a detailed study see Jürgen Kurtz, *The WTO and International Investment Law. Converging Systems* (Cambridge University Press, 2016); Jonathan Bonnitcha, Lauge Poulsen and Michael Waibel, *The Political Economy of the Investment Treaty Regime* (Oxford University Press, 2017) 97–100.

[198] *Asian Agricultural Products Ltd* v *Republic of Sri Lanka*, ICSID Case No ARB/87/3, Final Award (27 June 1990).

[199] See Jan Paulsson, 'Arbitration Without Privity' (1995) 10 *ICSID Review-Foreign Investment Law Journal* 232.

[200] The starting point of this important and still ongoing debate was the decision in *Maffezini* v *Kingdom of Spain*, ICSID Case No ARB/97/7, Decision on Jurisdiction (25 January 2000), para 64. On this issue see Zachary Douglas, 'The MFN Clause in Investment Arbitration: Treaty Interpretation Off the Rails' (2011) 2 *Journal of International Dispute Settlement* 97.

[201] See eg *SS Wimbledon*, PCIJ, Series A, No 1 (17 August 1923), 24–25; *SS Lotus*, PCIJ, Series A, No 10 (7 September 1927) 18; *Free Zones of Upper Savoy and the District of Gex*, PCIJ, Series A/B, No 46 (7 June 1932), 167.

[202] For an overview see Michael Waibel et al (eds), *The Backlash Against Investment Arbitration: Perceptions and Reality* (Kluwer, 2010).

where such use granted preferential title to compensation, as in the *Venezuela Preferential* case,[203] to the highly technical and legalised arbitration proceedings that are the rule today, much has been gained for the rule of law at the international level. But, at the same time, that may be too generous a comparator for the assessment of the current system. The current system is imperfect and needs reform. On the question of the rule of law, it has been argued that the development of investment arbitration may, in fact, undermine the development of rule of law institutions in host States.[204] In addition, the ability of States to regulate for the common good should not be subordinated or restricted by the erratic application of broad investment protection standards by 'ephemerous' arbitration tribunals, to borrow the adjective often used by Georges Abi-Saab. But such need is felt within a broader process whereby an important category of disputes is now heard and addressed in accordance with legal standards, which is no meagre achievement.

The second trend has been noted by Rudolph Dolzer in his Hague lectures. It concerns the actual achievement of what he calls the 'Permanent Sovereignty Movement' in connection with the assertion of powers over resources. Dolzer observes that, irrespective of one's assessment of the scope and influence of the legal principle of permanent sovereignty over natural resources, resource-rich countries control today a far larger share of their reserves than in the 1950s:

> Whereas 50 years ago, multinational companies held about 85 per cent of the rights to the global resources, their share has meanwhile been reduced to about 15 per cent. Today, about 85 per cent of these rights are held by the States with territorial jurisdiction over these reserves, including the rights in the exclusive economic zones adjacent to the land. According to the World Bank, national oil companies currently control about 90 per cent of the global reserves of oil and gas and about 75 per cent of the production. This dramatic reversal was effected by the States between 1960 and 1985. In other words, the change took place in the political climate created by the movement for Permanent Sovereignty over Natural Resources . . . The viewpoint, popular in Western States, that the movement for Permanent Sovereignty remained a paper matter of UN resolutions, because it did not achieve its goals to transform international law, fundamentally misunderstands the real purpose, and, more importantly, the real success of the movement. The central vehicle of the process of transformation was the establishment of national oil and gas companies of the States with territorial jurisdiction, which replaced the foreign companies.[205]

This perceptive observation must be kept in mind when assessing the balance between sovereign powers and international constraints. From a legal standpoint, the constraints imposed by international investment law certainly expanded over the reference period. But law is only one prism through which reality can be read and, in this case, it offers only a partial view.

Prospectively, although a significant recalibration of international investment law can be expected in the next years, the broad balance between sovereign powers and the international constraints imposed by the foreign investment system is unlikely to be fundamentally unsettled. The current reform proposals mostly concern the nature of the third pillar of the investment regime (the dispute settlement system), and it is therefore a change within the overall system, rather than a change of the system. The use of international agreements to promote and protect foreign investment and, more specifically, the core definition of investment, the standards of

[203] *The Venezuelan Preferential case (Germany, Great Britain, Italy, Venezuela et al)*, 22 February 1904, RIAA IX, 99–110.

[204] See Tom Ginsburg, 'International Substitutes for Domestic Institutions: Bilateral Investment Treaties and Governance' (2005) 25 *International Review of Law and Economics* 107.

[205] Rudolf Dolzer, 'International Co-Operation in Energy Affairs' (2014) 372 *Recueil des Cours* 395–503, 419–420.

investment protection, and the need for an international dispute settlement mechanism do not seem to be at stake. In this regard, there is significant convergence with the overall trends in the principles governing economic activity as a whole.

III CONCLUDING OBSERVATIONS: CHANGE 'OF' OR 'WITHIN' THE SYSTEM?

To conclude this survey of the foundational principles on which the post-1945 global economic order was built and their vicissitudes over the last seventy years, one simple question may be asked: has there been a change of the entire system or, instead, have new realities been tackled through variations within the system, as defined by the principles surveyed. The answer to such a question is necessarily normative, because it requires the selection of one or more benchmarks by reference to which the magnitude of the change is to be assessed, and it is only by reference to such benchmarks that the answer holds.

A first step is therefore to flesh out the benchmarks. The post-1945 global economic order was built on a balance between State powers and international constraints. From the perspective of trade, the liberalisation envisioned by the GATT left significant room for domestic trade policy, whether in the negotiation of tariff caps, or in the setting of a tariff level within such caps or, more generally, in the definition of a range of exemptions (e.g. public procurement) or exceptions (most notably Article XX GATT). Its main feature, however, was the multilateral character of the agreement, which had been unsuccessfully attempted in 1927 and now was achieved, despite the failure of its institutional component (the ITO). At the monetary and financial level, the approach was to stabilise the exchange rate of different currencies also at the multilateral level through a system of fixed but adjustable exchange rates pegged to the US dollar, itself convertible into gold. A key aspect was the avoidance of competitive currency devaluations, which was important both for trade liberalisation and which many saw as a major factor leading to the Second World War. The IMF's initial function was to step in and offer financial assistance when a country was unable to maintain the stability of the exchange rate. With respect to foreign direct investment, the post-1945 architecture essentially envisioned it from the perspective of lending for reconstruction and development, although as soon as the early 1950s the question of access to resources, particularly in the context of decolonisation, led to important assertions of self-determination, sovereignty and national development, which developed countries sought to tame through the conclusion of special agreements.

If such are the broad benchmarks selected to evaluate whether the system has changed, then a preliminary assessment is possible, subject to further, more granular, discussions of degree. With respect to the trade system, the establishment of the WTO in 1994 could be seen as a marked departure from the initial negative integration approach of the GATT. The WTO expanded the types of transactions governed (now including not only goods but also services and intellectual property rights), the sectors (e.g. agriculture or textiles) and types of State action (e.g. technical barriers to trade, sanitary and phytosanitary measures, government procurement, etc.). In several areas (e.g. IPRs, TBT and SPS), it emphasised a 'positive' integration approach, requiring the adoption of measures by States which introduce a significant level of harmonisation of certain policies, and it fundamentally changed the institutional architecture of the system providing, inter alia, for a sophisticated and compulsory dispute settlement system. Yet, this expansion could be seen as a matter of degree, rather than of nature. Indeed, the underlying core agreement remains the GATT, with its same conceptual architecture, and the key approach remains negotiated and progressive liberalisation (through reduction of tariffs) and non-discrimination. The rise of FTAs, whether bilateral or plurilateral, could represent a more fundamental departure from the post-1945 logic of multilateralism and, in many ways, a return to the bilateralism of the second half of the nineteenth century.

With respect to monetary relations, there was a major change from the fixed but adjustable exchange rates designed at Bretton Woods to the so-called 'non-system' of floating exchange rates, acknowledged through the 1976 reform of the IMF Articles of Agreement. The significance of this change is further supported by the reorientation of the IMF role from that of episodic intervention to a role of financial surveillance and long-term involvement in members' macro-economic policies, as a result of conditional lending. Together, these developments amount to a change 'of' the system itself rather than mere change 'within' the system. This conclusion is consistent with the demise of the concept that emerged in the 1980s to describe the approach followed by international financial institutions, namely the so-called 'Washington consensus'. The global financial integration that intensified in the 1970s and 1980s, with brisk shifts of massive amounts of capital from one currency to another and a series of financial crises, in particular the global financial crisis of 2008, undermined this consensus. The architecture established to deal with these challenges, although it relies partly on the IMF, is far from the initial Bretton Woods approach of fixed and adjustable exchange rates.

As regards international investment law, the answer to our initial question depends on the specific moment in time in which we situate the benchmark. This is largely because the legal conditions governing foreign investment in infrastructure and natural resource extraction underwent a fundamental change as a result of the decolonisation process. From a system of colonial privilege to one of sovereign equality, even if at times formal rather than material, the rules were clearly different. The transformation can be charted by following changes within each of the fundamental pillars of the system, the object, the law and the judge of foreign direct investment transactions. Within each of these, important changes took place in the post-1945 world, but perhaps the most noticeable change was the acceptance of national prerogatives on the basis of self-determination, permanent sovereignty and sovereign equality (hitherto denied to colonial territories) and its curtailment through extensive concessions granted by way of special agreements, both contractual and, most of all, in the form of bilateral investment treaties. The rise of bilateral investment treaties and investment arbitration can be seen as a change 'of' the system, particularly in the form that unfolded starting in the 2000s and which prompted a backlash from both developing and developed countries. Such backlash targets essentially the third pillar of the system (investor–State dispute settlement) and, although significant changes may be introduced in the years to come, they are unlikely to be of a nature and scale that would genuinely constitute a new system.

As a last word, going back to our point of departure in the introduction to this chapter, what remains striking when looking at the manner in which international law addresses the interlocked realms of trade, monetary and investment transactions, so closely connected historically, economically and politically, is their legal disconnection. More than seventy years after the post-1945 reorganisation, the legal approach of these three faces of the global economy remains separate, sectorialised and, at times, inconsistent.

15

The Friendly Relations Declaration at 50

Pierre-Marie Dupuy

I INTRODUCTION

The invitation to reconsider the principles of the Charter listed in the Friendly Relations Declaration obviously raises a fundamental question. Fifty years after their adoption, are these principles still valid or already obsolete in view of the radical changes affecting the political, technological, economic and social environment in which they had previously been reiterated? Here, we can see all the interest of the constitutionalist theses developed with regard to the Charter of the United Nations, despite the exaggerations to which they may have led.[1] From this point of view, and even if the Charter can in no way be reduced to the content of the Declaration itself, the reconsideration of the latter already raises the question of whether the world should radically change its global political constitution. We can see that it is difficult to respond lightly in a positive way! On the contrary, everything points to a response on the basis of two proposals: on the one hand, the nature and scale of the problems facing not only the society of States but also humanity as a whole provides a strong encouragement to reaffirm the need to respect, in particular, the seven principles enshrined in the Declaration as well as in the Charter as a whole; on the other hand, we are no longer in 1970 and each of these principles must be completed and reinterpreted in the light of the new challenges facing the entire international community, which is composed not only of States but also of the different components of civil society.

The purpose of this concluding chapter is to examine, successively, the contrast resulting from the comparison between the situation that prevailed in 1970 and the one we know today (section I) and then the content of the Declaration, whose principles, which are still valid, must be reinterpreted in the light of the contemporary context (section II).

II CONTRAST

1 *A historical review*

The Friendly Relations Declaration is largely the normative result of the Cuban crisis, resolved in extremis eight years earlier, when, after a global 'suspense', Nikita Khrushchev finally decided, on 28 October 1962, to order the dismantling of the offensive weapons installed in

[1] Thomas Kleinlein and Anne Peters, 'International Constitutional Law' in *Oxford Bibliographies in International Law* (Oxford University Press, 2018).

Cuba. As has since been confirmed, the world was then very close to a nuclear war between the Soviet Union and the United States. The conflict could only be avoided thanks to the composure of a few men, but also by the conviction shared by all that a nuclear conflagration would have been fatal to humankind as a whole.

The period between the successful resolution of the crisis and the adoption of the Declaration, eight years later, from October 1962 to October 1970, may seem too long to establish a direct link between the two. However, there is indeed a link. Between these two dates, the effective opening of the period known as that of 'peaceful co-existence' found expression in important normative achievements, including the 1963 Declaration of Legal Principles Governing the Activities of States in the Exploration and Use of Outer Space,[2] consolidated in the 1967 Outer Space Treaty,[3] the 1968 Treaty on the Non-Proliferation of Nuclear Weapons,[4] and, of course, in 1969, the Vienna Convention on the Law of Treaties,[5] whose famous Article 53 will be repeated as a direct reflection of the concerns of the time, not to mention the two United Nations Covenants on Human Rights, adopted in 1966.[6] However, all these legal instruments of cardinal importance for the development of the post-war international legal order lacked a major Declaration solemnly expressing the principles on which each of them found inspiration. The 1970 Friendly Relations Declaration, negotiated over little less than a decade, is thus the cornerstone of this period of so-called 'peaceful co-existence', whose normative productivity remains unparalleled.

The Cuban crisis had suddenly made the planet smaller; it had decidedly demonstrated how fragile the only one Earth we have could suddenly be. In the aftermath of the direct confrontation between Nikita Khrushchev and John F. Kennedy, the reference to the collective interest of *Humanity* was already demonstrated by the facts; it was then proclaimed in the texts, also in 1970, first with the UN Declaration on the Seabed.[7] In the aftermath of the 1962 crisis, the balance of terror was also validated, which in turn lay bare the fragility of the principle of collective security established seventeen years earlier in the UN Charter. However, the outcome of the Cuban crisis, which initially seemed resolved at the expense of the adventurism of the Soviet leader, also marked the development of a particularly active foreign policy of the Soviet Union. Led by Andrei Gromyko, this policy aimed to give a new dimension to 'peaceful co-existence', which was seen as a way of easing tension with the West in order to better prepare for the eventual victory of socialism. In turn, from 1973 and the beginning of negotiations within the framework of the Conference on European Security and Cooperation (OSCE), the Western countries confronted Soviet propaganda turning the invocation of human rights to their advantage.

Nevertheless, despite these strategic uses of legal norms, both sides had a clear interest in achieving the triumph of peace for themselves, in accordance with the letter and spirit of the Charter. Even if they did not necessarily fully subscribe to it, the leaders of both sides were thus forced to use the language of the constitutive act of the United Nations; the traumatism caused by the crisis resolved in 1962 inspired the idea that the content of the Charter should be

[2] Declaration of Legal Principles Governing the Activities of States in the Exploration and Use of Outer Space, UNGA Res 1962 (XVIII) (13 December 1963).

[3] Treaty on Principles Governing the Activities of States in the Exploration and Use of Outer Space, including the Moon and Other Celestial Bodies, 27 January 1967, 610 UNTS 205.

[4] Treaty on the Non-Proliferation of Nuclear Weapons, 1 July 1968, 729 UNTS 161.

[5] Vienna Convention on the Law of Treaties, 23 May 1969, 1155 UNTS 331.

[6] International Covenant on Civil and Political Rights, 16 December 1966, 999 UNTS 171; International Covenant on Economic, Social and Cultural Rights, 16 December 1966, 993 UNTS 3.

[7] Declaration of Principles Governing the Seabed and the Ocean Floor, UNGA Res 2749 (17 December 1970).

celebrated again by renewing the affirmation of its fundamental principles, as if to better demonstrate that none of these principles had suffered the corrosive effects of time. As in some religious rites, it was necessary to unite to reaffirm the belief in their authority. It is therefore important to understand that the restatement of the principles of the Charter was aimed both to refresh and revive the legitimacy attached to each of these golden rules.

Furthermore, the form of 'peaceful co-existence' that led, after a thorough process of distillation, to the adoption of the Friendly Relations Declaration can only be fully understood if one remembers the direct ideological dimension of the conflict that existed at the time. Contrary to what is happening in the current period, the Powers of the East, the Soviet Union and China, despite or because of the schism that had opened up between them, claimed to be defenders of the true Marxism-Leninism that would triumph over capitalism; whereas today, the confrontation between Russia and the United States or the United States and China no longer manifests more than the abrupt rivalry of mere nationalisms that are both exacerbated but largely secularised. On the other hand, the 'bracketing' of ideological and strategic contradictions between countries with different political regimes took on a more solemn dimension at the time because each of the two blocs claimed to be based on radically incompatible political principles. It was essential to demonstrate that they all wanted to consolidate peace.

It is because competition from East and West also had the challenge of attracting a third partner, then referred to, with some variations, either as the 'Third World', the 'non-aligned countries', or the 'group of 77'. Hence the importance of the renewed affirmation of the right of peoples to self-determination, which the three sides intended to affirm in connection with the classic principle of sovereign equality between States. Hence also the celebration of the need for development, an area in which the socialist countries clearly had an advantage, due to their declared ideology, while the United States (unlike the European countries, which were largely won over by social democratic ideas) only offered a laconic 'trade not aid' to the aspirations of developing countries expressed, in 1974, in the controversial Charter of Economic Rights and Duties of States.[8]

The major 'United Nations Declarations' of the time were adopted by the plenary organ of the 'World Organization' par excellence, the United Nations.[9] The General Assembly appeared as an organ whose prestige compensated, at least symbolically, for the paralysis of the Security Council induced by the veto of the Big Five, of which the Soviet Union remained the champion. From an institutional perspective, the Friendly Relations Declaration thus contributed to the designation of the General Assembly as the universal agora, a place predestined for the promotion of developing peoples. At the same time, the United States, placed on the defensive, denounced the 'automatic majorities' that it saw emerging in this Assembly.

The Cuban crisis had shown that in the nuclear age, the use of force between the two Super Powers could lead to global catastrophe. In the phase following the crisis, which lasted until approximately the end of the 1980s, Soviet diplomatic activism converged with the demands of developing countries, soon joined by the 'human rights diplomacy' coming from the West. Together with the efforts of the 'Third World' to invoke in its favour the principle of solidarity intended to animate the duty of co-operation of the rich countries with those who were just emerging from decolonisation, the globalising effect of the 1962 crisis would also contribute to the emergence of a new concept whose normative consecration was adopted the year before the adoption of the Friendly Relations Declaration. This is the concept that Article 53 of the Vienna

8 Charter of Economic Rights and Duties of States, UNGA Res 3281 (XXIX) (12 December 1974).

9 Following the expression of the late Michel Virally, *L'Organisation mondiale* (Armand Colin, 1972).

Convention on the Law of Treaties endowed with a normative power considered formidable by many observers: that of the 'international community of States as a whole' which can designate those general rules which are not only compulsory but also peremptory – that is, not subject to any derogation, by any State. The existence of *jus cogens* was affirmed by the largest majority, especially since the content of this *corpus juris* was not yet clearly determined (which is hardly the case today, contrary to what some authors may still say). However, *jus cogens* is composed of ethical norms established in law, in the name of the substantive and not only formal unity of the international legal order.[10] The ultimate consequence of the normative translations of 'peaceful co-existence' was thus the affirmation of a cohesion of this legal order, precisely because of the *content* and not only of the form of the norms that its right-holder, the 'international community of States as a whole', affirmed as having priority over all others.

2 A Striking Evolution

In the fifty years since the adoption of the Friendly Relations Declaration, major political changes have taken place on the international scene. To name but a few of them, the Soviet Union has disappeared; China has become the world's second largest power; Africa has affirmed an unprecedented potential for demographic but also economic development at the same time as it remains hampered by civil strife, epidemics and other daunting challenges; united Europe has expanded considerably but, at the same time, has lost much of its internal coherence; last but absolutely not least, the computer revolution and the digital age have introduced a radical revolution, particularly in the exchanges between people and communication techniques. As we have become acutely aware in the last decade, these technological changes enable, for good or evil, the direct expression of emotional and spontaneous reactions from large sectors of world opinion. The place of the State in international relations itself seems to be partly called into question, in view of the multiple flows of exchanges of all kinds directly established by private actors in international relations, some of whom confirm that they have actual resources that are often lacking for some State actors. It is the very definition of sovereignty that seems to be challenged in this way. The beginning of a fundamental movement towards the migration of large segments of the population from the South to the North has caused multiple tensions and anxieties in the latter hemisphere, fuelled by successive waves of terrorism from Islamist groups.

As a consequence, a generation of demagogic political leaders has risen, who are particularly ill-equipped to tackle the genuinely unprecedented challenges we face today. Radical mistrust of international institutions and, even more so, of multilateralism in general fuels the summary discourses of those thus placed at the head of a growing number of States. As the sheer complexity of the world reveals itself to the many, the choice of rulers who propose fallaciously simple answers becomes tempting. Populism is in vogue and it challenges the foundations of the rules-based international order which emerged from the ashes of the Second World War. One of its most direct manifestations are the short-sighted denial of climate change and of the massive loss of biodiversity. While the need for intensified co-operation by all members of the international community is thus becoming increasingly urgent, the expression of archaic nationalism competes each year in the UN General Assembly, with courageous stances which continue to advocate the virtues of multilateralism. While some reaffirm their commitment to the principles affirmed seventy-five and then fifty years ago, others do not hesitate to question or even ignore

[10] On this distinction, see Pierre-Marie Dupuy, '*L'Unité de l'ordre juridique international*. Cours général de droit international public (2000)' (2002) 297 *Recueil des Cours* 207 et seq.

the same principles, without realising the consequences attached to their irresponsible statements. Finally, it should be recalled that, speaking on 31 March 2020 of the Covid-19 crisis, the UN Secretary-General stated that 'the world is facing an unprecedented test. And this is the moment of truth … We must see countries not only united to beat the virus but also to tackle its profound consequences.'[11] The challenge posed by this unprecedented global health disaster will undoubtedly test the validity of at least some of the principles proclaimed in an entirely different context in 1970.

III CONTENT

1 *Is There a Hierarchy among the Seven Principles?*

After stating its seven principles, the Friendly Relations Declaration contains a 'General part' where the UN General Assembly '[d]eclares that: [i]n their interpretation and application, the above principles are interrelated and each principle should be construed in the context of the other principles'. It is true that, from a strictly legal point of view, each of these principles, all of which are already present in the Charter, were and remain endowed with the same authority.

However, when placed in the political environment that prevailed at the time of their adoption, they did not necessarily have the same dimension and, in reality, more importance was given to some of them than to others. The order in which the seven principles enshrined in the Declaration are set out does not exactly reflect the priority of the concerns of its promoters. For the Soviet Union, even more so than for the United States, the main goal was to achieve two objectives: on the one hand, to avoid the repetition of the Cuban scenario – that is, the direct confrontation of the two Super Powers with the immediate prospect of a nuclear confrontation; on the other hand, to ensure that the Western countries would not undertake an internal destabilisation of the bloc of socialist States (China being a case apart, since it was already in rupture with the USSR). These two objectives were in agreement so as to ensure the greatest possible stability between the Soviet Union and the United States in order to allow the former to consolidate their glacis and strengthen their internal cohesion. To this extent, one could go so far as saying that in 1970, the first and third principles – namely, the prohibition of the use of force and non-intervention in internal affairs – occupied a prominent place in this normative strategy. The second principle, on the peaceful settlement of disputes, is the direct substitute for the first principle, and it is the logical result of the repetition of the pair appearing in Article 2, paragraphs (3) and (4) of the UN Charter.

The fifth and sixth principles – namely, the principle of equal rights and self-determination of peoples and the sovereign equality of States – were of particular importance to the 'Third World' countries, while at the same time allowing the Soviet Union to gain an advantage over Western countries, some of which were (former) colonial powers. The principle of sovereign equality was decisive for the same developing countries, since it was supposed to guarantee their legal sovereignty vis-à-vis developed countries; its reaffirmation was (as it is) inherent in the very structure of the international legal order, and therefore unassailable by any country whatsoever.

The two remaining principles, the obligation of co-operation and respect for the principle of good faith, were a glue that enabled the respect and promotion of the other principles. The first of the two principles was, in particular, a way of moving from co-existence to co-operation, as

[11] www.un.org/en/un-coronavirus-communications-team/launch-report-socio-economic-impacts-covid-19.

captured by the famous formula of the late Wolfgang Friedman,[12] through multilateralism in international relations, particularly within international organisations. The second was a reminder of a principle stated in Article 2(3) of the UN Charter, which some saw as meta-legal and somewhere between law and international morality.

The General Part adds that:

> [n]othing in this Declaration shall be construed as prejudicing in any manner the provisions of the Charter or the rights and duties of Member States under the Charter or the rights of peoples under the Charter, taking into account the elaboration of these rights in this Declaration.

This sentence is complex and allows for different levels of understanding. By the time the negotiation was concluded in early 1970, it was clear to everyone involved that the statement of the right to self-determination went beyond the important, yet in hindsight embryonic, statement of self-determination in the UN Charter.[13] Although developing countries reluctantly accepted that no reference to Resolution 1514 (XV) was made in the Friendly Relations Declaration, the formulation of self-determination largely relied and elaborated on the text of that prior resolution, itself a significant expansion of the UN Charter and one of the major achievements of the decolonisation movement.[14] In this context, the reference in the General Part to 'or the rights of peoples under the Charter, *taking into account the elaboration of these rights in this Declaration*' is an attempt at consolidating the acquis.

At the same time, the earlier reference to '[n]othing in this Declaration shall be construed as prejudicing in any manner the provisions of the Charter or the rights and duties of Member States under the Charter' also implied a position of former colonial States, such as the United Kingdom and France, which had relied on similar language to reserve their position regarding the operation of the right to self-determination formulated in common Article 1 of the two 1966 Human Rights Covenants. The English text of the French reservation stated that:

> [t]he Government of the Republic considers that, in accordance with Article 103 of the Charter of the United Nations, in case of conflict between its obligations under the Covenant and its obligations under the Charter (especially Articles 1 and 2 thereof), its obligations under the Charter will prevail.

The British reservation singled out not only Articles 1 and 2 of the UN Charter but also Article 73. In this light, the saving clause contains a delicate balance between the positions of different States represented in the Special Committee which drafted the Friendly Relations Declaration.

In the last paragraph of the 'General Part', the UN General Assembly:

> [d]eclares further that: [t]he principles of the Charter which are embodied in this Declaration constitute basic principles of international law, and consequently appeals to all States to be guided by these principles in their international conduct and to develop their mutual relations on the basis of the strict observance of these principles.

This paragraph stresses the foundational character of these principles. It places all the principles of the Friendly Relations Declaration, including those that had been identified only as 'purposes' in the UN Charter (i.e. Article 1(2) referring to self-determination and Article 1(3) referring

12 Wolfgang Friedmann, *The Changing Structure of International Law* (Columbia University Press, 1964).

13 On self-determination see the chapter by MG Kohen in this volume.

14 Michel Virally had spoken of a Chapter XI bis to emphasise the normative development embodied in this and other resolutions on decolonisation. See Michel Virally, 'Droit international et décolonisation devant les Nations Unies' (1963) 9 *Annuaire français de droit international* 508, 526.

to co-operation), on an equal footing as 'basic principles of international law'. The discussion during the early stages of the drafting process concerning the distinction between 'purposes' (Article 1) and 'principles' (Article 2) is thus settled in favour of an integrative view which sees all seven principles of the Friendly Relations Declaration as 'principles' and 'appeals to all States' to observe them.

2 *What Future for the Friendly Relations Declaration?*

To answer this question, it is of course necessary to start by distinguishing the *negotium* from the *instrumentum*. The latter is the Friendly Relations Declaration itself, appended to Resolution 2625 (XXV) of the UN General Assembly, which only matters insofar as it can still serve as a reference text in public speeches. The *negotium*, on the other hand – namely, the content of the Declaration – remains the most important element and it is unavoidable. At least as long as the international community of peoples remains structured around independent States, both competing and increasingly interdependent, respect for the seven principles will remain essential.

Competition and rivalries among them will in particular continue to justify the cardinal principle of non-use of force more than ever, at a time when the number of countries endowed with nuclear weapons is increasing while, at the same time, Russia and the United States withdraw from – after largely disregarding – some crucial treaties on disarmament. Their lower level of compliance with the fundamental rule of non-use of force is particularly concerning. Specifically, the absolute prohibition of territorial acquisition by military means has suffered significant violations in the last decade, particularly in the relations between Russia and Ukraine, to the detriment of the latter. China's attempts to impose a totally unilateral approach to the delimitation of maritime areas in the South China Sea is also a cause for serious concern.

The growing interdependence of people in all fields, usually referred to as 'globalisation', will require more than ever the intensification of co-operation among States. It is here, however, that the scope of the fourth principle set out in the Declaration must be updated as it gains in scope and extension. Indeed, the gaps in the Declaration, which are also linked to the historical context of its adoption, should definitely be filled: it should be noticed, in particular, that the 1970 Declaration made absolutely no mention of the absolute need to strengthen international co-operation for the protection of the human environment; this gap may be explained by the decision to confine the work to the principles mentioned in the UN Charter, the novelty of environmental protection as a matter of international concern, the backlash against it from developing and newly independent States and the fact that, shortly before the last round of negotiation of the Friendly Relations Declaration, a separate process was launched to convene a Conference on the 'Human Environment' which took place in 1972.[15] In addition, throughout the 1970s, the protection of the environment was still a somewhat subordinate concern for most governments, and even more so in the East than in the West, both sides sharing in any case with the South, despite the Club of Rome's premonitory warnings, a profound underestimation of the dangers that had already long been threatening the human environment. Since then, however, despite the adoption of several dozen conventions relating to the various areas that require international co-operation, whether terrestrial, river, maritime, wetland, ozone layer, endangered species or the global climate as a whole,[16] environmental degradation has continued

[15] See the chapter by L-A Duvic-Paoli and JE Viñuales in this volume.

[16] See generally Pierre-Marie Dupuy and Jorge E Viñuales, *International Environmental Law* (2nd edn, Cambridge University Press, 2018), chs 4, 5, 6 and 7.

unabated. Governments are simply struggling to understand the scale of the catastrophes that lie ahead.

Another obvious gap in the Friendly Relations Declaration is the almost complete absence of any reference to the promotion of human rights[17] and humanitarian law,[18] which also reflects the position and influence of the Soviet Union. Since then, the spectacular expansion of international criminal law, essentially based on the individualised criminalisation of violations of the 'cardinal principles of humanitarian law', has brought attention to the gap between the situation prevailing in 1970 in much of the world and the period that began in the early 1990s with the establishment of the two ad hoc international criminal tribunals, for the former Yugoslavia and Rwanda, and then of the International Criminal Court. The direct link between respect for human rights and peacekeeping is constantly evidenced, particularly during the wars that followed the dissolution of the former Yugoslavia, as had been highlighted as early as 1992 in UN Secretary-General Boutros Boutros Ghali's *Agenda for Peace*.[19] The advanced age of the 1970 Friendly Relations Declaration is conspicuously manifested by these two shortcomings, namely the failure to refer to the need for co-operation to safeguard (and restore) the human environment and the scant references to human rights both in times of armed conflict and peace.

To take another field and broaden further the perspective of co-operation, whether or not still controllable by humankind in a thirty to forty-five year horizon, the rapid development of artificial intelligence already requires increased vigilance, which some good minds, including the late Cambridge professor Stephen Hawking and the prominent entrepreneur Bill Gates, called for several years ago. However, even if this vigilance were to be deployed through direct links and exchanges between researchers and concerned actors in the fields of interest, particularly in the areas of biological and health research and that of autonomous weapon systems (military drones), it would require the development of co-operation between States, particularly but not only in the military field. As an illustration of the interdependence of the seven principles, the prohibition of the use of force must also be revisited in the light of emerging issues, such as cybersecurity, the use of artificial intelligence for new types of weapons, or deployment of human activities in Outer Space, whose military use is prohibited, although some political leaders seem disinclined to remember it.

The advent of the digital age has also revolutionised the conditions under which 'the principle concerning the duty not to intervene in matters within the domestic jurisdiction of any State' can be violated. This principle has probably never been fully respected, but it is certain that, in recent years, the use of the Internet has amplified such disregard. This duty is a corollary of the principle of sovereign equality of States identified in the Declaration as the sixth principle, and its customary grounding was recognised by the International Court of Justice (ICJ) by reference to the Friendly Relations Declaration in the *Nicaragua* case.[20] Yet, it is now clear that some governments are deliberately using the increased access provided by the cyberspace to influence the outcome of electoral consultations, presidential elections and other democratic processes in other countries, although this is not necessarily the exclusive prerogative of Russia. The question

17 See the chapter by E. Riedel in this volume.

18 See the chapter by Bing Bing Jia in this volume.

19 Boutros Boutros-Ghali, *An Agenda for Peace: Preventive Diplomacy, Peacemaking, and Peace-Keeping: Report of the Secretary-General Pursuant to the Statement Adopted by the Summit Meeting of the Security Council on 31 January 1992* (UN, 1992).

20 *Military and Paramilitary Activities in and against Nicaragua (Nicaragua v United States of America)*, Merits, Judgment, ICJ Reports 1986, 14, paras 202–9.

then is how, if not to put an end to, at least to avoid the generalisation of this type of behaviour, which calls into question the normal functioning of democratic institutions in a foreign country. It is not for us to propose solutions but to highlight one of the major sources of the deliberate disregard for the third (non-intervention) and of the sixth principle (sovereign equality) and undoubtedly one of the areas in which reciprocal abstention, whether or not as a result of negotiations, seems essential.

As noted earlier, the period during which the Friendly Relations Declaration was adopted was characterised by the collective affirmation that there are a number of principles and rules that the international community as a whole considers so important for its survival that they are designated by it as peremptory or 'non-derogable'. Among such principles, the prohibition of the use of force is paramount and, yet, it has been greatly undermined in the last decades, particularly as some of its most recent violations are linked to the acquisition of territory. Generally, we can speak of a marked attenuation of the authority recognised by a certain number of States to these same principles.

So far, the history of the community of peoples shows that it has never been able to accomplish the scale of organisational and substantive change that is required to face the current challenges, except after unprecedented disasters. The twentieth century offers a particularly tragic illustration of this elementary observation: the League of Nations, despite its multiple imperfections, was in any case the result of an unprecedented global effort to structure international relations by trying to channel the use of force; it was the result of the millions of deaths caused by the First World War. The creation of the United Nations was in turn the result of an unprecedented tens of millions of deaths, including the victims of the Shoah, which remains the most horrific genocide in history. On its scale, fortunately a more modest one, the Friendly Relations Declaration resulted from a situation that led to stopping just at the threshold of what could have been the Third World War – this time probably the last, since it would be nuclear. The question today is perhaps whether the revival of the principles enshrined in the UN Charter and expanded in the Friendly Relations Declaration, can be achieved without first going through a new catastrophe affecting all humanity in an even more radical way than previous ones. Although many do not want to acknowledge it, the forces capable of triggering such catastrophic events may be already at work. This time, nuclear weapons are not even a necessary component of collapse. All it would take is for humanity to continue to systematically destroy the resources of the planet on which its survival is conditioned. Most recently, the pandemic caused by the sudden and totally unexpected expansion of Covid-19 has taken on such a dimension that one of the paradoxical ways of deriving some hope from it could be to see it as one of those global disasters that could lead to a new beginning, particularly in terms of increased international cooperation. But it can just as easily provoke the hegemonic enterprise of certain Powers that need not be mentioned here, if the spirit of mutual respect and cooperation advocated by Resolution 2625 is not given new impetus.

To conclude these observations, let me stress that we must not forget that international law and the very principles that underpin it are part and parcel of the great achievements of humanity; they are a prime example of a common heritage of mankind, which must be protected against reckless, petty and short-sighted nationalism and tribalism. The principles necessary for the collective and solidary organisation of the planet's survival have already been set out. It remains for us to ask ourselves how we can help revive our commitment to them and their normative pull. If there is a general mobilisation, there is still a chance we can make it happen. Hope is a risk. But it is a risk worth taking.

APPENDIX

The Friendly Relations Declaration (also available at www.un-documents.net/a25r2625.htm)

DECLARATION ON PRINCIPLES OF INTERNATIONAL LAW CONCERNING FRIENDLY RELATIONS AND CO-OPERATION AMONG STATES IN ACCORDANCE WITH THE CHARTER OF THE UNITED NATIONS, RESOLUTION 2625 (XXV) (24 OCTOBER 1970), ANNEX, OFFICIAL RECORDS OF THE GENERAL ASSEMBLY, TWENTY-FIFTH SESSION, SUPPLEMENT NO. 28, UN DOC. A/5217, AT 121

The General Assembly,

Recalling its resolutions 1815 (XVII) of 18 December 1962, 1966 (XVIII) of 16 December 1963, 2103 (XX) of 20 December 1965, 2181 (XXI) of 12 December 1966, 2327 (XXII) of 18 December 1967, 2463 (XXIII) of 20 December 1968 and 2533 (XXIV) of 8 December 1969, in which it affirmed the importance of the progressive development and codification of the principles of international law concerning friendly relations and co-operation among States,

Having considered the report of the Special Committee on Principles of International Law concerning Friendly Relations and Co-operation among States,[1] which met in Geneva from 31 March to 1 May 1970,

Emphasizing the paramount importance of the Charter of the United Nations for the maintenance of international peace and security and for the development of friendly relations and co-operation among States, *Deeply convinced* that the adoption of the Declaration on Principles of International Law concerning Friendly Relations and Co-operation among States in accordance with the Charter of the United Nations on the occasion of the twenty-fifth anniversary of the United Nations would contribute to the strengthening of world peace and constitute a landmark in the development of international law and of relations among States, in promoting the rule of law among nations and particularly the universal application of the principles embodied in the Charter,

Considering the desirability of the wide dissemination of the text of the Declaration,

1. *Approves* the Declaration on Principles of International Law concerning Friendly Relations and Co-operation among States in accordance with the Charter of the United Nations, the text of which is annexed to the present resolution;

[1] Official Records of the General Assembly, Twenty-fifth Session, Supplement No. 18 (A/8018).

2. *Expresses its appreciation* to the Special Committee on Principles of International Law concerning Friendly Relations and Co-operation among States for its work resulting in the elaboration of the Declaration;

3. *Recommends* that all efforts be made so that the Declaration becomes generally known.

1883rd plenary meeting,
24 October 1970

ANNEX

Declaration on Principles of International Law concerning Friendly Relations and Co-operation among States in Accordance with the Charter of the United Nations

PREAMBLE

The General Assembly,

Reaffirming in the terms of the Charter of the United Nations that the maintenance of international peace and security and the development of friendly relations and co-operation between nations are among the fundamental purposes of the United Nations,

Recalling that the peoples of the United Nations are determined to practise tolerance and live together in peace with one another as good neighbours,

Bearing in mind the importance of maintaining and strengthening international peace founded upon freedom, equality, justice and respect for fundamental human rights and of developing friendly relations among nations irrespective of their political, economic and social systems or the levels of their development,

Bearing in mind also the paramount importance of the Charter of the United Nations in the promotion of the rule of law among nations,

Considering that the faithful observance of the principles of international law concerning friendly relations and co-operation among States and the fulfilment in good faith of the obligations assumed by States, in accordance with the Charter, is of the greatest importance for the maintenance of international peace and security and for the implementation of the other purposes of the United Nations,

Noting that the great political, economic and social changes and scientific progress which have taken place in the world since the adoption of the Charter give increased importance to these principles and to the need for their more effective application in the conduct of States wherever carried on,

Recalling the established principle that outer space, including the Moon and other celestial bodies, is not subject to national appropriation by claim of sovereignty, by means of use or occupation, or by any other means, and mindful of the fact that consideration is being given in the United Nations to the question of establishing other appropriate provisions similarly inspired,

Convinced that the strict observance by States of the obligation not to intervene in the affairs of any other State is an essential condition to ensure that nations live together in peace with one another, since the practice of any form of intervention not only violates the spirit and letter of the Charter, but also leads to the creation of situations which threaten international peace and security,

Recalling the duty of States to refrain in their international relations from military, political, economic or any other form of coercion aimed against the political independence or territorial integrity of any State,

Considering it essential that all States shall refrain in their international relations from the threat or use of force against the territorial integrity or political independence of any State, or in any other manner inconsistent with the purposes of the United Nations,

Considering it equally essential that all States shall settle their international disputes by peaceful means in accordance with the Charter,

Reaffirming, in accordance with the Charter, the basic importance of sovereign equality and stressing that the purposes of the United Nations can be implemented only if States enjoy sovereign equality and comply fully with the requirements of this principle in their international relations,

Convinced that the subjection of peoples to alien subjugation, domination and exploitation constitutes a major obstacle to the promotion of international peace and security, Convinced that the principle of equal rights and self-determination of peoples constitutes a significant contribution to contemporary international law, and that its effective application is of paramount importance for the promotion of friendly relations among States, based on respect for the principle of sovereign equality,

Convinced in consequence that any attempt aimed at the partial or total disruption of the national unity and territorial integrity of a State or country or at its political independence is incompatible with the purposes and principles of the Charter,

Considering the provisions of the Charter as a whole and taking into account the role of relevant resolutions adopted by the competent organs of the United Nations relating to the content of the principles,

Considering that the progressive development and codification of the following principles:

(a) The principle that States shall refrain in their international relations from the threat or use of force against the territorial integrity or political independence of any State, or in any other manner inconsistent with the purposes of the United Nations,
(b) The principle that States shall settle their international disputes by peaceful means in such a manner that international peace and security and justice are not endangered,
(c) The duty not to intervene in matters within the domestic jurisdiction of any State, in accordance with the Charter,
(d) The duty of States to co-operate with one another in accordance with the Charter,
(e) The principle of equal rights and self-determination of peoples,
(f) The principle of sovereign equality of States,
(g) The principle that States shall fulfil in good faith the obligations assumed by them in accordance with the Charter,

so as to secure their more effective application within the international community, would promote the realization of the purposes of the United Nations,

Having considered the principles of international law relating to friendly relations and co-operation among States,

1. *Solemnly proclaims* the following principles:

The principle that States shall refrain in their international relations from the threat or use of force against the territorial integrity or political independence of any State or in any other manner inconsistent with the purposes of the United Nations

Every State has the duty to refrain in its international relations from the threat or use of force against the territorial integrity or political independence of any State, or in any other manner inconsistent with the purposes of the United Nations. Such a threat or use of force constitutes a violation of international law and the Charter of the United Nations and shall never be employed as a means of settling international issues.

A war of aggression constitutes a crime against the peace, for which there is responsibility under international law.

In accordance with the purposes and principles of the United Nations, States have the duty to refrain from propaganda for wars of aggression.

Every State has the duty to refrain from the threat or use of force to violate the existing international boundaries of another State or as a means of solving international disputes, including territorial disputes and problems concerning frontiers of States.

Every State likewise has the duty to refrain from the threat or use of force to violate international lines of demarcation, such as armistice lines, established by or pursuant to an international agreement to which it is a party or which it is otherwise bound to respect. Nothing in the foregoing shall be construed as prejudicing the positions of the parties concerned with regard to the status and effects of such lines under their special regimes or as affecting their temporary character.

States have a duty to refrain from acts of reprisal involving the use of force.

Every State has the duty to refrain from any forcible action which deprives peoples referred to in the elaboration of the principle of equal rights and self-determination of their right to self-determination and freedom and independence.

Every State has the duty to refrain from organizing or encouraging the organization of irregular forces or armed bands including mercenaries, for incursion into the territory of another State.

Every State has the duty to refrain from organizing, instigating, assisting or participating in acts of civil strife or terrorist acts in another State or acquiescing in organized activities within its territory directed towards the commission of such acts, when the acts referred to in the present paragraph involve a threat or use of force.

The territory of a State shall not be the object of military occupation resulting from the use of force in contravention of the provisions of the Charter. The territory of a State shall not be the object of acquisition by another State resulting from the threat or use of force. No territorial acquisition resulting from the threat or use of force shall be recognized as legal. Nothing in the foregoing shall be construed as affecting:

(a) Provisions of the Charter or any international agreement prior to the Charter regime and valid under international law; or

(b) The powers of the Security Council under the Charter.

All States shall pursue in good faith negotiations for the early conclusion of a universal treaty on general and complete disarmament under effective international control and strive to adopt appropriate measures to reduce international tensions and strengthen confidence among States.

All States shall comply in good faith with their obligations under the generally recognized principles and rules of international law with respect to the maintenance of international peace and security, and shall endeavour to make the United Nations security system based on the Charter more effective.

Nothing in the foregoing paragraphs shall be construed as enlarging or diminishing in any way the scope of the provisions of the Charter concerning cases in which the use of force is lawful.

The principle that States shall settle their international disputes by peaceful means in such a manner that international peace and security and justice are not endangered

Every State shall settle its international disputes with other States by peaceful means in such a manner that international peace and security and justice are not endangered.

States shall accordingly seek early and just settlement of their international disputes by negotiation, inquiry, mediation, conciliation, arbitration, judicial settlement, resort to regional agencies or arrangements or other peaceful means of their choice. In seeking such a settlement the parties shall agree upon such peaceful means as may be appropriate to the circumstances and nature of the dispute.

The parties to a dispute have the duty, in the event of failure to reach a solution by any one of the above peaceful means, to continue to seek a settlement of the dispute by other peaceful means agreed upon by them.

States parties to an international dispute, as well as other States shall refrain from any action which may aggravate the situation so as to endanger the maintenance of international peace and security, and shall act in accordance with the purposes and principles of the United Nations.

International disputes shall be settled on the basis of the sovereign equality of States and in accordance with the principle of free choice of means. Recourse to, or acceptance of, a settlement procedure freely agreed to by States with regard to existing or future disputes to which they are parties shall not be regarded as incompatible with sovereign equality.

Nothing in the foregoing paragraphs prejudices or derogates from the applicable provisions of the Charter, in particular those relating to the pacific settlement of international disputes.

The principle concerning the duty not to intervene in matters within the domestic jurisdiction of any State, in accordance with the Charter

No State or group of States has the right to intervene, directly or indirectly, for any reason whatever, in the internal or external affairs of any other State. Consequently, armed intervention and all other forms of interference or attempted threats against the personality of the State or against its political, economic and cultural elements, are in violation of international law.

No State may use or encourage the use of economic political or any other type of measures to coerce another State in order to obtain from it the subordination of the exercise of its sovereign rights and to secure from it advantages of any kind. Also, no State shall organize, assist, foment, finance, incite or tolerate subversive, terrorist or armed activities directed towards the violent overthrow of the regime of another State, or interfere in civil strife in another State.

The use of force to deprive peoples of their national identity constitutes a violation of their inalienable rights and of the principle of non-intervention.

Every State has an inalienable right to choose its political, economic, social and cultural systems, without interference in any form by another State.

Nothing in the foregoing paragraphs shall be construed as reflecting the relevant provisions of the Charter relating to the maintenance of international peace and security.

The duty of States to co-operate with one another in accordance with the Charter

States have the duty to co-operate with one another, irrespective of the differences in their political, economic and social systems, in the various spheres of international relations, in order to maintain international peace and security and to promote international economic stability and progress, the general welfare of nations and international co-operation free from discrimination based on such differences.

To this end:

(a) States shall co-operate with other States in the maintenance of international peace and security;

(b) States shall co-operate in the promotion of universal respect for, and observance of, human rights and fundamental freedoms for all, and in the elimination of all forms of racial discrimination and all forms of religious intolerance;

(c) States shall conduct their international relations in the economic, social, cultural, technical and trade fields in accordance with the principles of sovereign equality and non-intervention;

(d) States Members of the United Nations have the duty to take joint and separate action in co-operation with the United Nations in accordance with the relevant provisions of the Charter.

States should co-operate in the economic, social and cultural fields as well as in the field of science and technology and for the promotion of international cultural and educational progress. States should co-operate in the promotion of economic growth throughout the world, especially that of the developing countries.

The principle of equal rights and self-determination of peoples

By virtue of the principle of equal rights and self-determination of peoples enshrined in the Charter of the United Nations, all peoples have the right freely to determine, without external interference, their political status and to pursue their economic, social and cultural development, and every State has the duty to respect this right in accordance with the provisions of the Charter.

Every State has the duty to promote, through joint and separate action, realization of the principle of equal rights and self-determination of peoples, in accordance with the provisions of the Charter, and to render assistance to the United Nations in carrying out the responsibilities entrusted to it by the Charter regarding the implementation of the principle, in order:

(a) To promote friendly relations and co-operation among States; and

(b) To bring a speedy end to colonialism, having due regard to the freely expressed will of the peoples concerned;

and bearing in mind that subjection of peoples to alien subjugation, domination and exploitation constitutes a violation of the principle, as well as a denial of fundamental human rights, and is contrary to the Charter.

Every State has the duty to promote through joint and separate action universal respect for and observance of human rights and fundamental freedoms in accordance with the Charter.

The establishment of a sovereign and independent State, the free association or integration with an independent State or the emergence into any other political status freely determined by a people constitute modes of implementing the right of self-determination by that people.

Every State has the duty to refrain from any forcible action which deprives peoples referred to above in the elaboration of the present principle of their right to self-determination and freedom and independence. In their actions against, and resistance to, such forcible action in pursuit of the exercise of their right to self-determination, such peoples are entitled to seek and to receive support in accordance with the purposes and principles of the Charter.

The territory of a colony or other Non-Self-Governing Territory has, under the Charter, a status separate and distinct from the territory of the State administering it; and such separate and distinct status under the Charter shall exist until the people of the colony or Non-Self-Governing Territory have exercised their right of self-determination in accordance with the Charter, and particularly its purposes and principles.

Nothing in the foregoing paragraphs shall be construed as authorizing or encouraging any action which would dismember or impair, totally or in part, the territorial integrity or political unity of sovereign and independent States conducting themselves in compliance with the principle of equal rights and self-determination of peoples as described above and thus possessed of a government representing the whole people belonging to the territory without distinction as to race, creed or colour.

Every State shall refrain from any action aimed at the partial or total disruption of the national unity and territorial integrity of any other State or country.

The principle of sovereign equality of States

All States enjoy sovereign equality. They have equal rights and duties and are equal members of the international community, notwithstanding differences of an economic, social, political or other nature.

In particular, sovereign equality includes the following elements:

(a) States are judicially equal;
(b) Each State enjoys the rights inherent in full sovereignty;
(c) Each State has the duty to respect the personality of other States;
(d) The territorial integrity and political independence of the State are inviolable;
(e) Each State has the right freely to choose and develop its political, social, economic and cultural systems;
(f) Each State has the duty to comply fully and in good faith with its international obligations and to live in peace with other States.

The principle that States shall fulfil in good faith the obligations assumed by them in accordance with the Charter

Every State has the duty to fulfil in good faith the obligations assumed by it in accordance with the Charter of the United Nations.

Every State has the duty to fulfil in good faith its obligations under the generally recognized principles and rules of international law.

Every State has the duty to fulfil in good faith its obligations under international agreements valid under the generally recognized principles and rules of international law.

Where obligations arising under international agreements are in conflict with the obligations of Members of the United Nations under the Charter of the United Nations, the obligations under the Charter shall prevail.

GENERAL PART

2. *Declares* that:

In their interpretation and application the above principles are interrelated and each principle should be construed in the context of the other principles. Nothing in this Declaration shall be construed as prejudicing in any manner the provisions of the Charter or the rights and duties of Member States under the Charter or the rights of peoples under the Charter, taking into account the elaboration of these rights in this Declaration.

3. *Declares further* that:

The principles of the Charter which are embodied in this Declaration constitute basic principles of international law, and consequently appeals to all States to be guided by these principles in their international conduct and to develop their mutual relations on the basis of the strict observance of these principles.

Index